EVALUATION STUDIES REVIEW ANNUAL
Volume 7

Evaluation Studies

Review Annual

Richard J. Light, *Kennedy School of Government, Harvard University*
Katherine Lyall, *Director, Public Policy Program, Johns Hopkins University*
Laurence E. Lynn, Jr., *Kennedy School of Government, Harvard University*
Trudi C. Miller, *Applied Research on Public Management and Service Delivery, National Science Foundation*
David Mundell, *Education and Manpower Planning, Congressional Budget Office, Washington, D.C.*
Henry W. Riecken, *School of Medicine, University of Pennsylvania*
Peter H. Rossi, *Department of Sociology, University of Massachusetts, Amherst*
Susan E. Salasin, *National Institute of Mental Health, Rockville, Maryland*
Frank P. Sciolo, Jr., *Division of Advanced Production Research, National Science Foundation*
Lee Sechrest, *Director, Center for Research on Utilization of Scientific Knowledge, Institute for Social Research, University of Michigan*
Sylvia Sherwood, *Social Gerontological Research, Hebrew Rehabilitation Center for the Aged, Boston, Massachusetts*
Stephen M. Shortell, *Department of Health Services, School of Public Health and Community Medicine, University of Washington, Seattle*
Ernst W. Stromsdorfer, *Abt Associates, Cambridge, Massachusetts*
Elmer L. Struening, *School of Public Health, Columbia University*
Michael Timpane, *Teacher's College, Columbia University*
Carol H. Weiss, *Graduate School of Education, Harvard University*

Evaluation Studies

Review Annual

Volume 7   1982

Edited by

Ernest R. House
Sandra Mathison
James A. Pearsol
Hallie Preskill

SAGE PUBLICATIONS
Beverly Hills / London / New Delhi

H
1
E77
vol. 7
1982

For information address:

SAGE Publications, Inc.
275 South Beverly Drive
Beverly Hills, California 90212

SAGE Publications Ltd
28 Banner Street
London EC1Y 8QE, England

SAGE Publications India Pvt. India
C-236 Defence Colony
New Delhi 110 024, India

SO BaT LL 61571 12|8|82 $37.50

Printed in the United States of America
International Standard Book Number 0-8039-0386-3
International Standard Series Number 0364-7390
Library of Congress Catalog Card Number 76-15865

FIRST PRINTING

CONTENTS

For Glen, who never failed us.

ABOUT THE EDITORS

ERNEST R. HOUSE is Professor of Administration, Higher, and Continuing Education and Educational Psychology in the Center for Instructional Research and Curriculum Evaluation at the University of Illinois at Urbana. He has written and edited numerous works including: *School Evaluation: The Politics and Process* (1973); *The Politics of Educational Innovation (1974); Evaluating with Validity* (1980); and with S. Lapan, *Survival in the Classroom* (1978). He is currently editor (with R. Wooldridge) of *New Directions for Program Evaluation.*

SANDRA MATHISON is a doctoral candidate in educational psychology at the University of Illinois at Urbana. She received her B.A. in sociology from the University of Alberta (Canada). She has done evaluations of community college programs for several years and is currently a research assistant in the Center for Instructional Research and Curriculum Evaluation at the University of Illinois. Her areas of interest are evaluation of social programs and philosophical issues in program evaluation.

JAMES A. PEARSOL is currently a doctoral candidate in educational psychology at the University of Illinois. His major interest is in program evaluation, and he often wonders if formal evaluations have anything to do with "making sense" of educational and social issues. In the recent past, he has worked as a counselor in higher education settings, and as a researcher in an educational research center. He has published articles and reports in evaluation, career planning, and vocational education. Presently, he serves as a research assistant in the Center for Instructional Research and Curriculum Evaluation at the University of Illinois and is an evaluation team member for an evaluation of a national sex equity demonstration project.

HALLIE PRESKILL is a doctoral candidate in Vocational-Special Needs education and educational program evaluation. She has received a B.A. in Spanish, an M.S. in Elementary and Special Education, and presently holds an assistantship in the Center for Instructional Research and Curriculum Evaluation at the University of Illinois. Her current research interests include teacher evaluation, the career development and employability of handicapped students, special education program evaluation, and educational policy analysis. She has presented three papers and has published two articles in the area of vocational-special education and summative teacher evaluation.

Introduction
Scientific and Humanistic Evaluations

Ernest R. House

When my children were a bit younger, both went to Yankee Ridge Elementary School in Urbana. A few years prior to my oldest daughter Kristin's entering kindergarten there, Yankee Ridge had been a trial site for the teaching methods and materials that Bereiter and Engelman had been developing, the approach later known as Direct Instruction and commercially marketed as Distar.

The kindergarten teacher had been involved in the early try-outs. She was a vivacious, energetic woman, and she was enthusiastic about the choral reading of the Distar program. It was, she claimed, superior to any other reading program that she had encountered. She prided herself on running the only "academic" kindergarten in town and had inspired some of the other primary teachers to invest themselves personally in the Distar approach. There was a small devoted cadre of perhaps three teachers at that time.

My daughter responded well to this approach. She had always been small, shy, and quiet, a spectator at events rather than a participant. In nursery school she had enjoyed most the singing of songs and the nursery school teacher's guitar playing. She readily took to the group chanting of Distar. The dynamism of her teacher held her attention somewhat. There was a playful quality to some of the lessons. I would not say she was enthusiastic—she was never enthusiastic about school—but it was not bad.

I might also note that the Distar program (later called Direct Instruction and developed with a group of special education students) was employed there in an upper-middle-class school where the mean IQ was above 125 on the California Test of Mental Maturity. In Follow Through it was used with disadvantaged students and was advertised by its commercial publishers as a panacea for all students with learning problems. Opportunity knocks several times apparently.

Another part of the Yankee Ridge primary program was math, in which the teachers used Individually Prescribed Instruction (IPI) materials. Several years before, when I was a consultant with the Illinois Gifted Program, I had been partially responsible for introducing IPI materials into the Urbana Schools. In a search for new programs to exhibit in the Illinois demonstration centers, a team of us had visited Oak Leaf School before it was officially open to visitors. On return we prompted the Illinois Department of Education to grant $10,000 in seed money to five Illinois school districts interested in adopting the Pittsburgh materials. The Urbana district was one of these, and several years later the IPI materials were still in use at Yankee Ridge. Little did I know then that my own yet-to-be-born children would be instructed in a program I had helped import. Perhaps all educational reformers should be subject to such a fate.

From the beginning my daughter was not keen about the IPI materials. They consisted mainly of worksheets so that the students could work at their own pace, a feature that presumably motivated the student by providing successful experiences, a little "reinforcement" as they say. However, what my daughter saw was that as soon as she did one sheet, she had to do another one. This was not positive motivation for her. She resisted, lagged, and complained bitterly about the materials.

This program, I might add, was developed originally in a working-class school, transferred to such places as this demonstration center for gifted youth, and later used as a basic model for educating disadvantaged youths, in the Follow Through experiment. (Our curriculum development efforts seem to have great versatility, whatever else they may possess.)

Four years later my son entered Yankee Ridge, a different personality altogether—aggressive, highly motivated, intensely competitive. The previous semester we had spent in England, and there he had entered a classroom in which all the other children had been reading for some time. That classroom was very old-fashioned, taught the way I had been taught thirty years before with "Dick and Jane" readers.

Not wanting to be behind, my son resolutely set out to learn to read on his own, doggedly pursuing the teacher after school. (She had to see that he had mastered each little reader before he could advance to the next one, and she never had enough time during class hours to attend to him.) Within three months he learned to read and closed the gap between himself and the rest of the class.

"Too bad the girl hasn't had the same preparation the boy has had," said the bald English headmaster, who also made the tapioca pudding for the students' lunch everyday. In fact, both children had gone to the same nursery school, and both had had the same teachers there.

Back in Yankee Ridge in kindergarten and in the primary grades, Colby was well ahead of most of the other children in both reading and math. The pace of the choral reading bothered him. It was too slow. The dynamic teacher who had been the champion of the Distar materials had gone off to seek national office in a teacher organization. The remaining teachers followed the Distar prescriptions faithfully, but they were neither inspired nor inspiring. Something was missing. The lessons took on a routine, repetitive character for my son.

In math the better students used the linearly sequenced IPI materials as a race track. Everyone knew exactly where everyone else was on the track. The point was to race through the materials as quickly as possible. The materials had been introduced several years before, and since then the school district had fallen upon much harder financial times. There were too few clerks to score the tests, which were essential to progress in the curriculum. The teachers were becoming increasingly disenchanted because of the extra record keeping and their inability to keep up. The children were frustrated by having to wait so long for someone to examine their lessons so they could advance. They sat for long periods of time with their hands raised, trying to get someone to look at their papers. As a parent, of course, I was not entirely happy with any of these instructional arrangements for either daughter or son. For the middle-class parent, no education can be good enough for one's own child, short of the teacher devoting herself or himself exclusively to that child. The middle-class parent seeks not learning but advantage.

What do these personal reminiscences have to do with evaluation? It seems to me that a proper evaluation should capture some of the complexities of such a situation. Certainly, the individual differences among children are obvious. The different social contexts within which the programs operate are less so. That these programs will have subtle and profound effects not recorded by traditional achievement measures is highly probable. In implementation it is likely that schools will adopt part of a program, or in this instance, parts of two different programs. Furthermore, the programs will vary significantly in their implementation, depending upon the teachers themselves. Not even a program with a written script like Distar can escape variation. Finally, programs developed in one type of setting will be used in entirely different settings with quite different students, adding uncertainty to the implementation and the effects, if indeed such an entity as "a program" even exists. How do evaluations account for these complexities, and how do they inform us in such a way as to be meaningful?

Scientific Methods

Both of these curricula were part of the massive Follow Through experiment. How was the original Follow Through evaluation conducted? Thirteen models of early childhood education, including Direct Instruction and IPI, were compared to one another. Each sponsor or model was assigned several sites, i.e., school districts in which to implement its program. Within each site Follow Through and corresponding control classes were chosen at the end of third grade. Those children who were still left in the classes were administered four psychometric measures—the third grade Metropolitan Achievement Test, the Intellectual Achievement Responsibility Scale, the Coopersmith Self-Esteem Inventory, and the Raven's Coloured Progressive Matrices Test. Using previously collected data such as entry achievement scores as covariates, the Follow Through classes were compared to their controls to see which had statistically significant higher scores on the outcome measures. Findings for individual classes and sites were added together in a complicated way to provide a summary score for each Follow Through model. These summary scores could then be compared to those of other models to determine the winners and losers.

As is well known, the publication of the evaluation findings was greeted by a barrage of hostile criticism, most of which attacked the validity of the findings in some way. There were far more attacks than defenses of the study, and I think it accurate to say that the study is widely believed to be a bad example of evaluation. There is less agreement as to why the evaluation went wrong. Some critics point to technical deficiencies, others to political and historical factors. To this list of potential sources of error, I would like to add a more esoteric one. the particular notion of science upon which the evaluation was premised. Much of the evaluative reasoning was based upon the techniques and methods of mainstream social science, the aspirations of which have been to emulate the methods of the physical sciences.

Our notion of what science should be has evolved historically from the Enlightenment, from the birth of modern science in the seventeenth and eighteenth centuries. In their reaction against medieval scholasticism, which tried to discover the place of all things within God's purpose, the scientists and philosophers of the Enlightenment conceived the universe as a single, undifferentiated substance. Apparent changes within this substance, changes one could perceive with the senses, were actually changes in state, and these changes could be modeled by mathematical formulas. Newton's physics was the paradigmatic example for later generations.

Among visible phenomena, one could discover underlying and more fundamental relationships, and these discoveries would culminate in a coherent system of elements. Thus, underlying external appearances and differences, there was a logically connected structure of physical laws, and it was only a matter of time until scientists discovered what these laws were. Although Renaissance scientists had given up the notion of Divine Will ruling the universe, they had not given up the idea that there was an underlying order within it.

Given this conception of the nature of reality, it followed (particularly for those like Leonardo, Copernicus, and Galileo, who had rediscovered Plato and Pythagoras) that scientific explantion should be abstract, preferrably mathematical (Abbagnano, 1967). One could apply mathematical techniques to that which was measurable, and that which was measurable was a subset of what was observable. Application of the appropriate method would lead to the formulation of general laws. As mentioned, Newton was the supreme example of the scientist in action—observation leading to the mathematical formulation of universal laws of reality.

Success with these methods was rapid, and within the next few centuries, the confidence of science steadily increased. Observation and experimentation were advanced by some as the *sole* reliable method of knowledge. Exact measurement was important because some scientific propositions could be tested only by careful calculation. Science was conceived as a single coherent body of logical conclusions arrived at by universally valid principles of thought, such as deduction. These conclusions were founded securely upon controlled observation and experiment.

Ordinary language was viewed with suspicion. The goal of science, escaping from the clutches of religion, was to eliminate superstition, bias, and emotion from observations of the natural world. Ordinary language was laden with such baggage. Hence, scientific language should be shorn of biases and emotion. When possible, it should even be quasi-mathematical.

Isaiah Berlin (1980) has formulated three assumptions upon which modern science rests. First, science assumes that every question has one and only one true answer. If one does not arrive at such an answer, then one has asked the wrong question. Asking the proper one will yield the right answer. Second, there is one method or set of methods for discovering the answer, and this method is rational in character. Often the method is construed as observation and experiment or as the hypothetical-deductive process. Furthermore, this method for discovering truth is identical across all fields, although it may differ in detail somewhat. Third, the answers discovered by such a method are true universally, true for all people in all times and all places. Truth is not relative in any way. Underlying all three assumptions is the notion that the world consists of a single system explainable by the appropriate methods.

How do these ideas derived from physical science apply to the study of humans and human society? Within this Enlightenment tradition humans are seen as objects in nature. Human nature is regarded as being essentially similar in all times and places. Even though circumstances may change in detail, there are universal human goals and patterns, and these patterns are discoverable by proper scientific methods. Local and historical variations are relatively unimportant. In other words, human reality can be studied like physical reality.

Many of these features are seen in the science of linguistics, e.g., in Chomsky's search for a universal grammar. In spite of obvious differences in human languages, Chomsky believes that underlying these differences is a single specific universal grammar that enables all humans to speak and also limits how they do so (Chomsky, 1979). Furthermore, Chomsky believes that this universal grammar is biologically based, that is, grounded in physical principles. So even the most human of all characteristics—language—is subject to scientific investigation.

What does all this have to do with the Follow Through evaluation? The Follow Through evaluation was based upon the methods of mainstream social science, and through that, upon the notions of Enlightenment science, for mainstream social science has tried to emulate the methods of the physical sciences. The Follow Through evaluation shared similar presumptions.

Most fundamentally it was presumed that there was an underlying internally consistent reality to be discovered. There were different approaches to early childhood education, and these approaches could be tested against one another to see "which worked best" for disadvantaged children. There was an underlying set of relationships among the models to be discovered, and once they were discovered, policymakers would know how to act. After all, what would be the point of disobeying natural laws, as in physics, for example?

In order to discover these relationships, one had to conduct an experiment, a very large experiment. Careful calculation, measurement, and observation were called for. Only by the appropriate methods could the answer or solution be truly determined. Great attention was paid by the evaluators to the precision of their methods. When the relationships were discovered, they could be expressed in mathematical terms. Findings about each class, site, and model would culminate in a single, coherent set of findings to yield a clear picture of which model was best. The whole thing would add up.

Furthermore, the findings would be true universally, at least for disadvantaged children across the country. If Direct Instruction or IPI were the best models, they would be best in all sites and in other cities as yet untried, just as physical laws are true. They would also be true next year and last year, from cohort to cohort. In other words, local and historical variations from site to site or from time to time were relatively unimportant. A model would achieve similar effects in similar settings. Finally, the evaluation findings should be expressed in neutral, even quasi-mathematical language, so the results would be unbiased, unemotional, and clear to everyone.

In terms of Berlin's three assumptions, there was one answer to be discovered: "Which model works best?" When the evaluators waivered on this, they were aggressively sent back to the one question. There was one method for arriving at the answer. Pleas for other methods of investigation were resolutely rejected by the evaluators and government planners. The findings were taken to be universally true, good for all times and places.

Of course, the evaluation foundered badly. The findings were unclear. Local and historical variations proved to be quite important in both implementation and results. Findings were inconsistent from one site to another. Models did well in one setting but not in others. Results even changed from one year to the next with the same model on the same site. The methods did not yield clear, coherent, and consistent results. In fact, one could obtain dramatically different results by using slightly different methods of analysis. Even choosing the site, class, or student as the unit of analysis resulted in differences in what was seen. And the evaluation report itself, although largely statistical, capitalized upon emotional terms like "basic skills" to inscribe itself on the public consciousness.

Most critics said that the evaluators had chosen the wrong methods or that they had implemented the correct methods improperly or that they had generalized their results too far beyond particular sites. All of these may be true, but there is a more fundamental problem with the evaluation: The basic presumptions upon which the study was based proved to be incorrect. There is a sense in which social reality differs substantially from physical reality.

The nature of these differences I leave untouched here other than to suggest that if one evaluates an automobile for gas mileage, one will expect the gas mileage to be the same in other parts of the country (though even here there are conflicting methods of estimation). But if one institutes a new school program, one should not expect the results to be the same in other parts of the country.

Humanistic Methods

What does this mean? Should we abandon attempts to evaluate Follow Through? It seems to me there are other possibilities. The simplest is to constrain the reach of our scientific methods in various ways. We might apply these methods where we think they have a good chance of success. For example, there is no reason a priori to believe that Chomsky may not be correct about a universal grammar. It remains an unproved but empirical question. In scientific evaluation the closer one comes to physical phenomena, the more likely the success of these scientific methods. The less physical and the more cultural the entity being evaluated, the less likely the success with these methods. In other words, we might apply scientific methods more wisely, realizing that they do not generate the total truth or exhaust all possibilities. We need a broader notion of social science than that which prevails among many social scientists.

Rather than pursue that idea, however, in the rest of this introduction I would like to explore a mode of inquiry other than the scientific. What if one does not presume that there is one true method or that results are universal or even that there is only one true answer? Another way of investigating (and evaluating) is via the "manifest image" of humans, that is, by dealing with the world in terms of ordinary language, dealing with the world as it appears phenomenologically to individuals.

For example, evaluations might be case studies in which the evaluator constructs a narrative, a story as it were, as to what the program is all about. The story may be told in the words of the participants of the program. A major presumption of this approach is that one has to know what has happened and is happening within the program to know what is possible for its future. Every program, like every person, is bound to its past. To understand a program fully, one must see it through the eyes of its participants because it has a significance and meaning to them that only they understand. Even though the evaluator or investigator may not agree with the meaning that participants ascribe to their actions, the evaluator may believe it is vital to know what these meanings are.

One problem with the scientific mode of investigation is that it does not capture in any recognizable way the experience of the participants. Hence, one cannot fully appreciate the actions they might take. These experiences are recorded in ordinary, everyday language and concepts. If, on the one hand, the scientific mode of investigation emphasizes method as a way of controlling biases (a reasonable expectation derived from the historical conditions preceding the Enlightenment and certainly an invaluable aid in the pursuit of truth), the humanistic mode of investigation emphasizes *experience* as lived. For example, in the stories and anecdotes that I told about my children at the beginning of this introduction, one can discern bases for action that children, teachers, parents, and even program developers might take as a result of these experiences. There is virtually nothing in the original scientific evaluation of Follow Through that would give a hint as to the occurrence of such events. Science does not record experience in such ordinary terms. Yet it is undeniable that the nature of this experience determines action in a substantial way.

If the scientific findings of the original Follow Through evaluation really did reflect an underlying immutable, universal reality in the way that laws of physics do, then one might draw some basis for action from them. There is no sense in disobeying the laws of physics. But it is precisely this presumption of similarity between physical and social reality that I am questioning. The findings of the Follow Through evaluation do not have the necessity of the findings of physics even though elaborate quantitative methods were employed, and this is not simply because the wrong methods were employed.

What about the anecdotes about my children? Surely one cannot accept them at face value. They are undocumented and unsubstantiated. They may well be wrong. In fact, in the sense that they were conceived by a concerned parent, there is the possibility that they are distorted to fit the self-interests of the parent and the children. In accepting the ordinary language and experiences of participants, and hence provides an exceptional guide to their actions, its weakness is that it also mixes in their biases and those of the investigator. It is sometimes biased, subjective, and undisciplined.

There are ways of investigating such experiences in a disciplined manner, however, and these disciplines are called the humanities. The humanities share a concern for the "manifest image" of human beings and their actions. These actions were represented verbally, including the utterances of the individuals themselves. The humanities as fields of study also grew out of the Renaissance. Humanists also struggled for freedom from the hierarchy of the church and feudalism. This they hoped to achieve by resurrecting the study of the ancient manuscripts of Rome and Greece. This effort led to historical and textual studies. In a sense, the humanists tried to recapture the mental powers that they thought the ancients had acquired from poetry, rhetoric, history, ethics, and politics (Abbagnano, 1967).

The aim of the humanists was to assert the value and dignity of humans, to integrate humans back into the scheme of nature and history. "Man is the measure of all things" was their adopted motto. Aristotelianism, particularly the physics and logic, had long served as a cornerstone of medieval society, but the humanists preferred Aristotle's moral philosophy over his physics. Although both scientists and humanists started from the same origins, within a few centuries their paths diverged.

Against the extreme rationalism of scientific method, particularly as expounded by Descartes, who debunked studies like history altogether, came the Counter-Enlightenment. The main figure was Vico, who first denied some of the scientific presumptions as they applied to the social and cultural world. To study humans as natural objects in the scientific mode did not make sense, wrote Vico

(Berlin, 1980). Human activities were totally knowable from the "inside," as it were. Being human, one had insight into other people's motivations and purposes, thereby permitting a deeper and superior knowledge. There was no need to study humans as objects.

Furthermore, according to Vico, there was no unchanging human nature as presumed by the scientists. Humans changed with their culture, and it was deceptive to read current culture into that of the past. Cultures change, and the only way to understand the past was by an examination of past language, myths, and rites. In other words, one had to treat past societies as different in important respects. Scientific findings about humans were not necessarily true for all times and places. Nor was there only one true method for achieving such insights. Scientific methods were fine when applied to the natural world, but not when applied to humans.

Vico's analysis eventually led to theories of historical evolution and cultural relativism. The core idea was the notion of what a culture was, of its unity and uniqueness (Berlin, 1980). To understand a culture one must possess imaginative insight and be able to conceive of more than one way of categorizing reality. History should be an account of the variety of experience. Only by tracing the genesis and history of a culture could it be properly understood. In a sense there was not one great underlying coherent reality to be discovered but many. Knowledge was not cumulative in the scientific sense of progressively discovering the one underlying reality with one method. Also in contrast to scientific method, informed imaginative insight was necessary to understanding. One gained knowledge by experience or by imagination. There was no single structure of reality and no timeless "natural law."

As it has come down to us, the scientific mode of inquiry presumes to give us the world as an entity independent of our way of perceiving it, in other words, objectively. Since one can uncover the single underlying reality, scientific knowledge will be progressive (Scruton, 1980). The humanistic mode of inquiry, on the other hand, presumes to give us the world as it is experienced by other people, as seen through their cultural lenses. The essence of humanistic thought seems to be that human action is intelligible only when we see it through the eyes of the agent who does it, only when we see why he and she would do what they did. Only then do we see the order in the other person's experience. Science looks for causes as explanations; the humanities look for reasons. Meaning and significance are derived from the human context within which the action occurs. The significance of events is a "felt" significance. It is not independent of our ways of perceiving it. In fact, it is very much part of our way of perception and is, in that sense, subjective.

The humanities, however, are not simply collections of feelings. They presume to be disciplined inquiry. In this there is agreement that they involve the higher conceptual powers of humans, particularly the capacity to make comparisons and impose order on experience (Scruton, 1980) and the capacity for making distinctions of value, including moral distinctions (Olafson, 1979). Value, order, and coherence are terms one hears often from humanists. It is not difficult to see that the fundamental concepts of the humanities might be useful to formal evaluation. In fact, I would say that the humanistic mode of inquiry is *one* way of doing evaluation, and one that differs significantly from the scientific mode.

Besides seeing humans as the possessors of certain mental powers, the humanities portray individual persons and their actions in terms of their intentions and purposes (Olafson, 1979). Explanations are usually teleological, i.e., in terms of the agent's intentions. Actions are described narratively. The narrative conveys a "story" of what happens. Person, agency, purpose, value, and temporal continuity are key concepts. The agent's description of events is primary data, the object of the scholar being able to explain or understand the actions in the agent's own way (for an evaluation of a Follow Through model along these lines, see Zimiles and Mayer, 1980).

My thesis then is that the humanistic mode of inquiry is too seldom used in formal evaluations. Like the scientific mode it has a long disciplined tradition. It reveals a different aspect of social reality. Put more strongly, "The evaluator is essentially a historian: he helps individuals and organizations to learn from what has happened" (Cronbach et al., 1980, p. 221). One must caution, however, that humanistic methods have not yet been adapted to the purposes of evaluation nearly to the degree that scientific methods have been.

In all this I do not intend to demean the scientific mode of inquiry nor to suggest that it is invalid. There are many (perhaps most) situations in which scientific methods of evaluation are most appropriate. There are other situations in which evaluators would do better with different methods or with a combination of methods. It is important to realize that scientific methods are derived from particular historical circumstances and have particular limitations. They are not the sole path to truth. Too many evaluators cling to such a view. Especially in evaluating the social worth of something, one must sometimes take a broader view than scientific methods provide.

Consequently, in this volume we have included a different mix of articles than has been typical of past *Annuals*. There are more case study evaluations and related position papers. We have tried to effect more of a balance between qualitative and quantitative methods, since the latter have been emphasized so much in past volumes. (In a rough fashion quantitative methods correspond to the scientific mode and qualitative methods to the humanistic, although this is by no means a one-to-one correspondence. Quantitative methods are sometimes used in history and qualitative methods are often used in science. The differences between the scientific and humanistic are deeper than mere use of numbers.)

In addition, we have included a special section on ethics and several articles probing the value bases of evaluation. We think that these topics will receive increased attention in the future as evaluators become more conscious of the origins and value slant of their methods. After all, evaluation is by its nature value-embedded.

REFERENCES

Abbagnano, Nicola. *Humanism in The Encyclopedia of Philosophy* (Vol. 4). New York: Macmillan, 1967.

Berlin, Isaiah. *Against the Current: Essays in the History of Ideas.* New York: Viking, 1980.

Chomsky, Norm. *Language and Responsibility.* New York: Pantheon, 1979.

Cronbach, Lee J. and Associates. *Toward Reform of Program Evaluation.* San Francisco: Jossey-Bass, 1980.

Olafson, Frederick A. *The Dialectic of Action.* Chicago: University of Chicago Press, 1979.

Scruton, Roger. "Humane education." *American Scholar*, 1980, (Autumn), pp. 489-498.

Zimiles, Herbert and Rochelle Mayer with Elaine Wickens. *Bringing Child-Centered Education to the Public Schools.* New York: Bank Street College of Education, 1980.

I

THEORY

Evaluation has been largely perceived as a practical enterprise and it often moves forward with little regard for theoretical and philosophical issues that underlie the work at hand. There are assumptions inherent in any evaluation study that need to be recognized. The reasons for evaluating programs, the ways in which programs are evaluated, and the perceived benefits of evaluation have significant implications. This section contains articles that discuss general philosophical issues as well as those that address issues specific to evaluation studies.

The first article is the Summary from the Raizen and Rossi report, *Program Evaluation in Education? When? How? To What Ends?* The results and recommendations presented here are the work of the Committee on Program Evaluation in Education, but the impact of the report extends beyond education. Two findings permeate the report: (1) "evaluation must be viewed as a system that involves many organizations and many parties," and (2) "the quality and use of evaluations could be considerably enhanced through better management procedures." The second point is the most strongly stressed.

Recommendations are made for Congress and the Department of Education. The lack of utility of evaluations is seen largely as a mismatch between the information generated by evaluations and information needed to make decisions. Congress, they suggest, should be more specific about information needs and should manage evaluation funds in a responsible way. Changes in administrative and management procedures within the Department of Education are suggested as necessary reforms since the department has the power to make these changes. They do not ordinarily have such power over external forces and constraints.

Stake, in his response to Raizen and Rossi, considers this report "thorough, creative, and largely well reasoned," but he points out some flaws. The committee responsible for the report was dominated by social scientists and, not surprisingly, the recommendations (and more so the body of the report) rely heavily on social science methods. Stake points out that social science recognizes the great variance associated with local sites, but the main goal is the attainment of knowledge of the universal. This penchant for generalizations is a bias in the social science method that is harmful to the understanding of the instance, the particular arrangement.

Stake warns of the false promise in the tone of the report's recommendations. The expectations of what evaluation can accomplish are often beyond common-sense limits. Technical improvement, while necessary, will not lead to evaluation excellence. This emphasis on technical skills detracts from what Stake considers crucial concerns—educator skills and educational issues. Stake concludes his response to the committee report by encouraging the consideration of the report in spite of the flaws.

In a response to Stake's review of the NAS-NRC Committee Report, Rossi outlines several points of disagreement with Stake's interpretations. The major disagreement involves "fundamentally different views of social science and its contributions to evaluation activities." Rossi differentiates between evaluation and evaluation research on methodological grounds. A connoisseurial approach to evaluation is not evaluation research because it does not employ the methods of social science. The committee report was concerned only with evaluation research.

Before closing his response to Stake with several clarifications, Rossi defends the position of the committee report, which did not specifically address educational issues. Rossi feels the roles of evaluation, educator, and political agent should be kept distinct. The evaluator should be concerned with whether goals of programs have been attained and not with setting the goals for programs. Finally, the avoidance of educational issues is additionally justified because "the evaluation of educational programs is no different in form from the evaluation of any other program."

Fetterman's article outlines deleterious effects of evaluation design on participants in a youth employment program as an illustration of the potentially harmful effects of traditional research design. The treatment-control group design used in the evaluation of this program presents ethical, programmatic, and methodological problems. The ethical concern is an old one in using experimental designs for evaluating human services—how can the chance to help these youngsters be denied to some of them simply to create a control group? Trying to convince the parents and young people of the value of the program in light of the logistical, practical problems inherent in the design constitutes the programmatic problem. Fetterman suggests, "The application of this design to this population is methodologically bankrupt."

It is not only the evaluation design that Fetterman finds harmful to the program but also the federal intervention in the evaluation. Fetterman illustrates common criticisms of federal intervention in program evaluation. Because the federal government is seeking to maximize returns for money spent, the desire to weed out ineffective programs is implicit in demands for evaluating a program. Programs are consequently in a defensive position from their very inception. The added emphasis on replication of a prototypical model program carries the implication that any deviation or discrepancy is a negative characteristic of the program.

Fetterman concludes his discussion by outlining several organizational world views that harmfully influence the evaluation of this youth employment program. The research corporation, the educational research establishment, and the federal bureaucracy are organizational bodies whose world views inpinge upon the provision and evaluation of human services. The author closes with recommendations for conducting evaluations that encourage the consideration of the larger sociopolitical context of evaluation studies. This he hopes will "prevent misevaluations."

The article by Young, although not directly addressing evaluation studies, has some clear implications for the conduct of evaluations. His discussion illustrates the dominance of scientific methods and scientific knowledge in studies of social reality. Since evaluation studies clearly borrow this scientific method, the argument is germane to evaluation. Young's major point is that folk knowledge has been largely neglected and should be reinstated as a legitimate way of knowing.

Young describes the nature of both folk and scientific methods that lead to knowledge about the social world. The scientific methods encourage a monopoly over social knowledge by experts and professionals, while folk methods encourage particularism and involvement by all persons and groups in the production of social knowledge.

Young concludes by outlining what he calls norms of science, the purpose of which is to encourage the use of folk methods and indeed a diversity of methodologies in the creation of human knowledge. Young's view may be somewhat radical, but it is important to appreciate that more than one method of inquiry is necessary to understand the social world, a point that has direct implications for evaluation studies.

Modern social science presumes to produce knowledge that will allow a valid assessment of social reforms. Dunn suggests that such a presumption is questionable and the immediate issue is rather, "By what standards do policymakers, practitioners, social scientists, and other stakeholders in social reforms assess the adequacy of knowledge claims?" Much evaluation of social reforms has been based on Donald Campbell's "experimenting society" metaphor. Dunn feels that use of such a metaphor has added reasoned discourse about causal inferences but has failed to recognize social reforms as symbolically mediated constructions.

Dunn suggests that "reforms as arguments" is a more apt metaphor than the traditional one of "reforms as experiments." "Reforms as arguments" is elaborated by concepts drawn from jurisprudence and forensics. Dunn outlines three reasons why this is a better metaphor for social reforms: (1) data and evidence are only one of the several elements necessary for making successful knowledge claims, (2) truth is a social construction, and (3) the process of rational advocacy of stakeholders in the reconstruction of knowledge claims is emphasized.

Using Toulmin's analysis of arguments, Dunn provides a schema for the critical and reflective assessment of the presuppositions of knowledge claims. Standards for appraising knowledge claims are based on tests of truth, relevance, and cogency. Dunn outlines what each of these tests are and the related potential threats to validity of knowledge claims. The employment of such an analysis anticipates diverse challenges to knowledge claims that are the basis of reforms intended to alleviate practical social problems.

The response to Dunn's explication of social reforms as closer to arguments than experiments, Campbell agrees with the detail of the discussion while retaining a traditional scientific viewpoint. Even though he applies a dialectic notion to scientific knowledge, Campbell wants to uphold several of the tenets of a more traditional view of science. He suggests retention of a model of social science based on that of the physical sciences, the ideology of social experimentation, the concept of causality, a correspondence theory of truth, and the fact-value distinction. Campbell feels that his view of science has been ill characterized by the particular quotes Dunn has used. For example, he states that experimental variables and outcome measures are historically and dialectically indexed. To assume that scientists intend these variables and outcome measures as meaningful outside of a particular context or to all contexts is to distort the definition of experimentation.

Campbell spends a major part of his response arguing for the retention of the fact-value distinction, an issue that he suggests is mixed in Dunn's article. Campbell's position is to retain the distinction in order to expose value-biased distortions of knowledge claims. To retain such a distinction is to be aware of inevitable epistemological relativism and to use that notion to achieve objectivity, or so Campbell suggests. Otherwise one must abandon the quest for truth, a position that Campbell seems to attribute to Dunn. Campbell concludes by conceding most of Dunn's points although it remains difficult to discern what the marriage of the two sets of ideas might look like.

The last article in this section is a comprehensive and cogent discussion of the utilization of evaluation studies. These five vignettes demonstrate that use is a much broader and amorphous concept. Rather than identifying a specific use of evaluation, Weiss contends that it is more likely that a body of studies will converge on a theme and generalizations made as a result of this hazy, ill-defined body of knowledge. Weiss's suggestion is that use should be defined broadly in looking at evaluation studies.

Given this broad conception of use, Weiss outlines in the last half of the article how one might set about studying use. One can focus on studies, people, issues, or organizations to examine the utilization of evaluation. In each case the focus of attention implies a certain methodological strategy, and each strategy has its own limitations and sets of questions that can and cannot be answered. Her conclusion is that none of these strategies is sufficient alone and that the larger issue of use can be understood only through the employment of mixed strategies and multiple perspectives. Such advice probably applies to evaluation studies as well as to the study of utilization of evaluation findings.

1

Summary of
Program Evaluation in Education:
When? How? To What Ends?

Senta A. Raizen and Peter H. Rossi

Evaluation as an established field of applied social
science research has grown rapidly over the last 20
years, accompanied by the expectation that the empirical
knowledge resulting from evaluation studies would improve
the process of making decisions about social programs.
In education, more than $40 million is now spent per year
for evaluation activities by the Department of Education;
about $60 million more in federal funds is spent by other
federal agencies and by state and local agencies. But as
the number of evaluation studies and their sophistication
have grown, so has concern that evaluation work has not
lived up to its potential. In response to such concerns
on the part of Congress, the Committee on Program
Evaluation in Education examined four aspects of
evaluation in education: the varieties of evaluation and
their respective roles; the quality of evaluation
efforts; the use of evaluation results; and the
organization and management of evaluation activities. We
focused on these topics because they were identified to
be of greatest interest to the two primary audiences for
our report: members of Congress and their staffs and
high-level officials in the Department of Education.

FINDINGS AND CONCLUSIONS

Two major findings permeate the Committee's report.
First, evaluation must be viewed as a system that
involves many organizations and many parties. Attempts
to improve the quality of evaluation studies or to
increase the use of evaluation results must deal with

Reproduced from *Program Evaluation in Education: When? How? To What Ends?* National
Academy Press, Washington, D.C., 1981.

systemic problems rather than with the specific
shortcomings of any individual evaluation. Therefore,
much of this report deals with such systemic issues as
the role of evaluation, the context in which it takes
place, and the diverse interests of the many groups
concerned with federal education programs. Second, both
the quality and the use of evaluations could be
considerably enhanced through better management
procedures. At present, the processes for soliciting and
funding studies constrain creativity; quality controls
are insufficient; limited review procedures at all stages
inhibit the development of an active intellectual
marketplace--the most effective arbiter of quality and
use. Hence, most of our recommendations are designed to
improve the procedures that now govern federally funded
evaluations in education. Improvement in management
procedures is the single most important step that
Congress and the Department could take if they wish to
achieve better quality in evaluations and to increase the
likelihood that evaluation results will be used
appropriately.

The Role of Evaluation

To understand what evaluation can contribute to the
making of policy, one must understand its limited role in
affecting decisions that are largely shaped by other
forces. In any political decision, many parties with
diverse interests are likely to have a stake, and
evaluators are often asked to respond to several
audiences and competing constituencies. Even though
evaluations are frequently conducted at the behest of
governmental authorities making decisions about programs,
other audiences will respond to evaluation information as
well and use or not use it as it furthers their
objectives. Different audiences have need for different
types of information; different policy issues require
different types of studies. Unless the policy questions
to be addressed are clear to those who ask for
evaluations and to those who carry them out, the
perception that much evaluation work is irrelevant to the
policy process is likely to persist.
    The diversity of research activities all going under
the general name of evaluation has led to considerable
misunderstanding. The diversity has come about because
it has become evident that studying the effectiveness of

operating programs--the traditional focus of
evaluation--does not answer some important questions;
research is also needed in planning and implementing
programs. During the planning phase, there are questions
of need and how to meet those needs. Survey and
ethnographic studies can establish the extent and
distribution of an educational problem; controlled pilot
testing and field tests can determine the effectiveness
and feasibility of alternative interventions for
relieving the problem; and economic analyses can be used
to make cost estimates. Once a program is established
and operating, there are questions of fiscal and coverage
accountability. Analyses of administrative records can
determine whether funds are being used properly and
whether the program is reaching the intended
beneficiaries, although supplementary fiscal audits and
beneficiary studies are sometimes required. Finding out
whether the program is being implemented appropriately
requires, in addition to program administrative records,
special surveys of program services and ethnographic
studies. Finally, there are questions of program impact;
they can be addressed definitively only through rigorous
and often costly research methods. Consequently impact
evaluation should be undertaken only if the requisite
skills and resources are available.

Not all programs can be fully evaluated: that is, not
all questions can be answered for all programs. In
particular, meaningful impact evaluation is possible only
for programs for which intended beneficiaries and effects
can be clearly specified. There are two kinds of
programs for which such specification is extremely
difficult or impossible. For a program having vague
goals or many diverse goals, evaluators and those who
commission an evaluation must be able to agree on which
goal should be assessed and whether appropriate measures
are available to assess it. For a program in which local
sites are given autonomy to develop their own specific
objectives and means of reaching them, one cannot
evaluate for national impact by aggregating effects over
many diverse sites (though the effectiveness of
individual local projects may be evaluated). General
judgments about a national program become possible over
time, however, as knowledge from studies of individual
sites accumulates.

In an effort to increase the quality of information
furnished through local evaluations, Congress has sought
to encourage uniformity of methods and measurements in

evaluation. At this time, the Committee does not consider such uniformity an appropriate means for controlling quality, since requiring uniformity may prematurely inhibit further advances in methodology. Instead, evaluation methods should be subjected to the full test of the intellectual marketplace through intensive review and critique.

Improving the Quality of Evaluations

The few systematic or informal surveys of evaluation studies in education give some credence to the frequently voiced dissatisfaction with the general level of their quality. There appear to be several reasons that the quality of evaluations in education has been found wanting. First, the unrealistic expectation that complicated evaluation issues can be addressed by a wide variety of agencies has led to some inappropriate assignments of evaluation responsibility. For example, only a few large and sophisticated school systems and a handful of states have the capacity to carry out rigorous studies of program impact. In addition, the objectivity that is necessary for good evaluation is sometimes compromised at the state and local levels because much of the evaluation funding, though supplied by the federal government, is controlled by local program managers or state administrators. Evaluation requirements imposed on local and state authorities should match their capabilities, and fiscal and organizational arrangements should foster the integrity of local and state studies.

A second reason for the low quality of evaluations arises from the way in which federal evaluation activities in education are managed. Though the amount of money spent on evaluation represents only about 0.5 percent of the total federal support for education, it is a major source of income for private-sector research firms; moreover, evaluation work is heavily concentrated among the larger of those firms. This concentration has come about because of the current procedures for sponsoring and carrying out evaluations. Procurement documents are highly complex and often include detailed specifications on the various technical aspects of evaluation. Internal planning procedures and design of requests for proposals (RFPs) take so long that little time is left for response. Universities, minority firms, and small businesses, unlike large firms, are unable or

unwilling to compete under such conditions. The lack of
diversity among evaluation contractors reduces the
possibility of new ideas entering the evaluation system
and thereby improving it. Perspectives of beneficiary
populations, in particular, are underrepresented on both
the sponsor and the performer sides.

Flexibility in evaluation, which could contribute to
quality, has also been reduced because of emphasis in the
past on large studies. The restrictions on creativity
imposed by this approach are aggravated when a single
individual or small group within the Department develops
the main procurement instrument, as is usually the case.
An additional constraint on flexibility and creativity is
the current monitoring process, which makes it difficult
to adjust the course of a study because of changed field
conditions or because a different research direction is
warranted.

A third explanation for problems of quality is that
the intellectual marketplace for appraisal and scrutiny
of evaluations has yet to be fully formed. Generally,
there is no review by outside experts during the
procurement phase when the main elements of a study are
being designed; the lack of diversity among competitors
for evaluation work further inhibits opportunities for
the marketplace to operate; and, upon completion of a
study, external review of final reports happens only
sporadically. Institutional mechanisms for encouraging
ample discussion by experts and parties at interest of
plans for and findings of major studies are spotty at the
federal level; they are largely absent at the state and
local levels.

Using the Results of Evaluation

A frequently voiced criticism of evaluation is that
evaluation findings are seldom used. Implicit in this
criticism is the notion that utilization means direct and
often immediate changes in policy and program. In fact,
there are several different types of utilization, not all
immediately apparent. Moreover, the dissemination of
findings does not automatically lead to utilization, nor
is utilization synonymous with change.

Evaluation findings may be used for making specific
changes at a given time, as commonly envisaged in
discussions of utilization. Findings may also be used to
confirm that changes are not needed. But information may

also be considered and not used because it is inappropriate or because the indicated directions for policy are infeasible. Moreover, even when there is no immediately discernible use of knowledge derived from evaluations, it cumulates over time and is slowly absorbed, eventually leading to changes in concepts and decision perspectives.

There are important limits to the use of evaluation results in the short run. Social problem solving is and ought to be a political process; the forces and events impinging on decisions about programs are often more powerful than empirically derived evidence. The environment in which decisions are made seldom permits swift and unilateral action; new information may actually slow down the process, since it may make decisions more complicated. For these reasons, while evaluators and sponsors should do their best to disseminate evaluation findings, they cannot ensure utilization.

Dissemination can be improved in a number of ways, however. At the very least, evaluation results must be communicated to the primary audience. Copies of reports must be available; primary data should be accessible for reanalysis. Unfortunately, none of these minimal dissemination steps is now routine. Assuming that information is made available, other important factors affecting its use include whether it is perceived to be objective and whether it is structured and reported in a way that is relevant to potential users. Timeliness is also important, particularly when direct application to specific decisions is intended.

Because evaluation results are more likely to be used when they address issues of importance to specific audiences, concern with the use of evaluation findings cannot begin when final reports are ready to be disseminated. The primary audience and its information needs of a given evaluation should be identified at the inception of the study. Such initial identification will help define the type of evaluation to be undertaken, the issues to be addressed, the sort of information to be collected, and the form of reporting and communication that is likely to be most effective. The language of evaluation reports is often a barrier to use: reports must be intelligible to the intended audience(s) and should be augmented by more informal means of communication, including person-to-person interpretation of results. Linking mechanisms that mediate between researcher and audience can facilitate the spread of knowledge and the utilization process.

Organizing and Managing Evaluation Activities

The Department of Education has accountability and
oversight responsibilities with regard to federal
education programs and must carry out evaluation
activities that address those responsibilities. The
Department should also develop knowledge about programs
that can be used to improve both their management and
their contribution to more effective education. Finally,
the Department should be able to formulate new programs
based on tested alternatives that speak to unmet needs in
education.

At present, evaluation responsibilities are assigned
to several different units within the Department, and to
state and local agencies. Fiscal audits and
investigations on compliance with civil rights laws are
appropriately carried out by offices created specifically
for these functions. Similarly, local and state agencies
are appropriately responsible for supplying fiscal and
beneficiary information needed to administer federal
programs. However, the assignment of other types of
evaluation responsibilities among levels of government
and within the Department varies remarkably from program
to program, despite the existence of a central evaluation
unit.

Though some decentralization of activities is
appropriate, assignment of responsibilities should be on
a more systematic and purposeful basis. The Committee
suggests the following guidelines:

• Collection of information on beneficiaries served
and on allocation of resources should continue to be a
requirement for state and local agencies. When agencies
do not have adequate capability for accurate reporting,
technical assistance ought to be provided. An important
caveat is that reporting requirements should not generate
more information than can be digested at the level
(federal or state) receiving the reports. No requirement
should be imposed on all state and local agencies that
goes beyond the basic reporting needed for accountability
functions, such as studies of program effects and
cost-effectiveness analyses. Such studies should be done
on a national sample basis or by selected local or state
agencies of proven competence and with sufficient
resources.

• The Inspector General should continue to have
responsibility for fiscal audits. Coverage of
beneficiaries and program delivery should be monitored by
the officials who administer programs at the federal
level, but the central evaluation unit should, from time
to time, run independent studies as checks. As its major
responsibilities, the central evaluation unit should, in
cooperation with the program units, carry out studies to
establish whether and how specific programs can be
evaluated, sponsor documentation of program process and
implementation, and support studies aimed at the
improvement of existing programs or the development of
new ones. The research office of the Department should
help administer grant programs for evaluation studies and
support research on the methods and processes of
evaluation.

Decentralizing evaluation responsibilities to any
degree creates the problem of how evaluation dollars can
be used effectively when they are dispersed among three
levels of government and among many of the Department's
units. First, adequate reporting of evaluation
activities and expenditures must be instituted at all
levels and for all units. Second, the central evaluation
unit should be responsible for the coordination of
evaluation throughout the Department, particularly with
respect to planning and reporting procedures. The unit
should also provide technical assistance and review for
the design and procurement of individual studies done by
other units, and it should be responsible for a
systematic process of review of interim and final reports
by inside and outside experts. A special dissemination
branch within the central unit should help other offices
with dissemination of findings from evaluation studies.
The central evaluation unit will not be able to carry
out effectively the suggested evaluation and coordination
responsibilities as long as it is subsumed within the
management arm of the Department. The implicit message
of this organization is that only the management
perspective of evaluation is important. The Committee
believes that evaluation must address the substance of
policies and programs, not only their management.
Therefore, administrative arrangements should be changed
so as to give top decision makers within the Department
more direct access to the central evaluation unit.

RECOMMENDATIONS

The Committee has two sets of recommendations, one for Congress and one for the Department. The recommendations are presented and the discussion of them summarized in the following two sections; the chapter numbers in parentheses indicate where the more detailed discussions are found.

Recommendations to Congress

The first recommendation to Congress is concerned with obtaining a better match between the information that results from evaluation studies and the information that is useful in making decisions about programs. The next three recommendations, C-2, C-3, and C-4, are intended to improve oversight and accountability for evaluations carried out with funds from federal education programs. The last recommendation to Congress addresses management constraints external to the Department.

Recommendation C-1. When Congress requests evaluations, it should identify the kind of question(s) to be addressed. (Chapter 2)

   Given the diversity of evaluation activities misunderstandings about what information is needed have frequently arisen between Congress and the Department and its evaluation contractors. Congress should attempt to make more explicit whether it needs information about program services, about program coverage, about program impact, or about other program aspects. Such clarity will make it more likely that useful information will be delivered as a result of an evaluation effort. The primary audience(s) for the results of the requested evaluations should also be identified, since different audiences need different types of information.
   Clarity of congressional intent can be brought about in two ways. When specificity about questions and audiences is not possible ahead of time, evaluation staff within the Department need to engage in a continuing dialogue with members of Congress and their staffs to refine the policy issues to be addressed. Alternatively, legislative language can specify such issues when Congress wants specific information. Legislative

language regarding evaluation should refrain, however,
from specifying details of research method (such as
sampling procedure or use of control groups) or of
measurement. The choice of methods depends in part on
specific evaluation conditions and contexts and should be
done by technical experts only after careful
consideration of all facets of an evaluation.

Recommendation C-2. Congress should separate funding for
evaluations conducted at the state and local levels from
program and administrative funds. (Chapter 3)

Under present circumstances, the amount of money
invested and the kind of evaluation done at the state and
local levels is, in too many instances, controlled by
those who administer and run programs. This puts the
quality and integrity of state and local evaluation
activities in jeopardy. Moreover, the current
arrangement makes it impossible to know how much of the
federal funds potentially available for evaluation are
actually used for that purpose. Congress may also wish
to consider a percentage set-aside for evaluation of
programs at the state and local levels, as is now
legislated for a number of programs at the national level.

Recommendation C-3. Congress should institute a
diversified strategy of evaluation at the state and local
levels that would impose minimum monitoring and
compliance requirements on all agencies receiving federal
funds but allow only the most competent to carry out
complex evaluation tasks. (Chapter 3)

All state and local agencies receiving federal funds
for education programs should be required to provide an
accounting of the distribution of funds and of
beneficiary coverage for each program. When specific
services and procedures are mandated, these should also
be subject to reports to ensure compliance. The Congress
should require the Department to institute appropriate
quality control procedures to raise the quality of state
and local data. Evaluation tasks that go beyond
accountability questions, however, should only be
required of state and local units on a highly selective
basis. Congress may wish to consider authorizing a
competitive grants program, possibly administered through

the National Institute of Education, for school systems
and states that would provide for funding a few of the
most technically promising proposals for impact
assessments of local programs or for program improvement
based on evaluation of alternative program strategies.

Recommendation C-4. Congress should require an annual
report from the Department of Education on all evaluation
expenditures and activities. (Chapter 3)

The annual evaluation report currently required from
the Department should be expanded to cover all federally
funded evaluation activities in education, including all
of those in the Department as well as those carried out
by state and local agencies. Expenditures at all levels
should be specified; activities, findings, and their use
should be briefly described.

Recommendation C-5. Congress should authorize a study
group to analyze the combined effects of the legislative
provisions and executive regulations that control
federally funded applied research. (Chapter 5)

One of the causes of the lack of timeliness and
relevance of evaluation studies is the accumulation of
rules and regulations governing the whole process of
funding and carrying out applied research in the social
service area. While almost every provision now on the
books or enforced through executive practice is there to
provide some safeguard and may be reasonable when
considered in isolation, in the aggregate they have
negative effects. The trade-offs between the benefits of
the safeguards and the obstacles they create against
producing timely and relevant applied research at
reasonable cost deserve careful scrutiny. Simplification
and reform may be in order.

Recommendations to the Department of Education

The recommendations to the Department concentrate on
management issues for two reasons. First, as noted, we
believe that the quality of evaluations could be
considerably improved and the use of evaluation findings
increased through better management procedures. Second,

the Department has the power to change many of its current operating procedures, while it may be able to do relatively little about such external constraints as the development of the evaluation field, the size of its budget, or agency personnel ceilings. The recommendations on procedures are organized into those intended to develop better strategies for overall evaluation planning within the Department and for planning individual studies; those intended to increase the quality of evaluations, including three on training and technical assistance; and those intended to facilitate use. The last three recommendations speak to improvements needed in general management procedures.

On Evaluation Strategy

Recommendation D-1. In evaluations initiated by the Department of Education, the kinds of evaluation activities to be carried out should be specified clearly and should be justified in terms of program development or program implementation. (Chapter 2)

This recommendation is analogous to Recommendation C-1 to Congress. It emphasizes the need to think through what type of evaluation activity is appropriate to any given stage of planning or implementation of a proposed program or an existing program. For example, top-level Department officials need to specify what they wish to know about a program, why they wish to know it at some specified time, and what audiences other than themselves have information needs that must be satisfied through evaluation activities. All these needs must be coordinated with legislated requests for evaluation. (See also Recommendation D-10 on planning.)

Recommendation D-2. When pilot tests of proposed major programs are conducted, pilot tests of evaluation requirements should be conducted simultaneously to determine their feasibility and appropriateness. (Chapter 2)

While pilot tests of a program are being made, it is a relatively easy matter to pilot-test the proposed evaluation. Such a pilot test can be used to find out what measurements can and cannot be made of program benefits, how programs should account for and measure costs, which testing instruments and procedures are disruptive and which are not, how large a sample of beneficiaries is needed to get valid program measurements, and so forth. If a pilot test of an evaluation were carried out in conjunction with the pilot test of a program, the design of both the program and of the evaluation requirements would be strengthened.

Recommendation D-3. The National Institute of Education should continue and strengthen its program of support for research in evaluation methods and processes. (Chapter 2)

The advances made in the technical aspects of evaluation have been considerable, but uneven. The Committee believes that too much attention has been given to investigating problems in the use of randomized controlled experiments. Other important problems in methodology have not received sufficient attention, for example, methods for studying the delivery of services, for investigating the properties of achievement tests when used in the evaluation of programs, and for assessing the impact of programs that cannot be studied through the usual experimental paradigms. Another neglected area of research is the process of evaluation itself: how studies are commissioned and initiated, how they are managed, what laws and procedures impinge upon them. The Committee's work indicates that current procedures constrain the quality and the use of evaluations, but how these processes operate is poorly understood; therefore, it is difficult to design effective remedies.

On Quality, Training, and Technical Assistance

Recommendation D-4. The Department of Education should provide funds for training programs in evaluation to increase the skills of individuals currently charged with carrying out or using evaluations and to increase the participation of minorities. (Chapter 3)

The field of evaluation has grown more rapidly than the pool of skilled evaluators. As a consequence, there are many people working as evaluators whose training has been haphazard and inadvertent and who may not be fully familiar with more recent advances in techniques and methods. Others may lack adequate knowledge of the educational system or of the special needs of the groups to be helped by federal education programs.

A primary training need concerns the underrepresentation of minority group members in the educational evaluation enterprise. Well over half of all education programs target minority group persons as recipients of services. The Committee believes that the quality of evaluation would be improved by the employment of minority persons who are also well trained technically. For example, intimate personal knowledge of the circumstances of beneficiaries will help to define outcome measures that are more relevant to beneficiaries and more closely related to improving the effectiveness of programs. Hence, we believe that such perspectives should be represented to the fullest extent possible in the evaluation of such programs. Fellowships and internship programs in evaluation that include specific priorities for minority group persons would be doubly valuable; they would produce good researchers and they would enrich the evaluation system.

A second concern related to training is the relationship between the evaluator and the administrator or educator. The communication gap between the two that inhibits the use of evaluation may be narrowed by appropriate training on both sides. Executives and program staff would benefit from greater knowledge of the language of evaluation and how evaluation might be used; evaluators need exposure to the problems, procedures, and constraints of federal education programs. Evaluators also need to improve interpersonal and communications skills in order to convey evaluation information effectively.

Technical training for evaluation staff is also necessary, both within the federal government and at the state and local levels. There have never been sufficient numbers of staff trained in either rigorous evaluation methods or in research, and there have been rapid developments in the field. Evaluation is currently practiced by those from almost every type of background possible, including many with no more preparation than that of classroom teaching. Practicing evaluators need opportunities to upgrade and improve their skills. As one way of meeting this need, the Department should consider funding short-term institutes and conferences providing up-to-date knowledge to the evaluation

community. (See also Recommendation D-17 on training
opportunities for federal staff.)

Recommendation D-5. The Department of Education should
structure the procurement and funding procedures for
evaluations so as to permit more creative evaluation work
by opening up the process and allowing a period for
exploratory research. (Chapter 3)

The more complex the evaluation, the less likely is it
that one can spell out ahead of time the best methods for
addressing the questions that the evaluation is designed
to answer. The current RFP process in particular ignores
this fact. The Committee believes that the RFP process
can be made more flexible. RFPs for large studies should
include a period of exploratory research; they should
also provide for side studies that address questions
integral to the evaluation that emerge after it is under
way. Proposers should be given the freedom to specify
alternative methods and to suggest side studies. Most
important, sufficient time for developing proposals must
be allowed.

Mechanisms other than RFPs for funding evaluations can
also be used to open up the system. For example,
unsolicited and solicited proposals, 8-A contracting,
cooperative agreements, basic ordering agreements, and
grant awards are each appropriate to given evaluation
tasks. The Committee's recommendation that a greater
variety of funding methods be employed does not imply
that the use of RFPs be drastically reduced. Flexibility
in the award process, we believe, will permit the
introduction of new ideas that may contribute to
higher-quality evaluations. Flexibility will also allow
greater participation by minority organizations and
researchers.

Recommendation D-6. All major national evaluations
should be reviewed by independent groups at the design,
award, and final report stages. Review groups should
include representatives of minorities and other consumers
as well as technical experts. The results of their
review should be made broadly available. (Chapter 3)

This recommendation also is intended to open up the
process. There are three facets to it: improving the

technical quality of evaluations, assuring early
contribution and involvement from those most affected by
programs (beneficiary groups, teachers, etc.), and making
use of findings more likely through public exposure and
understanding.

When the RFP process is used, the agency itself should
solicit as much outside advice as possible, through
development of concept papers, planning conferences, and
other pre-RFP activities. Proposal evaluation and
selection procedures should include experts from outside
the sponsoring agency. After award of a contract, the
contractor also should solicit the views of outsiders.
Then, when the project is done, outsiders should again
review the work, its assumptions, its technical
ambiguities, and its policy implications. Reviews of
completed work should be widely disseminated in order to
encourage discussions of the findings. The Department
might sponsor an annual conference on important
evaluations that are at various points--design,
completion of final report, reanalysis. If this were
done, the educational community would know where to look
for the latest evaluation results and criticisms and be
apprised of impending work.

Recommendation D-7. All statistical data generated by
major evaluations should be made readily available for
independent analysis after identifying information on
individual respondents has been deleted. (Chapter 3)

When possible, ethnographic data and case study
material, similarly treated to protect privacy and
confidentiality, should also be made available.

Making primary data from evaluations available will
require support in major evaluation contracts for
documentation, storage, and dissemination of data and the
creation of explicit agency policy on access to data.
Since the objective is to generate adequate examination
of the methods and findings of major evaluation studies,
independent review and reanalysis should be supported by
the Department as part of its evaluation and research
programs.

Recommendation D-8. The Department of Education should
explore alternative approaches to technical assistance
for state and local evaluation needs. (Chapter 3)

The technical assistance needs of state and local
agencies are not uniform. They vary with the size of the
agency, the sophistication of the agency's evaluation
staff, and with the complexity of the federal program
activity in the agency. The technical assistance centers
associated with Title I are one approach to meeting such
needs. Another approach would be to identify or fund
exemplary models of monitoring and reporting and to
disseminate the procedures involved. A third approach
would be to develop the capability of state agencies to
provide technical assistance to less sophisticated local
agencies.

Technical assistance should also cover organizational
and personnel issues. In particular, state and local
agencies need to be aware of the desirability of
separating an evaluation unit from program administration
in order to avoid conflicts of interest. Work already
done by some state and local agencies on optimal
institutional arrangements, personnel requirements, and
procurement policies for extramural work can form the
basis of advice and assistance to others. (See also
Recommendation D-16 on minimum requirements for
monitoring and compliance reporting.)

On Utilization

Recommendation D-9. The Department of Education should
test various mechanisms for providing linkage between
evaluators and potential users. (Chapter 4)

The Department should consider establishing a unit
charged with studying, developing, and instituting
knowledge transfer mechanisms and evaluating their
effectiveness. Alternatively, outside experts might be
charged with this responsibility. Appropriate activities
would include assessing proposed dissemination plans,
performing needed translations of evaluation reports,
funding research on the communication and use of
evaluation information, and developing procedures
designed to improve the day-to-day use of evaluation
data, at least within the Department.

Recommendation D-10. The Department of Education should institute a flexible planning system for evaluations of federal education programs. (Chapter 4)

A workable planning system must provide for appropriate information to be available for recurring legislative decision cycles on education programs; it must accommodate an ongoing program of evaluation studies addressing problems that are poorly understood, and it must be sufficiently flexible to allow response to interesting but unanticipated questions that arise as a result of ongoing research, changes in policy, or development of new programs. The evaluation plan for any major education program should contain a series of linked studies, some of which furnish factual information in reasonably short time and some of which address issues of long-term interest.

Although planning does not necessarily lead to an agenda that is subsequently carried out in detail, planning almost always leads to an improved sense of priorities, provides a forum in which competing interests can reach accommodations, and induces an active as opposed to a reactive stance toward essential activities.

Recommendation D-11. The Department of Education should establish a quick-response capability to address critical but unanticipated evaluation questions. (Chapter 4)

In order to be fully responsive to the information needs of its primary audiences, the Department must be able to combine a deliberative planning process that allows time for field and constituency involvement with a quick-response capability that can address unanticipated but critical evaluation questions as they arise. Department staff charged with evaluation responsibilities should be able to respond within 2-6 months to evaluation-related questions to which Congress or top-level Department officials seek prompt answers. Several extramural mechanisms are available for this purpose, for example, maintaining lists of prequalified contractors who can be given specific task orders on short notice or using 8-A contracts and awards to SBA-eligible firms.

Recommendation D-12. The Department of Education should ensure that evaluations deal with topics that are relevant to the likely users. (Chapter 4)

In order to increase the relevance of evaluation results, primary audience(s) must be specified prior to the beginning of a study. When conditions change during the course of a study that might affect the usability of the findings, study objectives and design should be reconsidered to ensure that the study will remain relevant. Efforts should be made to deliver reports on time, especially when study results are intended for decisions that are made at specified times.

Recommendation D-13. The Department of Education should ensure that dissemination of evaluation results achieves adequate coverage. (Chapter 4)

All RFPs and grant announcements should include requirements for a dissemination plan oriented toward utilization, and proposal evaluation should give appropriate weight to the quality of the proposed dissemination plan. Dissemination plans should include specification of audiences and their information needs, strategies for reaching the audiences, provision for an adequate number of report copies and other materials, and mechanisms for adapting the dissemination plan as the study proceeds. Budget negotiations should recognize that adequate dissemination is costly and cannot be an afterthought.

Recommendation D-14. The Department of Education should observe the rights of any parties at interest and the public in general to information generated about public programs. (Chapter 4)

Findings from evaluations must be made available to those who are importantly affected by the programs being evaluated, including those who manage them, those who provide program services, and those who are intended to benefit (or their representatives). Since evaluations are paid for with public funds, they should also be made available to the public at large. The Committee is aware of the dangers in providing too much autonomy to evaluation units and contractors, but public interest

needs suggest that, at the dissemination stage,
evaluators should be guaranteed a certain degree of
autonomy. Appropriate changes should be made in contract
provisions to allow contractors and grantees the
necessary flexibility with regard to distribution of
reports and other dissemination strategies.

Recommendation D-15. The Department of Education should
give attention to the identification of "right-to-know"
user audiences and develop strategies to meet their
information needs. (Chapter 4)

   Perhaps the most neglected audience for evaluation
studies consists of program beneficiaries and their
representatives. We believe that this neglect is not so
much intentional as it is produced by the very real
difficulties of defining this set of audiences in a
reasonable way. In order to more closely approximate the
ideal that all those having a recognized interest in a
program should have reasonable access to evaluation
results, the Department should consider dissemination of
evaluation reports freely to groups and organizations
that claim to represent major classes of beneficiaries of
education programs. Positive, active dissemination to
such right-to-know groups may include such specific
activities as ascertaining their information needs prior
to evaluation design and during the evaluation, preparing
standard lists of groups and organizations to whom
evaluation results are routinely disseminated, and
seeking out comments and critiques of evaluation
reports. Since it is to be expected that such
right-to-know groups will be different for different
evaluations, careful consideration of the appropriate
right-to-know groups should be part of the dissemination
plans that contractors are asked to prepare as part of
their response to RFPs and grant announcements.

On General Management

Recommendation D-16. The Department of Education should
clearly spell out minimum requirements for monitoring and
compliance reporting and set standards for meeting the
requirements. (Chapter 5)

Such data items as distribution of funds, number and
types of beneficiaries being served, and specific program
services should be defined by the Department so that
local and state agencies will know exactly what reporting
is required of them. Quality control procedures should
be enforced so that adequate performance reports can be
made to Congress. Before setting the requirements,
however, the Department needs to examine its own capacity
to deal with local and state reports in order to avoid
collecting information that is never used because of the
sheer inability of federal staff to deal with the volume
of reports. The objective of this recommendation is to
improve the quality of data needed for accountability
without increasing the burden of response on local and
state agencies. To accomplish both ends, admittedly
somewhat difficult to reconcile, the Department should
consider appropriate development research on what kinds
of procedures would minimize response burden and at the
same time ensure sufficient data quality.

Recommendation D-17. The Department of Education should
examine staff deployment and should establish training
opportunities for federal staff responsible for
evaluation activities or for implementation of evaluation
findings. (Chapter 5)

The Department should consider alternative ways of
using the technical staff within the central unit and the
evaluation staff in other units. The greater the degree
of government involvement in an activity, the greater the
skills and the greater the number of personnel required:
grants and consultancies entail the least involvement,
contracts and evaluation teams configured of government
staff and outside experts more, and in-house studies the
most. The Department should examine the number and types
of positions assigned in light of responsibilities and
workload. It should also examine the academic and
experience background of personnel charged with
evaluation responsibilities. Such personnel should be

well grounded in the theory and methodology of relevant social science disciplines; they should be aware of the perspectives of the various parties at interest; and they should have practical program knowledge. Suitable training programs should be made available to prepare staff members adequately for their tasks.

Recommendation D-18. The Department of Education should take steps to simplify procedures for procuring evaluation studies, carrying them out, and disseminating their findings. (Chapter 5)

The Committee is aware that our recommendations for opening up the system and for involving minority groups and other parties at interest during various phases will complicate and prolong the evaluation process. However, we firmly believe that this can be more than compensated for by simplifying and improving internal management procedures now used by the Department.

The procurement process has become not only restrictive and inflexible but very costly in internal staff time and to proposers, though the cost to proposers is recouped eventually through overhead and in other ways, so that the government bears the double burden. Other sources of delay, once a contract or grant for a study has been awarded, must also be identified and addressed. This applies particularly to clearance procedures and to monitor and agency handling of requests for changes in study design, sampling procedures, testing, analysis, time frame, and the like. The Department should consider sanctions and incentives to encourage timely performance, and it should hold itself responsible for timely dissemination.

Our call for timely performance on studies that are intended to feed into a specific legislative or management decision in no way invalidates the need for a more deliberative approach in certain cases. There are times, especially when an effort is being made to remedy a problem that is little understood, when it is more important to promote a variety of studies that explore emerging leads than to mount a formal study designed to provide a definitive answer by a specified date. Even in such cases, however, the pace should be set by the research process and concerns for its quality rather than by overly cumbersome management procedures.

2

A Peer Response
A Review of Program Evaluation in Education: When? How? To What Ends?

Robert E. Stake

It is not necessary to be upset by the book's title. The remainder of this book review will appear as if the book had been properly titled, perhaps as "Recommendations to Congress and the Department of Education for the Improvement of Program Evaluation." The fact that there is little in it distinguishing educational evaluation from other types of evaluation will be noted.

THE ASSIGNMENT

In 1978, Congress directed the Commissioner of Education to conduct a study of evaluation practices across the country with respect to federal support of education and to make recommendations:

(1) to ensure that evaluations are based on uniform methods and measurements,
(2) to ensure the integrity and independence of the evaluation process, and
(3) to ensure appropriate follow-up on the evaluations that are conducted.

The Commissioner called for the assistance of the National Academy of Sciences, which invited fourteen persons, most of them applied social scientists, to serve on a Committee on Program Evaluation in Education to conduct the study. An empirical study was not undertaken. The committee commissioned two papers, one on federal evaluation activities and one on the evaluation research community. It circulated contributed statements by several committee members. Some thirty federal officials were interviewed.

The recommendations submitted to the Commissioner were based on these exchanges, drawing heavily, of course, on previous experience those social scientists had in evaluation. The chairman of the committee, Peter Rossi, a distinguished sociologist and specialist in survey research, was during part of this period, president of the American Sociological Association. Senta Raizen, a research specialist well known and respected on the federal scene, was named director of the study. The committee categorized the issues and drew up 23 recommendations, 5 to Congress and 18 to the Department of Education. (These have been presented in the previous pages.)

From Robert E. Stake, "A Peer Response," original manuscript.

Four topics were discussed at length as background for the recommendations:

(1) alternative evaluation procedures,
(2) improving evaluation quality,
(3) making use of results effective, and
(4) improving federal management.

In mid-1981 the report was presented so as to be most relevant to persons having responsibility for furthering federal evaluation studies.

THE ISSUES

The magnificent encounter to be found between the lines of this report features the relentless force of congressional aides, bureaucrats, and social scientists to develop a useful flow of information about federal programs— against the inexorable and often localized circumstances that override efforts to offer a generic program and to generalize about program quality. The committee was sensitive to both force and circumstance. It was loyal to the research community, steadfastly implying good research is doable, yet ably identifying endless obstacles and unrealistic expectations regularly met. The struggle was not reconciled. To Congress's first demand (for uniformity), the response was clear: Evaluation should not be uniform at this time. "While the goal of attaining uniformity in evaluation methods and measures is an extremely desirable one, it cannot be attained at the present time without prematurely inhibiting further advances in the field of evaluation and stopping it short of needed development" (p. 4). A third issue was that of *preferred* design. In a recently completed parallel review of evaluation studies, committee member Robert Boruch had pressed for congressional insistence on randomized controlled experiments, when possible (Boruch and Cordray, 1980). The committee here rejected this view, noting the need for methods best suiting the program, issues, context, and evaluation resources available (p. 58).

The committee suggested that the integrity of evaluation studies could be upgraded three ways: (1) by contracting with more competent researchers, (2) by making federal handling of contracts less constraining on researchers, and (3) by increasing the frequency of expert review of completed studies (p. 4). As to ensuring better use of evaluations, the committee voiced need for better knowledge of user problems, language, and deadlines; more reliance on persons (rather than reports) to convey findings; wider distribution of reports; and making data more accessible for reanalysis.

But the committee took a strong stand against simplistic notions of utility, particularly the expectation that subsequent program-governing decisions should conform to evaluation results. With a deference often missing in evaluation methodological literature, the authors indicated that evaluation "should not substitute for the political process. . . . The best one can do is to make sure that evaluation findings are available to those who might want them and that the findings address the issues of concern in an understandable and responsible way" (p. 97).

JUDGMENT

The views are sound. Most evaluation specialists would agree with the definitions, the positions taken, and the recommendations. That does not make them entirely right, of course. Insightful and reasoned as this report is, it is in some ways biased and self-serving—and indifferent to whether or not fundamental educational questions are raised in educational program evaluation. The 23 brief statements of recommendation did not each describe well what in detail the committee was recommending. For example, D-3 appeared to call for further development of evaluation designing, but in amplification was calling for more diversification of design. Furthermore, many of the recommendations need to be interpreted in terms of what the Congress, the Department of Education, and the evaluation community were doing at the time.

To reflect upon the import of these recommendations eight questions were raised. These questions, answered for each of the 23, are presented in Table 1. Please note the modal answer for each question before continuing.

Only a very few of the recommendations are of questionable merit, but almost all of them are in some ways problematic. For example, extra attention to specification can isolate evaluation undesirably from ordinary governance. A few recommendations seemed to ask more from government than it usually is prepared to give, but most did not. By and large, the committee followed the line of making government more rational, and probably more amenable to technocratic control. Unrealistic expectations of the evaluation community did not frequent these pages. The net effect appeared to require further federal support for the evaluation profession, with that and other recommended operations leading to a substantial increase in the overall cost of evaluating. Foreseeing whether or not the anticipated benefits would exceed the several additional costs was beyond the ambition of this review.

SOCIAL SCIENCE PERSPECTIVES

An aspect of the recommendations to be considered next is whether or not the advice of social scientists is likely to be fully in the best interests of education. Throughout this report the evaluation studies to be federally supported were presumed to be "social-science-based" (p. 35). Not just rigorous, disciplined, and empirical, but accommodated to the aims and standards of social science research.

In *Designing Educational Evaluations* (1981), Lee Cronbach described how social science methods are in some ways little suited to answering the questions of program evaluation, especially because they seek often to minimize the interaction of context with outcome. And at the 1981 Annual Meeting of the

TABLE 1 The Reviewers Analysis of the 23 Recommendations

Recommendations:	C-1	C-2	C-3	C-4	C-5	D1	D2	D3	D4	D5	D6	D7	D8	D9	D10	D11	D12	D13	D14	D15	D16	D17	D18
1. Is there *merit* in this recommendation?	?	Y	Y	N	Y	N	Y	Y	Y	Y	Y	Y	Y	Y	Y	Y	Y	Y	Y	Y	?	Y	Y
2. Would it probably cause some *problems* too?	Y	Y	Y	Y	Y	Y	Y	?	Y	Y	Y	?	Y	Y	Y	Y	Y	Y	Y	Y	Y	Y	Y
3. Is it *impractical* to expect government to do this at this time?	N	?	Y	N	N	N	N	N	N	N	?	?	N	?	N	?	?	N	?	N	?	?	N
4. Is it supportive of a "*rational management*" view of government?	Y	Y	Y	Y	Y	Y	Y	?	Y	?	?	N	?	Y	?	Y	?	Y	?	?	Y	Y	?
5. Is the evaluation community *ready and able* to fulfill its responsibility here?	–	?	?	–	?	?	Y	Y	Y	Y	Y	?	Y	?	Y	?	?	?	Y	?	?	?	Y
6. Would this provide substantial *support* to the evaluation community?	N	Y	?	?	N	?	Y	Y	Y	Y	Y	?	Y	?	?	?	Y	Y	Y	Y	N	?	?
7. Would this recommendation substantially raise the *overall cost* of evaluation?	N	?	Y	?	?	N	Y	?	Y	Y	Y	Y	?	?	Y	?	?	Y	Y	Y	?	?	N
8. Does this recommendation deal with a fundamental *educational* question?	N	N	N	N	N	N	N	N	N	N	N	N	N	N	N	N	N	N	N	N	N	N	N

Evaluation Research Society, Michael Scriven chided evaluators for following too narrowly the social science line. There are countless social science methods. The personalities of social scientists span the range. How might social-science-based evaluations be biased?

In *all* studies reality is multiply approximated. In evaluating single programs, errors of approximation have less chance to balance out. Social scientists draw from their disciplines constructs they have found to be powerful in research, worrying less as to whether they fit the educational program. They search for relationships among indicators chosen to represent constructs, which will be the relationships they propose to explain the phenomena of the program. They have a confidence, sometimes an imperious confidence, that they are the finders and keepers of knowledge of social affairs, and that the words they choose and the approximations (indicators, relationships) they generate will be an improvement. Sometimes they do a poor job of representing the central ideas of a policy, a program, or an event. That they work with approximations is acknowledged, but the representations are insistently set forth as better approximations than experiential knowledge. The validation of the representations is seldom pursued.

For example, an "equal opportunity" program might be objected to as lowering "educational standards." A typical social science evaluator, realizing that opportunity is nebulous and subjective, chooses to represent it in terms of proportionality of different ethnic groups in the total enrollment. Educational standards are allowed to be indicated by standardized achievement test scores. It is presumed that an increased representation of minority students accompanied by a lower mean test score indicates that the program is indeed having the alleged ill effect. Of course, it appears less misrepresentative if *three* indicators of each construct are used.

Since personal knowledge of phenomena is circumstantial, and since basic knowledge is defined as generalizable across circumstance, it is presumed that the scientists' general construct is an improvement over what generalization might be extracted from close scrutiny of personal experience.

A typical response to a skeptic claiming the representation does not "fit" the program or policy is that "the people involved need to be educated as to how these research variables consistently underlie their program. They need to know how to talk about their program in those terms." And administrators do become "educated" and work toward the *management of indicators*—believing it to be an improvement over their previous thinking about problems and possible solutions. In his book *Beyond the Stable State,* Donald Schon said this evaluation approach could work only if social affairs recurred in something of a "stable state." Though aware of repetition and even occasional order in our lives, Schon saw each important social affair marked more by uniqueness than commonality. He said we cannot rely on "indicators" for understanding social affairs.

The social scientist's quest for generalization did not create the federal appetite for general understandings. Here it appeared with the increased expectation that education was not merely the responsibility of the classroom teacher or local board of education. Distant administrators came under increased obligation to take programmatic initiatives. But even in cases of great remoteness from the classroom, those officials too have—as well as general interests—particularistic interests: which goals, which populations of students, which funding, and so on.

Whether treating local effects as error variance or as a new main effect, the social scientist does remain alert to the great variance associated with particular sites. But the aim of social science is to reshape understanding the instance into understanding the universal. And that is its bias.

The search for grand understanding is sometimes harmful to the search for understanding the worth of a particular arrangement. Federal officials and everyone else need to balance knowledge of the particular with knowledge of the general. Social scientists regularly press toward the general. The social science perspective, insight and bias all, is not as apparent in the committee recommendations as in the body of the report. The recommendations themselves reflect the preference of some social scientists for careful explication and deference to expert judgment.

Occasionally, the learning toward explication is extravagant: "A prime requisite for being able to evaluate the impact of a program is the existence of clearly designated, specific aims (p. 51). And "Meaningful impact evaluation is possible only for programs for which intended beneficiaries and effects can be clearly specified" (p. 3). And "Questions of program impact can be addressed definitively only through rigorous and often costly research methods" (p. 3).

These three statements are not only untrue, they hold forth false promise. We should not believe that explication and expense assure good evaluation. There are many situations where goals and audiences can be specified, but for which the evaluators lack critical (successful) experience. Evaluator promises often leap beyond what the proposer has previously accomplished, and also beyond the attainment of anyone in the field. These empty promises are disparaged in this report, but not without leaving the implication that somewhere there are truly competent evaluators who can accomplish what federal officials want accomplished. Emphasis on evaluator training, design integrity, and expert review are not inappropriate, but such emphasis on technical knowledge serves to enhance the role of the evaluation researcher in federal affairs, and of course, to enhance the incomes of evaluators.

As persuasively discussed by Joe Bailey in *Ideas and Intervention: Social Theory for Practice* (1980): "In general the appeal by professionals to their knowledge base operates to mystify the nature of their practice, their relations with their clients and with threatening groups" (p. 30). This report, I believe, has insufficient skepticism about the contributions of the social sciences.

EDUCATION'S ISSUES

Emphasis on social science may also be problematic if it distracts from what I will call "fundamental educational questions."

The study was undertaken for the National Academy of Sciences by a committee composed for the most part of social scientists. It was a scholarly group, but not one of the fourteen should be considered a scholar of education. They often have worked in education, studying educational processes—but not education as a whole. Most of them are educators, several work for educational departments, and several do research regularly in educational settings. But it was mostly a group of social scientists, apparently without a spokesperson for education.

That may not be important. They still could have talked about whether or not present evaluation strategies and procedures engage fundamental educational questions. By my reading of the report, they did not.

What are some fundamental educational questions unlikely to be raised by social scientists doing program evaluation? Here are a few:

- Are the ideas being taught those that should be taught?
- What is the optimum sequence of courses?
- Is there a critical mass of attention to the topic so that complexity, contextuality, and dominant patterns are learned and so that advanced reasoning skills can be practiced?
- Does the program have aesthetic sense, a historical perspective, and an interdisplinary rationale?
- Is care taken to assure an ethic of humane living as part of the program?
- Can the personal virtue sought by these educators be taught?
- How does this program contribute to undesirable stereotyping of youth?
- Why would a teacher want to teach this way?

This is not to suggest that only educationists would raise these questions. It is merely to remind us that some important questions are not typically raised by social scientists. Should they have been raised by this committee? Perhaps not. Congress did not ask the commissioner about them. The committee was not asked if evaluations of programs were somehow lacking in concern for the deepest meanings of education. If fundamental educational questions *have* been ignored in federally funded evaluations, however, it would have been a nice time to mention it. Had Harry Broudy or Maxine Greene or Madeleine Grumet or David Tyack been on the committee, such questions would have come up.

It is a sign of the technological times that neither evaluators nor administrators nor committee members need be expert in that over which they have jurisdiction, merely that they be jurisprudent. "A real expert can be brought into testify, if needed." This report on program evaluation in education, according to the authors, was not intended to be a comprehensive examination of program evaluation of education. Various ways of making evaluation of federal programs more meaningful, credible, and useful were deliberated, and recommendations made. Though not as well rounded as it could have been, the report was thorough, creative, and largely well reasoned. It deserves not to be ignored.

REFERENCES

Bailey, Joseph. *Ideals and Intervention: Social Theory for Practice.* London: Routledge & Kegan Paul, 1980.

Cronbach, Lee J. *Designing Educational Evaluations.* San Francisco: Jossey-Bass, in press.

Boruch, Robert F. and Cordray, David S. *An Appraisal of Educational Program Evaluations: Federal, State, and Local Agencies.* Evanston, IL: Northwestern University, 1980.

Schön, Donald A. *Beyond the Stable State.* New York: Norton, 1971.

Scriven, Michael. "History and Future Directions of Program Evaluation." Paper presented at joint meeting of Evaluation Network and Evaluation Research Society, October 2, 1981.

3

Some Dissenting Comments on Stake's Review

Peter H. Rossi

Stake's review of the NAS-NCR Committee's report on federal program evaluation in education contains many complimentary remarks about the report and is partially accurate in its view about the report's contents. Hence, it is tempting to lie low and hope that readers will only retain those features of his review. But to do so would be irresponsible because Stake's review contains several inaccuracies and many misunderstandings concerning the nature of the committee's mission and the nature of evaluation research generally. This rejoinder is intended to point out where Stake has gone wrong. The reader should be advised that I cannot speak here for the committee since members were not consulted about the contents of this rejoinder: There simply was not time enough to do so.

There are many points of agreement between Robert Stake and myself, usually on matters of substance, but there are also many points of disagreement, usually on matters of interpretation. Perhaps the major dispute centers around "social science." Stake characterizes the committee as being composed of social scientists and the Committee's view of evaluation research as the application of social science research methods to evaluation issues. With both these perceptions I agree; the disagreement arises over their interpretation, and involves fundamentally different views of social science and its contributions to evaluation activities.

First of all, evaluation research is not equivalent to evaluation. To the extent that an evaluation is based on empirical evidence collected in ways that are susceptible to replication and treated with due regard to issues of internal, external, and construct validity, then the evaluation in question is evaluation research. The disciplines that have concerned themselves with the methodological problems of empirical research on social systems have been the social sciences (from which I would not exclude parts of education). Whether or not a given individual or organization engaging in evaluation research regards her/himself or itself as doing social science, he/she/it is nevertheless doing so. The evaluation research in question may be conducted very well or very poorly, but it is social science research.

This is not to deny the possible validity of a connoisseurial approach to evaluation, in which expert judgments based on eccentric (but insightful) observations play major roles. Indeed, such evaluations may be worth more per resources expended. But they are not social science nor are they evaluation research.

From Peter H. Rossi, "Some Dissenting Comments on Stake's Review," original manuscript.

Stake also takes social scientists to task for seeking to generalize and for ignoring the richness of the real world with all its interindividual, interorganizational, and intersite variances. Here again we agree on the substance: Social science does try to generalize and a social scientist feels rewarded when he or she can move some of the error variance from the numerator into the denominator in calculating F. But doing so is not the primary goal of the social scientist. All the error can be removed by exhausting degrees of freedom, i.e., treating each unit observed as a distinct entity, a fatuous strategy leading only to the useless knowledge that every unit is a distinctly different entity.

There may well be many interaction effects out there in the real world, but there is not much evidence for that view of the world. True, there is a lot of unexplained variance, but that is not direct evidence for interaction effects. It may be easy to mistake error variance for interaction effects, but to do so is to obscure rather than to advance knowledge.

Stake takes the committee to task because it did not address itself to "fundamental issues" of education. Here again we agree on substance: The committee did not address such issues. But, I would regard this not as a fault but as a virtue. To do so would be to intrude into the policymaking sphere. It is not up to evaluators, as such, be they social scientists or connoisseurs, to decide what should be the goals of public education in the United States, but it is their responsibility to explicate what are existing goals as embodied in programs in the course of designing evaluations. Evaluators are not philosopher-kings, should not aspire to be such, nor have they been selected to perform such roles. As a citizen and as an educator, I have some strongly held ideas about what such program goals should be, but as an evaluator I properly am concerned only with whether or not policies, programs, and projects match and reach whatever goals that have been set for them. I want the goals of our institutions to be set by the political process, illuminated by debate that is enriched by the commentaries of social philosophers, and mindful of the constraints on institutions and their functioning as uncovered by social scientists, but I do not want philosophers and social scientists as such determining policy. Indeed the committee report is quite explicit on this point.

Although the major point of disagreement between Stake and myself centers around differing views of the role of social science as discussed above, there are a number of other issues that I will briefly discuss below.

(1) The "Relentless Force": Reading between the lines of the report, Stakes uncovered traces of a "relentless force of Congressional aides, bureaucrats, and social scientists . . . to offer a generic program and to generalize about program quality." I simply do not know what Stake means by this statement, especially since I wrote many of the lines between which he has apparently discerned this message.

(2) The "Preferred Design": Stake understands (and applaudes) that the committee rejected the view that randomized experiments are the preferred

design for evaluations. Indeed, we believe that the committee helped to contribute to the growing consensus that there are many evaluation research tasks, to only some of which are randomized experiments appropriate. But, we did say that randomized experiments are to be preferred for testing new programs and for impact assessments of ongoing programs that provide such opportunities. We also pointed out that such designs are expensive, call for highly technical skills, and should not be used unless the talent and resources are available and that the resulting information is deemed worth the expense by policymakers.

(3) "Integrity": The issue of assuring the integrity of evaluation research was not addressed in the report, as Stake suggests, by recommending that "more competent researchers" be recruited to evaluation research tasks. Rather, we suggested that the federal government fostered lack of integrity in evaluation research by imposing impossible tasks on evaluation units that could not do even possible evaluation research tasks. As we saw it, the federal government built into its ways of procuring evaluation research "structured strains toward hypocrisy and fraud" (this phrase was actually edited out of the report). In particular, Congress was not always clear in defining evaluation tasks, fostering misunderstandings on the part of the Department of Education that eventually were reflected in RFPs to which evaluators of high integrity could not easily respond without dropping their standards. In addition, evaluation tasks were often imposed on LEA and SEA evaluation units that were far beyond their capacities to undertake. Specifically, programs that did not have clear goals or clearly defined target populations were impossible to evaluate through impact assessments. And, complicated tasks imposed on units with no evaluation research talent only led to evaluations of unbelievably poor quality.

(4) "Self-serving": At several points, Stake claims that the committee made statements that were self-serving (given that we were social scientists). I have no doubt that we were self-serving, but not in exactly the fashion Stake intimates. Our statements about the expense of impact assessment were merely to warn the federal officials that to do such studies well requires a lot of resources, and hence should not be undertaken lightly. We did not suggest, as Stake states, that only more money would ensure better impact assessments. Nor did we state that all evaluation research problems can be solved by the employment of better researchers and more money, as Stake also implies. Rather, we pointed out that it was not productive to ask for more than can be delivered, because hungry researchers might be tempted to offer to deliver the impossible (either out of ignorance or out of greed).

A final point: The evaluation of educational programs is no different in form from the evaluation of any other program. To claim otherwise is to establish a special discipline and technical expertise particular to that field. It may be comforting to be evaluated by your friends and neighbors, but it does not advance our knowledge of how programs work to claim that some kinds of programs need the special knowledge that only those who are "in the know" can provide. The evaluation of educational programs is too important to be left in the hands of educators alone.

4

Blaming the Victim
The Problem of Evaluation Design and Federal
Involvement, and Reinforcing World Views in Education

David M. Fetterman

THE PURPOSE OF THIS ARTICLE is to show how evaluation design and federal involvement in demonstration projects may unintentionally cause a negative appraisal. In the study I present here, misuse of the treatment-control design and federal bureaucratic intervention represent a comedy of errors. The maladaptive behavior pattern is a manifestation of a system of values, and a function of three reinforcing world views: the contract research corporation, the educational research establishment, and the federal bureaucracy. It is the interaction of these world views, rather than a specific methodology or bureaucratic behavior, that is the source of the problem.

I am currently responsible for the ethnographic component of a national evaluation. One of the tasks included reviewing a large sample of discretionary demonstration projects. Congress approved the Youth Employment Demonstration Project Act (YEDPA) legislation in 1977. The act assigned $1.6 billion to manpower programs for youth, and approximately $110 million was to be spent in discretionary demonstration efforts that would foster "knowledge development" in the area of training and employment of "disadvantaged youth."

Informal interviews were conducted with more than 50 program directors across the country, with particular emphasis on their evaluation designs. One demonstration project evaluation typifies the experience of many programs. This demonstration project is based on an exemplary school for unemployed high-school dropouts. The objective of the program is to provide dropouts with a career orientation and a high-school diploma by replicating the original model school in four different parts of the United States.

A federal agency developed a proposal to test whether this program could be set up in different communities and show as much effectiveness with the additional youths admitted to the program to qualify as a demonstration project. The project would last for two years. It would be funded by one federal agency, managed by a second, and implemented and evaluated by two separate private agencies. The implementor (or disseminator) selected is the parent organization of the prototype school for unemployed high-school dropouts.

David M. Fetterman is a Research Associate at RMC Research Corporation, Mountain View, California. He is also an anthropology instructor at Stanford University. He has not identified any individual or agency involved in this study, in order to maintain their anonymity. For the same reason, he delayed publishing the findings until all significant parties had transferred to new positions. He is indebted to his colleagues at RMC, G. D. Spindler, and Deborah Waxman for their generous assistance.

Federal sponsorship of youth programs, e.g., Youth Employment Demonstration Project Act (YEDPA) legislation, testifies to the federal bureaucracy's commitment to programs for "disadvantaged" or disenfranchised youth. Some of the significant problems encountered by those in the demonstration project under study, however, can be traced to the unintentionally harmful effects of the research design, federal involvement, and the evaluation itself. These problems are discussed in detail because, according to program directors throughout the United States, they typify the problems found by many other YEDPA programs. (The names of all parties concerned have been changed to ensure their anonymity. I also believe that it is more important to understand the principles underlying this problem than it is to identify specific individuals or agencies, which generally produces more heat than light. Finally, individuals and agencies represent means by which policies and world views are stated—their actions are the symptoms, not the causes, of a greater disorder.)

The concept of blaming the victim was first drawn into the social-science literature by Ryan (1971). He begins his book with a brief and comic explanation of the concept:

Twenty years ago, Zero Mostel used to do a sketch in which he impersonated a Dixiecrat Senator conducting an investigation of the origins of World War II. At the climax of the sketch, the Senator boomed out, in an excruciating mixture of triumph and suspicion, "What was Pearl Harbor doing in the Pacific?" This is an extreme example of Blaming the Victim [p. 3].

The main thrust of the first two chapters of Ryan's work, however, was to demonstrate how the folklore of cultural deprivation has been used to blame "the miseducated child in the slum schools."

The cultural-deprivation theory attributes the poor performance of certain minority-group students (Jencks 1972; Coleman 1966) to a pathology of home environment. Programs based on this assumption attempt to change children's lives, e.g., their language and even their parents' patterns of child rearing. The child is often referred to as "disadvantaged" and "socially deprived." This is usually the reason cited for failure to learn in school. Ryan recognizes the parallel between this approach and Zero Mostel's Dixiecrat senator and elaborates further:

In pursuing this logic, no one remembers to ask questions about the collapsing buildings and torn textbooks, the frightened, insensitive teachers, the six additional desks in the room . . . the relentless segregation, the callous administrator, the irrelevant curriculum, the insulting history book, the stingy taxpayers. . . . We are encouraged to confine our attention to the child and to dwell on all his alleged defects. Cultural deprivation becomes an omnibus explanation for the educational disaster area known as the inner city school. This is Blaming the Victim. . . . Again by focusing our attention on the [Black]

Reproduced by permission of the Society for Applied Anthropology from *Human Organization* 40(1):67-77, 1981.

family as the apparent cause of social inequality, our eye is diverted. Racism, discrimination, segregation, and the powerlessness of the ghetto are subtly but thoroughly downgraded in importance.

In this study, the concept of "blaming the victim" involves the process whereby those in the demonstration project and those disseminating the programs are blamed for a misevaluation and/or misinterpretation of that evaluation. Attention is focused on the programs' deviations from the "model" and developmental problems as apparent causes of inadequate "replicability" (for those sites that have been less than successful in their adaptation). Once again our eyes are diverted. The nature of the research design and federal involvement (particularly in terms of inflexible timelines, threats of termination, and direct intervention) in the implementation process are "subtly, but thoroughly, downgraded in importance." The emphasis of this segment of the discussion will be on the role of the treatment-control component of the research design in this project—ethically, programmatically, and methodologically.

A Misapplication of the Treatment-Control Design: Ethical, Programmatic, and Methodological Problems

The Request For Proposal (RFP) required the four new sites to repeat the evaluation design used in the prototype site. This design is based on assumptions regarding the replication approach, which are discussed below. In addition, it tangentially represents what Mulhauser (1975) refers to as the "minor variation on what was done the last time something like this came up" approach. The original design had both psychometric and ethnographic components to answer different kinds of questions. The psychometric component of the evaluation (basically adopted by the current evaluation and the focus of this discussion) is described in the RFP:

The design involved three separate cohorts of applicants, applying at six- to eight-month intervals. Through over recruitment and a lottery process, known in advance to all applicants, three separate sets of experimental and control groups were selected in a ratio of about three students to one control. The ratio was selected to permit maximum entry into [the program] with the minimum N estimated to be needed for a group large enough to be sensitive to educationally meaningful effects.

A program staff member's remarks concerning this evaluation design echoed the sentiments of the disseminators, adopters, a few LEA (local educational agency) members, and community members (at the sites): "How many times are we going to be used as guinea pigs? . . . We have real problems that need help now, not more demonstration projects. . . . They already proved it was an 'exemplary' program. . . . Why aren't they just trying to help us make it work?" There are a variety of concerns expressed in this individual's remarks, including disillusionment with demonstration projects that disappear from the community as quickly as they arrive, alarm and resentment concerning the experimental terminology[1] of the evaluation, and most pertinent to this discussion, outrage regarding the ramifications of the treatment-control design itself.

Ethical Problems

First, the application of this design to dropouts and potential dropouts of urban high schools is unintentionally unethi-

cal. Briefly, the problem is that human beings are being denied a second chance—for many their last chance—to function productively within the system. In the federal bureaucracy's desire to present conclusive findings based on a rigorous research design—to present "absolute scientific proof" of success or failure—it failed to recognize the ethical consequences of applying this design to primarily low-income, minority high-school dropouts and potential dropouts. These teenagers decide to return to the school setting, but, through the lottery process, at least one-fourth of them are told to look elsewhere for assistance. Turning away an individual who has been "rekindled" with the desire to lead a productive life has numerous and profound effects. The tears of a young woman, heard over a transcontinental call, after she received a letter assigning her to the control group, only begin to scratch the surface of the problem. Interviews with rejected students and their parents at each of the sites reflect similar concerns about their children's patterns of behavior; they are "falling back into their old ways, not goin' to school, not working, just hanging around with—and—those hoodlums."

This is magnified by the entire process by which the individual is turned away. The individuals must first decide to give themselves or the system another chance. Then they must undergo approximately five hours of psychometric tests,[2] pass the reading test (at a fifth-grade level), and are then thrown into a lottery system where all of them are exposed to the possibility of nonacceptance or new failure. It is important to emphasize that this program represents their last chance, according to many of the potential students and their parents. Exposing these students to another opportunity to fail can inflict serious personal damage, as interviews with many rejected students suggest. Moreover, the application of this design to this population (dropouts) produces unintentionally harmful effects in two additional areas. First, it generates serious programmatic problems for the demonstration site. These problems are generally interpreted negatively by the evaluators and serve to blame the victim. Second, the application of this design to this population raises serious questions about the credibility of this segment of the evaluation or any evaluation that uses this design with similar populations.

Programmatic Problems

The most serious programmatic problems generated by this design concern recruitment. Program staff members faced an uphill battle to sell a program to potential students and their parents who considered it a risk: because it was a demonstration project, it was perceived by many as "a school for dropouts," and potential students needed to pass a test to gain admission to the program. When program staff members (or students who helped in recruitment) added that admission was further predicated on the youths' luck in being chosen by lottery to establish a control group, the appeal of the program was more than "just slightly tarnished." Basically, this design turns a number of students off before they even begin to understand the program—erecting almost impenetrable barriers to recruitment. (Simultaneously, the design raises almost impenetrable barriers for alienated youth interested in working within "the system.") This was compounded by the community's negative perception of the program. One director of another alternative program explained: "What kind of program asks for kids so they can turn one quarter of them away, back into the streets? Why should we recommend that kind of program?"

The implementation of this design had another unintentionally negative consequence for program operations—particularly for recruitment. The evaluation's impact on the program is directly related to the nature of the research corporation itself.

The evaluation corporation is a business concerned with producing a reputable research product, advancing the state of the art, and making a profit. Regarding the latter concern, professional testers were hired for this project in a manner that attempts to maximize their efforts (and minimize their costs). The professional testers were instructed not to test potential students unless 15 or more could be identified for testing at the sites. Consequently, staff members were unable to inform many students when testing would occur. Students waiting for about four weeks lost interest in the program. The attrition rates between the initial interview and testing ranged from 26 to 59%.

Similarly, the second cohort was held back because the recruitment figure was below the expected number (at least 75 youths). The evaluation design required that students enter as a block or cohort. Youths already tested were held in limbo for periods ranging between 1 and 14 weeks for information regarding program initiation. Once again, many lost interest and found other avenues of interest to pursue. Site D lost 49%, and sites A and B lost approximately 20% each of their potential students due to this waiting period. (Recommendations of an advisory panel were taken into consideration for the third cohort concerning this matter, and testing was conducted on a demand basis. This represented a more expensive procedure, but it reduced the attrition between testing and intake to a range of from 7 to 15%.

Methodological Problems

The application of this design to this population is methodologically bankrupt. In a classical treatment-control design (in educational and psychological experimentation), individuals are randomly assigned to treatment and control groups. The purpose of the control group is to determine what the treatment or experimental group would be like without the special treatment. One of the classical paradigms involving human beings, for example, is drawn from pharmaceutical studies of drug effects. A segment of the population is randomly assigned to a treatment and control group. The treatment group is given the drug or treatment and the control group is given a placebo.' Neither group is aware of who has been given the treatment since knowledge of group membership might significantly affect study outcomes. In this case, one segment of a biased sample is placed in the treatment (individuals who were not "turned off" by the rigorous examination and lottery system), and another segment is "slapped in the face"—told they could not enter the program. Here, the second group (representing the control group) is not a control group; it is merely a negative treatment group to compare with a biased sample of "treatment" students. (See Tallmadge [1979] for elaboration concerning the problems with treatment and control groups as applied to specific programs and populations.) The treatment sample is further biased by the type of students required to meet the demonstration project timelines. Only

students seeking a diploma and with sufficient credits to graduate from the program within the allotted demonstration period were initially accepted into the program (11th and 12th graders). This type of student is often referred to as "the cream of the crop" by local high school personnel. One administrator of a feeder high school said that he believed many of the students would have made it anyway. I disagree with this judgment. A more accurate assessment of these students would be: they are the best of the lowest achieving students in the public schools, e.g., bored, cutting classes, but still interested in graduating and with few serious legal or psychological problems. There are some indications that this administrator's comments represent a response to a perceived threat—if the program is successful with the students his school failed to work with, it would not reflect well on his school. The students, however, are clearly not the most disillusioned in the system.

The problems of the evaluation have, thus far, only focused on the role of the treatment-control design. The problems generated for the programs extend beyond this specific research design and involve additional facets of the evaluation itself, including the devil's bargain, reports, and deadlines.

The Devil's Bargain, Reports, and Deadlines

Evaluations customarily accompany large-scale implementation. This pattern represents one of the rules of the game in policy research. Clinton (1976) refers to this pattern as the devil's bargain. The potential adopter needs the funds for the program and must accept an evaluation as part of the package deal—even though the evaluation may serve potentially as a vehicle for their own demise. This pattern uniting the two elements is a product of the policy-maker/federal-agency world view—where accountability is stressed and required for survival, given the scarce resources allocated each year. Therefore, the program begins with a devil's bargain; the federal agencies seek to maximize their returns—and weed out the "weaker" programs—rather than focus their efforts on making a selected program work. The rationale for these rules is understandable and appropriate given the federal bureaucratic environment—with its scarce resources and high demands of accountability. This pattern, however, places the program in a defensive position, responding to another pressure before it is even on its feet.

From the federal perspective, the necessity to follow strict timelines is imperative. The inflexibility of timelines (often referred to as "the consequences of legislation"), however, causes a number of ramifications for the evaluation and consequently for the operation of the program. The formal issuing of the RFP for this study was delayed by approximately four months; however, the timelines for the evaluation and program start-up and operation were not altered. Therefore, much of the extensive preliminary work (e.g., building a "prototypical model," rescheduling site visits and work/study plans, and so on) were conducted in an insufficient period of time. In addition, the sites were to begin operation in October, and did not actually begin operating until December.

Similarly, the timelines and deadlines for results were not changed. As a consequence of this inflexibility, the first draft report was based on formal observations of one site (the only one in full operation), although formal observations of all the sites were required. The consequences of a cursory evaluation of the sites were detrimental: the bottom line of the report emphasized the fact that the other three had not "gotten off the ground." (Although the problems concerning extrinsic pressures—LEA negotiations and local politics—were clearly discussed, the message defacto stressed that only one site out of four had begun operations.) A draft of a second report was produced while members of the evaluation staff were still making site visits to meet deadlines. The report was sent to the manager of the demonstration project, and a copy was sent to the disseminator. The disseminator then read sections of the draft to both LEA officials and program staff, although the research corporation had asked them not to make any portions of the draft public. The sections of the report shared with the LEA officials only mentioned "their lack of cooperation," without mentioning the positive contributions reported in the draft. This created tremendous friction between the program staff and the LEA officials (as well as between the LEA and the research corporation). Similarly, the disseminator shared a portion of the draft with the program staff and only read the negative portion. When one staff member raised her hand after hearing each criticism and asked, "Well, didn't they say anything positive about us?" she was given the following reply, "It wasn't relayed to us." The effect of this highly edited disclosure further demoralized an already weakened staff.

The stress on maintaining deadlines for the program implementation has also had a direct effect on the start-up and operation of the program. The program's timeline is dictated by the legislature, rather than the timetable based on the same stage of development of the "prototypical" program. The late start of the program (primarily due to difficulties in securing a firm agreement with LEAs) forced the staff into a pattern of "always trying to catch up." This has led to great difficulties in hiring qualified staff and recruiting students. Most of the staff were interviewed and hired during the first day of training. In order to meet demonstration timelines, the recruitment for the first cohort took place in the middle of the second school semester toward the end of the academic year. The recruitment for the second cohort took place in the summer, once again to follow the demonstration guidelines—regardless of the local conditions. Neither time was suitable for a number of reasons: LEA personnel do not identify actual dropouts until September and potential dropouts until several months after the academic year begins; the schools are closed during the summer months and are occupied with their own agendas before they close; and recruiting students for school during the summer is especially difficult. Intensive recruitment periods often brought program operations to a screeching halt to meet the "numbers" and the deadlines. The effect of threats of termination, underlying directives to secure adequate numbers of students according to strict deadlines, inflicted much damage on program operations, and will be discussed in detail below. Finally, in September, indecision regarding the program's extension caused the staff at the sites to delay recruiting potential students until after the public schools' competing alternative programs began operation—effectively reducing the pool of eligible individuals.

The last aspect of the research design to be discussed in this analysis involves the concept of replication. An examination of this concept as it is applied to this study sheds light on how an evaluation can unintentionally create a damaging judgment of a program.

Replication

The central theme of the research design is replication. Can these programs be replicated in four sites? The very nature of the question, as well as its consequences for the program, bear examination. One of the ethnographic consultants to the evaluation presents his reaction to this question:

My first reaction . . . was, "Why would anyone expect four different programs in four different urban sites to replicate a model program in another site?" This expectation is against the first law of sociocultural systems—that all such systems (and a program of any kind is a sociocultural system) are adaptations to their environment. We should expect each program to show significant deviation from an initiating model, and from each of the other programs. The question should not be, "Do they deviate?" or even "How do they deviate?", but rather, "Are they adapting well (functionally) to their respective environments?" [Spindler 1979].

The emphasis on the replication concept has been problematic for the sites for a variety of reasons, and its influence on the evaluation design represents one of the most serious obstacles faced by the sites. The evaluation design employed the discrepancy-analysis approach (Provus 1971), which assumes that replicability is a desired and possible goal. Basically, discrepancy analysis consists of assessing the degree of congruence between model program standards and actual program performance. The Discrepancy Evaluation Model consists of five stages: design, installation, process, product, and cost. At each stage, a comparison is made between an ideal program design and reality. The difference between the program design and reality is called discrepancy. This information is then shared with the program staff, who are then to make appropriate adjustments in their program. The program design is constructed by the evaluator based on information elicited from all levels of the staff. The model is used as the standard.

In stage two—installation—the program operation is compared with the model to determine the fidelity of implementation. Stages three and four are concerned with measuring products. Stage three, according to Provus, measures "the relationship between process and interim products. The standard is the hypothesized relationships specified in the program design, and the reality is the degree to which interim products have been achieved" (ibid.:47). Stage four terminal products are compared with the products specified in the model or program design. Stage five uses a cost-benefit analysis—comparing the evaluated program with the cost of other similar programs. Provus revised the model in response to a number of objections to assumptions, operation, and benefits of the model. Many of these objections are still of concern to me; however, they detract from the body of this discussion (ibid.:155–57).

Provus' revised model follows the same basic stages, e.g., design, installation, process, product, and progress comparison (ibid.:183–214). One of the most important differences between his original and his revised model is that the program's design is compared with "performance" information. In addition, discrepancy between performance and standard is reported to those responsible for management of the program, rather than sharing the information with all levels of staff. The revised model was employed in the study under discussion. The standard program design was developed with the assistance of the parent organization of the prototype program. The use of the revised model had a profound effect on how evaluation feedback was received. Staff members were often "scolded" by management for not performing well enough. The staff resented this treatment and in turn were reluctant to provide evaluators with performance information in the future. The sponsor was attempting to replicate a program for dropouts, and potential dropouts. One begins to wonder, however, as one of my colleagues has pointed out, "whether it (the sponsor) was attempting to test a managerial control model—almost PERT-chart-like in its apparent authoritarian simplicity—but masking the incredible complexity of human difficulties in complex organizations." One of the problems with the discrepancy approach in general using the original and revised model is that it draws excessive attention to deviations from a prototypical model. The terms *deviation* or *discrepancy* carry a negative connotation. Although the evaluation team has repeatedly stated that deviations from the model are not necessarily good or bad, deviations have continuously been interpreted by all parties concerned as generally negative. The programs should be expected to "deviate" from the model of the program in adapting to their new environment. A more realistic and constructive approach would focus attention on "how well they adapt" to their new environment. Unfortunately, given all the caveats, values continue to be assigned—replication (adherence to model specifications) is considered good and deviation is viewed negatively. This becomes increasingly clear each time the finger is raised and members of one agency or another point to the fact that "[the program] is not replicating the model." Spindler also pointed out:

The problem is compounded when one realizes that the model is an ideal construct. That is, it is not an operational statement of an existing reality, it is a construction that is partly normative and partly empirical. Further, it is not a construction from an existing reality, for the initiating program in [deleted] was extinct before the construction of the model began. The model, therefore, is an ideal type reconstruction.

One of the major consequences of this approach is that it highlights deviations (which should be expected), and implicitly assigns a negative value to most deviations because they represent incomplete or inadequate replication. The staff at the sites have learned slowly to adopt themselves to this set of rules to survive; however, it has detracted from their fundamental mission—to successfully run the program.

Direct Federal Involvement

Federal agencies have a legal and moral obligation to see that the taxpayers' money is being used "appropriately" and efficiently. They must also operate their programs according to strict guidelines and timelines due to pressures of accountability—and to the realities of federal-agency vulnerability—which will be discussed in greater detail below. These pressures periodically force federal agencies to intervene in program operations. There have been at least four major points of intervention that have significantly affected the operation of the programs under study. Three of these were represented in terms of "threats of termination," and the last in the form of a national award. It is argued that the "hard line" approach often discussed in management literature can be effective in

producing desired outcomes; however, repeated tactics or manipulations of this nature generally produce undesirable—often demoralizing—results.

One of the first major forms of intervention by federal agencies involved in the study occurred during start-up. All of the programs experienced difficulties securing an agreement with the LEAs. As early as October the LEAs had expressed a general willingness to support the establishment of the program. The formulation of specific detailed agreements of cooperation took months to develop. Resolutions were required regarding the certification of program instructors, credits to be earned by electives and nontraditional classes, attendance procedures, mechanisms for referring student names and transcripts, and a plethora of more detailed matters. Formal agreements with the LEAs generally included only a few of the issues required to operate the program effectively. In site A the LEA formally signed an agreement in February incorporating the program into the LEA. (Site A is the only program that has been formally incorporated into the LEA and awards its own diplomas.)[1] In both sites B and C, the agreements with the LEA were not signed until July, primarily due to the opposition of the teachers' association.

At the request of the funding agency, the federal agency responsible for managing the implementation responded to the difficulties encountered in establishing agreements with the LEAs at sites B and C by taking the "hard line" and exercising pressure by threatening program termination. This is a logical step given the pressures of accountability in the federal bureaucracy. The disseminator became the bearer of the bad news during the early stages, and personnel at each of the sites indicated some confusion between the message and the messenger. (This also formally marked the beginning of estrangement between the disseminator and the staff of the programs due to the disseminator's conflicting role—serving the demonstration programs, the manager of the implementation, and the funding agencies.) Deadlines were communicated to the sites on three occasions. The initial deadline of April 26 was extended to May, then to June 16, and ultimately to July 16. During this time, the managing agency also informed the staff at the sites that "it was studying alternative courses of action" (regarding termination proceedings). The approach of threatening termination, rather than offering constructive assistance to remedy the problem, creates some questions regarding their overall orientation to the program. Nevertheless, in this case, the "hard line" approach appears to have significantly contributed to the desired outcomes—arriving at firm LEA agreements. One of the concomitant (negative) effects, however, is that it created much anxiety among the program's staff from the onset. This approach also generated a significant degree of anxiety among students, which then affected attendance; as one student said, "We didn't know if the program would even be here tomorrow, you know."

The funding agency became increasingly concerned about the "inability" of the sites to attract the anticipated number of youths—particularly with their failure to produce control groups. This should not have been surprising given student, community, and staff reaction to the design. Federal agencies generally operate according to contractual obligations—this requirement of "numbers" was initially viewed as such—a legal/contractual obligation. The funding agency examined the recruitment difficulties carefully and decided not to hold the sites to their contractual obligation to serve four cohorts—one was excluded. In addition, the funding agency required the last cohort to secure an experimental group of 90 students and a control group of 55. Failure to meet these goals would signify contract termination. The staff at the sites were told in early December that they had until the end of January to meet these targets.

The sites had been threatened with termination again—a pattern was beginning to emerge. Investigations suggest that staff turnover was partially due* to the instability and anxiety these threats produced in the program (staff turnover has been found to be directly related to attendance problems). The federal agencies were responding to delays—deviations from a set model—with termination rather than with constructive criticism and help. Since the programs represented part of a demonstration project to "learn if it can be done" in this abbreviated time span, repeated threats of termination were of questionable usefulness or appropriateness, and in addition, constituted a treatment to the "treatment" (program). During November and December, survival became the single most significant concern of the four youth programs. Fundamental program activities, such as instruction, counseling, and providing various nontraditional courses came to a screeching halt as the entire staff, and in three sites the students themselves, went door-to-door, canvassing the neighborhood and recruiting in the local schools. This particular case of intervention also represents one of the most obtrusive forms of interference between program implementation/operation and evaluation requirements.

The 90/55 figure had been required from each site, regardless of community size. This was extremely burdensome for site C, a rural site where five LEAs required canvassing, and for site D where youths did not perform well on reading tests. All of the sites met their goals by January 31; however, the cost was extremely high, particularly for sites C and D. In site C, the staff was forced to admit youths without the opportunity to examine their transcripts, and admitted students with insufficient credits to graduate within the allotted demonstration period. Thirty percent of the students had between 0 and 5 credits in LEA districts that required 16 credits for graduation. This produced a number of difficulties regarding rostering. Instructors had to teach a large variety of courses to meet student graduation requirements. In one of the sites (D), the greatest impact of the third cohort recruitment (when the minimum credit requirement and the minimum reading test score were lowered) was that staff members frequently found that students were unable to read the materials used by the last cohort; many were more difficult to motivate academically, and attendance patterns were irregular and of decreasing frequency.

The effects of the threat of termination also exacerbated existing internal problems, and further undermined the staff's morale. This cannot be emphasized enough because the consequence of a demoralized staff had tremendous impact on program operations. Staff members had already felt "persecuted, frustrated [due to internal problems], and underpaid." New threats of termination accentuated internal discord (endemic to most organizations) and disorders stemming from earlier evaluation and federal involvement.

The impact on staff morale was manifested in high staff turnover, poor staff attendance, routine lateness, early depar-

tures, and, for some, generally lowered interest in maintaining their former degree of commitment to a low-paying, developing program. This is a vicious cycle because as staff lose their commitment—however temporary—students lose their commitment to the program and attend less and less. Students have repeatedly reported that they come to the program to be with personalities—specific teachers, or counselors, or secretaries with whom they like to talk—not merely to acquire specific skills. When instructors or counselors are absent—because of a declining interest or commitment, or increasing frustration—students have less incentive to attend.

Federal agencies, concerned with their scarce resources and their accountability for taxpayers' money, then apply more pressure since the program is not serving a large enough group of individuals. This particular incident was compounded by what appears to be a form of interagency rivalry and poor communication through the cumbersome network of actors or acronyms (the funding agency, the managing agency, the disseminator, the evaluators, the LEAs, the local affiliate of the disseminator, and the demonstration program). The staff at the sites were informed of various ratios that they had to secure during the December-January period. This placed them in an even more precarious position—not knowing what ratio was sufficient to meet the "new" federal requirement and ward off termination threats. The staff at many of the sites were unaware of the appropriate number of individuals needed until mid-January, and the deadline was January 31. The managing agency submitted a ratio of 90/70, the funding agency countered it with a ratio of 90/50, and the managing agency returned with a submission of 90/55; eventually the ratio was settled at 90/55.

Another act of interagency rivalry almost brought all of the programs to a close. Although the programs were granted a contract extension for nine months, the delivery of monies was delayed for over four months due to a dispute regarding a debt of $60,000 between the funding and managing agencies. The managing agency refused to send the monies (received from the funding agency) to the programs until they received their $60,000. In the meantime, staff at the sites had to look for emergency local funding. The programs that succeeded in borrowing funds at a 22% interest rate were able to maintain stable program operations. Programs that were less successful showed many adverse effects as a result of the uncertain funding, such as loss of staff members, lower attendance rates, lower student and staff morale, and de facto poor evaluation ratings.

A third instance of federal intervention in the study occured when the funding agency visited site C to evaluate and possibly terminate the program. Members of the agency seem to have used this opportunity to make an example for the other sites—to let them know, according to one informant, "that this is the bottom line and that nobody is promised future funding" unless they meet minimum requirements, e.g., "numbers," attendance, and so on. The funding agency went looking for "the worst site," according to one high ranking official (confidential key informant). Two other informants stated that the funding agency personnel visited the program in the early afternoon after classes were being held. The building was clear, and they went directly to the director's office to express some of their concerns: "If only there was some show of community support." They also mentioned the lack of progress with the cafeteria and study-lounge construction. Later, at an interagency meeting, the agency personnel complained about not seeing any students at this site. According to the disseminator, "the staff had made a real effort to pull itself together" and "shine" for the visit. They also mentioned that "they cannot take another one of these . . . they have already been put through the mill."

The effect of one site being singled out—as an example, a test, and a display of power—has taken its toll at all of the sites. Repeated threats of termination and sponsor spot checks (used primarily as a warning for the rest) have contributed to the creation of a despondent or "overwhelmed" staff. The staff at this site was for the most part unaware that they served as a pawn in the larger chess game. Instead, staff members reacted to the surface manipulation—the moves that directly affected them (worsening existing internal disorders). According to one member, "When you don't know whether you're going to be here from day to day it's hard to get up and come to work, never mind planning ahead." This last event also contributed significantly to the already strained, however reparable, disseminator-program relationship.

Staff members at all of the other sites perceived the funding agency intervention as a threat to their own security and survival. The intervention placed program personnel on the defensive, emphasized the power relationship between various factions, and exaggerated the we-(site)/they-(other or antisite) dichotomy (Leacock 1977). The role the disseminator played in this display of power between the sponsor and the sites (and ultimately between the sponsor and the disseminator) further strained the disseminator's relationship with the sites.

The funding agency personnel periodically asked the disseminator to collect information about and from the sites that might jeopardize their survival—information that the disseminator is legally obliged to report (one of the elements of the "devil's bargain"). Staff members at the sites perceived the disseminator's actions, particularly in this last instance, as an expression of betrayal, placing the disseminator in the "they" category of the we-they dichotomy. (This amplifies the initial problem of the dual role of the disseminator.) At one point the staffs of the sites banded together, refusing to give information to the parent organization (disseminator) until a bond of trust was tenuously reestablished. The disseminator saw the action as a confusion of the message with the messenger; the problem is more accurately summed up as a double-bind situation. This specific intervention represents a test case for the sites, but it also represents a test of the disseminator. The funding agency must know whether the disseminators "know the problems" and are able and willing to "handle the problems." Simultaneously, the disseminator has an obligation to serve the sites in a nonthreatening, "protective" manner. If the disseminator is interested in the potential extension and expansion of the initial demonstration, it must respond to the sponsor's interest. At the same time, the disseminator serves another master—the sites—to ensure their survival and prosperity (which indirectly ensures the disseminator's own survival). These two roles conflict, and constitute a no-win proposition for any agency. The effect of the structure of the situation rather than the competency of any agency per se must be understood to accurately assess the situation and enable individuals to construct alternative means of accomplishing their objectives.

The last major form of federal intervention illustrates how the most well-intentioned efforts can produce undesirable effects—not unlike the case of steel axes for Stone Age men described by Sharp (1973). One of the sites received a special commendation from the White House for its overall excellence, and was assured of future funding. The site clearly deserved the award and the recognition for its superior service to dropouts and potential dropouts; however, the award did little for the other sites. The other sites served the same clientele as diligently but they remain uncertain about future funding. Staff members at one site that followed in the award-winning site's footsteps viewed the award positively—and it spurred them on to achieve similar success. The staff at the other two sites, although sincere in their admiration, were only reminded of their own lack of success in comparison to "the national award winning site."

The combination of a compliment, another threat, and further strained relations with the only formally supporting element in the system—the parent organization—significantly contributed to the demoralization of the staff at the last site visited. The effects of federal intervention were compounded when each of the sites was given a 9-month, rather than a possible 18-month extension, without any explanation. Most of the staff members at the sites had had the impression (unofficially) that they would be funded for approximately 18 months beyond the original contract because they were able to meet the last (90/55) requirement. The rationale for the shorter extension—to test the parties concerned and display the agency's power—is rarely recognized or discussed by staff members, and the staff and the disseminator were not even given superficial explanations for the agency's decision. The director of one site summed up the entire year of interagency rivalry and muscle flexing in the following manner:

"It's like two big elephants in the middle of the jungle ready for the fight, they run towards each other trampling everything in their path just to ram each other to show all the jungle who is the most powerful beast of all—but when the clouds of smoke clear away and the dust settles it is the earth that loses."

World Views: The Research Corporation, the Educational Research Establishment, and the Federal Bureaucracy

The key to understanding how the treatment-control design can be misused repeatedly and why such maladaptive federal behavior occurs routinely lies in the powerful role played by organizations with various world views.

As an example, the description of the research corporation's effect on program recruitment demonstrates how one world view influences behavior. As a business, the corporation was interested in maximizing its efforts and minimizing its costs. This orientation motivated the corporation personnel to instruct its testers to test no less than 15 students at a time. The result was that students lost interest in the program while waiting for a sufficiently large group to be assembled. The programmatic interference was unintentional; the disruption was simply the logical result of a research corporation's businesslike world view.

Another facet of the research corporation's perspective is related to the misuse of the experimental paradigm: the pattern of bidding for proposals with the problem, and in some instances the research design, defined in advance. This pattern encourages the adoption of research proposals and designs without sufficient scrutiny. Excessive protests jeopardize the corporation's chances of winning a contract. The businesslike world view promotes compromises that may contribute to the overall pattern of misused designs.

The educational research establishment's world view is an even more powerful influence contributing to the repeated misuse of this paradigm. This view is characterized by the experimental or quantitative approach to research. Campbell and Stanley (1966), and Riecken et al. (1974) are probably the most widely recognized or cited proponents of this approach. Campbell and Stanley wrote in their seminal work, *Experimental and Quasi-Experimental Designs for Research:*

This chapter is committed to the experiment: as the only means for settling disputes regarding educational practice, as the only way of verifying educational improvements, and as the only way of establishing a cumulative tradition in which improvements can be introduced without the danger of a faddish discard of old wisdom in favor of inferior novelties. [1963:2]

The fundamental elements of the paradigm are treatment and control groups, such as those used in the demonstration study under discussion.

Traditional educational researchers dominate (evaluation) research corporations. They have been socialized through graduate training to accept this orthodox credo. Educational researchers using alternative methods or perspectives are regarded as operating outside the mainstream of "acceptable" educational research. An overemphasis on the importance of the design has led to a situation in which the methodological tail wags the proverbial research dog.

I am aware of the recent modifications made by some of the leading proponents of the educational research establishment. For example, Campbell has written in "an extreme oscillation away from [his] earlier dogmatic disparagement of case studies" that

we should recognize that participants and observers have been evaluating program innovations for centuries without the benefit of quantification or scientific method. This is the common-sense knowing which our scientific evidence should build upon and go beyond not replace. But it is usually neglected in quantitative evaluations, unless a few supporting anecdotes haphazardly collected are included. Under the epistemology I advocate, one should attempt to systematically tap all the qualitative common sense program critiques and evaluations that have been generated among the program staff, program clients, and their families, and community observers. While quantitative procedures such as questionnaires and rating scales will often be introduced at this stage for reasons of convenience in collecting and summarizing, non-quantitative methods of collection and compiling should also be considered, such as hierarchically organized discussion groups. Where such evaluations are contrary to the quantitative results, the quantitative results should be regarded as suspect until the reasons for the discrepancy are well understood. Neither is infallible, of course. But for many of us, what needs to be emphasized is that the quantitative results may be as mistaken as the qualitative. [1979:52-53]

There is, however, a time lag between the deeply ingrained socialization patterns of the past and the acceptance of new ideas and views emanating from the center of the educational research establishment. The world of contract research is somewhat removed from and often antagonistic to the halls of academia, and requires additional time for the diffusion of new ideas.

The federal bureaucratic world view also contributes unintentionally to the misuse of the treatment control design, due primarily to environmental pressures. A brief examination of the federal agencies' viewpoint provides a rationale or logic for the misuse of the research design. The perspective of federal government policymakers is clearly presented in the literature by Mulhauser (1975) and Coward (1976), among others. One of the primary responsibilities of the sponsor or federal agencies is to produce the most credible and socially relevant research (Holcomb 1974) dictated by congressional mandate. Policy research, in contrast to basic research, however, represents another significant characteristic of the federal bureaucratic world view.

[Policy research in juxtaposition to basic research] is much less abstract, much more closely tied to particular actions to be undertaken or avoided. While basic [research] aims chiefly to uncover truth, policy research seeks to aid in the solution of fundamental problems and in the advancement of major programs. [Etzioni, 1971]

Policy research seeks immediate action in response to troubled situations such as unemployment, dropouts, and so on. It attacks a discrete part of the problem to "avoid turf problems." There is, according to Mulhauser (1975), "no search for a comprehensive understanding of the problem's nature or origin." There is simply a time pressure that requires immediate identification of politically viable "levers of action." Often, Mulhauser points out, "The action taken is a minor variation on what was done the last time something like this came up" (ibid).

Another responsibility of the federal agencies characteristic of a fundamental tenet of their world view is to provide timely input for policymakers. As Coward (1976) points out, "Evaluation data presented after a policy decision has been made can have little impact on the decision." In addition, federal agencies must maximize their returns in efforts with limited fiscal resources. The result of scarce resources combined with pressures of accountability produce a climate of interagency rivalry and thus the need to employ the maximization model (McClelland and Winter 1969). The maximization model suggests "that human beings everywhere tend to choose the personal action that they feel will gain them the greatest benefit [or avoid the greatest loss] with the smallest expenditure of resources" (see Barth 1963, 1966, 1967; Erasmus 1961; Bailey 1960; Kunkel 1970).

These fundamental elements of the federal agencies' perspective are required to successfully adapt to the federal environment. The federal agencies' survival literally depends on an adequate understanding of, adherence to, and manipulation of these norms. The fluidity of funding from year to year, political fluctuations and alliances, career concerns, and the acquisition-maintenance of power games contribute to the political instability of the bureaucratic hierarchy and world view.

The demands for data, according to strict guidelines and timetables, are generated from this environment. Knowledge is power, and information is required at prespecified periods to assist in the federal decision-making process, e.g., assessing the relative merits of competing programs. Coward (1976) warns, "Agencies place themselves in vulnerable positions if they sponsor a research effort that is unable to provide data under constraints imposed by policy deadlines." The inability to address these concerns in this fashion may leave an agency "out in the cold," with diminished or no future funding.

The generation of this demonstration project research design, its acceptance, and periodic federal intervention are appropriate, given the world views discussed above. However, the actions dictated by these world views often inhibit, rather than foster, the appropriate use of research paradigms and the growth of programs in operation.

Conclusion

The purpose of this discussion is to give a larger sociopolitical perspective of national program evaluation. The specific aim is to demonstrate how evaluation design and federal involvement can unintentionally generate a damaging evaluation. I did not write this article to lay blame on any single agency or set of agencies. Only the grossest injustice would be served if this analysis were to be used in such a manner.

Government agencies have traditionally equated the most credible research with the use of the experimental design, regardless of the nature of the task. Ethnographic evaluations are novel innovations that are presently regarded as secondary to traditional quantitative approaches. The traditional approach is adopted to make the strongest case before Congress—the source of future funds. The design is selected in accordance with the traditional canons of the educational research establishment. The federal climate of inflexible deadlines, interagency rivalry, and scarce resources forces bureaucrats to find the most convincing design for their audience, for their own political and economic survival. The federal bureaucrats then prepare the requests for proposal for research corporations, which in turn respond to federal interests. Therefore, we come full circle: the researchers are responsible for implementing the design as well as responding to RFPs, which explicitly or implicitly require the use of a specific research design, regardless of the task at hand.

The value of this design can be compared to the value of technology: it is neither good nor bad, useful nor useless per se—only specific applications are good or bad, useful or useless. The repeated misuse of the experimental design is a function of several mutually reinforcing world views. In theory, paradigms do not logically determine the choice of research methods, as Reichardt and Cook have demonstrated (1979:11-32). In practice, however, paradigms do lend themselves to the use of one research method more readily than another. I support the use of qualitative methods—specifically, ethnographic techniques—in social-policy research. These techniques respond more appropriately to certain evaluation concerns, e.g., process evaluation. In addition, the use of qualitative methods interrupts the chain of reinforcing world views that often blinds practitioners to the immediate situation. This does not suggest, however, that research strategies deriving from the qualitative world view are "superior to experimental design as a methodology for evaluating broad-aim programs," as my colleagues argue (Weiss and Rein 1972:243).

The appropriate use of both qualitative and quantitative design is required for social-policy research. I believe that Campbell's call for a clearer understanding of the relationship between qualitative and quantitative ways of knowing will contribute to an understanding of the larger problems facing educational research. Discussions of this nature reveal this chain of reinforcing world views, allowing us to break away from this chain and view the task at hand more clearly.

On one level, the problem has been the simple misapplication of the treatment-control design and federal intervention in program operation. On another level, the problem is the power of reinforcing world views that generate maladaptive behavior. An analysis of the research corporation, the educational research establishment, and the federal-bureaucracy world views shows how these parties can unintentionally produce undesirable effects on program operations. The application of the holistic perspective demands that our attention be drawn to the policy context of the program and program evaluation. This view, like Dali's painting of Dali's painting of Dali's painting ad infinitum, focuses on the importance of stepping back from the canvas to gain a more complete perspective of the portrait.

Fundamentally, however, the larger sociopolitical context of the study has been presented to prevent misevaluations, misinterpretation of evaluations, and hopefully the misuse of evaluations. I believe that by focusing on the situation's structural influence, and the world view of the agencies involved, attention will be drawn to the causes of the problem—not the symptoms. Hopefully, this information will be used to devise alternative means of accomplishing similar objectives; helping program participants; conducting respectable research; and making appropriate policy decisions for taxpayers. Finally, this analysis should help agencies avoid a repetition of some of these logical, albeit maladaptive, patterns of behavior. The purpose should not be to attack any one agency or set of agencies for their actions—not to blame the victim—but to remove unintentionally undesirable "treatments" from program operation and evaluation.

Recommendations

Briefly the recommendations are as follows:

1. Abandon treatment-control designs in projects with lower-socioeconomic-class participants. The reason for this recommendation is that it has unintentionally deleterious effects.

   a. It is unintentionally unethical. A dropout or potential dropout decides to give himself or herself or "society" another chance; comes to a program (representative of the larger society); passes a reading test; undergoes five hours of psychometric tests; and is then told, "I'm sorry but you have not been selected." The individual at the bottom of the socioeconomic ladder reaches out for help and is greeted with a slap in the face.

   b. Applying this design to this situation is "bad" research. The use of a treatment-control design can be useful; like technology, it is not good or bad per se, it is the application that is useful or not useful—good or bad. In this case, the control group is given a negative treatment—a slap in the face. The treatment group is aware that they have been selected and others have not—an additional treatment has been applied (e.g., the Hawthorne effect).

c. This design sheds an unfavorable light on the sincerity of the project to many community members, LEA officials, and the like.
    This is associated with previously existing perceptions of demonstration projects as "rip-offs" that "come and go . . . getting our hopes up and then letting us down." In fact, these associations and perceptions may contribute to recruitment difficulties presently experienced by demonstration projects throughout the country. Recruitment may represent a test of how communities are reacting to these types of demonstration projects (with their treatment and control constraints), rather than a test of how the community likes a specific program.

2. Comparison groups, static group comparisons, pretest/posttest paradigms, nonequivalent control-group paradigms, and systematic ethnographic approaches to evaluating education should be used in place of treatment/control designs.

3. Abandon efforts to replicate programs in favor of diffusing programs or traits of programs. The concept of replication is a biological not a sociological or anthropological concept. Genes and organisms reproduce themselves in a fashion quite unlike the replication of cultural patterns. Sociocultural systems and traits can be more constructively analyzed in terms of their diffusion from one plane to another—adapting to new environments. Focusing on the replicability of a program implicitly directs attention to the deviations rather than adaptations. Deviations, however carefully qualified, connote a negative step on the part of the adopters. Realistically, programs or sociocultural systems must adapt to their new environment, and can be evaluated on the basis of how successfully they adapt with different incentives and constraints.

4. Increased sensitivity to the unintentional effects of research-corporation, educational-research-establishment, and policymaker world views in program operations could mitigate future unintentionally deleterious treatments in program operation and evaluation. Accountability concerns need not be manifested in forms that may demoralize staff and students. Rational concern for accountability can be shown in a constructive, nonobtrusive assisting pattern.

5. Continue to support a qualitative/quantitative mix in future government-sponsored educational evaluation projects. This is recommended to enable evaluators to answer different kinds of questions, to place a check on each type of research, and to provide a routinized avenue for meta-evaluation or at least an analysis of the effects of federal and evaluation involvement.

6. Encourage the development of more channels of communication and feedback mechanisms between the various parties involved in an evaluation project.

NOTES

¹ A number of individuals associated with the experiment with experiments conducted with rats because of the treatment-control terminology.
² Potential students would periodically ask if the tests were designed

to "tell 'em if I were crazy or somethin'." Although the testers assured them that this was not the intended purpose, many students left the test sessions still under the impression that there was a hidden purpose.
³ See Matarazzo (1965) for elaboration of the "placebo effect" in educational and psychological experimentation.
⁴ This additional pressure, the presence of an evaluation, represents noise in the system, an intervening variable that would not normally be present in program operation. It represents a somewhat artificial situation, or at least a secondary treatment to program operations.
⁵ The single most important problem encountered by the program once a part of the LEA is that it is now in competition for the same students. Previously, if students were at high risk of dropping out, the local schools referred them to the youth program. The students would enroll in the program; however, they would remain on the local public school's rosters. When the students graduated from the youth program their diploma would be given to them from the local public school. Presently, the local school is reluctant to refer all of the high-risk students to the youth program. (The number of students on the rosters is translated into state and federal monies for the school.) An additional problem resulting from this new arrangement is that the program awards its own diplomas. Many students want to receive their diploma from their old high school. Therefore, many students complete all their graduation requirements at the youth program and transfer back to their old high school to graduate with their friends. This significantly affects the programs evaluation, for example in fewer graduates.
⁶ The overriding causes for high staff turnover are "weak" or "lax" management (e.g., supervisors or directors) and noncompetitive salaries. The program has become a training ground for many staff members. The program prepares them for roles in the public school, or as members of manpower training programs. The discrepancy between the program's salaries and the local school system's salaries represents the most serious flaw in the program model.

REFERENCES CITED

Bailey, F.
    1960 Tribe, Caste, and Nation. Manchester: Manchester University Press.
Barth, F.
    1963 The Role of the Entrepreneur in Social Change. Northern Norway, Bergen: Scandinavian University.
    1966 Models of Social Organization. Royal Anthropological Institute of Great Britain and Ireland. Occasional Paper, No. 23.
    1967 On the Study of Social Change. American Anthropologist, 69(6):661-69.
Campbell, D. T.
    1979 Degrees of Freedom and the Case Study. In Qualitative and Quantitative Methods in Evaluation Research. T. D. Cook and C. S. Reichardt, eds. Pp. 49-67. Beverly Hills, California: Sage.
Campbell, D. T., and J. C. Stanley
    1966 Experimental and Quasi-experimental Designs for Research. Chicago: Rand McNally.
Clinton, C. A.
    1976 On Bargaining with the Devil: Contract Ethnography and Accountability in Fieldwork. Council on Anthropology and Education Quarterly, 8:25-29.
Coleman, J.
    1966 Equality of Educational Opportunity. Washington, D.C.: U.S. Office of Education.
Coward, R.
    1976 The Involvement of Anthropologists in Contract Evaluations: The Federal Perspective. Anthropology and Education Quarterly 7:12-16.

Erasmus, C.
 1961 Man Takes Control. Indianapolis: Bobbs-Merrill.
Etzioni, A.
 1971 Policy Research. American Sociologist 6:8-12. Supplement.
Holcomb, H.
 1972 Tell Congress Results of Research. Education Daily 7(4):313.
Jencks, C.
 1972 Inequality: A Reassessment of the Effect of Family and Schooling in America. New York: Basic Books.
Kunkel, J.
 1970 Society and Economic Growth. New York: Oxford University Press.
Leacock, E.
 1977 Race and the "We-They" Dichotomy in Culture. Anthropology and Education Quarterly 8(2):152-59.
Matarazzo, J.
 1965 Psychotherapeutic Processes. Annual Review of Psychology 16:181-224.
McClelland, D., and D. Winter
 1969 Motivating Economic Achievement. New York: The Free Press.
Mulhauser, F.
 1975 Ethnography and Policymaking: The Case of Education. Human Organization 34:311.
Provus, M.
 1971 Discrepancy evaluation. Berkeley, California: McCutchan Press.

Reichardt, C. S., and T. D. Cook
 1979 Beyond Qualitative Versus Quantitative Methods. In Qualitative and Quantitative Methods in Educational Research. T. D. Cook and C. S. Reichardt, eds. Pp. 7-32. Beverly Hills, California: Sage.
Riecken, W. R., R. F. Boruch, D. T. Campbell, N. Caplan, T. K. Glenan, Jr., J. W. Pratt, A. Rees, and W. Williams
 1974 Social Experimentation: A Method for Planning and Evaluating Social Intervention. New York: Academic Press.
Ryan, W.
 1971 Blaming the Victim. New York: Pantheon Books.
Sharp, L.
 1973 Steel Axes for Stone-Age Australians. In To See Ourselves: Anthropology and Modern Social Issues. T. Weaver, ed. Pp. 457-64. Glenview, Illinois: Scott, Foresman.
Spindler, G.
 1979 Official Communication to [deleted] Research Corporation.
Tallmadge, G.
 1979 Avoiding Problems in Evaluation. Journal of Career Education 5(4):300-8.
Weiss, R. S., and M. Rein
 1972 The Evaluation of Broad-Aim Programs: Difficulties in Experimental Design and an Alternative. In Evaluation Action Programs: Readings in Social Action and Education. C. H. Weiss, ed. Pp. 236-49. Boston: Allyn and Bacon.

5

Sociology and Human Knowledge
Scientific vs. Folk Methods

T. R. Young

The kindest thing one might say about American sociology after 75 years of activity is that it has aided greatly the capacity of the human race to reflect upon its own behavior in undistorted ways . . . that it has provided people with the intellectual tools with which to assess and to assert that quality of life most congenial to the human process. The most unkind thing one might say is that American sociology has produced just those theories and just those methods and just that organization of research by which to legitimate and perpetuate oppressive forms of social life. The truth is more complex. One might rightly say that both views have merit. The fact is that American sociology has a history of considerable genius in the development of quantitative techniques and infuriating idiocy in such areas as criminology, urbanology, and rural sociology. It is the very genius of American sociology that I would like to critique in this paper. Briefly, I would like to offer the thesis that scientific methods subvert folk methods of knowlege constitution. This subversion is, I think, innocent enough in an enthusiasm to perfect its intellectual and research tools. With the end of innocence comes a more human task—personal and collective responsibility as well as the capacity to act upon that responsibility. The task requires that American sociology be understood as a knowledge factory and that this format be contemplated from a sociology of knowledge perspective.

The sociology of knowledge takes as its quest the relationship between human ways of understanding and different ways of organizing the knowledge process in society (Mannheim, 1936:264). In this paper, I would like to try to sort out the conflict of two ways of knowing: on the one hand there are folk methods for constituting positive knowledge and on the other hand there are scientific methods of acquiring accurate, positive knowledge. Both methods try to solve the problem of subjectivity: privately, individually held states of knowing and understanding. In this endeavor, the very existence of social reality is at stake. If persons have, internally, states of understanding that are different from each other in any persistent and significant way, their behavior will be at cross purpose or to no human purpose and gradually behavior will drift irreconcilably apart. There are, of course, social controls by which to resynchronize behavior but in these, too, folk methods are challenged by scientific methods. I wish to emphasize that the human project requires both folk methods and scientific methods of knowledge constitution. The former could ensure collective praxis; the latter could contribute to the authentic self-knowledge of a social life world. Together they could reunite the alienated divisions of the knowledge process. I suggest some canons in the last section that may promote such reunification.

Constituting Knowledge: Folk and Scientific Methods

I begin with the marxist point that knowledge does not exist objectively until there is an interactive (dialectical) process by which people understand social reality in the process of creating various forms of social relationship—indeed for Marx, this knowledge constitutive behavior was the

* This is an abridged version of a longer paper which is available from the author. [Address correspondence to: T. R. Young, The Red Feather Institute for Advanced Studies in Sociology. Route 1, Livermore CO 80536.]

uniquely human form of labor. The revolutionary animus in Marxian analysis is directed against all those forms of social organization that impair the knowledge constitutive process. In that the knowledge process involves insight, involvement, judgment, and wisdom as well as a share in the means of producing knowledge, the concept of praxis was a useful way to embrace the heart of the idea. In that certain social forms impaired praxis, revolution was necessary as a way to transcend those forms. Law, religion and morality were knowledge constitutive processes that, in the hands of a class, feudal (and certainly, bureaucratic) elite, systematically impaired the role of people in instituting—thus knowing intimately and collectively—work relations, family relations, political, and religious relations as well as market relations. The literature of critical sociology is filled with instances in which workers, voters, consumers, soldiers, and the residents of occupied countries resist the knowledge constitutive processes when that process is controlled by elites (Thompson, 1979).

Scientific methods for constituting knowledge are objective in that these methods take the subjective activity of human beings for granted just as folk methods take the objective structures produced by their highly sophisticated subjective activity for granted. Scientific methods (except for hermenuetical sciences) count marriage, citizens, crimes, divorces, children, votes, friendships, workers, mental patients, and such without reflecting upon the highly variable and greatly assorted ways in which these social facts are constituted as really-one-of-those-things. Scientific methods in "modern" sociology take mathematical models of human behavior as the first stage in perfecting the knowlege process. Actually, mathematical models are simple-minded representations of the very complicated process of constituting social reality. The primitive character of mathematical models can be seen by noting the rug-weaving patterns of the Navajo of North America or the basketweaving of the Baganda in East Africa. The mathematics in these two "primitive" art forms is more complex than the most sophisticated algebraic model of marriage, mobility, or crime found in "advanced" sociology today. That a sixteen year old Navajo woman can create in one medium a mathematical system more complex than a professional sociologist can in the written medium of numbers is not a matter of any great shame for the sociologist. What is of interest to note is that sociologists attempt to enforce a fairly primitive system of constituting knowledge over and set above very complex folk methods of knowledge constitution. One may well wonder why. We will return to that question in the next section.

In order to constitute a given statement as a scientific fact, sociology relies upon the authority of mathematical measures of concentration, dispersion as well as probability statements about variations from chance distributions. In this approach to knowledge constitution, interaction with the objects of study (not subjects) is unnecessary. And, even more interestingly, social control is not necessary. A fact is constituted outside the structure of social relations. Interaction and social control are not involved. It is a matter of some curiosity that sociology strips methodology of its social matrix.

Why is such knowledge once, twice, and thrice removed from its source? What advantage accrues to the user to such remoteness from the everyday activity of interacting persons? Why has scientific method replaced, in part, social/folk methods for determination of the facticity of given relationships? The answers to these questions require that we call into question the taken-for-granted aspects of scientific scholarship. Only by doing so may one contribute to the authentic self-knowledge of sociology and thus, returning to Marx and Mannheim, locate knowledge processes in the social matrix which produces them. The task is to restore its sociology to sociology.

Scientific Method as Social and Class Conflict

At some point in the course of social evolution, the various folk methods for establishing knowledge were supplemented and, increasingly, replaced by scientific methods. The history of this particular transition is precisely the history of sociology itself as a professional discipline—and the history of its allied disciplines; law, economics, geography, political science, psychology, and other knowledge institutions. What I would like to propose here is that scientific methods in sociology as well as other disciplines become of interest and are allocated resources *by those who control* resources, when the ordinary folk methods of knowledge constitution are an obstacle to the purpose of those who control the resources. Scientific methods replace folk methods when conflict relations obstruct naive, trusting, open interaction.

The first systematic "objective" study of a society which I am able to locate is one commissioned by Cromwell after the slaughter of Irish defenders of Dragheda and Wexford—"a righteous judgment of God upon those barbarous wretches" to put it in Cromwell's words. In order to repair the harm done to the knowledge process by ethnic, linguistic, religious, and economic cleavages between the Irish and the English that interfered with the subjective folk methods of constituting friend, law, justice, loyalty, commercial exchange, and political allegiance, Cromwell turned to objective methods and commissioned a study of Ireland. One can hypothesize that objective knowledge processes replace subjective processes to the extent that conflict relations grow between social entities. Conflict gives rise to professional sociology when violence fails to generate behavior *of the sort desired and defined* by the powerful outsider/enemy. There exists the distinct possibility that espionage (*Vide* Watergate), remote sensing, secret codes, signs and countersigns, private languages as well as esoteric social research arise under conditions of overt, sustained conflict in which one party has neither the interactive capacity nor legitimate right to shape the consciousness of another party. Social research as a knowledge constitutive process is but one of a whole set of indirect technologies by which to give form and shape to behavior when intimate, direct, and trusting modes are not possible. Part of the current interest in the ethics of the profession may arise from a dim awareness of the partisan character of sociological research.

The major thesis of this section of the paper then is that sociology—as well as law and other professional knowledge constitutive processes—are political devices by which one set of persons in conflict with another set of persons preempt folk knowledge constitutive processes in order to supplement and circumvent social cleavages to the private advantage of the research sponsor. It is necessary to study Irish, women, workers, Blacks, consumers, voters, "criminals," and such when the relationships between the sponsors of the research and the objects of research are so bad that interaction and social controls as knowledge constitutive activities are rejected or resisted by the object group.

When Cromwell could not get the Irish to comply to the British mode of constituting social (especially exchange) relations by force of arms, he turned to "objective" science. The same pattern is true for the first studies by Taylor of the work process. When persons who purchased the labor power of workers could not establish by interaction and by wage incentive the facticity of a more accelerated (and more profitable) work process, they turned to Taylor and his successors in order to study and, unilaterally, to get more production. The process by which workers (and others) are excluded from the knowledge process is called objectification in marxist analysis. It is a process which subverts praxis and, perhaps, the human enterprise itself. These are not nice things to say about sociology and research methods. The research done enables the sponsors of knowledge to quietly/secretly use the unshared knowledge to private advantage. Such social research, the more valid it is, better helps reproduce the social relations which are oppressive, exploitative, and unjust—relations which cannot stand open and undistorted processes of collective discourse.

The Ethos of Critical Methodology

American sociology, in the peculiar social context of American capitalism and corporate liberalism, has taken Merton as its mentor together with some lesser luminaries as Lundberg, Davis-Moore, and now, Blalock. In the next 75 years, it must delegitimate Merton, Weber, Lundberg, and others as the very model of sociological enterprise and install them as ordinary scholars who contributed something of value at the edges of human knowledge. Still more pressing is the need to reverse the growing monopoly over social knowledge claimed by the ASA membership and relocate that process in the public sphere rather than in the private sphere of market research, the state sphere of social problem research, or the professional sphere of academic symposia. This division of labor between those who study and know and those who are studied and vulnerable is a moral calamity (Young, 1980).

In a well known essay, Merton (1968:604–615) set forth four canons of a "democratic" scientific ethos. Of the four "canons" of science elaborated by Merton, only the canon of "Communism" is relevant to a critical sociology—and then only if one revises Merton's meaning of communism. In that meaning, communism is merely freedom of information—a bourgeois notion which makes information accessible in the marketplace of ideas to be chosen (purchased) by private individuals for private purpose (profit). This is, of course, a travesty on the notion of communism. In the marxist usage, and the one adopted here, the canon of communism holds that knowledge is collectively *produced*—and collectively *used*.

The other three canons of social research (skepticism, universalism, and disinterest) are directly, specifically, pointedly hostile to folk methods. Folk methods are not skeptical—they require faith, belief, innocence, and naivete in order to constitute social reality/knowledge. And, as Wunderlich (1980) points out, so does "normal" science. A little skepticism is necessary in a cooperative society. It is in a society of knaves, rascals, frauds, charlatans, public relations, and advertising executives where a full-blown skepticism is necessary.

Merton neglected to say that univer-salism creates a mechanical world in which all decisions, judgments, creativity, and rebellion are subjugated to the uniform application of impersonal rules. Universalism is in direct opposition to praxis in its moments of creativity and autonomy. Universalism creates the well-ordered world so necessary to sustain exploitative relations by asserting particularism as an antiquated folk method. It is this very particularism that brings history into human affairs. Each person, each group, each society, in order to function in its own socio-ecological niche, must be slightly/significantly different from all other such groups unless each entity lives exactly in the same environment and if the environment stayed exactly the same throughout eternity (Young, 1977). Universalism is the dream of a clock-maker.

Disinterestedness is the most dangerous advice Merton has given to American sociology. It makes moral cretins of us all. It puts us and our work in the service of whomever has the price to use social science methodology for whatever private interest comes to hand. Merton is properly concerned that one's interests do not lead one to slant one's research design or to falsify one's data in order to advance one's pet theory. The problem here is that one cannot be disinterested. The very act of conceptualizing problems, variables, and hypotheses is loaded with human history. If Pasteur, Salk, or Koch had been disinterested, they could have as easily worked on germ warfare as preventative medicine. In order to relocate sociology in a prosocial context, the norms adumbrated below are presented in opposition to those of Merton.

1. All social research should be in dialectical relationship with folk methods of constructing social reality. By this I mean that scientific methodology should be oriented in such a way as to facilitate democratic interaction and collective control of social facts. More particularly, research methodology should take as its proper domain the activities and vulnerabilities of the structures of domination: class, state, racist, and sexist power.

2. Qualitative analysis should take precedence over the quantitative. Social sci-

ence methodology in its quantitative mode should recognize the primitive character of its operations and not insinuate these as superior to folk methods. One should realize that quantification is a process by which the richness of everyday life is made progressively more barren as it proceeds. One discards information (variety) as human behavior is translated into word sets. Still more information is discarded as one transfers data from word sets into number sets—a number set simply is not as informative as a word set since word sets are not limited by the constraints on number sets—ordinality, intervality, and ratio-nality. One loses still more information as one converts descriptive parameters into summary statistics. Quantification, then, is a process by which information is systematically discarded. One must not assume that, since valuable information is obtained by such distillation, this knowledge surpasses that produced by symbolic interaction using words or by behavioral interaction.

3. Social science methodology should not be used to trump the legitimation processes of ordinary people. One should not accept as definitive the authority of social research in affirming the desirability of this system of work or that system of education. This strips human activity of its historical character; of its moral character; of its subjective (intentionality/praxical) character and establishes an oppressive structure of domination that benefits those who control the means of production of knowledge.

4. Sociological methodology should not take the development of formal theory as its goal but rather critique. Formal theory has some ugly characteristics. It must be complete, coherent, and universal. These characteristics define spontaneity, creativity, historicity, and discontinuity out of the system. A coherent system requires that one part of the theory be logically derivative from another part. It is this feature which makes prediction (hence control) possible. While regularity in human affairs certainly exists, one should pause before one assumes it must exist and pause again before one insists that *this* particular relationship endures for all time and place. One must admit into

one's theoretical model the possibility of revolutionary/radical change between elements of the system.

Were one to accept this very uncommon view of the goal of social research methodology; critique rather than formal theory, one must then proceed to analyze the forms of critique. There are two general forms of critique: immanent and transcendent. An immanent critique requires that one evaluate the behavior of a social formation in terms of what it promises to do. If a corporation promises to produce safe, necessary, economical goods in an efficient and safe way, one can critique it on those terms. If a society claims to be democratic, oriented to human rights, equal standing before the law, and personal privacy, all well and good, but the immanent question is to what degree does its performance match its prophecy?

A transcendent critique requires that one go outside the system and evaluate it upon standards that may be different from those the system employs itself. If one uses transcendent standards, one must be prepared to defend one's choices. Justification of critique must be a collective and uncoerced process if the critique itself does not become itself an instrument of alienation. Elsewhere I have argued that community, praxis, and ecological integrity are universally valid points of transcendent critique. Others use caloric intake, income inequality, and infant mortality rates together with other indices to compare and contrast differing social formations.

5. Sociological methodology should recognize that a wide diversity of methodologies by human knowledge is constituted, enriched, made more reflexive and more democratically based. Reporting of the sort done by David Halberstam should have equal footing to that done by G. William Domhoff. Literary criticism of the *New York Review of Books* should be seen as equally important to the Robust Estimation of Hoaglin. The work of *Telos* is vastly underrated when compared to the *AJS. Theory and Society, The Insurgent Sociologist,* NACLA, and MERIP are more oriented to the human project than are most of the mainline journals sponsored by the ASA.

6. Finally I would argue that the stilted, depersonalized, depoliticized, linguistic style of the ASA journals is itself hostile to the human condition—of those who write it if not those whose behavior is affected by the application of the findings. If the quality of human life is intimately connected to the quality of its symbolic systems (as indeed they are), then passion, anger, joy, disgust, hope, and rage should not be excluded from the pages of authentically human endeavor. The languages of business, mathematics, computers, and science are too small a vehicle in which to place the fate of human society. They are too meagre, too remote, and too barren a soil in which to plant ideas. I find the strident polemics of some left publications overblown and paranoiac—as bad as they are they are better oriented to human, social activity than the deadly, dull, and lifeless prose of American sociology.

One cannot speak of the range and scope of human endeavor with the narrow and dusty language of social science as now conceived—it is necessary to restore human forms of speech—folk methods of conceptualizing—to American sociology; that may be the most important task for the next 75 years.

REFERENCES

Mannheim, Karl
1936   Ideology and Utopia. New York: Harcourt and Brace.
Merton, Robert K.
1968   Social Theory and Social Structure (revised). Glencoe, IL: The Free Press.
Thompson, E. P.
1979   The Making of the English Working Class (1963 reissued). New York: Penguin.
Wunderlich, Richard and Camille Minichino
1980   Critical Dimensions in the Sociology of Science: Merton vs. Kuhn. Livermore, CO: The Red Feather Institute.
Young, T. R.
1977   "Radical dimensions in modern system theory." Western Sociological Review 8:2.
1980   "The division of labor in the construction of social reality." Urban Life 9(2):135–162.

6

Reforms as Arguments

William N. Dunn

The social sciences are an outgrowth of efforts to understand and alleviate practical problems through social reform. The development of social science disciplines is therefore practice-driven and not, as is mistakenly assumed by those who squat in the shade of the natural sciences, a product of "basic" research. This myth of the basic-to-applied research cycle, together with derivative misconceptions about the role of "social engineering," was challenged by Lazarsfeld throughout his career (Holzner et al., 1977). In his last published book he urged once more that we acknowledge the ordinary contexts of practical action which continue to drive the social sciences:

> The argument goes that applied research is radically different from basic scientific work and therefore detracts talent and resources from true progress in the discipline. This implies a false comparison with the natural sciences. It is true that technical engineers could not succeed without the knowledge provided by abstract research in mathematics and laboratory experiments of the "pure" sciences. But it is misleading to draw an analogy between the natural and social sciences. Nowhere in the social realm are there unconditional laws and basic theories already well established. Quite to the contrary, it is the study of concrete and circumscribed practical problem areas that has contributed a good part

Author's Note: An earlier version of this article was presented in June 1980 at an International Conference on the Political Realization of Social Science Knowledge and Research: Toward New Scenarios, a meeting held in memoriam of Paul F. Lazarsfeld at the Institute for Advanced Studies, Vienna, Austria. I would like to acknowledge helpful criticisms offered at that time by Thomas D. Cook, Burkart Holzner, Karin D. Knorr-

From William N. Dunn, "Reforms as Arguments," 3(3) *Knowledge: Creation, Diffusion, Utilization* 293-326 (March 1982). Copyright 1982 by Sage Publications, Inc.

of the present-day general sociological knowledge. Adopting a famous dictum by Lewin, one could say that nothing is more conducive to innovation in social theory than collaboration on a complex practical problem [Lazarsfeld and Reitz, 1975: 10].

While the social sciences are thus an outgrowth of attempts to understand and alleviate practical problems, they nevertheless represent more than "the growth of ordinary knowledge *writ large*" (Popper, 1963: 216). The social sciences have not only built upon but also transformed ordinary knowledge, frequently in ways that produce unhappy results. For every *Authoritarian Personality* or *American Soldier* there is at least one Project Camelot, while countless apparently innocuous or incompetent applied research efforts have legitimized bureaucratic interests in the name of "science." Indeed, the bulk of social science research appears to make little if any contribution to improvements in social theory or social practice.

We are therefore confronted by a paradox: Those very sciences that owe their origins to practice rarely produce knowledge which enlarges our capacity to improve that practice. For many this paradox is resolved by elevating social scientists at the expense of practitioners, typically by urging that canons of scientific reasoning displace the routines of politics (Bernstein and Freeman, 1975). For others, the paradox dissolves under the weight of arguments that the social sciences simply yield less usable knowledge than do various forms of interactive problem solving based on common sense, casual empiricism, or thoughtful speculation and analysis (Lindblom and Cohen, 1979). Here we are urged to displace the social sciences with ordinary knowledge that "is highly fallible, but we shall call it knowledge even if it is false. As in the case of scientific knowledge, whether it is true or false, knowledge is knowledge to anyone who takes it as a basis for some commitment to action" (Lindblom and Cohen, 1979: 12).

This radical juxtaposition of science and ordinary knowledge, while punctuating controversies surrounding the definition of usable knowl-

Cetina, Niklas Luhmann, and Herman Strasser. The article has since benefited from the comments and suggestions of Pittsburgh colleagues—Evelyn Fisher, Bahman Fozouni, Burkart Holzner, John Marx, Alex Weilenmann, Charles Willard, and Gerald Zaltman— *and from the reactions of Andrew Gordon, Duncan MacRae, Jr., Ian Mitroff, and Sam Overman.* Finally, I am grateful to Thomas D. Cook and Donald T. Campbell who, in a spirit of generous partisanship, supplied notes, materials, and references that challenged many initial assumptions and claims about philosophic and practical implications of quasi-experimentation. Portions of this article were prepared under grant NIE-G-81-0019 from the National Institute of Education.

edge, obscures important questions: According to what standards do policy makers, social scientists, and other stakeholders in social reform assess the "truth" and "utility" of knowledge (Weiss and Bucuvalas, 1980a)? Are such standards properly confined to "threats to validity" or "plausible rival hypotheses" invoked to assess social experiments (Cook and Campbell, 1979)? Can social science theory and research themselves be used to investigate the social origins and practical uses of knowledge that has been certified on the basis of competing standards (Holzner and Marx, 1979)? Can we raise these competing standards to an explicit level of consciousness where they may shape a genuinely critical public discourse (Habermas, 1975)? Finally, are reforms best viewed as reasoned arguments or debates, that is, "critical social transactions" aiming at improvements in knowledge and its social uses (Toulmin et al., 1979)?

In responding to these questions, this article offers five related claims. First, the metaphor of the "experimenting society" (Campbell, 1975b, 1971), since it is still burdened with residues of a positivist philosophy of science, places unnecessarily severe constraints on the range of standards available to assess and certify claims about social reform. Second, and in contrast, reforms are best viewed as arguments, a metaphor whose roots lie in the everyday social interaction of policy makers, scientists, and citizens-at-large. When we revisualize reforms as arguments, it is no longer possible to make facile distinctions between "science" and "ordinary knowledge," nor are we likely to reach the patently false conclusion that knowledge derived from one or the other source is inherently superior. Third, a transactional model of argument adapted from Toulmin (1958) provides a conceptual framework which not only accommodates the experimental metaphor—including "threats to validity" and their philosophic justification—but also permits a radical enlargement of standards for assessing and challenging knowledge claims. The transactional model is therefore appropriate as a central organizing construct for a new social science of knowledge applications, since it clarifies and specifies the notion of "frames of reference" by providing several classes of "tests" for assessing the adequacy, relevance, and cogency of knowledge claims. Fourth, and relatedly, these classes of tests may be transformed into threats to usable knowledge, that is, plausible rival hypotheses about the conditions under which knowledge claims will be accepted as a precondition of action. Finally, the transactional model supplies the contours of a critical social science of knowledge applications, that is, a social science which uncovers and raises to a level of explicit consciousness those unexamined prior assumptions and implicit standards of assessment that shape and also distort the production and use of knowledge. By making such standards transparent and public, a critical social science of knowledge applications may contribute to an expansion of individual and collective learning capacities and, thus, to emancipatory social reforms.

The Experimenting Society

Among the many perspectives available for exploring the nature of social reforms, Campbell's (1971) "experimenting society" has attracted great attention among applied social scientists in the United States (see Salasin, 1973). Drawing on analogies to physics, biology, psychology, and other laboratory sciences, this perspective is founded on an evolutionary epistemology which claims that the growth of individual and societal knowledge is a consequence of trial-and-error learning processes involving successive attempts to· compare hypotheses with experimentally induced outcomes (Campbell, 1959, 1974). This evolutionary view, partly based on Popper's (1959, 1963) natural-selection epistemology, claims that the aim of experiments is to achieve objective knowledge by challenging conventional scientific wisdom and current opinion. While experimentation is "the only available route to cumulative progress" in education and other domains of social reform, it is neither a panacea for social and scientific ills nor an inherently superior substitute for well-tested ordinary knowledge that has evolved over many centuries of trial-and-error learning by practitioners (Campbell and Stanley, 1963: 3-4). Indeed, the growth of ordinary and scientific knowledge is a cumulative product of evolutionary changes in human cognitive capacities for causal reasoning (Campbell, 1974; Cook and Campbell, 1979). Causation, therefore, is an inherited property of human cognitive evolution and not a special prize reserved for university people.

The experimenting society, while conditioned by ineluctable changes in human cognitive capacities, is nevertheless an active and critical society (Campbell, 1971). The experimenting society requires a critical posture toward all knowledge, since there are neither essential nor necessary and sufficient causes in nature. This critical posture is embodied in the principle of falsification, where "not yet disproven" points to the impossibility of ruling out all relevant alternative hypotheses (Cook and Campbell, 1979). While all data are theory-dependent, thus punctuating subjective properties of all human inquiry, the experimenting society avoids epistemological relativism by positing an external reality or "nature" against which hypotheses may be tested, notwithstanding the impossibility of fully testing causal claims against that nature. Moreover, theories of causation are understood in the sense of "nuisance factors" present in contexts of practice, while the most valid causal inferences are those involving factors that may be actively manipulated by experimenters. Grounded in ordinary language and everyday interaction, this practical and active theory of causation does not presume full and complete causal explanations, as does basic research in scientific disciplines. Partial explanations suffice. Thus, for example, manipulable causes (e.g., a light switch) may be activated to produce a desired effect (illumination) without understanding theories of electronics or particle physics.

The metaphor of the experimenting society is therefore an extension of an evolutionary critical-realist epistemology and not, as some critics would have it, a naive emulation of a natural science paradigm based on hypothetico-deductive methodology (Patton, 1975, 1978). A critical epistemological posture is evident in the distinction between "trapped" and "experimental" administrators, the latter of whom are urged to advocate reforms "on the basis of the seriousness of the problem rather than the certainty of any one answer and combine this with an emphasis on the need to go on to other attempts at solution should the first one fail" (Campbell, 1975b: 35). While acknowledging the vicarious, distal, and socially embodied character of knowledge (Campbell, 1959, 1979), the experimental metaphor is based on an ontologically realist posture that places primary reliance on experimentally induced outcomes that are independent of the desires of reform-minded social scientists and administrators.

The appropriateness of the experimental metaphor depends in part on our success in establishing that social systems in which reforms are carried out are analogous to physical systems in which laboratory experiments are conducted. While a major aim of writings on quasi-experimentation has been to show that laboratory experiments are not feasible in field settings—that "pure" experiments have been oversold and misrepresented—it is also true that the experimental metaphor retains an objectivist ontological platform appropriate to the study of physical systems. For example, describing a nested hierarchy of evolutionary learning processes of which science is the most developed, Campbell observes:

> What is characteristic of science is that the selective system which weeds out among the variety of conjectures involves deliberate contact with the environment through experiment and quantified prediction, designed so that outcomes quite independent of the preferences of the investigator are possible. It is preeminently this feature that gives science its greater objectivity and its claim to a cumulative increase in the accuracy with which it describes the world [Campbell, 1974: 434].

The characteristic feature of social systems, as distinguished from physical ones, is that they are created, maintained, and changed through symbolically mediated interaction (Holzner, 1969). Whereas physical systems may be presumptively characterized in terms of a stable external reality that *edits* experimental trials independently of the preferences of investigators (Campbell, 1974: 435), social systems may be characterized (again presumptively) in terms of a dynamic external reality that *edits and interprets* experimental trials on the basis of outcomes that are independent of the preferences of some investigators but quite dependent on the preferences of others. Social systems, therefore, cannot be satisfactorily characterized as either objective or subjective entities, or even as both. Social systems, as dialectical entities, are *more than both:* "Society is a human product. Society is an objective reality. Man is a social product" (Berger and Luckman, 1967: 61).

This dialectical claim does not simply affirm that social systems are cultural entities whose symbolic and self-reflective properties set them apart from physical ones; nor does it deny that social systems are perceived as objective entities by their members. Rather, it affirms that knowledge of social systems must, of necessity, be based on an understanding of the diverse meanings attributed to reforms by stakeholders who participate in the creation, maintenance, and transformation of humanly objectivated social structures. Social reforms are therefore symbolically mediated change processes the understanding of which requires that we uncover the action-motivating reasons which guide efforts to alleviate practical problems.

Therefore, the case for social experimentation as the only "truly scientific" approach to reform (Campbell, 1975b: 72) stands or falls on the persuasiveness of the claim that experimental data are *not* symbolically mediated—that is, that experimental outcomes constitute the sole source of knowledge that is not determined by the purposes of the experimenter. To make this claim Campbell asks us to imagine experiments as tribal rituals which are

> meticulously designed to put questions to "Nature Itself" in such a way that neither questioners nor their colleagues nor their superiors can affect the answer. The supplicants set up the altar, pray reverently for the outcome they want, but do not control the outcome [Campbell, 1979b: 198].

This tribal analogy, instructive because of its simplicity, raises several difficulties. First, it is unlikely that all tribal cohorts will accept the rule of empirical correspondence as an impartial standard for resolving problems that originally created a need for experimentation. In fact, it is not the reasoned acceptance of this or any other scientific norm that alone lends authority to experimental data. Also relevant are the diverse social sanctions, including disgrace and expulsion, that accompany the process of competitive experimental replication in scientific communities. "This competitive scrutiny is indeed the main source of objectivity in sciences (Polanyi, 1966, 1967; Popper, 1963) and epitomizes an ideal of democratic practice in both judicial and legislative procedures" (Campbell, 1975b: 80).

The social organization of inquiry implied by this ideal-typical community of experimenters, even if it reflected the practice of physicists (cf. Kuhn, 1971), fails to capture the behavior of policy-makers, practitioners, social scientists, and other stakeholders in social reform. The key participants in social reforms share neither the standards of appraisal nor the incentive structure of this ideal-typical community. For this reason, experimental outcomes are unavoidably mediated by diverse standards of appraisal which are unevenly distributed among stakeholders in reform.

Thus, claims about the appropriateness of the experimental metaphor are persuasive only if the nature of experimental results automatically forecloses options for symbolically mediated interpretation. While we might grant that experimental results "certainly are not speaking for one's hopes and wishes" (Campbell, 1979: 198), neither do they speak for themselves. Thus, for example, experimenters might share norms of competitive replication and experience disappointment with outcomes that run counter to their preferences, but nevertheless resist any inference that experimental results disconfirm a favored theory of reform. A principal reason for this resistance is that even well-socialized experimenters cannot be expected to share the same theoretical framework which elicited the choice of the particular (falsified) reform as a promising experimental intervention. Social theories, unlike physical ones, are difficult to falsify with experimental data because the interpretation of such data is mediated by the assumptions, frames of reference, and ideologies of social scientists and other stakeholders in reform.

The presence of symbolically mediated experimental outcomes is precisely what is at issue in social reforms whose aim is to alleviate problems that have been described as ill-structured (Mitroff, 1974), squishy (Strauch, 1976), or messy (Ackoff, 1974). Ill-structured problems are those where the main difficulty lies in defining the nature of the problem rather than determining through selective experimental interventions the most effective reform to alleviate it. Here the primary sources of invalidity are not those *first-order* threats to internal, external, and statistical conclusion validity detailed by Campbell and colleagues (Campbell and Stanley, 1963; Cook and Campbell, 1979), but *second-order* threats that call into question the appropriateness of problem definitions that create the need for experimental interventions and their assessment in terms of standard (first-order) threats to validity.

Second-order threats transcend or go beyond first-order threats (history, maturation, regression, instability, and so on) by providing metacriteria against which the formulation of a problem—as distinguished from constituent causal inferences that represent a solution within the boundaries of that problem—may be assessed and challenged. Second-order threats are sometimes defined as Type III errors by juxtaposing the formulation of the wrong problem (E_{III}) to setting statistical confidence limits too high (E_I) or too low (E_{II}) in testing the null hypothesis (Kimball, 1957; Raiffa, 1968; Mitroff and Sagasti, 1973). Since threats to validity have been explicitly invoked as a challenge to the error of misplaced statistical precision (Campbell and Stanley, 1963: 7), it is desirable to devise new terms that do not hinge on the dichotomy of errorful calibration (E_I and E_{II}) versus errorful conceptualization (E_{III}). Accordingly, first-order errors (E^1) involve the choice of the less valid of two or more causal inferences, while second-order errors (E^2) involve the selection of the less appropriate of two or more worldviews, ideologies, frames of reference, or problem definitions when instead the more appropriate one should have been selected (Mitroff and Sagasti, 1973; Dunn, 1981: 109-110).

Confronted by an ill-structured problem, the reform-minded administrator or social scientist might use "multiple measures of independent imperfection" (Campbell and Fiske, 1959; Webb et al., 1966) to ensure that measures are responsive to the diverse aims of stakeholders. Further,

> the loyal opposition should be allowed to add still other indicators, with the political process and adversary argument challenging both validity and relative importance, with social science methodologists testifying for both parties, and with the basic records kept public and under bipartisan audit [Campbell, 1975: 80].

These adversary procedures are relevant only where stakeholders cannot arrive at a common definition of reform. Yet to justify a reform "on the basis of the seriousness of the problem rather than the certainty of any one answer" (Campbell, 1975a: 35) begs the question: On the basis of what standards are we to assess the appropriateness of the problem? First-order threats do not assist in answering this question, since they are relevant and applicable only within a given problem frame. Required are second-order threats for critically challenging the appropriateness of the problem frame itself. To confuse these two levels is to violate a basic logical axiom: "Whatever involves *all* of a collection must not be one of the collection" (Whitehead and Russell, 1910: 101, cited in Watzlawick et al., 1974: 6).

Thus, while threats to validity provide a critical mechanism for reducing the probability of first-order causal errors (E^1), they do not deal satisfactorily with second-order conceptual errors (E^2). The experimental metaphor acknowledges the priority of pattern identification over knowledge of details, but only at the level of first-order causal errors: "Qualitative, common-sense knowing of wholes and patterns provides the enveloping context necessary for the interpretation of particulate quantitative data" (Campbell, 1974b: 11). Thus, while the experimental metaphor calls for the integration of qualitative and quantitative standards for assessing and challenging knowledge claims, this general plea simply exhorts social scientists to recognize the dependence of quantitative on qualitative knowing, for example, to recognize that several threats to validity (e.g., history) are based on common-sense knowing (Campbell, 1974b: 15). Even here, the loose translation of qualitative knowing into specific threats to validity excludes or ignores many varieties of qualitative knowing, including several forms of ethical and practical reasoning that are highly appropriate for understanding purposive social behavior (see von Wright, 1971). In short, qualitative knowing is not explicitly, formally,

and systematically incorporated into the critical methodological repertoire of social experimentation.

Jurisprudence as Metaphor

Any metaphor of reform should be assessed according to its capacity
"to produce satisfactory explanations of the type of events which it
investigates, rather than its success or lack of success in getting results by
the methods of natural science" (Levinson, 1966: 144; Dunn and
Fozouni, 1976). Because reforms are symbolically mediated and
purposive social processes aiming at changes in the structure and
functioning of some social system, they necessarily involve outcomes
which are valuative as well as factual in nature. The success of reforms
therefore depends on a rationally motivated consensus that some
projected future social state is both possible and desirable. In turn, any
applied social science which seeks to critically assess and improve the
process of reform must address competing ethical as well as explanatory
hypotheses (see MacRae, 1976). For this reason, reforms are appropriately viewed as a process of reasoned argument and debate where
competing standards for assessing the adequacy of knowledge claims
include, but are not limited to, rules for making valid causal inferences.
Here the appropriate metaphors are drawn from jurisprudence (Toulmin,
1958), law (Levine and Rosenberg, 1979), forensics (Brock et al., 1973;
Brown, 1976), and rhetoric (House, 1980), disciplines in which causal
inferences play an important but nonexhaustive role.

The appropriateness of the jurisprudential metaphor becomes evident
once we consider standards for appraising knowledge applied in the
course of social reforms. In the field of evaluation research, Suchman
(1972) alerts us to the pervasiveness of experimental outcomes which are
mediated by the worldviews, ideologies, and frames of reference of
stakeholders in reform. Collectively described as "pseudoevaluation,"
these forms of symbolic mediation include the selective use of data to
make a reform appear worthwhile ("eyewash"), the suppression of data
which run counter to the preferences of reformers ("whitewash"), the use
of data to subvert a reform ("submarine"), the ritualistic collection of
data on a reform for purposes unconnected with its consequences
("posture"), and the use of data to delay reform itself ("postponement").
Similarly, Rein and White (1976) call attention to several latent goals of
government-sponsored policy research, including the containment,
subversion, and policing of social reforms. Given the complexity of social
problems, scientifically popular recommendations for improving the

production and use of applied social research—including more rigorous research designs, better sampling procedures, and administrative centralization—are likely to be marginally effective, superfluous, or mystifying (Rein and White, 1976: 244-250).

These observations on the latent goals of applied social research suggest that we should begin with the *practice* of assessing knowledge claims made in the course of reforms, hoping to uncover concepts and standards of assessment which later might be used to develop theories of knowledge production and use. This aim can be facilitated by viewing reforms as reasoned arguments, rather than experiments which put questions to "nature itself." Arguments are like lawsuits, while conclusions are similar to claims put forth in court. Conflicts among stakeholders are analogous to cases in law where disputes are settled by invoking standards appropriate to different contexts, for example, criminal or civil disputes. Whereas the aim of jurisprudence is to study the variety of concepts and procedures used to resolve legal claims, the aim of the applied social sciences is to investigate concepts and procedures used to argue and settle practical claims. The applied social sciences may therefore be described as "generalized jurisprudence" or, alternatively, as "jurisprudence writ large" (compare Toulmin, 1958: 7).

The jurisprudential metaphor is particularly appropriate for investigating reforms, since the data or evidence introduced in a given case is only one of several elements necessary to make a successful claim. Equally important are the standards of appraisal employed to interpret data. Despite the belief that the applied social sciences produce conclusive fact and proof,

> they are instead engaged in producing inconclusive evidence and argument. Problem complexity denies the possibility of proof and reduces the pursuit of fact to the pursuit of those selective facts which, if appropriately developed, constitute evidence in support of relevant argument [Lindblom and Cohen, 1979: 81].

Argumentation is, therefore, a social process where all data or evidence is symbolically mediated. Whereas proof, demonstration, or validation holds that truth is directly and immediately attainable, argumentation sees truth entirely as a social construction (Phillips, 1973), as a product of natural social comparison processes:

> Put analogically, arguments are naturally occurring corollaries to research contexts. . . . It is rather as if we were to stand back and watch while our subjects framed their own hypotheses, selected methodological principles most appropriate to the hypotheses, utilized techniques

appropriate to both, and conducted their own research act . . . arguments give us more information than other kinds of research [Willard, 1980: 9-10].

The jurisprudential metaphor is closely tied to classical and modern philosophical traditions where reason serves a practical and critical function in assessing knowledge claims. The jurisprudential metaphor

> helps to keep in the centre of the picture the *critical* function of the reason. The rules of logic may not be tips or generalizations; they none the less apply to men and their arguments—not in the way that laws of psychology or maxims of method apply, but rather as *standards of achievement*. . . .
>
> A sound argument, a well-grounded or firmly-backed claim, is one which will stand up to criticism, one for which a case can be presented coming up to the standard required if it is to deserve a favourable verdict [Toulmin, 1958: 8].

The jurisprudential metaphor thus emphasizes that argumentation is a process of rational advocacy where stakeholders engage in the *competitive reconstruction* of knowledge claims. This competitive reconstruction, in contrast to the competitive replication of experiments, leads toward a pragmatic and dialectical conception of truth where social discourse plays a reflective and critical role in producing new knowledge. Knowledge is no longer based on deductive certainty or empirical correspondence, but on the relative adequacy of knowledge claims which are embedded in ongoing social processes.

A Transactional Model of Argument

Toulmin has operationalized the jurisprudential metaphor in the form of a structural model of argument (Toulmin, 1958; Toulmin et al., 1979). Extensions of this model to issues of public policy have recognized that the growing complexity of social problems demands increased reliance on persuasion, rather than formal logical certainty, and have called for systematic learning from practitioners as a major component of creative theory building in the applied social sciences (e.g., Brock et al., 1973; House, 1977, 1980; Kelly, 1980). In developing a reflective methodology for solving ill-structured problems, Mason and Mitroff (1981) have linked the structural model to a dialectical conception of knowledge and have attempted to develop appropriate technologies that may be employed by policymakers in concrete settings.

In his critique of positivistic ethical theories, Habermas (1975: 107) employs Toulmin's distinction between analytic and substantial arguments to argue that the growth of knowledge takes place through the rationally motivating force of substantial arguments, that is, arguments which abandon criteria of conclusiveness, demonstrativeness, necessity, certainty, justification, or validity and which rely, instead, on rational standards of achievement which enhance the persuasiveness of claims in particular social contexts (Toulmin, 1958: 234). Substantial arguments

> are based on logical inferences, but they are not exhausted in deductive systems of statements. Substantial arguments serve to redeem or to criticize validity claims, whether the claims to truth implicit in assertions or the claims to correctness connected with norms (of action or evaluation) or implied in recommendations and warnings. They have the force to convince the participants in a discourse of a validity claim, that is, *to provide rational grounds for* the recognition of validity claims [Habermas, 1975: 107; emphasis in original].

Toulmin's model of argument, since it accentuates the critical and socially transacted properties of knowledge production and use, is most appropriately described as a transactional model of argument. The transactional model is important for the applied social sciences because, first, it provides a visual representation or structural schema which may be used to systematically map arguments offered by applied social scientists, policymakers, and other stakeholders in social reform. Second, the transactional model permits and even compels a reflective and critical examination of assumptions which constitute the worldview, ideology, or frame of reference of stakeholders who advance and contest knowledge claims. Third, the transactional model may be extended and elaborated to yield a typology of standards, rules, or tests for assessing and challenging the "truth" and "utility" of knowledge (see Weiss and Bucuvalas, 1980a; Holzner and Marx, 1979). This same typology also yields a classification of threats to usable knowledge, that is, rival hypotheses about the adequacy, appropriateness, and cogency of knowledge claims. Finally, the transactional model affirms that processes of knowledge production and use are symbolic or communicative actions involving two or more parties who reciprocally affect the acceptance and rejection of knowledge claims through argument and persuasion. Thus, knowledge is not "exchanged," "translated," or "transferred," but transacted by negotiating the truth, relevance, and cogency of knowledge claims.

The transactional model contains six elements: data (D), claim (C), warrant (W), backing (B), rebuttal (R), and qualifier (Q). Together these elements provide a visual representation or structural schema that may be used to map arguments. The first triad of elements parallels those of the classical syllogism: minor premise (D), major premise (W), and conclusion (C). The model is nevertheless designed as a challenge to the classical syllogism and other analytic arguments. For this reason Toulmin introduces a second triad of elements: backing (B), rebuttal (R), and qualifier (Q). The backing (B)—which consists of additional data, claims, or entire arguments—certifies the assumption expressed in the warrant and is introduced only when the status of the warrant is in doubt. In analytic arguments the backings of warrants are tautological, since they include information conveyed in the claim itself. By contrast, the backings of warrants in substantial arguments do not contain information conveyed in the claim (Toulmin, 1958: 125). Practical arguments offered in the course of a social reform are seldom if ever analytic:

> If the purpose of an argument is to establish conclusions about which we are not entirely confident by relating them back to other information about which we have greater assurance, it begins to be a little doubtful whether any genuine, practical argument could *ever* be properly analytical [Toulmin, 1958: 127; emphasis in original].

The two remaining elements of the structural schema are the rebuttal and qualifier. The rebuttal (R) performs both a retrospective and an anticipatory role by specifying conditions under which the adequacy or relevance of a knowledge claim may be challenged. Finally, the qualifier (Q) expresses the degree of cogency or force attached to the claim and is typically expressed with such terms as "definitely," "very probably," or "at the one percent confidence interval (p = .01)."

The structural schema provides an explicit visual representation of these six elements and their role in making practical inferences, much in the same way that symbols used to depict different types of experimental, quasi-experimental, and preexperimental designs provide a visual image of the role of independent and dependent variables in making causal inferences (Campbell and Stanley, 1963). In contrast to experimental design notation, the structural schema surfaces and raises to a

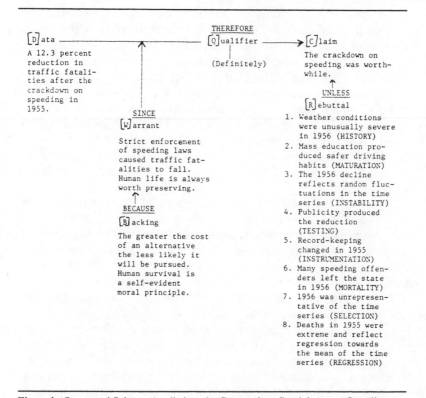

Figure 1: Structural Schema Applied to the Connecticut Crackdown on Speeding
SOURCES: Adapted from Campbell (1975b) and Dunn (1981).

level of explicit consciousness the assumptions and presuppositions which provide rational backing for substantial arguments. This critical function of the structural schema may be illustrated by borrowing from Campbell (1975b) a well-known example of quasi-experimental reform.

Following record high traffic fatalities in 1955, the governor of Connecticut implemented a crackdown on speeding violators. After one year there were 284 traffic deaths, a 12.3% reduction from the record high of 324 in 1955. On the basis of these data (D) the governor offered the following claim: "With the saving of 40 lives in 1956, a reduction of 12.3% from the 1955 motor vehicle death toll, we can say that the program is definitely worthwhile" (Campbell, 1975b: 75-76). Figure 1 illustrates the governor's argument, including suppressed warrants and backings and rebuttals based on threats to the validity of causal inferences (Campbell and Stanley, 1963; Campbell, 1975b).

The transactional model permits and even compels a reflective or critical posture toward the presuppositions of knowledge claims, whether practical or theoretical. For this reason it transcends overdrawn and facile distinctions between "professional social inquiry" and "ordinary knowledge" (Lindblom and Cohen, 1979), viewing both as potentially ideological in the classic sense of beliefs which originate in unexamined assumptions. The transactional model can also assist in transforming the empirico-analytic and hermeneutic sciences into critical ones (see Habermas, 1971), since the model forces the inspection of causal and ethical assumptions, as well as their underlying warrants, as part of a social process of interpreting qualitative and quantitative data.

Thus, the claim that "The crackdown on speeding was definitely worthwhile" might withstand all threats to validity but lack persuasive force. One or more stakeholders may question the adequacy of underlying causal assumptions ("Strict enforcement of speeding laws caused traffic fatalities to fall.") or moral principles ("Human life is always worth preserving."). If further support is required, certain axioms of economic theory ("The greater the cost of an alternative, the less likely it will be pursued.") might be introduced as backing for the warrant, as might ostensibly self-evident moral principles (human survival). The claim here is not that these particular axioms and principles are necessarily adequate ones, since they are certain to be challenged by stakeholders who hold competing theories, worldviews, ideologies, and frames of reference. The point, rather, is that adaptations of the empirico-analytic sciences (e.g., Cook and Campbell, 1979) and extensions of hermeneutics (e.g., Patton, 1975, 1978) do not address such questions in a systematic, critical, and self-reflective manner.

The transactional model thus accommodates all potentially relevant types of claims and forms of argument. Attention is not confined to descriptive and explanatory claims, the standard and exclusive focus of the empirico-analytic and hermeneutic sciences, but extends to claims which have ethical content insofar as their aim is to evaluate or advocate action. Further, arguments are not limited to a particular causal form (for example, deductive-nomological explanation) but include other forms of causal reasoning such as those represented by quasi-naturalistic (historical), quasi-teleological (cybernetic), and teleological (practical) explanations (see von Wright, 1971). This capacity to distinguish diverse forms of argument and types of claims clarifies a number of methodological inadequacies found in the applied social sciences, including the pervasive misconception that "evaluation research" evaluates and the regrettable tendency among public policy analysts to view claims which advocate or recommend courses of action as emotive or ideological appeals that are devoid of rational content. As Tribe (1972), Rein (1976), and MacRae (1976) recognize, this tendency reflects the implicit positivistic assumptions of policy analysis as an applied social science discipline that ignores or denigrates ethical discourse.

A related advantage of the model is its capacity to surface and make explicit the processes of reasoning used to make knowledge claims. Whereas applied social scientists and practitioners frequently suppress steps in the process of reasoning from data to claim—for example, by claiming that coefficients of association or so-called predictive equations speak for themselves as a demonstration of causal patterns or sequences —the transactional model surfaces implicit causal and ethical hypotheses alike. This critical function is by no means limited to hypothesis testing, since the model may be used to surface paradigms, worldviews, and frames of reference which unite epistemic communities (Holzner and Marx, 1979), to establish the boundaries of disciplinary matrices (Webber, 1980), and to distort the definition of social problems (Gregg et al., 1979).

By distinguishing analytic and substantial arguments, the transactional model provides the applied social sciences with a framework and methodology for transcending pseudo-ethical disputes whose resolution appears superficially to lie in greater logical consistency or better empirical data. In analytic arguments the major premise or warrant is taken for granted, and the main task is to demonstrate that conclusions or claims follow from the data with deductive certainty. Yet it is substantial arguments, and not analytic ones, which characterize the bulk of knowledge claims put forth in the course of social reforms. For this reason, disputes frequently turn on the presuppositions used to back warrants and not on surface assumptions or data such as those found in authoritative moral principles or empirical observations which have been validated through intersubjective agreement.

It is, therefore, insufficient to treat ethical hypotheses solely in terms of standards appropriate for analytic arguments, for example, metacriteria of logical consistency, clarity, and generality (MacRae, 1976: 90-98) or basic postulates of moral reasoning (Gewirth, 1979). Much less is it appropriate to confine ethical discourse to standards of appraisal appropriate for the empirical study of social determinants of knowledge or its applications (Holzner and Marx, 1979). The structural model, since it raises substantial arguments to a level of explicit consciousness, penetrates the rational content of ethical and nonethical assumptions which individually and jointly motivate the acceptance and rejection of knowledge claims.

Finally, the transactional model provides concepts and procedures of argument assessment which are reconstructable and public. The structural schema may be used retrospectively, to describe and evaluate different types of claims and arguments, and prospectively. While it is not possible "to list in advance the ingredients of a convincing argument" (Phillips, 1973: 178), the structural model can nevertheless be used prospectively to design arguments that withstand the diverse challenges or rebuttals which are commonplace in debates about reform. Mason and Mitroff (1981), for example, report the use of the transactional model to conduct an interactive dialectical debate among stakeholders engaged in resolving problems of public and business policy. Their interactive computer-assisted methodology not only permits stakeholders to attach ordinal plausibility values to each element of an argument and the argument as a whole but also, more important, enables them to challenge and revise assumptions in the course of a reflective debate. A similar dialectical methodology, also based on the transactional model, has been used to select maximally usable performance measures in the domain of evaluation research (Dunn et al., 1982). The aim of these procedures is not to "scientize" the model of argument, but to enhance prospects for its efficient use, recognizing that the capacity for reasoned debate and reflective understanding is a scarce resource.

Testing Knowledge Claims

Claims about social reform are products of frames of reference, that is, sets of systematically related assumptions that provide standards for appraising knowledge claims. A central component of frames of reference is what Holzner and Marx (1979: 103-111) call reality or truth tests and which Weiss and Bucuvalas (1980a) have investigated in the form of truth tests and utility tests. Truth tests are

decision points concerning evidence; the grounds for accepting or rejecting truth claims include . . . empirical as well as formal rational tests. Pragmatic tests rest on proof of workability . . . there are other tests of varying stringency and reliance on trust or authority [Holzner and Fisher, 1979: 233].

By contrast, utility or relevance tests are decision points concerning the delineation of an appropriate domain of inquiry or action. The basis for accepting or rejecting a relevance claim is the "potential significance of an item or line of inquiry . . . with regard to the inquirer's cognitive interests" (Holzner and Fisher, 1979: 233).

Concepts of truth and relevance tests pose practically and theoretically important distinctions. Nevertheless, it is now unclear how such tests are actually distributed among stakeholders in social reforms and, indeed, whether the existence and functions of such tests may be investigated empirically. Available typologies of such tests contain ambiguities that now impede directed empirical research. Pointing to the elusive nature of "relevance" and "utility," Holzner and Fisher (1979: 235) observe that "questions remain about the exact manner in which some information comes to the attention of a person and how it is sifted." Weiss and Bucuvalas (1980a), while calling for a new sociology of knowledge applications, call attention to the complexity of issues surrounding the concept of frame of reference and remind us of the many conceptual and methodological limitations facing those who wish to investigate the impact of truth tests and utility tests on individual and collective decisions.

The transactional model may be extended to generate a typology of knowledge claims and arguments which clarifies and specifies concepts of truth and relevance. Knowledge claims may be classified according to the explicit or implicit purposes of knowledge claimants or their challengers. Brockriede and Ehninger (1960), drawing from the fields of forensics and semiotics, classify claims into four types: definitive, designative, evaluative, and advocative. The purpose of definitive claims is to provide knowledge about the appropriate *definition* of some object (What is it?), whereas that of designative claims is to supply knowledge about *observed regularities* (Does it exist?). In turn, the aim of evaluative claims is to provide knowledge about the *value* of an event or object (Of what worth is it?), while the purpose of advocative claims is to supply knowledge about *policy* (What should be done?).

Relevance tests are closely related to these four types of claims. If relevance tests are decision points concerning the delineation of an appropriate domain of inquiry or action, policymakers and practitioners appear to be predisposed toward tests of relevance that reflect an interest in knowledge about what courses of action to pursue to resolve problems (advocative claims). Discipline-based social scientists, by contrast, are generally oriented toward tests of relevance that reflect an interest in definitions (e.g., definitive claims about poverty, health, or achievement) and in observed regularities in society and nature (e.g., designative claims about the sources of social inequality). These divergent purposes underlie contrasts between policy research and discipline-based research (Coleman, 1972), distinctions between "macronegative" and "micropositive" research findings (Williams, 1971), divisions within the "two-communities theory" of knowledge utilization (Caplan, 1979), and the pattern of factor loadings reported by Weiss and Bucuvalas (1980a) in their study of the frames of reference of mental health policymakers. In turn, evaluative claims often reflect tests of relevance shared primarily by philosophers and social critics, for example, those who see in policy analysis an ideology in disguise (Tribe, 1972). In each case the purposes of knowledge, as reflected in these four types of claims, affirm or diminish the relevance of that knowledge to different stakeholders.

The application of a relevance test does not guarantee that a knowledge claim will be regarded as sufficiently cogent or forceful. Tests of cogency are dependent on the relative force expected of a claim in particular circumstances. Hence, an advocative claim accepted as relevant to the aims of a particular stakeholder will not necessarily be viewed as cogent. Tests of cogency, which are an extension of Toulmin's qualifier, are evident in the practice of different professions. For example, members of the legal and medical professions use similar tests of relevance but different cogency tests (compare Holzner and Fisher, 1979: 235-236). Members of the legal profession typically employ a conservative cogency test (qualifier) for knowledge claims offered in criminal cases: Defendents are presumed innocent until proven guilty. By contrast, members of the medical profession often use a liberal test of cogency for claims surrounding the treatment of illness: Patients are presumed to be ill, and treated, until proven otherwise. In the first case the problem is to avoid "false positives," while in the second it is to avoid "false negatives." In other cases cogency and relevance interact, for example, when school officials set stringent confidence intervals in validating the results of achievement batteries which will be used to recommend students for jobs or further education, but apply liberal tests of cogency when assessing the effects of existing curricula on student achievement scores.

The appraisal of knowledge claims is not exhausted by tests of relevance and cogency. Knowledge claims, apart from their relevance, derive force or cogency from truth tests. Truth tests may be represented in terms of different sets of assumptions and underlying presuppositions used to transform data into claims in a practical or theoretical argument. Truth tests are standards for appraising the *adequacy* of knowledge claims, for example, by challenging the causal assumptions which underlie a claim. By contrast, tests of cogency and relevance are standards for appraising the requisite *force* and contextual *appropriateness* of a claim, respectively. Typically, tests of adequacy and relevance are discrete assumptions, standards, or rules, while tests of cogency are best represented in terms of varying levels of force required of a claim. Knowledge claims which are adequate and cogent may be irrelevant, while claims that are relevant may lack adequacy and cogency alike. For example, government-sponsored program evaluations may be regarded as relevant to the aims of reform-minded social scientists but nevertheless lacking in adequacy and cogency when assessed according to standards of research quality generally accepted by social scientists (Bernstein and Freeman, 1975).

Whereas tests of relevance and cogency appear to be comparatively simple, truth tests are complex. Many options for classifying truth tests are available in the writings of philosophers, anthropologists, sociologists, and other social observers and critics. For example, Peirce's contrasts among alternative methods of "fixing belief" (see Buchler, 1953) and Malinowski's (1948) essays on science, magic, and religion point to a range of truth tests used to assess the adequacy of knowledge claims. Similarly, Montague (1925) and Wallace (1971) distinguish alternative modes for generating and testing the truth of statements about the world, modes which differ along three dimensions: the status of knowledge producers; the use of approved methods to produce knowledge; and the reliance on observation as a check on knowledge claims.

The experimental metaphor, as we have seen, places primary reliance on the correspondence of claims to a stable external reality and secondary reliance on procedures for determining the coherence of such claims among multiple experimenters (Cook and Campbell, 1979). Authority is also important, since claims are partly certified on the basis of their having been derived from a learning process (scientific experimentation) that is believed to be unique in its penetration of a stable and objective external reality (Campbell, 1974). The danger is that (necessarily) presumptive ontological claims about what is real or natural may improperly authenticate or certify epistemological claims about what is true (Michalos, 1981). The ontology of objectivism, when used as a justification or warrant for science, may also result in the denigration of ethics on grounds that only science produces corrigible knowledge claims (Gewirth, 1960).

The limitation of these schema is that they do not incorporate a variety of potentially important truth tests which reflect alternative modes of explanation (von Wright, 1971), different knowledge-constitutive interests (Habermas, 1971), and competing standards for assessing ethical knowledge (MacRae, 1976). Any provisional classification of truth tests should therefore permit distinctions between naturalistic, quasi-naturalistic, and practical modes of explanation; enable distinctions among standards of knowledge adequacy appropriate for the empirico-analytic, hermeneutic, and critical social sciences; and foster an open consideration of possibilities for testing ethical hypotheses.

The classification of truth tests in Figure 2 attempts to build upon these diverse concerns with standards of knowledge adequacy. In contrast to Brockriede and Ehninger (1960), who employ Toulmin's model to classify artistic or rhetorical proofs, we use argument as a unifying construct to classify standards of knowledge adequacy. This extension of the transactional model proceeds from a recognition that the decisive element of most contested knowledge claims is not evidence or data (compare Campbell, 1974; Popper, 1961), but the underlying standards of appraisal which warrant the transformation of data into claims. Data themselves are rarely conclusive; most social theories are therefore radically undetermined by data (see Hesse, 1980).

Equally important for our purposes, contexts of practical action appear to be radically undetermined by generalizable standards or rules. As Knorr-Cetina (1981) argues, practical action is indexical and indeterminate insofar as "rules and decision criteria, and more generally definitions of the situation, are interpreted in context . . . it is the concrete, local translation of rules or decision criteria which determine the selections that are made, and which subsequently shape the outcomes of these selections." At the same time the underdetermination thesis, whether applied to theory or to practice, does not entail the conclusion that knowledge claims are properly explained solely in terms of externally imposed "sociological" factors (Laudan, 1981), since diverse standards or rules for certifying and challenging the adequacy of knowledge claims may hold as much or more explanatory import as do variables such as social structure (see Laudan, 1977).

Truth tests may be classified according to the general and specific functions they perform in knowledge transactions. These general functions are (1) *empirico-analytic:* knowledge adequacy is certified by assumptions about the logical consistency of axioms, laws, propositions, hypotheses, or principles and/or their correspondence to empirically observed regularities; (2) *interpretive:* knowledge adequacy is certified by assumptions about the action-motivating significance of purposes, intentions, reasons, or motivations; (3) *pragmatic:* knowledge adequacy is certified by assumptions about the effectiveness of past experiences in producing desired outcomes in parallel contexts; (4) *authoritative:* knowledge adequacy is certified by assumptions about the achieved or ascribed status of knowledge producers, the orthodoxy of knowledge, or the use of approved methods; and (5) *critical:* knowledge adequacy is certified by assumptions about the consequences of such knowledge in emancipating individuals and collectivities from unexamined or tacit beliefs that impede the realization of human potential.

Tests of truth, relevance, and cogency are distinct but interrelated standards for appraising knowledge claims. These three general classes of tests, together with specific variants, govern the adequacy, appropriateness, and requisite force of knowledge offering solutions for practical problems. Truth, relevance, and cogency tests are potentially independent, although the force of a knowledge claim (cogency test) frequently depends on prior assessments of relevance and adequacy. The reverse is generally not true, since various tests of cogency (for example, tests of statistical significance) seldom establish the relevance or adequacy of knowledge claims. These generalizations and the typology on which they are based are hypotheses, merely. With Weiss and Bucuvalas (1980a) we are now investigating these and other components of frames of reference in concrete settings of practice.

Threats to Usable Knowledge

In further extending the transactional model, we may view threats to knowledge claims as rebuttals (R) to practical and theoretical arguments which affirm, explicitly or implicitly, the adequacy, cogency, or relevance of knowledge. In contrast to other approaches which encourage the separate exploration of rival hypotheses about causation (e.g., Cook and Campbell, 1979), or those dealing with ethical norms (e.g., MacRae, 1976), the function of threats to knowledge adequacy, relevance, and cogency is to challenge both the substantial and analytic bases of empirical as well as normative claims. Therefore, while threats to adequacy, relevance, and cogency provide alternative interpretations of the same data or evidence, they are not limited to assessments of the validity of causal inferences.

Type of Warrant or Backing	Function of Truth Test
EMPIRICO-ANALYTIC	
-- Causal	A nomic connection (e.g., Boyle's Law) certifies that events described in data (D) are causally related.
-- Quasi-Causal	An apparent nomic-like connection (e.g., Toynbee's historical cycles) certifies that events described in data (D) are causally related.
-- Typological	A typology (e.g., Jung's theory of psychological types) certifies that events, actions, or persons described in data (D) are members of some class.
-- Representational	A representational rule (e.g., the Central Limit Theorem) certifies that events, objects, or persons described in data (D) are typical or representative of some wider population.
-- Analogical	An analogy or metaphor (e.g., the servomechanisms of systems theory) certifies that relations among events, objects, or persons described in data (D) are similar to those contained in the metaphor or analogy.
INTERPRETIVE	
-- Teleological	A statement about individual purposes, intentions, motivations, or reasons (e.g., goals of policymakers or social scientists) certifies that actions described in data (D) are causally related to such purposes.
-- Quasi-Teleological	A nomic connection (e.g., Ashby's Law of Requisite Variety) certifies that collective actions described in data (D) are causally related to collective purposes.
PRAGMATIC	
-- Clinical	A symptomatology (e.g., the F-Scale or the MMPI) certifies that symptoms described in data (D) are indicative of an abnormal or normal, deviant or healthy state.
-- Comparative	A parallel case or experience (e.g., socialized medicine in the United Kingdom or PPBS in the Defense Department) certifies that events or actions described in data (D) are similar in their effects to those of the parallel.

Figure 2: Classification of Truth Tests

Type of Warrant or Backing	Function of Truth Test
AUTHORITATIVE	
-- Personal	The achieved or ascribed status of knowledge producers (e.g., gurus, scientists, or expert commissions) certifies that information described in data (D) is accurate, precise, or reliable.
-- Ideological	An established belief or doctrine (e.g., scientism, capitalism, socialism) certifies that ideas described in data (D) are orthodox.
-- Ethical	A norm, value, or principle (e.g., Rawls' principle of justice or the Pareto Criterion) certifies that actions described in data (D) are justified.
-- Methodical	The use of an approved method (e.g., path analysis or phenomenology) certifies that information described in data (D) is accurate, precise, reliable, and valid.
CRITICAL	
-- Ontological	A presumption about the nature or reality of valid knowledge (e.g., objectivism or subjectivism) certifies that ideas described in data (D) are true or right.
-- Emancipatory	A presumption about the liberation of human potential (e.g., self-actualization, Theory-Y, homo laborans) certifies that ideas described in data (D) are true or right.

Figure 2 (Continued)

Figure 3 summarizes three classes of threats to usable knowledge. The majority of these threats reflect methodological and practical issues not addressed by Campbell and Stanley (1963) and Cook and Campbell (1979) in their listing of classes of threats to the internal, external, and statistical conclusion validity of causal inferences. Indeed, and as repeatedly noted, these validity threats are exclusively oriented toward standards of adequacy and relevance which are causal and designative, respectively. The one exception to this exclusive concentration on causal and designative standards is "irrelevant responsiveness of measures," a threat to external validity where the imperfect validity of measures in adequately representing experimental outcomes *valued* according to conflicting standards held by diverse stakeholders is overcome by multiple operationism and triangulation (Campbell, 1975b: 79-80; Campbell and Fiske, 1959; Webb et al., 1966). This threat to validity implies an interpretive test which is not easily reconciled with an experimentalist platform which contends that outcomes should be

Class/Type	Representative Threat
THREATS TO COGENCY	
-- Misjudged Cogency	Setting statistical confidence limits too high (Type I Error) or too low (Type II Error) in testing the null hypothesis
-- Misplaced Cogency	Correctly setting statistical confidence limits for the wrong problem (Type III Error)
THREATS TO RELEVANCE	
-- Misplaced Relevance	Production of cogent knowledge claims that are relevant to the wrong purpose
-- Untimely Relevance	Production of cogent and relevant knowledge claims too late
THREATS TO ADEQUACY	
-- Misplaced Adequacy	Use of less appropriate of two or more classes of truth tests when, instead, a more appropriate truth test should be employed
-- Subjectivity	Use of causal test when explanation should be supplemented or replaced with one based on subjectively meaningful action
-- Reflexivity	Use of quasi-causal test without recognition that social processes are subject to human reflection, initiative, and control
-- Misclassification	Use of typological test results in placement of events, actions, or persons in wrong class
-- Misrepresentation	Use of less appropriate of two or more representational tests, whether statistical or theoretical
-- Perspectivity	Use of analogical test as literal surrogate rather than perspective or metaphor
-- Objectivity	Use of teleological test when explanation should be supplemented or replaced by quasi-causal test which identifies humanly objectivated but unreflected law-like regularities
-- Spuriousness	Use of clinical test involving a set of symptoms which are less appropriate diagnostic or treatment indicators than another set of symptoms
-- Misplaced Comparison	Use of comparative test when two or more cases are not similar
-- Counterauthentication	Use of personal, ideological, ethical, or methodical test when some other person, doctrine, norm, or procedure is more qualified, orthodox, fair, or scientifically sanctioned
-- Substantiality	Use of a (necessarily) presumptive ontological claim to certify epistemological or ethical claims when, instead, such claims may be argued on substantial grounds
-- Misplaced Reflexivity	Claims about the emancipatory role of self-reflection and reasoned discourse are treated as if they refer to concrete contexts of practice when, instead, they are unrelated to ongoing practices

Figure 3: Threats to Usable Knowledge

independent of the preferences of different stakeholders (Campbell, 1979b).

Threats to the usability of knowledge may be divided into three classes: cogency, relevance, and adequacy (Figure 3). Threats to the cogency of knowledge claims are of two main types: misjudged cogency and misplaced cogency. Misjudged cogency, a topic of standard statistical textbooks, is illustrated by errors of practical judgment which occur when one sets statistical confidence limits too high (Type I Error) or too low (Type II Error) in testing the null hypothesis. By contrast, misplaced cogency occurs when one correctly sets statistical confidence limits but addresses the wrong problem. The threat of misplaced cogency is evident in John Tukey's admonition to applied social researchers: "Far better an approximate answer to the right question, which is often vague, than an exact answer to the wrong questions, which can always be made precise" (quoted by Rose, 1977: 23). This first-order threat has been generalized by Kimball (1957), Raiffa (1968), and Mitroff (1974) as Error of the Third Type (E_{III}) and discussed by Campbell and Stanley (1963: 6-7) under the heading of misplaced precision in one-shot case studies.

Threats to knowledge relevance are also of two main types: misplaced relevance and untimely relevance. Misplaced relevance involves the production of cogent knowledge claims which are relevant to one kind of purpose when, instead, cogent knowledge claims relevant to another kind of purpose should have been produced. This second-order threat is noted with great frequency in published literature on policy research (for example, Coleman, 1972; Rein and White, 1976). The threat of misplaced relevance is also noted by proponents of multiattribute utility analysis who contend that experimental program evaluations offer designative claims but not evaluative and advocative ones (Edwards et al., 1975: 140). By contrast, untimely relevance, a second-order threat that is more easily overcome, involves the production of relevant information too late to satisfy the needs of one or more stakeholders (see, for example, Weiss, 1977).

Threats to knowledge adequacy are more diverse and complex than those pertaining to relevance and cogency. Among the major threats to knowledge adequacy are:

(1) *Misplaced Adequacy:* This is the use of the less appropriate of two or more classes of truth tests when, instead, the more appropriate truth test should be employed. This second-order threat is found in theoretical and practical disputes surrounding the appropriateness of contending worldviews, paradigms, and frames of reference for policy research (for example, Tribe, 1972; Patton, 1975; Rein, 1976; MacRae, 1976).

(2) *Subjectivity:* A classical causal test is used to explain human behavior when, instead, the explanation should be supplemented or replaced by

one founded on subjectively meaningful action. Claims about the effectiveness of federally sponsored social experiments are frequently challenged on grounds of subjective inadequacy (e.g., Trend, 1978), another second-order threat.

(3) *Reflexivity:* A quasi-causal test is used to affirm the social or historical necessity of some process or event when, instead, such processes or events are subject to human reflection, initiative, and control. This second-order threat is sometimes applied to quasi-causal theories of revolutionary social change. Such theories are challenged on grounds that predictions of socio-historical events hold true if and only if reflection by stakeholders does not lead them to change their values or behavior or if unpredictable factors that arise through creative reformulations of social problems do not intervene (MacIntyre, 1973).

(4) *Misclassification:* This second-order threat may be invoked to determine whether a typological test results in the placement of events, actions, or persons in the wrong class. The creation of social pseudo-problems by labelling healthy persons as deviants reflects classificational inadequacies that derive from unexamined paradigms and social myths (see, for example, Lowry, 1974; Gregg et al., 1979).

(5) *Misrepresentation:* This is the use of a particular representational test, whether statistical or theoretical, when another more representative rule should have been employed. The underenumeration of minorities in the 1970 U.S. Census illustrates this second-order threat.

(6) *Perspectivity:* This is the use of an analogical test as a literal surrogate for some social process when, instead, the analogy is no more than a perspective or metaphor of that process. Challenges to the adequacy of quantitative policy models illustrate this second-order threat to metaphorical adequacy (e.g., Strauch, 1976).

(7) *Objectivity:* This is the use of a teleological test to explain action when, instead, the explanation should be supplemented or replaced by a quasi-causal test which identifies the operation of humanly objectivated but unreflected lawlike regularities. The concept of unanticipated social consequences and the "self-fulfilling prophecy" illustrate this second-order threat (Merton, 1976).

(8) *Spuriousness:* This is the use of a clinical test involving one symptom or set of symptoms to diagnose or treat a social ill when, instead, some other symptom or set of symptoms is a better indicant of the problem. Knowledge about the diagnosis and treatment of mental and physical illnesses is often subject to second-order threats of spurious symptomatology.

(9) *Misplaced Comparison:* This is the use of a comparative test to adopt a reform that has succeeded elsewhere when conditions surrounding the reform are not sufficiently similar to the case at hand. Misplaced comparison is a continuous second-order threat to knowledge claims about government-sponsored "exemplary" projects.

(10) *Counterauthentication.* This is the use of a personal, ideological, ethical, or methodical test when some other person, doctrine, norm, or procedure is more qualified, orthodox, fair, or sanctioned. Knowledge produced by mystics, seers, gurus, scientists, and expert panels and commissions is typically threatened by diverse forms of counterauthentication, as is knowledge which originates in ideological doctrines, ethical systems, and approved technical conventions of science.

(11) *Substantiality:* This is a (necessarily) presumptive ontological claim about the nature of social reality, human nature, or knowledge certifying epistomological or ethical claims when, instead, such claims should be argued on substantial grounds. This second-order threat is evident in Campbell's criticisms of the naturalistic fallacy (i.e., deducing ethical from nonethical premises) in contemporary sociobiology (Campbell, 1979a) and in efforts of critical social theorists (e.g., Habermas, 1975) to challenge presumptive ontological claims of logical positivism on grounds that such claims, since they represent conclusions of substantial arguments, are corrigible and redeemable through social discourse.

(12) *Misplaced Reflexivity:* Claims about the emancipatory role of self-reflection and reasoned discourse are treated as if they refer to concrete contexts of practice when, instead, they are unrelated to ongoing practices. Misplaced reflexivity is a standing threat to much work carried out in ethnomethodology, phenomenology, and critical theory.

These classes of threats to knowledge adequacy may stand in a contemporary relation, as when the threat of objective inadequacy induces the use of a combined teleological and quasi-causal truth test. In other cases, threats to knowledge adequacy expose fundamentally irreconcilable standards of appraisal, for example, when subjective inadequacy reveals that nomic connections (laws) appropriate to knowledge claims in physics are inapplicable to sociocultural systems. Finally, threats to knowledge adequacy may be extended in the form of additional classes. The framework described above makes no claim to exhaustiveness or universality.

Conclusion

Problems of knowledge production and use cannot be satisfactorily clarified or alleviated by making exaggerated and facile distinctions between professional social inquiry and ordinary knowledge; nor should we accept the patently false conclusion that knowledge derived from one or the other source is inherently superior. The task is rather to distinguish between approaches to knowledge creation and use which recognize the critical function of reason in appraising knowledge claims and those which do not. The metaphor of the experimenting society, while it has introduced reasoned discourse into the examination of causal inferences, fails to recognize that reforms are symbolically mediated social processes aiming at changes in the structure and functioning of some social system. Accordingly, experimental outcomes cannot be said to be independent of the preferences of stakeholders in social reforms.

The success of reforms depends upon rationally motivated consensus that some future social state is possible and desirable. Reforms are processes of reasoned argument and debate where competing standards for appraising knowledge claims include but are not limited to rules for making valid causal inferences. The jurisprudential metaphor not only captures these diverse standards for assessing knowledge claims but also directs attention to processes of knowledge creation and use as critical social transactions involving issues of the comparative adequacy, relevance, and cogency of knowledge claims.

The jurisprudential metaphor has been extended and specified in the form of a transactional model of argument. The transactional model, since it distinguishes between analytic and substantial arguments, is well-suited for critical inquiries into competing standards for assessing theoretical and practical claims alike. The transactional model provides a visual schema for mapping arguments; compels a reflective and critical posture toward presuppositions of knowledge claims; yields a classification of truth, relevance, and cogency tests; and permits a provisional listing of classes of threats to usable knowledge. The role of the transactional model is not limited to retrospective inquiries into standards of knowledge assessment employed by contending stakeholders, since an awareness of threats to usable knowledge helps anticipate diverse challenges to knowledge claims. By supplying the contours of a critical social science of knowledge applications—that is, a social science which uncovers and raises to a level of explicit consciousness those unexamined prior assumptions and implicit standards of assessment that shape and distort the production and use of knowledge —the transactional model may contribute to individual and collective learning capacities and, thus, to emancipatory social reforms.

References

ACKOFF, R. L. (1974) Redesigning the Future: A Systems Approach to Societal Problems. New York: John Wiley.

BERNSTEIN, I. N. and H. FREEMAN (1975) Academic and Entrepreneurial Research. New York: Russell Sage Foundation.

BROCK, B. L., J. W. CHESEBRO, J. F. CRAGAN, and J. F. KLUMPP (1973) Public Policy Decision Making: Systems Analysis and the Comparative Advantages Debate. New York: Harper & Row.

BROCKRIEDE, W. and D. EHNINGER (1960) "Toulmin on argument: an interpretation and application." Q. J. of Speech 46: 44-53.

BROWN, P. G. (1976) "Ethics and policy research." Policy Analysis 2: 325-340.

BUCHLER, J. [ed.] (1955) Philosophical Writings of Peirce. New York: Dover.

CAMPBELL, D. T. (1979a) "Comments on the sociobiology of ethics and moralizing." Behavioral Sci. 24: 37-45.

——— (1979b) "A tribal model of the social system vehicle carrying scientific knowledge." Knowledge 1: 181-202.

——— (1975a) "Assessing the impact of planned social change," pp. 3-45 in G. M. Lyons (ed.) Social Research and Public Policies. Hanover, NH: Public Affairs Center, Dartmouth College.

——— (1975b) "Reforms as experiments," pp. 71-100 in E. L. Struening and M. Guttentag (eds.) Handbook of Evaluation Research (Vol. 1). Beverly Hills, CA: Sage.

——— (1974a) "Evolutionary epistemology," pp. 413-463 in P. A. Schilpp (ed.) The Philosophy of Karl Popper. LaSalle, IL: Open Court Press.

——— (1974b) "Qualitative knowing in action research." Kurt Lewin Award Address, Society for the Psychological Study of Social Issues, American Psychological Association, New Orleans, September 1.

——— (1971) "Methods for the experimenting society." Presented at the meeting of the American Psychological Association, Washington, D.C., September 5.

——— (1959) "Methodological suggestions from a comparative psychology of knowledge processes." Inquiry 2: 152-182.

CAMPBELL, D. T. and D. W. FISKE (1959) "Convergent and discriminant validation by the multitrait-multimethod matrix." Psych. Bull. 56: 81-105.

CAMPBELL, D. T. and J. C. STANLEY (1963) Experimental and Quasi-Experimental Designs for Research. Skokie, IL: Rand McNally.

CAPLAN, N. (1979) "The two-communities theory and knowledge utilization." Amer. Behavioral Scientist 22: 459-470.

COLEMAN, J. S. (1972) Policy Research in the Social Sciences. Morristown, NJ: General Learning Press.

COOK, T. D. and D. T. CAMPBELL (1979) Quasi-Experimentation. Skokie, IL: Rand McNally.

DUNN, W. N. (1981) Public Policy Analysis: An Introduction. Englewood Cliffs, NJ: Prentice-Hall.

——— and B. FOZOUNI (1976) Toward a Critical Administrative Theory. Beverly Hills, CA: Sage.

DUNN, W. N., I. I. MITROFF and S. J. DEUTSCH (1982) "The obsolescence of evaluation research." Evaluation and Program Planning 4, 1.

EDWARDS, W., M. GUTTENTAG, and K. SNAPPER (1975) "A decision-theoretic approach to evaluation research," pp. 139-182 in E. L. Struening and M. Guttentag (eds.) Handbook of Evaluation Research. Beverly Hills, CA: Sage.

GEWIRTH, A. (1979) Reason in Morality. Chicago: Univ. of Chicago Press.

——— (1960) "Positive ethics and normative science." Philosophical Rev. 69: 311-330.

GREGG, G., T. PRESTON, A. GEIST, and N. CAPLAN (1979) "The caravan rolls on: forty years of social problem research." Knowledge 1: 31-61.

HABERMAS, J. (1975) Legitimation Crisis. Boston: Beacon Press.

————— (1971) Knowledge and Human Interests. Boston: Beacon Press.

HESSE, M. (1980) Revolutions and Reconstructions in the Philosophy of Science. Bloomington: Univ. of Indiana Press.

HOLZNER, B. (1969) Reality Construction in Society. Cambridge, MA: Schenkman.

————— and E. FISHER (1979) "Knowledge in use: considerations in the sociology of knowledge application." Knowledge 1: 219-244.

HOLZNER, B. and J. MARX (1979) Knowledge Application: The Knowledge System in Society. Boston: Allyn and Bacon.

————— and E. FISHER (1977) "Paul Lazarsfeld and the study of knowledge applications." Soc. Focus 10(2): 97-116.

HOUSE, E. R. (1980) Evaluating with Validity. Beverly Hills, CA: Sage.

————— (1977) The Logic of Evaluative Argument. CSE Monograph Series in Evaluation 7. Los Angeles: Center for the Study of Evaluation, University of California.

KELLY, E. F. (1980) "Evaluation as persuasion: a practical argument." Educ. Evaluation and Policy Analysis 2(5): 35-38.

KIMBALL, A. W. (1957) "Errors of the third kind in statistical consulting." J. of the Amer. Stat. Assn. 52: 133-142.

KNORR-CETINA, K. D. (1981) "Time and context in practical action: on the preconditions of knowledge use." Knowledge: Creation, Diffusion, Utilization 3: 143-165.

KUHN, T. S. (1971) The Structure of Scientific Revolutions. Chicago: Univ. of Chicago Press.

LAUDAN, L. (1981) "Overestimating underdetermination: caveats concerning the social causes of belief." Pittsburgh: Center for History and Philosophy of Science, University of Pittsburgh. (unpublished)

————— (1977) Progress and Its Problems: Towards a Theory of Scientific Growth. Berkeley: Univ. of California Press.

LAZARSFELD, P. F. and J. REITZ (1975) An Introduction to Applied Sociology. New York: Elsevier.

LEVINE, M. and N. S. ROSENBERG (1979) "An adversary model of fact finding and decision making for program evaluation: theoretical considerations," in H. C. Schulberg and F. Baker (eds.) Program Evaluation in the Health Fields (Vol. 2). New York: Human Sciences Press.

LEVISON, A. (1966) "Knowledge and society." Inquiry 9: 132-146.

LINDBLOM, C. E. and D. K. COHEN (1979) Usable Knowledge: Social Science and Social Problem Solving. New Haven, CT: Yale Univ. Press.

LOWRY, R. P. (1974) Social Problems: A Critical Analysis of Theories and Public Policy. Lexington, MA: D. C. Heath.

MacINTYRE, A. (1973) "Ideology, social science, and revolution." Comparative Politics 5(3).

MacRAE, D., Jr. (1976a) The Social Function of Social Science. New Haven, CT: Yale Univ. Press.

————— (1976b) "Technical communities and political choice." Minerva 14: 169-190.

MALINOWSKI, B. (1948) Magic, Science, and Religion and Other Essays. New York: Macmillan.

MARASCUILO, L. A. and J. R. LEVIN (1970) "Appropriate post hoc comparisons for interaction and nested hypotheses in analysis of variance designs: the elimination of Type IV errors." Amer. Educ. Research J. 7(3): 39-42.

MASON, R. O. and I. I. MITROFF (1981) "Policy analysis as argument," in W. N. Dunn (ed.) Symposium on Social Values and Public Policy. Policy Studies J. Special Issue 2: 579-584.

MERTON, R. K. (1976) Sociological Ambivalence and Other Essays. New York: Macmillan.

—— (1973) The Sociology of Science. Chicago: Univ. of Chicago Press.

MICHALOS, A. D. (1981) "Facts, values, and rational decision making," in W. N. Dunn (ed.) Symposium on Social Values and Public Policy. Policy Studies J. Special Issue 2: 544-551.

MITROFF, I. I. (1974) The Subjective Side of Science. New York: Elsevier.

—— and F. SAGASTI (1973) "Epistemology as general systems theory: an approach to the design of complex decision-making experiments." Philosophy of Social Sciences 3: 117-134.

MONTAGUE, W. P. (1925) The Ways of Knowing. New York: Macmillan.

PATTON, M. Q. (1978) Utilization-Focused Evaluation. Beverly Hills, CA: Sage.

—— (1975) Alternative Evaluation Research Paradigm. North Dakota Study Group on Evaluation Monograph Series. Grand Forks: Univ. of North Dakota.

PHILLIPS, D. (1973) Abandoning Method. San Francisco: Jossey-Bass.

POLANYI, M. (1967) "The growth of science in society." Minerva 5: 533-545.

POPPER, K. R. (1963) Conjectures and Refutations. New York: Basic Books.

—— (1959) The Logic of Scientific Discovery. New York: Basic Books.

RAIFFA, H. (1968) Decision Analysis. Reading, MA: Addison-Wesley.

REIN, M. (1976) Social Science and Public Policy. Baltimore: Penguin.

—— and S. WHITE (1977) "Policy research: belief and doubt." Policy Analysis 3: 239-272.

RIVLIN, A. M. (1973) "Forensic social science," in Perspectives on Inequality, Harvard Educ. Rev. Reprint Series 8.

ROSE, R. (1977) "Disciplined research and undisciplined problems," in C. H. Weiss (ed.) Using Social Research in Public Policy Making. Lexington, MA: D. C. Heath.

SALASIN, S. (1973) "Experimentation revisited: a conversation with Donald T. Campbell." Evaluation 1: 7-13.

STRAUCH, R. E. (1976) "A critical look at quantitative methodology." Policy Analysis 2: 121-144.

SUCHMAN, E. (1972) "Action for what? A critique of evaluation research," in C. H. Weiss (ed.) Evaluating Action Programs. Boston: Allyn and Bacon.

TOULMIN, S. (1958) The Uses of Argument. Cambridge, England: Cambridge Univ. Press.

—— R. RIEKE, and A. JANIK (1979) An Introduction to Reasoning. New York: Macmillan.

TREND, M. G. (1978) "On the reconciliation of qualitative and quantitative analysis: a case study." Human Organization 37: 345-354.

TRIBE, L. (1972) "Policy science: analysis or ideology." Philosophy and Public Affairs 2: 66-110.

von WRIGHT, G. (1971) Explanation and Understanding. Ithaca, NY: Cornell Univ. Press.

WALLACE, W. (1971) The Logic of Science in Sociology. Chicago: Aldine.

WATZLAWICK, P., J. WEAKLAND, and R. FISCH (1974) Change: Principles of Problem Formation and Resolution. New York: W. W. Norton.

WEBB, E. J., D. T. CAMPBELL, R. D. SCHWARTZ and L. B. SECHREST (1966) Unobtrusive Measures. Skokie, IL: Rand McNally.

WEBBER, D. J. (1980) "Conflicting worldviews, competing disciplinary matrices, and the utilization of systematic policy analysis." Presented at the meeting of the American Political Science Association, Washington, D.C., August 28-31.

WEISS, C. H. [ed.] (1977) Using Social Research in Public Policy Making. Lexington, MA: D. C. Heath.

—— with M. J. BUCUVALAS (1980a) Social Science Research and Decision-Making. New York: Columbia Univ. Press.

WEISS, C. H. and M. J. BUCUVALAS (1980b) "Truth tests and utility tests: decision makers' frames of reference for social science." Amer. Soc. Rev. 45: 302-312.

WHITEHEAD, A. N. and B. RUSSELL (1910) Principia Mathematica (Vol. 1) Cambridge, England: Cambridge Univ. Press.

WILLARD, C. A. (1980a) "Some questions about Toulmin's view of argument fields." Pittsburgh: Department of Speech, University of Pittsburgh. (unpublished)

—— (1980b) A Theory of Argumentation. Pittsburgh: Department of Speech, University of Pittsburgh. (unpublished)

—— (1978) "A reformulation of the concept of argument: the constructivist/interactionist foundations of a sociology of argument." J. of the Amer. Forensic Assn. 14: 121-140.

WILLIAMS, W. (1971) Social Policy Research and Analysis: The Experience in the Federal Social Agencies. New York: Elsevier.

ZALTMAN, G. (1979) "Knowledge utilization as planned social change." Knowledge 1: 82-105.

WILLIAM N. DUNN is Director of the University of Pittsburgh Program for the Study of Knowledge Use and Professor in the Graduate School of Public and International Affairs. He is author or editor of articles and books on participative management, planned social change, and public policy analysis and is currently principal investigator of a National Institute of Education-funded project devoted to methodological research on knowledge use and school improvement. His most recent publication is Public Policy Analysis *(Prentice-Hall, 1981).*

7

Experiments as Arguments

Donald T. Campbell

In his important article, "Reforms as Arguments," Dunn is attempting to help us achieve a gestalt switch into a new perspective on policy research. He is uncovering the implications that postpositivist theory of science has for applied social science. He has assembled an impressive array of relevant conceptual tools that are, for the most part, new to this application. These are missions I applaud and would like to participate in.

Scientific terms are typically indexical (Putnam, 1975: 229-235; Barnes and Law, 1976; Knorr-Cetina, 1981: 33-48) with meanings that are determined by and communicated effectively only in contexts of use. The key concepts in a conceptual revolution are dialectically and historically indexical. That is, they can only be understood in the context of the concepts they are intended to replace. To get across his new perspective, Dunn needs an explicit exemplar of the old paradigm and has done me the honor of choosing me for that role. Sharing a belief that we must try out and discard many new conceptualizations, and convinced of the clarifying role of vigorous dialogue, he has invited me to provide a comment, and our editor has approved. To best fulfill this role, I will somewhat suppress my own desire to be ultramodern and will defend such time-honored theses as the concept of cause, experimentation, a realist ontology, and "the scientific method" more generally. However, having been vigorously anti-logical-positivist for at least 25 years, and having a theory of knowledge that has always emphasized the indirectness, presumptiveness, and fallibility of all modes of knowing, I cannot be (as he recognizes in most passages) the exemplar for all that he wants to use as a contrasting background in current applied social

From Donald T. Campbell, "Experiments as Arguments," 3(3) *Knowledge: Creation, Diffusion, Utilization* 327-337 (March 1982). Copyright 1982 by Sage Publications, Inc.

science. Nor can I claim to be unmoved by the revolutions in theory of science which he represents. For example, my willingness to use dialectic concepts in describing the scientific method (which I do in print here for the first time) may be regarded as making a major concession to Dunn's point of view.

Reforms as Placebos

Dunn's title, "Reforms as Arguments," is a variant on my 15-year-old "Reforms as Experiments." My overall title for this commentary, "Experiments as Arguments," is a variant on his, intended to connote sympathetic agreement with his general epistemology. "Reforms as Placebos" is a second variant, intended as a warning against conflating the goal of truth with political linguistic usage. Dunn and I agree that most of what most governments offer in the name of "reforms" and "new programs" are symbolic gestures designed to indicate governmental awareness of problems and sympathetic intentions, rather than serious efforts to achieve social change. Abetted by us social scientists, there has been an escalation of rhetoric in our own Congress and administration so that funds needed for continuing welfare services to the needy have to be presented as new panaceas that are certain to cure the problems they alleviate. The underlying congressional intent is, for the most part, achieved when appropriations get spent locally. "Revenue Sharing" or "Problem-Specific Revenue Sharing" has long been a more appropriate description than "new program" or "reform." (The term *pork barrel* has similar connotations, but overemphasizes the role of diversionary interests and underemphasizes authentic goals of alleviating need, as distinguished from the rhetoric of curing the causes of need). Due to competing needs and limited budgets, most of the few genuine novelties get drastically underfunded and have no chance of producing demonstrable effects. The legislative requirement that such so-called programs be scientifically evaluated becomes just more empty rhetoric, a token to indicate that the money is being spent responsibly, on a par with the requirement of audited financial statements.

In stating this I have fallen into the popular usage of conflating "rhetoric" with deceptive persuasive efforts and vacuous promises. This should not be taken as a rejection of the current revival of the ancient disciplines of rhetoric, disputation, formal argumentation, and jurisprudence as models in theory of science. Rescher's (1977) use of them in his chapter on answering skepticism has been particularly illuminating for me. But the negative connotations of rhetoric are more than vulgar misunderstandings. They warn against uncritical acceptance of current practices of "symbolically mediating evidence." Conceptualizing "truth entirely as a social construction" reduces one's grounds for criticism of specific socially constructed beliefs as false consciousness, exploitative mystification, unwarranted reification, and the like (Keat and Urry, 1975). Substituting the goal of persuasion for the goal of truth, or defining truth as consensus, undermines our effective motivation for criticizing and changing the existing social order. The ontological nihilism (not a necessary accompaniment of our shared epistemological relativism) of the two quotations from Lindblom and Cohen (1979) seems to me particularly unfortunate, and while not unfairly taken out of context, something I had missed in my reading. Projecting onto them my ontologically realistic perspective, I had sympathetically understood them as criticizing the naive-realist arrogance of those quantitative social scientists who regard their latest study as standing alone as the unambiguous and sole basis for the relevant policy decision. Granted that we can never implement "correspondence" as a criterion for testing the validity of a specific belief, granted that we must use coherencelike criteria, testing beliefs only by comparison with the implications of other beliefs, "correspondence" still best expresses our goal of valid reference, the distinction between belief and valid belief. Once Dunn gets into his section on "Testing Knowledge Claims," he is utilizing as much of the correspondence theory of truth as I have intended.

The Ambiguity of the Outcome of Praxis

Even though I voluntarily "squat in the shade of the natural sciences" (in the sense of regarding the social and physical sciences as sharing yet-to-be-fully-explicated principles of scientific inference best exemplified in the physical sciences), I applaud Dunn's opening paragraph. The social sciences we are concerned with are and should be "practice-driven." There is no purified, validated social science from which we can derive sound principles for social engineering. In those cases where social change efforts have been inspired by a "pure" social theory, it is more true that the theory acquires validation from the outcomes of such theory-inspired practice than that the praxis acquires advance validity from the theory.

Intentionally induced change is close to the core meanings of both praxis and causality (Wright, 1971, and others reviewed by Cook and Campbell, 1979). Praxis is rightly conceived of as the optimal validation process, the optimal truth test for theories of society. Nonetheless, the outcomes of praxis or practice are profoundly equivocal and ambiguous in normal circumstances. The mode of implementation is never quite what theory called for, and these imperfections will be invoked if outcomes seem undesirable or absent. If practice seems successful, there will be interest in which aspect of the conglomerates was most responsible. "Seeming" success or "seeming" failure will be rendered equivocal because of other plausible change agents asserted to be present. The profound equivocality of praxis, be it revolutionary change or minor reforms, can be represented and clarified in argumentation, rhetoric, dialectical reasoning, and adversary process, particularly if well-funded parties in genuinely adversarial roles are permitted to participate (as in Habermas's "ideal speech community"). But these procedures do not in and of themselves remove the intrinsic ambiguity.

Logically this same equivocality exists for intentional causal interventions in the physical aspects of the world, even if not in such extreme degree. "Experiments" are deliberate intentional interventions in situations selected and contrived so as to reduce this equivocality. At their best, experiments do reduce equivocality, at least in regard to those plausible rival hypotheses articulated in the previous dialogue of competing theoretical interpretations and criticism. Even so, experiments at their best merely "probe" causal theories, they do not "prove" them (Campbell and Stanley, 1966: 35).

But even so again, deliberate intentional intervention greatly reduces equivocality of causal inference in contrast with efforts to infer causality from passive observation. Beginning explications as to why this is so are to be found in Bhaskar (1975) and Cook and Campbell (1979: Chapters 1 and 7).

In the physical sciences, experiments advance the argument but are never definitive. Dunn and I agree that a dialectical perspective does more justice to the history of experimental physics than does an image of the experiment as a window through which nature is seen directly. At each stage the "experimental variables" and the "outcome measures" are never "defined" for out-of-context or all-context meaningfulness. Instead, they are historically and dialectically indexical, acquiring their transient meaningfulness in the context of previous experiments and theories. In this important sense, *experiments are arguments* in a historical dialectic for the physical sciences and perhaps potentially for the applied social sciences.

This authentic continuity with the classic and medieval disciplines of dialectics, disputation, argumentation, and rhetoric should neither, however, lead us to undervalue the ideology of experimentation which founded the scientific revolution nor undervalue the dialectical importance of its self-conscious rejection of the disputation tradition. That older tradition was a part of a worldview which saw all of the ingredients for rational understanding as already present, needing only the spelling out of implications and clarifications which verbal disputation could produce. Such scholastic argumentation had reached a stalemate (of boredom if nothing else) and it was against this sterility that Galileo, Bacon, and the others rebelled. The new experimental science was to be exploratory beyond the limits of present knowledge and was to introduce physical acts and observations so as to settle the interminable verbal disputation. That the experiments and empiricism did not settle the arguments and could not in fact replace the verbal (theoretical, metaphysical) disputations but merely augment them should not blind us to the important advances made. Marx's call for a dialectic of praxis, not mere words and passive observations, and Dunn's call for employing "reforms as arguments" can be read as in keeping with the ideology of experimental science in this important regard.

Both Dunn and I are in favor of keeping open indefinitely the dialectic of practice through intentional efforts to change our social order accompanied by open criticism of these efforts. Our small disagreement centers around the role of the ideology of "social experimentation" in promoting this dialectic. For me, "experimentation" connotes a continuing iterative process, a self-conscious tentativeness precluding pretenses to having achieved finalization. But I join him and Lindblom and Cohen (1979) in decrying an image of social experimentation in which a single big national program evaluation or demonstration experiment settles a policy decision once and for all (Campbell, 1979a). We are also at one in regretting the miscarriages that occur when social movements supposedly committed to the dialectics of praxis try to stop this dialectic upon gaining political control.

Will a dialectic of experimental arguments ever be feasible in applied social science? I am in favor of our intentionally trying and of informing our efforts by an understanding of the social processes that have made science possible in the physical sciences. But although I favor trying, I share doubts that political conditions will ever make this possible. Even though in physics, too, the experimental data are also "mediated by assumptions, frames of reference, and ideologies," the stakes and motivational structures of political domination place the powerful participants farther from the "standards of appraisal and the incentive structure of the idealized scientific community." If, in his section, The Experimenting Society, Dunn is opposing the political mystification which comes from claiming scientific status for partisan rhetoric defended from competitive scientific criticism, I am happy to join him. If, on the other hand, he claims to be offering a more valid epistemology that would obviate the problems through other means than invoking more authentic experimental and scientific perspectives, I am in disagreement. (In passing, may I note that while the quotations from me in these pages are probably accurate, they are enough out of context to fail to communicate the profound fallibilism, epistemological relativism, and emphasis on presumptiveness characteristic of my view of science. In particular, Dunn's comments, following the quotation from my "Tribal Model" [Campbell, 1979c], advocate fallibilisms, all of which are contained and exceeded in my article.)

Going Beyond Threats to Cognitive Validity

The bulk of Dunn's article is devoted to expanding perspectives beyond the narrow set of cognitive concerns exemplified in the quasi-experimental design tradition. As he makes clear, this for the most part is a going-beyond, rather than a rejection. Thus Type III errors, ethical considerations, and relevance are all important, and I applaud the expanded perspective of concerns they provide. It is only in a few details that I demur from the 12 major threats to knowledge adequacy. Most of my objections could be avoided by rewordings Dunn would probably accept. Thus points 1, 5, 8, 9, and 10 are worded as though a second-best criterion were worthless, an unwitting council of perfection implicitly neglecting the fallibility of all such tests and our inevitable dependence upon fallible criteria. Thus point 6 is worded as though "literal surrogates" were sometimes available, rather than acknowledging explicitly that all similarity is metaphorical.

If Dunn's points 2 and 3 are read as denying causal efficacy to subjective meanings in determining human behavior, or denying that subjective meanings are themselves caused, or that either causal process can be demonstrated through experimental procedures, then we are in genuine disagreement. If, on the other hand, he is calling attention to the complex, multicausal settings of human action, and the common fault of neglecting causes other than the manipulator's intended cause, the failure to note "symbolically mediated meanings" other than the experimenter's intended one, then we are in complete agreement.

Most of any disagreements here are matters of wording and relative emphasis. The more important question is, "Are these 12 cautions needed in view of existing practice?" My answer to this is clear. Like Dunn, I can think of particular studies for which there has been neglect of each one of the considerations to which he calls attention.

The "Fact-Value" Distinction

To fill out my role as an old-fashioned epistemologist, I would like to make a case for maintaining, rather than abandoning, the fact-value distinction. Dunn's position on this is mixed, so I may be answering other young moderns and not him directly. While for at least the past 25 years I have been antipositivist, in particular where positivists have wanted to do away with the distinction between evidence and the reality to which the evidence refers, on the issue of the fact-value distinction I will use the analysis of the logical positivists and their predecessors, but without the value nihilism which often accompanied its expression (Campbell, 1979b). The tools of descriptive science and formal logic can help us implement values which we already accept or have chosen, but they are not constitutive of those values. Ultimate values are accepted but not justified. Most disagreements, however, are not about ultimate values but instead about mediating values, and for these the facts of the matter, the nature of the world and the nature of human nature, are all highly relevant. The theory of biological evolution predicts that we as a species will value human survival, and that is certainly a part of an ultimate value package which enough people will accept to make it worth the effort to develop mediational values in its service. Species characteristics are, however, so little fixed that probably in our ultimate value package we need more than genetic survival per se and need something more like "human survival under humane conditions" (Campbell, 1979b) and for me, at least, this would include the goal of survival with something like our present population level and urban residential patterns. In this perspective, one avoids value nihilism by assuming ultimate values or by discovering what values one has inherited and accepting them for purposes of mediational value clarification.

We are such pervasive valuers that almost none of the facts of the world can be apprised without valuational connotations, but this does not negate the fact-value distinction. It is characteristic of successful science, even in its dialectically and historically transient form, that its descriptions of the world are usable to implement widely divergent values. Thus, bacteriology can be used to control plagues or to design instruments of germ warfare. Thus, as immature a project as Adorno et al.'s (1950) *The Authoritarian Personality* (which both Dunn and I treat with respect) is usable not only to design modes of reducing ethnic prejudice but also to provide an excellent guide for a fascist rabble-rouser who would like to foment ethnic prejudice. The scientists who did the basic work may have been motivated by an extreme hostility to the disease, but this strong motivation will not restrict the usefulness of their approximative scientific achievements solely to those who share their motivation.

Our predicament as social animals who must achieve our sociality without inhibition of genetic competition among the cooperators (Campbell, 1972a, 1975, forthcoming), and as social animals with a fundamental disposition to individual and clique selfishness, puts us in a special predicament insofar as public belief assertion is concerned. Were science designed only to guide our own behavior, then the value neutrality of our scientific conclusions would be complete. The model of the world best-suited to implementing our own values would also have the validity optimal for guiding others with different values. However, the fact that we are in varying degrees in competition with those others provides a motive to keep our knowledge, or our beliefs, private. This motive to achieve secrecy is inevitably characteristic of applied science, social or physical, industrial or national. The norms of science and democracy are both against such secrecy. In paying lip-service to those norms, we generate public belief assertions. Individual-competitive and clique-competitive motives introduce in us a tendency to modulate these belief assertions so as to manipulate the beliefs of others in a direction favoring our interests. Dunn and I agree that in the social sciences, the norms that would inhibit this are particularly weak, and the feedback from experimental, quasi-experimental, passive descriptive, quantitative, or qualitative probes of reality are so ambiguous and inconsistent that they provide no discipline.

The role of the researcher as a consultant rather than an actor guiding his own action maximizes the belief manipulation interest in research reports. An established power structure with the ability to employ applied social scientists, the machinery of social science, and control over the means of dissemination produces an unfair status quo bias in the mass production of belief assertions from the applied social sciences. This will be fully as true in Marxist countries as it is in capitalist countries. The naively idealistic scientistically trained social scientist who enters this arena unaware of the belief manipulation component to the belief assertions produced by the research establishment which he is entering may indeed become an unwitting coconspirator in this mystification. This state of affairs is one which both Dunn and I deplore, but I find myself best able to express my disapproval through retaining the old-fashioned construct of truth, warnings against individually and clique selfish distortions, and a vigorously exhorted fact-value distinction, whereas he is tempted at points to abandon these old-fashioned tools of moral righteousness and to accept or even welcome the conflation of persuasive bias with descriptive accuracy. If not he, then there are others of his generation who, recognizing that published social science often constitutes advocacy of a partisan nature, accept this model for their own research. Rather than accepting for themselves the model of advocacy science focused on persuasion of audiences, it seems to me that out-of-power minorities would be better to maintain the traditional distinction and expose as false, the value-biased distortions of establishment belief assertions made in the name of science, and to devote their own research efforts, such as they can afford and squeeze in, to correcting those biases in the name of truth.

The occurrence of whistle blowing by members of bureaucratic structures gives testimony to the spontaneous occurrence of exposés in the name of truth by cogs in the establishment machine who have no ideological commitment of an antiregime nature. We have yet to fully explore the sources in human nature of the pain of continually lying, but the phenomenon no doubt exists, as Polanyi (1966) has noted in his analysis of the role of the privileged journalistic elite in the Hungarian revolution of 1957. Such pain is very plausibly involved in the leadership in the Dubchek regime in Czechoslovakia (Campbell, 1971). In our more pluralistic society, we would do better to expand the opportunities for whistle-blowing by redefining them normatively as the duty of multiple minority reports appropriate for every program evaluation and policy study, and open to every neurotic and disgruntled research assistant under extended freedom of information requirements, than to announce that all research is but persuasive advocacy.

Dunn agrees with the importance of the problem and wants to go beyond attention to deliberate deception in order to increase the social science research community's awareness of its unconscious co-optation into partisan paradigms. This is also the critical message of cultural relativism in the Boas/Herskovits tradition and the social class relativism of Marx and Mannheim (Campbell, 1972a, 1977). This effort to make us aware of biased-paradigm co-optation is again one best done by retaining a traditional fact-value distinction; it is a matter of becoming self-critically aware of our profoundly relativistic epistemologic predicament and using this awareness in the service of a more competent effort to achieve objectivtiy, rather than employing it to justify giving up the goal of truth.

Summary

Faced with Dunn's challenging and persuasive effort to introduce a new and broader epistemological paradigm for applied social science, I have nonetheless been able to convince myself that I should hang on to a number of old-fashioned points of view. These include acceptance for social research of a model of science shared with the physical sciences, an ideology of social experimentation, the concept of cause, a correspondence meaning for the goal of truth, a critical realist ontology, and the fact-value distinction. However, since I have long held a radical fallibilism and an emphasis upon the unproven presumptions underlying science, and in this essay have been willing to state this in the language of dialectics, I may in fact have conceded most of the points Dunn is making.

References

ADORNO, T. W., E. FRENKEL-BRUNSWIK, D. J. LEVINSON, and R. N. SANFORD (1950) The Authoritarian Personality. New York: Harper & Row.
BARNES, B. and J. LAW (1976) "Whatever should be done with indexical expressions." Theory and Society 3: 223-237.
BHASKAR, R. (1975) A Realist Theory of Science. Leeds, England: Leeds Books.
CAMPBELL, D. T. (forthcoming) "The two distinct routes beyond kin selection to ultra-sociality: implications for the humanities and social sciences," in D. L. Bridgeman (ed.) The Nature of Prosocial Development: Interdisciplinary Theories and Strategies. New York: Academic Press.

—————(1979a) "Assessing the impact of planned social change." Evaluation and Program Planning 2: 67-90.

————— (1979b) "Comments on the sociobiology of ethnics and moralizing." Behavioral Sci. 24: 37-45.

————— (1979c) "A tribal model of the social system vehicle carrying scientific knowledge." Knowledge: Creation, Diffusion, Utilization 2: 181-201.

————— (1977) Descriptive Epistemology: Psychological, sociological, and evolutionary. (Preliminary draft of the William James Lectures, Harvard University.)

————— (1975) "On the conflicts between biological and social evolution and between psychology and moral tradition." Amer. Psychologist 30: 1103-1126.

————— (1972a) "Herskovits, cultural relativism, and metascience," pp. v-xxiii in M. J. Herskovits (ed.) Cultural Relativism. New York: Random House.

————— (1972b) "On the genetics of altruism and the counter-hedonic components in human culture." J. of Social Issues 28: 21-37.

————— (1971) "Methods for the experimenting society." Presented at the meeting of the American Psychological Association, Washington, DC., September 5.

————— and J. STANLEY (1966) Experimental and Quasi-Experimental Designs for Research. Boston: Houghton Mifflin.

COOK, T. D. and D. T. CAMPBELL (1979) Quasi-Experimentation: Design and Analysis for Field Settings. Boston: Houghton Mifflin.

DUNN, W. N. (1982) "Reforms as arguments." Knowledge: Creation, Diffusion, Utilization 3: 293-326.

KEAT, R. and J. URRY (1975) Social Theory as Science. London: Routledge & Kegan Paul.

KNORR-CETINA, K. D. (1981) The Manufacture of Knowledge: An Essay on the Constructivist and Contextual Nature of Science. Oxford, England: Pergamon.

LINDBLOM, C. E. and D. K. COHEN, (1979) Usable Knowledge. New Haven, CT: Yale Univ. Press.

POLANYI, M. (1966) "The message of the Hungarian revolution." Amer. Scholar 35: 261-276.

PUTNAM, H. (1975) Mind Language and Reality. Cambridge, England: Cambridge Univ. Press.

RESCHER, N. (1977) Methodological Pragmatism. Oxford, England: Basil Blackwell.

DONALD T. CAMPBELL is New York State Albert Schweitzer Professor, Maxwell School, Syracuse University. He is Past President of the American Psychological Association. He is best known for this writings on social science research methodology. An extension of these interests into the social theory of science has appeared in Knowledge: Creation, Diffusion, Utilization entitled "A tribal model of the social system vehicle carrying scientific knowledge."

8

Measuring the Use of Evaluation

Carol H. Weiss

Studying the effects of social science research and evaluation used to be a problematic enterprise, and anyone writing on the subject had to justify its importance. Nowadays people in many places are concerned about the effects of research and evaluation on the development and improvement of social programs. It has become a matter of some moment to know *how much* contribution systematic research makes to effective programming and *how, when,* and *where* it has its major influence.[1] We can take the significance of the questions for granted. The challenge is to get on with the job.

This article addresses two issues that must be considered in getting on with the job of studying uses. The first is the definition of what we mean by research use, so that we can recognize it when we see it. The second is the design of how we study it, the entry point for inquiry and the tracers that supply evidence.

RESEARCH UTILIZATION: WHAT IS IT?

Research utilization sounds like a straightforward and obvious event. Particularly in a local agency, there seems little complexity in seeing whether a study has been used. Once a study has been done—say, an

From Carol H. Weiss, "Measuring the Use of Evaluation," in James A. Ciarlo (ed.) *Utilizing Evaluation: Concepts and Measurement Techniques.* Sage Research Progress Series in Evaluation, Vol. 6, pp. 17-33. Copyright 1981 by Sage Publications, Inc.

evaluation of one particular strategy of service—it should be clear whether the agency managers and program practitioners have adopted the strategy that was found successful, abandoned the strategy found unsuccessful, or modified existing strategy in accordance with the conclusions and recommendations of the study. To study use, one would think, you look at program managers' decisions about the program and see whether they have followed the import of the data and/or the explicit recommendations of the evaluator. That used to be the traditional formulation, and in some places it still is.

This article takes issue with that formulation of "research utilization." I suggest that it embodies an inappropriate imagery, and in fact goes so far as to abandon the term *utilization* because of its overtones of instrumental episodic application. People do not utilize research the way that they utilize a hammer. The whole process through which research penetrates the sphere of organizational decision making—the processes of understanding, accepting, reorienting, adapting, and applying research results to the world of practice—is more fluid and diffuse than the earlier image implied.

Let me give five examples of the interaction between the conclusions of an evaluation study and the acts of agency managers. Each of them illustrates that the traditional notion of research utilization, as supplying "answers" that program managers "adopt" to "solve" a problem, may be an inappropriate way to think about the subject.

ILLUSTRATIONS OF EVALUATION-PROGRAM INTERACTIONS

First, take the case of an evaluation study that does not produce forthright answers. It finds modest successes in some areas of program operation and modest shortcomings in other areas, without giving clear-cut direction for expansion, modification, or termination of the program. Many studies produce this kind of inconclusive evidence. There is "on the one hand," but there is also "on the other hand." What one does with findings of this sort is indeterminate.

Some evaluation studies discover an absence of expected effects, but cannot attribute the failure to any particular activities of the program or its staff. They do not reveal whether the basic theory of the program is wrong (i.e., that its activities are inherently unable to alter the behaviors that it aims to change) or whether the failings are due to the special conditions and disadvantages of the immediate setting. Therefore, the evaluation cannot say with any confidence whether the remedy is to abandon the program or to try to operate it more effectively.

In sum, evaluations do not always—or even often—come up with data that give explicit guidance for action. Therefore, it becomes difficult to study the "use" made of the study by monitoring the agency's adoption of the "answer" that the study supplied.

Because many evaluation studies—particularly those conducted in a single agency—do not have sufficient comparative data to specify the factors that contributed to program success or program failure, the evaluator makes a leap from the data in developing recommendations. She uses judgment—as well as science—in drawing implications for action. In the not infrequent case when outcomes are mixed (some indicators go up while others do not, or some clients benefit but others fail to benefit), the data may not lead to any direct lessons. The evaluator, in making recommendations, is inevitably guided by her own standards, beliefs, and predilections, her sense of what is possible and feasible, what costs too much or will encounter resistance, her knowledge of alternative possibilities and their likelihood of success. To study the "use" of evaluation by looking at the agency's adoption of the *recommendations* is in effect to study the use of the evaluator's judgment. It is not obvious that this is a study of the use of evaluation.

Consider a second case where one evaluation study comes up with one set of findings, while another evaluation of the same or a very similar program comes up with discrepant findings. Members of the program staff divide into two camps, one group advocating the implementation of the recommendations derived from the first study and a second group pushing for acceptance of the recommendations based on the second study. In such a situation, there will undoubtedly be people who insist on doing nothing until better information becomes available and the discrepancies are resolved. They are likely to prevail—at least for a time, while the agency searches for further data.

How does one assess the use of evaluation under these circumstances? No one can assert that the evaluations are not getting a hearing, but nothing seems to be happening in the program. No action is being taken that appears responsive to either evaluation. The person who is studying the use of evaluations by looking at program decisions is likely to conclude that the studies were not used. Perhaps two or three years later, after further evidence has accumulated from new evaluations or other sources, some of the findings from the earlier studies will be reinforced and gain in credibility, and significant changes will be introduced. But by that time, the student of the uses of evaluation will probably have come and gone.

These two examples indicate the frequent fragility of the "answer" that evaluation supplies. It is often incomplete, merged with nonresearch judgment, incompatible with or contradicted by other evaluation evidence, and only a partial guide to responsible action. This is not to say, of course, that it is valueless. The information from evaluation may well be the best information on program outcome around, and it usually has important implications for program managers. The significant point is that to study its use *only* in terms of immediate and direct impact on program decisions is unduly constricting.

Let us take a third case in which an agency encounters neither particular problems nor clearly defined decision points. The program has been operating and continues to operate. No decisions are pending about funding, staffing, clientele, or activities, or about expansion or contraction of the program. An evaluation is done that points out areas of potential improvement. People read the report and take it seriously, but there seems little opportunity to put the findings to work in obvious ways. They have a limited budget, staff with particular skills, a building not located in an optimal site but serviceable—and things are going pretty well. They have neither the motivation nor the opportunity to apply the evaluation findings; no decision has to be made and they make none. They tuck the suggestions away for future consideration when conditions change. But again, there is no visible effect on decisions.

The fourth illustration concerns an agency that confronts neither inconclusive evaluation results nor absence of decisional choices. Decisions about the future have to be made, and the evaluation study provides direction and recommendations for change. But the evidence that the study offers about program outcomes is only one kind of information that managers take into account. They also consider the costs of program modifications, the types of staff needed to implement the modifications, the wishes of client groups, the preferences of referring agencies, and the program emphases of federal sponsors. Let us suppose that some or all of these factors militate against the actions suggested by the evaluation. After weighing all the evidence, managers conclude that the other factors are more important and decide not to follow the prescriptions derived from evaluation. Anyone going in to study the use of evaluation according to the simple rule ("See if the decision followed the advice based on evaluation") would conclude that the study was not used. In fact, it stimulated significant review of the program. Even though its conclusions were outweighed by competing concerns of cost, staff capabilities, client demands, interagency relationships, or political feasibility, it illuminated problems, clarified trade-offs, and evoked new understandings of the possibilities and limits of program action.

Let us consider a final case. Program managers have developed plans to make changes in their program for reasons that have little to do with program effectiveness and much to do with the survival of their agency. An evaluation is done and points out shortcomings in the program. The managers take advantage of the opportunity to institute the changes that they have already planned. The action they take is not exactly what the evaluation report recommends, but it appears to be directed at problems that the evaluation has uncovered and responsive to evaluation conclusions. Is this a use of evaluation? The person looking at the outcome by the rule of thumb, "See if the decision followed the evaluation-based advice," might be misled. He would assume that the evaluation was used as a basis of decision, although in this case the change was contemplated long before the evaluation—and on other grounds. But in a different sense, the evaluation *was* "used": It provided an opportunity to bring about changes that the program staff wanted and it helped to legitimate their actions. Is that a legitimate use?

These kinds of cases are legion. They make the study of the effects of evaluation research a difficult enterprise. When the action that evaluation implies is unclear, or when different studies point in different directions, when organizational and political conditions leave little opportunity for implementing evaluation results, when competing constraints swamp evaluation evidence, when changes occur only after protracted periods of time, when staff use evaluation to legitimate changes they had already decided upon—how does the student of use of evaluation make sense of what is going on? To limit our attention to direct and immediate application of evaluation results to decisions forecloses the opportunity to understand how evaluations in fact affect program operation. We see only the small slice of the action that falls within our arbitrary definition of use and fail to examine the scores of subtle effects that may turn out to have cumulative consequences of major dimensions.

What makes the conventional approach to the study of use even more troublesome is the implicit assumption that use is good and nonuse is bad. Use of evaluation results seems to signify the triumph of science, reason, objective evidence, and dispassionate social scientists over the forces of inertia, agency politics, stupidity, and the self-servingness of managers and professionals. The notion that evaluations may be tinged with their own biases and that they do not always supply the final word gets little consideration—nor does the possibility that program managers and staffs have knowledge and judgment derived from sources other than evaluation. It is a myopic—and astigmatic—view of the agency world.

What often happens when agencies confront evaluations is even more complex than the five vignettes imply. In many cases, what evaluation research provides to program agencies is not so much specific evidence about the success or failure of particular programs as rich information about the contexts in which programs operate. Evaluation research can serve highly useful purposes by illuminating the backdrop against which choices must be made. It can provide information about clients (their problems, expectations, lifestyles, and motives), about programs (standards of selection of recipients, daily activities, resources, limits, modes of coping with obstacles, theories-in-use), about staff, and about the agency environment. Richly textured information of this kind can fill in pieces of what Patton et al. (1977) have called the puzzle of agency action.

Another major contribution that evaluation research often makes is to build up generalizations about program theory. It generates ideas about the kinds of interventions that work in given circumstances and the kinds of interventions that fail. It says something about which theories of programming are empirically supported and the conditions under which they hold. One study of one program (even of a program as administered at multiple sites) can be discounted on the basis of weaknesses in methodology. There is almost always some flaw that critics can find to justify disregarding the study's results—and often rightly so: The sample was too small, the time period too short, the study begun too soon after the program's start, the control groups corrupted, the measures too soft or too narrow or too remote from the program's central goals, the analysis inappropriate, or the recommendations too global or insufficiently supported by the evidence presented. One study, particularly a study that has had to make methodological compromises, is often fragile support for major programmatic revision.

But a body of evaluation studies, conducted by different investigators using different methodologies, often converge on a theme. And it is this theme, this orienting perspective, this generalization about programming that comes into currency. Some examples of ideas that have come from waves of evaluation studies would be: Released mental patients do not fare well in the community unless given intensive personal support services, in-school compensatory education programs for junior high and high school students do not overcome educational deficiencies, poor people use health services as extensively as other people when the services are available and convenient. And program managers and other decision makers use these kinds of ideas in making decisions about programs—even when the studies were not conducted on their own programs and *even when they cannot cite the studies from which the generalizations come.* They have absorbed the generalizations from diverse sources over a period of time, and these ideas become the taken-for-granted assumptions on which they base new plans and decisions. Social scientists studying the uses of evaluation research studies by traditional methods are very likely to overlook this kind of use entirely.

Students of research use have made a distinction between "instrumental use," in which research or evaluation conclusions are applied to a specific decision, and "conceptual use," in which research affects the understanding of issues more broadly (Caplan et al., 1975; Rich and Caplan, 1976; Weiss, 1977; Rich, 1977; Pelz, 1978). This is a useful distinction because it indicates that the use of research can take different forms. It recognizes that research can have consequences not only when people adopt its conclusions directly but also when they are influenced by its concepts and ideas.

As Caplan (1977), Caplan et al. (1975), Rich (1977), Patton et al. (1977), and others have shown empirically, conceptual use is likely to be more prevalent than instrumental use. It may also be more significant. Instrumental use is often restricted to relatively low-level decisions, where the stakes are small and users' interests relatively unaffected. Conceptual use, which does not involve immediate and direct application of conclusions to decisions, can gradually bring about major shifts in awareness and reorientation of basic perspectives.

While the categories of instrumental and conceptual use have served a useful purpose (they have helped in making the transition from our original exclusive preoccupation with instrumental use), I now believe that they are somewhat arbitrary. The use of research and evaluation is actually a continuum. At one end are those few cases where research actually switches a decision from A to B by the power of its evidence and analysis. In the middle are the many cases where research evidence is taken into account but does not drive the decision—cases where users filter research evidence through their knowledge, judgment, and interests, and incorporate much besides research into decision making. At the far end are the large array of issues on which research contributes more diffusely to an understanding of issues, the causes of problems, and the dynamics of intervention. For people who are concerned with the effects of research and evaluation on social programming, most of the phenomena of interest probably lie in the large and unbounded middle ground.

CONCEPTUALIZATION OF USE

Clearly a central issue for the study of the uses of evaluation, research, and analysis is: What constitutes a use? The direct implementation of specific evaluation conclusions in immediate decisions about the future of the program studied is only one kind of use—and it appears to be relatively infrequent. But there are many other kinds of uses where evaluation conclusions affect ideas about programming indirectly, over time, as part of a larger body of information, with less obvious consequences. To leave them out of our purview would represent a serious underestimate of the effects of research.

To clarify the concept of "use," we have to confront prickly questions. We have to specify such dimensions as these:

(1) *What is used.* Do we define the "what" as recommendations from one study, data and conclusions from one study, some *part* of the data, findings from a series of related studies, generalizations derived from a synthesis of studies, social science concepts used in the studies? Do we include findings that have been selectively plucked from research, or misunderstood, or distorted?

(2) *How direct is the derivation from the study.* Does "use" require that people read the original report, a summary written by the authors of the report, a description by someone else *about* the report? How about a conversation with the evaluator, a second-hand account from somebody who talked to the evaluator, or a staff person's recollection that there was "an evaluation on this"?

(3) *By whom it is used.* Decisions in organizations are rarely the province of one individual. Decisions require agreement and sign-offs at multiple levels. Do we limit certified users to the immediate program decision makers, include other staff in the agency, officials at other levels (federal, state, local)? How about direct-service staff who may modify some of their day-to-day behavior, or interest groups who may lobby for program change, or clients who learn from evaluation about the likelihood of program success and give or withdraw their support and attendance?

(4) *By how many people it is used.* Is it enough if one aide to a decision maker reads the report and forcefully propounds its lessons to her boss? Or is there some minimal penetration of the decision-making group that must be achieved?

(5) *How immediate is the use.* Does use have to take place shortly after the study was done? Is it a use if study conclusions are considered and

weighed over the longer term? What about the gradual percolation of evaluation results and ideas into agency deliberations?

(6) Most important of all, *how much effect is required*. To count as a "use" must every one of the evaluation recommendations be adopted? What if some recommendations are adopted but not others? Or suppose the evaluation stimulates review and rethinking but different changes from those recommended are adopted. What if evaluation results are given a thoughtful hearing but are purposely set aside under the weight of other factors? Or suppose the ideas from evaluation and research help people make sense of what they are doing and give them a new perspective on the program. Suppose they conclude that their current goals are excessively optimistic and unrealistic and scale down their goals. Or they begin long-range exploration of alternative agency missions. Or they find new grounds to justify what they are already doing. Are these "uses"? If evaluation results are given a hearing and affect opinions and ideas about programming, even in unintended ways, how do we rule some "in" and some "out" of the definition of use?

These are some of the conceptual issues that people who study the use of research and evaluation must grapple with. They are troublesome questions, particularly because some uses look "good" and others look "bad." To adopt evaluation recommendations looks "good," at least to evaluators. To cite evaluation as support for changes that would have been made anyway looks "bad," although it may be a highly effective merger of managerial experience and evaluation evidence. *Until we resolve questions about the definition of use, we face a future of noncomparable studies of use and scant hope of cumulative understanding of how evaluation and decision making intersect.*

In my view, the field should adopt a broad construction of the meaning of use at this time. (See also Cohen and Weiss, 1977; Pelz, 1978; Alkin et al., 1979; Rein and White, 1977; Patton et al., 1977; Knorr, 1977; Lindblom and Cohen, 1979.) We should look at the full range of ways in which research and evaluation influence the development of program and policy. To look small, to restrict ourselves to studying immediate applications of findings to decisions, takes for granted a rational theory of organizational behavior. It assumes that organizations make decisions according to a rational model: define problems, generate options, search for information about the relative merits of each option, and then, on the basis of the information, make a choice. As our colleagues who study organizational behavior tell us (Simon, 1976; March and Olsen, 1976; Meyer and Rowan, 1977; Weick, 1969; Mintzberg, 1973; Allison, 1971;

Thompson, 1967; Downs, 1967), this is a patently inaccurate view of how organizations work. When we implicitly adopt this as our underlying theory of organizations in studying research use, we inevitably reach distorted conclusions. Until we can develop better models of how organizations use information, we are best served by examining the spectrum of organizational uses of research and evaluation. We may like some uses and dislike others, but such judgments should not get in the way. We need to *understand* the consequences of research and evaluation for organizational practice. Only with a broad-gauge view will we make headway in this endeavor.

If an excessively rationalistic view of organizational decision making can constrict our understanding of the use of research and evaluation at the agency level, it is almost fatal to understanding at the policy level. Major policy directions taken by federal departments and their component agencies and the Congress are almost never the product of rational analysis alone. They are strongly influenced by legislative politics, bureaucratic politics, constituent interests, competing claims on the federal budget, pressure groups, public acceptance, and a host of idiosyncratic elements. To look only for the incorporation of research and evaluation results in the policies that emerge from the complex play of interests is to ignore almost all of the game. Such a narrow view also ignores the many diffuse ways in which research and evaluation affect, legitimate, and frame the positions that participants take and the bargains that they negotiate. Again, it seems sensible to look broadly at the ways in which research and evaluation help to shape the policy debate.

Once we have agreed on the definition of use, we have to look at the relation between the concept and the craft. How do we go about studying the complex and intricate patterns in which research and evaluation are woven into agency deliberations?

APPROACHES TO THE STUDY OF USE

Investigators who narrowly construe research use generally start with a *study* and try to trace its effects on subsequent decisions. Much has been learned by this strategy of investigation, and it deserves to be pursued further. But there are other approaches to the study of research use as well, some of which have significant potential for expanding our knowledge.

Basically, investigators have adopted four approaches for studying the consequences of research and evaluation. Each of them implies a distinctive type of question and typically uses a different data-collection method. Each of them is well-suited to exploring some issues and less appropriate for investigating others. Here are brief sketches of the four possibilities.

(1) Start with *studies* and follow the effects of the studies on subsequent decisions. This approach has been used to investigate the consequences of a single research study (e.g., Datta, 1976, on the evaluation of Head Start; Boeckmann, 1976, on the New Jersey negative income tax experiment; White, 1975, on evaluation of school performance in Atlanta; Rich, 1975, on the Continuous National Survey; Weiss, 1970, on the federal student loan program), and it has been used to study the effects of multiple studies (e.g., Alkin et al., 1979, studied the uses of five evaluations of Title I and Title IV-C educational programs; Patton et al., 1977, studied the uses of 20 health program evaluations). The basic assumption is that the investigator can ferret out the effects of the study on the people who make significant decisions.

(2) Start with *people* who are prospective users of research and evaluation studies. This is the approach that Caplan et al. (1975) used in their investigation of use. They sent interviewers to talk with federal officials in a wide range of federal departments and asked them about their uses of research—which studies they used, when they used them, how they used them, and the consequences of use (see also Caplan and Barton, 1976). The basic assumption is that people can remember the studies that influenced them and will be candid and accurate in their responses.

(3) Start with an *issue* and examine the ways in which research and evaluation help to shape the resolution of the issue. Aaron (1978) investigated the extent to which research helped to set the agenda, bound the discussion, and influence the direction of federal policy in three areas: poverty and discrimination, education and jobs, and unemployment and inflation. His analysis of the influence of research, evaluation, and policy analysis on the development of policy on these issues is a complex and fascinating study. In a somewhat broader vein, the National Academy of Sciences, panel on Study of the Policy Formation Process is currently studying the gamut of factors that shaped the Women, Infants, and Children nutritional program, the child care tax deduction, and federal interagency day care regulations. Research and evaluation studies are one of the formative factors that are receiving explicit attention. An underlying assumption of studies that focus on an issue, and examine the contribution of research to the progressive decisions on the issue, is that the investigator can separate the studies that actually had an impact on

decision makers from those that did not, and that he can unravel the special contributions that derived from research.

(4) Start with an *organization* and investigate the impact of research and evaluation on the life history of the organization. Studies of this type have to date been done mainly by social scientists concerned with organizational development and have focused on the effects of consultant intervention or the introduction of social-scientific innovations. Some examples[2] are the studies of the effects of social science research and experimentation in hospitals by Jaques's group in Britain (Rowbottom et al., 1973), the study of social scientists' involvement in research and action at the Glacier Metal Company over almost two decades (e.g., Brown and Jaques, 1965), and Klein's (1976) account of the effects of the employment of an in-house social scientist—herself—in the Esso Petroleum Company, Ltd.

These studies examine the changes and the processes of change in organizations that follow upon the introduction of social science research, analysis, and training into large organizations. They do not limit attention to effects on discrete decisions but range more widely over the consequences on structure, plans, priorities, communication, and programs. An assumption is that investigation can track the rippling effects of research on organizational behavior.

Methods of study tend to vary with the approach taken to the study of use. The method is largely determined by the locus of effect that is of primary concern.

Focus of Attention	Methodological Strategy
Studies	*Case studies* that trace the impact of the studies on decisions. While organizational records are usually reviewed, particular reliance is placed on interviews with informants.
People	*Surveys.* Interviews are conducted with a sample of potential users of research.
Issues	*Review of documents* (hearings, bills, reports, amendments) that mark the legislative and executive history of the issue. *Review of research studies* relevant to the issue. Documents that bear the

| | impress of research findings (testimony, references) are important for attesting to linkages. |
| Organizations | *Participant-observation.* Since the researchers generally have long-term involvement with the organization, their notes, records, and recollections are primary sources. |

The four approaches are directed at somewhat different questions about use. Although each of them can be used to answer a variety of questions, they are shaped by different conceptual and methodological constraints. By virtue of their internal logic, they appear to be best adapted to deal with particular questions.

Focus of Attention	*Questions best answered*	*Questions less well answered*
Studies	How much effect did the study have on decisions at the focal site?	What indirect effects did research have? Did it have effects at other sites? Were there long-term effects?
People	What kinds of people (by position, location, training, etc.) are most likely to use research? How much use do they make of research?	How does one person's use of research interact with others' uses (or nonuses) to influence events? Which available research leaves no impression?
Issues	What is the relative influence of research on the resolution of the issue compared with other information, interests, pressures, and demands?	Through what agents is research use mediated? How does research come to attention? Who promotes consideration of research and for what purposes?
Organizations	How much influence does research have on organizational behavior? Through what channels does research penetrate the organization? What are the consequences?	Why does research have the observed consequences? Are the processes of use unique to this organization?

Finally, let us look at some of the major limitations that attend each methodological strategy. Although some of the limitations can be mitigated by careful design and artful fieldwork, they tend to be the natural spawn of the method. Investigators have to make sedulous efforts to reduce their more serious effects.

Methodological Approach	Special Limitations Limitations
Case studies of the effects of research and evaluation	Short span of time under investigation. Informants' lack of knowledge about or sensitivity to the effects of research. Investigator's inability to interview all participants; overattention to the forceful or articulate informant.
Surveys of possible users	Respondents' poor memory of the research that has influenced them, their inability to disentangle research from all the other materials they read; inability to cite references, to recall the conceptual consequences of research, or to trace the steps of research use. Misreporting.
Documentary review of the resolution of issues	Lack of clear evidence of the linkages between research and official acts. Therefore, the investigator may attribute too much influence to a particular study or not enough. Research that influenced some participants may fail to surface.
Participant-observation of organizations	Bias of investigators, who are involved with the organization. Lack of generalizability of one organization's experience: idiosyncratic events, historical circumstances, personalities, time period.

To answer the gamut of unanswered questions about the uses of research and evaluation, none of these approaches is probably sufficient alone. To make progress in our quest for understanding, we need to employ mixed strategies and approach the question from multiple perspectives.

Above all, we need to come to consensus about the meaning of use, so that inquiries about the uses of research and evaluation can study the issue in comparable terms and build a cumulative body of knowledge. Only with clarity about the characterization of use can we proceed to learn (1) which kinds of people (2) in which kinds of contexts (3) make which kinds of uses (4) of which kinds of research and evaluation (5) with what range of consequences.

NOTES

1. The people who are interested in the uses of research and evaluation in policy and practice tend to be policy-oriented researchers and federal officials who fund research and evaluations. Both groups have a self-interested concern in legitimating their work, but they also tend to be professionally committed to the principle of research application for improving the caliber of program decisions. Relatively few policy makers or practitioners have yet paid serious attention to the question of research uses, except for the global, and skeptical, question of whether research and evaluation are ever used—or even usable—at all.

2. I thank Chris Argyris for bringing these studies to my attention.

REFERENCES

AARON, H. J. (1978) Politics and the Professors: The Great Society in Perspective. Washington, DC: Brookings Institution.

ALKIN, M. C., R. DAILLAK, and P. WHITE (1979) Using Evaluations: Does Evaluation Make a Difference? Beverly Hills, CA: Sage.

ALLISON, G. T. (1971) Essence of Decision: Explaining the Cuban Missile Crisis. Boston: Little, Brown.

BOECKMANN, M. E. (1976) "Policy impacts of the New Jersey income maintenance experiment." Policy Sciences 7: 53-76.

BROWN, W. and E. JAQUES (1965) Glacier Project Papers. London: Heinemann.

CAPLAN, N. (1977) "A minimal set of conditions necessary for the utilization of social science knowledge in policy formulation at the national level," pp. 183-197 in C. H. Weiss (ed.) Using Social Research in Public Policy Making. Lexington, MA: Lexington-Heath.

——— and E. BARTON (1976) Social indicators 1973: A study of the relationship between the power of information and utilization by federal executives. Ann Arbor: University of Michigan, Institute for Social Research.

CAPLAN, N., A. MORRISON, and R. J. STAMBAUGH (1975) The use of social science knowledge in policy decisions at the national level: A report to respondents. Ann Arbor: University of Michigan, Center for Research on Utilization of Scientific Knowledge, Institute for Social Research.

COHEN, D. K. and J. A. WEISS (1977) "Social science and social policy: Schools and race," pp. 67-83 in C. H. Weiss (ed.) Using Social Research in Public Policy Making. Lexington, MA: Lexington-Heath.

DATTA, L. (1976) "The impact of the Westinghouse/Ohio evaluation of the development of Project Head Start: An examination of the immediate and longer-term effects and how they came about," pp. 129-181 in C. C. Abt (ed.) The Evaluation of Social Programs. Beverly Hills, CA: Sage.

DOWNS, A. (1967) Inside Bureaucracy. Boston: Little, Brown.

KLEIN, L. (1976) A Social Scientist in Industry. New York: John Wiley.

KNORR, K. D. (1977) "Policymakers' use of social science knowledge: Symbolic or instrumental?" pp. 165-182 in C. H. Weiss (ed.) Using Social Research in Public Policy Making. Lexington, MA: Lexington-Heath.

LINDBLOM, C. E. and D. K. COHEN (1979) Usable Knowledge: Social Science and Social Problem Solving. New Haven, CT: Yale University Press.

MARCH, J. G. and J. P. OLSEN (1976) Ambiguity and Choice in Organizations. Bergen-Oslo-Tromsø, Norway: Universitetforlaget.

MEYER, J. W. and B. ROWAN (1977) "Institutionalized organizations: Formal structure as myth and ceremony." American Journal of Sociology 83: 340-363.

MINTZBERG, H. (1973) The Nature of Managerial Work. New York: Harper & Row.

PATTON, M. Q., P. S. GRIMES, K. M. GUTHRIE, N. J. BREMAN, B. D. FRENCH, and D. A. BLYTH (1977) "In search of impact: An analysis of the utilization of federal health evaluation research," pp. 141-163 in C. H. Weiss (ed.) Using Social Research in Public Policy Making. Lexington, MA: Lexington-Heath.

PELZ, D. C. (1978) "Some expanded perspectives on use of social science in public policy," pp. 346-357 in J. M. Yinger and S. J. Cutler (eds.) Major Social Issues: A Multidisciplinary View. New York: Free Press.

REIN, M. and S. WHITE (1977) "Can policy research help policy?" Public Interest 49: 119-136.

RICH, R. F. (1977) "Use of social science information by Federal bureaucrats: Knowledge for action versus knowledge for understanding," pp. 199-211 in C. H. Weiss (ed.) Using Social Research in Public Policy Making. Lexington, MA: Lexington-Heath.

——— (1975) "The power of information." Ph.D. dissertation, University of Chicago.

——— and N. CAPLAN (1976) "Policy uses of social science knowledge and perspectives: Means/ends matching versus understanding." Presented at the OECD Conference on "Dissemination of economic and social development research results," Bogota, Colombia, June.

ROWBOTTOM, R., J. BALLE, S. CANG, M. DIXON, E. JAQUES, T. PACKWOOD, and H. TOLLIDAY (1973) Hospital Organization. London: Heineman.

SIMON, H. A. (1976) Administrative Behavior. New York: Free Press.

THOMPSON, J. D. (1967) Organizations in Action. New York: McGraw-Hill.

WEICK, K. E. (1969) The Social Psychology of Organizing. Reading, MA: Addison-Wesley.

WEISS, C. H. (1977) "Introduction," pp. 1-22 in C. H. Weiss (ed.) Using Social Research in Public Policy Making. Lexington, MA: Lexington-Heath.

––– (1970) The Consequences of the Study of Federal Student Loan Programs: A Case Study in the Utilization of Social Research. New York: Bureau of Applied Social Research.

WHITE, B. F. (1975) "The Atlanta project: How one large school system responded to performance information." Policy Analysis 1: 659-691.

II

METHODOLOGY

The articles chosen for this section reflect both traditional and nontraditional approaches to evaluation. Historically, evaluators have relied upon experimental and quasi-experimental designs. However, as the field of evaluation has developed, evaluators have expanded their methodological perspectives. The authors of the following articles provide new insights into traditional strategies and also increase our understanding of the strengths of nontraditional methods.

The first article in this section is by Sechrest and Yeaton. Concerned with the number of ambiguous research outcomes, the authors reviewed different statistical approaches for determining effect size, being committed to the belief that estimating the size of effects is an important goal in research and evaluation. They decided that none of the procedures they reviewed (measures of proportion of variance) seemed adequate for studying effect size. As a result, Sechrest and Yeaton have developed two broad categories of empirical approaches: judgmental and normative. Both approaches are discussed with examples to illustrate inherent strengths and weaknesses. Provocative questions about small versus large effects are asked throughout the article. The authors conclude that measuring effect size is important in order to understand a phenomenon or problem under study, but they caution that ultimately, our most difficult task is to convince the audience of the meaningfulness of the solution to the problem.

The debate continues over the advantages and disadvantages of using case studies as an evaluation strategy. In a response to Miles (*Administrative Science Quarterly*, 24: 590-601, 1979), Yin writes that not only has case study emerged as an "accepted craft," but it has been used successfully in a number of studies in different disciplines. Yin believes that opponents of case studies have common misconceptions that case studies are the result of ethnographies and participant observation only. In this article he defines case study in terms of the evidence collected and the method of data collection. Yin argues that there is a difference between note taking and narrative. He suggests techniques for dealing with quantitative data and discusses the importance of building explanations. In the concluding sections he suggests two potential approaches to conducting cross-case analyses and recommends how case studies may be reported.

Researchers and evaluators have often relied on interview data to provide a more contextual and meaningful representation of an issue or situation. Numerous books and papers have been written on the methods and techniques of interviewing, but in the next section, MacDonald and Sanger discuss the paucity of manuals that describe good and bad interviewing techniques. Their article is an attempt to make explicit the debate over the epistemological, political, and technical differences among interviewing strategies used in program evaluation. The authors focus on the unstructured interview and discuss the strengths and weaknesses of note-taking versus tape-recording interviews. "Our intention is to expose the variables involved by elaborating two lines of reasoning, and to draw attention to some of the consequences of choice." MacDonald and Sanger include a chart that illustrates the consequences that result from a choice of using tapes or notes as the recording technique of the unstructured interview. The authors' final point is that the choice of recording technique is shaped by the evaluators' values and intents and has the possibility of affecting the complexion of the whole evaluation.

The fourth article in this section addresses the uses and abuses of intuitive data. Sadler's article attempts to sensitize naturalistic inquirers to potential problem areas. He discusses various forms of bias and asserts that even with the newer strategies that have been developed in naturalistic inquiry to eliminate or reduce bias (adversary hearings, improved training of evaluators, and the like), they are not sufficient for an unbiased investigation. Sadler assesses a person's performance as an intuitive data processor by describing thirteen specific conditions of intuitive thinking and judgmental processing. Some of the conditions discussed are data overload, internal consistency, uneven reliability of information, and confidence and consistency in judgment. Sadler concludes by affirming his optimism that if we have a better understanding of the ways data are intuitively processed, we might then be able to conduct evaluations of higher quality.

The critic-expert as evaluator was the method used for evaluating an arts program for physically impaired children. A panel of five people was selected based on their knowledge and skills in special education and their openness to and value of the arts. After reviewing the program's purpose and goals, each panel member viewed a performance of the *Living Stage*. They then wrote up their "impressions of the efficacy of the experience for handicapped children and their thoughts about the strategy as an evaluation technique." Anastasiow illustrates the use of this strategy for an operating program and provides an example of its implementation. His conclusions about the utilization of this approach when coupled with an experimental study of program goals are insightful.

The following article by Madaus summarizes his reactions and feelings as a team leader about various aspects of the events leading up to the MCT hearing, the hearings themselves, and the final videotape product. He discusses the strengths and weaknesses of using a modified judicial evaluation model (JEM) at the national level to explore education issues. Madaus analyzes various aspects of the judicial evaluation model including the process of selecting the team members, budget considerations and constraints, the critical time limits, the issue of labeling teams pro and con, and the role of the funding agency. He raises questions about the reality of expecting policymakers to view 24 hours of proceedings and the sensibility of participating in 24 hours of hearings for a finished product of 3 hours. He further discusses the power of television in presenting the teams' cases. In retrospect Madaus realizes how beneficial it would have been to have had witnesses who were credible to a TV audience, to rehearse certain pieces of testimony, and to have had a television consultant who would have helped the team make better use of the medium to present its evidence and technical arguments. Overall, Madaus feels that the clarification hearing model was illuminative, yet he cautions that this model may not be as productive for more divisive issues such as busing or abortion. He suggests treading carefully when selecting this method for evaluating controversial issues.

In the next article, Popham, who was the other team leader in the MCT clarification process hearings, describes his experiences in terms of the "process of the enterprise." He discusses the formulation of his team, the development of the hearing's issues, and the relationship between the pro and con teams at various meetings prior to the hearings. Popham outlines the strategies employed for recruiting witnesses and for constructing his team's arguments. He also addresses the difficulty of not "playing up to the television cameras" and the psychological impact of being readied for an appearance on national TV. Popham believes that the judicial evaluation model is a positive approach to evaluation by virtue of its ability to reach a greater number of policymakers than a written report would be able to do. However, he does see certain flaws in the model. The possibility that there may be "marked dissimilarity in proponents' prowess," and the "substantial costs" of this type of project lead Popham to conclude that this procedure may have limited use unless teams are carefully constructed and costs are kept to a minimum. Since the *Ed Researcher* (November 1981) article was published, Popham has modified his position regarding the overall usefulness of the adversary evaluation process. After viewing the videotapes months after the process hearings, Popham says he found them dull, and probably not convincing to those whose minds already made up on the issue of MCT. Considering the costs involved and the limited effectiveness of the adversary evaluation hearings, Popham now believes that this method of evaluation has no practical value for evaluators or decision makers.

The final article by Estes and Demaline describes the background, purposes, objectives, and results of the NIE-sponsored MCT clarification process hearings that explored issues related to minimal competency testing. Recognizing the social and political context of MCT, NIE decided to implement a modified version of the judicial evaluation model. Data from questionnaires, interviews, and observations were collected during and after each day's proceedings. In addition to the onsite data, approximately twenty individuals representing various education agencies viewed the hearings on videotape. Special interest groups, ERS/ENET conference participants, and instructional television programming managers also contributed to the data collected. The authors discuss the results of the hearings by addressing the five major evaluation questions regarding the appropriateness of the format and structure of the clarification process, the range of diversity of viewpoints on each issue, the degree to which the information presented added to an understanding of MCT, the audience's perceived usefulness of the information presented, and the viability of this approach for other NIE efforts. Based on the results of the data, Estes and Demaline offer their conclusions and recommendations concerning the efficacy and appropriateness of the clarification process model for evaluating educational issues.

9

Assessing the Effectiveness of
Social Programs
Methodological and Conceptual Issues

Lee Sechrest and William H. Yeaton

*The assessment of the outcomes of social programs should always
include estimates of the size of the effects produced.
Various approaches to this problem are discussed.*

When an evaluation's major purpose is to shed light on decisions having clear policy implications, it is difficult to imagine a choice regarding
the future implementation of programming being made *without* consideration of the magnitude of the effects involved. Some interventions
may produce effects that, however regular, are just too small to be of
any social importance.

Realistically, there is a host of plausible factors besides effect
size that are likely to influence a policy maker's decision about future `
implementation of programs; political, economic, and ethical issues
weigh heavily in the decision-making process. However, faced with
research outcomes of ambiguous or even unknown meaning, those
charged with responsibility for making decisions can rely only on intuitions, a highly undesirable state of affairs.

Reprinted with permission of the publishers and authors. Sechrest, L., and Yeaton, W. H.,"Assessing
the Effectiveness of Social Programs: Methodological and Conceptual Issues." In S. Ball (Ed.) *New
Directions for Program Evaluation: Assessing and Interpreting Outcomes,* no. 9. San Francisco:
Jossey-Bass, 1981.

Convinced of the importance of estimating the size of effects in research and evaluation, we began systematically to study existing ways of determining effect size (Sechrest and Yeaton, 1979b). We adopted the simple yet robust definition of an effect as the difference between means for two independent groups or conditions. We refined the definition for contingency tables, regression, and correlational analyses, though our simple definition will suffice for purposes of this discussion. A 20 percent difference between experimental and control groups in utilization of health services, a difference in attendance of 10.5 students per day during baseline and treatment conditions, and a salary differential of $1,250 between professional men and women all illustrate this definition of an effect.

Statistical Approaches

Unfortunately, we still lacked any direct information pertaining to the size of the outcome; it was not possible to say whether a 20 percent difference between groups, 10.5 students per day, or $1,250 represented, say, small, medium, or large effects. We turned, with eventual disappointment, to the existing statistical approaches to effect size estimation, namely, measures of proportion of variance accounted for. We have previously reviewed these statistical approaches to the size of experimental (or quasiexperimental) effects (Sechrest and Yeaton, 1979b). The considerations for choosing among the various estimators are numerous, but their shared limitations are worth elaborating upon. All the estimators are biased, and it is impossible to determine the extend of the bias involved. Depending on the circumstances (for example, number of subjects, proportion of error variance present, or kind of ANOVA model chosen), these estimators will tend to produce values that can differ substantially. Speaking in general terms, all suffer the deficiency of depending upon the specific features of the experiment and its implementation. For example, the percentage of variance accounted for by any of these estimators will vary as a function of how much variance is built into the experiment. A relatively homogeneous sample of subjects (for example, college students) would exhibit less variance in the dependent variable than a heterogeneous group (for example, people riding the subway in New York City). It should be easier to account for variance with a homogeneous than a heterogeneous sample. Since most of the estimators are expressed in terms of percentage of variance accounted for, we are in the rather uncomfortable position of estimating the size of an effect where the size depends upon (is confounded by) the choice of sample.

Similarly, the precision used in conducting an experiment would surely produce differing amounts of variance. Treatments implemented by different experimenters at different times of day in different rooms using slightly different cover stories should induce subjects to perform in rather disparate ways. Since mean values of experimental and control groups are not likely to change as a function of this experimental imprecision, experimental effects, as we have defined them, would remain constant. Experienced and inexperienced researchers should produce the same experimental effects but with different variances; hence, statistics estimating effect size will vary markedly. Since all the statistical estimates of effect size are ratio estimators, small changes in variance can greatly alter size of effects expressed in percentage of variance accounted for. Those features of an experiment that influence variance produced will also alter these estimates. For example, the number, strength, and range of treatments are other determinants of the amount of variance available to be accounted for. Effect size estimates will fluctuate as these determinants take on new values. For the same reasons, statistical significance is an inappropriate criterion upon which to gauge the size of an effect.

What then? As Benjamin Franklin said, "Necessity is the mother of invention," and we clearly wanted an offspring. We have begun to develop alternatives to statistical approaches to the effect size estimation problem; an elaboration of these initial efforts appears in a second paper (Sechrest and Yeaton, 1979a). We have considered several empirical approaches for estimating effect size, which we have classified into the broad categories of *judgmental* and *normative*.

Judgmental Approaches. The most common judgmental approach is probably intuitive. A policy maker examines the results of an evaluation, forms some subjective impression of the magnitude of impact, and takes this impression into account when making a policy decision. The impression of effect size the policy maker takes from reading the results of an evaluation may well be based on experience with similar problems using similar interventions. Unfortunately, this experimental background is likely to be different for different persons or even for the same person at different times. Consequently, judges are not apt to agree on their assessments of the magnitudes of an effect. Choose the appropriate judge and you can probably choose any desired answer to the question "How big would you describe this effect to be?"

There are instances, however, where disagreement is much less likely. McSweeny (1978) has reported on the effects of instituting a twenty-cent surcharge for each local directory assistance call per telephone per month (beyond three calls) for telephone subscribers in Cincinnati. The change of approximately sixty thousand calls per day in the experimental series after the charge was introduced is likely to be termed large by even the most conservative judge. The plausibility of the response cost procedure being responsible for the change demonstrated is greatly enhanced by the inclusion of a control series of long-distance directory assistance calls that did not receive the twenty-cent surcharge *or* decrease in frequency. Even without the control series, we are still much more likely to believe the functionality of the procedures, given the absolute change produced in this study. However, if one knew that a simple televised plea to cut down on local directory assistance calls would have decreased their frequency by fifty thousand per day, one would not be as likely to call the obtained decrease of sixty thousand calls a large effect.

We would go so far as to speculate that the production of large effects is on a par with the three factors cited by Cline and Sinnott in this volume as being necessary for adequate causal explanation in case studies. It is decidedly easier to argue away nonpreferred causal explanation in the face of substantial changes in dependent variable responding; small changes allow these rival explanations to become more believable, a point vividly illustrated by the McSweeny case study (assuming, for argument's sake, that the control series was not available).

Some judges are more likely to be convincing than others. Experts are often called upon when they are more informed sources of knowledge. Experts in an area of research and evaluation are more likely to be aware of similar work in the area of interest; in fact, their designation as expert may be owing to this greater awareness. Given the homogeneity of experimental backgrounds of experts in an area, we might expect a good deal of concurrence in their judgments about experimental effects. We have tested this notion, sending descriptions of smoking treatments to experts in the modification of smoking behavior. Judgments of probable success were correlated with reports of actual success reported in the results sections of studies from which the descriptions were taken. The average correlation was .47; several judges achieved correlations in the vicinity of .70. Judges were thus able to make reasonable a priori assessments of the size of the effects produced by the treatments as briefly described to them.

A similar strategy was utilized to assess the ability of experts in personality and social psychology to estimate the strength of manipulations from studies taken from the *Journal of Personality and Social Psychology*. Manipulation checks are frequently used to test the "take" of independent variables, and the results of these checks provide a standard to compare judgments of the strengths of treatment. When judges' estimates were averaged and the estimate for each manipulation was correlated with the actual manipulation check value, a correlation coefficient of .84 was obtained. Although these findings show only that judges can agree as to which treatments are likely to produce the largest effects, we believe they bear indirectly on judges' ability to agree in estimating effect sizes, even when, as with the social psychology manipulation checks, not all the outcome measures are in the same metric. We believe experts' judgments offer promise as a reasonable barometer of the magnitude of experimental effects.

Precedent exists within the behaviorist framework for making a posteriori judgment of the size of experimental effect demonstrated. Visual rather than statistical analysis is used as the general standard for acceptance into the *Journal of Applied Behavioral Analysis* (Michael, 1974). Reviewers expert in the given problem area judge whether a solution to a socially significant problem area has been demonstrated, paying particular attention to the graphic display in determining whether the effect "looks big." As Baer (1977, p. 171) has said, "If a problem has been solved, you can *see* that. . . . This, after all, was the major conclusion to be made, not whether an experimental effect had been uncovered." Regrettably, the factors influencing these judgments of outcomes have only recently begun to be studied (see DeProspero, 1976; Jones, Weinrott, and Vaught, 1978).

Normative Approaches. Evaluators are seldom in a position to employ absolute standards for assessing the applied significance of outcome measures. Medical interventions that save lives or increase life expectancy may represent instances where there is nearly universal agreement regarding treatment value, "nearly" because there are always the "what ifs?" What if the time and money spent on this intervention had been expended with an alternative treatment that saved more lives or saved the same number of lives with younger, smarter, healthier persons? What if the intervention extended the patient's life expectancy six years but produced recurring nausea and dizziness while an alternative treatment produced a three-year reprieve from death with few side effects? Clearly, issues of quality should be raised, as Ball has pointed out so forcefully in his contribution to this sourcebook.

More common is the case where some comparative standard is employed to gauge the size of an experimental effect. A novel approach to weight control is applauded when outcomes are larger than previous modification efforts; a treatment to increase compliance with a medical regimen is abandoned when results are smaller than existing treatments. A method of preventive dentistry is adopted if it is cheaper than other methods showing otherwise similar outcomes. Such comparative standards require data from other interventions with the same problem and outcome measure. It may be useful to know that a new approach to cigarette smoking control causes 50 percent of the participants to quit smoking if this quit rate is better than that achieved in most studies that attempt to induce participants to abstain from substance abuse if, and this is admittedly a big if, we can assume the problem areas are similarly resistant to change. It would be even more useful to know that this new approach to cigarette smoking control causes more participants to quit smoking than 90 percent of all other smoking modification methods. Policy decisions could be greatly simplified (but political, financial, and ethical considerations scarcely make them automatic) if this information were available.

Illustrations. An experiment by Jeffrey, Wing, and Stunkard (1976) utilized norms to assess the impact made in their efforts to bring about weight loss with obese participants. A mean weight loss of 11.5 pounds found in twenty-one previous studies compared favorably with the 11.0-pound average reported in their study. Should these methods of weight control be adopted by a community mental health clinic? Unless the treatment had secondary selling points (for example, delivered by paraprofessionals in large groups in sessions of limited duration), the magnitude of its effect is not particularly persuasive.

We have conducted a meta-analysis of forty-one recent smoking studies reporting percentage decrease in smoking. When the data from the experimental groups in these studies are averaged across all followup periods reported, the mean decrease in smoking was 53 percent, with a standard deviation of 27 percent. We might be inclined to call large those scores beyond one standard deviation from the mean, but such large standard deviations suggest marked disparity in the impacts of treatments as well as a nonnormal distribution. The standard deviation at the popular six-month follow-up point is still a rather substantial 22 percent. However, only 14 percent of the data points at six months were above 60 percent. We may be inclined to term a 70 percent decrease in smoking at the end of six months big simply because such decreases occur so infrequently. When the distribution of scores is not normal and cannot be legitimately abbreviated with a mean and standard deviation, a frequency distribution of the data offers a viable alternative as a standard to deduce large and small effect sizes.

Smith and Glass (1977) have utilized a similar technique to

aggregate the results of nearly four hundred psychotherapy and counseling studies. For their purposes, the authors defined effect size as the "mean difference between the treated and control subjects divided by the standard deviation of the control group" (p. 753). They reported a mean superiority of .68 standard deviations of experimental groups over control groups as their average effect size. Given an effect size standard deviation of .67 sigma, we would likely be no more than marginally impressed with a study demonstrating a .50 sigma experimental versus control group superiority. We might, on the other hand, be very enthusiastic about an innovative treatment showing an effect size beyond 2 sigmas.

The Smith and Glass meta-analysis illustrates a critical caution in effect size estimation studies. The point, also addressed in Ball's chapter in this volume, concerns the choice of comparison group or condition made by the researcher. It is foolish to imagine an experimenter would make decisions that would tend to diminish chances of producing a large experimental effect, should effect size become a new criterion to evaluate the worth of research. Therefore, a control group might be chosen solely to maximize the difference between experimental and control group scores. In the psychotherapy case, this might mean using a homogeneous control group (thus reducing the control group sigma in the denominator of the effect size indicator) that had never previously received psychotherapy (thus moving the control group mean in the numerator away from the experimental group mean). Campbell's (1975) notion of a corruptible indicator argues cogently for the very real possibility of this occurrence. Should our norms be periodically updated (as we maintain they should) by inclusion of this new psychotherapy study, it follows that the standard would become more stringent for the next researcher whose results are being compared to previous work in the field.

Quantity versus Quality of Change

Normative standards offer promise as a means of skirting otherwise subjective assessments of effect size magnitude. But subjective impressions of the change demonstrated in research may have greater clinical significance than the mere quantitative modifications made. For instance, a program that induces obese subjects to lose eleven pounds may not alter a subject's feelings of self-worth if no one else notices the change. A treatment to modify a husband's negative interactions with his wife may reduce the number of nagging statements to zero but go unnoticed by his spouse. We must distinguish carefully between qualitative and quantitative measures of change, a point made in another context by Ball (this volume), with which we would heartily concur. Said slightly differently, we must not be deluded into maintaining that we have produced large effects simply because the comparative size of the quantitative change is substantial.

Each study that reports the percentage decrease in hyperactive behavior of young children might also supply ratings of the extent to which parents and teachers notice the beneficial changes on rating scale assessments. Should a new intervention produce a three-point change (on a seven-point scale) in ratings by parents, we could reasonably term this a large effect, knowing that previous efforts had never produced more than a two-point change. Knowing that parents give more physical affection would further substantiate our claims for the importance of the change. If this study reduced the percentage of hyperactivity consistently below 5 percent, a change greater than 95 percent of previous studies, we should be further convinced this is a big effect, and we might strive for this quantitative standard as a goal in subsequent treatment programs prior to knowing the responses of parents and teachers.

The relationship between quantity and quality of change may often be inverse; small quantitative change may be associated with superior qualitative change while large quantitative change may be of inferior quality. The change in speech involved in dropping out racial slurs and implications of inferiority is a relatively small one, but the change in quality of interracial relations might be experienced as substantial. There have been reports on the coronary artery bypass operation that indicate the surgery does not prolong life but improves quality of life during the survival time (see Weinstein, Pliskin, and Stason, 1977). Presumably, also, there might be large quantitative changes of low quality. For example, a football coach might want some of his players to participate in a program to increase weight, but he would be dissatisfied if the increase were fat rather than muscle. A gain in reading ability reflected only in faster reading of comic books might not be regarded as much of an improvement.

Applied behavior analysts have always placed great stock in the quantitative assessment of behavior change but have only recently begun to recognize the importance of qualitative measures of change (see Wolf, 1978). This approach is termed *social validation*, to reflect directly the reliance upon pertinent members of society rather than the research audience as the appropriate group to substantiate presumed treatment benefits. For example, Fawcett and Miller (1975) asked judges to rate the public speaking ability of subjects before and after training. Clear differences in these pre–post ratings validated quantitative changes in public speaking; that is, the changes were sufficient to be discriminated by judges. However, a survey of several studies in the *Journal of Applied Behavior Analysis* (Yeaton, in press) suggests that rating scale changes are rather inelastic; large, absolute changes in the dependent variable are associated with small, absolute changes (less than three points) on a seven-point, semantic differential scale. Specification of other dependent variables may yield slightly smaller quantitative change but decidedly larger qualitative change. These results tend empirically to substantiate our caution that apparently large effects may be a wishful delusion.

We do not, unfortunately, know much about assessing quality of change, let alone know how to factor it into our judgments about the worth of interventions. Probably most persons assume there is a linear, and certainly monotonic, relationship between quantity and quality of change. Thus, for example, it is tempting to suppose improvement in reading ability is to be valued. But if, as seems likely, various kinds of reading materials are prepared deliberately for particular levels of reading ability, a modest change between levels might make little difference at all. For example, if most reading materials are programmed at, say, the fourth-grade level (comics) or the eighth-grade level (newspapers), improvement in reading ability from fourth- to fifth-grade level might actually make few new reading experiences available. For many variables, the relationship between quantity and quality of change will most likely not be linear and perhaps not even be invariably monotonic. The relationship between years of education and various indicators of quality of life may well be nonlinear, probably characterized by plateaus and step-wise changes. There may be very little advantage to having completed eleven years of school as opposed to ten but a large advantage to having completed twelve years of school as opposed to eleven. Similarly, the advantage of being able to read at the fifth-grade rather than the fourth-grade level may be negligible (even though that would be a 25 percent improvement) because no other changes flow from that one.

At present, we can do little more than urge investigators to consider carefully the quality of the changes they are investigating and to attempt to use their quality estimates to form their judgments about the importance of the quantitative changes they are able to demonstrate.

Dependent Variable Scaling Problems

Effect size may be difficult to determine accurately because the units in which the dependent variable is scaled may not be equal at all points on the scale. For example, Jencks (Yankelovich, 1979) has produced evidence on amount of education that suggests there are discontinuities in the meaning of increasing amounts of education. Thus, for black males, there is no advantage in completing high school if they are not going on to college. There may be little advantage in going on to college if they are not going to complete the bachelor's degree. Such findings suggest programs that produce increments in amount of education, for example, by keeping youth in school, have to be evaluated with great care lest seemingly large effects, for example, an additional year and a half of education, be the basis for policies ineffective in the long run. It is probable that inequalities in the units in which dependent variables are scaled are the rule rather than the exception.

One particular source of inequality is likely to be the point on the scale characterizing a target person or group, in that it will almost certainly not be equally easy to produce change at all points on the scale. It will, for example, certainly be easier to take a group of teenage males who run a hundred yards in 12 seconds and improve their running speed by .5 seconds than to take a group who run a hundred yards in 10 seconds and improve their speed by the same amount. Generally speaking, it will be easier to produce improvement in groups functioning below the population mean than to produce the same improvement in those functioning above the mean. Consequently, what would be a rather small gain for one group might be a large one for another, as assessed by the effort required to produce it.

Strength and Integrity. The development of a set of techniques to estimate the magnitude of an effect presupposes certain considerations of the strength and integrity of the treatment involved. Sechrest and colleagues (Sechrest and Redner, forthcoming; Sechrest and others, 1979) have elaborated upon strength and integrity issues in the context of research in criminal justice and evaluation, although our discussion must, of necessity, be much briefer. Strength refers to the a priori, planned intensity of treatment delivery. For example, therapy might be administered in a strong form by utilizing therapists in a one-to-one manner. Integrity of treatment, the degree to which the plan of delivery is implemented, can be ascertained only by careful monitoring and is free to vary independent of treatment strength. Since magnitudes of effects depend integrally upon both the strength and integrity of treatments, any assessment of intervention impact is open to question without knowledge of both strength and integrity.

Outcome measures expressed as norms offer a means for validating judged treatment strengths. We would be embarrassed if a strong treatment produced an effect estimated to be two standard deviations *below* the mean of other experimental groups treated for the same problem. Consistency of a priori judgments of treatment strength and a posteriori normative standards form a basis for ranking treatments classified along theoretical and process dimensions. For example, it is plausible to expect prompting procedures for fingernail biting to produce smaller habit decrements than, say, self-monitoring procedures, which may in turn be inferior to financial reinforcement contingencies. It would be insightful to discover the same ordinal relationship among these three treatments regardless of the problem domain. We would then be in the privileged position of recommending a treatment proportional to the judged severity of the presenting problem. Very strong treatments would not be recommended for mild problems. We are likely to apply a "weakest that works" principle both to preserve valuable resources and to avoid general client adaptation to strong doses of treatments.

Small immediate treatment effects might grow over time (Gilbert, Light, and Mosteller, 1975); an initial "nudge" might set a person off on a course that would produce large ultimate change just as a small force will set a ski jumper into motion. Indeed, many tested treatments seem implicitly to bank on the nudge notion, since they are, on the face of it, sufficiently weak as to make it scarcely imaginable that any profound change would be found immediately. Thus, for example, the group counseling program Kassebaum, Ward, and Wilner (1971) tested as an antidote to criminal recidivism involved only an hour or two of counseling per week by often not very well-trained counselors and often in large groups. However, the program was expected to reduce commitment to criminal life-styles and ultimately to reduce criminal behavior.

London (1977) has written about the twin but opposite processes of cumulative convergence and cumulative divergence. *Cumulative convergence* refers to any process that, once set in motion, tends to produce convergence toward some "normal" state. *Cumulative divergence* is an opposite process that tends to produce greater and greater divergence from normal. No matter how unusual the initial distribution of a set of numbers, integers, let us say, ranging from one to nine, additional randomly generated numbers will tend to produce a convergence of the distribution toward equal appearance of the nine integers. Similarly, the learning of speech is a cumulatively convergent process, since infants gradually come to sound more and more like the persons around them. An initial error in the trajectory of a missile, however, is a cumulatively divergent process, since the farther the missile travels, the farther off target it will be. In criminology, labeling theory describes a cumulatively divergent process in which the initially small act of identifying a youth as a delinquent is assumed to initiate a process that will produce greater and greater social deviation.

The implication of this discussion is that seemingly small treatment effects might really be large in their long-run implications, and, therefore, when nudges are achieved, they should be causes for elation (or despair if the change is in the wrong direction). The problem as we see it is that we do not often have a very good way of deciding when we have achieved a genuine nudge as opposed to a genuine small effect; the distinction is important. The optimism surrounding early Head Start programs, especially when it seemed there were some favorable outcomes, was based on the notion that a cumulatively convergent process that would cause experientially deprived children to become gradually more and more like their more favored classmates had been set in motion. In retrospect, the effects, such as they were, were less like nudges than just simply small, transient effects.

We do not know how to determine whether an effect is small but likely to grow as opposed to being simply small. Perhaps a careful study of effects that have proved to be of the nudge type would be informative and a basis for developing some expectations about cumulative processes. Assuming labeling theory to be correct, why does identifying a youngster as a delinquent have such profound effects, while labeling another as a bloomer (see the Pygmalion effect, Rosenthal and Jacobson, 1968) have a much more elusive and transient effect (see Lindgren, 1976)? We need to know.

Aggregation of Small Effects

There may be outcomes of interventions that, although small in a specific instance, may nonetheless be large when aggregated across a large number of units. For example, the improvement in gas mileage from reducing driving speed to fifty-five miles per hour might not be enough to effect savings that would be meaningful to most individual drivers, but the aggregated saving of gasoline would have a very important impact on this nation's oil consumption. Or relatively small changes in average sentence length for certain classes of criminal offenders would have large effects on the number of incarcerated persons in our jails and prisons at any one time. Charitable organizations such as the March of Dimes have successfully raised substantial sums of money by a plea to each individual to contribute only extra small change.

But not all small effects would necessarily become important even if aggregated, because at least some effects have implications only at the individual level. A small increase in reading ability, even if aggregated across large numbers of persons, would still remain a small increase in reading ability. Or if a nutritional rehabilitation program produced an average height increase of one centimeter in nutritionally deprived children (see McKay and others, 1978), those children would remain short, and the aggregated effects would be nil. We once encountered a newspaper article that referred to an estimate of the nationally aggregated loss in IQ points supposedly attributable to smoking. Somehow or other, the idea of a nation "losing" millions of IQ points does not seem to get at the nature of the problem.

However, even small effects at the mean could be large at the extremes if the effect were uniform across the entire distribution of values. Imagine, for example, a population of one million children with a mean IQ of 85 and assume a standard deviation in the IQ measure of fifteen. Assume also that an IQ of 125 is required as a minimum for successful completion of a premedical education. In that population, there would be only about 3,900 persons bright enough to complete a premedical education. Suppose, then, a compensatory education program were devised that would raise the mean IQ by five points and have a uniform effect throughout the distribution. There would then be more than 9,000 children bright enough to complete premedical education, a more than twofold increase. The effect of the program would have very limited implications at the mean of the population, but the practical implications at the extreme upper end would surely be accounted quite important.

Effects may also be aggregated across time at the individual level. If people are constrained from smoking by laws or customs limiting smoking in many places, and if they do not compensate by smoking when it is permissible, the aggregate effect across a lifetime could amount to many, many cigarettes. A reduction of food intake by one hundred calories per day would produce a weight loss of about ten pounds over the course of one year. The daily change in weight, or even the weekly change, would be undetectable, but the effect accumulated over time would be sizable.

Treatment Costs and Benefits

Had we the capacity to manufacture an inexpensive yet harmless pill that could cure cancer, we might term the magnitude of the effect, at the very least, gargantuan. More realistically, we would applaud a novel treatment for anorexia nervosa that produced greater benefits than standard treatments at the same cost or the same benefits at smaller costs. The cost-benefit basis for decision making is seldom so simple as this sketch implies, as Levine has articulated so cogently in this sourcebook. What dollar value would one place on the benefit of an overweight person losing forty pounds? It is difficult even to list all the benefits, let alone place a dollar value on them. What about the cost of a new wardrobe and a new diet and a divorce? A divorce? Perhaps! Neill, Marshall, and Yale (1978) report a retrospective interview study of the adverse material changes experienced by fourteen patients who underwent intestinal bypass surgery. Unintended side effects are at least as difficult to place a dollar value on as to predict.

Why should we bother to assess the effectiveness of research? At a fundamental level, we probably wish to demonstrate our understanding of the phenomenon or problem under study. An effectiveness measure may be a particularly convincing bit of evidence in making the case to the reader that we have located and perhaps controlled the most important variables associated with the phenomenon in question. Very often we wish to infer that a practical solution to a problem has been discovered. Such an inference is particularly plausible, should a large effect size be shown using either a judgmental or a normative approach. Furthermore, we assume staff and administrative personnel are more likely to initiate and maintain procedures that exhibit large rather than small magnitudes of effect. But even our preliminary efforts to articulate the conceptual issues that bear on the effectiveness assessment problem suggest the problem is not inclined to yield to a solution without relentless and sophisticated scrutiny. Even the most *potentially* convincing demonstration of our understanding of the functional relationship among critical variables and a hint of the discovery of an eminently practical solution to the problem may not be perceived to be of meaningful magnitude by the audience of relevance (see Sechrest and Yeaton, 1979a). This may be a simple matter of presentation of data and rhetoric of results, or a more basic deficiency in the public understanding of the logic of scientific questioning and answering. Our quest is then not so different from that of the artist who strives to produce a technically perfect work that expresses a beauty visible to all its beholders.

References

Baer, D. M. "Perhaps It Would Be Better Not to Know Everything." *Journal of Applied Behavior Analysis*, 1977, *10* (1), 167–172.

Campbell, D. T. "Assessing the Impact of Planned Social Change." In G. M. Lyons (Ed.), *Social Research and Public Policies: The Dartmouth/OECD Conference.* Hanover, N.H.: Public Affairs Center, Dartmouth College, 1975.

DeProspero, A. "A Comparison of Visual and Statistical Analyses of Intrasubject Replication Data." Paper presented at the meeting of the Association for the Advancement of Behavior Therapy, New York, 1976.

Fawcett, S. B., and Miller, L. K. "Training Public-Speaking Behavior: An Experimental Analysis and Social Validation." *Journal of Applied Behavioral Analysis*, 1975, *8* (2), 125–135.

Gilbert, J. P., Light, R. J., and Mosteller, F. "Assessing Social Interventions: An Empirical Basis for Policy." In C. A. Bennett and A. A. Lumsdaine (Eds.), *Evaluation and Experiment: Some Critical Issues in Assessing Social Programs.* New York: Academic Press, 1975.

Jeffrey, R. W., Wing, R. R., and Stunkard, A. J. "Behavioral Treatment of Obesity: The State of the Art 1976." *Behavior Therapy*, 1976, *9* (2), 189–199.

Jones, R. R., Weinrott, M. R., and Vaught, R. S. "Effects of Serial Dependency on the Agreement Between Visual and Statistical Inference." *Journal of Applied Behavioral Analysis*, 1978, *11* (2), 277–283.

Kassebaum, G., Ward, D. A., and Wilner, D. M. *Prison Treatment and Parole Survival.* New York: Wiley, 1971.

Lindgren, H. C. *Educational Psychology in the Classroom.* (5th ed.) New York: Wiley, 1976.

London, I. D. "Convergent and Divergent Amplification and Its Meaning for Social Science." *Psychological Reports*, 1977, *41*, 111–123.

McKay, H., and others. "Improving Cognitive Ability in Chronically Deprived Children." *Science*, 1978, *200*, 270–278.

McSweeny, A. J. "Effects of Response Cost on the Behavior of a Million Persons: Charging for Directory Assistance in Cincinnati." *Journal of Applied Behavior Analysis*, 1978, *11* (1), 47–51.

Michael, J. "Statistical Inference for Individual Organism Research: Mixed Blessing or Curse?" *Journal of Applied Behavior Analysis*, 1974, *7* (4), 647–653.

Neill, J. R., Marshall, J. R., and Yale, C. E. "Marital Changes After Intestinal Bypass Surgery." *Journal of the American Medical Association*, 1978, *240* 447–450.

Rosenthal, R., and Jacobson, L. *Pygmalion in the Classroom: Teacher Expectation and Pupils' Intellectual Development.* New York: Holt, Rinehart and Winston, 1968.

Sechrest, L., and Redner, R. *Strength and Integrity of Treatments in Evaluation Studies,* forthcoming.

Sechrest, L., West, S. C., Phillips, M. A., Redner, R., and Yeaton, W. "Some Neglected Problems in Evaluation Research: Strength and Integrity of Treatments." In L. Sechrest and others (Eds.), *Evaluation Studies Review Annual*, Vol. 4. Beverly Hills, Calif.: Sage, 1979.

Sechrest, L., and Yeaton, W. H. *Empirical Approaches to Effect Size Estimation.* Unpublished manuscript, Florida State University, 1979a.

Sechrest, L., and Yeaton, W. H. "Estimating Magnitudes of Experimental Effects." Unpublished manuscript, 1979b.

Smith, M. L., and Glass, G. V "Meta-Analysis of Psychotherapy Outcome Studies." *American Psychologist*, 1977, *32*, 752–760.

Weinstein, M. C., Pliskin, J. S., and Stason, W. B. "Coronary Artery Bypass Surgery: Decision and Policy Analysis." In J. P. Bunker, B. A. Barnes, and F. Mosteller (Eds.), *Costs, Risks, and Benefits of Surgery.* New York: Oxford University Press, 1977.

Wolf, M. M. "Social Validity: The Case for Subjective Measurement or How Applied Behavioral Analysis Is Finding Its Heart." *Journal of Applied Behavior Analysis,* 1978, *11* (2), 203–214.

Yankelovich, D. "Who Gets Ahead in America." *Psychology Today,* July 1979, *13* (2), 28–91.

Yeaton, W. H., "A Critique of the Effectiveness Dimension in Applied Behavior Analysis." *Journal of Applied Behavior Analysis,* in press.

Lee Sechrest is professor of psychology at Florida State University, where he teaches courses in research methodology and program evaluation. Previously he was at Northwestern University, where he was involved in the development of their training program in evaluation research. Sechrest is a consultant to a number of government and private agencies involved in development and evaluation of social interactions.

William H. Yeaton received his Ph.D. in psychology in 1979 from Florida State University. He served as an assistant editor for the fourth volume of the Evaluation Studies Review Annual *(1979). His research interests include program evaluation, empirical validation of procedures for diffusion of effective treatments, and behavioral community psychology.*

10

The Case Study Crisis
Some Answers

Robert K. Yin

In his *ASQ* article entitled "Qualitative data as an attractive nuisance," Matthew Miles (1979) has written a disarmingly candid rendition of the perils of qualitative analysis. Unfortunately, his candor in admitting the existence of these perils was matched by few suggestions for overcoming them. As a result, his article, based on a four-year study of six public schools, leaves the reader with a sense that qualitative analysis — and its implicit companion, the case study — cannot yet be regarded a rational, much less scientific venture.

Miles' principal problems were that: (a) within-case analysis was "essentially intuitive, primitive, and unmanageable" (1979: 597), (b) cross-case analysis was "even less well formulated than within-site analysis" (1979: 599), and (c) respondents objected to case study results much more frequently than to survey results, either threatening the research team with legal suit or attempting to rewrite history in order to appear more favorably in the case study (1979: 597). In conclusion, Miles states that, without renewed efforts at methodological inquiry, "qualitative research on organizations cannot be expected to transcend story-telling" (1979: 600).

The Miles article cannot be taken lightly. A well-respected researcher, frequently cited for one of the earliest contributions to the study of organizational innovation, Miles (1964) has indicated that there are grave problems with our craft. Furthermore, he leaves little hope for the immediate future, because the needed methodological research could require a decade or two (or three). Under these circumstances, what are the students of case study research to think? Indeed, what are the *funders* of social science research to think as they review new proposals for case studies? If Miles is correct, why should there be any further support for case studies as a research and development activity? These are the questions that raise the spectre of a case study crisis, and these are the questions that require some answers.

The purpose of this reply is to reaffirm the role of the case study as a systematic research tool. Although major improvements in case study research are still to be made, the goal is to show that an acceptable craft has already emerged.

© 1981 by Cornell University.
0001-8392/81/2601-0058$00.75

This material is based in part upon work supported by the National Science Foundation under Grant No. PRA 79–20580.

What is a Case Study?.

Miles began with a discussion of the advantages and disadvantages of *qualitative data*. However, about one-third of the way into the article, the fact that the research involved *case studies* emerged (1979: 592). Thereafter, the discussion intermingled

From Robert K. Yin, "The Case Study Crisis: Some Answers," 26(1) *Administrative Science Quarterly* 58-65 (March 1981). Copyright 1981 by Cornell University. Reprinted by permission.

the two topics and is an example of a frequent confusion regarding types of evidence (e.g., qualitative data), types of data collection methods (e.g., ethnography), and research strategies (e.g., case studies).

First, the case study does not imply the use of a particular type of evidence. Case studies can be done by using either qualitative or quantitative evidence. The evidence may come from fieldwork, archival records, verbal reports, observations, or any combination of these. An example of an organizational case study that combines qualitative with quantitative evidence is the research of Gross et al. (1971); in other examples, case studies have even relied solely on quantitative data, as in studies of the economic development of urban areas (e.g., Vietorisz and Harrison, 1970).

Nor does the case study imply the use of a particular data collection method. A common misconception is that case studies are solely the result of ethnographies or of participant-observation, yet it should be quickly evident that numerous case studies have been done without using these methods (e.g., Allison, 1971). Conversely, using these methods does not always lead to the production of case studies (e.g., the ethno-graphic and observational research on police behavior by Reiss, 1971; Rubenstein, 1973; and Van Maanen, 1979; none of which had typically been designed as case studies).

What the case study does represent is a research strategy, to be likened to an experiment, a history, or a simulation, which may be considered alternative research strategies. None of these other strategies is linked to a particular type of evidence or method of data collection, either. To cite two contrasting examples, there are some experiments — e.g., in biology and neuroanatomy — that use qualitative evidence and for which statistical analysis is irrelevant; at the same time, the field of history has been increasing its use of quantitative indicators (e.g., Furet, 1971). As a research strategy, *the distinguishing characteristic of the case study is that it attempts to examine:* (a) a contemporary phenomenon in its real-life context, especially when (b) the boundaries between phenomenon and context are not clearly evident. Experiments differ from this in that they deliberately divorce a phenomenon from its context. Histories differ in that they are limited to phenomena of the past, where relevant informants may be unavailable for interview and relevant events unavailable for direct observation.

These distinctions among type of evidence, data collection method, and research strategy are critical in defining case studies. Related clarifications also need to be discussed but can only be enumerated here: (1) The different types of case studies that are possible (exploratory, descriptive, and explanatory), (2) The types of research questions best addressed by case studies as opposed to other research strategies (explanations rather than incidence questions); and (3) The types of case study designs (all must cope with the essential problem that, because the context is part of the study, there will always be too many "variables" for the number of observations to be made, thus making standard experimental and survey designs[1] irrelevant).

How Can Within-Case Evidence be Analyzed?

Miles used two strategies to analyze within-case evidence, both of which met with difficulties. First, qualitative data were assembled into traditional narratives, but Miles found this to be a burdensome and unrewarding activity for his fieldworkers

[1] McClintock, Brannon, and Maynard-Moody (1979) are correct, however, in noting that these designs may be used for some subportions of a case study.

(1979: 593). Second, quantitative data were tabulated into 202 categories. Of this experience, Miles reported (1979: 593–594):

> At the beginning we developed an elaborate coding scheme. . . . Fieldworkers, including the coding specialist, hated the job. [Eventually] . . . the coding stopped, and the cards were not used for analysis.

Miles' experiences are typical of those encountered in many case study efforts. Although no easy formula exists, there are three ways in which these problems of within-case analysis can be reduced.

Distinguishing Note-taking from Narrative-writing. At the outset of any case study, there is an unfortunate tendency for the initial "write-ups" to be based on the *data elements* in the study. Thus, a common occurrence is for analysts to develop well-polished narratives for such items as individual interviews, specific meetings or other major events, logs of daily or weekly activities, and summaries of individual documents or reports.

The pitfall is in spending the inordinate time and effort to construct readable narratives for such data elements,[2] unless a study specifically calls for publishing these materials. Instead, any narrative accounts should be organized around the substantive topics of the case study. Each narrative portion should integrate evidence from different data elements, which therefore still need to be recorded precisely, but in the form of notes rather than narratives.

Two new problems now emerge. Around what topics should a narrative be organized and how should evidence be integrated? Although case studies may often begin with little conceptual framework, the narrative must nevertheless be organized around specific propositions, questions, or activities, with flexibility provided for modifying these topics as analysis progresses. As for integrating evidence, quantitative and qualitative data that address the same topic should be assembled together; similarly, interview segments from different respondents but on the same topic should be integrated (e.g., Jick, 1979; Yin, 1980).[3]

Both of these problems were surmounted in an organizational study that produced over 40 case studies of community organizations (National Commission on Neighborhoods, 1979).[4] The key to organizing the case studies, both in conducting the field inquiry and in writing the final report, was the initial enumeration of about 60 open-ended questions. The fieldworkers had to answer these questions by integrating the evidence they had collected, writing two or three paragraphs in response to each question. Thus, the final case studies resembled comprehensive examinations rather than term papers, and these products were written easily and within the constraints imposed by the commission's small budget.[5]

Tabulating Meaningful Events. A second technique deals with the problems of analyzing quantitative data. Although such data should be integrated with qualitative data throughout a case study narrative, the quantitative data themselves may first need to be coded and tabulated.

The major pitfalls occur when investigators use categories that are too small and too numerous. This situation creates difficulties for the case study analyst, who has neither the training nor

[2]
In fact, some textbooks mislead researchers by asking them to precede the construction of a case study by first writing, in acceptable narrative form, a full "case record" (e.g., Patton, 1980: 303).

[3]
Much more detailed advice needs to be given, but for now the reader is again referred to Gross, Giacquinta, and Bernstein (1971) as one of the best examples of this type of topic-by-topic integration of evidence.

[4]
The author designed the protocols and field guides for the commission's effort.

[5]
Miles does note, in passing, that his project turned to the use of "site summaries" and "site updates," which the field team found more pleasant to produce. One suspects that these documents were organized around integrating themes rather than data elements.

the inclination to serve as a mechanical recording device. Thus, one would not code all the elements of a Bales social interaction scale for every person attending organizational meetings, especially where such meetings were only one aspect of a case study. Similarly, many case studies begin with the naive assumption that "anything might be relevant, so one ought to observe and code everything." Indeed, there are phases in the research where such openness is warranted; but these phases should *precede* any formal coding effort, which would be initiated only when the scope of the study had been scaled down.

Instead, the quantitative data should reflect "meaningful events" in a case study. In one organizational study, for instance, life histories of innovations were the topics of 19 case studies (Yin, 1981). The quantitative data were based on tabulations of different organizational events, which were coded for each case study. Similarly, Pressman and Wildavsky's well-regarded study of implementation (1973) contains one dramatic set of quantitative information: the tabulation of the number of decisions needed to implement a policy. This information was used to support the major thesis of the entire study. Obviously, the determination of what is "meaningful" requires some sense of what the case study is all about. This does not imply a rigid conceptual framework, but the central questions of the case study do need to be identified beforehand. If, during the course of a case study, dramatically different conceptualizations arise, these should then lead to central questions for a new phase of the study, but new evidence may have to be collected.

Building Explanations. A third technique is relevant where case studies attempt to explain a phenomenon. An explanatory case study consists of: (a) an accurate rendition of the facts of the case, (b) some consideration of alternative explanations of these facts, and (c) a conclusion based on the single explanation that appears most congruent with the facts. Some of the best-known case studies in organizational research are of the explanatory variety (e.g., Allison, 1971; Gross, Giacquinta, and Bernstein, 1971; Pressman and Wildavsky, 1973). Thus, Allison's (1971) three models of foreign policy constituted alternative explanations for the facts of the Cuban missile crisis, and one of the models was found more satisfactory than the other two. Similarly, recent case studies of why research is useful (e.g., Yin and Heinsohn, 1980) attempted to compare the facts of a case against several competing models of the research utilization process.

There are no fixed recipes for building or comparing explanations. An analogous situation may be found in doing detective work, where a detective must construct an explanation for a crime.[6] Presented with the scene of a crime, its description, and possible reports from eye-witnesses, the detective must constantly make decisions regarding the relevance of various data. Some facts of the case will turn out to be unrelated to the crime; other clues must be recognized as such and pursued vigorously. The adequate explanation for the crime then becomes a plausible rendition of a motive, opportunity, and method that more fully accounts for the facts than do alternative explanations.

One of the few descriptions of the comparable research task may be found in Campbell (1975), which defends one-shot case

[6]
Several social scientists have called attention to this analogy. See, for instance, Truzzi (1976); and Cook and Campbell (1979: 97–98).

studies, a research design that had previously been discredited (Campbell and Stanley, 1966). According to Campbell, the search for an explanation is a kind of pattern-matching process. The process can be applied even if there is only a single case because the pattern must fit multiple implications derived from an explanation or theory.[7] Thus, it is incorrect to judge this situation by the norms of experimental design, which would stipulate that a single case study (or even a small group of cases) could never provide a compelling rationale for establishing the importance of a single factor (or variable). An explanation, and not a single variable or factor, is what is being tested, and this accounts for the frequent outcome where:

Even in a single qualitative case study the conscientious social scientist often finds no explanation that seems satisfactory. Such an outcome would be impossible if [single factors were being tested] — there would instead be a surfeit of subjectively compelling explanations. (Campbell, 1975: 182)

This interpretation may account for the later statement in Cook and Campbell (1979), in which the authors acknowledge that the one-group post-test-only design (still correctly regarded as an inadequate experimental design) is not to be considered synonymous with the one-shot case study (1979: 96). No explanation is offered for that statement, but our hunch is that the authors were beginning to recognize (but could not articulate) that a case study is not a data point that represents only a single observation. In fact, case studies as analytic units should be regarded on par with *whole* experiments, a realization that provides an important insight for cross-case analysis.

How Can Cross-Case Evidence be Analyzed?

Miles complains that there are few guidelines for conducting cross-case analysis. The analyst is caught in "... the steady tension between the unique, contextually specific nature of single sites, and the need to make sense across a number of sites" (1979:599). Under such conditions, Miles notes that accurate but thin generalizations across cases are likely to be the only result.

There are two potential approaches to cross-case analysis, though neither is so well-developed to serve as the formal set of rules whose need has been described by Kennedy (1979). The two approaches are a case-survey approach and a case-comparison approach.

The case-survey approach requires two conditions that cannot always be satisfied. First, isolated factors within particular case studies must be worthy of substantive attention; second, the number of case studies must be large enough to warrant cross-case tabulations. When these conditions exist, cross-case comparisons can be made by coding the single factors and establishing cross-case patterns. Illustrative applications have involved aggregations of 269 case studies of urban decentralization (Yin and Heald, 1975), of 140 case studies of urban innovations (Yin, Bingham, and Heald, 1976), and of 25 case studies of research utilization (DiMaggio and Useem, 1979). The Miles project itself attempted to follow this approach, but the results were difficult to interpret because there were only six cases (1979: 598).

In the long run, however, this approach may not be the most desirable. First, the number of factors worthy of examination is

---

[7]
Technically, Campbell claims that the multiple implications from a single pattern (or explanation) create multiple degrees of freedom. This differs from the interpretation of McClintock, Brannon, and Maynard-Moody (1979), who claim that Campbell's goal was to identify micro-units within a single case, for which multiple data points could be assessed. The two views, though different, are not incompatible.

often large relative to the number of case studies available, producing a shortage of sampling points for identifying any statistical interaction effects. Second, the extraction of single factors from a case study unduly simplifies the phenomenon being studied. Third, the approach treats case studies as if they were data points, with each case yielding an observation to be tabulated. For these reasons, the case-survey method should be used in highly selective situations, where, for instance, a critical factor or two appear to be of enormous importance. In contrast, the case-comparison approach is relatively new but is likely to prove more fruitful for cross-case analysis.

The craft of detective work again provides an analogous example. Assume that a detective has already produced a tentative explanation for a single crime (within-case analysis). Now the detective is confronted with another case, where the relevant conditions appear to be similar to those of the first case, and where the detective may be able to use the first explanation and establish that both crimes were committed by the same person. Modification may be necessary in applying the explanation to the second case, and the detective must learn to ignore irrelevant variations from case to case. How the detective carries out this work in (a) constructing an adequate explanation for each case singly, and (b) knowing the acceptable levels of modification in the original explanation as new cases are encountered, may be considered analogous to what confronts the researcher in doing cross-case analysis.

The successful application of this approach is not unlike more generalized theory-building. Thus, for instance, Martha Derthick (1972) reported on seven case studies, each of which was a site in a prominent federal program. When the lessons from each case study were compared, a common explanation emerged, which was used to characterize the problems of federal program implementation. Similarly, a study of 19 life histories of innovations was used to develop a more general model of the institutionalization process (Yin, 1981). In neither of these nor other potential illustrative studies, however, has the case-comparison approach been sufficiently documented to produce a specific set of guidelines for future researchers.

Premature criticism of the case-comparison approach should, however, be tempered by one important observation. In experimental science, the comparable analytic step — i.e., cross-experiment generalizations — has also not yet been reduced to an operational formula. On any number of occasions, an experimenter will conduct multiple experiments on the same topic. These experiments do not necessarily vary by single variables (otherwise they would be "groups" within the same experiment), but may differ along totally different and multiple dimensions (e.g., Latané and Darley, 1969). If we assume that an experiment is equivalent, as a unit of analysis, to a case study, the logic used to bring together a string of experiments is the same as that used to connect a string of case studies. At this time, neither logic has been specified in precise terms. Note, however, that whatever the approach, one does not tabulate the experiments in developing a general explanation or theory; neither should one tabulate the case studies.

Whether the case-survey or case-comparison approach is used, the case study researcher must preserve a *chain of evidence* as each analytic step is conducted. The chain of evidence consists of the explicit citation of particular pieces of evidence, as one shifts from data collection to within-case analysis to cross-case analysis and to overall findings and conclusions (Yin, 1979: *xii*). Most case study research has failed to establish an explicit chain, and critics can rightfully question how specific conclusions were reached.

How Can Case Studies be Reported?

The typical case study report is a lengthy narrative that follows no predictable structure and is hard to write and hard to read. This pitfall may be avoided if a study is built on a clear conceptual framework. Furthermore, a case study narrative may be replaced by a series of answers to a set of open-ended questions, as previously noted in the Neighborhood Commission study. This is easier to produce, and the reader can usually find the desired information or skim the entire text without difficulty. Or, where cross-case analysis is the major goal of the research, there may be no need for *any* single-case report; such a study might consist of brief summaries of individual cases, followed by the cross-case analysis.

One problem raised by Miles concerned the reactions of informants to case study results. Some informants disagreed with these reports, an outcome that Miles asserts does not occur when respondents are confronted with survey results. This problem, however, should not be attributed to the use of case studies. On the contrary, Miles' example confuses the reactions to individual versus aggregate evidence. In actuality, when survey respondents are given the results of their *own* interview and shown how these results have been interpreted by the researcher, similarly hostile reactions may also occur. Respondents may complain that they were forced to give oversimplified answers because questions were closed-ended, or that the researcher simply misinterpreted the answers. Conversely, reactions by informants may be minimal when they are asked to review cross-case results where case studies have been done. In summary, people are likely to react adversely whenever they are confronted with individualized data, but are likely to be more tolerant when confronted with aggregate data; this set of reactions occurs whether case studies, surveys, or other research strategies are used.

Future Work

This reply to Miles' article has attempted to show that case studies can be conducted systematically. No doubt, much further improvement in case study research is also needed. It is true, too, as Miles found (1979: 595), that the available methodological textbooks emphasize fieldwork and not case study design or analysis, although the most useful text was not cited by Miles: Barzun and Graff's *Modern Researcher* (1977). That text, though directed toward historians, contains some key guidelines for case study researchers. Its main shortcoming is that the emphasis is on historical and not contemporary events, and certain essential analytic steps are not covered. In all, the state of the art is not as impoverished as one might at first think, and case study practice can be dramatically improved by applying what is already known.

REFERENCES

Allison, Graham T.
1971 The Essence of Decision: Explaining the Cuban Missile Crisis. Boston: Little, Brown.

Barzun, Jacques, and Henry F. Graff
1977 The Modern Researchers, 3rd ed. New York: Harcourt, Brace, Jovanovich.

Campbell, Donald T.
1975 "Degrees of freedom and the case study." Comparative Political Studies, 8:178–193.

Campbell, Donald T., and Julian Stanley
1966 Experimental and Quasi-Experimental Designs for Research. Chicago: Rand McNally.

Cook, Thomas D., and Donald T. Campbell
1979 Quasi-Experimentation: Design and Analysis Issues for Field Settings. Chicago: Rand McNally.

Derthick, Martha
1972 New Towns In-Town: Why a Federal Program Failed. Washington, D.C.: The Urban Institute.

DiMaggio, Paul, and Michael Useem
1979 "Decentralized applied research: Factors affecting the use of audience research by arts organizations." Journal of Applied Behavioral Science, 15: 79–93.

Furet, Francois
1971 "Quantitative history." Daedalus, 100: 151–167.

Gross, Neal, Joseph B. Giacquinta, and Marilyn Bernstein
1971 Implementing Organizational Innovations. New York: Basic Books.

Jick, Todd D.
1979 "Mixing qualitative and quantitative methods: Triangulation in action." Administrative Science Quarterly, 24: 602–611.

Kennedy, Mary M.
1979 "Generalizing from single case studies." Evaluation Quarterly, 3: 661–678.

Latané, Bibb, and John M. Darley
1969 "Bystander apathy." American Scientist, 57: 244–268.

McClintock, Charles C., Dianne Brannon, and Steven Maynard-Moody
1979 "Applying the logic of sample surveys to qualitative case studies: The case cluster method." Administrative Science Quarterly, 24: 612–629.

Miles, Matthew, ed.
1964 Innovation in Education. New York: Columbia University Teachers College Press.

Miles, Matthew, B.
1979 "Qualitative data as an attractive nuisance: The problem of analysis." Administrative Science Quarterly, 24: 590–601.

National Commission on Neighborhoods
1979 People, Building Neighborhoods. Washington: U.S. Government Printing Office.

Patton, Michael Quinn
1980 Qualitative Evaluation Methods. Beverly Hills: Sage.

Pressman, Jeffrey L., and Aaron Wildavsky
1973 Implementation. Berkeley: University of California Press.

Reiss, Albert J., Jr.
1971 The Police and the Public. New Haven: Yale University Press.

Rubenstein, Jonathan
1973 City Police. New York: Farrar, Straus, and Giroux.

Truzzi, Marcello
1976 "Sherlock Holmes: Applied Social Psychologist." In William B. Sanders (ed.), The Sociologist as Detective, 2d ed. New York: Praeger.

Van Maanen, John
1979 "The fact of fiction in organizational ethnography." Administrative Science Quarterly, 24: 539–550.

Vietorisz, Thomas, and Bennett Harrison
1970 The Economic Development of Harlem. New York: Praeger.

Yin, Robert K.
1979 Changing Urban Bureaucracies. Lexington, MA: Lexington Books.
1980 Studying the Implementation of Public Programs. Golden, CO: Solar Energy Research Institute.
1981 "Life histories of innovations: How new practices become routinized." Public Administration Review (forthcoming).

Yin, Robert K., Eveleen Bingham, and Karen A. Heald
1976 "The difference that quality makes: The case of literature reviews." Sociological Methods and Research, 5:139–156.

Yin, Robert K., and Karen A. Heald
1975 "Using the case survey method to analyze policy studies." Administrative Science Quarterly, 20: 371–381.

Yin, Robert K., and Ingrid Heinsohn
1980 Case Studies in Research Utilization. Washington: American Institutes for Research.

11

Just for the Record?
Notes Toward a Theory of
Interviewing in Evaluation

Barry MacDonald and Jack Sanger

For the second time that day, deliberately now, Flavia said, "It takes two to tell the truth."

"One for one side, one for the other?"

"That's not what I mean. I mean one to tell, one to hear. A speaker and a receiver. To tell the truth about any complex situation requires a certain attitude in the receiver."

"What is required from the receiver?"

"I would say first of all a level of emotional intelligence."

"Imagination?"

"Disciplined."

"Sympathy? Attention?"

"And patience."

"Detachment?"

"All of these. And a taste for the truth—an immense willingness to *see.*"

"Wouldn't it be simpler," he said, "just to write it down?"

"Postulating a specific reader-receiver?"

"Casting a wider net: one or more among an unknown quantity of readers."

Quite cheerfully now, Flavia said, "You forget that I am a writer. Writers don't just write it down. They have to give it a form."

He said, "Well, do."

"Life is often too . . . peculiar for fiction. Form implies a measure of selection."

He pleased her by catching on, "At the expense of the truth?"

"Never essentially. At the expense of the literal truth."

Authors' Note: This article was originally presented to the Annual Meeting of the American Educational Research Association, March 19-23, 1982, New York, in a symposium entitled "Evaluation Methodology."

From Barry MacDonald and Jack Sanger, "Just for the Record? Notes Toward a Theory of Interviewing in Evaluation," original manuscript.

"Does the literal truth matter?"

She thought about that. "To the person to whom it happened."

(*A Compass Error*, Sybille Bedford)

This extract from a novel maps an area where social science methodologists seldom tread. The dynamics of the interview process still await sustained treatment, though Guba and Lincoln (1981) have made a beginning. In educational research and evaluation, where an increasing reliance on the interview method is evident, there is little by way of guidance for the novice in an otherwise comprehensive literature. Even fieldwork manuals talk around the interview, not about it. We cannot find books where examples of good and bad interviews are discussed. One is tempted to conclude that the interview process is indescribable or unjustifiable, apparently self-taught, probably idiosyncratic, perhaps not worth talking about. Even if one pieces together the relevant fragments from the voluminous output of a methodologist like Lou Smith, who more than anyone else has described his fieldwork behavior in terms of its underlying intellectual purposes, structures, and processes (see particularly Smith, 1981), the impression remains that a rather important instrument of evaluative enquiry is characterized by an unusual degree of normative latitude.

The odd thing about this is that whenever evaluators get together to discuss how they do their work, or when the try to induct newcomers to the field, interviewing practices and skills feature prominently on the agenda. In an evaluation center like ours, for instance, which has built a tradition of naturalistic program evaluation, the ends and means of interviewing are the subject of extensive and often heated debate. From this debate, different profiles of interviewing practice begin to emerge and take shape, the blooms of a hitherto secret garden. And what becomes immediately evident is that this secret garden is no collective farm. Even in a group like ours, with a shared rhetoric of intent and consensual canons of criticisms, the varying prosecutions of intent and interpretations of the canons reveal a disturbingly wide range of modi operandi. Sure, we all agree that interviewing should be consistent with the naturalistic imperative—to generate public knowledge of educational action that derives from, consists of, or is coextensive with private knowledge. And sure, we all agree that interviews, the best method we have for getting access to this private knowledge, should be effective, fair, and valid (leaving aside House's [1981] collapse of fairness and validity into a single category). Such agreements do go some way toward defining the boundaries of the permissible, but they fall short of resolving our epistemological, political, and technical differences. These differences shape our procedures, our roles, and ultimately our products, in ways that are not widely understood. This paper is an attempt to provide for some a window, for others a door, to what has been a private debate. In the course of writing it, one reason for the paucity of public debate has become quite clear. The issues are complex and interpenetrating, and the range of practice is so wide as to defy unchallengeable categorization for purposes of comparison and contrast. We have, we think necessarily, limited the coverage of the paper in several ways. In the first place, it is about the so-called unstructured interview, for reasons we will shortly elaborate. In the second place, the discussion is organized around one seemingly limited issue, whether the interviewer should take notes or tape record the interview. And finally, only two profiles of interviewing are described, compared, and assessed in terms of their strengths and weaknesses. These profiles are not, of course, the only choice open to the would-be interviewer, nor are their logics the only logics available. Our intention is to expose the variables involved by elaborating two lines of reasoning, and to draw attention to some of the consequences of choice.

Before embarking upon that task, it may be useful to locate the topic within the still evolving field of program evaluation. It would now be rare to find a program evaluation that did not at some stage use interviews to obtain data. Ever since Stake (1967) convincingly argued for a much more comprehensive range of information needs than had previously been recognized, evaluative investigations have increasingly included interviewing in methodological packages designed to cope with an expanding matrix. Evaluation has become a complex methodological task. As those who use and shape evaluation become more sophisticated about information needs and more realistic about the prospects of immediate program success, the demands made of evaluation stretch both the resources and skills of teams and individuals. Relatively simple input-output models of program effectiveness, calling for specification at one end and measurement at the other, have given way, in the sober aftermath of a succession of reformist misadventures, to concerns that stress program understanding, reception, variation, and impact in the broadest sense. The "why of the outcomes" (Hastings, 1966) has become an important provision in evaluation designs. It is this broad change that underlies the emergence in the last decade of a naturalistic school of program evaluators, field-based chroniclers, and interpreters of the participant constituencies generated by programs. For this school the interview, even more than direct observation, is the predominant means of data gathering. Its flexibility and negotiability make it uniquely attractive to evaluators who usually need to gather many different kinds of data in a short span of time. But even traditional evaluation studies whose main focus is still aims achievement now supplement their test batteries with interviews designed to yield contingency data. In other words, the interview is now a commonplace instrument of program evaluation studies.

A great deal of this interviewing is known as "unstructured." The term has no consensus meaning. At the one end of the spectrum of users are those who, armed with a range of program interests, problems, issues, perhaps even conclusions, mean by it only that they do not know what line of questioning they will pursue until they have a chance to see what kind of information is available. "Unstructured" in this sense means no more than tactical opportunism. At the other end, where most of the "naturalists" are located, are for those whom the term "unstructured" connotes an epistemological sensitivity to the terms in which interviewees understand their experience, and an intent to in some sense keep faith with these "structures." Again, what is meant by keeping faith is not always clear. There is a big difference between those for whom validity inheres in the subjective, individualized organization of affect and cognition, those whose claims rest upon the strength of a literal interpretation of the term "interview," and those metatheorists who seek reconstructions of experience that account for the self-knowledge of others. All would agree that validity depends upon intersubjective agreement but would differ about the parts played by interviewees, interviewer, and audiences in securing and validating the data of educational experience. Some invoke scientific labels to indicate where they stand on this rather daunting issue, but it is not all clear how evaluative interviewers of, say, phenomenological persuasion would differ from, say, symbolic interactionists, ethnologists, ethnomethodologists, existentialists, linquistic ethnoscientists, or ethnographers of communication. But as evaluators of educational programs, concerned with the acquisition and transfer of knowledge of human action, we all have at least a sense of the problematics of enquiry that shapes and sensitizes our practice.

For the evaluator, the intrinsic problems of interview data are compounded by the sociopolitical circumstances in which he or she tries to resolve them. The evaluator operates in a context of persuasion, a contest for resources in which his or her role is to provide knowledge for allocation decisions. With truth and consequence so intertwined, disinterest, which might help, is a scarce commodity. And that's not all. The evaluator has to be fair to those whose interests are at risk, and this commitment can seriously restrict the pursuit of private knowledge. When an evaluator constructs an interview sample, that sample has to represent the constituency of interests generated by the program if he or she is to avoid the charge of taking sides. Program constituencies tend to be large and varied and so must be the sample. The evaluator rarely has the time, resources, or freedom to develop the kind of intimate, friendly relationship with respondents that is commonly advocated by social scientists as a precondition of productive and valid interaction. Prominent program actors apart, the evaluative interview tends to be a one-off, hit-or-miss encounter between relative strangers. Can it do more than offer the stakeholders a chance to be heard? Can it do even that?

At some point a program evaluator needs to know what it is like to take part in the program, what meanings and significance it holds for participants, why they respond to it in the ways they do. The evaluator is an outsider looking in, trying to find out what it is like to be an insider. Not merely for his or her own satisfaction; he or she has to tell others. These others may be nonparticipants, the evaluator's various "publics." Or they may be the participants themselves, users and receivers as well as givers of this knowledge. The evaluator has therefore both outsider and insider audiences in mind. He or she already knows a lot about the surface features of program experience—roles and responsibilities, observed behaviors, self-reports, and other indices of program involvement and impact. The evaluator knows a lot too about patterns of interaction between program participants, which participants have had opportunities to observe and judge other participants, who is likely to know what about the program. But the evaluator knows too that these surface features are more constitutive of public performance than of private experience, and are heavily shaped by program scripts, professional norms, personal image management, and structures of accountability. The evaluator wants, assuming that his or her audiences need, a better understanding than these indices give of why the program in action is the way it is. In these circumstances, the evaluator looks to the unstructured interview to reveal the dark side of the program moon.

Unstructured interviewing is peculiarly appropriate for such a purpose, as well as being arguably indispensable for those evaluators who seek to represent the concerns and interests of evaluatees. In principle it allows both parties to participate in the generation of an agenda and permits the interviewee to be proactive in that process. The extensive and effective use of such interviews could help evaluators to redress the imbalance of interests that invariably ensues from the circumstances and sources of their commission. But unstructured interviewing promises more; it appears to offer a means of getting to the nub of the "information for understanding" problem. With rare exceptions, and to greater or lesser extent, the programs we evaluate fail to deliver the goods. They stumble, they seize up, they get subverted, emasculated, rejected, diverted, diluted, or otherwise run out of steam. Even those program evaluators who preconceive their major task as the demonstration of goal accomplishment end up casting around for unanticipated benefits and trying to explain shortfalls in targeted outcomes. The development of more sensitive and durable models of intervention has much to gain from efforts to map and understand what happens to programs, and the unstructured interview is the means by which underestimated or unanticipated dimensions of program experience may be probed.

As we have indicated, there is very little help as yet in the growing literature of evaluation for those who seek guidance on good practice in unstructured interviewing. Even the naturalistic school of evaluators, for whom the evocation of the personal experience of public life is a required strand in program portrayal, has had little to say about the principal means by which this evocation is achieved.

This presentation will explore one seemingly insignificant variable in unstructured interviewing, the choice between tape recording and note taking as the means of recording. We say "seemingly insignificant" not because it seems so to us, but because the few published guides that make reference to it pay scant attention. To quote the most recent of these (Guba and Lincoln, 1981), "For most of this kind of interviewing we recommend notepads and written notes; tape-recorders can make one a victim of the 'laters'—'later I will listen to these tapes, later I will analyse these data.'" Here, typically, tape recording and note taking are treated as if they were alternative means of generating an identical product rather than, as we will argue, generators of different kinds of encounters with divergent products.

We launch our analysis from a penetrative observation from a cognate field. Johnson (1975), reviewing his field study of social welfare offices, notes briefly two phenomena that are central to our analysis of interviewing options. At one point in his research he had the opportunity to compare written field notes with cassette recordings of the observed events. He writes: "First, the master field notes reflected an attempt to recapture all the statements of a particular worker as he presented the facts of a case and the diagnosis reached. Grammatical and syntactical structures, as I recalled them, had also been recorded. The transcripts, however, illustrated my illusions. They revealed only my grammar and syntax." If this degree of discrepancy is characteristic of a committed and sensitive observer, what can we reasonably expect of the notes of the more involved interviewer? Does it matter? One distinguished sociologist, questioned on this issue at a gathering of naturalistic enquirers, shrugged off the problem as a pedantic quibble, with words to the effect, "I don't care if he actually said what I say he said. The point is he might have said it." (We leave to the reader the enigma of the status of a recalled exchange that was neither taped nor written down.) Some of those present were shocked by the response, others nodded knowingly. Whose truth is it, anyway? Later in the same review Johnson returns to the comparison, this time to attack the taped record. "When I listened to the cassette recordings of home visits, on several occasions I realised that I knew certain things about the actions that had not been stated in so many words. This is not to imply I had to read between the lines of the transcripts or review them in an ironic or metaphorical manner to understand them. It is to say some of the crucial features of the action were not expressed verbally." Such observations and reactions introduce one set of issues and possibilities that need to be taken into account when we choose how and what to record when we interview. Fidelity, accuracy, validity, even authenticity are at risk. But there is another set of issues and possibilities, linked to the first set but not addressed by the comments we have cited. A decision to take notes or to tape record significantly influences the nature of the social process of interviewing, in particular the generative power of the encounter. In what follows we explore both the necessary and the arguable differences between a conversation in which one participant writes things down and a conversation that is automatically recorded.

From this point on we attempt to pursue these issues by describing, justifying, comparing, and contrasting two models of interviewing, both offered as responses to the naturalistic aspiration, both conceived and practiced in a context of program evaluation concerns. One favors tape recording, the other, note taking. Since one of the authors is committed to the first of these models, and the other to the second, we are jointly committed to not taking sides in this presentation.

For the evaluator the unstructured interview poses three serious problems. The first is how to achieve a penetrative conversation with relative strangers in a short space of time. The second problem, given a "solution" to the first, is how to be fair to the interviewee whose interests are at stake. Striking a balance between the "right to know" and the individual's right to some measure of protection is a central issue in the politics and ethics of evaluation practice. In unstructured interviewing the individual faces the maximum risk of personal exposure, and this means that the two problems referred to are at least uncomfortably juxtaposed and arguably indissolvable. The third problem, given a "solution" to the first two, is "what claims to truth are associable with the results?" The case for any system of conducting, recording, interpreting, and reporting such interviews must therefore address these problems and offer a resolution.

Although the choice between tape and notes can be seen as a discrete issue of ad hoc preference, we believe that the choice is better understood as an issue embedded in differing evaluation rationales, and we begin our dissection of two interviewing practices by outlining the reasoning that we invoke in their defense. The case for tape recording is made within a particular view of the evaluator's role in a liberal-democratic society. The case for note taking takes account of this view, is sympathetic to its concerns and values, but offers an alternative response to the problems of evaluative action. The two positions are comprehensive in that they address the purposes, values, and aspirations of evaluation and try to show how procedures and methods are related to these. At the same time, the overall advocacy is tempered by consciousness of deficiency. We want more attention to the issues, not converts to a particular practice.

THE CASE FOR TAPE RECORDING

The unstructured interview is the means by which, throughout a constituency of stakeholders in a particular program, the evaluator promotes the manufacture of a trading commodity (private data, personal experience, individual evaluations) that will constitute the basis of his or her subsequent efforts to achieve exchange (reporting). Within this perspective the autonomy of the interviewee is respected, and the principle of reciprocity guides the evaluator/broker of trade-offs between constituents. The separation of the data generation and data reporting phases of the process is essential to the operation, as is the construction of an interview sample that represents program "interests." In its strongest form this conception of evaluation derives from a political philosophy that stresses the individual as decision maker and the dangers of both bureaucratic and academic control of educational enquiry. Let us expand that position a little. All evaluation is formative. The question that evaluators address is, "What should be done next?" All evaluators would agree with that. What divides them is the substructure of that question. Whose next step matters most? Whose evaluation of what has happened so far should count? How should decisions about the next step be reached? Evaluators part company on these questions, and do different things as a result (see MacDonald, 1976).

Choosing priorities—of focus, of issues, of audience—is clearly a headache for evaluators. After all everybody has an "interest" in educational programs. Everybody evaluates education in the light of that interest and with whatever available information they choose to make use of. Everybody acts on the basis of that evaluation in so far as it is compatible with their other interests and evaluations. In this sense everyone is entitled to consideration as an evaluative actor with respect to social policy, entitled to a share in the evaluation service. But, of course, not everybody has equal potency of action or accountability for consequence. Some are more responsible than others for the allocation of resources to education and for their effective use. Some have more to gain and lose. Potency of and accountability for action are prime factors in the evaluator's response to the problem of whose next step he or she should address. So is demand, positive and negative. Evaluators are not short of advice or free of direction toward this, away from that. So is access. Evaluators can only look at what they are allowed to see, and visas can be hard to get. They have to honor their contracts too, and these may preempt both initial and emergent options. The independence we like to associate with evaluation is difficult to secure and maintain in this context of multiple constraints.

Nevertheless, all evaluators carry into their work an ideal of their service that determines how they exploit the available or negotiable areas of discretion. The particular conception of the evaluation service that we have outlined here is one to which one of the writers (MacDonald, 1976) has attached the label "democratic," a deliberately provocative title intended to focus attention on the political function of evaluation. Democratizing evaluation (making the service more consonant with the principles of the liberal democratic state) commits the evaluator to a particular political view of what he or she is about. It makes central and problematic the means by which and the degree to which private knowledge should become public knowledge. It means respect for persons as both givers and receivers of information. It means enhancing the possibility of the widest possible debate about matters of common interest and consequence. In this sense an evaluation report can be seen as fulfilling the function of foreshadowing (rather than preempting or concluding) a debate about what should happen next. That is the justification for evaluation reports being inconclusive accounts of programs.

Given these aspirations, and focusing now on the unstructured interview, we can say that words are important, what the interviewee says. Nonverbal communications are interpretations of the observer. Creating the conditions in which the interviewee says what he or she means, means what he or she says, says what he or she thinks, and thinks about what he or she says, are the major tasks of the interviewer. Self-representation in transportable form is the aim.

The case for the tape recorder is embedded in these concerns and values. At one level it rests upon a conception of the interview as a creative process that demands of the interviewer full commitment to the generation of data. The use of the recorder allows postponement of those roles (processing and reporting) that would seriously limit this commitment or otherwise inhibit the interchange. A procedural corollary of this aspiration is that the data so generated belongs in the first instance to the interviewee. Its subsequent use by the interviewer for the purpose of informing others has to be negotiated with the interviewee-owner. The presence of the recorder means that the interviewer is free to concentrate on one task—production. Relieved of any immediate need to edit the communication, to select, marshall, and codify what he or she hears and sees, the evaluator can listen to all that is said, observe all the nonverbal communications, and develop a person-to-person dynamic without the hindrance of constant reminders of ultimate purpose and role. The tape recorder in this sense seems to offer the best opportunity of realizing the intentions of the unstructured interview, to evoke and develop the interviewee's affective and cognitive experience of the program. Precisely because the encounter is not experienced by the interviewee as instrumental to the purposes of others, precisely because he or she is not compelled to produce the immediately negotiable public account, the interview offers a rare opportunity to explore, with an unusually attentive and interested listener, his or her own realms of meaning and significance. It is these realms of meaning—the private experience and evaluation of public life—that the program evaluator needs to represent in the dialogues of educational policy.

The record is essential for subsequent phases of the evaluation. It guarantees the availability of an accurate chronicle of the verbal component of the interview, a total record of what both participants said. Although it is unlikely to be reproduced in full in an evaluation report, the record is the basis of subsequent representations of the interview and negotiations about its use. For the interviewee and for other parties who may wish to challenge or corroborate the use in context or the interpretive selection of the data, it constitutes an independent and undeniable resource. Depending upon the agreed rules governing control of the interview data, the tape may be seen as a first draft, a basis for further development as well as negotiation. Given unqualified interviewee control over the use of the interview the evaluator does of course risk the loss of revealing data, but interviewees may exercise this power by demonstrating a correspondingly greater sense of responsibility for securing the validity and adequacy of the data. Experience shows that program participants who have had this opportunity to ensure that their experience, concerns, and perspectives are adequately represented in the evaluation report (i.e., that they have had a say, not just a hearing) are much more receptive to critique of their actions and less hostile to the reporting of alternative perspectives. In short, the use of the tape recorder in the generation of a data base enables the tasks of the evaluator to be more effectively shared with many of those who are most vulnerable to the consequences. Since we have argued that the taped interview frees the interviewer to develop a more penetrative discourse, the provision of these checks and balances constitutes a necessary safeguard against misuse of the product.

WEAKNESSES OF TAPE RECORDING

It is only a partial record of the interaction and the communication—the sound component—and even this partial record will be reduced if, as usually happens, subsequent use of the record is based on transcript-words only. These verbatim accounts reveal the extent to which communication depends upon the synthesis of sound, gesture, expression, and posture. In extreme cases the word residue of the communication is unintelligible. In every case it underrepresents the communication. The experienced interviewer can to some extent minimize this problem by prompting verbalization ("That's an interesting shrug, what does it mean exactly?"). Note-taking interviewers have a similar problem but rely on their own reading of the communication to round out incomplete sentences and nonverbalized intimations of states of mind. Facility with language, experience of self-representation, and a preference for the kind of discourse that best survives the recording filter are important variables in any program constituency, and there is a danger that tape-based representations will be skewed in favor of the most articulate. This skew can be compounded by uneven take-up on the part of interviewees of opportunities to improve the accounts they have given and to monitor their use. In many educational programs, these characteristics of interviewees will correlate with the interviewee's location in a hierarchical system and can lead to a serious distortion in evaluation reports in favor of superordinate perspectives.

That would-be democratic evaluator will do his or her best to counter these threats to the validity and fairness of the reports. This evaluator must make sure that his or her principles and procedures are understood by all interviewees, that all have reasonable opportunities to exercise the rights accorded to them, and that those who have most difficulty in fulfilling their tasks are given most assistance. These obligations upon the evaluator leads us into consideration of a major weakness of the approach—the demands it makes of the evaluator's time and resources. It is a slow method and one that is costly in terms of secretarial support. It invokes a complex system of separate stages in the execution of the evaluation task and the maintenance over a period of time of a participant network. It is ill-suited as a major instrument of enquiry in circumstances of urgency, where information about one part of a constituency is needed quickly by another. It is messy, complicated, and exasperatingly subject to delays, even where the evaluator has negotiated agreed deadlines with evaluatees. For these reasons alone it is unpopular with those who commission evaluation studies, and can often only be successfully advocated in circumstances where the inadequacy of managerial assumptions and forecasts is either evident or anticipated, where there is enough time to learn, or where programs are so politically sensitive that a democratic evaluation is a necessary concession to hostile stakeholders.

THE CASE FOR NOTE TAKING

Historically, and in disparate disciplines and paradigms, note-taken accounts of interviews have been preferred to other forms of recording in that they aspire to serve two basic functions for which other techniques are inadequate. These functions are unobtrusiveness and economy of effort. Any reference to the technology of recording by authors of case-study manuals or naturalistic inquiry methods usually prefaces a choice for note taking with some such declaration. However, note taking has a broader basis for use than just these two criteria.

The note-taking interview should be seen as a joint act of making. The evaluator is a representative of near and distant audiences and enables the interviewee to develop a case for those audiences. The fact that the data is generated in note form maintains least transformation in the process of creating the final vehicle of communication in which the data will reside. At all stages there are words on paper. By encouraging the respondent to be privy at the outset to these stages of production, the evaluator's operations are given high and contestable profile and his or her authority, conversely, is diminished as the respondent discovers an equal control of opportunity. If, as would be ideally the case, the evaluator is able to complete his or her notes and present them the same day for comment to the respondent, then the evaluation *process* will become much more meaningful to the respondent. And the respondent gains shared control over his or her products.

What is this mysterious process? It comprises the usually hidden, reflexive acts of interpretation, analysis, and synthesis that convert data into draft reports. These acts are evidenced in the written words, themselves, the syntax, the metaphors, the juxtaposition of information, the special highlighting of data, and the very act of overall simplification. They combine to form the groundwork of theory building. Essentially, they are interwoven in a story that communicates the "essence" of the constituency's experience. It is as a storyteller that the notemaker achieves greatest impact.

Note taking should aspire to make the interviewee aware that he or she is not merely a source of so much recondite information but that he or she is an instrument of education in the evaluator's operations. The personal constructs of the interviewee are to be afforded the important significance owing to him or her by the deference exemplified in the conduct of the interview.

The interviewee becomes the subject of thoughtful effort on the part of the evaluator to be placed carefully in the unravelling scheme of the program. Note taking, at best, draws interviewer and interviewee closer in the mutuality of the event. Their developed intimacy imbues both words and syntax with information (the substantive nature of the interviewee's account) and with the character of the interviewee. Properly recorded notes thus become acutely analogous to the interview in its social and psychological context. For the recorder, the notes are meaningful coding, a mnemonic arrangement of evaluation history. Providing the evaluator manages to engage the respondent in joint action, there is then every possibility that the interview can proceed to the penetrative levels that the interviewer requires. The notebook acts as a symbol of the interest and concern of the interviewer and the importance he or she ascribes to the interaction.

There is an overall pragmatic reason for preferring notes to other forms of recording during evaluation: economy. On-site data processing and the collection of summarized information enable the evaluator to keep in constant touch with the pulse of his or her operations. Analysis and synthesis leading to theory are kept within the event and are not imposed at a temporal distance in the manner of a jigsaw construction of discrete pieces of cold data. In the best of circumstances this keeps the evaluator focused upon the properties of the field of study, explaining them in terms of idiosyncratic context rather than as part of an imposed grand design. Patterns of explanation that make up eventual reports, case studies, or portrayals must take account of these disparately processed, obstinately extant interview events, rather than seeking postevent coherence for a mountain of raw data and treating it piecemeal.

And what of the practical criteria that facilitate the successful interview? When to write and what to write provide the interviewer with his or her greatest challenge. Given that eye contact and general nonverbal encouragement provide the basis of sympathetic listening, recourse to notes should be minimized. Notes are generally effective in/for the following circumstances:

- When previously undiscovered data of importance arise from the testimony of the witness.

- Data that would be difficult or impossible to triangulate in the testimonies of other witnesses.

- Metonymic statements, though obviously seriously intended, seem at variance with the expected or consistent viewpoints of individual or group.

- Statements that politically, theoretically, or situationally seem to define significant insights or attitudes of an individual or group.

- Key words whose currency gives insight to individual or group thinking.

- Key words that, for the interviewer, allow reconstruction of the depth and breadth of the interview.

The purpose of those notational forms is to make the respondent conscious of the evaluator in a service role, at ease and in control of the technology of recording. The service role becomes experientially amplified for the interviewee in the course of that event. The role is one that facilitates the respondent in developing a most articulate and just explanation of his or her thinking concerning all areas of mutual and public interest.

Note taking and note making will always be a matter of highly developed skill. Every act of recording involves meaningful transformations of data. Words have strong contextual clothing. Verbatim accounts do not necessarily provide accurate representation of what occurs in interviews. However, through the broad strokes of the note-taken account, much nuance, implicit and explicit, is retained, rather as in the words of impressionism; stand too close and the meaning's gone. In this way, note recordings are ideally suited to protecting the respondent against the kind of retaining mud that context-bound statements often produce. Note taking attends to the fluid process of people-in-charge. It does not hold them to particular states or attitudes or final statements but reflects the daily choices and changes that people have to make in their daily lives.

WEAKNESSES OF NOTE TAKING

Note taking has some very obvious problems associated with it. In many ways these problems combine to demonstrate that, at the stage of recording data, factors such as accuracy, fairness, and appropriateness may be largely decided by the evaluator's skill with the technology.

The most obvious practical difficulty to the smooth generation of data that note taking presents is in its capacity to be distracting to the respondent. Handled badly: breaks of eye contact to rush to the note pad, a slow scrawl holding back a respondent's flow or even the pained look of the evaluator realizing that he or she is suffering data overload; and the interview devolves into nonpenetrative irritation. If the respondent does not dry up, then he or she may become "coopted" to the needs of the interviewer by picking up cues from pen movement, speaking selectively and pausing dramatically to allow assimilation and record-ing. Lack of penetration becomes heightened because the evaluator's eyes, fixed to his or her writing, misses facial contact and other nonverbal referencing that together help to tune the meanings of spoken words. An interpretation that is heavily ear-dependent is likely to be very different from an interpretation employing the usual mix of senses.

If the evaluator does not coopt, then he or she may dominate. Note taking is an activity that can lend itself to massive infusions of the evaluator's own attitudes, interests, and needs. Unconsciously, as the fingers write, the evaluator may be grasping for the tightest control of the type and ordering of data. Improperly handled, notes become the coded instrument of a dominant interviewer and the respondent's case becomes perverted to fulfill the evaluator's goals. In terms of the three styles of evaluation posited by MacDonald (1976)— bureaucratic, autocratic, and democratic—note taking would always seem more naturally suited to the former two. In the latter case, the most stringent discipline is needed in order to come near to upholding a democratic mode.

A major concern in note taking is the sheer loss of hard information. There is inevitable reductionism in its use. Babies may be thrown out with bathwater, underlying threads missed, and facts mislaid. Because it tends to focus on the highlights of the respondent's case, background detail, contextual evidence, and powerful, though illogical or not immediately apparent influences may be omitted as extraneous noise. Data that depend entirely upon note recordings will remain questionable until the quality of the writer can be vouchsafed.

A last problematic area is the lack of leverage that notes afford in presenting cases. Because they can always be called into question as "mere interpretation," they do not represent a means by which an evaluator can hold a respondent to witness in the development of his or her case. Without the actual words, what is there to barter with? The undoubted consequence of this lack of hard currency is the tendency for notes to provide ample evidence of the interviewee's public status rather than his or her personal understandings.

GENERATING, PROCESSING, AND REPORTING INTERVIEW DATA—TWO PROFILES

We will now attempt to illustrate the consequences that flow from a choice of tapes or notes as the recording technique of the unstructured interview by offering a detailed breakdown of two practices with recording technique as the key variable (Tables 1 and 2). In these tables we address the question, "What do the cases for tape or notes mean in terms of concrete operations, procedures, and products?" Evaluation interviews are shaped by individual theories of evaluative action, personal views of purpose and possibility in which philosophical, moral, ethical, political, social, and psychological ingredients are combined. We have argued that it is a mistake to assume that techniques of recording are so malleable and adaptive that they can be harnessed to any intent. Different techniques make different processes and products possible.

The organizational rationale of the profiles makes the conventional distinction between data generation, data processing, and data reporting, dealing with each as a separate, though not always separable, phase of interviewing practice. Following our earlier argument that interviews need to be penetrative, fair, and valid, we have used the criteria of effectiveness, fairness, and validity to examine the claims made for each practice at each stage of the operation. Finally, we have used the columns of the tables to separate the formal properties of the interviews from the claims and criticisms we think are associable with them.

The result is a highly condensed but we hope not impenetrable codification of two uses of the unstructured interview. We apologize for the dense and cryptic form of the entries in each of the 54 boxes, and for the large number of entries. We wanted to make it possible for the reader not just to compare and contrast the profiles, but to reconstruct the realities they attempt to represent. The rest of this paper assumes that the reader has familiarized himself or herself with the charts.

No profile is offered of an approach to interviewing that combines both recording technques. It might be argued that duplication of technique could mitigate weaknesses, but the strength of counterarguments based on the compounding of constraints, mutually exclusive benefits, or simply the labor

(text continued page 195)

TABLE 1 Tape Recording

	Characteristics	Strengths	Weaknesses
DATA GENERATION			
Effectiveness	Personalized relationship. Conversational style. Continuous discourse. Sustained multisensory communication. Interviewer as listener.	Naturalistic. Prolific. Penetrative of experience. Tolerant of ambiguity, anecdotalism, inconclusiveness.	Selective but mindless record. Data overload. Favors the articulate. Machine-phobia. Visible data lost.
Fairness	Confidential but on-the-record. Interviewee control emphasized, but hazards unknown, and minimal indication of the value or likely use of the data.	Testimony as "draft." Authority vested in objective record. Emphasis on generation maximizes opportunity to testify.	High-risk testimony encouraged. Consequences of disclosure difficult to estimate. Overreliant on interviewer integrity and interviewee judgment.
Validity	Insulated from consequences. Structured by the truth holder. Told to a person.	Raw data preserved in verifiable form. Stimulus as well as response recorded. Time to search for truths. Freedom to tell. Safe responses quickly exhausted and superseded. Dissimulation hard to sustain under continuous observation.	Off-the-cuff data. Freedom to lie. Pressure on interviewee to be "interesting." Machine-phobia. Overreliant on interviewee self-knowledge.

(continued)

Table 1 (continued)

	Characteristics	Strengths	Weaknesses
DATA PROCESSING			
Effectiveness	Record transcribed. Transcript sent to interviewee for improvement and release. Interviewee invited to: (a) amend or delete, (b) extend, develop, (c) prioritize, indicate high-risk data. Uncontentious data may be summarized. Deadline for return stipulated.	Data retains much of its original form. Considered testimony. Inaccuracies corrected. Additional data obtained. More clues to interviewee's values and valuables, a guide to negotiable reporting. Interviewee's responsibility for the product is explicit.	Costly. Time-consuming. Obsolescent. Loss of valuable data. Inadequacy of verbal record.
Fairness	Negotiation confidential. Interviewee the arbiter. Access to record. Governed by agreed rules, but "release" can be seen as a "chicken run" test for the foolhardy.	Interviewee rights respected. Time and opportunity given to change testimony, to calculate risks and benefits. Interviewee free to consult others, to take advice. Possession of transcript and agreement constitute insurance against abuse.	Interviewee asked to release not knowing: (a) how the data will be reported, or (b) norms of disclosure. Interviewee may be poor judge of own interests. Transcripts lower self-esteem.
Validity	Characterized by set sequence of moves open to scrutiny. Based on objective record.	Depends on the argument that, given the power and the responsibility for making known their own truths, interviewees will make more effort to do so.	No data on the context of response. Relies overmuch on the interviewee's belief in and commitment to the evaluation mission.

190

Effectiveness	Aspires to theatrical form of oral history. Interviews provide subscripts in program drama, interwoven in chronological, scene-by-scene construction. Draft showing data in context negotiated simultaneously with interviewees. Draft rewritten in response to respondent critiques. Final report public.	Naturalistic autobiographical data has inherent dramatic form. Rashomon effect—multiple perspectives. Dramatic imperative overrides interviewee's discretionary impulse. Surrogate experience for the reader. Yields better understandings of what has happened, challenges social beliefs underlying program policy and action.	Slow delivery. Lacking in scientific respectability. Inconclusiveness. Overlengthy due to irreducible obligations to individuals. Costly to produce and disseminate.
Fairness	Draft report confidential to interviewee group. Rewritten to satisfy interviewee criticism. But in negotiation the evaluator presses: (a) audience concerns and needs, (b) dramatic values.	Interviewee participation. Form of the report foreshadowed by the form of the interview. Individual testimony highly valued. Natural language maximizes accessibility to nonspecialist readers and to subjects.	Evaluator allocates "star" and "support" status. Evaluator alone has all the data. Interviewee cannot retract released data.
Validity	Individual bias, censorship, inaccuracy subject to correction through consultation with knowledgeable and multivariate constituency. Account open to external challenge based on cited testimony or back-up tapes, but—artistic values may intrude.	"Pluralist" endorsement of account as accurate, relevant, balanced. Triangulation of oral histories. Autobiographical emphasis. Appeals to reader's own experience.	Context of generation disappears. Role and influence of evaluator underemphasized. Formal imperatives override substantive. Genre makes the account dismissable as factoid.

TABLE 2 Note Taking

	Characteristics	Strengths	Weaknesses
DATA GENERATION			
Effectiveness	Structured roles. Working relationship. Question/Answer style. Episodic discourse. Interviewer as informed questioner and ethnographer of communication.	Only what is "finished" and valued is recorded, so interviewee's stumbles, confusions, incoherences, irrelevances are weeded out or improved and polished. Professional control of the record. Penetrative of meaning and salience. Parsimonious.	Reductionist. Interviewee deference to recording task constrains natural discourse, invites closure and conservatism and resultant lack of penetration. Reduced nonverbal contact.
Fairness	Private except for what is noted—and remains so. Open notebook offers interviewee cumulative evidence of data value. (Even closed notes indicate selection criteria.) Time out to write and check entries enhances interviewee control of testimony.	Low-risk testimony the norm. Affords the security of the conventional recording medium. Emphasis on role performance rather than role experience protects the person.	No chance to reconsider testimony or its representation. Tendency for interviewer's structures to organize the data. Reliance upon interviewer's skill with shorthand/encoding.
Validity	Emphasis on public outcomes minimizes lazy, careless, or unsupportable testimony. But—no objective record; limited verbatim data.	Nonverbal as well as verbal components of communication taken into account. Interviewer uses knowledge and skills to cross-check, represent other viewpoints, challenge testimony.	Little raw data survives. Most data has been treated at source in some way. Difficult to respect informal, non-propositional forms of knowledge and understanding.

DATA PROCESSING

Effectiveness	Negotiation of noted summary in biographic form for improvement and release. Interviewee invited to: (a) authorize the representation, (b) rewrite, and (c) add.	Summaries facilitate faster data negotiation and clearance. Economical in time and cost. Clearance facilitated as summary approximates to recall of event.	Difficult to use data except in individual interview packages. Paucity of raw data. Understandings of data prematurely fixed. No reselection of raw data possible.
Fairness	Absence of high-risk data reduces need for confidentiality. Joint arbitration of processed accounts. Interviewee can totally reject the account as inconsistent with his recall of event.	Nature of summary affords less threatening accounts. Summaries evidence evaluator's style and likely use of data—signals that inform and "arm" respondent against later abuse. Economical, intelligible forms facilitate interviewee task in negotiating clearance.	Packaged nature of summaries deters from deleting/adding to accounts. Respondents private interests under-represented. Empathy/sympathy with interviewee at mercy of writer's skill. Lack of independent record may lead (a) strong interviewees to disclaim account; (b) weak interviewees to accept account.
Validity	High premium placed upon interviewer's skill and integrity in selection, analysis, and synthesis of data. Accounts of particular testimony structured in terms of their contribution to generalized validity of program overview.	Rich data on context of response. Interviewer's skill, interests and overall knowledge enable valuation, validation, and rationalization of data.	Interviewer error/bias in generation compounded at advanced processing stage. Lack of objective evidence to substantiate analysis. Vulnerable to facile causal interference. Autobiography treated as biography.

(continued)

Table 2 (continued)

	Characteristics	Strengths	Weaknesses
DATA REPORTING			
Effectiveness	Biographical portrayal or narrative account of the program experience, with individual cameos. Thematic or issues organization. Interviews treated piecemeal or as epitomes of the program story.	Condensed and susceptible to summary. Complex features noted but integrated. Commonalities emphasized. Parsimonious use of raw data to support or illustrate. Offers a synthesis of understanding.	Individuals submerged in overview or lost in "group" perspectives. An outsider's account of insiders.
Fairness	Deemphasis on individual testimony. Opportunities to comment, adverse comments noted and reported, usually as addenda.	Individuals protected because their testimonies are subsumed in framework of understanding.	Interviewees dependent on sympathetic evaluator as spokesman for their realities. Importance of individuals as actors diminished. Interviewees deskilled as critics by literary construction and by lack of source data record.
Validity	Emphasis on contextualization, coherence, contingency. Inherent logic forms in summarizing afford critique. Constucts explicit.	Interviewer, with skills, interests and knowledge, is the most qualified to judge authenticity, relatedness, and resulting hierarchies of data importance. Interviewer's commitment is to the "greater truths." Interviewer accountable to academic peers.	Loss of individual voices. Final reports are summaries of summaries—high possibility of gross reductionism, compounded error, and heavy skewing. Reliance on interviewer as storyteller increases systematic bias. No objective raw data to support the account.

intensity of such an approach probably explains why interviewers choose one or the other. That such a choice about the nature of the data itself is what we have tried to establish.

Note taking is the traditional tool of many fields of research and has, consequently, become strongly associated with the researcher's freedom to investigate, analyze, and theorize. Time and usage have largely conspired to reduce the debate over its appropriateness. Tape recording, on the other hand, is by comparison, a relative upstart. Its inception in research was, and still is, attended by misgivings over the ethics of surveillance, its appropriateness, and its sensitivity. While the tables examine one comparative usage of the instruments with particular regard to effectiveness, fairness, and validity, they do so within the boundary of an overall concern for democratizing influences each may have upon evaluation. In this context there is an interesting dichotomy between some of the leading exponents of each technique. Whereas notes have, in themselves, not suggested a strong and consistent model of practice and the ethics of note taking appear to be rewritten by each evaluator, in tape recording, if the interests of respondents are to be upheld, certain principles and practices seem to be required. In many ways, exploiting the properties of the tape to mitigate the dangers of misrepresentation ensures a certain democratic procedure. It would seem that whereas for the democratic model, principles and procedures create an actively participative constituency and a restraint of academic or bureaucratic usurpation (as much a constraint upon the evaluator as anyone else), within note taking democracy must reside in the intent of the evaluator.

We have then divergent political forms, one in which the evaluator assumes personal responsibility for the integrity, validity, and appropriateness of the account and one in which the evaluator, faced with this problem, tries to devolve some of that responsibility upon all the constituency members of the evaluation process because it provides complete texts of participant accounts that remain as objective data throughout the program to its completion and beyond. It remains a protection and defense for each participant and enables him or her to assume first-person, direct-action status within the evaluation. Thus the possibility of evaluator control appears to be restricted. But is it merely delayed? In the tape-recording interview we have profiled it can be argued (see Jenkins, 1980) that the stage-by-stage transfer of power from interviewee to interviewer maximally disadvantages the respondents. In this sense the whole procedure can be seen as a flytrap of the patient spider. Notes, on the other hand, produce a more complex infusion of evaluator influence. Decisions cannot be delayed but are the stuff of transaction. Note taking is a continuous process of synthetic transformation and must always face major problems of systematic error and bias.

Lou Smith, a note taker, approaches these pitfalls by invoking the collected viewpoints of insider groups and individuals as safeguards against a hardening and monolithic interpretation of the case. However, these viewpoints—these diverse rationales—are not kept in their intact syntactical forms by the note taker but require "attending and conceptualising styles similar to those audience uses" (Smith, 1981). Here is one way in which note taking may shape the language of evaluation reporting. A note taker is more likely to think in terms of "vicarious experience" and "false consciousness" than a tape recordist, because such terms are part of the genre of literature. A tape recordist need only say, "Attend to the actual words." Literary forms and devices provide a number of useful guidelines for the note taker. Take Smith's description of the overall product: "Eventually we have an outline which holds. It has a structure reflecting three major dimensions: integrity, complexity and creativity. By integrity I mean it has a theme, a thesis, a point of view." And he goes on to compare the development of an evaluation with that of a picture, poem, or novel, which "seems to develop something of a life of its own."

While the same pressures are on the tape recorder user to find communicable forms, he or she has fewer options if he or she is committed to preserving the epistemologies (political structures) of respondents. The tape recorder user's prime concern is exploring live evidence with the reader. He or she must hold to heterogeneity. Thus the natural outcome of the tape is theater (Tom Stoppard: "Writing plays is the only respectable way you can contradict yourself in public.") But notes, while wishing for similar outcomes, have the added complication of providing a product in a traditional narrative form that must uphold its integrity through the quality of its language. Like it or not, the pressure is on the evaluator to tell a good, coherent story. At the negotiation phase of a democratic evaluation what is negotiated by the note taker must invite, implicitly, an approval of narrative quality and style. In all but the final stage of negotiation of tape-based extracts, there are no such features to tax the respondent. He or she is asked to authenticate live data. The respondent retains control over a unitary form. In final drafts the literacy confusions remain for the note-taken summary of summaries, but it is only at this stage that tape-based accounts become as perplexing for the negotiating respondent. Now, a text is supplied in which the respondent's words are embedded, displayed in arrangement with the words of others in a form whose meaning for and impact upon an audience is extremely difficult to judge. In both cases final drafts are, as often as not, faits accomplis of form and substance (see House, 1981) that may do little to deliver promises of respondent control.

Despite their more overt denial of democratic process, note-based accounts conform to the expectations of literate audiences in a way that the more documentary forms suggested by tapes do not. For naturalism read narrative-imperative. Style seduces. We all want to be part of a good story. The writer retains favor through literary largesse.

On a more practical level, the evaluator is often part of a team or, if working alone, he or she may have adopted a plan of action that requires feedback and advice to a project. Lou Smith writes about sitting with the rest of the team and brainstorming, using read-out notes as a stimulus to provide a profile of a program. Notes here can be seen as relatively frictionless compared with tapes. Tapes are caught in time-locked confidentiality until the process of transcription and negotiated use have been completed. In any case they take a lot of listening to and are not easy to skim. Tapes lack the flexibility of use that makes notes attractive. Notes remain the best communication device within the action of a program. Exactly *what* is communicated and its ad hoc validity, is what is at question.

Glaser and Strauss (1967) in their grounded theory work defend the investigator's right to "analyse his data and decide(s) what data to collect next and where to find them, in order to develop his theory, as it emerges." Translated to evaluation such an assertion needs to be qualified by the evaluator's responsibility for program-specific theories and understandings take primacy. Nevertheless, we have a sense here of what Smith (1981) following Malinowski, means by extolling foreshadowing in preference to preconceiving in naturalistic evaluation. The task is more daunting for the note keeper than the tape user. Note-taken interviews have necessarily a greater interrogative edge and a greater reliance on what is already known (conceptualized). The need for concise mnemonics on paper and the requirement for progressive refinement in the interests of the final synthesis increases the chances of slippage from foreshadowing to preconceiving. In comparison, the very obduracy of tapes in terms of processing and the respondents' control over them together delay the evaluator's ability to get on with discovering and organizing emergent issues and establishing priorities.

CONCLUDING COMMENT

There are no absolute distinctions in the nature and quality of interviews based on different recording techniques. The influence of evaluator values and intents is such that the distinctions become blurred with greater skill and experience. Nor would we imply an inescapable partition between evaluations resulting from use of one or the other technique leading to totally distinct accounts. But, at different stages in the conduct and use of interviews, each technique has sufficient inherent idiosyncracy for it to constrain or enhance what evaluators are trying to accomplish. The complexion of the whole evaluation may be affected by the choice of recording technique.

It should be emphasized finally that we have dealt here with only one evaluation instrument, the unstructured interview, and with one focus, the gathering and representation of the participant experience of educational programs. The extent to which the priorities and values we have emphasized in this context lose their force in the broader, arguably less problematic canvass of the total evaluation mission we leave to another time.

REFERENCES

Glaser, B. and Strauss, A. (1967) *The Discovery of Grounded Theory.* Chicago: Aldine.

Guba, E. and Lincoln, Y. (1981) *Effective Evaluation.* London: Jossey-Bass.

Hastings, J. T. (1966) "Curriculum Evaluation: The Whys of the Outcome." *Journal of Educational Measurement,* 3: 27-32.

House, E. R. (1980) *Evaluating with Validity.* Beverly Hills, CA: Sage.

Jenkins D. (1980) "An Adversary's Account of Safari's Ethics of Case Study." In Helen Simons (ed.) *Towards a Science of The Singular.* Norwich, England: Centre for Applied Research in Education, University of East Anglia.

Johnson, J. M. (1974) *Doing Fieldwork Research.* London: Collier Macmillan.

MacDonald, B. (1976) "Evaluation and the Control of Education." In D. Tawney (ed.) *Curriculum Evaluation Today: Trends and Implications.* Schools Council Research Studies. London: Macmillan Education.

Smith, L. (1981) "An Evolving Logic of Participant Observation, Educational Ethnography and Other Case Studies." In L. Shulman (ed.) *Review of Research in Education.* Chicago: Peacock.

Stake, R. (1967) "The Countenance of Educational Evaluation." *Teacher's College Record,* 68 (7).

12

Intuitive Data Processing as a Potential Source of Bias in Naturalistic Evaluations

D. Royce Sadler

Whatever its other strengths, the mind is apt to make errors of judgment and inference. To most of us, this statement comes as no surprise. As one might expect, there has been a long history of attempts to identify and understand the nature and extent of these tendencies. Francis Bacon in the 17th century, for example, rebelled against the influence of Aristotelian thinking and the methods of acquiring knowledge (especially about the physical universe) current in his own day. In particular, he warned against a number of sources of distortion which he called *Idols*. Those associated with sensory perception and intuitive methods of analysis he called the "Idols of the Tribe," since he believed them to be "inherent in human nature, and the very tribe or race of man" (Bacon 41).

Recent research in human perception and cognition has given substance and specificity to many of Bacon's concerns. In addition, there has been growing interest in the implications of this type of research in various social settings, in particular, to courtroom testimony (Yarmey, 1979) and to decision making in business (Wright, 1980).

Because bias threatens an evaluation, it is not surprising that there is considerable literature on the topic. It is possible to group various forms of bias under three broad headings. First, there are *ethical compromises*, actions for which the evaluator is personally culpable. Second are what may be called *value inertias*, unwanted distorting influences which reflect the evaluator's background experience.

The first part of this paper is a brief survey of these two categories, mainly to indicate the scope of each and so distinguish them from the third category, *cognitive limitations* in dealing with data.

The major purpose of the paper is to elaborate the third category. This takes the form of a survey of faulty intuitions which have been identified in empirical research. Only those aspects which appear to have direct relevance to evaluation (in particular, naturalistic evaluation) are included. This is not to suggest that current naturalistic approaches to research and evaluation are undisciplined and merely impressionistic. They are not, of course. But such a catalog of commonly-found intuitive biases is justified even if it is not accompanied by concrete proposals as to how each may be eliminated or reduced. To be sure, the presentation may appear to be somewhat negative (after all, it is a list of defects) but if it helps sensitize naturalistic inquirers to potential problem areas, its contribution will be positive.

Ethical Compromises and Value Inertias

Potential sources of bias in the first category include (1) conflict of interest between the evaluator (or the agency) and the program evaluation itself (Scriven, 1976); (2) reactivity between the providers of information on the one hand and the evaluator as consumer of information on the other, because of the purposeful, goal-oriented activity of both parties (Cochran,

From Sadler, D. Royce, "Intuitive Data Processing as a Potential Source of Bias in Naturalistic Evaluations." *Educational Evaluation and Policy Analysis*, July-August 1981, pp. 25-31. Copyright 1981, American Educational Research Association, Washington, D. C. Reprinted by permission.

1978); and (3) sloppiness in the way the evaluation is carried out (shallowness, prejudice, capriciousness, and the intrusion of unsubstantiated opinion). Page (1979) refers to evaluations with some or all of these characteristics as self-serving, flexible, politicized, and compliant.

Taken together, ethical compromises are associated with one of the two meanings of the term "subjectivity" distinguished by Scriven (1972). The second has to do with values, preferences, and personal meaning; in this sense, subjectivity is, as Scriven (1967) and Krathwohl (1980) argue, a natural and necessary element of evaluation, which calls for no apology.

Some biases can be traced to a particular evaluator's background knowledge, prior experience, emotional makeup, or world view. Although these may affect what data are collected and how they are interpreted, they are not so much sinister and morally reprehensible as simply natural characteristics of a person *as a person*, hence the label *value inertias*.

Scriven (1973), for example, warned against the possible biasing effect of knowing a program's objectives. This knowledge may cause an evaluator to attend to goals as they are stated to the virtual exclusion of important side effects. Or an evaluator's attention may be captured by an incident known to have had great significance in another context (perhaps in a previous evaluation, or in the evaluator's own experience). A different evaluator may miss it altogether.

There is a sense in which knowledge and values are inseparable. Consciousness acts selectively on a great mass of stimuli, sorting out "what is and what is not worth noticing, what is important and valuable and what is insignificant or valueless" (Najder, 1975, p. 5). Granted that we all have different *sensory* thresholds, it is clear that there remain many idiosyncratic dispositions and presuppositions linked with our backgrounds of values.

To reduce the impact of ethical compromises and value inertias, a number of strategies have been developed or suggested. These include new methodologies (e.g., Wolf, 1975, on adversary proceedings), improved training of evaluators, periodic checks on the independence of evaluators, choosing an evaluator with a proven track

record, requiring evaluators to disclose their interests (Scriven, 1976), the externalization of value positions (Hammond & Adelman, 1976), and openness in providing a rationale for subjective judgments (Goodrich, 1978). Elimination of the biases mentioned so far, by whatever methods can be devised, is a necessary *but not sufficient* condition for an unbiased inquiry. It is necessary as well to identify and deal with biases due to the limitations of our information-processing capacity.

Naturalistic Approaches to Evaluation

Among the developments in evaluation methodology over the past decade has been a growing interest in *in situ*, naturalistic approaches and a reduced emphasis on quantification, controlled experiments, and multivariate analyses. However, naturalistic modes of inquiry are susceptible to a hazard not normally a problem when researching in the positivist tradition. It is this: naturalistic inquirers typically do most of their data reduction and analysis using a marvelously designed piece of apparatus, the brain. No device or system so far devised, irrespective of size or complexity, can match its ability to extract information from noisy environments. But, of course, any inferences drawn from data can be only as good as native cognitive mechanisms allow.

Studies over the past 40 years into the processes of human decision making, clinical judgment, and problem solving have shown that the human mind as information processor frequently draws incorrect inferences about the nature of the world and that there are certain recurring patterns. Fortunately, our natural tolerance for ambiguity, together with our adaptive ability, allow us in everyday living to recover from the consequences of a partially incorrect judgment (unless it is a devastating one), to revise an opinion, or to salvage some pieces. Initially vague conceptions need to be clarified only to the extent that makes the next step possible.

The situation is more serious when it is the evaluator who stands between the program and the audience, and when policy decisions that may affect the lives of many people may depend on the outcome of an evaluation. The audience must of necessity reconstruct a conception of what the program is, how it operates, and what its effects are, by drawing upon what the evaluator as intermediary is able to convey. Direct access of the audience to the program for verification purposes is frequently inappropriate or impossible.

Information-processing Limitations

Incorrect inferences are broadly due to our inherent incapacity to deal effectively with large masses of information at once, our intuitive ignorance of notions of natural variability (randomness and probability), and our tendency to seek meaning in or impose meaning upon the world around us.

Man's performance as intuitive data processor (hereafter IDP) is certainly impresive, but it is still somewhat fallible. There is considerable consistent evidence of misperception, misaggregation, and defective inference, leading to suboptimal assessments. These biases appear to be in some fundamental way linked to our natural processes of cognition, though this is not to suggest that all of the weaknesses occur all of the time, or that any is invariant over persons, tasks, and contexts. Many of them are of lesser importance in positivistic evaluations because of the methods of analysis. Naturalistic inquirers, on the other hand, pursue their tasks sensitively and sequentially. It is these same characteristics that make the naturalistic inquirers more vulnerable.

The listing of IDP biases which follows draws from the review of Shulman and Elstein (1975) together with more recent material. Only one or two references are given for each item, and depending on how the headings are construed, there may be some overlap and interdependence among the items. Some of the research evidence comes from laboratory experiments (in particular those of Tversky & Kahneman, 1974) and some from investigations of actual clinical judgments. There appears to be no empirical evidence indicating the importance of IDP biases relative to those in the other two categories, nor is it clear how often they occur in naturalistic evaluations. It should be noted that some of the data-analytic techniques described in the literature on ethnography and natur-

alistic research methods implicitly recognize these cognitive limitations.

1. *Data Overload*

In his classic paper, Miller (1956) showed that an informational bottleneck exists which places severe limitations on the amount of data able to be received, processed, and remembered by the human mind. By reorganizing the way the information is structured, the limits can be stretched but there remain upper limits to capacity.

This is especially important when evaluators not only describe or portray (something which can be done serially), but make inferences as to cause and effect, or valuations as to the worth of a program's means and ends (processes which involve aggregation). Summers, Taliaferro, and Fletcher (1970) showed that in making judgments where there were many aspects to be considered simultaneously, evaluators actually used less information than they thought. When some information which judges *said* they were using was experimentally varied over wide limits while other information remained fixed, there was no change in the judgment.

2. *First Impressions*

Poulton (1968) found that for physical stimuli judges effectively calibrated themselves on the first few stimuli received, and that this early baseline was persistent. Wason (1968) found the same for informational stimuli. The *order* in which information was received turned out to be important.

Tversky and Kahneman (1974) called the phenomenon "anchoring," and noted that estimates of simple quantities such as proportions tended to "creep" upwards or downwards from an initial starting point, and resisted adequate revision in the face of evidence. This effect is possibly more noticeable when an original estimate is provided by someone the evaluator regards as likely to be knowledgeable, for example, a program administrator or participant. But an evaluator's own first impression might be just as enduring.

3. *Availability of Information*

The impact of information for both evaluator and audience depends on whether it is easy to retrieve instances, to search for examples, or to understand reasons (Tversky & Kahneman, 1974). For example, if the researcher comes to a certain understanding of events (perhaps formulating a tentative hypothesis), but finds it difficult to find concrete supporting examples (even if they exist) or suitable analogies, that understanding is less likely to find its way into a report. Even if it does, a reader may judge the plausibility of a hypothesis by the ease with which instances can be recalled or imagined and these in turn depend on the reader's previous experience. Even the manner in which information is displayed (numerical, graphical, anecdotal) is important. Hawkins, Roffman, and Osborne (1978) found that decision makers often obtained their important evaluative information by word of mouth and personal contacts and tended to rely on this even when comprehensive evaluative information became available.

4. Positive and Negative Instances

When tentative hypotheses are held during the gathering of data, evidence is unconsciously selected in such a way that it tends to confirm the hypothesis. In other words, what is noticed, or what counts as a fact, depends in part on what is to be verified (Feyerabend, 1978). Wason (1968) found that people tended to ignore information which conflicted with an already held hypothesis, and that even intelligent individuals adhered to their own hypotheses with remarkable tenacity when they could produce confirming evidence for them.

It is not that people try to "save face" by deliberately ignoring disconfirming instances; the negative instances are simply not perceived at all, apparently because that aspect of the cognitive detection apparatus is not switched on. (The converse, of course, also applies: if one consciously looks for disconfirming evidence, the positive instances may go undetected.)

A related phenomenon sometimes occurs in analyzing taped conversations between researcher and informant. Some word with a certain folk meaning is discovered after listening to maybe an hour of tape; replay of the first hour of recording may show that the term was in fact being used all along, but simply escaped notice.

5. Internal Consistency, Redundancy, and Novelty of Information

Two sets of data about a particular phenomenon, from different but equally credible sources, might tell stories that are conflicting and unbalanced (that is, one is more extreme than the other). Wyer (1970) found a tendency to discount the importance of the less extreme data, leading to a more extreme evaluation overall. Novelty (which is, of course, a relative term because of the differing backgrounds of evaluators) tended to be impressive. Redundancy, on the other hand, reduced the likelihood of an extreme assessment. Thus, an aspect which appears novel at first may eventually be perceived as unimportant, merely because there is enough redundancy to change the way an evaluator looks at it.

In passing, it is worth noting that balanced conflicting information does not "cancel out" and leave one with no knowledge at all. To be aware of ambiguity is not the same as being entirely ignorant.

6. Uneven Reliability of Information

Unreliability in the data is often ignored—people treat data from a poor source as though it has almost the same diagnostic power as reliable data (Kahneman & Tversky, 1973). More recently, Beach et al. (1978) found that people discounted information when the sources were discovered to be less credible than at first thought, but that revision of an early hypothesis occurred by successively smaller amounts as the sources were found, one by one, to be fallible. Even when all sources were finally discredited, there appeared to be a residue of evidence for the hypothesis.

7. Missing Information

Slovic and MacPhillamy (1974) found that judges, in comparing two different phenomena, attached more importance to dimensions where commensurability was easy. In evaluations, the availability of a baseline (perhaps from previous evaluations) may result in a stronger emphasis on a particular dimension even when direct comparison of two programs is not the aim.

In a complementary study, Yates, Jagacinski, and Faber (1978) found that judges tended to devalue a dimension not fully described, but that some "filled in" the missing information in unpredictable ways: some assumed it to be at a desirable level, some at an "average" level, and some at an undesirable level. Their experiments also showed that one's evaluation is affected not only by what is considered "important" in the abstract but by what is actually attended to at the time of analysis.

Further, Johansson and Brehmer (1979) found that subjects who were told that certain key information necessary to successfully complete a predictive task was missing proceeded as though that condition made no difference.

8. Revision of a Tentative Hypothesis, Evaluation, or Diagnosis

When new information is received, revision tends to be either conservative (that is, not enough notice is taken of the new information), or excessive (overadjustment). There is clear evidence for conservatism in single-stage inference (Edwards, 1968; Peterson & Beach, 1967). On the other hand, when an inference is based not on raw data but on a previous inference drawn from data (multistage, or cascaded inference) there is less conservatism, and sometimes overcompensation (Youssef, 1973; Youssef & Peterson, 1973) but the reason is obscure. It appears that only the most salient of the information from the first stage is utilized in the second stage, the rest being ignored (Gettys et al., 1973a, 1973b). Under certain circumstances this may result in a better diagnosis, but through a partly invalid chain of inferences.

9. Base-rate Proportion

By base-rate is meant the underlying proportion of a population which falls into a particular category (e.g., an ethnic group). Difficulties arise when the inquirer receives both base-rate and (say) clinical data. When base-rate information alone is available the impression of proportion or incidence is, as one would expect, simply the base-rate. However, when data which does not contribute at all to a knowledge of incidence is available, the base-rate information may be suppressed or even ignored in favor of a simplistic expectation: "no" information may be interpreted as a 50–50 proportion (Tversky & Kahneman, 1974). On the other hand, if the evaluator finds clinical information relevant, it tends to take precedence over base-rate information in forming an impression of incidence (Carroll & Siegler, 1977), even if the clinical data applies only to a very small number of exceptional cases. Of course, a single exceptional case (such as the misuse of funds) may be critically important for policy decisions but is not relevant in making an assessment of relative frequency.

Insensitivity to base-rate frequency is a persistent characteristic of intuitive data processing (Kahneman & Tversky, 1973; Peterson & Beach, 1967). Only under special conditions (such as a small number of cases with complete enumeration) does it seem that people can intuitively combine base-rate with other information.

10. Sampling Considerations

For a given base-rate, the proportions observed in small samples vary to a more marked degree than in large samples. Even experienced users of statistics intuitively expect less variation than probability theory would suggest. Tversky and Kahneman (1971) investigated this tendency by asking people to estimate the likelihood of replicating an initial result, other things being equal. They found that judgments were made in terms of how representative the sample or case seemed to be of the population, and so neglected to take adequate account of natural variability. Their research also showed that people expected a local result to hold true for a population, and for global characteristics to be evident in a sample, provided that the sample was thought to be representative of the population.

Bar-Hillel (1979) showed that in judging the accuracy of information obtained from a sample, people are less sensitive to the absolute size of the sample than to the ratio of sample size to population.

11. Confidence in Judgment

Once an assessment is made, people have been shown to have an almost unshakable confidence in the correctness of their decisions, even in the face of considerable, relevant, contrary evidence (Einhorn & Hogarth, 1978; Oskamp, 1965; Tversky & Kahneman, 1974).

12. Co-occurrences and Correlation

Observed co-occurrences are frequently interpreted as evidence of a strong correlation. Smedslund (1963) described it this way: "Normal adults with no training in statistics do not have a cognitive structure isomorphic with the concept of correlation. Their strategies and inferences typically reveal a particularistic, nonstatistical approach, or an exclusive dependence on ++ [double positive] instances" (p. 172). Chapman and Chapman (1969) provided corroborative evidence in a study of the use of illusory correlations among diagnosticians. It may sometimes be necessary, Einhorn (1970) suggested, to unlearn preconceived correlations between certain cues and start again.

It is possible that the type of preferential detection mentioned earlier in item 4 is responsible in the case of co-occurrences as well.

13. Consistency in Judgment

Repeated evaluations of the same data configurations are frequently different (Goldberg, 1970; Meehl, 1954). In particular, (1) if A is preferred to B, and B to C, then we should expect A to be preferred to C (the transitivity condition), and (2) if A is preferred to B at one time, it should, other things being equal, be preferred at a later time. Tversky (1969) demonstrated that, under experimental conditions involving uncertainty, consistent and predictable intransitivities occurred. Thurstone (1927) and Guilford (1928) actually based a theory of scaling on this phenomenon.

Conclusion

This article began by classifying potential sources of bias into (1) ethical compromises, or distortions due to the possibility of payoffs and penalties, (2) background experience, the idiosyncratic trappings an evaluator brings to the task, and (3) limitations in human information-processing abilities. Thirteen specifics from the literature on intuitive thinking and judgmental processes were described under the third category. These specifics covered how people intuitively deal with such characteristics of the information as quantity, order, and availability (items 1-3), with mixed information (items 4-8), with revision of tentative inferences (items 9-10), and with variability in the data (items 11-13).

The purpose of the paper has been to draw the attention of naturalistic evaluators to some common failings, in the belief that better understanding of the ways data are intuitively processed will lead to better evaluations. The listing can serve as a checklist in the business of reducing, integrating, and drawing inferences from field data.

References

BACON, F. Novum organum. 1620. Book I, Aphorisms 41, 45–52.

BAR-HILLEL, M. The role of sample size in sample evaluation. Organizational Behavior and Human Performance, 1979, 24, 245–257.

BEACH, L. R., ET AL. Information relevance, content, and source credibility in the revision of opinions. Organizational Behavior and Human Performance, 1978, 21, 1–16.

CARROLL, J. S., & SIEGLER, R. S. Strategies for the use of base-rate information. Organizational Behavior and Human Performance, 1977, 19, 392–402.

CHAPMAN, L. J., & CHAPMAN, J. P. Illusory correlation as an obstacle to the use of valid psychodiagnostic signs. Journal of Abnormal Psychology, 1969, 74, 271–280.

COCHRAN, N. Grandma Moses and the "corruption" of data. Evaluation Quarterly, 1978, 2, 363–373.

EDWARDS, W. Conservatism in human information processing. In B. Kleinmuntz (Ed.), Formal representation of human judgment. New York: Wiley, 1968.

EINHORN, H. J. The use of nonlinear, noncompensatory models in decision making. Psychological Bulletin, 1970, 73, 221–230.

EINHORN, H. J., & HOGARTH, R. M. Confidence in judgment: Persistence of the illusion of validity. Psychological Review, 1978, 85, 395–416.

FEYERABEND, P. K. Against method. London: Verso, 1978.

GETTYS, C. F., KELLY, C., & PETERSON, C. R. The best guess hypothesis in multistage inference. *Organizational Behavior and Human Performance*, 1973, *10*, 364–373. (a)

GETTYS, C., ET AL. Multiple-stage probabilistic information processing. *Organizational Behavior and Human Performance*, 1973, *10*, 374–387. (b)

GOLDBERG, L. R. Man versus model of man: A rationale, plus some evidence, for a method of improving on clinical inferences. *Psychological Bulletin*, 1970, *73*, 422–432.

GOODRICH, T. J. Strategies for dealing with the issue of subjectivity in evaluation. *Evaluation Quarterly*, 1978, *2*, 631–645.

GUILFORD, J. P. The method of paired comparisons as a psychometric method. *Psychological Review*, 1928, *35*, 494–506.

HAMMOND, K. R. & ADELMAN, L. Science, values, and human judgment. *Science*, 1976, *194*, 389–396.

HAWKINS, J. D., ROFFMAN, R. A., & OSBORNE, P. Decision makers' judgments: The influence of role, evaluative criteria, and information access. *Evaluation Quarterly*, 1978, *2*, 435–453.

JOHANSSON, R., & BREHMER, B. Influences from incomplete information—A note. *Organizational Behavior and Human Performance*, 1979, *24*, 141–145.

KAHNEMAN, D., & TVERSKY, A. On the psychology of prediction. *Psychological Review*, 1973, *80*, 237–251.

KRATHWOHL, D. R. The myth of value-free evaluation. *Educational Evaluation and Policy Analysis*, 1980, *2*, 37–45.

MEEHL, P. E. *Clinical versus statistical prediction*. Minneapolis: University of Minnesota Press, 1954.

MILLER, G. A. The magical number seven, plus or minus two: Some limits on our capacity for processing information. *Psychological Review*, 1956, *63*, 81–97.

NAJDER, Z. *Values and evaluations*. Oxford: Clarendon Press, 1975.

OSKAMP, S. Overconfidence in case-study judgments. *Journal of Consulting Psychology*, 1965, *29*, 261–265.

PAGE, E. B. More objective! *Educational Evaluation and Policy Analysis*, 1979, *1*, 45–46.

PETERSON, C. R., & BEACH, L. R. Man as an intuitive statistician. *Psychological Bulletin*, 1967, *68*, 29–46.

POULTON, E. C. The new psychophysics: Six models for magnitude estimation. *Psychological Bulletin*, 1968, *69*, 1–19.

SCRIVEN, M. The methodology of evaluation. In R. W. Tyler, R. M. Gagné, & M. Scriven (Eds.), *Perspectives of curriculum evaluation* (AERA Monograph Series on Curriculum Evaluation, No. 1). Chicago: Rand McNally, 1967.

SCRIVEN, M. Objectivity and subjectivity in educational research. In L. G. Thomas (Ed.), *Philosophical redirection of educational research* (71st Yearbook Part I). Chicago: National Society for the Study of Education, University of Chicago Press, 1972.

SCRIVEN, M. Goal-free evaluation. In E. R. House

(Ed.), *School evaluation: The politics and process*. Berkeley, Calif.: McCutchan, 1973.

SCRIVEN, M. Evaluation bias and its control. In G. V Glass (Ed.), *Evaluation studies review annual* (Vol. 1). Beverly Hills, Calif.: Sage, 1976.

SHULMAN, L. S., & ELSTEIN, A. S. Studies of problem solving, judgment, and decision making: Implications for educational research. *Review of Research in Education*, 1975, *3*, 3–42.

SLOVIC, P., & MACPHILLAMY, D. Dimensional commensurability and cue utilization in comparative judgment. *Organizational Behavior and Human Performance*, 1974, *11*, 172–194.

SMEDSLUND, J. The concept of correlation in adults. *Scandinavian Journal of Psychology*, 1963, *4*, 165–173.

SUMMERS, D. A., TALIAFERRO, J. D., & FLETCHER, D. J. Subjective vs objective description of judgment policy. *Psychonomic Science*, 1970, *18*, 249–250.

THURSTONE, L. L. A law of comparative judgment. *Psychological Review*, 1927, *34*, 273–286.

TVERSKY, A. Intransitivity of preferences. *Psychological Review*, 1969, *76*, 31–48.

TVERSKY, A., & KAHNEMAN, D. Belief in the law of small numbers. *Psychological Bulletin*, 1971, *76*, 105–110.

TVERSKY, A., & KAHNEMAN, D. Judgment under uncertainty: Heuristics and biases. *Science*, 1974, *185*, 1,124–1,131.

WASON, P. C. On the failure to eliminate hypotheses: A second look. In P. C. Wason & P. N. Johnson-Laird (Eds.), *Thinking and reasoning*. Baltimore: Penguin Books, 1968.

WOLF, R. L. Trial by jury: A new evaluation method. *Phi Delta Kappan*, 1975, *57*, 185–187.

WRIGHT, W. F. Cognitive information processing biases: Implications for producers and users of financial information. *Decision Sciences*, 1980, *11*, 284–298.

WYER, R. S., JR. Information redundancy, inconsistency, and novelty and their role in impression formation. *Journal of Experimental Social Psychology*, 1970, *6*, 111–127.

YARMEY, A. D. *The psychology of eyewitness testimony*. New York: The Free Press, 1979.

YATES, J. F., JAGACINSKI, C. M., & FABER, M.D. Evaluation of partially described multiattribute options. *Organizational Behavior and Human Performance*, 1978, *21*, 240–251.

YOUSSEF, Z. I. The effects of cascaded inference on the subjective value of information. *Organizational Behavior and Human Performance*, 1973, *10*, 359–363.

YOUSSEF, Z. I., & PETERSON, C. R. Intuitive cascaded inferences. *Organizational Behavior and Human Performance*, 1973, *10*, 349–358.

Author

D. ROYCE SADLER, Lecturer, Department of Education, University of Queensland, St. Lucia, Brisbane, Australia 4067. *Specialization*: Educational evaluation and research.

13

Panel Review Strategy (PRS)
A Methodology for Evaluating the Arts

Nicholas J. Anastasiow

This article describes the development and trial of the technique of "panel review strategy" as an evaluation strategy.[1] What will be examined in this article is the development and rationale of the strategy, and its trial use with the Living Stage improvisational company's work with physically impaired children in two school settings. The reader should keep in mind the two separate themes: the first is the trial of an evaluation strategy; the second is the use of this strategy to evaluate the Living Stage's work with physically impaired children.

INTRODUCTION

The rationale for the use of a panel review strategy (PRS) is based on the difficulty of assessing the effect of an artistic endeavor on those who participate in or experience the endeavor. For example, consider these questions: What impacts can be measured for the million people who viewed the Picasso retrospective at the Museum of Modern Art? What behavioral measure can be designed to determine the artistic value of the "Baryshnikov on Broadway" television special? What knowledge can be determined for those who read the novel *JR* by William Gaddis? Do these experiences have entertainment value only, or do they provide the difficult-to-define, illustrative constructs of aesthetic satisfaction, insight, creativity, inspiration, and human affirmation. Most human beings will attest to the value of the arts, although society spends only a minute share of its income on such activities. The task of making operational the impact of the arts by systematic behavior indices that are practical, and from which cause-effect inferences can be drawn, is not impossible but it is exceedingly difficult and costly. For example, it may not be cost-effective to measure heartbeat deceleration as an indication of attention, relaxation, and involvement of every individual who views the Picasso exhibit. However, it is technically possible and could be managed by devising an electronic measure that could be assembled with the portable audio tour guides available in most museums. One could test the relative effects of Picasso's blue period versus his rose or abstract periods. However, few artists seek such data.

There have been some attempts to render emotional and aesthetic constructs behaviorally observable. For example, Ken Majer is currently assessing the

From Nicholas J. Anastasiow, "Panel Review Strategy (PRS): A Methodology for Evaluating the Arts," original manuscript.

impact of a Carl Rogers training session on physicians. Through the arduous technique of Gagne's "task analyses," Majer's techniques include paper-and-pencil evaluations, telephone interviews, and on-site interviews with patients and health care staff (Majer and Meyers, 1980).

To those who practice the arts, the accepted means of evaluating the artistic endeavor of experience has a long history. Art can be evaluated, for example, by how many individuals purchase tickets, view the exhibit, but the record, turn to the appropriate channel, buy the hardcover copy, and by over how long a time period this takes place. However, above all, the arts depend upon and seek the expert opinion or evaluation of the critic. Art is viewed and reviewed. It is analyzed and critiqued. The artist may chafe at a bad review, but the system appears to work. It is this model of critic-expert on which the concept of panel review has been founded. In some other recent work, Eisner (1977) examines the role of the connoisseurship in the evaluation of teaching. Grier (1973), a student of Eisner, distinguishes between the connoisseur who is an appreciator of art and the critic who makes public in linguistic terms the impact that the work had on the critic, and thereby, its potential cultural relevance. Pepper (1956) suggests that it is the repeated and multiple observation of man by man that not only corroborates the value of work, but would reduce error that a single observation would hold. The panel review strategy described here offers multiple observations by critics who assess both the worth of the activity and the activity's impact on the child.

Another justification for the panel review strategy can be noted. Policy decisions are sometimes determined from a position paper developed by one or more professionals. These papers set forth the logic of a position and recommendations for policy action. The paper is then reviewed by "experts" who respond to the logic set forth. The experts eventually present their views and recommendations. This technique is often referred to as the "Delphi technique."

In both cases, it is to the expert-critic that the decision maker turns for assistance in establishing policy. This traditional mode of evaluating the arts, the critic-experts, will next be related specifically to the theater and drama.

THE CRITIC AS EVALUATOR

In the art of the theater and drama, the critic brings to bear his or her expertise to evaluate the achievement of the performance. In some cases, plays are critiqued before a performance, but usually, it is the performance that is evaluated. The performance itself is a gestalt of the talents of many professionals who are experts: the author, director, actors and actresses, set designer, and lighting designer, to name a few. Purposes of plays may vary, but it has come to be expected that plays include dramatic action, dialogue and attention to the use of language, dramatic characterization, emotional intensity, and a guiding idea or theme. The playwright has responsibility for providing these constructs in a particular written form. The role of the director is to bring his or her unique vision with the greatest possible artistic integrity. The actor brings life and his/her own interpretation to the character. The play is critiqued by the reviewer who utilizes a special set of criteria for evaluating the above aspects of the performance. The critic may describe the play as "well-written," "beautifully conceived," "disjointed," "unimaginative," "poetic," and so forth. The critic will most likely attribute to the director the blocking, pacing, ensemblege coordination, dramatic intensity, and possibly, character interpretations. It is the actor/actress who more probably will be credited with character interpretation. Usually, an individual actor or actress is singled out for his or her performance, but in some cases, the "ensemblege" is noted for ensemble acting. Critics may differ on how they perceive the play, some favorably, some unfavorably, however, the sum total of all the critics or the unique power of a single critic, serves to evaluate all of the elements of the entire production, thus determining its "success" or "failure." A single actor may be mentioned for an outstanding performance in a "weak" play. In a "strong" play, the writer, director, and actor or actress may all be credited with distinction. Although the ultimate judgment of the play's worth may reside with scholars and historians, the critic's evaluation is its initial assessment.

Let us now examine the Living Stage goals and objectives and review the application of the panel review strategy. It is important to note that Living Stage has been operational for fourteen years. It has been evaluated by critic-participants who have sent letters, evaluation forms, and importantly, have asked the company to return to the participants' settings. The company has hundreds of letters on file documenting the value of their talents. A wide set of critic-participants have offered support for the company on a wide set of dimensions.

The Living Stage director also evaluates every session during "note sessions" following a performance. These sessions include the director's critiques directed toward evaluations of child performance and participation. Goals are established for each child for the next performance. A running record is maintained on each child.

LIVING STAGE

The following description of Living Stage was prepared by Living Stage personnel.

"Every child—disabled or not—has the potential for creative genius." This belief forms the philosophical basis of the Living Stage, an improvisational theater troupe dedicated to turning its audience on to their own creativity.

For the past 14 years, the company, an outreach component of Washington, D.C.'s Arena Stage, has worked with the disabled, the elderly, juvenile delinquents, and prisoners to awaken self-expression, communication, and confidence. The national acclaim received from educators and others who work with disabled children led to a 1977 Bureau of Education for the Handicapped

(BEH) grant. The purpose of the 12-month grant was to demonstrate the troupe's capacity to work with handicapped children in Fairfax County, Virginia. The program was so successful that in October 1978, the company received funding for a 3-year project to develop a model for working with young multiply handicapped children (ages 3-8) at Sharpe Health School in Washington, D.C., and at Fairhill School in Fairfax, Virginia.

Twice each week, for two-and-a-half hours, the troupe conducts a workshop at each school to encourage self-expression and self-discovery among handicapped students at the school. The philosophy of the program is to use the troupe as a tool to promote a greater sense of self-worth and positive thinking.

The company consists of three actors/actresses, a musician, stagehands, and the director, Bob Alexander. There are no written scripts. However, members of the troupe have a repertoire of over 80 songs and 500 poems and phrase passages to deepen the content of the performance. In addition, the musician accompanies the dramatizations with an electric piano. He changes the style of the music according to the action flowing from each scene.

A participational rather than presentational format is used for each workshop. Each scene evolves from the emotions and thoughts of the actors. The program consists of four separate stages: (1) the jam, (2) a performance session, (3) warm-up exercises, and (4) the open play.

Even before the children enter the room, they can hear the sounds of music emitted from the workshop area. This "jamming" continues as the children arrive with troupe members playing congo drums, the electric piano, and various percussion instruments. The environment pulsates with sounds and colors from the bright blue, red, and yellow collapsible boxes used as props.

The children are drawn into a carpeted area where musical instruments are laid out for their use in the jam session. At this point the actors/actresses slowly draw each child into musical and verbal improvisations until everyone is participating.

Each child gets the opportunity to direct the sound and action from the rest of the group. He/she has control of the environment. The purpose is to live out one's true feelings—whether they express love, hate, loneliness, fear, or joy.

According to Wendy Hanes, project coordinator, the process inspires "creative play." "Each child develops listening skills which lead to new and improved learning and communication skills." This motivates increased action and motor participation. Imagination and abstraction exercises are inherent in the process. A chain reaction is set off, with the impact increasing motivation and learning capacity.

The final result is that the handicapped child loses consciousness of his or her disability and reaches a new creative environment where he/she feels confidence and greater self-esteem.

For the children who participate in Living Stage, the role they play is that of both actor and playwright, for they create their own characters and in general, are encouraged to create a stronger personality. The children, participating in the presence of the actors, are encouraged to use their faces, their voices, and their limbs to express ideas and emotions. As was noted above, the company has divided the experience into four major components, but each component contains a repertoire of techniques that the artists bring into play in an improvisational manner. They model the techniques and encourage the children to improvise, thereby, becoming actors/actresses, playwrights, and the characters they invented.

PANEL SELECTION CRITERIA AND COMPOSITION

The panel review strategy was designed to serve as critic-expert to view and evaluate the achievement of Living State with physically impaired children. In selecting the panel the author sought two prominent characteristics in the reviewers: one, the person had to be knowledgeable and skilled in special education, and two, the member had to be open to and value the arts. Five panel members were selected.

PANEL PARTICIPATION ACTIVITIES

Prior to the panel members' actual viewing of Living Stage, they were acquainted with the company's purpose and concept through telephone and written communication. These materials included written descriptions of Living Stage. Before the observation, the panel members met with the director of the company and heard his presentation of the goals of the company. The panel members were scheduled in pairs since the space in the elementary school setting could not accommodate more than two adults at a time. One setting was in a suburban area where the program occurs once a week after school. The second setting was in an inner-city school where the program is presented once a week for two-and-a-half hours. Each panel member viewed a complete performance and then wrote up his or her impressions of the efficacy of the experience for handicapped children and his/her thoughts about the strategy as an evaluation technique. A brief summary of panel's impressions of the company is included below followed by each member's thoughts about the PRS as a method of evaluation for the arts.

One member saw great possibility in Living Stage assisting nonhandicapped children in accepting the body movements and facial expressions of handicapped children, which are offensive and frequently rejected. Another member felt that the program offers a superior educational experience particularly for handicapped children. This member noted that the actors in the Living Stage Theater Company offer humane, compassionate, and empathetic experiences to the participant child. Enthusiasm of the children seemed high with students finding most activities involving and worth doing. The program is overall a quality learning experience that meets broad educational goals for the handicapped child.

A third panel member noted that throughout the entire performance, the children's behavior was characterized by a strong and persistent positive affect. This affect was noted in circumstances in which children were engaged in solitary activities as well as when they were participating in groups. There was a high degree of group cohesion. The strength and positive nature of these peer interactions was surprising, given the type and severity of the handicaps manifested by these children. Correspondingly, the attention spans of the children were continuous and long. He stated in summary, that the experience can produce a unique contribution to the development of handicapped children.

A fouth panel member commented that there was substantial positive peer interaction evident throughout the two-hour session. Children functioned as a cohesive "group" with cooperation and facilitation among group members. Although the Living Stage actors clearly were a source of great attraction and joy to the children, child-child interactions appeared to be equally as frequent as child-actor interactions.

The group interaction was remarkable for its noncompetitive and nonjudgmental quality, which extended not only to the physical and other impairments of the children but to the more general factors that inhibit creative expression in a group context. His overall impression was that the group was "chaining" to one another's ideas, each new idea building upon or elaborating the previous ideas, such that divergent thinking and ideational fluency were occurring at a group level and were being facilitated by the group context.

The presence of *group* mediational thought, or "chaining," indicates that: (1) the children were listening to each other, (2) the children valued each other's responses sufficiently to incorporate them into their own flow of thought, (3) there was no rejection of novel or divergent ideas, and (4) the group showed quite good attention span and capacity for sustained concentration and involvement with an activity (in one instance this included 45 minutes of continuous improvisational dramatic play, where an entire and complex plot was created and acted by the group).

Children switched flexibly between the role of leader and follower during the group activities. Most of the children spent at least some time as activity leader (i.e., suggesting an activity component for the group to follow) and then smoothly transferred to the leadership role to another child or Living Stage actor. Each child's contribution was valued and accepted, and my impression was that a genuinely nonjudgmental context was achieved.

In summary, this panel member's observations in the areas of social skills, group problem solving (and group problem formulation), emotional development, self-image and body-image, self-esteem, and facilitation of individual and group creative processes all were extremely favorable to the Living Stage program.

The fifth member commented that the cast, in particular the lead actress, are excellent teachers. They prepared children for transitions, they anticipated, they were inventive, imaginative, and extremely flexible. The children demonstrated a great deal of joy, happiness, and emotional release during the morning. Yet there was very little out-of-control behavior. The mood was calm: intense, yet not overstimulating. The music was marvelous, and added greatly to the mood and the ambience of the otherwise dull classroom.

The children, and the adults, were on task most of the time. The children demonstrated repeatedly that they were aware of what was taking place, anticipated the next event, and looked forward to participation.

In summary, the panel review members found the Living Stage to be a valuable contribution to the lives of handicapped children on a broad set of cognitive and affective dimensions. In order to support the idea of Living Stage one must value the development of social skills and creativity. Clearly the impact is profound; but profoundity, like beauty, is found in the eye of the beholder. The panel found cognitive and social skill development, but they also found joy and beauty.

ASSESSMENT OF THE PANEL REVIEW STRATEGY

All of the panel members agreed that the panel review strategy is an effective means of evaluating an artistically oriented program. One member wrote, "I applaud Gary (McDaniels) for both his creativity and his viking spirit."

Another stated, "The difficulties in evaluating the impact on handicapped children of a performance of Living Stage are certainly substantial. Despite my initial apprehension regarding an ability to define appropriate dimensions for such a naturalistic evaluation, I feel confident that, within limits of such a methodology, my observations reflect an accurate assessment of Living Stage performance." The others expressed confidence that they were able to observe difficult-to-define constructs while sitting in the classroom.

The panel members' observations of Living Stage are concrete evidence that constructs which are difficult to define, whether they be cognitive or affective, can be observed, and following their observation, can be defined. The limitation of the strategy is that specific growth of individual children is not captured by the single viewing of panel members. Growth or development is best captured through systematic gathering of data over time.

Case studies offer a great deal of insight into a program's potential effectiveness. However, most case studies are questioned by researchers who fear that the writer's bias may not be controlled, particularly when the writer is a member of the program.

The panel review strategy appears to provide insight into program effectiveness and what may be happening as part of the program's impact on particular children. They are essentially inductive processes, but induction, no matter how highly valued, is not proof. They are as Pepper (1956) notes, corroborations, and can be used as empirical evidence.

What should be added to induction is an experimental test designed to verify the insight and hypotheses or theory that was arrived at inductively. For example, Einstein's great theory, arrived at inductively, still had to be subjected to empirical test.

Thus, this author proposes that case study data and panel review strategy reports form the basis for selecting constructs that can then be studied through systematic observations of a child over time. Newer advances in research have resulted in methods of "controlled induction" that give greater credence to potential cause-effect statements derived from induction. These newer methods are referred to as time series or single subject designs (Glass, Willson, and Gottman, 1975; Bentler, Lettieri, and Austin, 1976).

SUMMARY

The panel review strategy is an effective means of evaluation for the arts. It would appear to be most useful after the program has been established and fully operational. In this case, the Living Stage had several years experience in other school settings and had been in operation in school settings with disabled children for three years. One should not discount the major difficulty of operating in a setting under the control of others and the period of time required to learn to work within such a situation. After the program has been established and operational, a selected review team can gain credible information and can generate potential constructs for further study.

Panel review strategy is not intended to be a total evaluation of a program. It is designed to offer some validation, much like content, and possibly construct validation, for test constructors. Expert opinion has a place in evaluation and can reassure the funding agency that the project is achieving its goals and that monies are not being wasted. A single subject research design can demonstrate which goals are being achieved, in what manner, and by which child. The power of the design to allow for causal claims should not be diminished. For example, the panel review strategy coupled with single-subject research can translate the joy observed in the Living State performance, to the inferred growth of the child's efficacy and self-competence by demonstrating through systematic observation his or her increased participation in verbal interactions, in imaginative play, or in other constructs valued by the field.

NOTE

1. The idea of utilizing a panel of experts to evaluate a program's objectives, achievements, and impact grew out of conversations with Gary McDaniels when he was Chief of the Division of Innovation and Research, in the Bureau of Education for the Handicapped. In all honesty, I cannot recall whether the idea was originally his, mine, or both. In any case the author assumes responsibility for its execution. Thanks to Drs. Joseph Bleiberg, Michael J. Guralnick, Samuel J. Meisels, Herbert Goldstein, and Gayle Mindes who served as panel members.

REFERENCES

Bentler, P. M., Lettieri, D. J., and Austin, G. A. [Eds.] *Data Analysis Strategies and Designs for Substance Abuse Research.* Washington, DC: U.S. Government Printing Office, 1976.

Eisner, E. On the Uses of Educational Connoisseurship and Criticism for Evaluating Classroom Life. *Teachers College Record,* 1977, *79*(3): 345-358.

Glass, G. V, Willson, V. K., and Gottman, J. M. *Design and analysis of time-series experiments.* Boulder: Colorado Associated University Press, 1975.

Grier, W. D. The Criticism of Teaching. Unpublished dissertation, Stanford University, University Microfilms International, Ann Arbor, Michigan, 1973.

Majer, K. and Myers, C. *Human Dimensions in Medical Care.* La Jolla, CA: V.A. Hospital Program, The Consulting Group, 1980. (mimeo)

Pepper, S. C. *The Basis of Criticism in the Arts.* Cambridge, MA: Harvard University Press, 1956.

14

The Clarification Hearing
A Personal View of the Process

George F. Madaus

Editor's Note: The following two articles represent the authors' perceptions and suggestions about the process—a modified judicial evaluation model—used in the National Clarification Hearings on Minimum Competency Testing.

It was early morning of the second day of the Clarification Hearings in Washington, D.C. I was seated in front of the makeup table cluttered with bottles, tins and brushes of all sorts, my new TV-compatible suit and blue shirt carefully protected by a bib. As the makeup artist was applying a brown fluid to my face, and undoubtedly wishing she had the skills of a plastic surgeon, Bob Ebel happened by the door. Seeing Bob, the incongruity of the situation hit me. How did I, and a number of my colleagues in the next room waiting their turn in front of the lightbulb-studded mirror, get involved in this alien world? While I had my doubts from the beginning, Bob's appearance triggered the realization that 11 months earlier, when I agreed to serve as team leader for the negative side in the Clarification Hearings on Minimum Competency Testing (MCT), I really had no idea what I had let myself in for. I was again brought up short about the implications of the whole process, and my part in it, 2 weeks ago after viewing, along with students and colleagues here at Boston College, the edited version of the hearings on public television. In what follows I have attempted to describe my reactions and feel-

ings, both positive and negative, to various aspects of the process leading up to the hearings, the hearing itself, and the final TV product developed by Maryland Public Broadcasting (MPB).

I will not get into the specifics of either case except where it might illustrate a more general point about the process itself. This paper does not rehash the pros or cons of MCT. Interested readers can find the outline of both cases in the *Phi Delta Kappan*, October 1981 issue, and the tapes of the full 24 hours of hearings and the 3-hour edited version are readily available.

Instead of specifics about MCT, I will concentrate on the strengths and weaknesses—as I see them—of the clarification process itself—as I experienced it. Further, in a more general sense, I have set down my reflections about the strengths and weaknesses of using a modified judicial evaluation model at the national level to illuminate and clarify education issues.

The Model

We employed a modified version of the adversary of judicial evaluation model (JEM). The principle modification was the elimination of a jury or panel whose purpose was to hand down a decision or make recommendations about the object being evaluated. There were very good reasons for this deletion. By eliminating a "verdict" or a set of recommendations, NIE avoided the unpleasantness

and controversy that would have certainly followed on a federally sponsored panel declaring one side or the other the "winner," or promulgating a set of recommendations on how to structure a MCT program. If the verdict or recommendations favored the negative side it would have surely unleashed a raft of criticism and complaints about unwarranted federal intervention in state programs. If the pro side was the beneficiary then NIE would have had to deal with the enmity of those adversary groups opposed to MCT. By eliminating the panel or jury component from the Clarification Hearing process NIE avoided this no-win situation. "Winning" or "losing" was left to the eyes of the beholders; *de gustibus non est desputandum.*

This modification, made in August, took on added significance after the November election. The Clarification Hearing mode was viewed as an acceptable, nonintrusive federal presence in education; it provided information to state and local policymakers which they could use or ignore as they saw fit.

From the beginning, NIE insisted that we were engaged in a clarification process; our task was to illuminate the issues surrounding MCT. Winning and competition between the teams were not to be part of the process leading to the hearing. Therefore, one of my main criterion in evaluating the clarification process is the extent to which I feel it effectively and efficiently clarifies and illuminates issues.

The Audience and the Model

From the outset the plan was to make the videotaped proceedings of the hearing, along with written

George Madaus is Director of the Center for the Study of Testing, Evaluation and Educational Policy, Boston College, Chestnut Hill, MA 02167. Specializations: Educational testing and program evaluation.

From Madaus, George F., "The Clarification Hearing: A Personal View of the Process." *Educational Researcher*, January 1982, pp. 4, 6-11. Copyright 1982, American Educational Research Association, Washington D.C. Reprinted by permission.

transcripts, available to interested policymakers at all levels. These products were to help inform their decisions concerning the design or modification of MCT programs. Initially there were no plans to produce a television program to be aired nationally by the Public Television System (PBS), but this feature was added to the process in the late fall.

Staying with the original, more limited goal for a moment, one must ask how reasonable it is to expect policymakers, or even their surrogates, to view the full 24 hours of proceedings? I thought then, and nothing has happened to change my mind since, that it was preposterous to expect legislators or board members to find the time to view unexpurgated tapes.

The next question was, how reasonable is it to extract a 1- or 2-hour executive summary tape which policymakers might be more apt to view and that truly reflects the complexity of the issues? I did not know the answer to this question initially. However, after viewing the 3-hour edited version of the tapes, I feel that altogether too much clarity and illumination is lost through the editing process. These doubts about the validity of the summary tapes are not a reflection on the work done by MPB. Based on material recommended by both teams producer Frank Batavick did a superb job of putting together the edited version for the series "Who's Keeping Score?" The difficulty is that you necessarily do violence to a carefully constructed, 12-hour case when you are forced to reduce the testimony and evidence to 75 minutes.

This leads me to my next question: Why go through 24 hours of exhausting hearings if the product that will receive the widest circulation and viewing is a 3-hour summary tape? If I had been more clever perhaps I could have structured each witness' testimony so that a piece could have been lifted intact for the expurgated version. But had I been that shrewd why ·bother with the rest. Unlike a real trial we were not building a record for an appeal.

Here I also must record my pessimism about the possibility of policymakers taking the time to read a more traditional, written evaluation of MCT. In hindsight— and I would caution the reader that mine is not always 20/20—I think that the TV medium has the potential of reaching and affecting more policymakers than does our more traditional evaluation reports. However, I also feel that the clarification hearing mode does not exploit the potential of that medium to reach and educate viewers. I am convinced now that the expertise of the participants, the TV time allocated to the project, and the funds expended for the series "Who's Keeping Score" would have been better used to produce a three or four-part documentary on MCT, not a flashy but shallow, commercial-type documentary, but one of more substance and visual power, perhaps a NOVA or COSMOS type product.

If such a 4-hour documentary had been our goal at the outset, the two teams could have worked cooperatively with the TV experts to put together a TV production that could have more effectively exploited the medium in presenting the pros and cons of MCT. Such a series would have been a more effective, efficient and dramatic way to illuminate the issues than the static question-and-answer format employed in the hearings. Also, more public television outlets might have picked up the product, than to have the date elected to show "Who's Keeping Score."

When NIE informed us of the decision to involve MPB in producing a series of three 1-hour excerpts for each day of the hearing, to be aired on public television, and to be preceeded by a 1-hour documentary produced solely by MPB with very little input from the team, the whole enterprise was transformed. We had a new audience, the general public or that segment of it that watched PBS. We were repeatedly admonished not to alter our efforts to continue as before; nonetheless, the spectre of the nationally aired product had considerable psycho-

logical impact. We certainly sensed that the process had been changed but did not appreciate until after the editing process to what extent the medium had altered the process. The announcement did change the way we chose some of our witnesses. For example we wanted some witnesses who would be recognized as creditable by a more general audience than the education, testing/research communities. We also asked the question "how will this witness come across on TV?"

Presented with NIE's decision to seek funds for the public broadcasting component, our team requested that part of that budget include a TV expert for each team. This request, like several others, was ignored. However, if a similar process is ever repeated it is crucial that each team have a TV person working closely with it to help the team utilize the power of the medium in presenting their case. Of course, such an addition adds to the cost.

If I had it to do again—God forbid—and the hearing mode was still the vehicle, then I would want to rehearse witnesses before a TV consultant and a small panel of lay people. The lay panel could provide feedback on whether technical points were properly translated and presented and whether the material and testimony were understood. Some evidence and testimony that I understood because of my background were clear neither to educators without a research background nor to those outside the field. The extent of this problem was not evident to me until the hearing and the editing process. A lay panel watching a rehearsal of the evidence and testimony would have helped us avoid this problem. But again, this would have added to the cost of the project and necessitated cooperation on the part of the witness that might not always be forthcoming from busy public personalities.

A TV consultant could offer advice on how the witness might better come across on TV. For example, two witnesses read a great deal of their testimony. If you read the transcript the testimony is very powerful. However, it does not make for good TV viewing; eye contact was not maintained and the testimony lost spontaneity. Perhaps I should have anticipated this problem but I did not.

More importantly, the TV consultant would have been invaluable in helping us better utilize the visual medium to present some of our evidence and technical arguments. Technical matters are difficult to present to a general audience through the question-and-answer format of the JEM. While both teams used graphics to illustrate material, these were static renditions of drawing supplied by the teams. Nonstatic graphics such as those seen on Wall Street Week, and other visual devices such as short film clips or animations could have helped to make some of the arguments more understandable to a general audience. Here again there are budget implications. The TV person could also have helped us to anticipate the editing process in structuring the testimony of each witness. In short, if you are going to reach a large audience to clarify an educational issue by using TV, don't go into the process with one hand tied behind your back. While I knew a fair bit about the issues surrounding MCT, I knew nothing about the medium.

The Issue and the Model

My perception is that NIE was very happy with the Clarification Hearing. The hearings and NIE's effort were received favorably by the public. The process resulted in a NIE-sponsored product that may be seen by a very large audience of both professional educators and lay people, depending on how many PBS affiliates choose to air it. The hearings were seen as an acceptable federal presence in education—informative but not intrusive. I have heard since that NIE was considering using the model with other issues and this gives me pause. Care needs to be taken in using the clarification hearing model with some issues.

In some respects NIE was lucky that MCT was the subject of the first national use of the clarification hearing model, lucky in the sense that MCT is not a highly di-

visive issue encompassing deeply felt ideological or value-rooted positions. Moreover, it is not a burning issue in the minds of the public. You do not see bumper stickers that say "Toot if you're against MCT." You are not accosted in airports by people with signs that say "A Little MCT Never Hurt Anyone." Further, the possible positive and negative effects of MCT are rather easy to document and technical issues of testing are fairly straightforward.

I have serious reservations, however, about using the model for highly divisive issues such as busing or abortion. I also have my doubts whether it should be used for clarifying the issues surrounding bilingual education. I think that a federally sponsored clarification hearing on such ideologically based issues, which affect deeply held beliefs on both sides, could cause great mischief. The composition of the two teams and the selection of the hearing officer could touch off protests from groups on the right and left of the issue. Cooperation and data sharing would be difficult. I would anticipate severe and bitter fights over the admissability of evidence and witness testimony.

Thus, while I feel that the clarification model or some variant on it has the potential to illuminate a number of issues for various stake holders and publics not reached through more traditional evaluations, I think the issue needs to be chosen with care, particularly if federal funds are involved.

The Team

The first task I faced after agreeing to be the team leader for the con or negative team was to build a team. This is a crucial step in the process. In choosing team members I tried to select peers who could serve an outreach function to the various constituencies concerned about MCT. I was blessed with a superb team. Ours was truly a team effort from beginning to end.[1]

Unfortunately because of budget limitations, we met as a team only twice prior to the hearing. The first occasion was a meeting in Washington to orient both

teams. Our second meeting in January was devoted to the development of strategy for case building and identifying potential witnesses and groups to contact. While subsets of the team met from time to time, the whole team never came together again until the hearing. Further, the budget did not cover very much in the way of the team members time once the days for the two meetings, the hearings, and the editing were deducted. If the model is ever used again the budget should accommodate at least three or four team meetings prior to the hearing and sufficient funds to cover the team members' work during the case-building process. There was altogether too much "contributed service" on the part of generous team members. Both teams should come together for the two final data-sharing sessions and for both sessions with the hearing officer. Once again, these recommendations would increase the cost of the project. However, it does little good to have an excellent team but not be able to optimally utilize their talent.

There were disagreements on some details of strategy and on a few issues and there was one that is worth recounting. What part should team members play at the actual hearing? Originally I was not comfortable with handling all the direct and cross-examination myself. I felt that each team member, if he or she wished, should participate to some extent in both of these functions. Some team members disagreed. They felt that if all eight of us were directly involved in examining witnesses it would be confusing to the TV audience viewing the edited copies (another example of how the spectre of the TV production influenced us). Further, there was some sentiment that the direct and cross-examination should be handled by someone with trial experience. However, most of us felt that if the JEM was to work non-lawyers should be able to handle those functions. After polling the team it was agreed that the task of direct and cross-examination would be split between Diana Pullin and myself. Instinctively I was troubled by the decision. A few weeks before the hearing I reconsidered after one team member asked what the team would do during the hearing other than sit and take notes. At the 11th hour I decided that all team members would participate in either the direct examination and/or cross-examination of witnesses. I would recommend this course to anyone using the model. People in the audience and those who viewed the TV version commented on the team participation and involvement. We looked and acted like a team. Those who originally had reservations also agreed that this involvement was beneficial.

Budget

One serious reservation about applying the JEM on a national scale is the cost. Each team had a budget of $107,000 with which to work. An additional $100,000 went to a subcontractor for project management and for the hearing. About $250,000 (I do not know the exact amount) went to MPB for the TV component.

One hundred thousand dollars is simply not sufficient to do the job correctly. Travel for the team to meet before, during, and after the hearing, and for data sharing and meeting with the hearing officer; travel for 30 witnesses to come to Washington, and for case development—all this took a large chunk out of the budget. In keeping a daily log of my activities I found the job to be nearly a full-time one from December through July, although I was budgeted for quarter time. As I mentioned earlier, the budget for team members was stingy and only their generosity made some of the work possible.

The budget did not permit us to do research, as originally planned, nor did it permit a first-hand investigation of the sites chosen by the opposing team. On the first point we had to rely pretty much on what was out there and much of that was simply testimony or hearsay. There were a number of issues on which we would have liked to have gathered data, but we could not because of the costs. Bob Linn did the analysis of extant data tapes to illustrate points about the cut score, measurement

error and item bias, but that was the extent of our original research. For the rest we collated the data, testimony and hearsay that we found, primarily by mail and phone.

Not being able to visit the opposing teams sites was a major disadvantage. While we had a very broad outline of what each of their witnesses was going to say, the best we could do was to call them or contact individuals who might help us develop a line of cross-examination. This approach was not very beneficial. Our cross-examination was by far the weakest aspect of our case. However, if we had had the funds to go to each site, and could have gotten the necessary cooperation to interview and observe for a week or so I am confident that we could have turned up rebuttal witnesses or at least better lines of cross-examination. Whether those rebuttal witnesses would have felt free to testify is another matter to which I will return.

A national Clarification Hearing is not cheap and the funds expended on this project do not reflect what is needed to do the job adequately. I have already made a number of suggestions that would increase the costs. As Jim Popham said to me at one point, it's a matter of a 15-watt bulb for illumination instead of 100 watts. The basic question is whether additional wattage can be justified through a cost benefit analysis.

Time

One major difference between the JEM and the actual judicial process is that the JEM has sharp time limits for practical reasons related to budget and audience. Direct, cross, redirect and recross are all constrained by a fixed time limit.

A good deal of witness preparation involved timing. A major decision we had to make was how much of our time should be allocated to direct and how much to cross-examination. At one point we felt that we would cross only a few witnesses husbanding our time for our case in chief. Eventually I think we cross-examined all but two witnesses. However, in editing the tape for "Who's Keep-

ing Score" we selected very little cross-examination, using our precious 75 minutes for direct testimony.

We employed two stop watches to keep track of time. The cross-examination of one witness was progressing very well but we were forced to cut it short because we had gone over our allotted time. Another 5 to 10 minutes and we might have made some very telling points. Whether they would have been included in the edited version is another question. If we had turned up a witness to directly rebut a pro witness we would have been faced with an interesting time trade off between rebuttal and direct testimony.

Considerations related to time influenced the kind of case we chose to develop. There were two strategies. The first was to develop only a few points and have all witnesses hammer repeatedly at the same theme. The pro team selected this strategy and it was very effective. It is easier for the audience to follow the more limited arguments, and repetition hammers the points home.

The second strategy and the one we followed was dubbed by Wade Henderson as "the death by a thousand cuts." We felt that in addition to the three issues there were a number of important contentions that also had to be developed—for example, the technical limitation of tests when used for certification—if the issues surrounding MCT were to be truly clarified and illuminated. Further, as far as possible, the views of various concerned groups had to be represented. This involved allocating time across many points and constituencies.

I did not have a good solution to the problem of the time constraints associated with the model. However, two teams jointly developing a documentary with a TV crew would, I feel, have been able to clarify the issues and contentions more effectively and efficiently with less time than was needed for the 3 days of hearings.

The Negative or Con Label

The label con or negative team was a difficult burden to carry for a number of reasons. First, being against competency testing is akin to being against motherhood. The adjective "competency" in front of the noun "test" puts the opposition in a difficult position. Second, it is always difficult to argue against the status quo, not to mention trying to prove a negative. Certainly our side was the more threatening one to established programs. This, in turn, made it difficult to gain entry to programs or to obtain data we wanted to investigate. Why should an administrator collaborate on a process that might involve dirty linen appearing on national television?

Third, we had to repeatedly emphasize that our team was not antitesting or against standards. Fourth, we felt that we had to spend part of our time and resources presenting an alternative to MCT. In short, I felt our side had to carry a heavier burden of proof.

Perhaps the most difficult aspect of the negative label was trying to get school people to testify. Very often we were told of problems endemic to MCT but the person did not feel free to testify because either district or state administrators were sold on the program. For a while we even wrestled with ways witnesses might remain anonymous. We were very explicit in warning people that there might be a backlash associated with their public appearances. Further, we decided not to have students relate their problems with MCT because they might later be embarrassed by their TV appearance.

If the goal is to clarify and illuminate issues through TV then using the documentary approach might help to lessen the problem and the difficulties associated with the negative or con label. In fact, using such an approach might involve only one team with different views represented.

Project Management

Future uses of the model should involve one major change. After providing the funds directly to the teams, rather than going through the red tape of monthly billings to a third-party contractor, the fund-

ing agency should withdraw from the management of the project. Day-to-day project management should be in the hands of the hearing officer and his or her staff. Alternately analogous to a court appointed monitor, an independent group or individual appointed by the hearing officer could manage the mechanics of the project. The funding agency should not be involved in directly telling or even suggesting to a team what it thinks the team should or should not do; nor should the agency intervene with its view of what should be, in debates or arguments between the two teams. Such disagreements should be adjudicated by the hearing officer, or a designate, without either the explicit or implicit intrusion of views on the part of the funding agency staff.

At the very least the whole issue of the funding agency's role in the process needs more discussion. The JEM is held out as one that presents an opportunity for impartial pursuit of the "truth." When the funding agency or its representatives have an implicit or explicit agenda of their own related either to the substantive area being evaluated or concerns about backlash that might ensue, then it is no longer an impartial party in the process.

The Issues

A key ingredient in the process is the framing of the issues and the definitions of key terms. This is a place where I felt we went awry. Both sides thought that they understood the boundaries of the debate and the terms as defined. It turned out that they meant different things to the two teams. For example, we thought we were debating programs where, if a pupil did not pass a test, he or she was not promoted, could not graduate, or was automatically put in a remedial program. After examining them we felt that the South Carolina and Detroit programs did not fit these parameters. In South Carolina they do not use the test results as a sole or primary determiner for promotion or graduation. Further, the State's regulations forbid using the test score

alone to classify students for remediation. In Detroit pupils who fail the test still receive a regular diploma, but if they pass they receive an endorsed diploma. There was a heated, even bitter, debate over the inclusion or exclusion of these two sites. In the case of Detroit the pro team considered the endorsed diploma a form of classification. We were not aware of this variant when we agreed to the definition of classification and hence we objected. We did not know if we were opposed to endorsed diplomas. In the case of South Carolina, they argued that the test information was part of a classification procedure. We argued that it did not fit the sole or primary determiner criterion. The point is not to revisit these arguments but to recommend that a fuller discussion of the boundaries of the debate and definition of key terms should include specific reference to the actual sites to be used. This type of discussion, moreover, should not be put off but should come very early in the data-sharing process.

Data Sharing

Data sharing is a key component in the JEM. Unfortunately, there were weaknesses in this process, part of the problem being related to distance. The training tape showed a project at the University of Indiana where the two teams were on the same campus and worked closely together. It is very difficult to collaborate when you are 3,000 miles apart and only a small portion of your time is supposedly covered by the contract. True we did have meetings in which we were able to share data, but discussions of the TV process ate into the available time, and there were not a lot of data to share until about 10 weeks or so before the hearings. Rather than inundating the other team with all the material and leads we were following it was agreed that we would wait until the case was more or less firm before sending essential material. This was to keep the reading down to an acceptable level.

I do not know exactly how to overcome these problems except to say that the teams need more, or at least longer, joint meetings in which the actual evidence, testimony and cross-examination of each witness are discussed in detail. Exposing your hand completely at a joint meeting like a dummy hand in bridge is a difficult concept psychologically when deep down you often feel you're in a poker game. A joint effort at building a TV documentary might alleviate this problem. Another interesting variant might be to have one team develop and present both sides of the case.

The Hearing

The hearing itself was both stimulating and exhausting. Eight hours a day of hearings for 3 days coupled with nightly preparation is a fatiguing experience. Before the hearing some sort of introduction to the TV cameras is needed. Also, during the hearing a TV monitor should be provided for each team to give the team feedback on such basic matters as eye contact, posture, positioning and delivery.

On the hearing mode itself, I think once you eliminate the panel, decide to televise the proceedings, and are not evaluating a particular program with its direct acquiescence and cooperation, then, at least on a national scale, the hearing format is not the most efficient or effective way to clarify or illuminate issues. The hearing mode is probably effective and efficient at the state or local level when you are assured that the stake holders to the evaluation will be in attendance, and when a panel is constituted to make recommendations about a program that has agreed to this form of evaluation. Furthermore, limiting the hearing to the state or local level greatly reduces costs.

An interesting variant in the present model would be to have the two teams come together after the hearings to cooperatively make recommendations to design a MCT program taking into account evidence and testimony introduced at the hearing.

The Hearing Officer

This project was indeed fortunate to have as its hearing officer Barbara Jordan who was very ably assisted in her task by Paul Kelley of the University of Texas. There were at least two possible roles for the hearing officer. The first, and the one Professor Jordan chose, was that of neutral arbitrator: She set the stage for the hearings by describing the process, purpose and procedures; she introduced witnesses, ruled on objections, and acted as a referee. The second option was for the hearing officer to intervene directly by questioning witnesses. A minor problem with this second option was the already tight time constraints built into the process. A more troubling problem would have been that questions put by a nationally respected hearing officer could tip a case in favor of one side or another. The tone of the questioning might implicitly signal to the viewing audience a "decision" by the hearing officer in favor of one side. This would negate the benefits of eliminating the jury or panel from the proceedings. For this reason, I would recommend the first role as the most appropriate one when the model is used in a national context.

The Product

After the hearings each team had the job of editing their 4 hours of each day's proceedings down to 25 minutes. Several things became apparent immediately. First, the written transcript was not a particularly good guide for editing; material that read well did not necessarily view well. Second, our evaluation of witnesses made at the hearings did not necessarily hold up when we saw the tapes. It was very difficult to edit 15 or 20 minutes of testimony down to 2 or 3. Basically, this involved making sure that all of our arguments were covered by quick snippets. This, in turn, resulted in a final product that lacked depth and clarity. We were forced to ask

"Why 3 days of hearings if the most widely disseminated product is a bastardized version?"

There is a wealth of material in the full 24 hours of tapes, which could be excepted to develop into short tapes for specific audiences dealing with focused issues. For example, tapes dealing with all of the evidence and testimony concerning MCT and the handicapped would make excellent viewing for concerned groups and for pre- and in-service teachers. Similarly, the testimony on reading or on technical issues could be excerpted for teaching purposes. These potential spin-off tapes for special audiences or for pre- or in-service teaching could be a very desirable side effect associated with the full 3 days of hearings.

Conclusion

The model, with its public television component, has the potential to reach and educate audiences that would not ordinarily be reached through more traditional evaluation reports. Research on the model, or variants of it, should be pursued. Evaluations of the process now in progress should shed additional light on the model's strengths and weaknesses.

At the local and state level, with a specific program that agrees to the process, the model may be very useful, although it might tax the attention span and retention powers of the audience. When the model is used nationally costs go up substantially and the issue to which the model is applied must be chosen with care. Further, a panel to hand down a verdict is probably not desirable. More importantly, if the purpose is to clarify and illuminate issues for the general public and for various stakeholders through the television medium, then the question-and-answer, basically aural mode of the model may not be the most effective or efficient use of available time. Going through 3 days of intensive hearings using the question-and-answer format and then editing out 90 percent of the proceedings makes little sense to me. Rather it would be better to start out with the final product in mind and utilize the medium and its technology to its best advantage.

My experience with the Clarification Hearing was like my experience in the Army. After it was over and I was out I was glad I had the experience. I had learned all kinds of new things and met some wonderful people, but no way would I re-up.

Footnote

[1] The team members, who helped to develop arguments, located and prepared witnesses, helped with both direct and cross-examination of witnesses during the hearing, and assisted in the editing of the TV tapes were: James Breeden, Senior Manager, Office of Planning and Policy, Boston Public Schools; Sandra Drew, Chicano Education Project, Denver, CO; Norman Goldman, Director of Instruction, New Jersey Education Association, Trenton; Walter Haney, National Consortium on Testing, Huron Institute, Cambridge, MA; Wade Henderson, Executive Director, Fund for Public Education, Council on Legal Education Opportunities, American Bar Association, Washington, D.C.; Robert Linn, Chairman, Department of Educational Psychology, University of Illinois at Urbana-Champaign; Renee Montoya, Chicano Education Project, Denver; and Diana Pullin, Staff Attorney, Center for Law and Education, Washington, D.C.

While not a member of the team, Simon Clyne of Boston College was invaluable as an administrative assistant to the team.

15

Melvin Belli, Beware!

W. James Popham

Most children love to play "make-believe." Preschoolers often spend endless hours pretending that they are doctors, explorers, or—more recently—astronauts. Perhaps it is because I still possess these toddler tendencies that, when recently invited to play lawyer for a year, I readily accepted.

An Invitation Arrives

More accurately, in the spring of 1980 a representative of the National Institute of Education (NIE) inquired if I would be willing to serve as team leader for the "pro" side in an adversarial appraisal of the merits of minimum competency testing (MCT). The project would result in a 3-day Washington, D.C. hearing concentrating on the strengths and weaknesses of MCT. Although the hearing was to be conducted in a quasi-judicial manner, complete with testimony from witnesses, cross-examinations, and a judge (referred to as a hearing officer), there was to be no verdict. No jury would decree which side had won or lost. The thrust of the project was to *clarify* the issues associated with MCT for those policymakers who were considering the initiation, modification, or termination of an MCT program.

Several years earlier I had participated in a large-scale adversarial evaluation and had found a fair number of flaws in the approach (Popham & Carlson, 1977). This new project, fashioned more closely along the lines of the judicial evaluative model propounded almost a decade ago by

Robert Wolf (1975) appeared capable of remedying some of those weaknesses. Thus, I accepted the invitation to be the pro team leader because (1) I was positively disposed toward the potential payoffs of MCT programs, (2) I wished to learn more about adversarial evaluation approaches, and (3) perhaps subconsciously, I yearned to play lawyer.

In the remaining paragraphs I wish to describe, from an unabashedly personal perspective, the NIE-sponsored project which culminated in a July 1981 clarification hearing on minimum competency testing. Although the chief arguments that we produced in favor of minimum competency testing will be touched on in passing, the focus of this analysis will be on the *process* of the enterprise rather than its product. (For articles focusing on the pro and con team's positions see the October 1981 issue of *Phi Delta Kappan*.) I shall conclude by offering an overall appraisal of this project's version of adversarial evaluation, that is, the clarification hearing model, as a vehicle for dealing with public policy issues.

Team Choosing

One of the initial tasks facing each team leader was the assembly of a group of individuals who would carry out the project. I had spoken with my counterpart George Madaus, who would be leading the con team, and he indicated an intent to form a team of senior professionals drawn from various parts of the country. George's plan was to select indi-

viduals representing various constituencies concerned with MCT, for he anticipated that his team members would thus be able to aid in securing witnesses representing such constituencies.

As I contemplated the possible strategies that might be employed to defend the raptures of minimum competency testing, I concluded that we were apt to rely heavily on witnesses who were familiar with on-going MCT programs. Being unable to anticipate from whence such witnesses would be drawn, I sensed the probable need for our team to do a good deal of searching for our witnesses. I also wanted to work closely with my team members, thinking through our strategy, tactics, and witness-gathering schemes. I chose, therefore, to enlist a predominantly local team consisting of (1) an experienced attorney conversant with the conduct of informal arbitration hearings (Professor Reginald Alleyne of the UCLA Law School), (2) a seasoned school administrator familiar with the nuts-and-bolts of competency testing programs (Anthony Trujillo of California's Tamalpias School District), and (3) two junior professionals who, as trained researchers, would be able to play prominent roles in the data-gathering and strategy-formula-

Jim Popham is Professor, Graduate School of Education, UCLA, and Director of the International Objectives Exchange (IOX), Los Angeles, CA 90024. Specializations: Educational evaluation and policy analysis.

tion process of the project (Carol Bloomquist of UCLA/IOX and Celia Rodrigo of IOX).

Throughout the project's duration, particularly in its earliest strategy-formulation phases, the geographic proximity of our team members permitted frequent meetings of the team. As the project entered its data-gathering and witness-preparation stages, the geographic proximity of team members again proved invaluable. Because of our frequent meetings we were, indeed, able to function as a team.

Issues Formulation

Early in the project, all members of both teams met in Washington, D.C. with NIE officials and representatives of the hearing officer, Barbara Jordan, former U.S. Representative for Texas and currently a professor at the L.B.J. School of Public Affairs, University of Texas at Austin. (Paul Kelley of the University of Texas, Professor Jordan's representative, performed most ably throughout the project's duration.) The chief purpose of the meeting was to formulate the issue statements around which the clarification hearing would revolve.[1] Even though the 2-day meeting was initiated with a clear reaffirmation of the project's commitment to clarification rather than victory-oriented adversarialism, it was at this issues-clarification meeting that I first sensed the emergence of partisanship tendencies that, in time, would do serious violence to all participants' hopes that clarification rather than conflict would be the guiding spirit of the project.

Professor Madaus and I had met earlier with NIE officials to discuss the general thrust of the project. We had both agreed to carry out our respective teams' activities in such a way as to illuminate the issues associated with MCT. We agreed to share information, strategy, and tactics throughout the project—until the 3-day hearing itself. In other words, we had committed ourselves and our teams to eschew petty competitiveness aimed at winning rather than clarifying.

Yet in spite of this resolve, at the issues-formulation meeting I detected in both teams clear leanings toward one-sidedness in a dispute over the wording of issues statements. It was as though members of both teams could not squash societally spawned yearnings to *win*. At least some members on each team were, perhaps without clearly understanding why, attempting to couch the project's issue statements in a form that could be more readily defended by their team.

Although I could understand why it was that such tendencies were developing, given the early stage of the project, the surfacing of such partisanship did not bode well for the future of our ostensibly nonpartisan venture in clarification.

To summarize briefly the results of the issues-formulation meeting, it was agreed that the hearing would focus on the effects of MCT programs with respect to (1) students, (2) the curriculum and teaching, and (3) public perceptions of schooling. Having agreed to these three foci, our team set out to isolate an effective strategy to defend the position that minimum competency testing would yield more dividends than deficits.

Thickening Our Plot

As our team members appraised the situation, we were obliged to defend an entity that existed in multiple forms. The task we faced was somewhat akin to defending "government." Clearly, there are good governments and bad governments. We could no more support all forms of MCT than we could support all forms of government. We quickly concluded, therefore, that we would organize our case in support of *high-quality* MCT programs. Indeed, we conceived of our mission as informing educational decision makers about the attributes of MCT programs that would render them delightful rather than dismal.

We believed that our opponents, the con team, would be required to demonstrate that there were *inherent* drawbacks in MCT, drawbacks so profound as to preclude its yielding positive effects. All we

had to do was show that a properly conceptualized and well-implemented MCT program could yield positive effects. It seemed to us that, having cast the contest so that we were obliged to support only high-quality MCT programs, we really had the easier side of the case to defend.

We agreed that the bulk of our witnesses would be drawn from MCT programs that were currently working effectively. Although we knew that we would have to do some solid searching to come up with a set of witnesses from high-quality MCT programs, we were convinced that this would be possible. Although we planned to sprinkle our witness list with occasional nonschool experts, for example, measurement and evaluation specialists, from the very outset we planned to draw most of our witnesses from the real world of schools—from MCT programs that were working.

Another major strategy decision was drawn from our analysis of the core construct under analysis, that is, minimum competency testing. As we saw it, the public had thrust MCT on the schools because of citizen doubts regarding the honesty of public school promotion/graduation practices. MCT laws were frequently fashioned as a reaction against "social promotions" or the awarding of diplomas based on students' "seat time" rather than the possession of basic skills. Accordingly, we decided to organize a major thrust of our case around the *restoration of honesty in public school promotion practices.*

As any experienced debater will tell you, you're in pretty good shape if you end up defending motherhood, liberty, or truth. We believed that by casting our arguments so that we would be defending honesty, we would be aligning ourselves with the forces of virtue. And, of course, if the pro team was supporting *honesty,* then the con team would be seen as defending. . . .

The Arrival of Television

From the very outset of the project, it had been planned that the hearings would be videotaped, edited, and made available via videocassettes to interested parties. After Barbara Jordan had agreed to participate, however, there began to be talk about securing funds so that edited versions of the hearings would be televised nationally via the Public Broadcasting System (PBS). And then it became official. In addition to a 1-hour documentary TV program which would kick things off, three 1-hour programs drawn from the hearings would also be broadcast nationally. Participants found themselves preparing for a television "event."

As soon as the TV decision was confirmed, team leaders met with the PBS personnel who would be producing the programs. We were admonished not to "play to the cameras" in our efforts to develop a case. On the contrary, we were told to direct our efforts at the hearings for the live audience attending the hearings. The PBS folks were to cover the affair as though it were a news conference.

Well, as much as I would like to report that we were able to take these admonitions seriously, we could not. Both teams knew full well that the real payoff in the project would be the national TV audience. When our team, for instance, contemplated the size of the live audience likely during a muggy July in Washington, D.C., we sensed that the affair might be somewhat less well attended than a Rolling Stones concert. Thus, as much as we strained to adhere to the mandate "don't be influenced by television," we found ourselves ,definitely organizing our case around the contemplated television programs.

For example, we realized that only a small amount of the hearings per day could be used in a 1-hour television program. As it turned out, each team could choose only 25 minutes per day from over 6 hours of testimony. Accordingly, because my opening remarks were slated for 20 minutes—much too long for TV purposes—I incorporated a readily *excerptible*, 4-minute capsule statement in my opening remarks. At a number of points along the way, we also tried to anticipate the like-

ly editing process by building editable segments of witness testimony.

During the hearings themselves, the impact of national TV was nothing short of heady. Imagine yourself, for example, being readied for TV at a make-up table across from Ralph Nader. (He was, of course, using only consumer-approved cosmetics.)

And how would you feel being powdered and pancaked every hour or so? One make-up girl used so much pancake make-up on my sparsely haired head that she began calling me "Buckwheat"!

In short, although we tried to keep the impact of television to a minimum, we weren't all that successful. Perhaps, given the likely influence of the TV programs, it was folly even to attempt to downplay the TV end of the project.

Witness Recruiting

The fundamental strategy of the pro team was simple. We wanted to defend the proposition that high-quality MCT programs would yield positive effects on students, the curriculum, and public perceptions of schooling. Our task was to gather a group of witnesses who could offer convincing testimony on those three points.

We initiated our quest for witnesses by contacting officials in a half-dozen departments of education in states where we had reason to believe that some effective MCT programs were under way. These officials identified local school districts and individuals whom we could contact to discuss possible site visits. At this point Celia Rodrigo and Carol Bloomquist, two of our team members, played a prominent role as they arranged to visit school districts in eight states during a 3-month period. Face-to-face interviews were conducted with more than 325 potential witnesses. These would-be witnesses were usually teachers, administrators, school board members, students, and interested citizens.

All the interviews with potential witnesses were tape-recorded. Carol and Celia identified their "best bet" witnesses, then I listened to the tapes involving these

individuals. Subsequently, the actual set of witnesses for the hearing was selected by the total team. In addition to approximately 30 school-based witnesses, we chose a half-dozen expert witnesses who could address key technical or philosophical points related to the case. Included in the latter group were Professor Michael Scriven, Professor Robert L. Ebel, and syndicated newspaper columnist William Raspberry. All witnesses were then interviewed by telephone to discuss the thrust of their testimony. We subsequently prepared a set of questions for each witness and, in most cases, the essence of a probable answer. After mailing these documents to all witnesses, a second telephone preparation session was held with most witnesses.

In selecting questions for different witnesses, we took cognizance of the hearing's three issues, attempting to support each issue with the testimony of two or more witnesses on each of the hearing's 3 days. In matching witnesses and issues, of course, we were attentive to the experience and perceived credibility of the witness.

Our Issue-oriented Contentions

Although we attempted to put forward a series of general contentions, such as the adequacy of current measurement technology for the requirements of MCT programs, we attempted to organize the bulk of our case around the hearing's three issues. More specifically, our witnesses offered testimony on the following points.

Effects on Students. In general, MCT programs of high quality will have positive effects on students. These effects will be yielded chiefly for low-achieving students, but even average and high-achieving students will benefit from high-quality MCT programs. Positive effects on students will occur because of:

● *Mastery of basic skills.* More students will master basic skills as reflected by their performance on competency tests.

- Positive attitudes toward self and school. Many students will acquire more positive self-concepts and more positive attitudes toward school as a result of becoming proficient in basic skills.
- Mastery of skills other than the basics. Students will learn far more than the basics because those basic skills that are mastered will serve as stepping stones to the acquisition of other skills and knowledge.

Effects on Curriculum and Teaching. In general, MCT programs of high quality will have positive effects on curriculum and teaching. These curricular effects will prove beneficial for students at all levels of ability. The positive effects on curriculum and teaching will occur because of:

- Worthwhile curricular emphases: Clearly defined competencies, selected by an open decision process, will be more defensible than many current curriculum emphases which have often been unthinkingly inherited rather than rationally selected.
- Increased teacher effectiveness. Clearly defined competencies will permit teachers to enhance their instructional effectiveness by providing students with more time-on-task; that is, practice relevant to the competencies.
- Broadened curriculum coverage. Increased efficiency in promoting an MCT program's target competencies will result in more available time for other instruction, and thus lead to expanded curriculum coverage.

Influence on Public Perceptions. In general, MCT programs of high quality will have a beneficial influence on public perceptions of educational quality because of:

- Abandonment of social promotions. Performance-based indicators of student accomplishments constitute a move toward honesty in promotion practices, thus eliminating the awarding of "seat time" promotions and diplomas.

- Demystification of the school's curricular emphases. The clarity of competencies and the ease of interpreting the meaning of criterion-referenced test results will demystify the school's curricular targets and thereby heighten public confidence in the aspirations of the educational system.
- Improved pupil performance. Test-based evidence of improved student attainments will reassure an incredulous public regarding the schools' educational effectiveness.

We attempted to hammer away at these points throughout the hearing, not only because they dealt with the hearing's issues, but because we believed that our witnesses would be able to supply convincing testimony on each point.

The Hearing

The 3-day hearing itself constituted, for me, an unforgettable experience. I can never recall a setting in which I was obliged to be as intellectually alert for such an extended period. (The experience may be sharply contrasted with the intellectual challenges of a UCLA faculty meeting.) At the conclusion of the hearing I was both physically and mentally enervated. I have gained a new respect and compassion for trial lawyers.

Barbara Jordan ran a tight ship throughout the 3 days. (In passing, I must note that one of the most significant aspects of the whole project was the opportunity to work with this warm and wonderful woman.) We had to attend to time allocations and procedural rules zealously. Given our team member's careful monitoring of time allotments, for the 3 days we used up all but 48 seconds of our approximately 10-hour allocation.

I found the con team's members, in spite of the outright adversarialism called for in the hearing itself, to be cordial and fair. George Madaus was a living example that even an Irishman, under pressure, can be a nice person. The hearings, in short, were enjoyable.

Retrospect

In reviewing the adversarial model embedded in the NIE clarification hearing I have attempted to identify high-strength reactions to the whole enterprise. Briefly, I shall conclude by recounting these.

First, I am more positive toward this version of adversarial evaluation than I was to versions with which I have worked earlier. That there are problems with the model is clear. But that there is inherent virtue is even more clear. The single most important advantage of this approach is that its adversarialism permits the attraction of a far greater audience of concerned policymakers than would ever be the case were a written evaluation report to be made available to those individuals. Interest in the contest can corral a vastly greater and, potentially, influential audience. Would a written evaluation report about the virtues of MCT, even if issued in multicolored reports by NIE, attract as much interest as televised hearings? Hardly.

Second, I am still troubled by the possibility that there will be marked dissimilarity in proponents' prowess. In this instance the teams, as well as the team leaders, were well matched. What if they are not? Policymakers might erroneously reach a decision in favor of a weak position merely because it was well defended.

I believe that some technical adjustments might be employed to dodge this defect, at least to some extent. I propose that although there would be two teams just as we saw in the MCT hearing, that those two teams work in total unity during the case development, witness-gathering, and witness preparation phases. This effort would be to develop the best two cases that both teams could collaboratively construct. This total collaboration would be possible because until a week or so before the hearings, neither team would know which side it was defending in the hearings themselves. In other words, both teams would strive to produce the best possible case for each side of the issue since, via a coin-flip, a team might end up defending either position. Collaborative case building would reduce any skill disparities, at least until the hearing itself, when both teams would at least be working with the best strategic position and witness array that the aggregated team members could produce.

Finally, I am troubled by the substantial costs of the NIE project. Each team received a budget of roughly $100,000. There was approximately $100,000 more allocated for other aspects of the project. Our team ended up spending $85,000 for all phases of the operation. I am convinced we could have done the job for under $50,000 with a loss in quality of less than 10 percent. To make these sorts of adversarial ventures worth their costs, we must reduce costs to the minimum.

Policymakers will not continue to support evaluative endeavors

that appear to be more costly than necessary. While I believe that NIE officials made no major error in their allocation of funds for this project, since all of us were learning about the nature of the enterprise, hindsight permits me to see that we could have done a reasonably good job with much less money.

On balance, then, I found the NIE clarification hearing project a useful one—both from the perspective of learning more about MCT as well as about the adversarial evaluation process. It was an exciting 12 months from project's initiation to the final editing of the videotapes. I await with interest the results of an external evaluation of the entire enterprise.[2] But even if that evaluation made the whole project look tacky, I'd jump at another invitation to do the same thing. The 3 days in Washington, D.C. hooked me completely. I found that I *do* like to play lawyer.

Notes

[1] I was distressed with how little we seem to know about framing issues for such adversarial hearings, hence have attempted to write a brief speculative piece about the problem; see Popham (in press).
[2] An external evaluation of the NIE clarification hearing project, under direction of Gary Estes of the Northwest Regional Educational Laboratory, will be released in early 1982.

References

Popham, W. J. Framing issues for educational decision-makers. *Newsletter* of the Research Evaluation Program, Northwest Regional Educational Laboratory, in press.
Popham, W. J., & Carlson, D. Deep dark deficits of the adversary evaluation model. *Educational Researcher*, 1977, 6(6), 3–6.
Wolf, R. L. Trial by jury: A new evaluation method—I. The process. *Phi Delta Kappan*, 1975, 56(3), 185–187.

POST-TV SCRIPT

As can be seen in my foregoing remarks, I left the MCT Clarification Hearing Project with a fairly favorable disposition toward adversary evaluation based chiefly on the *audience-attracting potential* of that evaluative approach. I was particularly optimistic about the widespread audience that the PBS-televised programs might attract. In spite of a formidable array of defects in this version of adversary evaluation, I thought that its inherent capacity for snagging a large audience would override those shortcomings.

But, unlike George Madaus, I wrote my article without having seen the four videotapes based on the hearings. I finally saw the programs when they were shown during January in Los Angeles, over four months after they were initially available for screening from PBS. I believe the essence of my concern is aptly reflected in the selected Los Angeles viewing time, namely, Saturday mornings at eight o'clock in the morning—opposite *Woody Woodpecker* re-runs!

Distressingly, that wasn't a bad choice by the local L.A. station because, in all honesty, the programs represented something less than exciting TV fare. Contrary to my hopes, the edited one-hour videotaped versions of the MCT hearings were pretty dull viewing. My guess is that the programs would only be of interest to those who were already fairly conversant with the MCT scene, and most of those folks had probably made up their minds about MCT already.

Thus, my one big plus for adversary evaluation evaporated while I sat benumbed in front of my TV set of three Saturday mornings in January.

For me, adversary evaluation has been like a person whom I've tried hard to like, but ended up disliking. I genuinely believe that, in spite of its seductive appeal, adversary evaluation is too costly and too inefficient to warrant its widespread use.

16

Outcomes of the MCT Clarification Process

Gary D. Estes and Randy E. Demaline

BACKGROUND AND PURPOSE FOR
CLARIFICATION PROCESS PROJECT

The National Institute of Education (NIE) sponsored a project designed to clarify issues related to Minimum Competency Testing (MCT). The MCT clarification process was adapted from adversary evaluation methodologies, in particular, the judicial evaluation model. A brief background to the Clarification Process, its purposes, and its objectives, as outlined by NIE, are given below.

The NIE initiated a study in 1978 of MCT programs. The first part of the study was to collect descriptive information on the MCT programs across the country, resulting in program descriptions and typologies of program characteristics. The documents that were produced provided descriptive information on factors such as whether tests were locally or state developed; whether tests were used for graduation, promotion, or retention; whether remedial programs were mandated; and areas in which tests were administered (Gorth and Perkins, 1980). Although these data were valuable resources in characterizing MCT programs, it was not the intention of Phase I to evaluate or study major issues related to MCT programs and their policy or programmatic implications. It was too early in the MCT programs to undertake an evaluation of their effects. Phase II was initially intended to be a three-year evaluation. NIE determined that an evaluation of MCT as a good or bad phenomenon was not responsive to the current information needs or a most appropriate role for a federal agency. An appropriate role was to address the major concerns about MCT programs. These included (a) identifying the major issues related to MCT programs and (b)

Authors' Note: This article is based on work completed pursuant to NIE Contract No. 400-80-0105, P-13. The opinions expressed do not necessarily reflect the position of the National Institute of Education, and no official endorsement should be inferred. This article is a revised form of a presentation made at the Annual Meeting of the American Educational Research Association, New York, March 1982.

From Gary D. Estes and Randy E. Demaline, "Outcomes of the MCT Clarification Process," original manuscript.

providing information that might be useful to individuals concerned with MCT program issues.

The NIE (Herndon, 1980) identified three concerns that guided the planning of the clarification process.

(1) In spite of the rapid and continuing growth of Minimum Competency Testing, the quality of information available to decision makers is limited and tends to be clouded by the complexity of the issues and by the demands of different and competing interests.
(2) In order to clarify these issues, it is essential that the framework for the study recognize the social and political context of MCT and provide a structured forum for the presentation and examination of different perspectives on the issues.
(3) In order for the results of the studies to be meaningful and valid, it is essential that both the decision-making audience and other vested interest groups have an integral role in its design, implementation, and dissemination.

A traditional evaluation approach was not viewed as directly addressing these concerns. The judicial evaluation methods described by Wolf (1979) offered many strengths compared with the traditional evaluation process. Specific advantages cited by Herndon (1980) were that the judicial process:

(a) provides a public forum for the examination of these issues from different perspectives;
(b) allows for public participation in the process through the presentation of testimony;
(c) permits introduction of a wide range of evidence (documentary evidence, human testimony, quantitative data), the clarification of which can occur immediately through cross-examination, rebuttal testimony, and the like; and
(d) provides a forum for including the perceptions, opinions, and judgments of those affected by policy and program decisions through the use of human testimony. Often the more subjective forms of evidence can help put facts into proper perspective. Testimony can then be examined within the context of facts and situations.

The materials and information from the clarification process were targeted for a broad audience. Herndon (1980) indicated that the project was

to provide decision makers and other interested audiences a clear understanding of the dynamics of MCT, and to provide a vehicle for the involvement of parents, teachers, students, citizen groups, administrators, school board members, legislators and other interested parties in a process that will help inform policy at the state and local levels.

Five questions were agreed upon by the NIE and the Northwest Regional Educational Laboratory (NWREL) as the focus for the evaluation of the clarification process.

(1) How appropriate are the format and structure of the Clarification Process in Presenting MCT issues, i.e., in what ways does the Clarification Process help or hinder the presenting of MCT issues?
(2) Does the information presented represent a fair diversity of viewpoints on each issue?

(3) Does the information presented add to the current understanding and knowledge of Minimum Competency Testing?

(4) Do the audiences perceive the information to be useful in terms of pending policy or program decisions?

(5) What is the viability of this approach for other NIE efforts?

This article reports information on these evaluation questions.

Evaluation Criteria

A discussion of the criteria or the framework used to address the evaluation questions listed above will be helpful in reading or interpreting the results of this evaluation. Specifically, the questions above basically focus on the utility of the clarification process as an approach for studying MCT issues. The framework by which one judges the utility of an evaluation or study can substantially influence the degree to which it is judged to be useful or not. One concept that might be proposed is that there needs to be direct observable evidence that information from an evaluation or study directly influences program or policy decisions. This view might be characterized as reflecting a rational or systemic approach to decision making. This approach risks an insensitivity to the reality of decision making in which evaluation or study results will be only one of several forms of input. Obvious other key factors include political concerns, logistical constraints, and interpersonal variables. Patton (1978), in describing the results of studies assessing the utility of federal program evaluation, stated:

> None of the impact described is of the type where new findings from an evaluation led directly and immediately to the making of major, concrete program decisions. More typical impact is one where that evaluation findings provided additional pieces of information in a difficult puzzle of program action, permitting some reduction in the uncertainty within which any federal decision maker inevitably operates.

The orientation used in this evaluation of the MCT clarification process is similar to that described above by Patton (1978) and is consistent with the perception of Alkin et al. (1979), who offer that evaluation often has "incremental" rather than "major" influences in decisions. Specifically, the criterion used in judging the utility and information value of the clarification process was the degree to which it appeared to facilitate, influence, or modify the perceptions or ideas of the intended users. It might be helpful to outline explicitly a criterion that was not applied. A restrictive criterion that was discarded in judging the effectiveness of the clarification process information was the necessity of evidence demonstrating that the information from the clarification process was directly applied in making decisions about MCT. If evidence were available that the information was useful in discussing or deliberating MCT issues *or* in making decisions, then the clarification process would be judged by us to have an impact and utility.

METHOD

Hearings

Three primary data sources were used for obtaining information on the hearing conducted in Washington, D.C., July 8-10, 1981. First, a questionnaire was distributed and participant responses collected during the third day of the hearing. Initial plans in the NWREL evaluation design were to collect responses following each hearing day. However, at the suggestion of the NIE, NWREL agreed to limit data collection at the hearing to the third day. The primary concern for reducing the data collection from each day to the third day was to not overly burden observers at the hearing.

Three or four small-group interviews of five to six individuals attending the hearing were conducted following each day of the hearing. Reactions to the effectiveness of the hearing and information gained at the hearing were discussed. Participants were encouraged to provide reactions to the process used to clarify the MCT issues. The interviews were unstructured and lasted for approximately 30 minutes.

Finally, the evaluation teams' observations based on the three hearing days were an additional source of data. The evaluation team attempted not only to observe the hearing process, but also to note the number of people attending the hearing and other audience reactions, e.g., the degree to which participants stayed for the entire day, or came and went during the day, or the extent to which some staff preferred to observe the hearing on the TV monitors located in conference rooms outside the main hall.

State Data Collection

The NWREL evaluation design included plans to collect data from videotape audiences within states. Data were collected in the following states: California, Florida, Illinois, Montana, Texas, and Wisconsin. These states were selected based upon reviews by Gorth and Perkins (1980) and Pipho (1980) and through interactions with the NIE and the clarification process team leaders. An attempt was made to obtain variety in geographical representation, types of MCT programs, and stage of MCT implementation across states. Stage of MCT implementation was important since the MCT concerns are likely to vary as a function of whether there is a state test, local tests, or options, or whether MCT is still under consideration.

Each state was informed that a one-day session was planned in which the videotapes and written materials from the clarification process would be reviewed. Each state was asked to organize a group of approximately twenty, which would include representatives from the state education agency, i.e., the chief state school officer, or representative and other state department staff, and LEA representatives including administrators, teachers, and school board members. Additionally, it was requested that legislative representatives and representatives from special interest groups also be invited. A questionnaire was administered during the state data collections, and brief discussion sessions of approximately one-half hour were held following each of the one-hour videotapes. These discussions were tape recorded and transcribed for analysis.

Special Interest Group Session

A session like those held within the states was held in Washington, D.C. for representatives of special interest groups or national organizations.

ERS/ENET Meeting

The first day's edited videotape was shown to a group of 18 participants at the Evaluation Research Society/Evaluation Network meetings held in Austin, Texas, October 1-3, 1981. The group was composed primarily of individuals directly involved or concerned with evaluations, and it represented multidisciplinary backgrounds. Written and tape-recorded reactions were obtained.

PBS Data Collection

The Southern Educational Communication Association (SECA) distributed a questionnaire to approximately 125 directors of instructional television and programming managers for PBS stations across the country. The major purpose for collecting data from these sources was to estimate the extent to which PBS stations broadcast the clarification process videotapes. Follow-up phone calls were made on December 2, 1981 to a random sample of 28 PBS stations to assess the representativeness of the limited response to the written questionnaire from SECA.

NWREL evaluation plans initially were to obtain PBS viewer responses from interactive systems such as the one at QUBE in Columbus, Ohio. Stations in Omaha, Nebraska and San Diego, California, were contacted in addition to the QUBE station. The interactive systems were not in a sufficient number of households within either Omaha or San Diego to warrant collecting data. The QUBE station decided not to broadcast the clarification process series due to low interest and adequate other programming.

RESULTS

Attendance at the Hearing

On July 8, 9, and 10, the MCT clarification process hearing was held as planned. It was anticipated that 500 persons per day might attend. Tickets were distributed on the basis of this limitation and procedures were set that would allow only those persons with tickets to attend.

The actual attendance at the hearing was much less than had been expected. Audience counts were taken at different times during the three days. Attendance ranged from 140 during the morning of the first day to 42 near the end of the third day. The audience appeared to be evenly distributed across federal, state, and national organizations with relatively fewer local agencies present.

How appropriate were the format and structure of the clarification process in presenting MCT issues? Audiences agreed that testimony and cross-examination enhanced the presentation of the issues. Eighty-two percent of the audience at the last day of the hearing and 83 percent of the site-visit audiences agreed to some degree with the statement. Of the state visits, the most negative reaction came from California where 31 percent (10 of 32) disagreed with the statement. In Florida and Illinois, there was no disagreement with the statement.

Audience interpretation of "enhanced" should be considered. In California, there were several negative comments in the open-ended responses about the use of emotional data and the lack of factual or back-up data. This could account for the negative response to the question. On the other hand, in Florida, which had no negative responses, there were remarks about the discomfort with "bleeding heart" testimony and the concern with misrepresentation of facts. The relatively high ratings in Figure 1 combined with individuals' comments imply that the word "enhanced" was probably interpreted as adding to interest level but not necessarily providing valid data.

Finally, comments at the hearing and in state visits about the effectiveness of cross-examination and to a lesser extent the direct examination suggested that simply presenting evidence without the adversarial connotation might be effective. That is, the adversarial nature of direct examination with cross-examination appeared to enhance the interest value but not necessarily "sharpen" the information produced from the clarification process.

The clarification process offered the situation where a witness was allowed to expand on his/her own beliefs and was not necessarily required to produce hard data to back up statements. At the same time, many evaluation procedures fail to gather these subjective data that can provide important additional information. The question of whether the use of personal judgments enhances the presentation of issues was asked at the hearing and after showing all three tapes at the state visits. The data collected are summarized in Figure 2.

The data collected here are very similar to the data mentioned earlier concerning the use of direct examination and cross-examination. The audience appears to have equated the use of personal judgments with the use of direct examination and cross-examination in the hearing. Again, comments support the finding that personal testimony contributes to the interest value but not necessarily to the quality of information gained from the clarification process. Although the adversarial process of direct and cross-examination is intended to bring into clearer focus the points under discussion, little evidence was found that this occurred in the clarification process, even though viewers agreed that personal judgments and examination enhanced the presentation of information.

As will be elaborated later, the criterion used to evaluate the usefulness of the clarification process greatly affects how these comments are interpreted and the subsequent utility of the clarification process. We proposed a criterion that information rated as useful by the audiences could be a criterion for utility. In this sense, the aspects of personal testimony and direct/cross-examination were

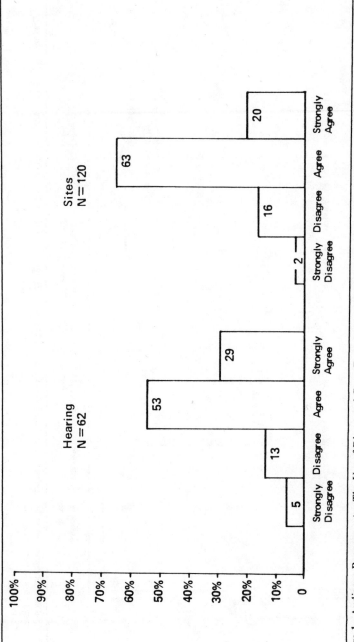

Figure 1 Audience Responses to: The Use of Direct and Cross-Examination Enhanced the Presentation of the Issues (responses in percentages)

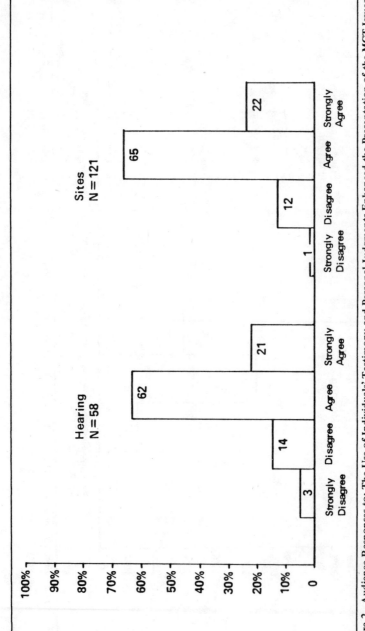

Figure 2 Audience Responses to: The Use of Individuals' Testimony and Personal Judgments Enhanced the Presentation of the MCT Issues (responses in percentages)

seen as strengths—strengths not necessarily proposed for the adversarial approach as described by Wolf (1979). In addition to interest, a perceived benefit of using personal testimony within an adversarial format is that individuals' "biases" are more clearly discernible than might otherwise be possible. Highlighting issues and variety of persons were also cited most frequently as strengths of the clarification process.

The question of the comprehensiveness of each team's arguments was asked at the hearing and after all three tapes had been shown at the state visits. The data from the question are summarized in Figure 3 for the hearing and Figure 4 for the state site visits.

It appears from the data in Figures 3 and 4 that the audiences saw the pro team as presenting a more comprehensive case than the con team. This was true throughout the site visits except for Montana where neither team was rated superior to the other. Finally, both teams, and thus the clarification process, were rated as providing comprehensive cases. Comments support that the comprehensiveness is largely felt to result from the variety of witnesses, MCT programs, and testimony/evidence that was presented. No strong consensus existed as to why the pro team was felt to present a more comprehensive case than the con team. Comments included that the con team's case was focused more on technical issues related to setting cut scores or unreliability of tests. It also is our opinion that this was partly a function of the ease with which the pro team's arguments could be identified with the issues under debate. The pro team's case was generally clearly related to effects on students, curriculum, or perceptions.

One of the last questions about the shows concerned the strengths and weaknesses of the clarification process. The major comments from the audiences concerning the strengths were:

	Number of Comments
Highlights the major issues and gives a sense of the pro and con biases.	32
Presents a variety of persons and opinions from various regions and experiences (the most mentioned category at the hearing).	27
More interesting and will make a better impact than written material.	22
Involved expert witnesses and people who have a sense of personal, emotional commitment to a viewpoint.	16
Good use of limited time.	7
Lively, exciting, dynamic presentation.	7
The give-and-take promoted discussion.	4
Dramatic quality.	4
Allows for probing questions and cross-examination.	4

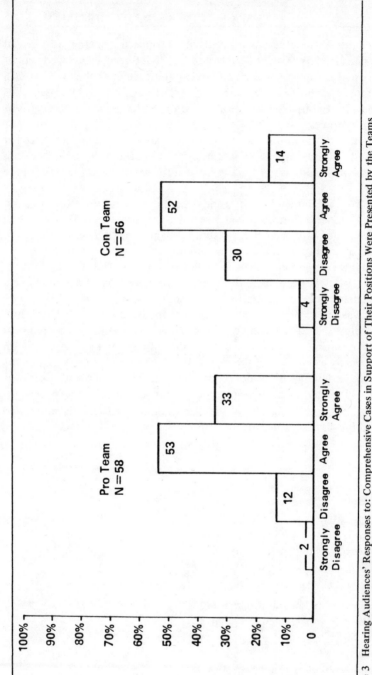

Figure 3 Hearing Audiences' Responses to: Comprehensive Cases in Support of Their Positions Were Presented by the Teams (responses in percentages)

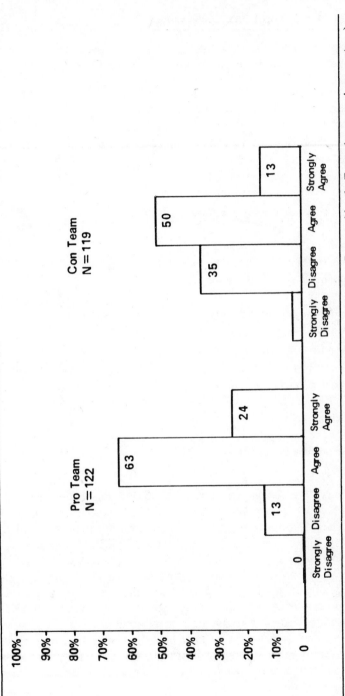

Figure 4 Site Audiences' Responses to: Comprehensive Cases in Support of Their Positions Were Presented by the Teams (responses in percentages)

The audiences were also asked to identify the weaknesses of the Clarification Process. The major comments concerning the weaknesses were:

	Number of Comments
Personalities can be more persuasive than facts.	14
Opinions without data and documentation.	13
Lack of structure and wavering from the issues (also mentioned at hearings).	12
Need fewer people, more experts, more depth.	11
Variation in quality of questioning and cross-examination.	8
Editing eliminates some clarification, truncates arguments.	7
Dichotomizes the argument; avoids middle ground.	5
Desire to win not necessarily to present valid arguments.	5
Superficial, oversimplification of a complex topic.	4
Lack of definition of MCT; not uniform nationwide.	4
Allows for possible inaccurate statements.	4
Too long.	4

In summary, the format and structure of the clarification process were generally viewed as appropriate in presenting MCT issues. Appropriate is best interpreted, based upon comments, as presenting information that highlights important MCT issues, makes good use of personal judgments, and provides an interesting format for presentation. Factors such as direct/cross-examination specifically, or adversarial format in general, were not cited as particular strengths or advantages for the clarification process. The strength of the adversarial process might be that presenting pro and con so that "both sides are heard" enabled the audiences to benefit from interesting personal testimony with some check on a major weakness, i.e., personalities can be more persuasive than facts. Finally, the number and nature of strnegths and weaknesses that were cited indicate an overall positive reaction to the clarification process *with* some concerns or reservations.

Did the information presented represent a fair diversity of viewpoints on each issue? Both the hearing and state audiences were asked to agree or disagree with a statement that the clarification process offered a variety of viewpoints. For the state audiences, the question was asked after each show. The audience felt that they were being presented with a variety of viewpoints that the average around 3.2 (Agree = 3). At least 81 percent of the responding audiences agreed with this statement and this was a frequently cited strength. A similar response was observed in relation to the question of whether there was a fair discussion of the issues. It should be remembered that one of the major reasons for undertaking the clarification process was for the NIE to sponsor a study that would not appear to support or decry MCT, but would provide information in a fair manner so others could make MCT decisions.

Respondents at the hearing and after each show at the site visits were asked to agree or disagree with a statement that the two teams presented clear arguments. The results are summarized in Figure 5. The edited tapes produced a more favorable response to the con teams' arguments than did the hearing. There was around a half a standard deviation difference between the rating of the pro and the con arguments at the hearing with the audience stating that the pro team presented clearer arguments. This difference was not quite as great in the opinion of the state audiences, even though the pro team rated consistently higher than the con team on all three shows. Even the lowest rating of 2.8 for the con team's arguments at the hearing is evidence that most viewers felt the arguments were presented clearly.

The audiences at the site visits were asked to list the information in that show which they felt was not useful. Table 1 lists the most frequent responses to this question. It is interesting that even though on previous questions the audience felt that the personal testimony enhanced the presentation of issues and offered a variety of viewpoints, it was the one element that caused the most concern when it came to useful information. This same concern appeared in the interviews after the shows. Also, the attack on multiple-choice tests, although considered valid by some, did not seem to be an MCT issue to the audiences during the interviews. Attacking multiple-choice tests did not seem equivalent to attacking minimum competency tests.

The listing of the special education students' parents in the second and third show is indicative that members of the audiences felt that special cases should not be used to attack MCT programs in general. Others in the audience seemed to find the use justified for the purposes of alerting viewers to potential problems that could be faced or needed to be avoided.

In summary, subjective testimony or personal judgments are viewed to add interest and to clarify *how individuals "feel" about their MCT programs* but doubt exists as to the value of the information in clarifying the issues. It appears these personal judgments are viewed as best for *highlighting* rather than *clarifying* issues.

Did the information presented add to the current understanding and knowledge of Minimum Competency Testing? The audiences at the hearing and in the state visits were asked to rate the amount of knowledge gained. The results are displayed in Figure 6. At least half of the site-visit audiences gained some

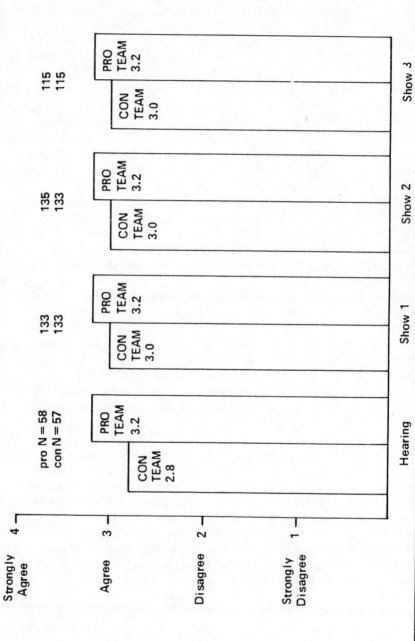

Figure 5   Audience Response to: Arguments Were Presented Clearly by the Teams (average responses)

TABLE 1   Responses to Question: Which Information Was Not Useful?

	Number of Responses
Show 1	
Subjective ("I feel" type) testimony	15
Attack on multiple-choice tests	10
Show 2	
Special education parent	9
Standard setting and technical material	5
Redundant testimony	5
Show 3	
Handicapped issue	7
Subjective testimony	5

knowledge from each of the shows, but the number decreased from 63 percent saying at least "some new knowledge" for the first show to 50 percent for the third show. This was substantiated by interview comments about the redundancy of the information contained in the third show. The major comments are listed in Table 2. In order to see what points the audiences were picking up in the hearing and the shows, a question was asked that had them identify the most persuasive points made by each of the teams.

From the hearings. Responses to pro and con team points were clearly targeted to issues of effects on students. Statements about the pro team also frequently cited effects on curriculum and public perceptions of education. Statements about the con team did not as often contain evidence for effects on curriculum or public perception, but appeared to focus more on specific effects or factors about MCT, e.g., cut-score unreliability and other cautions about using tests. Other points, even though not frequent from the con team, appear to be that resource allocations on curriculum/improvement strategies would be better than resources going to MCT. Combined pro and con team points might be characterized as providing information about (a) potential for MCT given some *actual* cases of positive MCT programs and (b) pitfalls to avoid in undertaking an MCT program. Little evidence was gathered to suggest that strong information about how to implement a program was presented.

From the state visits. Table 3 lists the major points that were mentioned by the respondents. Specific knowledge gained from the pro team's case appeared to be easily related to the three hearing issues. Individuals felt that the pro team points included that MCT could (a) assist to identify students in need of remedial instruction, (b) facilitate in assessing individual students' strengths and weaknesses, and (c) reduce discrimination in schools by identifying students' educational deficiencies and thus reveal any potential discrimination that might have led to the deficiencies. Effects on curriculum were related to arguments that

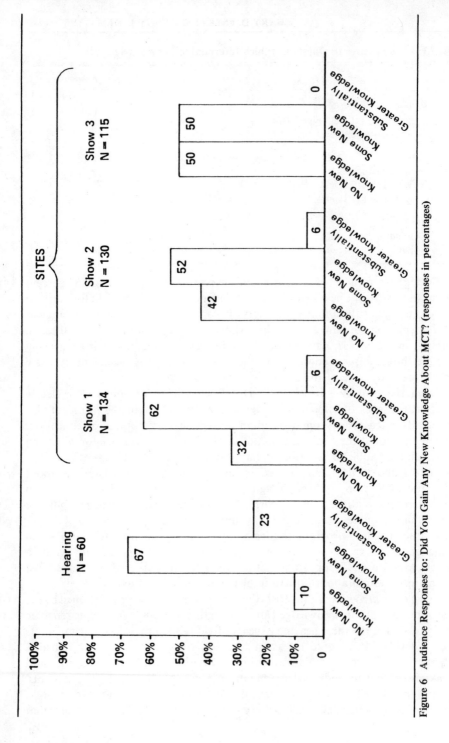

Figure 6 Audience Responses to: Did You Gain Any New Knowledge About MCT? (responses in percentages)

TABLE 2   Responses to Question: Did You Gain Any New Knowledge
About MCT?

	Number of Responses
Show 1	
Specific information about particular MCT programs	18
MCT may lead to less local control	5
Effect on curriculum–standardized vs. individualized	3
Show 2	
Specific practices and results of state and local districts	9
Impact on special categories of students (handicapped, non-English speaking, mobile)	8
Chance of undue failure on repeated testing small	7
Concerns of test validity	3
Relationship of MCT to life success	3
Show 3	
The variation among MCT programs	3
38 states already have MCT	3
Effect on "high risk" students	3

(a) MCTs were useful for identifying instructional objectives, (b) they helped to focus curriculum across schools, districts, or a state, and (c) standardized instruction resulted in more efficient remediation of basic skills and thus greater flexibility in other areas. Finally, the above points appeared to be somewhat persuasive in convincing viewers that MCT would have a positive influence on the public perception of education. An example is several viewer comments related to the fact MCTs might assist in reducing discrimination and in improving educational programs.

Information gained from the con team's case can also be classified around effects on students, curriculum, and public perception of education. However, the points were addressed through a different perspective and were not seen to be as clearly related to the hearing issues as was the pro team's case. Arguments about effects on students focused on negative effects of labeling students who fail MCT, effects of unreliable tests, and cut scores and effects due to lost educational opportunities if students were retained in grades or denied high school diplomas. Effects on the curriculum included reduced curricular emphases due to overly focused attention on minimums, teaching to the test versus teaching toward skills or objectives, and reduced number of courses available as a result of the increased number of remedial classes. Effects on public perception appeared to center on the above issues and on the fact that MCTs would not by themselves have a positive impact on education or on the public's perception of education.

Although the cases can be related to the three hearing issues, comments from both the edited videotapes and the hearing indicated that the audiences did not

TABLE 3   Major Points in Presentations Identified by Respondents

	Number of Responses
SHOW 1	
Pro	
MCT identifies individual needs for remediation.	31
MCT programs increase accountability, credibility, and public confidence.	26
MCT focuses objectives and improves the curriculum.	26
MCT assures that necessary skills are being mastered.	13
Con	
No single test should be a sole criterion.	39
Tests and test items are imperfect.	22
MCT reduces local control of curriculum.	10
Tests do not match what is taught.	10
Tests are redundant sources of information.	8
Minimums can become maximums.	7
SHOW 2	
Pro	
Districts can have positive results.	25
MCT increases accountability, credibility, and public confidence.	10
Passing levels can be made with informed judgment.	9
There is a better chance of students receiving instruction and remediation.	8
Minority children also need the skills.	8
Making choices (as in multiple-choice tests) is a way of life.	7
There is a low chance of repeated undue failure.	7
Teachers should be involved with MCT development.	5
Expect high, get high.	5
Con	
MCTs are culturally biased.	15
Misclassification and labeling of students is dangerous.	14
Curriculum can be narrowed.	13
Tested skills do not imply success in life.	10
Cut-off scores are arbitrary.	9
Evaluation should not be based on a single criterion.	8
Tests often do not have curricular validity.	5
SHOW 3	
Pro	
Some school districts have been successful in upgrading.	16
MCT increases accountability, credibility, and public confidence.	13

TABLE 3 (continued)

Minorities support MCT.	8
There is an increase in positive attitude.	7
Con	
Schools can improve without MCT.	21
Tests determine the curriculum.	9
There will be teaching to the exams.	6
Cut-off scores are arbitrary.	6
Decisions should not be based solely on the test.	5
There needs to be special treatment for the handicapped.	5

perceive the pro and con teams to address the same issues, and that neither team was directly addressing the issues. Thus, although subsequent analyses of the cases and testimony reveal that it is possible to organize the teams' cases around the issues debated in the clarification process, this was not apparent to the audiences. This is probably a characteristic of the personal testimony approach to presenting information. This approach is characterized by individuals giving their reactions (which generally cut across issues). In the pro team's case, the general impression often was that MCTs are good, have helped focus programs, and generate public support. The con team's case was more often perceived as focusing on technical issues such as the effects of using a single test for high school graduation or grade promotion/retention. The pro team's contention that MCT was only one of several criteria did not result in a clarification of this specific issue since the audience expressed confusion about the issue, i.e., individuals felt no case was made that the MCT was used as a "sole criterion." In this case the audiences felt that the pro team had "defeated or won" this point by showing that the MCTs were never used as a sole criterion. The purpose of this example is to illustrate that the viewers gained knowledge that was not necessarily related to the specific phrasing of the issues debated.

Did the audiences perceive the information to be useful in terms of pending policy or program decisions? In the site visits, after all three shows had been viewed, the audience was asked to identify what MCT issues were of most concern to them and if the information in the shows might be useful to them. Table 4 shows the major issues that the audiences listed as the ones they were most concerned about.

After identifying the issues that were important to the audiences, they were then asked if and how the information would be useful to them. The three most frequent responses to this question were:

Being aware of what practices are going on	(6)
Identifying issues for discussion	(6)
Informing public about processes and practices	(6)

TABLE 4   Responses to Questions: What MCT Issues Are You Most
Concerned About? (5 or more responses)

Issue	Number of Responses
Impact on curriculum	17
Diploma attachment	11
Remedial program	10
Cut-off scores/standards	8
Loss of control for development	8
Criterion validity	7
Impact on minority students	6
Use or misues of MCT results	5
Emphasis on one test	5

From the comments, the information will be primarily useful for making persons aware of what is presently happening and the issues that need to be addressed. It will also be useful for stimulating discussion in meetings and workshops. Few responses indicated that the information was directly useful in making a decision or choosing a direction. However, the statement, "I plan on becoming more active to see that Illinois retains a local control policy," is an example of a decision or position facilitated by the clarification process. Again, it is positive that individuals who viewed the tapes felt they were useful for awareness or general discussion purposes. Seldom are decisions or judgments based upon "revelations" obtained from a single experience or source of information, but the clarification process can assist with discussions, deliberations, or decisions about MCT.

Four possible functions were identified for the information from the hearing and shows. Viewers were asked to rate the usefulness of the information for performing four functions.

(1) Formulating a policy about adopting an MCT program.
(2) Assisting with the implementation of an MCT program.
(3) Informing the general public about MCT.
(4) Revising or dropping an MCT program.

(The fourth function was rated only on the questionnaire given at the site visits.) Figures 7 and 8 contain responses for the hearing and state audiences, respectively. The findings are very important in that they reflect the overall utility of the product for the states. Some very interesting patterns can be seen from Figures 7 and 8.

First, the audiences in the states and at the hearing saw the information as more useful in the areas of formulating policy and informing the public, and less useful in the areas of assisting implementation and revising or dropping a program. For areas of general informational need, the audiences saw the information as useful. When specific information is needed, such as in the

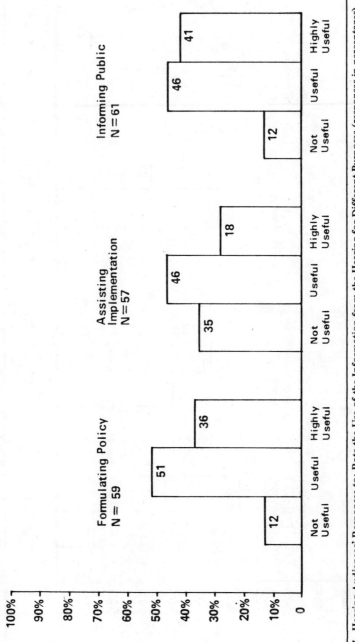

Figure 7 Hearing Audiences' Responses to: Rate the Use of the Information from the Hearing for Different Purposes (responses in percentages)

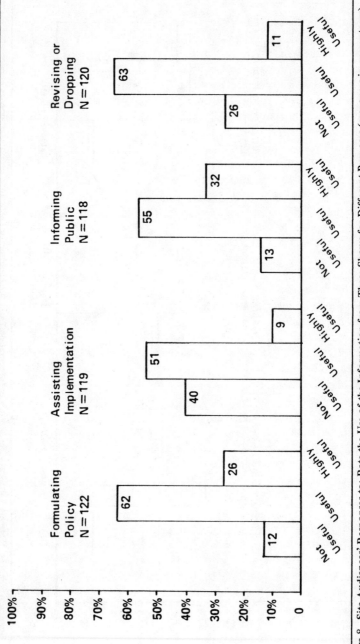

Figure 8   Site Audiences' Responses to: Rate the Use of the Information from These Shows for Different Purposes (responses in percentages)

implementation or revising/dropping functions, the information was not seen as useful.

Audiences also rated watching the video presentation as more interesting than reading a report. Their main concern was their inability to analyze and check the validity of the data for themselves. The negative response from the Florida audience could be because this question came after the third show. During the final arguments of the con team in the third show, a strong point is made that if the cut-off score for the Florida test were lowered by three points, 11,000 more students would receive their diplomas. The Florida concern stemmed from the fact that no Florida student to date has been denied a diploma based on the test. This led then to comments concerning the clarification process's proneness to "gross misrepresentation of facts."

For the parts of the audience that responded positively to the video presentation method, the main emphasis was the appropriateness of the tapes for a variety of audiences that specifically included parents and school board members. It was felt they might be willing to spend a few hours viewing and discussing the tapes but would probably be unwilling to invest even the same time in reading a report.

The results in Figure 9 to the question about the usefulness of the *User's Guide* differ from the results obtained when the audience was asked the same question about the edited tapes. The mean answer for all three uses is around 2.1 where "2" is "useful." Therefore the *User's Guide* was rated as equally useful in all three categories, although somewhat greater variability was noted for responses to informing the public. Additionally, ratings of 2.1 for the *User's Guide* were higher than videotape ratings for assisting with implementation (1.7) and revising or dropping (1.9) and they were lower than those for informing the general public (2.4). This supports the conclusion stated earlier that the written materials support areas cited as weaknesses about the videotapes. The audiences responded that the *User's Guide* would be a useful resource after viewing the videotapes and would be more useful than the videotapes in actually making program or policy decisions.

One caveat is needed in concluding that the clarification process accomplished its objectives. Specifically, a high level of "self-generated" interest in using the clarification process information has not been evidenced to date in information obtained within this evaluation. Six states declined to participate in a one-day meeting and, within states, individuals did not express overwhelming interest. In summary, once the information is viewed, positive responses are made. It is important that dissemination-type efforts such as those initiated by the NIE be continued and that support, fiscal and personnel, be provided for these efforts.

It is important to note that the viability and attractiveness of the clarification process rests largely on the fact that a video format was rated superior to a written format in generating audience interest and in being useful for stimulating discussion on issues. This statement does not negate the need for written materials like the *User's Guide* to support the videotapes. The written materials

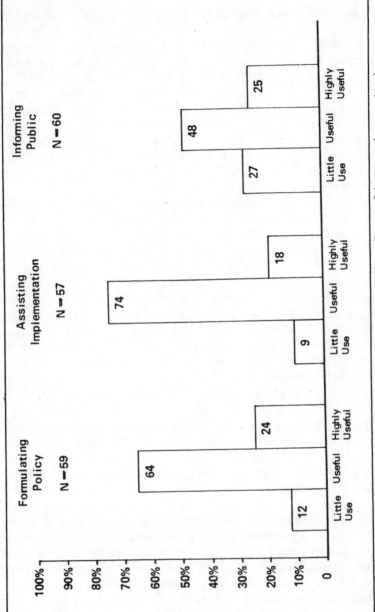

Figure 9 Site Audiences' Responses to: How Would You Rate the *User's Guide* for Different Purposes? (responses in percentages)

address some of the criticisms related to checking data mentioned above. Finally, it is less clear that the adversarial aspect of the clarification process was felt to be a strong contributor to the interest in the materials.

Information from Public Broadcasting Services (PBS) Stations

One of the anticipated outcomes was that PBS stations across the country would broadcast the documentary and the three hearing tapes. They were originally scheduled to air September 17 and the three successive Thursdays thereafter. It was left up to the individual PBS stations whether they would broadcast the shows then, at a later time, or at all. Questionnaires regarding the broadcasting of the shows and their comments concerning the quality were sent by the Southern Educational Communication Association to the PBS stations across the country.

Twenty-eight questionnaires were returned. Of the 28, 19 (68 percent) planned to show at least the documentary. To get an idea of the representativeness of this sample, a random sample of 28 PBS licensees from the *Directory of Information Sources for Public Television CPB* were contacted to find if they had shown or were going to show the programs. Of this sample, 14 (50 percent) responded positively. This implies that the sample of questionnaires seems to overrepresent the percentage of stations that will air the programs.

The stations were asked to identify the dates and times that they would be showing the tapes. This information is presented in Table 5. Although some of the stations are showing the programs during evening hours, the majority are showing them during nonprime hours. It appears that the stations did not consider the MCT material to be of sufficient interest to warrant prime-time broadcasts. Two of the stations are providing a follow-up session.

Comments concerning the length of the programs and the series primarily noted that it was too long. Most stations (and this was also mentioned in the telephone calls) said that 30-minute segments are easier to schedule than 60-minute segments. Comments concerning the production quality of the programs were also collected. For the documentary, only one station replied "average" while the rest stated "good" to "excellent." Comments were made that the content could have been condensed and that the documentary seemed biased toward the con viewpoint.

For the edited tapes, the comments were not as positive, although six stations responded "fine" to "very good" and four said they had not seen the tapes yet. Comments ranged from "ho-hum," "uninspired and uninspiring," and "not as good as *Advocates*," to constructive comments such as "many edits," "too much data," and "content could have been condensed."

CONCLUSIONS AND RECOMMENDATIONS

This discussion is organized around the five major evaluation questions. The viability question is addressed first with responses to other questions viewed as

TABLE 5 Responses on Dates and Times Shows Were Aired

Respondent	Documentary			Program 1			Program 2			Program 3		
1	10/13	(11:00 p.)	3	10/24	(noon)	7	10/31	(noon)	7	11/17	(noon)	7
	10/17	(noon)	7									
2	10/25	(5:00 p.)	1	10/25	(6:00 p.)	1	11/1	(6:00 p.)	1	11/8	(6:00 p.)	1
3	TBA			TBA			TBA			TBA		
4	9/27	(7:00 p.)	1	10/4	(9:00 a.)	1	10/11	(9:00 a.)	1	10/18	(9:00 a.)	1
5	TBA			Working with schools								
6	9/17	(9:00 p.)	5	9/24	(9:00 p.)	5	10/1	(9:00 p.)	5	10/8	(9:00 p.)	5
7	10/8	(11:00 a.)	5	10/8	(noon)	5	10/9	(11:00 a.)	6	10/9	(noon)	6
8	12/20	(6:00 p.)	1	—								
9	9/20	(3:00 p.)	1	9/27	(3:00 p.)	1	10/4	(3:00 p.)	1	10/11	(3:00 p.)	1
10	10/3	(5:00 p.)	7	10/10	(5:00 p.)	7	10/17	(5:00 p.)	7	10/24	(5:00 p.)	7
11	9/17	(8:00 p.)	5	10/1	(8:00 p.)	5	10/8	(8:00 p.)	5	10/15	(8:00 p.)	5
12	9/24	(6:00 p.)	5	10/1	(6:00 p.)	5	10/8	(6:00 p.)	5	10/15	(6:00 p.)	5
13	10/8	(10:00 p.)	5	—								
	10/13	(1:30 p.)	3									
14	9/29	(10:30 p.)	3	9/30	(10:30 p.)	4	10/1	(10:30 p.)	5	10/2	(10:30 p.)	6
15	9/24	(10:30 p.)	5	10/1	(10:30 p.)	5	10/3	(10:30 p.)	7	10/5	(10:30 p.)	2
16	12/19	(11:00 p.)	7	12/26	(11:00 a.)	7	1/2/82	(11:00 a.)	7	1/9/82	(11:00 a.)	7
	12/21	(6:30 a.)	2	12/28	(6:30 a.)	2	1/4/82	(6:30 a.)	2	1/11/82	(6:30 a.)	2

NOTE: 1 = Sunday; 7 = Saturday.

support and elaborations to it. Findings and recommendations on the process of the clarification hearing are reported elsewhere (Bourexis, 1981, Estes, 1982).

What Is the Viability of This Approach for Other NIE Efforts?

The question of viability of the clarification process or variations of it for future efforts by NIE or others might be characterized as a summative question. Based upon results of information collected for this evaluation, the clarification process appears to be a viable approach for providing information to audiences concerned with major education or policy issues.

Clarification process characteristics. In recommending the clarification process as a viable approach, it is critical to consider what constitutes the clarification process. Aspects of the judicial or adversarial evaluation approach include direct and cross-examination and use of this approach is characterized by stages in a case development process. These characteristics are intended to produce a variety of information that is more comprehensive than traditional evaluation approaches. However, the clarification process is distinguished from traditional evaluation approaches in another important dimension. Specifically, the use of videotapes to present personal testimony is a major dimension on which the clarification process differs from traditional evaluation approaches. In fact, it is not possible to disentangle the effects of using videotapes as a primary reporting and dissemination technique from the effects of using the adversarial approach in the clarification process. Future studies might attempt to look at these factors. One way might be to use written documents from a clarification process or adversarial approach as a primary means for communicating the evaluation information, and compare this to the more traditional written evaluation report. Another variation would be to present the results and findings from a more traditional evaluation report by videotape. Finally, fewer witnesses testifying in greater detail might increase audience participation, decrease the adversarial nature that did not appear to strengthen the information gained, and decrease the redundancy of testimony.

Given these caveats, information from this evaluation supports some areas of the process and provides cautions that might be helpful in future applications. Audiences found the videotapes to be quite valuable in generating discussion and identifying issues related to MCT. They felt that the videotapes were much better than written evaluations. "Better" was interpreted as more interesting. Additionally, participants or potential users felt that the materials were more useful for policy or general information purposes and less useful for program implementation or revision purposes. Thus, responses to the utility of the clarification process are consistent with findings of Worthen and Rogers (1977) and Wolf (1979) in which adversarial approaches were more useful for summative than formative type decisions. Respondents indicated that areas such as bilingual education, school finance, tax tuition credits, curriculum issues, special education and mainstreaming and competency based education are issues that might be addressed by the clarification process.

Timeliness. Given a recommendation that the clarification process is a viable approach, it is important to offer comments separately for the edited videotapes, written materials, and the hearing. First, those who participated in the sessions conducted for this evaluation provided positive reactions that the videotapes were an interesting information source. However, it is also notable and significant that twelve states were contacted to obtain a sample of six who were interested in participating in the sessions. While it is possible that factors other than their interest in the materials affected the decision not to participate in these sessions, the expressed reason in each state except one was the "untimeliness" of the information. Specifically, five states declining either (a) felt that they had already addressed the issues related to MCT or (b) did not wish to use the clarification process materials because they might raise sensitive issues given the current political or policy factors within the state.

It will generally be necessary to have a movement such as MCT somewhat underway before sufficient information will be available for a study. On the other hand, if the study is conducted after most decisions and policies have been implemented, then it is less likely that the study can have an impact. MCTs have been established in approximately 38 states, and it is likely that other states have considered MCT. Thus, much information exists related to the MCT programs and many MCT decisions and policies are in place. Given this factor and the evidence that the clarification process information is more useful for general information in making policy-level decisions, it appears that materials from the clarification process would be most useful in reviewing policy and informing audiences about MCT and its possible ramifications.

Use of materials. Although the clarification process materials appear to assist in highlighting issues that might need to be addressed in implementing or revising an MCT program, they do not provide specifics on MCT implementation-type decisions. These might include how to maintain student records in MCT programs, how to ensure test security, how to handle reciprocity of MCTs across school districts, steps to take in developing MCTs, and setting standards. The *User's Guide* will be more useful than the videotapes in this area. Thus, the combination of *User's Guide* and videotapes appears to have value even in states or areas where MCT programs are established. This use ranges from reviewing current policy or implementation decisions to identifying issues that have not been adequately addressed to simply informing audiences, e.g., a school board, about the range of issues in MCT.

The hearing. The hearing, which was an integral part of the clarification process, was not well attended. The strongest explanation appears to be the fact that individuals are not able or interested in committing three days to attending a hearing. Rather, the information in the shorter edited videotapes and *User's Guide* appears to have more interest. Given that individuals who attended the hearing and viewed the videotapes felt that some additional information was attained in the hearings, future applications should maintain some interest in the audience for the hearing. Interest in attending a hearing will be greater if the hearing is less than three days, i.e., a one- or at most two-day hearing. Attendance at a hearing might increase if earlier invitations were sent or if regional hearings were held in major population areas, e.g., Wolf's handicapped hearings.

Finally, the actual hearing might be critical for state or local applications of the clarification process in which local audiences were the primary focus. For a national study such as the clarification process, it is possible that the hearing can simply be the vehicle to get the edited videotapes. Given these factors, the NIE should not maintain the hearing audience as a *major* target for the outcomes of future clarification process applications without implementing a strategy to increase interest and attendance. These strategies could include (a) sponsoring regional meetings or hearings and (b) opening the hearing to inquiries or responses from the audience to increase the participation and potential pay-off for any attending the hearings.

Did the Information Presented Add to the Current Understanding and Knowledge of MCT?

Results from this evaluation provided evidence that individuals gained awareness-type knowledge as a result of attending the hearing and viewing the edited videotapes. The knowledge gained can be characterized as either reinforcement of existing ideas or identification of new issues to consider. Numerous examples of misinformation were cited by viewers, although there was no consensus as to specific items. It appears the clarification process is best described as having synthesized existing information that is helpful in understanding and discussing MCT. As elaborated earlier, knowledge from the pro team's case was more easily and directly identified with the three MCT issues debated in the clarification process. Other evaluation approaches will likely be as efficient if the objective is to generate new knowledge about an area rather than to summarize or highlight existing information.

Did the Audiences Perceive the Information to be Useful in Terms of Pending Policy or Program Decisions?

Audiences clearly felt the information from the clarification process was more useful for general information or discussion than for implementation or program revision decisions. The *User's Guide* was more useful than the videotapes for the latter. General interest in using the information was expressed. However, it is important to note that those participating in the hearing, state visits, or PBS survey represent those most interested in using the information.

It appears that the three one-hour edited videotapes are somewhat redundant and, in any event, too long to be used with SEA or LEA audiences. Several participants suggested that a one-hour tape summarizing the key points would be more useful. A one- or at most two-hour tape will be more helpful in training sessions. The reduced time in viewing edited videotapes can be used more productively to review materials in the *User's Guide* and to facilitate discussions and interactions among the audience in the session. In summary, the audiences felt (a) the information from the videotapes was useful, (b) three hours of videotapes were not needed and (c) the *User's Guide* is a valuable addition to the videotapes.

Finally, it is recommended that a greater proportion of attention or resources be provided to promoting use and dissemination of shorter videotapes and a *User's Guide* to capitalize on the potential benefits. If few individuals or agencies actually use the materials, it will not much matter that they would have liked them if they had used them. Recommendations included providing the materials directly to state education departments and providing training support for disseminating those materials.

Did the Information Present a Fair Diversity of Viewpoints?

The audiences felt that a variety of viewpoints was presented during the hearings and that a fair debate of the issues was provided. Thus, the proposed advantage of the clarification process to provide a diversity of viewpoints that fairly represents both sides of an issue was accomplished. Although individuals felt that both cases were presented clearly, the pro team's case was rated slightly stronger than the con team's in clarity of presentation. As discussed under information learned, this is partly attributable to differences in arguing for or against an issue as well as any factors related to the team's effectiveness. Finally, it appears, based on experiences from the clarification process and other applications of the adversarial approach, that pro and con sides of issues will generally rest on different assumptions and arguments or at least on differing values assigned to these. These differences are likely to leave viewers or an audience with the impression that slightly different issues were posed by the two sides. This appears to be a neutral characteristic that will be associated with pro- and con-type arguments.

A recommendation for the case development stages of the clarification process is to use the experiences from the clarification process in assisting to focus arguments on issues and to anticipate that arguments will not be perfectly "responsive to each other." Again, presenting information through individuals testifying versus through written documentation will probably affect the degree to which the arguments are perceived to be directly responsive to each other. That is, it is easier to lay out arguments in a point-counterpoint fashion when communicating in written form than in a hearing setting.

Audiences also felt that comprehensive cases were provided by the pro and con teams, with the pro team's case viewed as more comprehensive. Responses as to whether important data were presented or omitted, or whether misinformation was conveyed also support the contention that the clarification process resulted in comprehensive information at the policy or general information level.

As specified earlier, gaining information related to actual program implementation issues and more discrete level decisions as *not* cited as a strength of the clarification process. The focus was on the more general questions rather than on the specifics. One can hypothesize that issues framed on operational aspects of MCT programs might not be clarified by the clarification process. An example is, "Should alternate forms of an MCT be developed to facilitate test security and repeated assessments of students?" The clarification process is best suited for the larger issues, and more traditional approaches will probably *be at least as well* suited for the operational, formative-type decisions. On the question on alternate test forms, it might be effective to simply gather information and present advantages and disadvantages that would need to be considered in deciding whether to use multiple test forms. Given the advantages and disadvantages, it is likely that a decision could be made.

How Appropriate Were the Format and Structure of the Clarification Process in Presenting MCT Issues?

Respondents in this evaluation valued as interesting the use of individual testimony and personal judgment in presenting MCT issues. This aspect of the hearings and videotapes is a strength. The use of individual testimony is not necessarily a characteristic associated with the clarification process or adversarial approaches. It might be equally possible to present evaluation data using other approaches by incorporating video presentations.

Although the process of using direct and cross-examination was rated to enhance the presentation of issues, comments suggested that cross-examination was not particularly effective in some cases. Since no advantages were cited for the attorneys who conducted direct and cross examination, it does not appear that legal training necessarily increases the effectiveness of direct or cross-examination. This statement is made in light of the fact that several persons at the hearing and in state visits cited that the clarification process participants were not experienced in direct and cross-examination. At the same time, there was no indication that the participating attorneys were more effective than the nonattorneys.

Finally, it is recommended that future studies or efforts attempt to begin addressing the extent to which the adversarial nature of the clarification process, rather than the use of individual testimony and presentation through videotapes, contributed to the positive evaluations of the clarification process. It was not clear in the study that the positive outcomes were dependent upon the adversarial aspect of the clarification process or that they were more a function of the videotapes and individuals' testimony. Efforts for studies in this area will enhance evaluation utilization and impact.

REFERENCES

Alkin, M. C., Daillak, R. D., and White, P. *Using evaluation: Does it make a difference?* Beverly Hills, CA: Sage, 1979.

Bourexis, P. *Phase I Report: Process evaluation of minimum competency testing clarification process.* Northwest Regional Educational Laboratory, Portland, OR, December, 1981.

Estes, G. "An evaluation of the adversarial approach to clarifying MCT issues." Paper presented at the Annual Meeting of the American Educational Research Association, New York, March 1982.

Gorth, W. and Perkins, M. "A study of minimum competency testing programs: final typology report." Amherst: National Evaluation Systems, 1980.

Herndon, Enid. "NIE's study of minimum competency testing: a process for the clarification of issues." Unpublished, circa March-April, 1980.

Patton, M. Q. *Utilization-focused evaluation.* Beverly Hills, CA: Sage, 1978.

Pipho, C. "Analysis of state minimum competency programs" (Final Report for NIE #6-79-0033). February 28, 1980.

Wolf, R. L. "The use of judicial evaluation methods in the formulation of educational policy." Educational Evaluation and Policy Analysis. 1979(1), 3, pp. 19-28.

Worthen, B. R. and Rogers, W. T. "Uses and abuses of adversary evaluation: a consumer's guide." Paper presented at Annual Meeting of the American Educational Research Association, New York, April 1977.

III

ETHICS

The ethical and value basis of evaluation has been seriously neglected. Evaluators are not generally aware of what values are implicit in their techniques nor how different assumptions lead to quite different outcomes in evaluation studies. We have included a section on ethics in this *Annual* to draw attention to this important aspect of evaluation. There are not many such papers written each year, but there are a few worth reading. Perhaps in the years ahead evaluators will attend as closely to their own behavior as they do to that of the people they evaluate.

In the first article, "Risk in Benefit-Cost Analysis," Schulze and Kneese argue that benefit-cost analysis, at least as typically practiced, is based upon the philosophy of utilitarianism. Utilitarianism allows one to trade off the benefits and costs to one person in exchange for those of another. Only the total benefits and costs really count. Hence, building a dam that benefits one person is justified if the total benefits exceed the risk to a different person living below the dam, regardless of what the latter may think.

Other ethical systems call for a different weighting of benefits and costs. For example, a libertarian ethic demands that each person accepting a risk be compensated for that risk. Uncompensated risks are not permissible. By contrast, an egalitarian ethic would demand that the well-being of society be judged by the position of the person worst off in society, or an elitist ethic by those best off.

Schulze and Kneese's article illustrates that some of our most common methodological tools are embedded, usually unknowingly, in particular philosophical systems. These philosophical systems have different ethical consequences, often consequences we would not like. The authors suggest that benefit-cost analysis be broadened to include alternative weightings that are consistent with a variety of ethical views.

In "Handling Value Issues," Eraut offers practical advice to the evaluator. He contends that evaluators are generally unaware of the values held by the community in which they work, a condition he labels "value complacency." The evaluator usually promotes the values implicit in the evaluator's roles and procedures or else those derived from the evaluator's personal views. Eraut contends that most evaluators would agree that such unintentional transmission of values is undesirable.

He distinguishes between the intrinsic and extrinsic purposes of evaluation. Intrinsic to evaluation are estimations of worth and the pursuit of truth. Extrinsic purposes include the uses to which evaluation is put, such as for accountability and guiding decision making. Eraut accepts the idea that the evaluator must make judgments but rejects the notion that all data can be summarized by a good or bad label. Rather, the evaluator should recognize divergent value positions where they exist, help develop arguments for these positions, and examine how well these arguments are supported by the evidence.

For extrinsic purposes the deeper question is, what is the source of authority in an evaluation? Eraut sees two potential sources: the authority the evaluator has as a member of a research community and the authority participants have, which is derived from their specialized knowledge of a particular context. Eraut's resolution is for the evaluator to negotiate an evaluation brief as the basis for the evaluation, based upon four principles that he enunciates.

The article by Carter and Deyo, entitled "The Impact of Questionnaire Research on Clinical Populations," is unusual among these in that it is a report of an empirical study. Reservations about the effect of a questionnaire, the Sickness Impact Profile, on respondents led to a study to determine what effect the questionnaire had. Even though the SIP had been in development for several years and had cleared the usual procedures, some members of a review committee feared the instrument would depress the ill patients who were the respondents.

To resolve this issue the SIP was administered to a sample of patients and these patients were surveyed to determine what effects the SIP had on them. The overwhelming majority of patients reported that the effects were positive; only a few reports were negative. Hence, the ethical issue about this particular questioning was resolved empirically.

In "Confidentiality in Criminological Research and Other Ethical Issues," Wolfgang catalogs and briefly discusses several ethical problems faced by the social researcher. Although many of the examples cited are not those of evaluation research, most of the problems discussed are encountered by evaluators at some time or another. And, since the examples are drawn from criminology, they are rather more dramatic and extreme cases than those encountered in most evaluations.

Should the researcher go to jail to protect data? Should written consent from informants be required? Is the researcher obligated to report criminal infractions to the authorities? These are some of the sensitive questions that Wolfgang addresses. He ends by discussing the role the researcher/evaluator should take in making public policy pronouncements, an issue critical to evaluators. How far from his/her data can the evaluator go in making policy recommendations? Wolfgang cites his own court testimony in Arkansas as to the frequency with which blacks are sentenced to the death penalty for raping a white, but the issue surfaces later in the education section of this volume when one examines the conclusions of Coleman et al.'s comparison of public and private schools.

Finally, in his article on "Policy Evaluation," Fischer emphasizes the lack of attention to normative issues in current evaluation efforts. He notes the connection between the political form of governance known as technocracy and the epistemology that researchers in such a technocracy espouse. In a technocracy, those who govern are legitimated primarily by an appeal to technical expertise and scientific knowledge. Decisions are correct because they are scientifically based. A positivistic epistemology fits such an authority structure.

Unfortunately, within such a positivist framework, ethical and value premises are seldom examined. They are seen as being beyond the reach of scientists and hence not their concern. Only the means to predetermined ends are the subject of scrutiny and not the ends themselves. Discovering the most efficient means to preset ends is called "technical rationality." The scientist/evaluator is confined to this rationality in a technocratic/positivist framework.

Fischer discusses three ways of introducing normative considerations—a forensic approach, policy argumentation, and practical reason. Each has some advantages and liabilities. Unfortunately, each also leaves the basic fact/value dichotomy essentially intact. Nonetheless, Fischer's article provides a provocative discussion of one of the most formidable problems facing evaluation—the role and justification of particular values within evaluation.

17

Risk in Benefit-Cost Analysis

William D. Schulze and Allen V. Kneese

Received August 11, 1980—revised October 9, 1980

In recent years, benefit-cost analysis has been increasingly applied to large societal decision problems (such as developing a fast breeder energy economy) which involve both risks to society and analysis of very long-term consequences possibly extending over many human generations. This paper examines the philosophical underpinnings of the technique which is a special case of utilitarianism, and compares implications of the technique to those arising from alternative ethical systems in analyzing questions of public safety. Ethical systems which emphasize the good of the whole, such as utilitarianism, are shown to differ sharply in decision outcomes from those which emphasize the rights of the individual, such as libertarianism. It is suggested that benefit-cost analysis should be broadened to include alternative weightings of benefits and costs consistent with a variety of ethical views.

KEY WORDS: benefit-cost analysis; risk; enthics; public safety

1. INTRODUCTION

Benefit-cost analysis has long been used to evaluate public works, especially water-resource investments. A large amount of literature exists on this mode of applied economic analysis. This literature treats both conceptual and empirical problems, but for the most part does not question the basic philosphical underpinnings of the technique, which is a special case of an ethical doctrine called utilitarianism.

In recent years, benefit-cost analysis has been increasingly applied to large societal decision problems such as the disposal of nuclear waste, the costs and benefits of developing a fast breeder energy economy, and the desirability of storing helium for the benefit of future generations. These problems have two characteristics which tend to set them apart from the more conventional applications. First, they involve uncertainty and risks to society in a central way. In the case of nuclear wastes there are possible

risks to health and in the case of failure to store helium there is the risk that certain energy technologies cannot be developed for the long-term future. Second, they involve the analysis of decisions which may have very long-term consequences, possibly extending over many human generations.

In the case of these issues, concepts and techniques that were developed to help evaluate issues of the shorter term and less uncertain and risky nature are not obviously suitable for large societal decision problems. Ethical questions as to justifiability of imposing risks to life and health on people, possibly people in future generations, and whether it is proper to apply conventional discounting procedures when it would effectively wipe out any consideration of the long-term future, assert themselves strongly.

In view of this, the authors set out to examine the ethical foundations of benefit-cost analysis and what effect the application of alternative ethical criteria would have on the outcome of such analysis.[3] We proceeded by defining some ethical systems suffi-

[1] Department of Economics, University of Wyoming, University Station, Box 3985, Laramie, WY 82071.
[2] Resources for the Future, 1755 Massachusetts Avenue, N.W., Washington, D. C. 20036.

[3] We would like to acknowledge the help of a group of economists at the University of New Mexico and Philosophers at the University of Maryland.

ciently simply and rigorously to permit formal quantitative analysis. Then the criteria were used to "weight" benefits and costs in such a way that the outcome would conform to the particular criterion specified. By using this technique, we completed several illustrative case studies, including helium storage and nuclear waste disposal.[4]

We should be clear that we are not the first to apply distributional weights to benefit-cost analysis [see, for example, refs. (1 and 2)]. But so far as we know, we are the first to link these weights both to issues of public safety and to ideas emerging from the formal philosophical field of ethics. Some criteria emerging from this literature, as we will see, emphasize the good of the whole (utilitarianism), and some the rights of the individual (libertarianism).

We should also be clear that this paper contains material from what is essentially an ongoing research project. We plan to continue this line of inquiry and to try to deepen our understanding of the relationships between ethics and economics.

In this paper, we briefly, perhaps cryptically, outline the ethical systems we have examined so far. We then present a theoretical analysis of their implications for handling risk in the context of benefit-cost analysis.

2. ETHICAL SYSTEMS

As just indicated, to examine benefit-cost analysis from the ethical standpoint, it was necessary to define a set of ethical systems in such a way that they could be used as "weights" on the benefits and costs of proposed actions. The following were identified.

2.1. Utilitarian (Benthamite)

A utilitarian ethical system requires "the greatest good for the greatest number," based on ideas put forward by Jeremy Bentham,[3] John Mill,[4] and others. The social objective is to maximize the sum of the cardinal (measurable) utilities of all individuals in a society. For an individual to make an ethically "correct" action, all consequences of that action must be considered. As translated to a social decision rule,

the criterion requires that the government should act in such a way as to maximize utility of society as a whole. Depending on beliefs about the nature of individuals' utility functions, any distribution of income can be justified, ranging from a relatively egalitarian to a relatively elitist viewpoint. Benefit-cost analysis can be regarded as a very special subcase of the utilitarian ethic where individuals' utility functions are linear with identical constant marginal utilities across individuals and where future utilities are identically discounted.

In summary, utilitarianism argues that for a two person society with individuals A and B, where utility is denoted U, the social objective should be to maximize $U_A + U_B$.

There do exist ethical systems which are totally egalitarian and totally elitist. These diametrically opposed systems are described next.

2.2. Egalitarian

The egalitarian view holds that the well-being of a society is measured by the well-being of the worst off person in that society. This simple notion would lead, if fully adopted, to a totally egalitarian distribution of utility.[5]

The egalitarian criterion can be expressed mathematically as follows: For two individuals A and B, where utility is denoted U, if $U_A < U_B$, we maximize U_A subject to $U_A \leq U_B$; if $U_B < U_A$, then we maximize U_B subject to $U_B \leq U_A$. If we reach a state where $U_A = U_B$, then we maximize U_A subject to $U_A = U_B$. The implication of this for redistribution of income in a many-person society is that we begin by adding income to the worst off individual (taking income away from wealthier individuals) until he catches up with the next worst off individual. We then add income to both individuals until their utility levels (well-being) have caught up to the third worst off, etc. Eventually, this process must lead to a state where $U_A = U_B = U_C = U_D \cdots$ for all individuals in a society, where all utilities are identical, or to one where further redistributions will make everyone worse off, e.g., through negative impacts on incentives. This criterion can be written more compactly for a two person society as max min $\{U_A, U_B\}$, so we are always trying to maximize the utility of the individual with the minimum utility. Implicit also in the arguments is the assumption that individuals' utility

---

[4] A relatively full report on this work is found in a working paper of the Department of Economics at the University of New Mexico entitled *A Study of the Ethical Foundations of Benefit-Cost Analysis Techniques* by Shaul Ben-David, Allen V. Kneese, and William D. Schulze (August 1979).

[5] Contemporary egalitarianism is often associated with the writings of John Rawls [see Ref. (5)].

functions with respect to income are about the same. Thus, this ethical criterion would work towards a relatively equal distribution of income based on need.

2.3. Totally Elitist

An elitist criterion can be derived as the precise opposite of the egalitarian criterion. The well-being of society is measured by the well-being of the best off individual. Every act is "right" if it improves the welfare of the best off and "wrong" if it decreases the welfare of the best off.[6]

Lest the reader dismiss the elitist criterion as irrelevant for a Western democratic society, some elitist arguments should be mentioned. The gasoline shortage of the summer of 1979 moved Senator Hiyakawa of California to comment, "The important thing is that a lot of the poor don't need gas because they're not working." Economic productivity can in this sense rationalize a defined "elite." Thus, concepts of merit can be elitist in nature, e.g., those who produce the most "should" have the largest merit increases in salary (even though they may already have the highest salaries).

The income distribution implied by this criterion is not simply to give all the society's wealth to the best off. This is true because, if between two individuals A and B we are attempting to

$$\max \max \{ U_A, U_B \}.$$

or to maximize the utility of the individual who can attain the greatest utility, we must first find the solution for $\max U_A$ and then separately for $\max U_B$. and then pick whichever solution gives the greatest individual utility. Obviously, it will usually be better to keep B alive to serve A, i.e., to contribute to his well-being than to give B nothing if A is to be best off. Thus, subsistence is typically required for B. Similarly, if we have two succeeding generations, it may well be "best" for the first generation to save as much as possible to make the next generation better off. This attitude has been manifest among many immigrants to the United States with respect to their children. Thus, an elitist viewpoint may support altruistic behavior.

----
[6] The elitist view is often associated with the writings of Friedrich Nietzsche [see ref. (6)]. But, as noted in the text, less objectionable arguments for the elitist view can be made.

2.4. Libertarian

The fourth ethical system is an amalgam of a number of ethical principles embodied for example in the viewpoint of the U.S. Constitution that individual freedoms prevail except where others may be harmed. These views which emphasize individual rights have been formalized by Nozick[7] in a strict libertarian framework. We are not concerned here with changing the initial position of individuals in society to some ideal state, but rather in benefiting all or at least preventing harm to others, even if they are better off. This ethic has been imbodied often by economists in the form of requiring "Pareto superiority," that all persons be made better off by a change in resource use or at least as well off as before. Any act is then immoral or wrong if anyone else is harmed. Any act which improves an individual's or several individuals' well-being and harms no one is moral or "right."

The libertarian or Paretian ethic does not define a best distribution of income. Rather, the criterion requires that any change from the existing social order harm no one. If, for example, Mr. A and Mr. B initially have incomes Y_A^0 and Y_B^0, then we require for any new distribution of wealth (Y_A, Y_B) — for example, more wealth becomes available — that

$$U_A(Y_A) \geq U_A(Y_A^0)$$

and

$$U_B(Y_A) \geq U_B(Y_B^0)$$

or each individual must be at least as well off as he initially was. Any redistribution, e.g., from wealthy to poor or vice versa, is specifically proscribed by this criterion. Thus, this criterion, while seemingly weak — i.e., it does not call for redistribution — can block many possible actions if they do as a side effect redistribute income to make anyone worse off, however, slight the effect may be. Often, then to satisfy a libertarian criterion requires that gainers from a particular social decision must actually compensate losers [for a discussion of compensation, see ref. (8)].

3. ECONOMICS OF RISK

The economics of risk (or safety) has developed rapidly over the last several years. Unfortunately, earlier attempts at measuring the value of safety programs have given economists a "black eye" for supposedly advocating that individual human lives could be valued as the lost economic productivity associated with a shortened life span. This view, pursued in great detail by Dorothy Rice[9], and used by Lave and Seskin[10] and others, implied that the value of life of, for example, a 50-year-old carpenter would be the remaining earnings to retirement age. The value of life of a retired female (someone's grandmother) was by the same argument taken to be zero. Similarly, small children, since many years would pass before they could begin to earn productive income, were valued at next to zero, discounting future earnings at a market rate of interest. Elaborate calculations were made for different individuals on the basis of age, occupation, sex, etc. to determine the value of remaining earnings as a measure of the "value of life." On economic theoretical grounds, all of these calculations have been shown to be nonsense. [For a correct economic-theoretical treatment of safety see Mishan[11] or Conley[12].] However, permanent harm remains in that many decision makers now shy away from any attempt to value the benefits of safety programs in dollar terms.

The economist's notion that individuals do voluntarily trade off safety for monetary compensation in no way attempts to value life. Rather, the question is asked, how much do individuals require as *a priori* compensation to voluntarily accept a small additional risk of death? Note, then, that in correctly studying the problem of risk (as opposed to the value of life approach mentioned above), economists utilize data on behavior where monetary compensation is actually paid for accepting risk. We will find in analyzing ethics and risk, that the economist is utilizing a rather special situation to derive estimates of the value of safety. But, for the moment, let us follow through on the notion of a trade-off between safety and monetary compensation.

Imagine a game of Russian roulette in which an individual is offered sums of money to participate voluntarily. If, for example, the risk of the gun firing when the trigger was pulled were only one in ten thousand, and the compensation for accepting the risk was $1000, current economic studies would suggest that most people would accept the risk (this is a much better proposition—risk versus compensation—than driving to work for a typical day's pay!). However, economic theory suggests that as the probability of death increases, monetary compensation would have to increase dramatically. Figure 1 shows the expected kind of relationship between compensa-

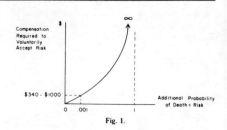

Fig. 1.

tion and risk. Clearly, as the probability of death approaches one, compensation approaches infinity—odds are that the participant will not survive the game to enjoy the proceeds, so, absent of some bequeathement motive, no amount of money is sufficient. Note, however, that for small increases in annual risk of death, such as those associated with risky jobs (typically less than 0.001 per year), annual job compensation is increased by $340–$1000 as shown in Fig. 1 [see Smith[13] and Thaler and Rosen[14]]. Thus, economists now focus on the far left-hand side of Fig. 1, only dealing with the dollar values necessary to compensate individuals for small voluntary risks. Total benefits for a safety program may, of course, sum up to a large dollar figure if many people obtain small reductions in risk through a public policy action.

However, this method of valuing risk seems at least in part out of accord with observed human behavior. Just as the old value of life measure used by Rice and Lave and Seskin leads to counterintuitive results, (e.g., grandmothers do not take up hang gliding because their lives are "worthless," nor does society place a near zero value on the lives of children), the new measure of the value of safety seems to ignore the special importance many individuals place on involuntary or uncompensated risks. The risks associated with nuclear reactor accidents or nuclear waste storage, risks associated with public transportation including airlines, risks of flood, fire, earthquakes, or other disasters, all seem to be treated differently both in a social and individual perspective than do voluntary-compensated risks. Economic theory, and consequently empirical estimates of the value of safety, have notably failed to account for these differences. Rather, economists have argued that placing a different value on safety in different situations is economically inefficient.

The logic behind this argument is as follows: Given a fixed safety budget, if we have a program that can save one life for $50,000 and another program which can save 10 lives for $50,000 we should pick the second program. Further, given a larger total budget, we would wish to pick the combination of programs which we would expect to save the greatest number of lives. We should pursue each of the programs to the extent that each additional life saved by a program cost the same at the margin.

4. ETHICS AND RISK

The obvious counter to the argument just raised is that individuals may well value safety differently in different settings. Are uncompensated risks less ethically acceptable than compensated risks?

We can use the four ethical systems presented above to analyze uncompensated risk as follows: assume we have two identical individuals, A and B, with the same utility functions. If A imposes a small risk on B and receives a benefit equal to B's incremental or marginal value of safety, we have a situation which satisfies traditional benefit-cost analysis, i.e., benefits to A are equal to cost imposed on B in dollar terms, so the situation is accepted. However, from an ethical perspective, A is imposing an uncompensated risk on B.

Technically, we define A's expected utility as

$$E_A = \left(1 - \Pi_A^0\right)U_A\left(Y_A^0 + G\Delta\Pi_B\right),$$

where Π_A^0 is A's risk of death, U_A is A's utility which is a concave function of his initial income Y_A^0 plus the monetary gain G, for imposing a unit of risk on B, times the increase in risk imposed on B, $\Delta\Pi_B$. An example of this situation would be Mr. A building a dam upstream of Mr. B for his own gain. Mr. A receives a net benefit of G for each unit of risk (of failure of the dam which could drown Mr. B), which he imposed on Mr. B. This net gain might result from the value of irrigation water net of the cost of constructing the dam. In this context, benefit-cost analysis, as traditionally practiced, would argue that if incremental net benefits to A equal or exceed incremental costs (of risk) to B, the dam is acceptable.

Mr. B's expected utility, where he is not compensated for risk imposed by A, is then defined as

$$E_B = \left(1 - \Pi_B^0 - \Delta\Pi_B\right)U_B\left(Y_B^0\right),$$

where Π_B^0 is Mr. B's original risk of death, $\Delta\Pi_B$ is the additional risk imposed by A, and U_B is Mr. B's utility, a concave function of his income, Y_B^0.

If we were to compensate Mr. B for voluntarily accepting risk from Mr. A at a rate of C dollars per unit risk, Mr. B would maximize his compensated expected utility,

$$\left(1 - \Pi_B^0 - \Delta\Pi_B\right)U_B\left(Y_B^0 + C \cdot \Delta\Pi_B\right),$$

with respect to $\Delta\Pi_B$ which implies

$$C = \left. \frac{U_B}{U_B'\left(1 - \Pi_B^0\right)} \right|_{\Delta\Pi_B = 0}$$

or that C equals B's marginal value of safety, the economists definition for the right-hand side of the expression above. (Note that the prime in the expression above is used to denote the derivative and we evaluate the expression where additional risk, $\Delta\Pi_B$, is zero.) Thus, traditional benefit-cost analysis requires that G, Mr. A's marginal gain, exceed or equal C, Mr. B's marginal loss, to start construction of the dam, both valued in dollar terms. However, Mr. A does not have to actually compensate Mr. B at a rate equal to or exceeding C, as defined above. Note the criterion that $G \geqslant C$ is only necessarily consistent with the utilitarian criterion when utility functions are linear and constant marginal utilities are equal for A and B.

How, alternatively, would the four ethical systems described above view the situation where B's risk is uncompensated? Where social welfare, W, for the first three criteria is defined as follows:

Utilitarian: $W = E_A + E_B$
Totally Egalitarian: $W = \max\min\{E_A, E_B\}$,
Totally Elitist: $W = \max\max\{E_A, E_B\}$,

the condition for acceptability is that $[dW/d\Delta\Pi_B]_{\Delta\Pi_B = 0} \geqslant 0$. If $[dW/d\Delta\Pi_B]_{\Delta\Pi_B = 0} < 0$, then the risk, $\Delta\Pi_B$, is rejected. Note that the term $[dW/d\Delta\Pi_B]$ is the slope (rate of increase) of social welfare with respect to an increase in risk to Mr. B. If this slope is positive at the origin ($\Delta\Pi_B = 0$) then an increase in risk to B is justified. For the Libertarian ethic, we require

Libertarian: $E_A \geqslant E_A^0 \equiv (1 - \Pi_A^0)U_A(Y_A^0)$
                $E_B \geqslant E_B^0 \equiv (1 - \Pi_B^0)U_B(Y_B^0)$.

or that both parties be better off than before the initial state preceeding consideration of the risk $\Delta\Pi_B$ on Mr. B.

Table I presents a summary of an analysis for uncompensated risk using the social welfare, W, criteria established above where we assume that A's incremental gain, G, is equal to B's incremental cost, C, in dollar terms; that the *a priori* risks Π_A^0 and Π_B^0 are identical and that utility functions U_A and U_B are identical as well.

The example is, of course, structured so that traditional benefit-cost analysis just accepts the imposition of an increment in uncompensated risk. However, the utilitarian ethic with identical strictly concave utility functions rejects the situation if Mr. B is initially worse off than Mr. A, i.e., B has a lower income, $Y_A^0 > Y_B^0$, since the risk is not distributed across society in a way that moves towards maximizing total utility. Similarly, the totally egalitarian or Rawlsian ethic rejects the imposition of risk by Mr. A on Mr. B if B is worse off initially since the risk of the dam failing makes the distribution of utility less equal in this case. The totally elitist ethic implies the converse: that if Mr. A is better off, he has the ethical right to impose a risk on Mr. B. Finally, the libertarian ethic rejects the notion of uncompensated risk no matter what the initial distribution of wealth since, by definition, an uncompensated risk makes someone worse off.

Table I is surprising in several respects. First, it is often supposed that benefit-cost analysis can be justified, or at least is supported generally by the Utilitarian ethic. Clearly, at least for uncompensated risk, this is not always the case.

Second, all of the four ethical systems examined reject uncompensated risk at least some of the time. This may in part explain the failure of the traditional economic view of a uniform-smooth risk trade-off, as expressed in Fig. 1, to predict the observed societal aversion to uncompensated public or social risks. All of the ethics consider some uncompensated risks "wrong," at least some of the time, implying no trade-off exists at all! Individuals may, of course,

adopt "ethical" preferences in accordance with the ethical systems we have described. In cases where individual preferences reject uncompensated risks as "wrong," the preferences of individuals become lexicographic. This term implies, in the case of safety, that among a set of alternatives, the alternative with the most public safety (least uncompensated risk) is always preferred to all other alternatives. Figure 2 shows a mapping of the preferences of an individual with lexicographic preferences between public and private (uncompensated and compensated) safety. If the individual initially has a combination of public and private safety denoted z^0, all points to the right of z^0, marked as the shaded area, are preferred because they have more public safety, i.e., less uncompensated risk. Thus, any point like z^2, which has less private safety but more public safety than z^0, is preferred to z^0. The only points which do not increase public safety but which are still preferable to z^0 are those marked above z^0 by the solid line, i.e., those which maintain the same level of public safety, but which increase private safety. Thus, with lexicographic preferences, private safety is still desired, but only secondarily to public safety. Clearly, where an individual or society invokes an ethical objection to uncompensated risks, preferences are lexicographic. Economists have always used the assumption of preferences of the sort shown in Fig. 3, where points such as z^1 (or those in the shaded area) which are all preferred to z^0, are bounded below by a smooth curve (or straight line) as shown, implying a continuous trade-off exists. Note, however, that if Table I were to be reworked on the assumption of *a priori* compensation for risk imposed on Mr. B by Mr. A, we would find all of the ethical systems considered accept compensated risk. Thus, the economists' notion of a money-risk trade-off seems perfectly acceptable if *a priori* compensation *actually* occurs.

Table I. Uncompensated Risk A imposes risk on B^a

Ethic	$Y_A^0 > Y_B^0$	$Y_A^0 < Y_B^0$
Traditional B/C (utilitarian with linear utility)	accept	accept
Utilitarian (strictly concave utility)	reject	accept
Totally egalitarian	reject	accept
Totally elitist	accept	reject
Libertarian	reject	reject

$^a A$'s gain equal to B's loss.

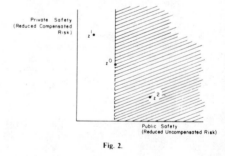

Private Safety (Reduced Compensated Risk)

Public Safety (Reduced Uncompensated Risk)

Fig. 2.

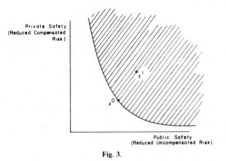

Private Safety
(Reduced Compensated
Risk)

Public Safety
(Reduced Uncompensated Risk)

Fig. 3.

Thirdly, the libertarian ethic, with its close relationship to a constitutionalist viewpoint is of special importance for Western democracies. This ethical system, although seemingly weak in not requiring redistribution of income, rejects all uncompensated risks, implying lexicographic preferences as described above.

It is perhaps this last point, when applied in a broad context, which goes furthest in explaining the opposition that benefit-cost analysis has received in analyzing certain issues. For example, in many cases, lawyers and environmentalists have argued that polluting the environment is "wrong" and that economic policies such as selling permits for the right to pollute or taxing pollution are unethical. Similarly, advocates of public safety argue that no amount of effort on the part of airlines, operators of nuclear reactors, or large hydroelectric dams is sufficient when uncompensated risks are involved for the general public. These attitudes, which are reflected in enormously higher expenditures per life saved in some safety programs as opposed to others, seem consistent both with a libertarian ethic and with lexicographic preferences.

5. CONCLUSION

Although the libertarian ethic seems inconsistent with the way economists treat risk in benefit-cost analysis, this view is not inconsistent with an economic perspective. Consider the example of the dam once again. However, let us now take construction of the dam as a public project which would provide benefits of recreation and availability of water to the general public. Also, assume the risk of failure of the dam is imposed on many people. In a libertarian-free market framework we could imagine a perfect world

in which *a priori* compensation would take place for all risks. Risks would be commodities traded in perfect markets. Thus, to build the dam, the right to impose risks on those below the dam would have to be purchased. Such a market for risk would, of course, require perfect information on the part of all parties. Further, since all market transactions would be voluntary—the dam builders would have to pay enough to all affected parties to get them to voluntarily accept any associated risks—no real ethical issues would be raised. This conclusion holds because, in the extreme, an individual could demand infinite payment to accept the dam, hence preventing its construction above that individual. Note then, that this particular arrangement protects each individual's rights—no one is forced to accept risk involuntarily—analagous to the perfectly competitive private market case wherein, for example, a worker may voluntarily accept a higher wage to work at a riskier job, but is free not to accept the offered compensation and risk. (The assumption of competitive markets, of course, implies full employment with consequent free choice of occupation, i.e., no one is forced to take a risky job *or* starve. Our society, with actual unemployment, effectively prevents forced employment with welfare programs.) In the private risk case, however, if one individual in the wage market is very risk averse and does not wish to accept a risky job, then another less risk averse individual will likely take the position. Thus, tenth story windows are washed without raising ethical questions or creating a societal crisis over *private* risk. Alternatively, our example of the dam points out an unfortunate problem with public as opposed to private risks. Construction of our example dam might be blocked by *one* very risk averse individual objecting to the imposition of a *public* risk; that is, if the market we proposed for risk were in existence. The distinction between public (joint) risk and private (separable) risk is then an important one, because, if a private market existed for public risk, one risk averse individual could then block joint action.

Another example may be useful in this context. Imagine that the passengers on an airliner are informed that by flying "low and fast" they will arrive at their next stop on time, making up for previous delays.' Clearly, a joint decision by the passengers is necessary. Those less risk averse will likely approve the divergence from standard procedures. Those fear-

---

' This situation actually occurred some years ago in Texas. Passengers voted for low and fast.

ful of flying in the first instance would likely resist. Airline risk is thus a public as opposed to private risk, since risks are joint—indivisible—as opposed to separable.

Different ethical systems will view such a situation in very different ways. Those focusing on the good of the whole including democratic or utilitarian viewpoints or benefit-cost analysis would all approve of "flying low and fast" if: (1) the majority voted for this alternative (democratic); (2) the summed utility gain to those less risk averse exceeded the utility loss to those more risk averse (utilitarian); or (3) the willingness to pay of those passengers wanting to fly low and fast exceeded the willingness to pay of those opting for "standard procedures" (benefit-cost). All three are roughly consistent with utilitarianism or benefit-cost analysis from a philosophical perspective in that a very risk averse individual could be out-voted, out-"utilitied," or out-payed by other individuals. Thus these criteria in themselves—including benefit-cost analysis—do not protect individual rights against some concept of majority rule or benefit.

A number of ethical systems alternatively focus on individual rights. These include those proposed by Kant,[15] Rawls[5] and the libertarian view as formalized recently by Nozick.[7] These ethical systems all would reject the imposition of uncompensated risk by the majority onto an objecting minority or individual. Each of these ethical systems might then reject benefit-cost analysis as it is traditionally performed. An alternative to traditional benefit-cost analysis is to weigh benefits and costs in a manner consistent with a number of alternative ethical systems. Clearly, outcomes may be vastly different under ethical systems which look to the "good of the whole," as opposed to those which focus on protecting "individual rights."

ACKNOWLEDGMENTS

The research upon which this paper is based was supported primarily by the National Science Foundation (NSF). The authors, however, take full responsibility for the study, and the results should not be taken to represent the views of NSF or any other sponsoring agency.

REFERENCES

1. B. Weisbrod, "Income Distribution Effects and Benefit-Cost Analysis," in *Problems in Public Expenditure Analysis*, S. Chase, ed. (Brookings Institution, Washington, D.C., 1968).
2. T. Page, *Conservation and Economic Efficiency* (Johns Hopkins, Baltimore, 1977).
3. J. Bentham, *An Introduction to the Principles of Morals and Legislation* (1789).
4. J. Mill, *Utilitarianism* (1863).
5. J. Rawls, *A Theory of Justice* (Belknap Press, Cambridge, 1971).
6. F. Neitzsche, *Beyond Good and Evil* (1886).
7. R. Nozick, *Anarchy, State, and Utopia* (Basic Books, New York, 1974).
8. E. Mishan, *Introduction to Cost Benefit Analysis* (Praegar, New York, 1971).
9. D. Rice, *Estimating the Cost of Illness*, U.S. Department of Health, Education, and Welfare, Public Health Service, Home Economics Series No. 6 (May, 1966).
10. L. Lave and E. P. Seskin, Air pollution and human health, *Science* **109** 723–732 (August 1970).
11. E. J. Mishan, Evaluation of life and limb: A theoretical approach, *Journal of Political Economy* **79** (December 1971).
12. B. Conley, The value of human life in the demand for human safety, *American Economic Review* **66** 45–57 (March 1976).
13. R. Smith, The feasibility of an injury tax approach to occupational safety, *Law and Contemporary Problems* (Summer–Autumn 1974).
14. R. Thaler and S. Rosen, "The Value of Saving a Life: Evidence from the Labor Market," in *Household Production and Consumption*, D. E. Terleckys, ed. (Columbia University Press, New York, 1975), pp. 265–297.
15. I. Kant, *Fundamental Principles of the Metaphysic of Morals* (1785).

18

Handling Value Issues

Michael Eraut

INTRODUCTION

This paper was first given to an ongoing seminar of British evaluators that met to discuss ethical issues in evaluation. It was revised in the light of comment from colleagues at that seminar, and subsequently formed part of a symposium presented by that group to the Annual Meeting of the British Educational Research Association in September 1980. It discusses several theoretical, methodological, and practical problems in handling value issues and negotiating evaluation goals. A divergent approach to evaluation is suggested that allows values external to a situation to be introduced alongside those of the participants, and that is appropriate in situations both of value conflict and of value complacency.

VALUE TRANSMISSION IN TEACHING AND EVALUATION

Whether teaching is regarded as a repressive or a subversive activity, it involves the transmission of values. Anyone who is not prepared for that responsibility should avoid becoming a teacher. But how far should a teacher be aware of the values he or she is responsible for transmitting? The answer, I would suggest, must depend on the extent to which these values are shared with other interested parties. If values are so embedded in the culture of a community that they are taken for granted by all its members, it is not the responsibility of a teacher working within that community to be uniquely aware of them. But if values are only shared by one section of the community, and the teacher is not aware of this, there is a problem. Such lack of awareness of values held by other sections of either the local community or the professional community is commonly found in evaluation studies. I call it value complacency. This complacency may sometimes be attributable to a particular group of teachers who "choose" not to think about certain issues; or it may be the more general result of professional socialization. Some values are taken for granted in schools and teacher education, while others are treated as problematic; and it is open to debate whether the boundary has been appropriately drawn. However, whether value complacency is general to the education service or specific to a particular teacher or group of teachers, it raises problems for the evaluator.

From Michael Eraut, "Handling Value Issues," original manuscript.

Simple logical analysis suggests that a teacher may handle values in three different ways: (1) by assuming them or taking them for granted (implicit transmission); (2) by advocating them or refuting them and taking up a definite value position (explicit transmission); or (3) by making them the subject of his or her teaching with the intention of promoting pupils' value awareness while still preserving their autonomy (explicit discussion). Promoting value awareness as a teaching goal implies that values should be explicitly discussed but not imposed by the teacher, but this aim is difficult to achieve in practice. So we have to consider a further possibility, that of the unintentional transmission of values. Each of these four situations demands a different response from an evaluator. The first may signal value complacency. The second and third will often indicate value conflict—which values should be handled by transmission and which values by discussion? The fourth shows a failure to achieve intentions in a sensitive area.

The same analysis can also be applied to the evaluator's own activities. Both his/her actions during the evaluation and his/her final report may involve implicit, explicit, or unintentional transmission of values. These values may come from participants in the evaluation, from sources external to the evaluation or from the evaluator him- or herself. In this last case the values may derive either from the way the evaluation is conducted, i.e., they are built into the evaluator's role and procedures, or from personal views held by the evaluator.

Some of the principles suggested by this analysis will command general agreement among evaluators. For example, unintentional transmission of values by evaluators is undesirable though difficult to avoid in practice. Other principles may be more debatable. Can respect for evidence be treated as an assumed value? If value neutrality is claimed, should it be explicitly discussed? We might agree that an evaluator should avoid promulgating his or her personal values in the sense of explicit or implicit transmission; but would we agree that he or she should not introduce them for explicit discussion? I do not believe that these issues can be resolved by using facile labels like "democratic" or "bureaucratic," or by trying to oversimplify the complex web of influences, power relationships, rights, and responsibilities that characterize our educational system. But I shall be returning to discuss some of these problems later. Here it is sufficient to note that ethical issues arise when an evaluator is confronted with value complacency as well as when he or she is confronted with value conflict.

THE GOALS OF EVALUATION

The idea of evaluation as a goal-oriented activity has been much neglected in recent British debates about methodology and it also has a bearing on the much-debated distinction between evaluation and research. I do not wish to deny the importance of seeing evaluation as a process or discussing its principles of procedure; and I will be returning to this theme later on. But evaluations also have purposes and outcomes, and these too are relevant to the discussion of value issues. My own experience is largely in small-scale evaluation studies within single institutions where questions of purpose and outcome are unavoidable; and I am constantly surprised at their apparent neglect in large-scale public evaluations where goals often seem to be taken for granted. Though the analysis that follows is based on such small-scale studies, much of it may well be equally applicable to the others.

The first distinction I wish to make goes to Scriven's (1967) classic paper "The Methodology of Evaluation," but I hope to use less confusing terminology. What Scriven has called "goals" and "roles" I prefer to call *intrinsic purposes* and *extrinsic purposes*. Under intrinsic purposes I include both philosophic goals—estimations of worth, merit, and value—and scientific goals—pursuit of truth, collection, and presentation of data.[1] Under extrinsic I include goals such as accountability and guiding decision making. Both types of purpose are present in all evaluations, and this is why the evaluator's role is so difficult.[2] On the one hand, the evaluator has to pursue the truth according to the criteria of the research community, while on the other, he or she is expected to have some effect and this is judged according to the criteria of the practitioner community. Lack of resources will severely limit what the evaluator can do, so he or she will probably be unable to fully satisfy either community. The evaluator has to choose what he or she does, and justify it in strategic as well as absolute terms, to show that it was the best that could be done with the resources available in the circumstances that existed at the time.

I find it useful to distinguish three main categories of intrinsic purpose: (1) examining the realization of intention, (2) interpreting what is happening, and (3) ascribing value to actions, activities, and programs. Although all three categories will normally be present in an evaluation to at least some extent, their relative importance will vary. The first two are concerned with descriptive data, and hence include the elucidation and interpretation of values embedded within a program or its context. The third concerns the value judgments that are or might be made about such a program and about its intended or observed effects.

VALUES EMBEDDED WITHIN A PROGRAM

My first type of intrinsic purpose, *examining the realization of intention*, includes the classical notion of assessing the achievement of objectives but is broader in conception. It does not assume that intentions are precisely formulated, that all participants have the same intentions, or that intentions only relate to outcomes. There are many situations when intentions are conceived primarily in terms of participation, motivation, and involvement; and it is assumed that beneficial outcomes will naturally follow. Stake (1967) provides a useful framework for examining the realization of intention in the descriptive half of his Countenance of Evaluation Model, though one has to recognize that the distinction between a transaction and an outcome may depend on the level of analysis. For example, if a film is shown and written about for homework, that homework would be an outcome if one were evaluating the lesson or the film, but a transaction if one were evaluating the whole course.

For the purposes of this particular paper, I shall focus primarily on problems associated with describing values that are implicit or explicit in the entity being evaluated; and this should not be taken as implying that other types of problem are any less significant when one is examining the realization of intention. Beginning with observed values rather than intended values, I shall follow the Countenance Model's distinction between Antecedents, Transactions, and Outcomes. Observing *values as outcomes* is usually taken to mean assessing the extent to which pupils have come to hold certain values that the program is intended to promote.[3] Methods of investigation include observation of pupil behavior, interview, and questionnaire—each with its attendant difficulties. One has to recognize that the validity of instruments purporting to measure values will always be rather limited, because there is a considerable gap between talk and action and between action in one context and action in another context. Moreover, many intended value outcomes are long-term, with a time span beyond that of most evaluation studies. Both these problems are found in normal education and social studies programs. Other value outcomes are expressive rather that instructional (Eisner, 1969). For example, a school may seek to promote artistic or recreational activities without being particularly concerned about which particular activities pupils eventually favor. Despite these problems, however, the question of values as outcomes is usually too important to be neglected. The evaluator has to make the most of the limited evidence at his/her disposal.

Observing *values as antecedents* presents similar methodological problems so I will not discuss it further. Again, considerable caution is needed in interpreting the evidence. Indeed, the difficulty of assessing what values people hold suggests that values can only be reliably observed when they are revealed by *transactions*. This perspective also accords with the notion that teachers do not often have specific objectives when communicating values because they are not sure what it is possible to achieve. When value goals are aspirations rather than expectations, the realization of intention can be investigated only by examining the congruency of the observed transactions of a program with what are often very long-term aims. The principal methods for collecting such evidence are direct observation and analysis of the material that teachers and pupils see, read, and write; and the relationship between transactions and outcomes has to be argued logically rather than measured empirically.

Further problems arise when one seeks to determine what values are intended by teachers. *Intentions* can be uncertain or ambiguous and value awareness is often limited. Some intended values may be revealed in interviews, and others inferred from a teacher's behavior or selection of material. But how about the values that are embedded in common forms of professional practice? Does the fact that the practice was intended necessarily imply that the values are also intended? When a teacher uses a book because it is "good literature," does he or she necessarily intend that the values in it should be transmitted without question? One could hardly call these pupils' encounter with those values accidental. Issues such as these cannot be handled at the level of simple empirical description, they demand penetration beneath the surface; and this involves attempting to interpret what is happening.

A second question—"How is it that some values come to influence a teacher more than other values?"—is equally significant but less frequently asked. It involves trying to understand how conflicts of intention are resolved, and making the important distinction between intentions embedded in practice and the rhetoric of justification. Thus it is closely intertwined with the problem of discovering intentions that was raised a little earlier. The methodological difficulties of pursuing these questions are considerable, especially when techniques such as participant observation are ruled out by lack of time and opportunity. Hence I have been experimenting with a technique that I like to call "instance interviewing."

Instance interviewing involves basing an interview on the discussion of two or three instances.[4] It needs some object or some shared experience to provide a starting point, as questions about ordinary events are likely to be treated with suspicion or amazement. Day (1981) used video recordings of classroom events as a source of incidents. I have used students diaries and pupil exercise books. Such an interview can reveal factors affecting particular decisions and the way in which potential conflicts of value are resolved, by probing intentions in a context where the rhetoric of justification is inappropriate. The "theory of action" (Argyris and Schon, 1974) that is thus disclosed is largely tacit and implicit, taken for granted, and embedded in personal practice. A more general interview, on the other hand, would be conducted in the language of "talk about teaching," which has been carefully developed to preserve teachers' autonomy and to justify their actions. The linguistic difference can be seen by comparing the kind of teacher intentions revealed by Smith and Geoffrey (1968) with those of the recent Schools Council "Aims of Primary Education" Project (Ashton, 1975).

VALUE JUDGMENTS ABOUT A PROGRAM

Hitherto we have been primarily concerned with descriptive data, with intended and observed values in the program being evaluated and the problems of elucidating and explaining them. My third category of intrinsic purpose, *value ascribing*, is not so much concerned with values embedded within a program as with value judgments about a program. Again, I have found the debate about the handling of judgmental data somewhat impoverished, with little discussion of the validity problem or of how value issues should be treated in evaluation reports. There is even a tendency to ignore judgmental data altogether or to confine its collection to a narrow range of respondents. Indeed, the popular preference for formative rather than summative evaluation may be an attempt to escape from this kind of responsibility.

Perhaps the main reason for this retreat from discussing judgmental data has been a reaction to Scriven's (1969) declaration that:

> His (the evaluator's) task is to try very hard to condense all that *mass* of data into one word: *good* or *bad.*

This overestimates what can be achieved with any reasonable degree of intellectual humility. Conflicting values cannot be "condensed" without imposing some superordinate ethical framework. Few evaluators are prepared to accept this role of "philosopher king." Still fewer believe it would be acceptable to others. But it is also recognized that the traditional positivist ideal of a scientific value-free evaluation is equally unattainable. Hence the notion of an evaluation report that finishes with a clear set of recommendations has been abandoned by many evaluators, although it is what many of their clients still expect. Such *convergent evaluation* can only be achieved by imposing values, either those of the evaluator or those of the people who commissioned him or her; or, in situations of value complacency, by some form of collusion between these two parties.

In Britain there have been two main responses to this dissatisfaction with convergent evaluation. One reaction has been the development of *neutral evaluation*, where the evaluator aims to be purely descriptive so that each of his/her audiences can draw their own independent conclusions, untrammelled by the evaluator's own interpretations. It looks a useful recipe for conflict avoidance, but I see three main drawbacks. First, data selection and interpretation are intimately connected processes so there is danger of unfocused accounts embodying hidden principles of selection that preempt the possibility of independent interpretation. Second, such evaluations are inevitably rather lengthy and structureless so they are difficult to read, interpret, and use. The evaluator saves his/her own conscience at the expense of not helping the clients. Third, I find the role of evaluator incompatible with that of pure empiricist, irrespective of whether he or she uses positivistic or naturalistic methods. Evaluation involves ethical as well as empirical enquiry almost by definition, and that is why I have emphasized its value ascribing purpose.

Illuminative evaluation has rather different aspirations, and its progressive focusing strategy leads to concise reports that are easy to read (Parlett and Hamilton, 1972). Its use of client-defined issues as a basis for selection is both practical and honest, but also brings disadvantages. It cannot import values that are not identified by the respondents, and this makes it of little use in situations of value complacency.[5] If one is concerned with what Habermas (1976) refers to as "suppressed interest" or what Lukes (1974) has called the "third dimension of power," then one has to recognize that an evaluator may have an ethical responsibility to introduce values that have not been identified by the respondents. But can this be done in a manner that avoids imposing the evaluator's own personal views?

DIVERGENT EVALUATION

This section should be read rather differently from the rest of this paper as I am temporarily departing from my commentator role to explore an evaluation model that I have used with some success in small-scale evaluation studies and in the intrinsic analysis of curriculum materials (Eraut, Goad, and Smith, 1975). I am not yet sure of its range of application, but it represents a constructive attempt to respond to some of the problems of handling judgment data that we were discussing earlier. In particular, I find its ethical stance an attractive compromise between an evaluator's accountability to his/her immediate clients, the evaluator's accountability to the wider public, and his/her standards and values as a professional person working in education.

The process, which I like to call *divergent evaluation*, recognizes that there are likely to be several different value positions and that some of them are potentially conflicting, and then attempts to relate the empirical evidence to these value positions without according priority to any of them. One of the tasks of the evaluator is to explore the connections between empirical evidence and the various values that might provide criteria for judging it. The evaluator thus places his/her ability to think and argue at the service of the different audiences as well as his/her ability to collect data. By showing linkages between the empirical evidence and certain values, the evaluator is aiding those who espouse those values toward the judgments they are most likely to support: but since the same service is offered for rival values, all audiences are also reminded of the judgments that others are likely to make. This procedure also allows the evaluator to introduce values not heeded by any of his/her respondents without giving them any special priority. Thus divergent evaluation aims to increase sensitivity to other viewpoints, to represent all the value positions of involved parties, and to introduce additional values where appropriate.[6] Moreover, those who lose out on any final decision will find that their position has been treated with respect and that the evaluation has not been biased against them.

Some of the key questions that underpin this divergent approach to evaluation are as follows:

- How is the program viewed from divergent value position?
- By what criteria do people decide whether it is worthwhile?
- Are there any additional criteria that it would be appropriate to introduce?
- What arguments could be used to justify or criticise the program?
- What value judgments and empirical judgments would these involve?
- How well supported by evidence are the arguments?

Possible sources of additional values or criteria are the education literature, the views of people other than those consulted as participants, alternative forms of practice, and the views of the evaluator.

Before moving on to look at some of the practical difficulties, let us explore the logic of evaluative argument a little further without claiming that people actually use the logic in practice. Arguments have to be justified as well as invented, and then logic does become important. When somebody makes a judgment about an educational program, that judgment entails criteria or standards. The extent to which the program meets each of these criteria is a separate empirical judgment, not necessarily independent because many criteria overlap. The selection and relative weighting of these criteria, however, is mainly a value judgment; though this too is not totally independent of some technical considerations.[7] Judgment is inherently complex, and I would argue that simply collecting people's judgments without seeking to explore their underlying structure is too narrow an approach for evaluators to readily adopt. It is closely analogous to confining empirical data collection to the measurement of outcomes. It may indicate whether people approve of certain programs, but that is all.

In practice, few people make rational judgments in the logical way I have just described. The process is usually less deliberate, and people often have difficulty in explaining how they arrive at their judgments. They also tend to take "short-cuts" by making judgments on one point on the basis of evidence that relates to quite a different point.[8] This need not prevent an evaluator from exploring some of the possible criteria being used: It just warns him/her not to assume that doing so will build up a rational coherent picture or a fair representation of someone's standpoint.

The opposite situation can be equally problematic. People do not necessarily hold coherent sets of values with clear priorities between them. They may not even hold fixed views on a particular educational program. So it is often easier to explore possible components of a judgment without forcing people to decide on their relative weighting. That is why I am suspicious of many attitude question-naires and opinion scales. Often they do not reveal judgments that have already been made, but force people to make snap judgments there and then. However, their validity can be checked by interviewing a sample of respondents. Indeed, I have found the interview follow-up of a questionnaire to be a valuable procedure, with the questionnaire providing a useful starting point for discussion. What difficulties did the respondent encounter when filling it in? What did he or she think the question meant? Was it the right question to ask? Was he or she thinking of any particular incident. It becomes yet another approach to instance interviewing.

Another practical problem is the context and timing of any attempt to gather people's opinions on a course. The views expressed can be heavily influenced by the context in which the relevant questions are asked. For example, one of the interesting things I discovered when evaluating university science courses was that if you give students course evaluation questionnaires, this immediately puts them in a "mastery learning" frame of mind with the result that they show preference for a highly structured program. However, if you talk to them about their degree course as a whole, their changes in attitude over the years, the place of academic work in university life, and their career prospects, they are more likely to assume an "intellectual development" frame of mind and show preferences for a weakly structured program. The timing of an interview can be equally important. Consider talking to a teacher about the value of teaching multiplication tables by rote when any of the following events had occurred on the previous day: (1) an argument with an older colleague who teaches very formally about the handling of a child with behavioral problems; (2) a discussion with a probationer who does not believe in teaching tables at all, and who still has difficulty in keeping his/her class in order; (3) a parents' evening in a highly aspirant white-collar catchment area; (4) a test that showed his/her pupils performing badly in mechanical arithmetic; (5) an in-service course that examined children's misunderstanding of arithmetical processes; (6) a talk from a personnel officer from a large local firm, complaining of the standard of arithmetic shown by his apprentices. I hope you will forgive the stereotypes, but I think they make the point that the response is unlikely to be the same in each case.[9]

For all these reasons, I am prepared to argue a case for exploring components of value judgments rather than seeking final summary opinions. If the latter exists, they will soon be revealed; if they do not exist, why try and force them? I would argue that people's selection of criteria and their empirical judgments on the basis of those criteria are likely to be more stable and reliable than their final judgments. The relative weighting of criteria is more likely to be influenced by context and timing, and forcing judgments in order to get hard data is likely to be counterproductive. Surely an evaluator hopes that people will suspend judgment until after they have read his/her report. So why encourage them to firm up their views in advance?

An alternative to the detailed mapping of separate criteria is to analyze judgmental data with the aid of ideal types. These are logically derived but empirically chosen, by a process that a colleague once described as a kind of naturalistic cluster analysis. Three stages are involved.

(1) Values are explored in open interviews in order to establish the range of criteria used by the evaluator's audiences.

(2) This evidence is used to construct three or four ideal types that encompass the full range of criteria, with each type being based in a position that emphasizes a particular set of criteria to the virtual exclusion of all others.

(3) The empirical evidence is examined from the standpoint of each ideal type in turn, and rival arguments about the merits of the course assembled.

For example, when evaluating the curriculum of a middle school I found that most of the relevant criteria could be derived from one of three ideal types— integrated day man, basic skills man, and traditional subject man. The arguments for and against the observed practice could then be presented from each of these three different viewpoints. This covered the full range of opinion without forcing any respondent to make a final summary judgment.

(1) Ideal types are seen as extremes so everyone else becomes "a moderate."

(2) Arguments can be presented sharply enough to be clearly understood and free of pretense (thus avoiding the current vogue for trying to say all things to all men and effectively saying nothing!).

(3) The evaluation can be seen as unbiased, in the sense of not being based on one particular value position.

(4) The whole range of opinion is catered for.

(5) Nobody is placed in a position of having to defend some previously ascribed position.

The technique allows one to protect both confidentiality and divergency, and this is a considerable asset in situations of potential or actual conflict. But it is not universally applicable, and I have not always found it to be the most appropriate way of analyzing judgmental data.

Extrinsic Purposes of Evaluation

The extrinsic purpose of an evaluation concerns the uses to which the information collected will be put; and again the situation is more complicated than many writers suggest. Consider, for example, the temporal aspect. All evaluations are *of* the past, *in* the present, and *for* the future. Not only will most of the events being studied be past events, but even the evaluation itself will be a past event by the time it is concluded. The evaluation is "in the present" in the sense that it affects current events and is in turn affected by them; the interaction between the evaluator and the situation being evaluated can never be ignored. Then the most often quoted purpose of evaluation, namely "to guide decision making," belongs in the future. Any actions taken as a result of an evaluation will be in the future and for the future. All three temporal elements are necessarily present but their respective importance may vary. For example, an emphasis on accountability will tend to concentrate on the past, an emphasis on contextual understanding or problem diagnosis will be primarily concerned with the present, and an emphasis on decision making will be oriented toward the future.

The dominant image of evaluation is still "retributive," not primarily, I believe, because of lingering memories of "payment by results," but because most evaluations are "commissioned" by those "in authority." Hence those "under authority" who are subjected to evaluation see themselves as potential victims (Elliott, 1978). They also suspect, with good cause, that information that reflects badly on their work will be more "newsworthy" than information that reflects well—one of those facts of human life of which the popular press are only too well aware. Some evaluators try and escape this "retributive" image by denying their link with the past and emphasizing that their sole purpose is to guide decisions in the future, but I personally do not believe that this attempt to sever the connection between evaluation and accountability is ethical. Most evaluations have an element of accountability in them somewhere, and it is dishonest to disguise it. Hence possible forms of reporting and access to information have to be discussed when arrangements about confidentiality are being negotiated.

The "threat potential" of evaluation can be treated more constructively if one takes a more professional view of accountability. Teaching is rarely a matter of total success or total failure and a competent professional will always fail to achieve some of his or her goals; so the grounds for external concern cannot just be that teachers are not wholly successful. Far more reprehensible, it might be argued, would be the failure to monitor one's teaching. However, even making a careful distinction between the evaluation of teaching and the evaluation of teachers does not resolve the problem of how to present negative information about teaching in a manner that is likely to have a constructive outcome. My usual response is to seek to legitimize the teaching by identifying it with some form of common professional practice, while at the same time making it abundantly clear that the teaching is not having the desired effect. The issue then ceases to be one of incompetence and becomes one of choosing the appropriate form of practice for the particular situation. This does not relieve the teachers concerned of any responsibility for taking action, but it may prevent them from dismissing the evaluation as biased against them. For similar reasons I have always held the view that evaluative information about individuals should either be anonymous or remain confidential.

Our recent research into *accountability* has been exploring, among other goals, the implications of the general proposition that evaluation should be an integral part of normal professional conduct and that teachers shuld be held accountable for seeing that it is properly done. In particular, we found it useful to distinguish between general monitoring or trouble-shooting and long-term accountability for policies, performance, and procedures (Becher, Eraut, and Knight, 1981). Monitoring is concerned with keeping things going by spotting any obvious signs of trouble and taking appropriate action. It usually takes existing policies and procedures for granted because its purpose would be defeated if it became too reflective or too time-consuming. Long-term accountability, on the other hand, would seem to imply some kind of program or periodic reviews. These would not only be more systematic but more concerned with the appropriateness of policy and the general style of its implementation. The underlying question must be, "Are we doing what is best?" and this inevitably involves judgments of value.

Unlike monitoring, which is universal, reviews are relatively rare. Unavoidable decisions take precedence over avoidable decisions, regardless of their respective importance (Eraut, 1970). However, there is a growing view that school-based reviews are a professional responsibility that derives from the practice of delegating decisions to individual schools. Such reviews must involve at least some consideration of alternative policies and their respective merits and values (Eraut, 1978), if the question, "Are we doing what is best?" is not to be totally ignored. But this suggests a need for teachers to be aware of different policy options and the values they entail. Hence I would argue that an evaluator participating in such a review has an obligation to develop option and value awareness.

Similar obligations arise when we consider the second extrinsic purpose of evaluation, that of guiding decision making. It has become fashionable to claim to follow this goal as it conveniently avoids connotations of measurement or accountability. But what does it mean to take it seriously? At the very best careful consideration should be given to the precise nature of the decision that could follow the evaluation. Does one envisage course changes or minor improvements within a fixed curricular pattern, or is the pattern itself to be subjected to scrutiny? Will there be changes in aims as well as changes in the way the aims are being implemented? What range of policy options is likely to be examined? I have already argued that if there is a limited awareness of options it could be part of an evaluator's task to extend the range; and I would now like to add that he or she may need to collect evidence relevant to all the options being considered, and not just the existing state of affairs. The evidence relevant to untried options may be limited, so this could involve visits to see how other approaches are working elsewhere. Such visits would not normally seek to collect performance data, as antecedent factors would render any direct comparison invalid. But they could reveal different value priorities, implementation problems, and unexpected side-effects.

A third extrinsic purpose of evaluation is the *development of contextual understanding.* This goal is shared with organizational development and institutional research and cannot properly be considered as the only goal of an evaluation as opposed to a research study. But it could be an important subsidiary goal and often turns out to be more significant than was originally envisaged. Contextual understanding is important if one is seeking to predict the effect of proposed policy changes. It may also help people to improve the quality of their work within an existing policy framework; and it may help an organization in a state of rapid change to keep some tabs on where it is going and what is happening to it. It is closely related to the intrinsic purpose of interpretation, the key distinction being that for extrinsic purposes the understanding needs to be shared by the participants and not confined to the evaluator and the research community.

Evaluation as problem diagnosis also belongs in this tradition, because its purpose is to get behind the symptoms and disclose the underlying factors. Though the need for speed and the atmosphere of crisis make this an unusually difficult and delicate task, the advantage of a short, sharp investigation by a trained evaluator can be considerable. Not only should his/her experience prevent him/her from being immediately satisfied with the obvious explanation, but the evaluator also has a potentially important role as a diplomat at a time when people's ability to communicate with each other is usually rather low.

NEGOTIATION OF THE EVALUATION BRIEF

The emphasis that I have given to goals in this paper has been partly an attempt to redress the balance in response to current preoccupations with evaluator roles. But it also reflects a belief that goals need to be discussed much more; and I would argue that the relative priority to be given to the various intrinsic and extrinsic goals I have outlined should be part of the negotiation.

Earlier I drew attention to the inevitable influence of an evaluator on the situation he or she is studying. This influence is much greater than the well-known experimenter-effect in classical research designs, both because evaluation is more threatening than research and because an evaluator has a greater need to build good relationships. He or she needs not only cooperation, but access to information as well. Thus evaluation cannot be considered as a purely intellectual process in which an evaluator plans his/her work, collects evidence about remote events, and then reports. It is also a social process during the course of which people may feel threatened, annoyed, troubled, bored, concerned, interested, or even excited. How can an evaluator handle it? Does he or she attempt to maintain an aloof independence, or does he or she become involved? Who does he or she see as his/her clients?

Behind these questions lies a deeper issue—what is the source of authority in an evaluation? Apart from the question of who commissioned the evaluation with whose consent and under what conditions, there is the important question of generalizability. The authority that an evaluator derives from membership of the research community relies on his/her access to generalizable knowledge and precise research techniques, whereas the authority of the participants derives from their specialized knowledge of a particular context, especially those aspects of it that are not readily described in terms of generalized knowledge and precise measurement. It would appear that the evaluator has to choose between (1) precise measurement, independence, reliance on external authority, and low access to contextual information, and (2) involvement, shared authority, reliance on situational validity, and high access to contextual information.[10]

Each of these approaches has its disadvantages. The "independent" evaluator

- has to rely on either authority or good salesmanship to gain cooperation;
- need to use relatively structured instruments;
- appears remote and threatening;
- gains little understanding of the context;
- gets little interest in his/her report;

whereas the "involved" evaluator

- gets drawn into disputes between client groups;
- finds it difficult to criticize, or in any way to represent "the public interest";
- is liable to be accused of bias;
- invests so much time in building and sustaining relationships that he or she has little left for other activities.

Moreover, while the "independent" evaluator is in danger of overemphasizing his/her research role, the involved evaluator is in danger of ceasing to be an evaluator altogether and becoming a change-agent. Somewhere we have to find a balance.

I believe that the key to this problem of "independence versus involvement" lies in the notion of negotiated purpose and process; and I propose to base such negotiations on four main principles, two practical principles:

(1) The evaluator will find it difficult to develop relationships and gain access to information without declaring his/her purpose and procedures; and a willingness to negotiate will usually improve his/her chances.

(2) Increased participation in evaluation policy is likely to result in increased attention to evaluation results.

and two moral principles:

(3) People have a right to know what an evaluator is doing and why.

(4) All those who might reasonably be considered as clients have a right to some stake in the evaluation enterprise.

Let me suggest how I think this approach to evaluation as a social process might work in practice. After a brief period of familiarization, the evaluator embarks on a fairly lengthy negotiation phase. First he or she asks his/her various client groups to contribute from their own perspectives to an initial agenda of issues, i.e., to say what they think the evaluation ought to be about. Second, he or she expands the agenda to include important issues that he/she feels have been omitted, and formulates it in a way that will allow new issues to emerge during the course of the evaluation. Third, the evaluator uses the expanded agenda to negotiate agreement on the general purpose of the evaluation and invites comment on his/her proposed data-gathering procedures. Fourth, he or she gets a promise of cooperation, and asks for additional help where he or she feels he/she can get it. For example, the evaluator may invite some of his/her clients to assist in the development and analysis of questionnaires—a process that brings them together in a situation where they can learn from each other, as well as involving them as "co-evaluators"—or to go through a file of student work and note the major difficulties and misunderstandings. I have tended to work fairly informally with only a short written agenda (about one side of a page), but in conflict situations greater formality may be necessary. Rippey (1973), for example, who describes evaluation studies of highly controversial urban education programs, gives several cases where each rival client group has been invited to contribute items to a questionnaire and the detailed wording has been formally negotiated. He claims that this has not only helped to reduce the threat of evaluation, but also helped client groups to develop more constructive relations with each other. At an individual level consultation over the agenda is a useful method for involving the type of client who leaves the evaluator to get on with it and then ignores the results if they displease him/her; while the "co-worker" approach provides a constructive role for clients who wish to vet every move the evaluator makes.

CONCLUSION

This paper has been an attempt to explore a large number of both theoretical and practical problems associated with the handling of value issues in evaluation studies. The goal analysis has helped to give it coherence but should not be regarded as authoritative, nor should the occasional digressions to consider personal approaches to the solution of methodological problems. The paper is intended to be exploratory and I hope people will read it and discuss it in that frame of mind. If at times my position seems a little firmer than it really is, that is because I have tried to be constructive. Being constructive is part of my ethical stance as an evaluator; and, however difficult the problems under discussion, I would not want this paper to contradict that message.

NOTES

1. I would argue that this and following statements have meaning without assuming a positivistic role for social science, an absolutist approach to values, or an objectivist attitude to truth.

2. I also recognize that the distinction between instrinic purpose and extrinsic purpose is not absolute. Habermas, for example, would claim that truth is not unrelated to utility. However, the distinction draw attention to likely areas of conflict and I find it a useful aid to thinking about evaluation strategy.

3. Assessing whether the pupils value the program, i.e., their attitude toward it, would be collecting judgmental rather than descriptive data and it is therefore discussed later. However, it must be acknowledged that value outcomes and judgments cannot be entirely separated.

4. The method bears some resemblance to Flanagan's (1954) Critical Incident Technique, but seeks to focus on typical incidents at least as much as critical incidents.

5. A somewhat similar point, but without this specifically ethical dimension, is made by Parsons (1976).

6. The argument here is that insofar as evaluation is concerned with the pursuit of truth, there is an obligation for an evaluator to help people see values as problematic. Making them aware of other people's values may help, even when those other people are not immediate participants. It also reduces the likelihood of the evaluator unconsciously adopting the values of one particular group.

7. Some values may turn out to be commonsense beliefs that can be empirically tested. But such testing is rarely feasible within an evaluation study and the research literature suggests that it would only rarely lead to a conclusive outcome. So while beliefs can be clearly labeled as empirical, they have to be treated almost as if they were value judgments.

8. The well-known "halo" effect by which judgments of goodness (or badness) get overgeneralized is but one example of this phenomenon.

9. In our recent accountability study, we found that the context of meetings and their timing with respect to press reports on sensitive issues caused considerable variation in teacher opinion. So also did a period of industrial action.

10. There is, of course, a socioanthropological research tradition that involves both unstructured techniques and independence, but I do not believe that this position could be sustained by anyone formally labeled as an "evaluator."

REFERENCES

Argyris, C. and Schon, D. (1974) Theory in Practice: Increasing Professional Effectiveness. San Francisco: Jossey-Bass.

Ashton, B. et al. (1975) Aims into Practice in the Primary School. London: University of London Press.

Becher, T., Eraut, M., and Knight, J. (1981) Policies for Educational Accountability. London: Heinemann.

Cronbach, L. (1963) "Course improvement through evaluation." Teachers College Record 64, 8: 672-683.

———and Suppes, P. [eds.] (1969) Research for Tomorrow's Schools: Disciplined Inquiry for Education. New York: Macmillan.

Day, C. (1981) Classroom Based In-Service Education: the Development and Evaluation of a Client Centred Model. Occasional Paper 9. Sussex, England: University of Sussex.

Dreeben, R. (1968) On What is Learned in School. Reading, MA: Addison-Wesley.

Eisner, E. (1969) "Instructional and expressive educational objectives: their formulation and use in curriculum," in W. J. Popham (ed.) Instructional Objectives. AERA Curriculum Evaluation Monograph 3. Skokie, IL: Rand McNally.

Elliott, J. (1978) "Classroom accountability and the self-monitoring teacher," in W. Harlen (ed.) Evaluation and the Teacher's Role. New York: Macmillan.

Eraut, M. (1970) "The role of evaluation," in G. Taylor (ed.) The Teacher as Manager. London: Councils and Education Press.

———(1978) "Accountability at school level," in T. Becher and S. Maclure (eds.) Accountability in Education. NFER Publications.

———Goad, L., and Smith, G. (1975) The Analysis of Curriculum Materials. Occasional Paper 2. Sussex, London: Education Area, University of Sussex.

Flanagan (1954) "The critical incident technique." Psychological Bulletin 51: 327-358.

Habermas, J. (1976) Legitimation Crisis. London: Heinemann.

Hastings, T. (1966) "Curriculum evaluation: the why of the outcomes." Journal of Educational Measurement 3: 27-32.

Lukes, S. (1974) Power. London: Macmillan.

Parlett, M. and Hamilton, D. (1972) Evaluation as Illumination: A New Approach to the Study of Innovatory Programmes. Occasional Paper 9. Edinburgh: Centre for Research in the Educational Sciences, University of Edinburgh.

Parsons, C. (1976) "The new evaluation: a cautionary note." Journal of Curriculum Studies 8, 2.

Rippey, R. N. [ed.] (1973) Transactional Evaluation. London: McCutcheon.

Scriven, M. (1967) "The methodology of evaluation," in R. W. Tyler, R. M. Gagne, and M. Scriven, Perspectives of Curriculum Evaluation. AERA Curriculum Evaluation Monograph 1. Skokie, IL: Rand McNally.

Scriven, M. (1969) "Evaluating educational programs." Urban Review 3: 20-22.

Smith, L. M. and Geoffrey, W. (1968) The Complexities of an Urban Classroom. New York: Holt, Rinehart & Winston.

Snyder, B. R. (1971) The Hidden Curriculum. New York: Knopf.

Stake, R. E. (1967) "The countenance of educational evaluation." Teachers College Record 68: 523-530.

19

The Impact of Questionnaire Research on Clinical Populations

A Dilemma in Review of Human Subjects Research Resolved by a Study of a Study

William B. Carter and Richard A. Deyo

Concern about the safety of invasive techniques in medical research is common, and potential benefits and risks are often closely scrutinized. Aside from informed consent and assurance of confidentiality, the safety of noninvasive measures, especially interview and questionnaire instruments, is often taken for granted. Nonetheless, review committees for human research consider the impact of such instruments on respondents and the risks of noninvasive research have received considerable attention both in the literature[1] and in the formulation of national policy for the protection of human subjects.[2] Recently, we were confronted with a dilemma about a human research committee's objection to the proposed use of a *health status questionnaire*. Careful resolution of this problem was important to future research efforts because of the widespread use of questionnaires and interviews in medical, behavioral, and epidemiological research.

The types of risks involved in noninvasive research are primarily psychological rather than physical, but there is substantial similarity in assessing risk/benefit ratios.[3] Concern about potential risks of such research is apparent from studies of the human research review process. In one study, Barber[1] examined human research committee reviews of 90 behavioral research proposals. Approximately 19% of committee reviews raised questions about informed consent, 32% about risks, and 19% about confidentiality. Examples of potential harm identified by the committee included embarrassment, loss of privacy, disclosure of confidential information,

danger of arrest, adverse family or social consequences, anxiety, fear, self-incrimination, or harmful new self-awareness. Despite such concerns, actual assessment of the impact of noninvasive measures has been exceedingly rare, apart from a few reports of psychological harm resulting from stress,[4] deception,[5] and sensory deprivation experiments.[6] Since little information is available for assessing risks, human research review committees must rely largely on their own intuition and judgment in weighing the potential risks of noninvasive measures against the possible knowledge to be gained from their use.[7]

The present study arose from such circumstances. In the review of one of the authors' (W.B.C.) research projects, a study of factors influencing influenza vaccination and other preventive health behaviors, a human research review committee expressed concern over the possible adverse effects of asking elderly or chronically ill patients to self-administer one of the proposed questionnaires, the Sickness Impact Profile (SIP). The SIP is one of a group of new health status instruments developed for use in assessing the outcomes of health care services. Such instruments are being used both for programmatic evaluation and in clinical therapeutic trials. For example, the SIP has been used in trials of therapy for chronic obstructive lung disease[8] and cancer[9] conducted by the National Institutes of Health. The SIP is designed to reflect a subject's perception of health-related changes in his/her daily activities. Changes are operationally defined in terms of behavioral dysfunctions

From William B. Carter and Richard A. Deyo, "The Impact of Questionnaire Research on Clinical Populations: A Dilemma in Review of Human Subjects Research Resolved by a Study of a Study," 29(4) *Clinical Research* 287-295 (October 1981). Copyright 1981 by the American Federation for Clinical Research. Reprinted by permission.

Table 1: Sickness Impact Profile Categories.

Behavior Category	Selected Items
1. Sleep and Rest	I sit during much of the day. I sleep or nap during the day.
2. Eating	I am eating no food at all; nutrition is taken through tubes or intravenous fluids. I am eating special or different food.
3. Work	I am not working at all. I often act irritably toward my work associates.
4. Home Management	I am not doing any of the maintenance or repair work around the house that I usually do. I am not doing heavy work around the house.
5. Recreation and Pastimes	I am going out for entertainment less. I am not doing any of my usual physical recreation or activities.
6. Ambulation	I walk shorter distances or stop to rest often. I do not walk at all.
7. Mobility	I stay within one room. I stay away from home only for brief periods of time.
8. Body Care and Movement	I do not bathe myself at all, but am bathed by someone else. I am very clumsy in body movements.
9. Social Interaction	I am doing fewer social activities with groups of people. I isolate myself as much as I can from the rest of the family.
10. Alertness Behavior	I have difficulty reasoning and solving problems; for example, making plans, making decisions, learning new things. I sometimes behave as if I were confused or disoriented in place or time; for example, where I am, who is around, directions, what day it is.
11. Emotional Behaviors	I laugh or cry suddenly. I act irritably and impatiently with myself; for example, talk badly about myself, swear at myself, blame myself for things that happen.
12. Communication	I am having trouble writing or typing. I do not speak clearly when I am under stress.

rather than symptoms or capacities. The SIP is comprised of 136 items that broadly cover 12 categories of activities involved in carrying on one's life (Table 1).

The reviewing human research committee was concerned that the wording of the instrument might cause patients to reflect negatively on their state of health, which could lead to undue psychological stress, anxiety, or even depression. The focus of their concern was on self-administration by respondents who were usually at home and often in isolation. The committee's conviction regarding possible risks was great enough that it decided the study could proceed only if the SIP were administered by an interviewer or dropped from study procedures.

In a number of respects, this judgment was surprising. The SIP had undergone rigorous development at this institution over a six-year period.[10,11] Furthermore, it had been applied in a variety of settings and to patient populations similar to that of the proposed study. Testing and clinical applications had involved both an interviewer-administered format and a self-administered format in which an interviewer gave only the instructions. In addition, interviewers generally reported favorable reactions on the part of participating subjects. These factors were brought to the committee's attention, but the decision was firm. The proposal in question was a small developmental study preceding a two-year research project. While the use of the interviewer-administered SIP format would have had minimal impact on this preliminary phase, such a modification had major implications for the feasibility of the larger project. The SIP has shown considerable promise in clinical settings, and the restriction of administrative format would have far-reaching consequences for future applications.

The pilot nature of the proposed research appeared to provide a good opportunity for assessing possible adverse effects of self-administering the SIP. An empirical study of impact was proposed and accepted by the committee as an integral part of the project. During the early phases of this study, a colleague (R.A.D.) was initiating a clinical study that required rheumatoid arthritis patients to self-administer the SIP several times during a six-month period. Interestingly, this proposal initially had been reviewed and approved without difficulty by a second human research review committee at this institution. His study provided an opportunity to extend observations regarding self-administration of the SIP. The principal investigator (R.A.D.) concurred and obtained human subjects approval to incorporate into his study an evaluation of SIP impact on respondents.

The research described here represents a study of two studies, aimed at identifying adverse effects of self-administration of the SIP or of administration of other interviews and questionnaires included in the studies.

Procedures

Both projects were conducted in the outpatient clinics of the Seattle Veterans Administration Medical Center; the arthritis project also included outpatients from the U.S. Public Health Service Hospital. From the two studies a total of 110 patients (95 men, 15 women) were interviewed by a research assistant who was experienced in both structured and open-ended probe techniques. Interviews were conducted over the telephone; a summary of specific items utilized in assessing adverse impact is shown in Table 2. The research assistant recorded patient responses verbatim and was instructed to probe carefully for details of any possible adverse effects. To simplify reporting, the two studies are labelled Study I and II.

Study I

This study was designed to examine patients' understanding of preventive care, their preventive health practices, and to characterize the process by which they decided whether or not to undertake a specific physician—recommended preventive activity, influenza vaccination. All patients were considered to be at high risk for the complications of influenza and were either 65 years of age or older or had diagnoses of diabetes, chronic lung disease, or chronic heart disease. The 58 patients in this study had a mean age of 66 years, and on the average had completed a high school education. In addition to the self-administration of the SIP, study activities included a personal interview, a decision-making questionnaire (administered by telephone), and a self-administered health opinions questionnaire. Instructions for the self-administered questionnaires were given by telephone. This study required a substantial time commit-

Table 2: Summary of Questions Utilized to Assess the Impact of the Study and the Questionnaires.

Overall Study Impressions

Do you have any general impressions, thoughts, or feelings you would like to share with us about our study?

Thinking about the entire study, do you feel it was a positive, neutral or negative experience?

What did you like most about the study?

What did you like least about the study?

Has this study affected the way you think about your health in any way? For example, has the study made you think more about your health, worry more about your health, helped clarify health issues, identified new health practices, etc.?

The Consent Process

Was the study adequately explained to you?

Were there any questions asked that you didn't expect or that surprised you?

Was anything asked that bothered you?

The Sickness Impact Profile*

Do you have any general impressions about this questionnaire?

Did you have any difficulty filling out this questionnaire?

Did filling out this questionnaire cause you any distress or discomfort?

How do you feel about this questionnaire (positive, neutral or negative)?

If your doctor had access to information like this, do you think it would be helpful?

Recommendations

Did we leave out anything that you wished we had asked about?

Knowing what you know now, if a close friend were asked to participate in our study, would you recommend it to him?

*In Study I a similar set of questions was asked for the decision-making and health opinions questionnaires.

ment on the part of subjects (approximately four hours) over a three-month period, for which they were reimbursed $25. Patients were encouraged throughout the study to comment freely on study procedures. Enclosed with the self-administered questionnaires was a solicitation of any "thoughts or feelings" regarding them and specifically of any bothersome aspects. Finally, within 48 hours of receiving the self-administered questionnaires, subjects were contacted by telephone and the impact interview (Table 2) was conducted.

Study II

This project was designed to examine the clinical utility of SIP data in managing rheumatoid arthritis patients attending rheumatology specialty clinics. Following in-person instructions at the beginning of the study, patients were asked to self-administer the SIP at home several times over a six-month

Table 3: Patient Ratings of the Entire Study and Individual Instruments.

Impressions of SIP (Studies I & II)

		Impressions of Entire Project			
		Positive	Neutral	Negative	Totals
Sickness	Positive	76	2	0	78
Impact	Neutral	9	20	1	30
Profile	Negative	1	0	1	2
Questionnaire	Totals	86	22	2	110

Impressions of Other Instruments (Study I only)

		Impressions of Entire Project			
		Positive	Neutral	Negative	Totals
Health	Positive	34	2	0	36
Opinions	Neutral	13	5	0	18
Questionnaire	Negative	3	1	0	4
	Totals	50	8	0	58
Decision-	Positive	45	1	0	46*
Making	Neutral	6	5	0	11
Questionnaire	Negative	0	1	0	1
	Totals	51	7	0	58

period. SIP responses were forwarded to the investigators prior to each clinic visit and the results were made available to half of the participating physicians and withheld from the other half. Various aspects of the questionnaire's measurement characteristics and of physician and patient behaviors were observed. The telephone impact interview was conducted during the course of the study, in all cases within a month of SIP completion. Of 60 enrolled subjects 52 could be contacted by telephone and are included in this report. Their mean age was 58 years and their educational level was similar to subjects in Study I.

Results

The vast majority of patients in both projects reported favorable impressions of the entire study. As shown in Table 3, 86 of the 110 patients reported that their participation in the study as a whole was a positive experience, 22 a neutral experience, and only 2 felt it was a negative experience. Further, even those patients with negative impressions of a specific questionnaire frequently had a positive view of the entire study.

Table 4 summarizes the reactions of those patients who offered specific comments about study activities. Again, the majority of reactions to the overall study were positive. Regarding what they liked most about the study, 50 patients offered responses. Factors most frequently cited included the opportunity for health self-appraisal, specific questionnaires, or "everything" about the project. Only 35 comments were

elicited about what patients liked least. Most of these reflected administrative difficulties such as those shown in Table 4.

It can be seen from the marginal totals in Table 3 that more negative comments were elicited by questions concerning specific study instruments than by questions about the overall project. The same trend is apparent from the distribution of specific comments shown in Table 4. The difficulty in eliciting adverse reactions with general questions is further demonstrated by responses to the written question included with the self-administered instruments in Study I. In response to this solicitation of adverse effects, only 12 subjects returned comments. Of these, 7 were positive remarks about the study, 3 concerned the SIP format, 1 included a lengthy self-description, and 1 was an apology for delay in returning the questionnaires.

While most reactions to the SIP were favorable (Table 3), some adverse effects were reported. However, similar results were observed for all study instruments and by comparison the SIP appeared to elicit no greater negative reaction.

Finally, at the end of each impact interview patients were asked whether they would recommend this study to a close friend and if there was anything the patient wished we had included.

Table 4: Summary of Statements Elicited by General Questions Concerning Study Activities.

	COMMENT CATEGORIES						
	Positive Reactions		Administrative Difficulties		Psychological Distress		
Did You Have Any General Impressions About:	Number of Responses	Examples	Number of Responses	Examples	Number of Responses	Examples	Total Responses # Interviews
The overall study? (combined projects)	62	good study worthwhile nice to have some- one ask opinions	9	format wording too many questions difficulty deciding	1	too psychological	72 110
The SIP? (combined projects)	5 (4)*	clear cut enjoyed it	19 (8)	didn't understand some words too long a lot didn't apply to me	3 (1)	a little negative too many questions and very stressful	27 110
The health opinions questionnare? (study 1 only)	2	liked it gives you middle- ground	8	couldn't understand too long poor wording hard to decide	2	"trick" questionnaire, depressing made uneasy	12 58
The decision-making questionnaire? (study 1 only)	6	to the point thorough liked it	5	questions nebulous too long	1	nervous on phone	12 58

*Numbers in parentheses are responses from Study 1 only. These are included to allow comparison with other Study 1 instruments.

Reflecting on the entire experience, 99 subjects reported they would recommend the study and only 2 would not. The remaining individuals were uncertain. With regard to the latter question, 17 individuals offered specific suggestions that included requests for more items concerning mental health, stress, depression, loneliness, sexual activities, what bad days are like, and finances. These comments were interesting because they represent content areas often considered "sensitive" or "offensive" by human research review committees.

While these data provide some measure of the frequency of a negative impact of study activities, they provide little assessment of the severity of this impact in subjects who experienced adverse effects. We therefore used certain responses as a screen for those individuals who might be cause for concern, and attempted to characterize those individuals in more detail. First, we asked if patients thought they had received adequate information about the studies at the time of enrollment. All 110 patients said they had received adequate explanations. Next, we carefully reviewed the responses of any patient who indicated that study procedures caused him to think more about his health; who indicated surprise, annoyance, discomfort, distress or difficulty; or who rated any study activity negatively. Patient responses to specific questions are shown in Table 5. Though there are few affirmative responses to any one question, a total

Table 5: Screening Questions for Adverse Impacts.

			Subject Responses		
Study Activity	Specific Inquiry*	No	Yes, not Specific+	Yes, Specific	Total
Overall study (combined projects)	Has this study affected the way you think about your health?	66	35	9	110
	Were there any questions that surprised you?	98	6	6	110
	Were there any questions that bothered you?	106	1	3	110
Sickness Impact Profile (combined projects)	Did you have any difficulty filling out the SIP?	99	0	11	110
	Did filling out the SIP cause you any distress or discomfort?	104	2	4	110
Other questionnaire instruments health opinions and decision-making (Study I only)	Any difficulty, distress or discomfort?	49	0	9	58

*See Table 2 for exact wording.
+Could not recall specific items, or made only general remarks (questions were "vague" or "stupid").

of 55 individuals answered yes to at least one question. Of these 55, 22 had indicated only that study activities caused them to think more about their health. There was no evidence from responses to the entire inquiry that this experience had any adverse consequences, and the vast majority indicated a positive overall experience with the study. Twenty-one additional subjects indicated either administrative problems or nonspecific surprise with some aspect of the study. Again, there was no other indication of distress and other responses were positive.

Ten of the remaining 12 individuals appeared to experience distress with a specific activity, but this apparently was not generalized to other study activities. One of these patients did not like flu shots or the decision-making questionnaire, but appeared to make light of these negative feelings and rated other study activities as neutral. Also included here are the four patients (Table 3) who viewed the health opinions questionnaire negatively. One of these was insulted and angered by the wording, but all viewed other aspects of the study positively. Five patients indicated some distress or annoyance with the SIP, but again had positive or neutral impressions of other study activities. For all 10 patients, the distress appeared to be transitory.

In exploring adverse reactions, the interviewer was unable to identify any continuing anger or distress.

Finally, there were two individuals who did exhibit a consistent pattern of distress which may represent the type of reaction that was anticipated by the review committee. One of these patients was a Japanese-American with limited facility in English. This patient viewed the SIP as "too psychological" and exercised the option to withdraw from the study. Further follow-up revealed that the patient and spouse had invested great effort in translating the SIP. The second patient had recently suffered a stroke and his wife had assisted with all study activities. The impact inquiry was, in fact, answered by the wife who felt that her husband had difficulty concentrating and was upset by the length of study activities. While distress was associated with each of the instruments used in Study I, the entire study was seen as a positive experience. Only the SIP was given an overall negative rating. The wife indicated that specific SIP items upset the patient by reminding him of stroke-related disabilities. Even so, the distress was apparently transitory. In retrospect, both of these cases represent failings in the initial study enrollment procedures.

Discussion

This report is an attempt to address the concerns of a human research review committee about whether specific questionnaire procedures might result in undue stress, anxiety, or depression. Any attempt to measure such effects must rely on self-report and is subject to a number of inherent limitations. In our study, patients may have wished to avoid offending the interviewer or investigators. They may have rationalized what were in reality adverse emotional effects, or subdued their criticisms in the face of special attention and or reimbursement. Conversely, the strengths of this method were that patients were questioned a short time after their participation in research activities, a number of general and specific questions were posed, and the interviewer was allowed to explore in detail any hint of adverse reactions.

On the basis of our observations, the safety of noninvasive research procedures cannot be taken for granted. A small incidence of adverse reactions was reported for all of the questionnaire procedures examined. However, these reactions were in most cases narrowly focused and transitory.

The Sickness Impact Profile certainly appeared to pose no greater risk than several other questionnaire instruments used in these studies. This finding should provide reassurance to both human research review committees and to investigators interested in applying health status measures like the SIP to clinical populations. Self-administration of this instrument, and presumably similar instruments, appears to impose very little emotional burden on respondents and most find it a positive experience. These results resolved the original human research review committee's concern about self-administration of the SIP and provided a firm empirical basis for allowing the larger, two-year project to continue as designed.

We found that this evaluation was relatively easy to implement, inexpensive and of value to the investigators as well as the human research review committee. The study provided insights into the strengths and limitations of all the instruments examined, clarified patient misunderstandings, and pointed to potentially valuable changes in wording and measurement strategies. It should be noted, however, that adverse reactions identified in this study were elicited only through detailed questioning. No adverse responses were identified by written solicitation included with the self-administered questionnaires and general questions posed by an interviewer provided very little yield. Only by asking questions directed at specific study instruments and specific negative reactions were most of the adverse effects identified.

The specific issue raised by this review committee concerned possible adverse emotional effects experienced by elderly or impaired individuals as a result of self-administering the SIP in isolated settings. Of the three patients who viewed either the SIP or the entire study negatively, none were living alone, and two had help from their spouses in completing the SIP. Two had relatively mild degrees of dysfunction and were relatively young (52 and 32 years of age). A third had difficulty with all the study activities but the adverse impact was apparently transitory. These cases did not appear to typify the patients or situations that were of specific concern to the reviewing committee. However, these findings are consistent with those of other investigators who found that anticipatory judgments about subjects' behavior in research settings are often inaccurate.[12]

It is difficult to adopt the viewpoint of subjects whose experience is widely different from our own. What is viewed as disturbing or offensive questionnaire content may vary considerably across subject groups. Instruments like the SIP may not be perceived as offensive if the content of the instrument accurately reflects common illness-related experiences encountered by subjects. Thus, in assessing adverse effects, it is important for review committees to conceptualize potential risks in terms of subjects' experiential frame of reference, remembering that if the content of an instrument is congruent with that experience it is unlikely to be disturbing.

In light of such difficulties, decisions regarding the appropriateness of questionnaire content are often left to the subject as part of the informed consent process. However, when review committees are concerned that this process may not afford adequate protection of subjects, they must directly attempt to assess risk. It seems clear that attributions based on intuition and personal experience are often erroneous in identifying adverse impacts. Based on our observations, there appear to be several available sources of information that may assist human research review committees in assessing the fit between instrument content and subject frame of reference. We offer these as suggestions for future considerations of this type.

Origin and Intent of the Questionnaire

The method used in developing the content of the instrument in question may be of some assistance in determining whether that content reflects the probable experience of intended research subjects. For example, items included in the SIP were obtained empirically from diverse samples of healthy and ill individuals. These items, then, may reflect commonly experienced behavioral dysfunctions resulting from illness.

Technical or Performance Characteristics of the Questionnaire

Reliability and validity data will be available for many formally developed instruments. While it may be difficult to predict how offensive content would influence questionnaire reliability, construct or criterion-related validity estimates may be adversely effected. These assessments correlate instrument scores with other independently determined measures that are thought to reflect the same subject experiences. If such correlations are relatively good, then it is likely that the instrument accurately reflects respondent experience. Available data for the SIP demonstrated highly reproducible results that correlated strongly with measures of health care utilization, other measures of health status, and physiologic measures. These characteristics alone would be insufficient to judge an instrument's appropriateness, but they do offer objective evidence that the questionnaire may reflect actual experiences of respondents.

Expert Opinion

Experts representing a number of disciplines could be called upon to evaluate the potential impact of a given instrument, but it may be unclear who would be the best judge of such impacts. Principal investigators, experts in various disciplines, or even those who developed the instrument in question may not be the best groups for advising human research review committees. In our view, a more appropriate group may be those individuals who have

actually administered the instrument. Such individuals may be available in large institutions and may provide useful opinions and information about subject reactions to the instrument.

Empirical Assessment

Finally, if all other forms of resolution fail, review committees may want to request an empirical study to evaluate the impact of the instrument in question. As we have shown, this can be accomplished in a pilot study employing telephone contact and should include detailed questions about specific research activities and about specific potential impacts. Such evaluations, if thoughtfully designed, can be fruitful for investigators as well as their reviewing committees.

References

1. Katz J: Experimentation with Human Subjects. New York, Russell Sage Foundation, 1972.
2. The National Commission for the Protection of Human Subjects of Biomedical and Behavioral Research: The Belmont Report: Ethical principles and guidelines for the protection of human subjects of research. DHEW Publication No. (OS)78-0012, 1978.
3. Barber B: Some perspectives on the role of risk benefit criteria in the determination of the appropriateness of research involving human subjects. Chapter 19, Appendix Vol II of The Belmont Report. DHEW Publication No. (OS)78-0014, 1978.
4. Berkun MM, Bialek HM, Kern RP, Yagi K: Experimental studies of psychological stress in man. Psychol Monog 76(15):1-8, 1962.
5. Ring K, Wallston K, Corey M: Mode of debriefing as a factor affecting subjective reaction to a Milgram-type obedience experiment an ethical inquiry. Rep Res Soc Psychol 67:68-85, 1970.
6. Bressler B, Silverman AJ, Cohen SI, Shmanovian B: Research in human subjects and the artificial traumatic neurosis where does our responsibility lie? Am J Psychiat 116:522-526, 1959.
7. Kimble G: The role of risk benefit analysis in the conduct of psychological research. Chapter 20, Appendix Vol II of The Belmont Report. DHEW Publication No. (OS)78-0014, 1978.
8. Nocturnal Oxygen Therapy Trial Group: Continuous or nocturnal oxygen therapy in hypoxemic chronic obstructive lung disease. Ann Int Med 93:391-398, 1980.
9. Barofsky I, Sugarbaker PH: Health Status Indexes: Disease specific vs general population measures. The Public Health Conference on Records and Statistics. The People's Health. Facts, Figures and the Future. DHEW Publication No (PHS)79-1214:263-269, 1979.
10. Bergner M, Bobbitt RA, Kressel S, et al: The Sickness

Impact Profile: Conceptual formulation and methodology for the development of a health status measure. Int J Health Serv 6:393-415, 1976.

11. Gilson BS, Bergner M, Bobbitt RA, Carter WB: The Sickness Impact Profile: Final development and testing

1975-78. Final Technical Report, Department of Health Services, University of Washington, 1979.

12. Milgram S: Some conditions of obedience and disobedience to authority. Hum Relations 18:57-75, 1965.

This paper was awarded the 1981 Nellie Westerman Prize for Research in Ethics.

William B. Carter, PhD, is Associate Director, Health Services Research and Development Affiliation Program, Veterans Administration Medical Center, 4435 Beacon Avenue, South, Seattle, Washington 98108; and Assistant Professor, Department of Health Services, University of Washington, Seattle, Washington.

Richard A. Deyo, MD, is Veterans Administration Fellow in the Robert Wood Johnson Clinical Scholars Program,

University of Washington and Veterans Administration Medical Center, Seattle, Washington.

Requests for reprints should be addressed to Dr. Carter.

This project was supported by the Health Services Research and Development Affiliation Program, Veterans Administration Medical Center, Seattle, Washington. The opinions expressed are those of the authors and not necessarily those of the Veteran's Administration or of the Robert Wood Johnson Foundation.

20

Confidentiality in Criminological Research and Other Ethical Issues

Marvin E. Wolfgang

I. INTRODUCTION

This article is intended to stimulate discussion of ethical issues involved in research in criminology and criminal justice. I will touch on related issues bearing on the teaching of those subjects as well, for many who face moral dilemmas in acquiring knowledge also face such dilemmas in attempting to impart knowledge.

Criminology is the systematic, scientific study of crime, criminals, and society's reaction to both. The belief system of the canons of science inheres in my reference to research. The acquisition of knowledge, for its own sake or for some other utilitarian end, is achieved by means of relatively detached and dispassionate perspectives. I suppose that in Austin Turk's[1] terms, this approach is predominantly empirical, although not necessarily devoid of or insensitive to the legal or polemical definitions of reality. Applied in its common sense to the actions of the professional researcher in criminology, the term "ethics" refers to the set of principles governing conduct. I am applying that term to the professional researcher in criminology. Some of the issues I shall raise are also issues in other disciplines of research and teaching; some are peculiarly specific to criminology; all, I am asserting, are ethical issues. But some observers may challenge their ethicality and claim instead that these

---

* An earlier version of this paper was presented at the Conference on Ethics, Public Policy and Criminal Justice, Center for the Study of Values, University of Delaware, Newark, Delaware (Oct. 23-25, 1980).

** Director, Center for Studies in Criminology and Criminal Law, University of Pennsylvania.

[1] A. Turk, Legal, Polemical, and Empirical Definitions of Criminality (paper presented at the Conference on Ethics, Public Policy and Criminal Justice, Center for the Study of Values, University of Delaware, Newark, Delaware, Oct. 23, 1980).

From Marvin E. Wolfgang, "Confidentiality in Criminological Research and Other Ethical Issues," 72(1) *The Journal of Criminal Law and Criminology* 345-361 (Spring 1981). Copyright 1981 by Northwestern University School of Law. Reprinted by permission.

may be only dilemmas of decisions that have no right or wrong, good or bad quality. I think they do, else I would not raise them.

The most common and classical issues have been addressed many times in essays, in litigation, and in codes of ethics drawn up by professional organizations like the American Sociological Association and the American Psychological Association, to which codes I shall refer later. The classical issues relate to protection of human subjects, invasion of privacy, confidentiality of records and interviews, accessibility to data, and immunity of researchers from prosecution. I will expand on one or two of these familiar issues and raise others that are less widely discussed.

II. RESEARCH STYLES

Research style raises a variety of classical ethical issues. Four episodes of court cases involving social scientists illustrate the serious issues of legal protection of rights of investigators to protect their sources of information and of immunity from being questioned by public agencies.

Case 1.[2] In November, 1972, Samuel Popkin, a Harvard political scientist, became the first American scholar jailed for not revealing his confidential sources of information about the unauthorized release of the Pentagon Papers. When he declined to identify his sources to a federal grand jury before which he appeared for ten hours, he spent one week in jail until the jury was dismissed.

Case 2.[3] A private research firm conducted a major social experiment designed to measure the impact of various negative income tax plans on labor force behavior and other activities of low income families in New Jersey for the Office of Economic Opportunity (OEO). Respondents filled out detailed questionnaires with information about their income, expenditures, and living arrangements after researchers had promised absolute confidentiality. The Mercer County prosecutor subpoenaed the research firm to submit individual case records to ascertain which recipients of federal aid programs had received illegal double payments from New Jersey Welfare. A U.S. senator crusading against welfare reform demanded individual files from researchers, and the Government Accounting Office wanted the same for reanalysis of the data. Researchers convinced some of these agencies that they did not need identified case histories and substituted the aggregate data instead.

---

[2] Nejelski & Finsterbusch, *The Prosecutor and the Researcher: Present and Prospective Variations on the Supreme Court's Branzburg Decision*, 21 Soc. Prob. 3 (1973).

[3] Kershaw & Small, *Data Confidentiality and Privacy: Lessons from the New Jersey Income Tax Experiment*, 20 Pub. Pol'y 257 (1972).

Researchers had, however, no legal grounds for denying the requests if the government agencies insisted on this information.

Case 3.[4] A commission appointed by the Governor of New York to investigate the riot and deaths which occurred at Attica Prison in 1971 interviewed thousands of witnesses under a pledge of confidentiality and published its report. The New York State Attorney General's office, which had been investigating criminal liability resulting from the riot, issued a subpoena for the commission's complete records. A trial court granted the commission's motion to quash the subpoena. However, in a future criminal trial, another court might compel disclosure of a witness' statements.

Case 4.[5] Lewis Yablonsky, a criminologist/practitioner, while testifying in defense of one of his main informants in his hippy study, was asked by the judge nine times if he had witnessed the informant smoking marijuana. Yablonsky refused to answer on fifth amendment grounds. Although he was not legally sanctioned, he said the incident was humiliating and suggested that researchers should have guarantees of immunity.

Along these same lines, I have a more personal example, fortunately not one that has gone, or is likely to go, to court.[6] *Delinquency in a Birth Cohort*[7] was a study of approximately ten thousand boys born in 1945 who lived in Philadelphia from ages 10 to 18. No ethical problems in collecting and analyzing data were encountered, for we had complete cooperation from the Board of Education, the Archdiocese, and private schools with regard to access to school records. Moreover, the Philadelphia Police Department and Selective Service granted us permission to compare names and birthdates in order to determine which boys who registered for selective service had a delinquency record.

In 1970 we obtained a research grant from the National Institute of Mental Health (NIMH) to study a ten percent sample of the birth cohort and to interview those members we could locate. After diligent investigative work we located approximately sixty percent of the sample and asked them questions requiring interviews of an hour or more. None whom we found refused to be interviewed. We had no informed consent form in those days. We asked many questions concerning their

---

[4] Nejelski & Finsterbusch, *supra* note 2, at 4-5.

[5] Irvin, *Participant Observation of Criminals*, in RESEARCH ON DEVIANCE 128-29 (J. Douglas ed. 1972).

[6] Wolfgang, *Ethical Issues of Research in Criminology*, in SOCIAL RESEARCH IN CONFLICT WITH LAW AND ETHICS 25 (P. Nejelski ed. 1976). The account here is an abridged and modified version.

[7] M. WOLFGANG, R. FIGLIO & T. SELLIN, DELINQUENCY IN A BIRTH COHORT (1972). *See also* Wolfgang, *Crime in a Birth Cohort*, 117 PROC. AM. PHILO. SOC'Y 404 (1973).

education, occupation, family, military service, gang memberships, and other personal history. Of special interest to us in analyzing their histories up to age twenty-six were self-reporting of both delinquencies prior to age eighteen and crimes committed from ages eighteen to twenty-six. We asked if they had committed any of thirty offenses before and after age eighteen and whether the crimes they committed resulted in their arrest.[8]

Many of the young men revealed to the interviewers that they had committed a variety of crimes. This study did not mark the first use of the self-report technique.[9] However, most previous studies in the United States had drawn subjects from juniors and seniors in high school who reported in mostly anonymous questionnaires or protected interviews relatively innocuous juvenile status offenses such as stealing from their mothers' pocketbooks, truancy, or petty larceny. Even the relatively sophisticated studies conducted in Denmark, Norway, and Sweden dealt mostly with petty offenses. The birth cohort follow-up in Philadelphia explored a much wider range of criminal offense behavior, including serious crimes such as robbery, burglary, rape, and even criminal homicide.

---

[8] The questions related to the following offenses:
1. Been out past curfew.
2. Played hookey from school.
3. Run away from home.
4. Made an obscene phone call.
5. Hurt someone badly enough to require medical treatment.
6. Used heroin.
7. Taken a car for joyriding.
8. Disturbed the people in a neighborhood with loud noises.
9. Set off a fire alarm for the fun of it.
10. Threatened to hurt someone if he didn't give money or something else.
11. Taken some money from someone without his knowing it.
12. Had heroin in your possession.
13. Smoked pot.
14. Stolen something from a store.
15. Passed a bad check.
16. Forced a female to have sexual intercourse with you.
17. Broken into a residence, store, school, or other enclosed area.
18. Used a weapon to threaten another person.
19. Helped a girl to have an abortion.
20. Purposely damaged or destroyed property.
21. Gone to a house of prostitution.
22. Killed someone not accidentally.
23. Been drunk in public.
24. Carried a gun without a permit.
25. Carried a switch-blade or other big knife.
26. Had pot in your possession.
27. Hurt someone in a minor way, like knocking him down.
28. Bought or accepted property which you knew was stolen.
29. Had sexual intercourse before you were married.
30. Had sex relations with another male.

[9] McClintock, *The Dark Figure*, in COLLECTED STUDIES IN CRIMINOLOGICAL RESEARCH 13-27, 31-34 (Council of Europe 1970).

Many of the young men in the Philadelphia study revealed to the interviewers that they had committed a variety of crimes. Four respondents informed us that they had been involved in criminal homicide—one before reaching eighteen—and seventy-five respondents claimed to have committed forcible rapes. Neither these offenses nor the other less serious admitted offenses resulted in any respondent's arrest.

There are several major ethical, scientific, and legal issues involved in the collection of these offense data:[10]

A. SHOULD WE HAVE HAD WRITTEN INFORMED CONSENT?

Each cohort member who was located for an interview generally cooperated. Interviews were conducted in 1971, a period just prior to the intensive concern for research using human subjects, prior to the requirement of the Department of Health, Education and Welfare that research proposals contain forms about such research, before university committees in research ethics were established, and before screening commitees at HEW were functioning formally. Interviewers informed members orally that responses would be strictly confidential, used only for research purposes, and analyzed in the aggregate, with no single individual identified or identifiable in the final research report. We interpreted cooperation in replying to questions, many of which were personal and sensitive, as consent to the uses we announced at the outset. Laws on privacy, informed consent, confidentiality, and accessibility to records were yet undeveloped. Nevertheless, there were sound reasons against requesting written consent.

Consider the psychology of the interview. Although researchers generally contacted cohort subjects first by mail or telephone, sometimes initial contact was at the subject's front door. In that event had the

---

10 As with the cohort study, a myriad of ethical problems arise with other styles of research in deviance and crime. Participant observation in juvenile gang research may involve, as it did for John Wise who worked for James Short and Fred Strodbeck in Chicago, direct observations of delinquent and criminal activities followed by result tabulation and recordation. J. SHORT & F. STRODBECK, GROUP PROCESSES AND GANG DELINQUENCY (1965). In a study soon to be published, Bernard Cohen observed, *not* as a participant, the street network activity of heterosexual female prostitutes in about 30 street locations in New York City for several years. He described his qualitative naturalistic ethnomethodology and then kept count and blended in his quantitative analyses. He observed solicitations and other offenses, but he contends that because observation took place only in public places, the acts would have occurred whether or not he observed them from his car or some other post. He claims that he did not intrude into the lives of his subjects and that he did not have an obligation to report offenses, despite his giving no one assurances of confidentiality. Nor did he obtain informed consent to view the public performances of the prostitutes. B. COHEN, DEVIANT STREET NETWORKS: PROSTITUTION IN NEW YORK CITY (1980). Under these circumstances, Cohen contends, he violated no ethical restraints of scientific inquiry. I think he is right. Carl Klockars also experienced these dilemmas about disclosures of crimes that came to his attention in *The Professional Fence*. C. KLOCKARS, THE PROFESSIONAL FENCE (1974).

interviewer asked for written consent, the subject might have wished to be more fully apprised of the mechanics and ultimate use of the interview. For example, he could have asked to see the interview schedule. Compliance with such a request would have nullified the advantages of proceeding gradually from neutral to sensitive questions. It is impossible to know how many refusals such a process would have promoted.

Moreover, the form of the written consent could or could not have contained reference to the refusal of the research staff to reveal information to the police. We did not know then and still do not know whether a court order could indeed impound the records, whether any member of the staff who had access to specific information could suffer prosecution and imprisonment for protecting records, or whether any effort to conceal data would be successful. Without the reference, the form would have been inadequate and therefore misleading. With the reference, without admitting that one or more of these agencies might have the authority to confiscate, or impound our records, the form again would have been misleading. If the form admitted that justice authorities could impound our records refusals to participate would have been so abundant that the project would have been impossible. Either lies or agnostic replies would have been the interviewees' responses to a variety of hypothetical questions. The former would be unethical; the latter would invite refusals to be interviewed.

On the other hand, the oral request for participation in a sociological research maintained a minimum of formality, permitted the respondent to refuse to answer any specific question (of course, a written consent does not preclude specific question refusals), and permitted employment of the pretested question positioning intended to maximize the likelihood of response. The result was rapport and cooperation.

B. SHOULD THE RESULTS OF THE INTERVIEW BE PUBLISHED?

Our Center unequivocally supports publication of the results with the protections announced in letters and orally by the interviewers. No single individual will be identified or identifiable and all data will be aggregated. Undeniably, publication in professional journals or books produces a new layer of visibility of the research. Newspapers and other media summarizing our earlier original birth cohort study thereby made the police and courts aware of the character of the study. The same certainly will occur with publication of the follow-up reporting not only many of the personal, sociopsychological variables in the lives of cohort members, but also the self-reported delinquencies and crimes. At that point, police and other agencies could exert pressure on the research team[11] at the Center to reveal the names of those cohort members who informed us of their crimes. The danger of publication would then become a function of the degree to which threats of such pressure are real.

We still intend to publish, under the assumptions that (1) pressure to disclose names is an unlikely event, and (2) our Center can effectively function as a buffer between our research subjects and the acquisition of our files by outside persons.

C.   ARE MEMBERS OF THE RESEARCH STAFF ACCESSORIES AFTER THE FACT?

Having obtained information about criminal offenses from identified subjects, the researchers stand in a posture of harboring information, if not hiding individuals or abetting escape. The researcher does not have the mantle of the clergy or of medical practitioners for protection. Probably the "crime," if any here, is misprision of a felony, which is obsolete in most jurisdictions but still an offense under federal law.

The traditional research response to the charge of being an accessory is that he or she is a neutral, disinterested recipient of data collected only for scientific research purposes. The purpose for obtaining the information is to aid the scholarly enterprise and to provide guidance for a rational social policy. Data obtained that could have direct untoward consequences to subjects are not the possession of the state but of science. Research is not designed to treat, help, or harm individual subjects, and the social scientist is not a representative of any branch of government with an obligation to execute certain police or judicial duties. It may be argued that technically he *is*, but the social definers do not perceive or define him as such. The scientist might contend that he is not even sure that the information given him is valid or correct; the rebuttal is that it gives cause for official investigation.

D.   ARE MEMBERS OF THE RESEARCH STAFF OBSTRUCTING JUSTICE?

To the extent that notions of justice relate to the punishment of offenders, anyone who has information about crimes and fails to report it denies the system of justice its capacity to function relative to those crimes and their perpetrators. Courts, however, generally construe obstruction of justice more narrowly and require obstruction of proceedings actually pending, with specific intent to do so.

---

[11] Researchers are not granted judicial protection based on the first amendment. In Branzburg v. Hayes, 408 U.S. 665 (1972), the Court rejected a reporter's privilege based on that amendment. However, there are some narrow areas of protection, as in the case of research on the effect and use of drugs, according to the Federal Comprehensive Drug Abuse Prevention and Control Act of 1970, 21 U.S.C. § 872 (1970).

Unwillingness to report reflects an uncompromising respect for the conditions of scientific research that explicitly provide for confidentiality. Moreover, the research neither helps nor hinders the police and prosecutory functions of society for were it not for the scientist's inquiry, the information would not be available to authorities anyway.

E. IS THERE, NONETHELESS, AN OBLIGATION TO SOCIETY AND
    CRIMINAL JUSTICE TO REPORT THIS KNOWLEDGE,
    TRANSCENDING THE ETHICS OF CONFIDENTIALITY OR
    THE INTERESTS OF SCIENCE?

Putting aside questions of legality, this question asks whether the scientific researcher has broader moral responsibilities than his research perimeters. Does the absence of written informed consent minimize the impropriety of revealing criminal behavior by respondents, or would revelation be ethically worse than not revealing the information? The scientist may be viewed as ethically accountable only to the myopic limits of his scientific vision. Over its long history, science has created codes of conduct possessing deep traditions. Thus, in the Philadelphia study the scientist values protecting the individual used for his research above the interests of capture for criminal justice. Society until now has generally permitted the scientist his priority allocation. Again, the scientist seeks neither to help nor harm the individual respondent per se, nor to help nor hinder the criminal justice system. His role is neither benevolent nor malevolent.

If a medical laboratory research project unrelated to cancer research inadvertently discovered that a volunteer subject had cancer, the researcher might feel rightly obligated to inform the subject, because such information might save a diseased person's life. Many other examples are imaginable in which revelations to the research subject and to others could have beneficial effects. Is it conceivable that a piece of information about a research subject may be discovered that would be harmful to him but of considerable benefit to many others? If so, no such situations exist in the criminological research under discussion. It may be said that if any researcher doubts the moral obligation to maintain confidentiality, he should abstain from this kind of research. He would thereby satisfy his sense of ethics that lie outside the framework of those of science.

F. WHAT SHOULD A RESEARCH CENTER DO IF THE POLICE,
    PROSECUTOR, OR COURT REQUESTS THE FILES?

Our position is clear: we would not honor the request. We would make every effort, short of using aggressive force, to prevent the files from being examined or taken from the Center's premises. We would, if necessary, enter into litigation to protect the confidentiality of the records. There is no United States Supreme Court case affirming or rejecting this position.

Even if the staff is not viewed as accessory after the fact or as obstructing justice for refusing to identify subjects, a court may still hold staff members in contempt if they do not submit the files to examination or impounding upon a court order. Whether a research staff is immune from contempt remains undecided in the caselaw. Nevertheless, were our Center's staff declared by the courts as not immune from prosecution, we would still maintain a posture of unwillingness to reveal names.

G.   CAN A RESEARCH STAFF DEVELOP A TECHNIQUE THAT CAN
     PROVIDE A FAIL-SAFE PROTECTION AGAINST IDENTIFICATION
     OF INDIVIDUAL SUBJECTS IN A RESEARCH FILE?

There are techniques that surely would delay, if not forever prevent, subject identification. Researchers might use computer tapes on cards that show only identification numbers representing names for the file that is to be analyzed statistically in the aggregate.[12] Number-name combinations might be on a separate computer tape which can be deposited in a bank account in a foreign country where accounts are secret. Although no law prohibits this procedure, the account owner (in our example the Center) may still be subject to charges of contempt for failing to produce the tape.[13] Nevertheless, considering the paramount purpose of confidentiality, such a process is both pragmatically expedient and ethical. However researchers decide to catalogue their data, in studies such as that conducted in Philadelphia they should not record the names of victims or other identifying facts about specific crimes unless absolutely essential for the research. Without such details, the files are less useful to law-enforcement officials.[14]

---

[12] This suggestion was made in Blumstein, *Science and Technology*, in TASK FORCE REPORT OF THE PRESIDENT'S COMMISSION ON LAW ENFORCEMENT AND ADMINISTRATION OF JUSTICE (1967).

[13] Similar issues have been raised in Wolfgang, *The Social Scientist in Court*, 65 J. CRIM. L. & C. 239 (1974).

[14] Recently, the Northern District of California stressed the need to preserve confidentiality in Richards of Rockford, Inc., v. Pacific Gas and Electric Co., 71 F.R.D. 388 (N.D. Cal. 1976). Plaintiff, seeking final payment for delivery of 135 spray cooling modules for use in one of the gas company's power plants, brought an action for breach of contract against Pacific, which withheld final payment because the spray modules allegedly did not perform as guaranteed. Plaintiff deposed a professor who, under a pledge of confidentiality, had interviewed employees of the gas company as part of a research project which involved inquiring into the decision to install the spray cooling facility. On the advice of counsel, the professor,

III.   PUBLIC POLICY STATEMENTS

Another ethical issue pertains to the issuance of public or social policy statements. Increasingly, public decisionmakers are listening to social scientists in general and criminologists in particular. Even if these officials do not always take our advice, they often request our testimony. The efficacy of such testimony is unclear. Having been involved in some of these dramas, I have felt keenly the pressure of considering the ethics of presenting scientific evidence vulnerable to criticism before bodies that intend to act on the testimony. Scientific evidence is presentable in a relatively bland, descriptive fashion without explicit leaps to interpretation beyond the data. Absent interpretation, however, an audience usually will receive the data in ways that conform to their own predilections. If the researcher offers his own conclusions, he should do so with a clearance to his conscience that he has done his best work with the available material at his command. If the testimony bears on social policy, the researcher must struggle with determining when a Sumnerian (William Graham Sumner) description moves to a Wardian (Lester F. Ward) prescription.

The scientific issues of reliability and validity can reach the threshold of an ethical issue when statements relating to crime and punishment could affect the lives of many thousands of persons: how many replications of one good study are required for firm prescriptive conclusiveness? This and similar questions continue to disturb the scientific community, especially in light of conflicting and contradictory findings on such topics as deterrence, incapacitation, plea bargaining, and the death penalty. If one has a posture on a particular policy issue and the scientific evidence is equivocal, should the researcher avoid offers to testify? Is self-imposed silence an ethically acceptable position to science? I think not, even if there is fear that the presentation of findings may be abusively employed or distorted in interpretation by others.

Allow me again to give an example from my own research experience on the topics of race, rape, and the death penalty. Science deals with probabilities, not certainties. At what point a probability state-

---

and later his research assistant, refused to disclose either the identity of the gas company employees interviewed or the content of the interviews.   .

According to the court, the issue was "whether on these facts, plaintiff's interest in satisfying its discovery request outweighs the public interest in maintaining confidential relationships between academic researchers and their sources." *Id*. at 389. Noting that neither the professor nor his assistant were parties to the proceeding, that they initiated their research with no view to this litigation, that the central subject of the litigation was not central to the study, and that factual issues dividing the parties were resolvable without recourse to statements of the gas company employees, the court stated that "[c]ompelled disclosure of confidential information would without question stifle research into questions of public policy, the very subjects in which the public interest is the greatest." *Id*. at 390.

ment can become morally prescriptive is not clear, despite our reliance on tests of statistical significance. In one instance research was performed to determine whether there was *differential* sentencing based on race of the offender and victim. When the carefully collected data revealed differential treatment by race, I finally concluded in official judicial testimony that such a differential was inferentially *discriminatory*. The difference between these two terms—"differential" and "discriminatory"—signified a prescriptive leap.[15]

Most people's attitudes about the death penalty rest fundamentally upon one or more ethical assertions. Teachings from social or behavioral science may be a factor in these determinations, but research from these disciplines is often selectively used to buttress pre-existing beliefs and moral postures. The judiciary, especially at the federal level, has increasingly admitted social science research in testimony by expert witnesses and in Supreme Court briefs.

Over ten years ago, Michael Finkelstein traced the history of judicial reasoning in jury discrimination cases and showed that for some time the Supreme Court had been reasoning according to its intuition of probabilities.[16] Finkelstein argued that statistical support should replace intuition in judicial reasoning. The Court later cited him in its *Whitus v. Georgia*[17] decision which, as de Cani noted,[18] marked the beginning of the Court's "willingness to listen to a probabilistic argument that the group from which the jury was chosen was not a representative cross-section of the community."

My own initial involvement in the presentation of social science research was in the *Maxwell v. Bishop*[19] case in the Arkansas district court, which involved a black convicted of raping a white and sentenced to death. Research had demonstrated that out of twenty-eight legal and extralegal variables concerned with the offense of rape, the offender, and the victim, the only variable that emerged as overwhelmingly statistically significant was that of blacks raping whites, relative to the sentence of death. Now, permit me to refer to my previous account:

> I was asked under cross-examination if I had ever been in Arkansas before my appearance as an expert witness for the Legal Defense Fund. I

---

15 Some of the following has been adapted from my article, *The Death Penalty: Social Philosophy and Social Science Research*, 14 CRIM. L. BULL. 18 (1978).

16 Finkelstein, *Application of Statistical Decision Theory to the Jury Discrimination Cases*, 80 HARV. L. REV. 338 (1966).

17 385 U.S. 545, 552 n.2 (1966).

18 de Cani, *Statistical Evidence in Jury Discrimination Cases*, 65 J. CRIM. L. & C. 234, 235 (1974).

19 257 F. Supp. 710 (E.D. Ark. 1966), *denial of appeal rev'd and remanded per curiam*, 385 U.S. 650 (1967), *aff'd*, 398 F.2d 138 (8th Cir. 1968), *vacated and remanded per curiam*, 398 U.S. 262 (1970).

responded in the negative. The Assistant Attorney General used this re-
ponse to imply that I did not fully understand the social conditions or the
litigation processes in Arkansas. It was further brought out under cross-
examination that Garland County, in which Maxwell had been tried, was
not included in the survey sampling of Arkansas counties. The state argued that failure to include Garland County was a fatal error, that the
generalized conclusions drawn from the Arkansas rape-death penalty
study could not apply to the *Maxwell* case.

Based upon my research, this conclusion was absurd. We had taken a
carefully drawn random sample of counties in Arkansas, as well as in the
other ten Southern states, without attention to the counties in which specific cases for litigation may finally occur. Our primary interest had been
to determine whether there had been a customary, institutionalized, systematic process of differential sentencing to the death penalty based on
race; hence, the specific litigated cases were of no consequence to our random selection. If we had drawn our sample counties purposefully to pick
counties in which cases like *Maxwell* had occurred, we would have destroyed the statistical randomness of the selection of counties and would
also have distorted the character of the scientific inquiry. Yet, this fact
and this kind of reasoning had little impact on either Assistant Attorney
General Fletcher Jackson or Judge J. Smith Henley.

The social scientist who becomes involved in testifying and displaying
research evidence must also be prepared for opinions that contravene the
traditional specific canons of response. For example, Judge Henley accepted my conclusion that sentencing patterns of Arkansas Negroes convicted of raping white victims "could not be due to the operation of the
laws of chance." He accepted the conclusion that a black convicted of
raping a white woman had about a 50 per cent chance of receiving a death
sentence, and that any man convicted of raping a woman of his own race
stood only a 14 per cent chance. But Judge Henley thought the difference
could be explained on grounds other than race, and contended that the
imposition of the death sentence might be due to some factor for which
statistical analysis had not been possible or presentable. He announced in
his decision that the "variables which Dr. Wolfgang considered are objective . . . broad in instances . . . imprecise . . . . Discrimination moreover
is a highly subjective matter [and might not] be detected by a statistical
analysis . . . . Statistics are elusive things at best, and it is a truism that
almost anything can be proven by them." These are common assertions
made by persons who are not social scientists trained in statistics. Yet, the
social scientist who becomes involved in testifying in this area must be
prepared for arguments and decisions that are political or that reside in
legal vicissitudes outside the framework of social science inquiry and evidence.[20]

Upholding the conviction in *Maxwell*, the United States Court of
Appeals for the Eighth Circuit[21] acknowledged the extensive and sophis-
ticated research, yet concluded that "nothing has been presented in
Maxwell's case which convinces us, or causes us to seriously wonder,

---

[20] Wolfgang, *supra* note 13, at 244.
[21] Maxwell v. Bishop, 398 F.2d 138 (8th Cir. 1968).

that, with the imposition of the death penalty, he was the victim of discrimination based on race." The court's resistance to social science research is blatant:

> Whatever value [the statistical] argument may have as an instrument of social concern, whatever suspicion it may arouse with respect to southern interracial rape trials as a group over a longer period of time, and whatever it may disclose with respect to other localities, we feel that the statistical argument does nothing to destroy the integrity of Maxwell's trial. Although the investigation and study made by Professor Wolfgang in the summer of 1965 is interesting and provocative, we do not, on the basis of that study, upset Maxwell's conviction and, as a necessary consequence, cast serious doubt on every other rape conviction in the state courts of Arkansas.[22]

The court was unwilling both to accuse a state of discriminatory conduct in sentencing proportionately more blacks than whites to the death penalty over a twenty-year period and to acknowledge that Maxwell may have been a victim of such a practice, despite its statement that "we do not say that there is no ground for suspicion that the death penalty for rape may have been discriminatorily applied over the decades in that large area of states whose statutes provide for it. There are recognizable indicators of this."[23] Michael Meltsner recounted in his book *Cruel and Unusual* that "if race were not related to capital sentencing in Arkansas, the results observed in the twenty-year period study could have occurred fortuitously in two (or less) twenty-year periods since the birth of Christ."[24] Juxtapose this statement against the court's use of such phrases as "we do not say that there is no ground for suspicion" and "there are recognizable indicators." How different the language of science and the court! A probability of 0.02 becomes "recognizable indicators."

Although recognizing social science research in its 1976 death penalty decisions, the Supreme Court was careful to minimize its use.[25] As

---

22 *Id*. at 148.

23 *Id*. at 147.

24 M. Meltsner, Cruel and Unusual: The Supreme Court and Capital Punishment 100-01 (1973).

25 As Meltsner also shows, the Supreme Court reflected an increasing receptivity to social science research in the *Furman* decision. The basis for inferring cruel and unusual punishment in the imposition of the death penalty hinged on the interpretation and relationship between the eighth and fourteenth amendments. Both Justices Douglas and Marshall accepted the social science research that showed discrimination in the imposition of the death penalty. But in the brief before the Supreme Court in the *Fowler* case in 1974, Solicitor General Robert Bork inserted the following statement about research: "In any event, we do not think that the meaning of the Eighth Amendment should turn on the results of the latest social science research." Brief for the United States as Amicus Curiae at 37 n.13, Fowler v. North Carolina, 428 U.S. 904 (1976).

Moreover, the abundance of research on deterrence introduced to the Court has resulted in no definite judicial conclusionary statements. The testimony of Thorsten Sellin that the

Hugo Bedau noted:

> One of the most galling features of the *Gregg*, *Proffitt*, and *Jurek* decisions is the way the court reacted, or rather failed to react, to the social science research published in the years since *Furman*. With perhaps one exception, the court passed it by without significant acknowledgement, discussion, or rebuttal. This was especially conspicuous in the *Gregg* ruling. . . . For social scientists and jurists who had expected that this round of death penalty cases would find the Supreme Court resting its decision, at least in part, on the results of careful and relevant empirical investigations, the *Gregg* decision can be viewed only as a bitter disappointment. Four years ago, in his dissent in *Furman*, Chief Justice Burger complained of the 'paucity' of evidence relied on by the majority ruling in favor of abolition. This year's ruling in *Gregg* rests on even less.[26]

Until the Supreme Court can come to grips with probabilistic and inferential statistics, intuitive, clinical, and vague judgments will continue, as will *ethical* decisions.

IV.   EVALUATION RESEARCH AND THE P < .05

Norval Morris raised an interesting question about the "burglar's nightmare."[27] We ordinarily think of random representative samples or assignments as scientifically acceptable, even ethically proper. But suppose burglars alike in all important particulars were assigned randomly to experimental and control groups, the experimentals to be released six months or a year earlier than they ordinarily would be and the controls at their regularly appointed time. How would the burglar assigned to the control group respond? He could say that it is unjust and unethical to be put into the control group and that he deserves to be released early also. Can science, for the sake of determining whether early release pro-

---

death penalty has no ascertainable deterrent effect led to its abolition in England. Isaac Ehrlich's econometric analyses, suggesting that eight lives were saved by such execution was quickly challenged by a series of other econometric studies that denied the correlation between executions and the homicide rates. *See* Bailey, *Murder and Capital Punishment*, 45 AM. J. ORTHOPSYCH. 669 (1975); Bailey, *Rape and the Death Penalty*, in CAPITAL PUNISHMENT IN THE UNITED STATES 336 (Bedau & Pierce eds. 1976); Baldus & Cole, *A Comparison of the Work of Thorsten Sellin and Isaac Ehrlich on the Deterrent Effect of Capital Punishment*, 85 YALE L.J. 170 (1975); Bowers & Pierce, *The Illusion of Deterrence in Isaac Ehrlich's Research on Capital Punishment*, 85 YALE L.J. 187 (1975); Forst, *The Deterrent Effect of Capital Punishment: A Cross-State Analysis of the 1960s*, 61 MINN. L. REV. 743 (1977); Passell & Taylor, *The Deterrence Controversy*, in CAPITAL PUNISHMENT IN THE UNITED STATES 59 (Bedau & Pierce eds. 1976); Peck, *The Deterrent Effect of Capital Punishment*, 85 YALE L.J. 164, 359 (1975-76); B. Forst, V. Filator & L. Klein, The Deterrent Effect of Capital Punishment (unpublished manuscript).

A recent panel of the National Research Council of the National Academy of Sciences has carefully reviewed the literature on deterrence and provided new models of analysis. As mentioned earlier, the panel concludes that the evidence is currently inconclusive because of the inadequacy of the data.

26 Bedau, *New Life for the Death Penalty*, 223 NATION 144, 146-47 (1976).

27 Morris, *Punishment, Desert, and Rehabilitation*, in EQUAL JUSTICE UNDER LAW 137 (U.S. Dep't Justice 1976).

duces no more recidivism, justify retention of some subjects in prison? The burglar says no, the scientist says yes.

Evaluation research presents a whole series of ethical issues, far more than we can explore here. But there is at least one overriding commentary I wish to make. Scientists and researchers have an ethical obligation to know about the most robust and sophisticated research techniques available, else their findings may be faulty and fall far short of a conclusion on the basis of the best available evidence. The newest and most complex techniques are not always applicable to certain kinds of data; hence, the researcher should seek to fit his analyses to the quality of his material. Moreover, as probability statistics have become increasingly admitted into litigation both in civil and criminal proceedings, some judges have come to accept the P value of .05 as nearly sacred in determining what is acceptable and what is unacceptable science. Neither scientists nor judges should be so rigorously wedded to the notion of .05 to ignore consistent patterns and trends of P values a bit more than .05. The ethics of our findings are not bound by an invariable obedience to such limited notions of reality.

V.   RESEARCH FUNDS

The source of research funds may not pose a moral dilemma for many recipients. Nevertheless pressure to adopt unpalatable suggestions, unmanageable time constraints, or politicization of the funding agency may put into question the ethics of accepting funds from that source. It is unlikely that the researcher will seek or accept funds from a group whose views he considers unacceptable or intolerable, irrespective of the imposition of those views on the research.

Some researchers would not accept funds from major corporations because of presumed unethical practices in the acquisition of wealth. Others, opposing the power of government, may likewise refuse government funds for research, however free from interference in the research. In either case the danger of manipulation of research findings by the funding agency often provides an additional disincentive to accepting research funds. Where the agency does impose its views on the research, say by conditioning publication of results on their conformity with the agency's views, the scientist who values freedom of publication and scientific inquiry prostitutes his integrity by accepting such conditions. Recognizing the possibility that research will facilitate the misuse of power in both the private and public spheres, the Code of Ethics of the American Sociological Association affirm[s] the autonomy of sociological inquiry.

The sociologist must be responsive, first and foremost, to the truth of his investigation. Sociology must not be an instrument of any person or group which seeks to suppress or misuse knowledge. The fate of sociology as a science is dependent upon the fate of free inquiry in an open society.[28]

VI.   TEACHING CRIMINOLOGY

I am indebted to Professor Jerome Hall for the provocative suggestion that it is ethically good and sound for a criminology professor to disclose to new students his ideological preferences within the subject matter to be discussed. Such disclosures permit the students to take those perspectives into account when digesting hypotheses, findings, and interpretations offered by the professor. An instructor controls the interactive dynamics of the classroom through the choice of topics, selection of readings, and the approaching and concluding of a topic. I should think that topics such as free will and determinism, consensus versus conflict, correctional treatment versus retribution, and the just deserts model and others are proper candidates for the presentation of one's perspectives. _ Whether the perspectives are based on the best available scientific evidence may be of some consequence; but, however they are derived, teachers should display them explicitly. Scientists and teachers in other disciplines such as astronomy, biology, and even mathematics must sense this same disclosure obligation. But in criminology and criminal justice, where the law, ethics, and science converge on so many topics, disclosure is vital.

Revealing personal biases in a textbook may fulfill a teacher's obligation to disclose. But can a professor ethically require his own students to purchase the textbook? The book is, after all, nothing more than the written, usually more elegant and comprehensive, presentation of the professor's learning. Arguably, the process of putting such a book together is itself a claim that the book is the best in the field. Moreover, students need not elect to take the course. Therefore, requiring its purchase is reasonable and logical. To further insulate the ethical propriety of requiring one's own textbook, the professor might divest himself of the royalties and thereby reduce the cost to students.

VII.   CONCLUSION

I conclude by referring to a reply by Professor Stephen J. Morse to Judge Bazelon's argument for more welfare programs in order to reduce poverty and ultimately crime. Professor Morse argues against what he calls "welfare criminology" and for a firm sentencing policy in criminal justice. He raises a number of ethical issues:

Is it immoral to ask that the cost of reducing crime be borne by the mor-

---

[28] *Toward a Code of Ethics for Sociologists*, 3 AM. SOC. 316, 318 (1968).

ally responsible agents who have been convicted of crimes beyond a reasonable doubt, rather than by innocent persons? If mandatory sentences of humane duration significantly reduce the crime rate (in contrast to poverty programs which have not done so), can it reasonably be claimed that such a program is amoral or immoral? To be sure, we cannot be certain which would be more effective, increased social welfare or criminal justice reform. But given this uncertainty and the past failures of social justice solutions, it does seem clear the social justice adherent is not entitled to claim that his position is *the* moral one, and that alternative analyses and suggestions are immoral.[29]

The *Report of the Task Force on the Role of Psychology in the Criminal Justice System* speaks eloquently about the reasons for the importance of ethics in this field:

> While other institutions, such as mental hospitals, also restrict individual freedom, the criminal justice system is the principal locus of legitimate force in American society. The consequences of its misapplication may be severe and irreversible. An additional reason for placing a high priority on ethical consensus in criminal justice is that the people processed by that system are likely to be poor or minorities and thus to have little access to conventional means for redressing their grievances.[30]

Scientific research and ethics are interrelated, especially in criminal justice. Ethical decisions are made and changed based on subjective perceptions of good and evil, right and wrong. Changes in science are mostly cumulative and, within the sustained value system of the canons of science, change is improvement in the understanding and the acquisition of knowledge. When ethics and science intersect, the historical moment is important. For when the qualitative difference of our ethics meets the quantitative maturation of our science, each impinges on the other in ways that require constantly new interpretations. The ethical issues of justice today are little different from those raised by Plato, Aristotle, Kant, and others. The science of today is little understood by a demographic generation removed from today. To mesh the two is our perennial problem.

29 Morse, *The Twilight of Welfare Criminology: A Reply to Judge Bazelon*, 49 S. Cal. L. Rev. 1249, 1265 (1976).

30 *Report of the Task Force on the Role of Psychology in the Criminal Justice System*, 33 Am. Psych. 1099, 1100 (1978).

21

Policy Evaluation
Integrating Empirical and Normative Judgments

Frank Fischer

Traditionally, the dominant theme in policy evaluation has been the quest for scientific rationality. As an ideal, the scientific approach to evaluation has its material and intellectual origins in the convergence of primary forces that have shaped modern society, namely industrialization and technological development. The impact of this convergence was first clearly reflected in the canons of scientific management and today is embodied in the theory of its stepchildren—operations research and systems analysis.

The steady development of these decision-oriented sciences has given rise to the modern conception of technocracy. As a form of decision making, technocracy is legitimated through an appeal to scientific expertise, beyond which further appeal is neither necessary nor permissible (Ferkiss, 1969). Its influence on the conduct of contemporary policymakers is difficult to overstate. There can be little doubt that the technocratic value system has emerged as one of the dominant ideologies of the twentieth century (Habermas, 1970).

Fundamentally, technocracy derives its legitimacy from two sources. The first is the material progress that has resulted from a pragmatic adherence to its methodological principles. Modern bureaucratic organization, as the institutional embodiment of technical rationality, has made possible unprecedented levels of economic growth. Second, technical rationality is legitimated by the dominant epistemological theory that has governed scientific progress, namely positivism. Technical rationality is essentially the handmaiden of positivism's instrumental orientation to action, emphasizing the selection of "efficient means" to given ends and values (Fischer, 1980).

Under the methodological prescriptions of positivism, only technical decisions about the instrumental relationship of means to ends lend themselves to the rules of rational assessment (Weber, 1949). Value judgments, as decisions about which ends or goals to choose, are ruled beyond the reach of scientific methodology and, therefore, must be relegated to philosophy and metaphysics. Unlike factual questions (such as, "What is the most efficient means to pursue that which is to be done?"), the answers to value questions must ultimately be based on emotional judgments of personal conviction, taste, or faith. Discussion of normative

From Frank Fischer, "Policy Evaluation: Integrating Empirical and Normative Judgments," original manuscript.

principles and assumptions in this view can only lead to a hopeless morass (Meehan, 1975).

These methodological principles provide the framework for a policy science that emphasizes empirically oriented technical criticisms of means designed to efficiently achieve goals or ends taken as given. When carried to a logical extreme, technical efficiency tends to emerge as the essence of rational action.

As one ardent advocate of the positivistic orientation put it, "The economic principle is the fundamental principle of all rational action, and not just a particular feature of a certain kind of rational action—all rational action is therefore an act of economizing" (von Mises, 1960: 148). The policy scientist functions as a social engineer whose task is to calculate the costs and benefits of alternative means for achieving goals. In the process, the value-laden political dimensions of policy tend to be denigrated. Frequently, they have been portrayed as irrational interruptions that impede the methodological requirements of efficient decision making (Wildavsky, 1966).

As long as the central economic problem of society remained the production of the basic necessities of life, as it did for most of history, a technical orientation toward the means of achieving economic goals successfully served as the legitimate source of standards for rational action. Not only did such standards facilitate an unprecedented level of economic development; they also secured political stability through the satisfaction derived from increasing levels of consumption. However, as the central economic question has begun to shift in the second half of this century from production to the question of "production for what?" the canons of technical rationality have come under increasing criticism from a variety of quarters (Weisskopf, 1971). As talk of the "limits of growth" and a "zero-sum" economy intensify, the pressing problem becomes less a matter of determining efficient means to ends than a question of which ends to choose (Thurow, 1980).

At this juncture, technical rationality itself becomes part of the problem. Insofar as it leads to the denigration of the value-laden political dimensions of normative deliberation, it leaves us with a profound dilemma. We are provided with rational procedures for dealing only with the secondary aspect of life. We can talk about how to get to specific goals but not about what these goals should be. Technical rationality thus denies the possibility of the methodology necessary to pursue the most pressing issues of the times (Habermas, 1970). Diesing has succinctly summed up the dilemma: "It seems unfortunate to have rational procedures available for the relatively less important decisions of life and to have none for dealing with the most important decisions" (1961: 1).

Labeling the problem as an "administrative crisis," Hart and Scott (1973) trace it to the instrumental orientation of the value system of the technocratic elites. To bring out the unarticulated premises that inform their decisions and behavior, they advocate the introduction of normative discourse in organizational policy-making and evaluation.

THE PROBLEM OF METHODOLOGY

These issues have renewed methodological exploration in the social and policy sciences. Policy theorists such as Dror (1969) and Rein (1976) have begun to recognize the necessity of studying the normative political dimensions of policy evaluation and decision making. Beyond the emphasis on efficiency, these theorists understand the need to include the political assessment of policy goals. Policy analysts must devote more effort to the normative aspects of political decision making, particularly problems concerned with the recognition of diverse goals and values, political accommodation to contradictory goals, and recruitment of normative support for particularly policies. Specifically, this raises the question of how a particular policy relates to the existing structure of social and political values. For the policy analyst, it poses the problem of how to evaluate the normative acceptability of proposed policies to various relevant participants—political decision makers, interest groups, administrators, and so on—whose consents are required for policies to be translated into political action. For Arnold Meltsner (1972: 859), focus on this political dimension of policy "will be the lever by which the analyst achieves some measure of usefulness and success."

From a positivistic perspective, the logic of the task is clear. The analyst must empirically sort out the political norms and values that bear on a particular policy problem and relate them to a causal model of the social processes that underlie the policy issue. The policy scientist can turn here to techniques such as value mapping (Rein, 1976: 43). The task is first to determine the logical compatibility of a desired goal with other accepted goals in the larger normative framework or ideology that are then to be integrated into the policy model as causal variables related to specific empirical conditions and consequences. A methodology of political acceptability is translated here into a scheme for modeling and prediction. The ideal, according to Meltsner (1972), is an analytical integration of political categories and data into the structure of a mathematical policy model. Similarly, Dror (1969) and Majone (1975) state that political feasibility should be expressed as a "probability distribution" of each policy alternative. As an equation, political acceptability (Y) could be expressed as a product of $W_1X_1 \ldots W_nX_n$, where W_1 represents a value judgment about the importance of X_1 to the participants and X_1 designates the magnitude of a specific causal variable (Hammond and Adelman, 1978). Conceived within the framework of a stochastic model, the influence of political knowledge will depend on political science's ability to quantify political factors.

There is a large body of comparative policy output research aimed at establishing such causal linkages (Hofferbert, 1974). These efforts search for causal connections between the determinants of policymaker behavior, including the influence of specific normative decision rules, and public policy outputs (Rae and Taylor, 1971). For policy mapping, such findings provide an important beginning for further refinements. This, however, does not affirm the operational potential of the scientific approach for policy decision making. It only points to the theoretical or logical possibility of the project.

Writers such as Meltsner (1972), Dror (1968), and Majone (1975) are aware of the major operational dilemmas posed by the scientific ideal. Even if theoretically possible, a subject still open to debate, the scientific ideal suffers the empirical limitations of a scientific value theory in general. Given both the state-of-the-art of quantification and the enormous complexity of the linkages between values expressed in the phenomenological world of policymaking and their statistical designations in an abstract causal policy model, the positivistically based approach is far removed from the realm of practical decision-making techniques, especially when it comes to the normatively complex problems that press for policy solutions. In statistical terms, it requires first the ability to quantify normative political variables without distorting their fundamental or essential characteristics. Generally, analysts must rely on the use of indirect proxy variables designed only to estimate normative characteristics. Values usually emerge from the process as conceptually static and noncomplex.

Second, the scientific approach implies the possibility of integrating these quantified normative variables in an empirically grounded theoretical model of the underlying social process, a model capable of connecting a complicated web of cause-and-effect relationships with means-ends (input/output) relationships (Arrow, 1967). The explanatory power of the available policy models is far from the level needed to provide the foundation for the design and development of effective intervention strategies. Such models can retrospectively isolate variables that assist in explanation, but are far too imprecise to generate predictive or causal knowledge. While such decision models have *heuristic* value in a range of social problems, they generally can provide *solutions* only in well-defined technically oriented problems that lend themselves to quantification and calculation. In social policy, answers can be calculated only under restricted circumstances—such as uncomplicated, simple situations with quick and easy formation, or perhaps where calculations are based on preemptory values (Frohock, 1979: 23-63). The more sophisticated and compelling the mathematical formulation, as Dahl (1975: 130) puts it, the more it tends to apply to less controversial technical problems.

Equally important, the failure of the analytical process is fostered by the overly simplistic conception of values and value clarification that lies behind it. Brown (1976) and Rein (1976) attribute this failure to misleading positivistic assumptions, based on the fact-value dichotomy, which underplay the complexity of the nature of values and the character of normative relationships. Under positivistic assumptions, the task of normative analysis, borrowed from Weber, is limited to the explication and elaboration of the consistency of value judgments and the examination of their logical implications for action. For the policy analyst, this means tracing out the relationship of an established goal to a fixed or static web of values that surrounds a social problem. Once accomplished, normative variables are to be quantified and plugged into the larger empirical model, which specifies the causal relationships that underlie the desired social action. Beyond these formal tasks, which are to a large degree technical in character, little further reflection about values is required.

Examination of the actual policy research process, however, shows the approach to be a misleading simplification, if not a fundamental epistemological mistake. Value positions in policy research seldom prove to be static conceptions that remain fixed and unchanging. Instead, they tend to shift iteratively as the analyst moves through the phases of data collection, analysis and interpretation. New data and knowledge frequently have a direct impact on the content and desirability of normative policy goals. Normative analysis, therefore, becomes an ongoing process that continues to occur throughout the phases of empirical policy research. This reality tends to call into question the scientific formulation of political acceptability ($Y = W_1X_1 \ldots W_nX_n$), as the values of W would tend to change throughout the empirical and deliberative processes. New data (X), as well as technical refinements in research design and quantification, introduce qualitative shifts in value judgments (W). This suggests that value perspectives are as much internal to the policy processes as they are fixed entities "out there" in the social world.

The policy analyst has a dilemma here. The methodological tools for both the empirical and normative dimensions of the policy mapping process are underdeveloped. Causal models can locate variables that assist in explaining social observations, but their margins of error are too wide to be useful in policy decision making. At the same time, the methods of normative analysis rest on simplistic assumptions about the role of values in the social process. In recognition of these limitations, writers such as Meltsner (1972) and Dror (1978) have attempted to provoke discussion about the development of an alternative methodology. They maintain that the policy sciences must develop less rigorous, but more practical, approaches to normative policy analysis such as scenario writing or the Delphi method, techniques based on the use of trained insight, imagination, and conjecture. At least during the interim period of methodology with training in the art of "political judgment." The success of such alternatives will depend upon their ability to relate qualitative data about political norms and values to quantative information about program performances and to bring it to bear on practical questions that confront policymaking problems.

PRACTICAL DISCOURSE

The question, thus, is how to develop a practical framework capable of incorporating the full range of empirical and normative judgments. The importance of the problem has led some writers to renew epistemological investigation in the policy sciences. For some, the solution can only be found outside of the conventional modes of thinking (Mitroff and Pondy, 1975). Policy methodologists must turn to the philosophy of the social sciences and other areas traditionally conceived to be far removed from policy analysis (Churchman, 1971; Anderson, 1978) in an effort to reconstruct policy evaluation as an alternative mode of inquiry with its own rules and procedures (Lindblom and Cohen, 1979; House, 1980).

An important clue as to how a practical logic of policy discourse might be constructed can be gleaned from the work of ordinary language philosophers, concerned with the explication of the logic and purposes of practical discourse. The question posed here is quite similar to the one that concerns ordinary language philosophers such as Toulmin (1958), Baier (1959), Taylor (1961), and Perry (1976). The similarity of concerns, in fact, is significant enough to suggest the study of practical reason as a potential avenue of methodological exploration for policy theorists (Fischer, 1980; Dunn, 1981).

Influenced by ordinary language philosophy, a number of political theorists have begun to seek knowledge about values through the meta-ethical analysis of the structure of normative arguments in politics (Dallmayr, 1976). The primary purpose of meta-ethics is to explicate the distinctive logic of practical discourse to determine how people make reasoned judgments—i.e., how they choose and systematically employ rules and standards as criteria to arrive at conclusions. The basic aim is to come to a clear understanding of what it means to be rational in the process of dealing with values and norms, particularly in relation to empirical statements (Taylor, 1961). Where conceptual linguistic analysis focuses on the definitions and meanings of concepts employed in practical discourse, meta-ethics examines the nature of the judgments in which normative concepts are used; it inquires about the logic of practical discourse that governs reasoning about values; and it asks whether value judgments can be justified, proven, or shown to be valid.

An outgrowth of the later work of Wittgenstein, the ordinary language approach to practical deliberation represents a loosely connected set of orientations characterized as much by ambiguity as by unity and agreement. On the most general level, however, these orientations share a common response to positivism and the fact-value dichotomy. Fundamentally, the study of practical reason represents an effort to circumvent the methodological pitfalls of the fact-value separation without necessarily resolving the underlying epistemological problem that it poses. Instead of emphasizing the failure of attempts to validate fundamental ideals, ordinary language writers focus on the rational elements that make normative practical discourse possible in everyday life. Accepting the fact that values may in the final analysis rest on irrational components, they reject the positivistic conclusion that all normative discourse must be relegated to an intellectual limbo. They point to a number of dimensions of practical discourse that militate against such a conclusion. For example, in everyday life, actors are seldom faced with the lofty intellectual task of establishing the validity of fundamental values. Also, they have succeeded, at least to a degree, in explicating the outlines of an "informal logic" that governs practical deliberation. Such theorists argue that positivists, in their overemphasis on the irrationality of fundamental values, overlook the normative inferential methods that mediate the wide range of normative discussion about practical world affairs carried on within a framework of fundamental values. As most of the deliberation about practical affairs is conducted within a general social consensus about ideal values, it is possible from this view to argue that positivistic philosophers, and mainstream social scientists, have thrown the proverbial baby out with the bathwater.

The analysis of practical reason begins with the recognition that normative and scientific discourse are two distinct types of reason, each with its own logic and purpose. Writers such as Stephen Toulmin (1958) argue that the fundamental distinction between the two rests on purpose or function: the function of scientific judgment is to alter expectations about what will happen, while that of normative judgment is to alter attitudes, behavior, and decisions about what should happen. Scientific judgments are based on the formal logic of the hypothetical-deductive model of causal demonstration. In contrast, normative judgments follow an informal logic that can be better understood in terms of something akin to a "jurisprudential analogy." Drawing attention to the similarities between normative arguments and those used by lawyers in a courtroom, Toulmin demonstrates that a good lawyer does not simply present the facts of the case but rather marshals them to stress those aspects of the situation that favor his or her client. The lawyer selects language and structures arguments designed to persuade or convince a jury to decide in favor of the client. Similarly, moral and political judgments are statements in support of decisions that can be forcibly or poorly defended. They are neither factual nor emotive statements, but rather "like records of practical decisions or positions taken which can be defended or supported much like a lawyer defends his client" (McDonald, 1953: 52). They are rationally, constructed but not proven inductively or deductively like a scientific proposition.

POLICY DELIBERATION

For present purposes, the contribution of a practical logic rests on its ability to provide the logic structure of the rationally persuasive argument. The task is to present standards for decision making that can serve as guides to asking deliberative questions about policy judgments. Such questions can be used as pointers or direction finders, turning attention to facts, values, and norms that might not otherwise be seen (Barry, 1976). They should, as Wayne Leys (1952: 11) puts it, "help voters, administrators, judges, and anyone who participates in the determination of policy by providing a 'rational-analytic' for reviewers, investigators, auditors, surveyors, and consultants, who are asked to pass judgment upon what others have done." Organized as a framework of questions, it can "improve and systemize practical judgments by finding out whether the right questions are being asked" (Leys, 1952: 11).

The identification of such a framework has clear implications for policy analysis. As a metanormative guide for probing the acceptability of policy judgments, it would provide each participant in policy debate with a common framework for laying out his or her arguments. All parties would be subject to the same methodological questions and rules of judgment. Where agreement or concensus proves beyond reach, it should be possible to specify the exact points of tension and disagreement and suggest the kinds of evidence, if any, that might resolve these conflicts (Rivlin, 1973).

Such work has been initiated by writers such as Hambrick (1974) and Brock et al. (1973). Hambrick, for example, has delineated the following ten propositional components that must be included in the logical structure of a policy argument.

(1) *Action Proposal:* A statement specifying a proposed policy action.
(2) *Policy Proposition:* A statement indicating both the action(s) and goal(s) believed to lead to the policy action.
(3) *Grounding Proposition:* A definitional or conceptual statement stipulating a proven or assumed empirical claim that lays a foundation for the policy proposition.
(4) *Normative Proposition:* A statement specifying the positive or negative value derived from the policy goal.
(5) *External Impact Proposition:* A statement describing the policy action's impact on other than the intended goal.
(6) *Causal Proposition:* A statement specifying the immediate cause-and-effect relationship that results in the goal.
(7) *Instrumental Proposition:* A statement that turns the independent variable in the causal proposition into a dependent variable in the evaluation.
(8) *Time-Place Proposition:* A statement establishing the temporal and spatial configuration of variables providing an empirical base for assessing the need for policy intervention.
(9) *Constraints Proposition:* A statement of factors that potentially alter the instrumental or causal propositions.
(10) *Comparative Proposition:* A statement about the efficiency or effectiveness of the policy action.

Hambrick's scheme, however, is limited by its emphasis on the empirical questions that underlie policy arguments—questions about cause and effect, cost and benefits of alternative means, and unanticipated impacts. Such questions fail to deal adequately with the normative dimensions of analysis. Still missing is a statement of the logical structure that relates factual evidence to normative deliberation.

As a preliminary step toward the development of an informal logic of policy questions, the purpose here is to suggest twelve points or loci around which empirical and normative judgments might be organized. Offered as a rationalanalytic guide, the questions are drawn from Taylor's (1961) study of the logic of evaluation and an examination of specific policy arguments (Fischer, 1980). They are presented as a framework of component parts that constitute a complete policy judgment rather than a normative calculus. Instead of supplying information per se, these questions serve as a guide to the kinds of empirical and normative questions that require examination.

A Logic of Policy Questions

- *Program Objectives:* Is the program objective(s) logically derived from the relevant policy goal?

- *Empirical Consequences:* Does the empirical analysis uncover secondary effects that offset the program objective(s)?

- *Relevance:* Is the policy goal(s) relevant? Can it be justified or grounded by an appeal to a higher principle(s) or established causal knowledge?

- *Situational Context:* Are there circumstances in the situation that require an exception be made to the policy goal?

- *Multiple Goals:* Are two or more goals equally relevant to the situation?

- *Precedence:* Does the decision maker's value system place higher precedence on one of the conflicting criteria? Or does it make contradictory prescriptions in this situation?

- *System Consequences:* Do practical consequences resulting from a commitment to the decision maker's basic value system facilitate the realization of the ideals of the accepted social order?

- *Social Equity:* Do other value systems, which reflect interests and needs in the social system as a whole, judge the consequences (as benefits and costs) to be distributed equitably?

- *Ideological Conflict:* Do the fundamental ideals that organize the accepted social order provide a basis for an equitable resolution of conflicting judgments?

- *Alternative Social Order:* If the social order is unable to resolve value system conflicts, do other social orders equitably prescribe for the relevant interests and needs for the conflicts reflect?

These questions are designed to point to unperceived angles and forgotten dimensions that need investigation. The task of the policy analyst is to tease out the answers to each of the questions and formally organize them in such a way that the strengths and weaknesses, inconsistencies and contradictions, of a policy are revealed.

In addition to probing policy arguments, this approach makes it possible to give some shape to the characteristically general discussions that typify the fact-value problem in the social science literature. One way to illustrate the role of factual evidence in normative deliberation is by relating this scheme to the naturalistic conception of ethical theory, which emphasizes the empirical dimensions of normative discourse.

Naturalists point to six types of factual knowledge that can be brought to bear on value judgments: (1) knowledge of consequences that flow from alternative actions, (2) knowledge of alternative means available, (3) knowledge of established norms and values that bear on the decisions, (4) the particular facts of the situation, (5) general causal conditions and laws relevant to the situation, and (6) knowledge about the fundamental needs of humankind (Kurtz, 1965). These six types of facts, and their methodological counterparts in policy evaluation (such as comparative input-output and means-ends analyses, situational and political feasibility studies, causal and systems analysis), can be located across the twelve components of the logic of evaluation. Information about consequences and alternative means are the principal objectives of the questions concerning empirical consequences, unanticipated effects, and alternative means (see above). Knowledge of existing norms and values and the particular facts of the situation are the central focus of relevance and situational context. Causal conditions and laws bear directly on the investigation of system consequences; and knowledge about fundamental human needs is the ultimate source of standards for evaluating alternative social orders. Also, for comparison, Hambrick's empirical questions can be fitted to specific points in the framework. The following diagram shows that all of the factual elements (identified by number) are incorporated in a practical scheme that accompanies the full range of normative inquiry.

Policy Questions Practical Reason	Role of Empirical and Normative Analysis	Hambrick's Policy Questions
Program Objectives	Logical Rules of Normative Analysis	
Empirical Consequences	Empirical Knowledge of Consequences (1)	Causal Proposition Instrumental Proposition
Unanticipated Effects	Knowledge of Alternative Means (2)	Comparative Proposition
Relevance	Knowledge of Established Norms (3), Causal Conditions Laws (5)	Normative Proposition Grounding Proposition
Situational Context	Particular Facts of the Situation (4)	Time-Place Proposition
Multiple Goals	Normative Logic	
Precedence	Normative Logic	
System Consequences	Causal Conditions, Laws (5) and Consequences (1)	
Social Equity	Normative Logic Knowledge of Norms (3) and Consequences (5)	

Policy Questions Practical Reason:	Role of Empirical and Normative Analysis	Hambrick's Policy Questions
Ideological Conflict	Normative Logic	
Alternative Social Orders	Knowledge of Fundamental Needs (6) Normative Logic	

Some policy scientists will argue that questions about ideological conflict and alternative social systems are beyond the scope of the trade (Meehan, 1975). To a large extent this is true, at least in terms of the prevailing definitions of policy science. The point here is not to argue that the policy scientist should turn political philosopher, but rather to show the logical relationship between empirical policy research and the full range of normative inquiry. Even though policy scientists are not directly concerned with the construction of alternative social systems, they are consumers of the ideological framework of the society they are working within. Utilization of the full range of normative questions provides the analyst with a framework for exploring the value conflicts and contradictions operating within the system (Anderson, 1979). Such information may not be the primary objective of policy science, but it is essential to policymakers who must translate policy research into language of the political process.

As a final word, it is important to say that the methodological sketch presented here can only be offered as a tentative beginning. Much more is needed if the logic of practical discourse is to be translated into the language and concerns of policy evaluation. The objective here has only been to point to the normative problem and suggest an alternative direction. At this stage, the issue is less a matter of arguing the merits of a specific approach than of encouraging others to help nurture the much needed dialogue about normative methodology.

REFERENCES

Anderson, Charles W. (1979) "The Place of Principles in Policy Analysis." American Political Science Review 73: 711-723.
——— (1978) "The Logic of Public Problems: Evaluations in Comparative Policy Research," in Douglas E. Ashford (ed.) Comparing Public Policies. Beverly Hills, CA: Sage.
Arrow, Kenneth J. (1967) "Public and Private Values," in Sidney Hook (ed.) Human Values and Economic Policy. New York: New York University.
Baier, Kurt (1959) The Moral Point of View. Ithaca, NY: Cornell University Press.
Barry, Brian (1976) Political Argument. Atlantic Highland, NJ: Humanities Press.
Brock, Bernard et al. (1973) Public Policy Decision-Making: Systems Analysis and Comparative Advantages Debate. New York: Harper & Row.
Brown, Peter G. (1976) "Ethics and Policy Research." Policy Analysis 2: 259-274.
Churchman, C. West (1971) The Design of Inquiring Systems. New York: Basic Books.

Dahl, Robert A. (1975) Modern Political Analysis. Englewood Cliffs, NJ: Prentice-Hall.
Dallmayr, Fred R. (1976) "Beyond Dogma and Despair: Toward a Critical Theory of Politics." American Political Science Review 52: 64-79.
Diesing, Paul (1962) Reason in Society. Urbana: University of Illinois Press.
Dror, Yehezkel (1969) "The Prediction of Political Feasibility." Futures 1: 282-288.
——— (1968) Public Policymaking Reexamined. San Francisco: Chandler.
Dunn, William (1981) Public Policy Analysis: An Introduction. Englewood Cliffs, NJ: Prentice-Hall.
Easton, David (1969) "The New Revolution in Political Science." American Political Science Review 58: 1051-1061.
Ferkiss, Victor (1969) Technological Man. New York: George Braziller.
Fischer, Frank (1980) Politics, Values, and Public Policy: The Problem of Methodology. Boulder, CO: Westview.
Frohock, Fred M. (1979) Public Policy: Scope and Logic. Englewood Cliffs, NJ: Prentice-Hall.
Habermas, Jurgen (1970) Toward a Rational Society. Boston: Beacon Press.
Hambrick, Ralph (1974) "A Guide for the Analysis of Policy Arguments." Policy Sciences 5: 469-478.
Hammond, Kenneth R. and Leonard Adelman (1978) "Science, Values and Human Judgment," in Kenneth R. Hammond (ed.) Judgment and Decision in Public Policy Formulation. Boulder, CO: Westview.
Hart, David and William Scott (1973) "Administrative Crisis: The Neglect of Metaphysical Speculation." Public Administration Review 33 (September-October): 415-422.
Hofferbert, Richard I. (1974) The Study of Public Policy. New York: Bobbs Merrill.
House, Ernest R. (1980) Evaluating with Validity. Beverly Hills, CA: Sage.
Kramer, Fred (1975) "Policy Analysis as Ideology." Public Administration Review 36: 509-517.
Kurtz, Paul (1965) Decision and the Human Condition. New York: Dell.
Leys, Wayne A. R. (1952) Ethics for Policy Decisions. Englewood Cliffs, NJ: Prentice-Hall.
Lindblom, Charles E. and David K. Cohen (1979) Usable Knowledge: Social Science and Social Problem Solving. New Haven: Yale University Press.
MacRae, Duncan (1971) "Scientific Communication, Ethical Argument, and Public Policy." American Political Science Review 56: 38-50.
Majone, Giandomenico (1975) "On the Notion of Political Feasibility." European Journal of Political Research 3: 259-274.
Meehan, Eugene J. (1975) "Science, Values, and Policies." American Behavioral Scientist 17: 53-100.
Meltsner, Arnold (1972) "Political Feasibility and Policy Analysis." Public Administration Review 32: 859-867.
Mitroff, Ian and Louis Pondy (1975) "On the Organization of Inquiry: A Comparison of Some Radically Different Approaches to Policy Analysis." Public Administration Review 24: 471-479.
Perry, Thomas D. (1976) Moral Reasoning and Truth. Oxford: Clarendon.
Rae, Douglas W. and Michael Taylor (1971) "Decision Rules and Policy Outcomes." British Journal of Political Science 1: 71-90.
Rein, Martin (1976) Social Science and Public Policy. New York: Penguin.
Rivlin, Alice (1973) "Forensic Social Science." Perspectives on Inequality. Cambridge: Educational Reprint Series, No. 8.
Taylor, Paul W. (1961) Normative Discourse. Englewood Cliffs, NJ: Prentice-Hall.
Thurow, Lester (1980) The Zero-sum Society. New York: Basic Books.
Toulmin, Stephen (1958) The Uses of Argument. Cambridge: Cambridge University Press.
——— (1950) An Examination of the Place of Reason in Ethics. Cambridge: Cambridge University Press.
Von Mises, Ludwig (1960) Epistemological Problems of Economics. Princeton, NJ: Van Nostrand.
Weber, Max (1949) "The Meaning of Ethical Neutrality," in Edward Shils and Henry A. Finch (trans. and eds.) The Methodology of the Social Sciences. New York: Macmillan.
Weisskopf, Walter (1971) Alienation and Economics. New York: Delta.
Wildavsky, Aaron (1966) "The Political Economy of Efficiency: Cost-Benefit Analysis, Systems Analysis, and Program Budgeting." Public Administration Review 26: 292-310.

IV

EDUCATION

The widely discussed study conducted by Coleman, Hoffer, and Kilgore on the effects of public and private schools is summarized in the first article in this section. "Cognitive Outcomes in Public and Private Schools" addresses the principal issue of whether private schools bring about higher achievement in basic cognitive skills. The report is one of the first based on the data collected for the "High School and Beyond" longitudinal study of U.S. high school seniors and sophomores, funded by the National Center for Educational Statistics (NCES). In this article, the authors provide a brief discussion of the sampling procedures and the instruments used to collect the data.

Possibly the most debated issue in this study is that of the cognitive outcomes of education. The authors' overall conclusion is "that students in Catholic and other-private schools score better on these achievement tests than do students from public schools." The authors use three different analysis strategies to examine the differences. They conclude that only minimal differences occur in reading but greater differences occur in vocabulary and mathematics. According to the authors, if public schools were able to institute education policies similar to those in the private school sector, the achievement of the students would be comparable.

The next article is a critique of the Coleman, Hoffer, and Kilgore study. Bryk discusses the methodological difficulties and questions the use of a survey research design as the basis for the analysis of private and public schools. He wonders whether the sample size, particularly for ethnic groups, is adequate. Bryk is further troubled by the lack of discussion of standard errors and tests of statistical significance.

In terms of the study's major finding that "private schools produce better cognitive outcomes than do public schools," Bryk notes the conflicting purposes of the report. He questions whether the report was intended to be a social science study or whether its purpose was to muster support for a particular policy. He concludes that the evidence presented in "Public and Private Schools" is plausible, but due to insufficient information provided for the technical reader the study's conclusions must be viewed with caution. Because of the study's methodological weaknesses, Bryk claims that the report in its present form does not conform to his definition of disciplined inquiry. He describes the study as a policy argument that supports a particular policy recommendation.

A rejoinder to the criticisms of Bryk and five other scholars by Coleman, Hoffer, and Kilgore is the next article in this section. The authors admit that

"Public and Private Schools" does have some technical deficiencies as Bryk asserts. Due to the small sample size of non-Catholic private schools, the authors admit that one should not generalize to the total universe of private schools. They also agree with Bryk that the report should have included more information about sampling error and potential biases in the data and plan to include the standard errors and alternative analyses in their final report. However, aside from the caveat about non-Catholic schools, the authors suggest that the omitted technical information "has little effect on these substantive conclusions."

Regarding the issue of cognitive outcomes, Coleman, Hoffer, and Kilgore respond to Bryk's criticism of selection bias that "background differences between students in the private and public sectors . . . lead to the higher achievement . . . in private schools." The authors provide additional evidence that disputes the critics' claims of uncontrolled selection factors that might affect achievement.

They also address the issue of comparing private and public school program comprehensiveness and reiterate their finding that "general program policies and curriculum practices may be a central factor in achievement in secondary education." In response to Bryk's assertion that the Coleman, Hoffer, and Kilgore study is a policy argument and not disciplined inquiry, the authors claim that the study was not designed to be relevant to tuition tax credit legislation and explain the purposes and policy questions the study was designed to explore.

In terms of Bryk's criticism that the study is not disciplined inquiry, the authors assert that the issue is more complex than "including or failing to include information on sources of error." The difference between disciplined inquiry and policy-related research, according to the authors, is that in policy research the "various interests, values and conception of reality will be more favorable to certain interests and values than to others." The authors agree that questions about the researchers' backgrounds and biases are relevant but feel that Bryk is unfair "to prejudge the motivational origins of the results" and that he has an incorrect image of disciplinary research in relation to policy research.

In the last five years, the use of computer-assisted instruction (CAI) has flourished in the public schools. The decreasing hardware cost, increasing availability and quality of software, and the opportunity to obtain federal grants have all encouraged school systems to invest in computer-assisted instruction. Levin and Woo discuss the results of a study that assessed the costs of CAI in a Los Angeles School District Title I program. They discovered that not only could the costs of CAI be calculated reliably, but CAI could be afforded within the funds allocated by Title I. The authors suggest that further studies be conducted analyzing the merits of different CAI approaches and that effectiveness and cost estimate data be included in these studies.

To date, reports on evaluations of special education programs have been noticeably absent from the literature. Six years into the Education for All Handicapped Children Act, few evaluations of special education programs have emerged. The article by Maher describing an evaluation of a special education day school for conduct problem adolescents is an example of one possible approach. In this case the school decision makers wanted to know how effective their school was in terms of individual students' achievement. By using Goal Attainment Scaling and Program Satisfaction Questionnaires, in addition to interviews, observation, and document reviews, the evaluator was able to provide useful information to the school's administrators.

The following article addresses local school district use of Title I evaluation information. In her article, David asserts that most Title I evaluation studies have been directed to the needs of the federal government and not to the local school system. The author reports on a study that attempted to find out how local staff used Title I evaluation results and what factors explained the use of results. By conducting structured interviews, analyzing related documents, and observing Title I programs in six states and fifteen districts, David discovered that the evaluation results consisted of standardized test scores. The primary purposes were to meet the federal guidelines, provide feedback to teachers, and to indicate program effectiveness.

David found that the evaluation findings did not lend themselves to program improvement because of the lack of contextual information, inattention to measuring program goals, and the lack of trust in standardized test scores. In order for the evaluation results to be useful, she contends that attention must be paid to the "underlying reasons for lack of use, including individual attitudes and beliefs about the program and evaluation."

The last article in this section addresses the question of "How valid are the estimates of the impact of Title I on student achievement that are derived from TIERS (Title I Evaluation Reporting System)?" While David found in the preceding article that the federal requirements of reporting evaluation data formed the basis of program evaluation information, Linn et al. discuss the validity of the estimates of impact on student achievement. They focus on the cumulative effects of statistical artifacts, unrepresentative norms, conversion errors, student selection, test administration procedures, attrition, and practice effects from one of the norm-referenced models included in TIERS. The authors reach several conclusions and make recommendations to improve the validity of the testing system. Their conclusion that Title I students should be tested annually rather than on a fall/spring cycle is based on the belief that it would reduce the testing burden for Title I students and would eliminate the bias inherent in fall/spring testing. Linn et al. caution local users of the TIERS data that the many small sample sizes lead to larger variability in estimates of gain. They state that once a year estimates of performance level "are apt to be more testworthy and more useful than the estimated gains."

22

Cognitive Outcomes in Public and Private Schools

James Coleman, Thomas Hoffer, and Sally Kilgore

Three types of analysis are carried out in this paper and provide strong evidence that there is, in vocabulary and mathematics, higher achievement for comparable students in Catholic and other-private schools than in public; the results are less consistent in reading. The last portion of the analysis shows the elements of school policy that can account for these differences—account for them by showing that achievement is just as high in the public sector when the policies and the resulting student behavior are like those in the Catholic or other-private schools

There are a number of specific issues which provide grounds for the argument that attendance at private schools should be facilitated, as well as a number which provide grounds for the argument that attendance at private schools should be restricted. Some of these, such as the relative rights of the parents and of the state in control over the child, are wholly in the realm of values; others have a factual component, and it is these for which social research can be valuable. In the report, "Public and Private Schools" (Coleman, Hoffer, and Kilgore, 1981), a number of these issues, on both sides of the debate, were identified. In this paper we will briefly discuss the results relating to several of these issues and then discuss one of them at length. First, though, it is important to identify what the major issues appear to be.

On each side of the debate there appears to be one principal issue that can be addressed with empirical data. On the side of restricting attendance at private schools, the principal argument is that private schools bring about social separation which can lead to divisiveness: for example, separation of the upper economic classes from the lower (perhaps the earliest argument against private schools, and in England it is still the one most frequently made), separation of different religious groups (the argument that has historically been used in the U.S.) and separation of racial groups (the argument that is most often made currently in the U.S.).

The principal issue addressable by empirical data on the other side of the debate is that private schools provide better education than that provided by public schools. The argument as made by individual parents is an argument about particular schools and particular children: A private school available to them gives better outcomes for their children than does the local public school to which their children would be assigned. But if the argument holds in a sufficient

From James Coleman, Thomas Hoffer, and Sally Kilgore, "Cognitive Outcomes in Public and Private Schools," 55 *Sociology of Education*, 65-76 (April/July, 1982). Copyright 1982 by the American Sociological Association. Reprinted by permission.

number of cases, and if parents are good judges of the question, then the argument follows that education for American children in general will be improved by facilitating greater enrollment in private schools. On the other hand, if public schools in general do as well or better with comparable students than do private schools, such facilitation will not improve education for American children.

This argument can refer to several specific outcomes of education. One is achievement in the basic cognitive skills. Another is in the area of moral development, ranging from escape from the influence of gangs and drug pushers to the inculcation of religious moral values. Still another is in post-high school activity, in particular college attendance—or going to a more preferred college.

In this paper we examine in detail the evidence for only one of these principal issues: the question of whether private schools bring about—for comparable students—higher achievement in basic cognitive skills. The results of this analysis have implications not only—or perhaps not even primarily—for the public school-private school policy question, but also for the functioning of schools in all sectors. But, before we examine this evidence, we will briefly describe the data base and review some results on other issues.

THE DATA

The data used in the "Public and Private Schools" report and thus this paper, are from the first (1980) wave of the National Center for Education Statistics (NCES) study, "High School and Beyond," a longitudinal study of U.S. high school seniors and sophomores. This study was conducted for NCES by the National Opinion Research Center at the University of Chicago.

A detailed report on sample design and sampling errors, "High School and Beyond: Sample Design Report," is available, so the sample will be described only briefly here. The sample was a two-stage stratified probability sample with schools within a stratum drawn with a probability proportional to their size. Once a school was selected, up to 36 sophomores and 36 seniors were drawn randomly from the students enrolled in each selected school.

Several special strata were included in the sample design. Schools in these special strata were selected with probabilities higher than those for schools in regular strata to allow for special study of certain types of schools or students. The following kinds of schools were oversampled:

- Public schools with high proportions of Hispanic (Cuban, Puerto Rican and Mexican) students.
- Catholic schools with higher proportions of minority group students.
- Public alternative schools.
- Private schools with high proportions of National Merit Scholarship finalists.

Substitutions were made for noncooperating schools in those strata where it was possible. Out of 1,122 possible schools, students at 1,015 schools and school administrators from 988 schools filled out questionnaires.

In many schools the actual number of seniors and sophomores was less than the target number for several reasons. First, in some schools fewer than 36 sophomores or 36 seniors were enrolled. This reduced the number of eligible students from 73,080 (72 students in each of 1,015 schools) to 69,662. Second, 8,278 students were absent on the survey date. Third, 1,982 students, or in some cases their parents, declined to participate, exercising their right in a voluntary survey. Substitutions were not made for noncooperating students. Finally, 1,132 cases were deleted because they contained very incomplete information. Thus, data are available for 30,030 sophomores and 28,240 seniors. This represents a completion rate of 84 percent: 58,270 out of 69,662 eligible students. In addition to the students in the regular sample, data were collected from friends and twins of participating students.

Weights, which are used in all the analyses reported here, were calculated to reflect differential probabilities of sample selection and to adjust for nonresponse. Use of appropriate weights yields estimates for high school sophomores and seniors in the United States and separate estimates for schools or students classsified in various ways, such as by geographical region or school type.

Information of several sorts was obtained in the survey. Students completed questionnaires of about one hour in length and took a battery of tests prepared by the Educational Testing Service with a total testing time of about one and one-half hours. School officials completed questionnaires covering items of information about the schools. Finally, teachers gave their perceptions of specified characteristics of students in the sample whom they had in class, to provide information beyond the students' own reports about themselves. Many of the items in the questionnaires as well as the entire test battery for seniors replicate the items used in NCES's study of the 1972 senior cohort.

Details on coding procedures, relevant descriptive statistics and regression coefficients will be available in the revised publication of the report (Coleman, Hoffer, and Kilgore, 1982).

A Brief Review of Some Results

When considering how much the private schools contribute to the separation of children of different races, of different income levels and different religions, there are two components to the question. One is between-sector segregation and the other is between-school segregation *within* a sector. For example, if private schools enrolled only a few black children, but they were distributed evenly across all private schools, then the between-sector racial segregation would be great, while the between-school segregation within the private sector would be

TABLE 1   Proportions of Students in U.S. High Schools and
Separate Sectors from Different Subpopulations

	U.S. Total	Public	Private Total	Private Catholic	Private Other Private
Blacks	.13	.14	.05	.06	.03
Hispanics	.07	.07	.06	.07	.04
Income above $20,000	.43	.41	.60	.58	.63
Catholics	.34	.31	.66	.91	.17

small or non-existent. Or if at the other extreme, private schools enrolled students of each religious group in exactly the same proportions as do the public schools, but every private school had students of only a single religious group, then the between-sector segregation would be zero, but the between-school segregation within the private sector would be complete.

Obviously, the private sector's contribution to segregation along the lines of income, religion or race depends not on one or the other of these components, but rather on the combination of the two taken together. One useful way to assess the combined effects of between-sector segregation and between-school segregation within the private sector—and thereby to estimate the overall contribution of private schools to segregation in U.S. high schools—is to compare the average amount of segregation for all U.S. secondary schools to that found in the public sector alone. If there were no private schools and their students were reabsorbed into the public sector in exactly the same way current public school students are distributed among schools, then the degree of segregation in all schools would be that of the public schools. Thus, the difference between the degree of segregation for all secondary schools and that found in public schools can be seen as the contribution of the private sector to segregation along the various dimensions.

As shown in Tables 1 and 2, the results for segregation by race and ethnicity, income and religion are rather different. We discuss here only race and religion. In terms of between-sector segregation of racial groups, the data show that only about one-half as high a proportion of blacks are in the Catholic sector as in the public, and about one-quarter as high a proportion are in the non-Catholic private schools (referred to here as "other-private" schools). But the between-school segregation within the private sector is much less than that in the public sector (seen by comparing columns 2 and 3 in Table 2). The impact that these two countervailing segregation patterns have on racial segregation in American secondary schools can be seen by comparing the overall racial segregation (column 1) with the racial segregation found in the public sector (column 2). In the case of racial segregation, this impact is negligible—indicating that the much lower level of segregation within the private sector has an integrative effect that

TABLE 2   Between-School Segregation for U.S. High Schools and Within Separate Sectors

	U.S. Total	Public	Private Total	Catholic	Other Private
Black-White	.49	.49	.29	.31	.21
Hispanic-Anglo	.30	.30	.34	.25	.55
Low-High Income	.23	.21	.16	.18	.14
Catholics-Non-Catholics	.30	.22	.63	.11	.28

just counterbalances the segregative effective of the smaller proportions of blacks in private schools.[1]

For religion, which in this analysis is restricted to Catholic religious background versus all others,[2] the matter is quite different. In the public sector, about 30 percent of the students are from Catholic backgrounds, compared to 65 percent in the private sector (in the Catholic schools themselves, about 90 percent are from Catholic backgrounds and in other private schools, 17 percent). But the separation of Catholics and non-Catholics in the private sector is much higher than that in the public sector—as might be expected, since most students in the private sector are in a religiously sponsored school. Again, comparing the total segregation (column 1) with religious segregation within the public sector (column 2) we can assess the effects: In contrast to the case of racial separation, the private schools do contribute to religious separation of secondary school students.

Two outcomes of education deserve brief mention: post-high school plans and affective outcomes. Using the students' responses to the question: "How far in school do you think you will get?" we are able to compare the educational plans across sectors. About 25 percent more of the students in Catholic and other private schools expect to finish college or go beyond than are found in the public sector. When family background characteristics were taken into account, the differences between the sectors were reduced, very sharply for other private schools and less so for Catholic schools. Both this, and evidence from retrospective questions which show greater self-reported increases in the proportion of students planning to attend college, indicate that Catholic schools, and other private schools to a lesser degree, more often lead to plans for high levels of post-secondary education than do public schools.[3] While private school students generally plan to attain higher levels of education, for seniors planning to take a full-time job immediately after high school, slightly *more* of those in public schools had a job already lined up than did those in the Catholic schools, and those in the other-private schools were least likely, by about 10 percent, to have a job lined up.

Only suggestive evidence was obtained with regard to affective outcomes. For two sets of items, one set related to self-esteem and the other to fate control, sophomores in public, Catholic and other-private schools showed about the same levels of self-esteem and fate control. In all three sectors, the seniors showed higher levels of both. But in both, the senior-sophomore difference was greater in the other-private schools than in either the public or Catholic schools. The possibility that this does represent greater growth in the other-private schools is reinforced by an additional comparison between two sets of "high-performance" schools, public and private.[4] Here too, the private schools (which were nearly all non-Catholic) showed a greater senior-sophomore difference than did the public schools on both affective dimensions. Two differences in the functioning of the other-private schools on the one hand, and the public and Catholic schools on the other, may be worth mentioning because of their possible relation to these affective differences: First, the student-teacher ratio in both Catholic and public schools is over twice that in the other-private schools (and slightly higher in the Catholic schools than in the public). And second, in the Catholic and public schools, participation of seniors in extra-curricular activities was at the same level or below that of sophomores, while in the other-private schools the participation of seniors was higher.

COGNITIVE OUTCOMES IN PUBLIC AND PRIVATE SCHOOLS

Of the battery of tests given sophomores and seniors, three tests had subsets of items that were identical for both grades: eight items in reading, eight items in vocabulary and eighteen items in mathematics. Scores on these subtests are reported in Table 3.

The table shows, as might be expected, that students in Catholic and other private schools score better on these achievement tests than do students from public schools. The table shows that in both types of high performance schools the averages are higher than in any of the other sectors, and that the average scores for the high performance private schools (which are generally small, homogeneous and highly selective) are higher than the higher performance public schools (which are generally large, comprehensive, upper-middle class suburban schools—the "elite" public schools in their respective metropolitan areas).

Comparison of the public, Catholic and other-private sectors shows that the private sector sophomores are about at the level of the public sector seniors (less in reading, more in mathematics). The public-private differences at the sophomore level are one-third to one-half of a standard deviation. The differences at the senior level seem about the same. The question, of course, is what these differences mean.

As with any non-experimental comparisons, that is, in any comparisons where there is non-random assignment to treatments, there are two possible explanations for differences. One is that the treatments have had different effects; the

TABLE 3 Mean Scores and Standard Deviations for Items that are Identical for Seniors and Sophomores in Public and Private Schools: Spring 1980

	U.S. Total		Major Sectors						High Performance Schools			
			Public		Catholic		Other Private		Public		Private	
	Grade		Grade		Grade		Grade		Grade		Grade	
Subtest	10	12	10	12	10	12	10	12	10	12	10	12
Means:												
Reading (8)[a]	3.67	4.54	3.60	4.48	4.34	5.00	4.32	5.34	4.85	5.77	6.06	6.71
Vocabulary (8)	3.78	4.58	3.69	4.48	4.59	5.35	4.78	5.56	5.11	6.24	6.65	7.22
Mathematics (18)	9.56	10.80	9.40	10.63	11.05	12.10	11.28	12.74	12.53	13.76	15.09	16.38
Standard Deviations:												
Reading	2.01	2.10	2.00	2.10	1.92	1.96	2.05	2.04	2.12	1.94	1.49	1.18
Vocabulary	1.90	1.97	1.88	1.97	1.84	1.74	2.00	1.94	1.86	1.65	1.24	.97
Mathematics	4.04	4.24	4.04	4.24	3.56	3.82	4.17	4.14	3.80	3.62	2.33	1.70

a. Numbers in parentheses refer to total number of items on subtests.

other is that there are no effects, and instead the differences are due to initial selection into the treatments. This is important to reiterate because selection of schools by parents, and in some cases of students by schools, means that non-random selection is of potentially great importance in accounting for these differences.

For this reason, we attempted three different strategies in attempting to discover what part, if any, of the achievement differences between schools shown in Table 3 is due to differences in the "educational treatments" provided by schools in the three sectors. The first approach is a variant of a standard statistical technique, controlling differences in student input in an attempt to statistically control for the initial selection. This, of course, is always subject to the objection that not *all* the input differences have been controlled for, leaving some of those differences masquerading as effects of the treatments. To reduce this problem, possibly at the cost of attributing to selection of some treatment effects, we also included statistical controls on some variables that, while most would argue are largely initial differences, might also have been affected by the treatments, that is, by the schools. Listed below are the set of variables used as statistical controls that are clearly prior to and unaffected by the school, along with those others which are at least partly prior, but possibly also affected by the school.

Clearly prior
    Family income
    Mother's education
    Father's education
    Race
    Hispanic/non-Hispanic
    Number of siblings
    Number of rooms in the home
    Both parents present
    Mother's working before child was in elementary school
    Mother's working when child was in elementary school

Not clearly prior
    Encyclopedia or reference books in home
    More than 50 books in home
    Typewriter in home
    Owns pocket calculator
    Frequency of talking with mother or father about personal experiences
    Mother thinks student should go to college after high school
    Father thinks student should go to college after high school

In this first analysis, the three achievement subtests were regressed by sector and grade on the 17 background variables listed above. Table 4 shows, for students with the same measured background characteristics, the additional increments on the sophomore scores in reading, vocabulary and mathematical subtests that may be attributable to being in the Catholic or other-private sector.

The increments in achievement were estimated for each grade within the public and private sectors by taking differences of standardized achievement estimates. The standardized estimates of achievement ($\hat{Y}$) were calculated as follows:[5]

$$\hat{Y}_{ij} = a_{ij} + \sum_{k=1}^{17} b_{ijk} X_k + b_{ij} D_{ij} \qquad [1]$$

where $\hat{Y}_{ij}$ is the standardized score for the ith grade in sector j, a_{ij} is the intercept and b_{ijk} are the coefficients for the background variables in that sector and grade. X_k is the mean for the public school sophomores on the k th background characteristic and D_{ij}, the sector increment. The increments shown in Table 4 are the differences of each $\hat{Y}_{ij}$ from the public school sophomore mean achievement for each subtest. Estimates of $\hat{Y}_{ij}$ for the other private sector were obtained by adding the dummy coefficient (D_{ij}) for that sector onto the estimate for the Catholic sector, since a single equation was used for the private sector.

The last three rows of the table show the raw differences between sophomores in the three sectors, and between sophomores and seniors in the public sector. Thus the comparisons of rows 2 and 3 with rows 5 and 6 of Table 4 show how much of the differences between public and private school sophomore achievement are accounted for by the selection into private schools as reflected by the 17 background characteristics. The results indicate that between three-fifths and two-thirds of the raw differences between Catholic and public schools are accounted for by these selection differences, and between two-thirds and four-fifths of the raw differences between other private and public schools are similarly accounted for. This leaves, however, substantial differences remaining: from a low of one-fifth of the initial difference to a high of about four-fifths of the initial difference. Comparison with the background-controlled senior increment (that is, a two-year increment) on line 4 of the table shows that this is from something over a grade level difference in vocabulary and mathematics (for both the private sectors) to something less than a grade level in reading.

This analysis suggests, then, that although more than one-half of the raw differences between public and private schools are due to initial differences in the 17 background characteristics, substantial differences remain unexplained by these selection factors and may be attributable to "treatment" differences in the schools. The objection of course remains that perhaps an unmeasured factor affects both selection into the school and the achievement level.

The second mode of analysis uses a different way of separating out the selection effects. The survey covered sophomores and seniors in each school, and with the subtests of identical items, it is possible to compare senior scores with sophomore scores. This controls for differences in the input level of achievement (or rather, the sophomore levels of achievement) in examining the senior levels of achievement. It does not depend on background controls which are always subject to the possible objection mentioned earlier. It has, however, another

TABLE 4   Estimated Increments to Test Scores in Public and Private Schools
with Family Background Controlled: Spring 1980[a]
(standard error of difference in parentheses)

	Reading	Vocabulary	Mathematics
Public school sophomores	3.60	3.69	9.40
Standardized sophomore increments for:			
Catholic schools	0.32	0.36	0.58
	(.048)[b]	(.045)	(.091)
Other-private schools	0.14	0.33	0.56
	(.064)	(.060)	(.121)
Senior increment in public schools	0.73	0.63	0.88
	(.018)	(.018)	(.037)
Raw increments (from Table 3)			
Sophomore increments for:			
Catholic schools	0.74	0.90	1.65
Other-private schools	0.72	1.09	1.88
Senior increment in public schools	0.88	0.79	1.23

a. Family background refers to 17 subjective and objective background characteristics which are listed in the text. Relevant regression coefficients and sector means are given in the appendix to Coleman et al. (1982).
b. Numbers in parentheses are standard errors of sector differences in predicted achievement. The standard error is calculated by taking the square root of the sum of variances of the predicted means (estimated by standardization of each of the sector-grade specific regression equations to the average background of public sophomores),

$$\sqrt{\text{var } (\hat{Y} \text{ public}) + \text{var } (\hat{Y} \text{ private})}.$$

The variances are estimated by pre-multiplying the variance-covariance matrix of the regression coefficients, V(b) by the transpose of the public sophomore background mean vector, X', and post-multiplying this product by the vector of public sophomore background means; that is,

$$\text{var } (\hat{Y}) = X'V(b)X.$$

See Draper and Smith (1966) for a discussion of estimating variances of point estimates such as these.
      Regression equations were estimated using frequency-weighted pairwise deletion. In the variances calculated here, estimates were readjusted to reflect the sample size, which in this case is taken to be the number of students in a given grade and sector who had completed the respective test.
      Given the two-stage probability sampling design used in "High School and Beyond," one may want to know about possible design effects. The method for calculating standard errors described above assumes a simple random sample and follows from the work of Kish and Frankel (1974) showing that the design effect for sampling designs such as those used in "High School and Beyond" approaches unity for complex statistics (such as regression coefficients). More recently, we have thought it important to verify this finding for the specific estimates made in this table. Following the Balanced Repeated Replication method for empirically deriving sample variances—developed at the U.S. Bureau of Census—we calculated empirical variances for the private sector. Four of six estimates of design effects for the Catholic increment approach unity and the other two effects (sophomore vocabulary and senior reading) were close to two (2.071 and 2.118, respectively). For the other private sector, design effects were uniformly found to be greater than two, with four of the six between values of 2.9 and 3.4 (these four were sophomore vocabulary and mathematics, senior reading and vocabulary).

defect: if achievement growth is correlated with initial achievement levels in the same treatment setting, then a higher level in the sophomore year would mean a higher level in the senior year, even if there were no treatment differences.

Although this is a statistical problem (again possibly producing a bias toward the private schools), it is a different one than in the preceding analysis, so that it will give another estimate of the differences between sectors. There is, however, a problem that creates another possible source of error: The sophomore and senior classes are not the same students, but two different cohorts, and there is selection between sophomore and senior years due to dropouts. Different dropout rates for different sectors, or different correlations of dropout with achievement in different sectors, would lead to differential distortions in the apparent sophomore-senior growth.

The dropout rates from sophomore to senior year (which is the period during which most dropout occurs in high school) is very different in the public and private sectors. According to our estimates (which may be slightly high) this is 24 percent over that period in the public schools, 12 percent in the Catholic schools and 13 percent in the other private schools. If we make the assumption that the dropouts in each sector came equally from each point in the lower one-half of the distribution of tests scores, and that if they had remained in school they would maintain their same place in the distribution, then it is possible to calculate what *would be* the test scores of seniors if there had been no dropouts between sophomore and senior year. Obviously, this will bring the apparent growth rate in the public schools down more than that in the private sectors.

The estimated gains from sophomore to senior year, adjusted for dropouts, in the three sectors is given in Table 5. In addition, in the bottom three rows estimated yearly learning rates (based on the average number of items learned and the number remaining to be learned[6]) are shown for each sector in each of the three tests.

The results show that the estimated learning rate in reading in the Catholic schools is only slightly above that in the public schools, but that in all other cases, the estimated rates in the private sectors from sophomore to senior are at least twice those in the public sector. In contrast to the estimates of private-public differences based on sophomore scores shown in Table 4, here the other-private school gains appear larger than those in the Catholic schools. Both methods agree, however, in showing that both private sectors are above the public, and both agree in suggesting that there are less public-private differences in reading than in the other two areas of skills.

A variant upon the method of assessing differential gain is shown by another analysis, in which the estimated sophomore-to-senior growth is calculated not by

TABLE 5   Estimated Sophomore-Senior Gains in Test Scores and Learning Rates, with Corrections for Dropouts Missing from Senior Distribution

Item	Public			Catholic			Other-Private		
	10	12	Est. Gain	10	12	Est. Gain	10	12	Est. Gain
(1) Estimated gains[a]									
Reading	3.57	4.05	0.47	4.33	4.81	0.47	4.30	5.11	0.81
Vocabulary	3.68	4.09	0.41	4.58	5.19	0.61	4.73	5.35	0.62
Mathematics	9.39	9.77	0.38	11.04	11.73	0.68	11.28	12.26	0.98
(2) Estimated learning rate[b]									
Reading		.06			.07			.12	
Vocabulary		.05			.10			.10	
Mathematics		.02			.05			.08	

a. Numbers are rounded to two decimals independently so that some rounded "estimated gains" differ from the difference between rounded sophomore and senior scores.
b. Learning rate refers to estimated proportion of items learned in a given year from those items not known.

correcting for dropouts, but by standardizing the senior achievements in each of the private sectors on the 17 background characteristics, to obtain an estimated achievement for a student like the average public-school sophomore. Then an estimated growth for this "standard sophomore" is obtained by comparison with the analogous sophomore scores in the two private sectors. This estimated growth is compared with that shown in line 4 of Table 4. The results are shown in Table 6.

This table shows slightly *less* gain in reading and mathematics in the Catholic schools than in the public schools and somewhat more in each area in the other private schools. The size of these other-private extra gains is, taken over all tests, about one-quarter of the background-standardized sophomore-senior gain in the public schools, or about an extra one-half a year.

These extra private-school gains, around zero for the Catholic schools and about one-half a grade level in the other private schools, are considerably lower than those estimated in Table 5, suggesting that the dropout correction may have been too great. Other analyses[7] taken together with the analyses shown in Tables 4, 5 and 6, suggests the following general conclusions, based both on the initial sophomore levels and the estimated gains from sophomore to senior years:

(a) There is higher achievement and greater sophomore-senior growth in both the Catholic and other-private sectors than in the public sector in vocabulary and mathematics. The differences are substantial, on the order of magnitude of one grade level.

(b) Reading achievement in the other-private schools appears only slightly above that in the public schools for comparable students, but the sophomore-senior growth appears considerably greater. The reverse pattern appears for Catholic schools: greater sophomore achievement, but no more, and perhaps less, growth in reading achievement from sophomore to senior than in the public

TABLE 6   Estimated Sophomore-to-Senior Achievement Growth in Catholic
and Other Private Schools Beyond that in Public Schools
for Student with Average Background:[a] Spring 1980
(standard error of difference in parentheses)

	Reading	Vocabulary	Mathematics
Catholic	−0.07	0.19	0.01
	(.072)	(.066)	(.136)
Other-private	0.27	0.17	0.17
	(.095)	(.087)	(.180)

a. Estimates are obtained from separate regressions for sophomores and seniors in each sector, obtaining predicted achievement in each sector and grade standardized to mean public school sophomore background characteristics for 17 objective and subjective characteristics. "Extra growth" is obtained by comparing these standardized achievements between grades and then across sectors. Standard errors for the differences between Catholic and other private sophomore-to-senior growth and public sophomore-to-senior growth are calculated by taking the square root of the sum of variances of the sophomore-to-senior differences for the sectors under comparison. The variances of the sophomore-to-senior differences are obtained by the method described in the footnote to Table 4. Regression coefficients, standard errors of the slopes and R^2s are given in the appendix to Coleman et al. (1982).

schools. These inconsistencies suggest only very small private-school effects in reading.

It is useful to note that the National Assessment of Education Progress reports, in comparing 17-year-olds in public and private schools in reading achievement, show that there are initial differences in favor of private schools, but that these nearly vanish when controlled statistically on family background (NAEP, 1981). This is reasonably consistent with our results. (NAEP did not separate Catholic school students, who constitute about two-thirds of the private school total, from the other private students.)

WHAT MAKES THE DIFFERENCE?

The third method for studying the differential effects of public and private schools takes a completely different tack. It asks: What are the measured ways in whch public, Catholic and other-private schools are especially different, atter student background differences are statistically controlled, and what difference do these factors make for achievement, wholly within the public sector or alternatively within the private sector? If we find that certain characteristics on which Catholic and other-private schools are higher are associated with higher achievement *within* a sector, where family background characteristics of students are statistically controlled, then this does two things:

(a) It provides a strong reinforcement to the inference that the average Catholic or other-private school does bring about higher achievement for comparable students than does the average public high school.

(b) It shows just what things about a school—whether in the public sector or the private sector—make a difference in cognitive outcomes. This, of course, does not show everything that makes a difference, but only those on which public and private schools characteristically differ.

If, on the other hand, we find that those measured factors on which Catholic and other-private schools differ from public schools when student background is controlled are *not* associated with achievement within a sector when student background is controlled, this implies two things:

(a) First, it shows that these factors are not themselves important for achievement;

(b) Second, it throws doubts on the inference that public-private differences in achievement are due to effects of the school rather than selection of students, by implying that if there are such effects, they must be through other unmeasured factors that differentiate public and private schools.

This analysis is especially important in the test for private school effects. It makes the public-private differences that remain after student background is controlled less subject to the alternative interpretation that additional selection effects remain and are responsible for these differences. For that interpretation would depend upon selection effects operating (over and above the 17 background factors which are controlled) for the school factors themselves, *within* each of the sectors. This becomes a much more tenuous hypothesis to maintain than the original selection-into-private-school hypothesis.

The factors on which both Catholic and other-private schools differ most sharply from the public schools, among those measured in the research, are discipline and student behvior. Some of this is due to differences in student input. For example, the average difference between Catholic school and public school sophomores in the amount of homework is the difference between 5.56 hours per week in the Catholic schools and 3.75 in the public schools. For Catholic school sophomores, like the average public school sophomore on the background characteristics discussed earlier, the 5.56 hours is reduced to 4.92. This leaves a difference of 1.17 hours per week which can be attributed to something about school organization or school policy. Similar background-controlled differences between Catholic and public high schools and between other private and public high schools can be calculated for other variables. The results of such calculations are shown in Table 7 for five types of variables: coursework taken by the student, homework, absenteeism, school disciplinary climate, and student behavior in the school. The last two of these are fundamentally different from the first three, for they characterize the school as a unit, rather than the student. They are least susceptible to the alternative selection hypothesis, which for them must become especially tortured.

As the table shows, there remain substantial differences in most of these variables in the direction of a more orderly school and more academic demands in the private sector.

TABLE 7   Differences Between Private and Public Schools in Student Behavior and School Climate. Standardized to Family Background Characteristics of Public Sophomore Students:[a] Spring 1980   (standard error of difference in Parentheses)

Item	Catholic Minus Public		Other-Private Minus Public	
	Sophomore	Senior	Sophomore	Senior
a. Coursework completed by students				
Proportion taking honors in English	−.02	.01	−.018	.08
	(.011)	(.013)	(.014)	(.017)
Proportion taking honors Mathematics	.02	.02	.06	−.03
	(.011)	(.012)	(.015)	(.017)
Average number of advanced mathematics	DNA	.71	DNA	.34
courses		(.034)		(.045)
b. Homework completed by students				
Average number of hours per week	1.17	0.78	1.31	1.27
	(.092)	(.100)	(.123)	(.133)
c. Attendance by individual students				
Absent from school	−.43	−.39	−.06	−.16
	(.028)	(.033)	(.037)	(.043)
Cut class now and then	−.20	−.21	−.04	−.08
	(.009)	(.013)	(.013)	(.017)
d. Disciplinary climate as perceived by students[b]				
Teacher interest	.39	.40	.49	.51
Fairness of discipline	(.008)	(.009)	(.011)	(.012)
	(.008)	(.007)	(.009)	(.010)
Effectiveness/strictness of discipline	.59	.59	.31	.31
	(.008)	(.008)	(.010)	(.011)
e. Student behavior in school as perceived by sophomores[c]				
Absenteeism	.65	.66	.55	.56
	(.007)	(.008)	(.010)	(.010)
Cutting class	.79	.80	.54	.53
	(.010)	(.011)	(.014)	(.014)
Students fighting each other	.39	.38	.55	.56
	(.007)	(.007)	(.009)	(.010)
Students threatening teachers	.17	.16	.18	.17
	(.002)	(.002)	(.003)	(.003)

a. Family background characteristics controlled are the 17 used in Table 4. The numbers in the table are obtained by first multiplying public school sophomore background means by regression coefficients from the regression of the variable in question on family background to obtain the expected level of the variable in question for that population, using regressions carried out on private school sophomores, private school seniors and public school seniors, then subtracting the public school value from the private school value.
b. Climate variables aggregated to school level.
c. Behavior variables to school level; a high value implies that students perceived this as happening rarely or never.

TABLE 8   Achievement Differences Between Private and Public Schools
Due to Various Areas of School Functioning, for Students
with Family Backgrounds Like that of the Average
Sophomore in Public Schools:[a] Spring 1980

	Catholic			Other-Private		
	Reading	Vocabulary	Mathematics	Reading	Vocabulary	Mathematics
Sophomores						
Coursework	−.02	−.02	.05	−.06	−.06	−.13
Homework	.06	.04	.13	.06	.04	.15
Attendance	.04	.03	.15	.01	.01	.02
Disciplinary climate	−.03	−.08	−.18	.06	−.01	.12
Student behavior	.33	.12	.47	.33	.19	.57
Total accounted for	.38	.10	.63	.40	.17	.75
Overall (from Table 4)	.32	.36	.58	.14	.33	.56
Seniors						
Coursework	.01	.01	1.09	−.06	−.06	.48
Homework	.04	.03	.02	.07	.05	.03
Attendance	.02	.00	.04	.01	.00	.01
Disciplinary climate	.01	.00	.02	.10	.07	.01
Student behavior	.20	.01	.26	.18	.11	.40
Total accounted for	.28	.05	1.42	.30	.17	.95
Overall (from Tables 4 & 6)	.24	.56	.60	.40	.51	.74

a. The standard errors of the difference for Table 8 are not presented because of the particular problems involved
in estimating var(Y). The method outlined in the footnote to Table 4 assumes fixed values for X, the vector of
background means. In Table 8 this assumption is not appropriate, since the values for the school functioning
variables (obtained from the equations represented in Table 7) are random variates.

With these differences as a starting point, the question can be asked, based on
a regression of achievement on these school variables (controlling on student
background) just how much difference in achievement these differences in school
characteristics make *within* any sector. In effect, if we ask that question for the
public sector, we ask what would be the difference in achievement between the
average student in the public sector and a student whose own coursework, study
habits and absenteeism were like that of a student who was in one of the private
sectors but whose background characteristics were like the average public school
sophomore—and whose school had a disciplinary climate and student behavior
environment like that of the school in the Catholic or other private school
attended by such a student. Or to put it more simply, we ask about achievement
differences within the public sector associated with the behavioral and school
differences that remain between private and public schools when student backgrounds are controlled (see Table 8).

Comparing the last two lines for sophomores and seniors shows that in four
out of six comparisons among sophomores, and in three out of six among
seniors, the predicted achievement for the public high school student in a school
with these characteristics is *higher* than that in the Catholic or other-private
sectors. It appears that these *are* school factors through which the average private
school brings about greater achievement than does the average public school.

Looking at the five different areas, the one that seems to make the most difference is what we have called "student behavior." This is not the student's *own* behavior but the behavior of students in the school as a whole, with his own (i.e., homework and attendance) controlled. The effect is especially strong for sophomores, but this is probably due to the fact that most of the variables making up that behavior are perceptions on the part of sophomore students about their school—and those perceptions will be most accurate for their grade. The student's own homework and attendance make some difference (and it should be remembered that these are only the differences in homework and attendance that can be attributed to school policy), with homework generally making more difference. Policy-related differences in so-called honors courses make little difference, and in fact inspection of Table 7 shows that there are few sector differences in these policies; but the policy-related difference in frequency of taking advanced mathematics courses (which is present only for mathematics in the senior year) makes a great deal of difference.

The one set of variables that makes little difference or is even slightly negative is the school "disciplinary climate." That seems at first peculiar; but once we recognize that disciplinary climate affects student behavior, then we can see that it may certainly have an effect, but *through* these variables. A further analysis not reported here (Table 6.3.6 in the original report) shows that this is indeed the case. The apparent absence of an effect of disciplinary climate on achievement is merely the absence of a *direct* effect; it does have an effect on student behavior which in turn affects achievement.

It is important to recognize that all the analysis just discussed (Table 8) is within public schools, examining how these differences in school policy affect the achievement of public school students. The results indicate that the policy differences affect public school achievement just as they do private school achievement. It would be possible to do a similar analysis within the private sector, showing how achievement is *reduced* by policy changes that would bring these variables—for comparable students—down to the level found in the average public student.

CONCLUSION

The three types of analysis carried out in this paper provide strong evidence that there is, in vocabulary and mathematics, higher achievement for comparable students in Catholic and other-private schools than in public; the results are less consistent in reading. The last portion of the analysis shows the elements of school policy that can account for these differences—and can account for them by showing that achievement is just as high in the public sector when the policies and the resulting student behavior are like those in the Catholic or other-private schools. The first question that arises is what is it that prevents the public schools from instituting such policies, from being similar to private schools in these respects and thus—according to our analysis—bringing about equal or higher levels of achievement? Public schools once demanded and got higher levels of homework, better attendance, minimal frequency of cutting classes, and generally better student behavior than is now the case. Why are they not able to do so now? Or more to the point, what is different about those that *are* able to do so—for some do—and those that are not? It would be sad to have to conclude* that the constraints placed on public education are so harmful to academic achievement that a movement to the private sector is necessary for such achievement to flourish. Some parents have arrived at such a conclusion in their own local situation; it remains to be seen whether changes will come about in the public sector.

NOTES

1. Subsequent analysis shows that these findings hold at a regional level, except in the case of the South, where enrollment patterns in the private sector do contribute to racial segregation. It should be noted however that public schools in the South continue to be the least segregated of any region in the country.

2. No other religious group was sufficiently represented in the private sector sample to permit analysis of other religious groups.

3. Subsequent analyses using more elaborate controls for family background differences have led to revisions of these conclusions. The two analyses mentioned in the text above employed controls for family income, mother's and father's educations, and race and ethnicity. The subsequent analyses introduced the additional controls for the variables listed on page 9. With these additional controls, the public sophomore background standardized differences between private and public school students on the educational plans variable ("How far in school do you think you will get?") still show that the reductions from the uncontrolled differences are greatest for the other private school students and smallest for Catholic school students. When background standardized sophomore-to-senior differences are compared between sectors, though, the subsequent analyses indicate that growth is lowest in the Catholic schools. These findings suggest, then, that Catholic high schools do not generate higher levels of planned attainment from the sophomore to senior years. When the additional background variables are introduced into the equations modeling retrospective accounts of when plans for college were first formulated, the results again show that little effect on growth appears attributable to Catholic high school.

4. This includes 11 public schools selected from the sample for having the highest proportion of graduating seniors as National Merit Semi-Finalists, and 12 private schools selected from the universe of private schools by the same criterion.

5. Separate regressions for public and private school sectors at each grade were done, rather using a single regression equation with dummy variables for sectors, to allow for different effects of background characteristics in different sectors. The Catholic and other-private sectors were combined for a single regression, because of the smaller numbers of cases in these sectors. A dummy variable for the other private sector was included in the equation. The estimated increment at the sophomore level due to the Catholic sector is obtained by first calculating the predicted test scores for public and Catholic sophomores with background characteristics standardized to that of the average public school sophomore, and then finding the difference between the Catholic sector and the public sector. The increment for the other private sector is found by adding to this the value of the other private dummy variable. Regression coefficients, standard errors of slopes and coefficients of determination for each of the equations used in this article are included in the appendix to Coleman et al. (1982). All the regression analyses reported in this article were done with pairwise deletion of cases.

6. The equation for this is learning rate = $-t^{-1}\log(P_1/P_0)$, where p_0 is the probability of not knowing an item as a sophomore, and p_1 is the probability of not knowing it as a senior.

7. One of these analyses involves the same kind of approach as that on which Tables 4 and 6 are based, but with only one overall equation for sophomores and one for seniors, with the private sectors entered as dummy variables. The regression coefficients for the dummy variables have the same interpretation as lines 2 and 3 in Table 4, and if interaction terms between each of the two dummy variables and each background variable were included, the values should in principle be the same. Without the interaction terms, this analysis (reported below) is inferior to the one reported in Tables 4 and 6, since one is assuming that the family background variables have the same effect for all students. The coefficients for sophomores and seniors are given below (standard errors are in parentheses):

		Reading	Vocabulary	Mathematics
Sophomore:	Catholic	.26 (.05)	.41 (.04)	.46 (.09)
	Other-Private	.02 (.06)	.31 (.06)	.22 (.12)
Senior:	Catholic	.13 (.05)	.46 (.04)	.46 (.10)
	Other-Private	.22 (.07)	.33 (.06)	.51 (.13)

These show (except for two cases) greater coefficients for seniors than sophomores and least effects of the private sector in reading. While there is consistency in these results, statistical significance is not strong: For each test, using a standard t-test for the significance of the differences between the coefficients of sectors at each grade level, the only significant difference is between coefficients in the sophomore and senior years for reading in the other-private sector.

The reason for the differences between these results and those of Tables 4 and 6 is that the estimated effects of family background are different in the private sectors than in the public. Here the private school effects are estimated in the presence of background effects that are averages weighted heavily in favor of the public schools, which constitute 91 percent of the school population. This difference is especially important in the case of the Catholic Schools, where the effects of family background are much smaller than in the public or other private sectors.

REFERENCES

Coleman, J., T. Hoffer and S. Kilgore
    1981   Public and Private Schools. Report submitted to the National Center for Education Statistics. Chicago: National Opinion Research Center.
    1982   High School Achievement: Public, Catholic and Other-Private Schools Compared. New York: Basic Books.
Draper, N. and H. Smith
    1966   Applied Regression Analysis. New York: John Wiley and Sons, Inc.
National Assessment of Educational Progress
    1981   "Reading and Mathematics Achievement in Public and Private Schools: Is There a Difference?" Denver, Colorado: Education Commission of the States.
National Center for Educational Statistics
    1982   High School and Beyond: Sample Design Report. Washington, D.C.: National Center for Educational Statistics.

23

Disciplined Inquiry or Policy Argument?

Anthony S. Bryk

Public and Private Schools has brought considerable visibility to the comparative study of public, Catholic, and non-Catholic private schools. This general area has been too long ignored, and it represents rich ground for inquiry about the organization and effectiveness of schools. The work of James Coleman, Thomas Hoffer, and Sally Kilgore provides a valuable first step. The descriptive analyses of the public, Catholic, and non-Catholic private school sectors substantially extends our understanding in these areas.

Among its most interesting findings are the reported relationships of measures of organization and ethos to school effectiveness. These analyses contribute to a growing body of literature (see, for example, Edmonds, 1979; Rutter, Maughan, Mortimore, & Ouston, with Smith, 1979) aimed at improving schools through a better understanding of school climate. We have come a long way since the motto "Schools don't matter much" and the general pessimism which followed the earlier Coleman Report, *Equality of Educational Opportunity* (Coleman, Campbell, Hobson, McPartland, Mood, Weinfeld, & York, 1966).

Unfortunately, these important aspects of *Public and Private Schools* have attracted little attention to date, and, in fact, are somewhat peripheral to its central purpose: to examine policy questions concerning the appropriate role of the federal government in private education and to inform current policy debates about the likely consequences of federally supported tuition tax credits and educational vouchers. It is along these lines that Coleman, Hoffer, and Kilgore compare the relative effectiveness of public and pri-

The ideas presented in the concluding section have been stimulated by conversations in several meetings of a research seminar at The Huron Institute, Cambridge, Massachusetts, that is examining the utility and productivity of recent educational evaluations. This research is being conducted in collaboration with the Center for Instructional Research and Curriculum Evaluation at the University of Illinois, Champaign-Urbana; it involves David Cohen, Eleanor Farrar, Ernest House, Richard Light, Steve Raudenbush, Robert Stake, Carol Weiss, and Lauren Jones Young, and is supported by the National Institute of Education under contract 400-80-0008. While I am indebted to all of the above, I alone am responsible for any flaws in the logic of the argument presented.

vate schools. Controversy surrounds these analyses, and a new motto suggested by Cronbach (1981) — "Private schools do it better" — seems likely to emerge.

Coleman and his colleagues use a survey research design as a basis for their analysis of private and public schools. In examining the validity of their conclusions, we must distinguish between two different purposes for a survey, both of which appear in this study. The first is enumerative, addressing "what is" questions, such as "What is the racial composition of Catholic schools?" The second is analytic, attempting to identify causal relationships and to answer "what will happen if" questions, such as "What will happen to achievement if students who attend public schools decide to enroll in the private sector?"

While surveys are ideal for examining the first type of question, they are not a strong means of answering the second. Surveys are frequently used to *explore* causal relationships, but both the true experiment and the quasi-experiment are generally viewed as a more rigorous method of *validating* causal relationships (see, for example, Bryk & Light, 1981; Cook & Campbell, 1979). In the *experiment* we manipulate the context, and then wait to see what occurs. In this manner we obtain limited but direct evidence about "what will happen if?" In the *survey* we gather data on existing phenomena and look for relationships that occur naturally. By applying statistical models to survey data we can obtain only indirect evidence about the "what will happen if" question, since no manipulation of variables has actually taken place. Further, since each statistical model relies on a set of both substantive and technical assumptions about the data, the validity of the answers to "what will happen if?" questions will depend on the validity of those assumptions.

As I began my analysis of the *Public and Private Schools* study, I assumed that this essay would develop out of a general set of complex technical issues that confront any effort at causal analysis of survey data. While some discussion of such issues occurs, the most salient concerns are quite basic — as, for example, are the sample sizes adequate to sustain the conclusions offered? What are we comparing under the terms "public," "Catholic," and "other private schools" and how does this relate to educational policy?

> *Finding:* Facilitating use of private schools through policies such as tuition tax credits and educational vouchers would bring a greater proportion of blacks and Hispanics, rather than whites. into private schools. (p. xxvii)

In general, the sample sizes for Catholic and other private schools in the *High School and Beyond* (1980) survey, the data base for *Public and Private Schools*, are small when disaggregated by ethnic group. While probability sampling techniques were employed in order to assure a nationally representative sample *overall, High School and Beyond* was not designed in order to assure representativeness for all *subgroups* within the overall sample. This is particularly troublesome in the non-Catholic private school sector where the total sample consists of 1,832 students, of whom 1,622 are white, and only 76 black and 70 Hispanic.[1] Further, over half of the Hispanic students come from only one

---

[1] Other than information on the total sample size for each sector, the study provides no description of the *High School and Beyond* sample. The numbers cited here on the ethnic composition of the non-Catholic private sector were provided by Thomas Hoffer in a personal communication to the author. I wish to acknowledge his assistance and express my gratitude.

school. Making national generalizations, as Coleman et al. do, seems quite inappropriate in this case.

In terms of the specific finding cited above, the evidence for this was drawn from estimated relationships between family income and percentage enrollment in Catholic and other private schools for whites, blacks, and Hispanics. In general, blacks and Hispanics are underrepresented in Catholic and other private schools, which Coleman and his colleagues suggest is in large part a function of income differences across the three ethnic groups. The authors observe that when they control for these income differences in their analyses, the enrollment rates for blacks and Hispanics are quite similar to those for whites. Policies which involve federal support for private education should therefore reduce the effect of income differences and actually encourage racial integration.

Criticisms of this analysis have come from many sources.[2] One of the most basic involves the adequacy of the sample size for supporting reliable enrollment rate estimates for the various ethnic groups. Although neither standard errors nor tests of statistical significance are reported in *Public and Private Schools*, it is possible to piece together approximate standard errors and tests of significance using data from the report, information on the survey design presented in Appendix A, and supplemental information provided by the authors.[3] Depending upon the particular income level, the standard errors for black and Hispanic enrollment rates range from about .5 of 1 percent to about 3 percent with a typical value of about 1 percent. The estimated standard errors for the enrollment percentages are in many instances about the same size as the estimated differences among the ethnic groups. Further, these standard errors are large relative to the absolute size of the estimated enrollment rates, which are typically about 3 to 4 percent. This is particularly important in the current situation because it implies a very wide margin of error in the enrollment shifts predicted on the basis of these estimates.

It would be appropriate in a situation like this to adjust the estimated rates through a process called statistical smoothing or shrinking, rather than using the raw estimates for prediction. The idea is that some of the variation in the estimated percentages is associated with the extreme values represented in this particular sample. The estimated percentages provide valuable but fallible information about the underlying relationship between income and probability of enrollment in private schools.

The findings reported by Coleman and his colleagues would still emerge if the relationship between income and the probability of enrollment in private schools were a

[2] Goldberger (Note 1), for example, has raised questions about the reliability of students' reports on their family income. Murnane, in another essay in this volume, has taken Coleman et al. to task for failure to consider supply-side consequences of a tuition tax credit policy.
[3] The standard error (s. e.) of a proportion is estimated as follows: $s.e.\ (p) = D\,[p(1\cdot p)/n]^{\frac{1}{2}}$ where p is the estimated proportion; n is the sample size; and D is a design factor that takes into account the manner in which the probability sample is drawn.
For a random sample, the design factor is 1.0. For the two-stage cluster sample used in *High School and Beyond*, Table A.1.1 in *Public and Private Schools* reports D values ranging from 1.509 through 2.689, depending upon the particular subgroup for analysis. Unfortunately, design factors are not presented in the report for the separate ethnic groups. On the basis of a personal communication with the authors, I have used an approximate value of 1.5. Information on the sample size broken down by income level and ethnic group does not appear in the draft report. They were, however, provided by Thomas Hoffer in a personal communication.

line. However, if the relationship is best represented by a curve with an increasing slope as a function of income, then the findings could easily reverse: a larger proportion of whites rather than blacks and Hispanics would be predicted to shift into private schools. In fact, the estimated relationships presented in *Public and Private Schools* provide some indication of such curvature. Without actually computing adjusted rates, it is impossible to predict the results. Nevertheless, it seems clear that the findings offered by Coleman et al. on this point are on very shaky ground.[4]

Finding: Private schools produce better cognitive outcomes than do public schools. (p. xx)

This is perhaps the key finding of the study, and has certainly attracted the most attention. In examining the credibility of this finding, we need to consider "what is being compared," as well as the adequacy of the statistical analysis used in making the comparison.

A Basic Noncomparability Across Sectors

High School and Beyond was designed as a general purpose survey. The decision to compare public, Catholic, and non-Catholic private high schools came after the survey had been conducted and therefore was not a specific consideration in developing the design.

A central function of a general purpose survey is simply to describe a group or some set of groups. Several chapters of *Public and Private Schools*, for example, engage in description of public, Catholic, and non-Catholic private high schools and the students enrolled. For this purpose, one designs the survey in order to assure representation of the various types of high schools that exist.

In other sections of the report, the authors move beyond simple description to a more analytic function. For example, by comparing data from public, Catholic, and non-Catholic private schools, they seek to draw inferences about the relative effectiveness of these sectors. Under tuition tax credits or educational vouchers it seems clear that some increased number of families would view private education as both attractive and financially viable, and some shift of students across sectors would follow. This would occur as the aggregate effect of individual families choosing among the options available to each of them. Thus a primary purpose of the current research is to illuminate what might be the consequences of such policies and the shifting of students that would result. By comparing, for example, cognitive achievement across sectors, the authors are attempting to predict whether, in aggregate, student performance is likely to improve or decline under a federal policy that encourages students to shift from one sector to another. When designing a survey to inform this issue, the comparison embedded in it must be defined in such a way as to assure consistency with the framework of choice available to individ-

---

[4] The relationship between income and probability of enrollment for the non-Catholic private sector is surprisingly flat. Two possible explanations for this readily occur. First, since the other private sector includes special education schools, the relationship for this portion of the sector is likely to have negative slope the higher the income group, the less likely a student is to be enrolled in a special education school. Considerable past research indicates disproportionate numbers of poor and minorities in special education. Second, the estimated relationship does not take into account the variable cost of the commodity – other private education in question here. Since the cost of education in the Catholic sector is partially subsidized through the religious orders, we can expect higher tuition costs in the non-Catholic private sector that should diminish the overall demand. Further analysis of the demand for private education should take tuition levels into account.

ual families which in aggregate might produce the enrollment shift. The sectors compared in this research, however, do not meet this criterion.

Few, for example, who currently enroll their children in an academic program in a public school would consider, even under the most generous voucher system, enrolling that same child in a special education school. Most would judge it an inappropriate option. Yet, population statistics for the non-Catholic private sector indicate that approximately 16 percent of the schools in this sector are special education schools, although we do not know how many of them are represented in the sample because the draft report does not describe it.[5]

The non-Catholic private sector also includes the more extreme religious schools such as Christian fundamentalist academies. Parents who enroll their children in these schools are likely to be motivated primarily by religious concerns. Including these schools in an assessment of the academic effectiveness of the non-Catholic private sectors seems misdirected. Again, a parent who is concerned about promoting high academic achievement is unlikely to choose this option. In fact, this concern applies in varying degrees to almost any religious-based private school. Defining an appropriate comparison group within the non-Catholic private sector for academic public school programs involves a certain ambiguity that cannot be easily resolved.

Similarly, the sector comparisons do not take into account the different curricular emphases of public and private schools. According to *High School and Beyond* 27 percent of public school students are enrolled in vocational education programs, compared to 9 percent of the students in all private schools. Similarly, approximately 70 percent of the private school students are enrolled in academic programs, in contrast to only 34 percent of those enrolled in public schools. Therefore, to compare public and private schools in aggregate is to ignore an important difference between them: private schools offer primarily an academic curriculum whereas public schools offer a more diverse program. It would make more sense, for example, to compare the cognitive achievement of students enrolled in academic programs in public schools with that of students enrolled in similar programs in Catholic schools than simply to compare the sectors in total. Similar problems occur when comparing public schools to non-Catholic private schools because of the diverse set of purposes represented among non-Catholic private schools. While defining an appropriate comparison group in the non-Catholic private sector is a difficult task, simply to compare the public and non-Catholic private sectors in aggregate does injustice to both.

Adequacy of Statistical Adjustments

Public and Private Schools reports that there are substantial differences in the family background of children who attend schools in the different sectors. Briefly, students in Catholic and other private schools are more likely than public school students to be

---

[5] The statement that 16 percent of the schools in the non-Catholic private sector are special education schools is based on data presented in Table 2.2.2. Of the 18,951 secondary schools in the United States, 4 percent or approximately 758, are designated special education schools. Of the 13,429 public high schools, 0.1 percent or about 13 are designated special education schools. Of the 1,688 Catholic high schools, 7.3 percent or approximately 123 are special education. Putting these numbers together yields 622 special education schools in the non-Catholic private sector. Since the non-Catholic private sector consists of 3,841 schools, special education schools constitute 16.2 percent of the sector.

white, have higher family incomes, and have parents with more education. Some adjustment for these differences should be made before comparing academic outcomes across sectors. Statistical methods, such as those utilized by Coleman et al., are traditionally employed for this purpose.

The adequacy of using such approaches to compensate for preexisting differences between groups has been the subject of considerable debate. Some methodologists (see, for example, Campbell & Erlebacher, 1970) have suggested that when applying regression-based techniques, underadjustments are to be expected. For *Public and Private Schools*, this argument suggests that the effects of public schools have been underestimated. More recent research (see, for example, Bryk & Weisberg, 1977; Cronbach, Ragosa, Floden, & Price, 1977; Weisberg, 1979) has clearly demonstrated that statistical adjustments may result in either over- or underadjustment of preexisting differences between groups. Since no empirical procedure exists for determining whether a data set has been adjusted correctly, we cannot be certain that Coleman, Hoffer, and Kilgore's estimations of school effects are correct.

However, careful examination of the data in *Public and Private Schools* can provide some clues about the adequacy of the analysis performed. There is strong evidence that, although statistical adjustments were carried out, underestimation of public school effects may still persist. The clearest indication of this is reported in the analysis of future education plans. One set of questions in *High School and Beyond* asks seniors to recount whether they had expected to attend college when they were in grades 8, 9, 10, and 11. Sophomores were asked the same questions about their college expectations in grades 6, 7, 8, and 9. Although there may be some question about the reliability of these retrospective accounts, Coleman and his colleagues deem them adequate for inclusion in their study. Statistical adjustments were made on these data for preexisting differences in family background variables[6] among the public, Catholic, and other private school groups. The findings are quite illuminating. For high school seniors, 48 percent of the public school students, 62 percent of the Catholic school students, and 53 percent of the non-Catholic private school students said that when they were in eighth grade they intended to go to college. The high school sophomores' retrospective accounts to eight grade indicated that 52 percent of the public school students, 65 percent of the Catholic school students, and 56 percent of the other private school students said they intended to go to college. Thus, even after statistical adjustment, 14 percent more Catholic students than public school students (based on the seniors' data) and 13 percent more (based on the sophomores' data) said they planned to attend college. What do these findings mean? Differences in college aspiration that appear in the eighth grade clearly cannot

---

[6] The data on this point can be found in Table 6.2.7. The adjustment variables used in this analysis consist of information on family education, income, race, and ethnicity. In most analyses of cognitive achievement, these constitute the major explanatory background variables. In addition to these four variables, some of the outcome analyses employed an additional set of 13 other adjustment variables. Included in this latter group is information on family size, mother's work experience, educational resources such as books in the home, and parental attitudes about their children's future educational plans. It is possible that the residual selection effects present in Table 6.2.7 might attenuate or even disappear if additional adjustment variables, such as these, were included in the analysis. Attenuation of the effects seems likely, but elimination does not. The differences reported in this table after the first set of statistical adjustments remain quite large (13 percent to 14 percent), and further adjustments could actually increase the size of these effects.

be due to effects of secondary schools, but can only reflect family background and the cumulative effects of schooling up to the eighth grade. These differences suggest that a selection bias exists which has not been accounted for by the analyses conducted to date. Since the statistical model employed here is used for all the analyses of educational outcomes, this finding raises serious questions about its adequacy and the effect estimates based upon it.

What additional analyses should be conducted in light of these problems? *Public and Private Schools* presents few descriptive statistics on the analytic sample, such as means, standard deviations for various subgroups of students within each sector, and correlations. A more extensive exploratory analyses of these data will provide the technical reader a better basis for understanding the likely behavior of statistical adjustments in this case.

Beyond exploratory analysis, two relatively new techniques merit investigation. The analysis of covariance structures, which is derived from a psychometric orientation (Jöreskog, 1970; Jöreskog & Sorbom, 1978), focuses on developing more complex and more adequate measurement models for all variables. Relationships can then be modeled in terms of the underlying constructs for which the observed variables are assumed to be indicators. Alternatively, economists suggest building models of how individuals select into groups, and then use these selection models for purposes of adjustment (see, for example, Barnow, Cain, & Goldberger, 1980; Heckman, 1979). In principle, either approach may lead to unbiased estimates of sector effects conditioned upon the appropriateness of the model assumptions.

These analyses are conditional — this point can not be overemphasized. In each case, we must first make some assumptions about the processes generating the data and then, based on these assumptions, derive estimates for the parameters of the model. Because these models are more complex than traditional regression-based techniques they require more assumptions. On the technical side, these models require assumptions about the multivariate distribution of independent and outcome variables, and in many applications, we must also assume that the values of certain parameters — for example, an error variance component — are known. On the substantive side, we must specify many unidirectional relationships among individual variables and in some cases make assumptions about underlying constraints. How statistical techniques should then be applied to a model will depend on our assumptions; a slight change in the model, adding a variable or posing some constraints, may alter considerably the estimated effects. While certainly these techniques should be attempted, alone they provide only weak evidence about sector effects. Because they require so many assumptions, the process can be somewhat akin to building a superstructure without worrying that its foundation may be quicksand. As a companion to the more traditional regression analyses reported by Coleman et al., and in the context of extensive exploratory analyses suggested above, these techniques can be valuable and could have strengthened their analysis. Alone, they must be approached with a great deal of caution.

> *Finding:* Private schools encourage higher educational aspirations than public schools.
> (p. xxii)

For the purpose of analyzing the effects of school sector on future educational plans, Coleman and his colleagues use a scale that ranges from "less than high school graduation" (with a value of 1) through "vocational, trade, or business school of two years or more beyond high school" (with a value of 4), to "a Ph.D. or equivalent" (with a value of 9). This scale is quite appropriate for indicating the amount of education a student receives. However, it is an inadequate method of measuring the educational production of high schools because it fails to incorporate information on the ways secondary schools differ, particularly public secondary schools, which have a multiple set of goals. For example, an appropriate score on the future educational-plan scale for a student enrolled in a high school vocational education program might be a value of 3 or 4. For those enrolled in an academic program, scores would probably range from 6 (2 years of college or more) to 9 (the Ph.D. or equivalent). Clearly, this scale is biased in favor of careers involving academic preparation, and implies that vocational education aspirations are inferior to college aspirations. Therefore, averaging all students' scores without regard to their high school program misrepresents the effectiveness of schools that offer a vocational curriculum. Since most vocational training occurs in public schools, those schools will appear less effective than private schools, even if their vocational programs are of high quality and are successful in advancing the public schools' educational objectives. Using this type of scale to compare schools violates a basic principle of program evaluation — the necessity for examining a program's effectiveness in light of its goals.

Vocational education programs, some critics might argue, serve as a "dumping ground" for the failures of public schools, and as a result these students' reduced educational aspirations should be viewed as a negative effect of public schools. This argument, while perhaps assumed by Coleman and his colleagues, is never actually presented in the study. Moreover, in making such an argument, one must remember that admission to vocational educational programs is often selective, that students in vocational education programs give their schools ratings comparable to those given by students in general programs,[7] and that job opportunities, as well as incomes, for some vocational education graduates exceed those for some college graduates.

Finding: Catholic schools best fulfill the ideal of the "common school." (p. xxviii)

Coleman et al. report that the achievement levels and educational aspirations of students from different parental education backgrounds, of black and white students, and of Hispanic and white students are more nearly alike in Catholic schools than in public schools. This conclusion was reached by running separate regressions by sector for each educational outcome on a limited set of background variables, and then using the estimated regression equations to predict expected differences for representative cases. Central to this analysis is the adequacy of the estimated regression equations.

At least in part, these findings result from the definitions of public and private schools adopted by Coleman and his colleagues. Public high schools, by design, encourage more diversity than Catholic high schools, which focus primarily on academic preparation.

---

[7] Table 12 in *High School and Beyond* (p. 21) presents data on the percentage of high school seniors rating various school characteristics as "good" or "excellent" by curriculum and school type. The characteristics are: school reputation, library facilities, quality of instruction, condition of buildings, school spirit, and teachers' interest in students. While the reports from students in public school vocational education programs are somewhat less positive than those from students in academic programs, vocational education students are more positive than their counterparts in the general curriculum.

Similarly, non-Catholic private schools also reflect a varied range of purposes. An alternative, far simpler generalization here is that institutions with diverse objectives produce diverse results. This conclusion is certainly consistent with the analyses reported by Coleman et al., and it more fairly represents the diversity of schools' purposes that exist within both the public and non-Catholic private school sectors.

From a more technical point of view, the fact that the public and non-Catholic private samples are more heterogeneous than the Catholic sample does not necessarily explain the differences in the estimated regression equations that underlie the finding that Catholic schools embody the "common school" ideal. It is possible that similar regression equations would emerge and the same results occur by using revised sample definitions (for example, comparing only students enrolled in academic programs). We know, however, that a few extreme values in a sample exert considerable leverage in determining the estimated regression coefficients. For example, data from severely handicapped students in non-Catholic private schools, though relatively few in number, could substantially influence the estimated coefficients. Thus, the analyses that support the common school theme could shift dramatically under alternative sample definitions.

> *Finding:* Private schools have higher rates of engagement in academic activities because these schools encourage better attendance, demand more homework, and encourage enrollment in more rigorous subjects. They also create a climate more conducive to achievement by maintaining standards for student behavior, reducing incidents of violence, and hiring teaching staff with a greater overall personal commitment to students. (p. xxviii)

Coleman and his colleagues present these analyses of school effectiveness, which are the most intriguing and interesting aspects of the study, not to illuminate the effects of alternative school policies, but to defend their general thesis that private schools produce better educational outcomes than public schools. They argue that since public and private schools have different educational outcomes and school policies, being able to demonstrate that the school policies that distinguish public from private schools are related to outcomes within each sector will provide additional evidence to support their general thesis about the effectiveness of private schools. Their goal is to validate the observed private school effects by providing an empirically-based explanation for their occurrence.

The study's findings should be viewed with caution because the basic analysis problem is quite complex. The task consists of simultaneously analyzing data on individual students, such as their family background and educational experiences, as well as organizational data on the character of the school, its resources, and climate. Methodologists have not resolved satisfactorily how best to analyze data from multiple levels — the student and the school. The analyses reported in *Public and Private Schools* are fragmentary, assembled into a kind of patchwork quilt to support the findings, and presented without sufficient information for the technical reader to adequately judge the conclusions. At this point, all we can say is that the evidence presented so far is plausible.[8]

---

[8] Additional analysis of the school effectiveness issue might draw on ideas suggested by Cronbach, Deken, and Webb (1976) and Burstein, Linn, and Capell (1978). A conceptually adequate plan might proceed as fol-

Concluding Comments

Public and Private Schools reflects fundamental ambiguities about social science, the information it generates, and its appropriate role in the formulation of social policy. As Lindblom and Cohen (1979) have argued, using social science as a basis for social policy rests on the assumption that the knowledge it produces is special, different, and apart from the ordinary or common knowledge that each of us possesses. The physical sciences achieve this authoritativeness in part through the use of technical procedures, such as sophisticated instrumentation, which allow the scientist to "see" what the ordinary observer cannot. Applied social science research has no similar technology. To the outside observer, the data collection methods of social science, such as the interview or observation, look very much like the procedures of inquiry each of us uses routinely in the conduct of our daily lives.

If there is an argument for the special character of applied social science research knowledge, it can not rest primarily on technical aspects of method. Rather, it must draw on the basic character of the research process — a commitment to *disciplined* inquiry (see Shulman, 1981). While researchers may use varied methods, they share a core of values that distinguishes the practice of social science from other activities, such as use of political rhetoric. These values include a concern for specificity in the definition of terms, the systematic collection and examination of evidence, the identification, control, or reduction of bias — both personal and from other sources — and a manner of argumentation based on the principle that knowledge advances by disproof.

From this vantage point — applied social science research as disciplined inquiry — *Public and Private Schools*, at least in its draft form, is incomplete. The weaknesses of its method raise serious doubts about its conclusions. In terms of the manner of argument, the study's analyses and alternative hypotheses appear to be selective, and generally limited to advancing the motto that "Private schools do it better." At its most basic level — the quality of the design and data collected — the draft report simply does not provide adequate information for assessing its technical merit. Several very basic elements are not presented:

— descriptive statistics of the samples used in the various analyses. We do not know what is being included under the labels "public," "Catholic," and "other private schools."

— sampling errors for the various statistics presented in the report. We have no standard for judging whether the reported findings constitute anything more than sampling variation.

— a description of possible nonsampling errors associated with the implementation of the survey and their likely effect on the reported results.

---

lows: at the first level, we consider how family background characteristics and educational experiences of individual children relate to the outcomes for these children in individual schools. It is reasonable to expect differences across schools in these production functions. At the second level, we relate the characteristics of the schools, such as organizational climate and disciplinary structure, to various parameters in these production functions. Thus, the model represents both the differences in outcomes across individuals within schools, as well as how these differences are related to school characteristics. Strenio (1981), using an empirical Bayes approach and drawing on theoretical work on hierarchical models advanced by Lindley and Smith (1972), provides an illustration consistent with this idea.

— a description of the conditions under which the survey and test data were gathered.

— an analysis of subject non-response and missing data.

— a description of the reliability and validity of the tests used as well as a full description of the tests themselves.

— an examination of errors of measurement associated with each survey question. This is particularly important for those survey items (such as family income) used as adjustment variables in the school effects analyses.

Thus, we lack considerable information fundamental to any judgment about the adequacy of the research reported. The possible biases involved are numerous and conceivably run in both directions. At this point, the margin of error on any finding, whether favoring private or public schools, is very large, and the study's credibility for policy purposes highly suspect.

What, then, should we make of *Public and Private Schools?* It seems appropriate to characterize the current study as a form of policy argument. While numerous caveats about the research appear in the text, the summary and concluding sections — those directed toward a policy audience — are much less cautious. While the findings are wrapped in a mantle of social science research, the report is inconsistent with the notion of disciplined inquiry. However, it is consistent with emerging canons for improving the utility of evaluation and policy research. It is timely and succinct. *Public and Private Schools* is organized to address a particular policy issue, and the evidence is assembled to support a particular policy recommendation. The findings are presented quite plainly and have been disseminated with much fanfare. In contrast to disciplined inquiry, which by its nature may be viewed as too cautious to be useful for policy purposes, this research will indeed be used in the current policy debate.

Social scientists are faced with a dilemma. In striving to make applied social science research more useful for social policy, we run the risk of stripping the research process of its fundamental character and the only basis for claiming that the results should be accorded special status in the policy debate. While we may have figured out how to catch the policymaker's ear, we may have nothing special to say. This is not to denigrate the value of *Public and Private Schools*, but rather simply to understand it as a form of argument not unlike the social portraiture of life in the urban classroom, or the political rhetoric on the plight of the poor. In the hands of a distinguished individual such as Coleman it can be a powerful instrument. While it may not constitute disciplined inquiry, we must note in fairness that disciplined inquiry itself is limited. It cannot resolve the inherent ambiguity in the nature of much social science knowledge. Some conflicts can be settled — for example, we can in fact determine whether the data in *High School and Beyond* are sufficient to permit reliable distinctions among the income demand curves for private education for whites, blacks, and Hispanics — but others will persist. Survey research, for example, by its nature involves a high degree of uncertainty when used for analytic purposes. Different assumptions can lead to different conclusions, and reasonable social scientists will disagree about the reasonableness of the various assumptions. Applied social scientists cannot resolve most of these differences since they involve alternative theoretical and value premises, both of which are external to the analysis.

Nevertheless, disciplined inquiry serves a valuable function when it helps us to identify differences in assumptions and the possible consequences associated with each. It would be a misfortune if disciplined inquiry turned away from such questions as "What is the relative effectiveness of public versus private schools?" To claim that such questions are invalid or unworthy of study defies common sense. Yet we must recognize that the results of such inquiry will frequently lead us away from simple policy answers to an understanding of the complexities inherent in an apparently simple question. Information gained from careful inquiry can change the way we think about social problems (Weiss, 1980), and ultimately may be the most powerful way social science can influence social policy.

Reference Note

1. Goldberger, A. *Coleman goes private (in public)*. Unpublished manuscript, University of Wisconsin, Madison, 1981.

References

Barnow, B. S., Cain, G. G., & Goldberger, A. S. Issues in analysis of selectivity bias. In E. Stromsdorfer & G. Farkos (Eds.), *Evaluation Studies Review Annual* (Vol. 5). Beverly Hills: Sage, 1980.

Bryk, A. S., & Light, R. J. Designing evaluations for different program environments. In R. A. Berk (Ed.), *Educational evaluation methodology: The state of the art*. Baltimore: Johns Hopkins University Press, 1981.

Bryk, A. S., & Weisberg, H. I. Use of the nonequivalent control group design when subjects are growing. *Psychological Bulletin*, 1977, **84**, 950-962.

Burnstein, L., Linn, R. D., & Capell, F. *Analyzing multilevel data in the presence of heterogeneous within-class regressions*. Los Angeles: Center for the Study of Evaluation, University of California, 1978.

Campbell, D. T., & Erlebacher, A. How regression artifacts in quasi-experimental evaluations can mistakenly make compensatory education look harmful. In J. Hellmuth (Ed.), *Compensatory education: A national debate* (Vol. 3), *Disadvantaged child*. New York: Brunner-Mazel, 1970.

Coleman, J., Campbell, E., Hobson, C., McPartland, J., Mood, A., Weinfeld, F., & York, R. *Equality of educational opportunity*. Washington, D.C.: U.S. Government Printing Office, 1966.

Cook, T. D., & Campbell, D. T. *Quasi-experimentation*. Chicago: Rand McNally, 1979.

Cronbach, L. J. Remarks in response to an invited address by James Coleman on *Public and Private Schools*. 1981 Annual Meeting of the American Educational Research Association, Los Angeles, April 1981.

Cronbach, L. J., Deken, J. E., & Webb, N. *Research on classrooms and schools: Formulation of questions, design, and analysis*. Occasional papers of the Stanford Evaluation Consortium, Stanford, Calif., July 1976.

Cronbach, L. J., Ragosa, D. R., Floden, R. E., & Price, G. G. *Analysis of covariance in nonrandomized experiments: Parameters affecting bias*. Occasional papers of the Stanford Evaluation Consortium, Stanford, Calif., 1977.

Edmonds, R. Effective schools for the urban poor. *Educational Leadership*, October 1979, pp. 15-24.

Heckman, J. J. Sample selection bias as a specification error. *Econometrica*, 1979, **47**, 153-161.

High school and beyond. Chicago: National Opinion Research Center, 1980.

Jöreskog, K. G. A general method for analysis of covariance structures. *Biometrika*, 1970, **57**, 239-251.

Jöreskog, K. G., & Sorbom, D. *LISREL IV: Analysis of linear structural relationships by the method of maximum likelihood: User's guide*. Chicago: International Educational Services, 1978.

Lindblom, C. E., & Cohen, D. K. *Usable knowledge: Social science and social problem solving*. New Haven: Yale University Press, 1979.

Lindley, D. V., & Smith, A. F. M. Bayes estimates for the linear model. *Journal of Royal Statistical Society*, 1972, **34**(1, Series B), 1-41.

Rutter, M., Maughan, B., Mortimore, P., & Ouston, J., with Smith, A. *Fifteen thousand hours: Secondary schools and their effects on children*. Cambridge, Mass.: Harvard University Press, 1979.

Shulman, L. S. Disciplines of inquiry in education: An overview. *Educational Researcher*, 1981, **10**(6), 5-12.

Strenio, J. *Empirical Bayes estimation for a hierarchical linear model*. Unpublished doctoral dissertation, Harvard University, 1981.

Weisberg, H. I. Statistical adjustments and uncontrolled studies. *Psychological Bulletin*, 1979, **86**, 1149-1164.

Weiss, C. *Social science research and decision-making*. New York: Columbia University Press, 1980.

24

Questions and Answers
Our Response

James Coleman, Thomas Hoffer, and Sally Kilgore

The reviews of our draft report, *Public and Private Schools*, ask four kinds of questions: (1) Is the study itself satisfactory on technical grounds? (2) Do the study's results, which are generally more favorable to private schools than to public schools, appear correct? (3) What inferences can be drawn from results such as these about the effect of policy changes on educational outcomes? (4) Is this the way social policy research should be done?

The first point is addressed primarily by Bryk, whose general conclusion is that the study is not technically satisfactory because information about various sources of error is not presented. The second point is addressed by both Bryk and Murnane, who argue that statistical difficulties associated with elimination of possible biases due to selection into the private sector make it impossible to validate the result of higher achievement in the private sector. Bryk also declares other results "not proved," basing his conclusions both on technical grounds and his own calculation of sampling variation. Heyns, Braddock, Bryk, and Murnane discount the achievement differences we find, insisting that comparisons within school program — academic, general, and vocational — are more appropriate.

The third point is addressed by most of the reviewers. Braddock argues that higher education, which currently has a public/private mixture and shows a rather high degree of racial segregation, offers a better example of what would be the segregative consequence of facilitating private schooling than any scenario we propose. Murnane says that no inference can be drawn about the effects of facilitating enrollment at private schools because this would change the internal composition of the private sector, as well as the distribution of available private school offerings (the "supply response"), and would bring about government regulation of the private sector to an unknown degree. Heyns agrees with this conclusion, adding that the study provides no information about the ways a facilitating policy such as tax credits would affect movement into the private

From James Coleman, Thomas Hoffer, and Sally Kilgore, "Questions and Answers: Our Response," 51(4) *Harvard Educational Review* 526-545 (November 1981). Copyright © 1981 by the President and Fellows of Harvard College. Reprinted by permission.

sector, nor about its cost-effectiveness. Guthrie and Zusman make a similar point, arguing in addition that the study's results have no implications for policies in public schools because of the constraints under which they operate. Finn, in contrast, argues that the study's principal implications relate to public schooling, focusing on the finding that public school students do as well as those of comparable backgrounds in private schools when the public schools have disciplinary standards and academic demands comparable to the average private school.

Finally, on the fourth point, two of the authors, Bryk and Murnane, imply that this is not the way social policy research should be done. Others are silent on this point, except for Finn, whose response implies that he feels this is the way such research should be done. We will respond to each of these points, though our responses will be more detailed in some areas than others. And, in conclusion, we will place this study into the larger context of secondary education issues in the 1980s.

Technical Deficiencies

Public and Private Schools does have several reporting deficiencies, at least one of which would have led, if more fully addressed, to a much greater tentativeness in our generalizations. The sample of non-Catholic private schools is small (27 schools), the sample of students within them is small (631 sophomores and 551 seniors), and the nonresponse rate of these non-Catholic private schools was higher than in any other sector. The schools in this sector are also very diverse. These sampling limitations imply that any generalization from the study's sample of schools to the total universe of private schools is very shaky, and should probably not be done. Although few of the study's generalizations were specific to the non-Catholic private sector, those which were should be given little, if any, weight in the overall conclusions. Apart from the validity of the study's conclusions regarding those non-Catholic private schools actually sampled, the questions about this sample's representativeness of the total population of such schools are sufficiently great that little can be said from the study about this sector as a whole.

We also agree that there could and should have been fuller reporting of sampling errors and potential biases in the data. Calculation of standard errors was particularly complicated for some of our analyses. In lieu of calculation of standard errors, we depended upon consistency of results from alternative analyses, such as different sets of background variables, different assumptions about constancy of regression coefficients in different sectors and different grades. These were not reported, however, and thus could not give a reviewer a basis for confidence in the robustness of the results. Thus, the criticism is well taken; we are reporting standard errors as well as some of the alternative analyses we conducted in the final report (and in a revised draft[1]). In general, the standard errors show that the achievement results reported in the draft can be generalized to the system as a whole, with the caveat about non-Catholic schools mentioned earlier. Thus, the inclusion of the omitted information on standard errors has little effect on these substantive conclusions.

---

[1] A revised draft will be published by Basic Books under the title *High School Achievement: Public, Catholic, and Other Private Schools Compared.* The final report of *Public and Private Schools* will be submitted to the National Center for Education Statistics (NCES) on November 30, 1981.

In the section concerned with policy changes directed toward making private educa tion more affordable to minorities and low income groups, the calculation of standard errors suggests that our original generalizations do need to be qualified. Bryk correctly points out that the standard errors for our estimates of the proportions of blacks and His panics who are enrolled in private schools are quite large at some income levels. How ever, the problem is not as severe as Bryk's comments suggest. At the lower-income lev els, the increases in the proportions of blacks and Hispanics in Catholic schools are sta tistically significant. The confidence that one can place in the comparison of point esti mates at the middle- and upper-income levels does decline where the proportions en rolled increase and the relative numbers of minorities decline.[2] Yet, in terms of a more limited question we proposed — how to account for black underenrollment in Catholic schools — the technical deficiencies do not alter our conclusion: once income is taken into account, the differences in black and white enrollment are reduced. We will discuss this in greater detail in the subsequent section. What seems important to stress then is that the evidence is quite strong that the lower income of blacks constrains their entry into Catholic schools, but given the technical limitations, the evidence is unclear regard ing precisely how much a reduction of the income constraint would improve their rela tive representation in Catholic schools.

Other criticisms of the study made by the reviewers which fall partly under the "tech nical deficiency" heading are more closely related to the substantive results. Thus, we will examine them in the next section.

Are the Results Correct?

In one sense, reviewers are in an advantageous position when they ask this question, for they can raise doubts without having to resolve them. In another sense, the authors are in an advantageous position, for we are in a better position to carry out analyses that go beyond those in the report in resolving those doubts. Just as the reviewers have used their advantage, we will use ours, making use of some of these additional analyses along with those of the study itself to address this question.

Analysis of Cognitive Outcomes

A major issue posed by several reviewers, particularly Bryk and Murnane, is that of se lectivity: the possibility that residual background differences between students in the private and public sectors (beyond the background characteristics controlled in our analysis) lead to the higher achievement we found in private schools. If this criticism is correct, achievement differences are not caused by schools, but are due to backgrounds responsible for selection into the sector. And as Bryk states, the error could be in either direction: toward an overestimate of the effects of the private schools, as assumed by a number of critics, or toward an underestimate.

The reviewers raise several points. One is that the retrospective evidence from the 8th grade students from comparable backgrounds (presented in Table 6.2.7 of *Public and*

---

[2] While statistical significance is not especially strong here, the consistency of results provides another guide to interpretation. In the analysis in question, there are no exceptions across the seven income levels to the gen eral pattern of a reduced black-white enrollment difference (pp. 36-38).

Private Schools) shows higher expectations in the private sector, suggesting uncontrolled background differences. Two points are relevant to this. First, only 5 background factors were used in Table 6.2.7; when reanalyzed with the 17 factors used in studying the achievement effects, the differences in 8th grade expectations are reduced.[3] More important, when we look at the retrospective 6th grade expectation from sophomores, the public/private differences almost entirely vanish when these 17 background factors are controlled: 40 percent in the public sector report having expected to go to college; 42 and 43 percent are the comparable figures in the Catholic and non-Catholic private sectors. These new data, then, provide evidence contrary to the critics' claim of uncontrolled selective factors that might affect achievement. The evidence is in the reverse direction: the 17 background factors used in our analysis control for those selection factors affecting educational aspirations and, by extension, achievement.

Another point made by reviewers is that additional statistical techniques should be used, such as one which explicitly models the selection process into the private or public sector and then accounts for achievement of students from different backgrounds conditional upon selection into the sector. Both Murnane and Bryk are dubious about the merits of techniques that follow this approach because they depend greatly on the model specification for selection and achievement. Nevertheless, the reviewers consider the approach helpful, if not conclusive. We concur with both the reservations regarding this type of analysis and with the importance of exploring what information these techniques may provide. In the final report, we will discuss in full our use of two different models for one of these techniques, developed by Heckman (1979), but it seems helpful to briefly summarize them here.

In one case, the estimate of the selection bias effect on achievement was not significantly different from zero; in the other, it was significantly different from zero.[4] But

---

[3] An extensive search for relevant background variables was conducted in an effort to minimize the effects of differences in initial selection that could masquerade as organizational causes of differences in achievement. In the end we selected 17 background variables, measuring both objective and subjective differences in the home. Some of these subjective differences may not be prior to the student's achievement, but may in part be consequences of it. We thought it desirable to do this so as to compensate for possible unmeasured differences in family background. The 17 background characteristics are the following:

Clearly prior to student achievement	*Not clearly prior*
1. Family income	11. Encyclopedia or reference books in home
2. Mother's education	12. More than fifty books in home
3. Father's education	13. Typewriter in home
4. Race	14. Owns pocket calculator
5. Hispanic non-Hispanic	15. Frequency of talking with mother or
6. Number of siblings	father about personal experiences
7. Number of rooms in the home	16. Mother thinks student should go to
8. Whether student lives with two parents	college after high school
9. Mother's working before child was in	17. Father thinks student should go to college
elementary school	after high school
10. Mother's working when child was in	
elementary school	

[4] For this analysis, only sophomores have been included, using the full mathematics test (with 38 items) as an achievement measure. This test, along with all others used in this analysis, was prepared by the Educational Testing Service for NCES's longitudinal studies. The first model used all but 3 of the 17 variables from the analysis specified in Footnote 3 (these were eliminated to reduce the number of cases lost in a listwise deletion necessary for the program), and dummy variables for religious background (Catholic non-Catholic) and re-

both results are negative, indicating that controlling for the selection bias operates *in favor of* the private sector. This implies that our original estimate of achievement difference is lower than the true difference for comparable students.

Thus, results from the Heckman model suggest that, if anything, the private-school effects are greater than estimated in our report. However, the problem with these results is their dependence on model specification and their instability, for the actual achievement estimates from these two specifications differed greatly.[5] The main import of these results is not to provide strong corroborating evidence for private-school effects, but to still the criticism that use of such a technique would properly eliminate selection bias. At the same time, any evidence the results do provide is in the direction of confirming the greater achievement in private schools than in public schools.

A more serious selection-bias criticism of the achievement results of the study is based on a "comprehensive versus academic" argument made by several reviewers. According to this argument, the public school is comprehensive, while the Catholic and other private schools provide only academic education for college-bound students. Heyns and Bryk, for example, state that it is inappropriate to compare the entire public sector, where only 30 percent of sophomores and 35 percent of seniors report being in an academic program, with the Catholic schools where 62 percent of sophomores and 70 percent of seniors are in an academic program, or with the non-Catholic private sector, where 57 percent of sophomores and 70 percent of seniors are in an academic program. Thus, for them, the question is whether or not one can appropriately compare schools with different curriculum structures. This is a legitimate question, but the critics have overlooked certain points.

First, Heyns asks why we should expect young people who are engaged in work-study and vocational programs to acquire the reading, vocabulary, and mathematics skills measured by tests used in the analysis. Yet these tests measure basic skills — elementary literacy and numerical skills. These are skills that should be held by high school graduates whatever program they are in. If students in a vocational or general program fail to learn these skills, their program is not a legitimate reason.

Second, the criticisms, such as those of Bryk and Heyns, imply that the program a student is in is wholly determined by background and ability, not by school policy. Yet we

---

gion (northeast versus other). The same variables were used for both the probit analyses predicting entry into the private or public sector as in the Ordinary Least Squares (OLS) equation predicting achievement in mathematics.

For the second model we decided to incorporate some exclusionary rules (implying that some variables had an effect on entry into the private or public sectors, but no direct effect on achievement). The probit model included the following variables: (1) income, (2) region, (3) religious background, (4) mother's education, (5) number of siblings, (6) number of rooms in home, (7) educational aspirations in the 8th grade, (8) frequency of talking with parents about personal experiences, (9) encyclopedia or reference books in home, (10) more than 50 books in the home, (11) owns pocket calculator, (12) two parent family, (13) mother's expectations regarding college, (14) race, and (15) ethnicity. The OLS equation predicting achievement deleted variables 1, 3, and 7, and added the variable regarding mother's working prior to elementary school. This modified model stabilized the results considerably in comparison with the first model, and yielded a significant selection bias effect in the achievement equation. The effect, however, was negative, suggesting that the bias of unmeasured student characteristics is in the opposite direction of effects due to measured characteristics. (The covariance selectivity coefficient was − 3.01 with .586 as the adjusted standard error for the private sector achievement equation.)

[5] The differences in achievement estimates from the two equations exceed 20 points.

know this is not true, as Braddock has mentioned. For example, compare the sopho-more and senior years in the public and private schools. At the sophomore level, 31 per-cent of the students are in an academic program in the public schools, 62 percent in the Catholic schools, and 57 percent in the non-Catholic private schools. To give the critics the benefit of the doubt, assume that these differences are due solely to differences in background and ability, and are not caused by policy differences in the sectors. Then what do we say about the seniors? The percentage in an academic program in the public schools is 35 percent, in the Catholic schools 70 percent, and in the other private schools 70 percent — an increase of 5 percent, 8 percent, and 13 percent, respectively. Since the dropout rate between sophomore and senior years is larger in nonacademic programs and is about twice as high in the public than the private sector,[6] we would expect to see a greater increase in the percentage in an academic program in the public schools. But the reverse is true. Obviously, students move into an academic program from their soph-omore to their senior year in the private sector, but comparable students in the public sector are not making that move. The point can be illustrated by an analysis we carried out but did not present in the study. When being in an academic program as a senior was itself taken as a dependent variable in the public and Catholic schools, with the 17 back-ground characteristics and school sector as independent variables, school sector was the strongest predictor. With all these background characteristics controlled, a student in a Catholic school was still 25 percent more likely to be in an academic program than a stu-dent in a public school. This additional analysis corroborates much of the earlier school program research (see Alexander, Cook, & McDill, 1978) and suggests that general pro-gram placement policies and curriculum practices may be a central factor in achieve-ment in secondary education.

The assumption that we grant to the critics in the preceding paragraph — that the sophomore program is purely a function of background and ability, and independent of school policy — is a very dubious one. If being in an academic program is taken as a de-pendent variable with the 17 background factors which include both parents' expecta-tions about college attendance and school sector as independent variables, enrollment in a Catholic or other private school is significantly and positively related to being en-rolled in an academic program as a sophomore.

But let us suppose for a moment that being in a given program was not dependent on school policy and that students from comparable backgrounds in the same program (academic, vocational, or general) have the same potential for performance in cognitive skills. If we again allow our critics the assumption that placement in a given program is independent of school policy, we can then ask how students in the same program and from comparable backgrounds perform in public and private schools. This assumption will introduce a bias against the private sector because the data discussed above strongly suggest that some students who would be in a general or vocational program in the public sector are in an academic program in the private sector.

We conducted such an analysis only for the academic and general programs since vo-cational programs are infrequent in the private sector, and only for the public and Cath-olic schools. Using the same procedures and background variables we have used in pre-

---

[6] The dropout rate as estimated in *Public and Private Schools* (p. 182) is 24 percent for the public sector, 13 percent for the Catholic sector, and 15 percent for the other private.

vious analyses, and adding dummy variables for enrollment in vocational or general programs, we estimated achievement for students in academic and general programs in both the Catholic and public sectors, for students with backgrounds standardized[7] to the average public school sophomore.

We find that sophomores in academic programs in Catholic schools achieve at higher levels than their counterparts in the public sector, and that the differences for students in academic programs are significant for all three tests. At the senior level, the differences are in the same direction, but are statistically significant only for vocabulary. In the general programs, students in Catholic schools achieve more highly than those of comparable backgrounds in public schools in all three tests in both grades; and in this case, the differences are statistically significant for all three tests in both grades. Furthermore, the differences between the sectors are consistently greater for students enrolled in the general program.[8]

Thus, while there is evidence that students from comparable backgrounds in an academic program achieve somewhat more highly in Catholic schools than in public schools, the greater gap appears to exist in the general program. Consistent with this, students in a general program appear to be subjected to greater demands in Catholic schools than in public schools. For instance, when comparing coursework for seniors with comparable backgrounds in general programs, those in the Catholic sector take an average of 2.3 advanced mathematics courses, as compared with 1.6 such courses taken by seniors in the public sector (Coleman, Hoffer, & Kilgore, in press). Absenteeism, cutting classes, and homework also show sharp differences for the general program students. In all these areas, the differences between Catholic and public schools are greater for students in a general program than in an academic program.

Thus, the matter of school program is not the simple one suggested by our critics. It is not that academic students go to private schools and non-academic students go to public schools. Differences in school program placement policies make it more likely that students, whatever their background characteristics, will be placed in an academic program if they attend a Catholic school rather than a public school. Second, even though this is the case, students who are in academic programs in Catholic schools do better than students from comparable backgrounds in public schools in most comparisons, and at least as well in the others. Third, it is for the students in the general program that being in a Catholic school makes the most difference in achievement — exactly the oppo-

[7] For each test, standardization is performed as $\hat{Y}_{ij} = a_{ij} + \sum_{k=1}^{n} b_{ijk}\bar{X}_k$: where $\hat{Y}_{ij}$ is the standardized score for the ith grade in sector j, a_{ij} is the intercept and the b_{ijk} are the coefficients for the background variables in that sector and grade. X is the mean for the public school sophomores on the kth background characteristic.

[8] Table A
Estimated Achievement Within School Program[a]

| | General Program | | | | | Academic Program | | | |
| | Sophomore | | Senior | | | Sophomore | | Senior | |
	Public	Catholic	Public	Catholic		Public	Catholic	Public	Catholic
Reading	3.43	3.68*	4.06	4.24*	Reading	4.11	4.25*	4.91	5.04
Vocabulary	3.52	3.82*	4.09	4.48*	Vocabulary	4.17	4.41*	4.90	5.30*
Mathematics	9.00	9.64*	9.54	10.06*	Mathematics	10.62	10.83*	11.94	11.94

Note. *Significantly different from comparable public school achievement at .05 level.
[a]Achievement tests are the same subtests used throughout our study. The regression equations for each grade and sector include all the background variables listed in Footnote 3 and dummy variables for general and vocational program enrollment. Standardization procedures follow those described in Footnote 7.

site of what the critics would suppose. Such results seem associated with the greater academic and disciplinary demands made upon general program students in the Catholic schools than in the public schools.

The argument that program differentiation should be included in analysis of public private achievement has been extended by some critics to the finding we call the "common school" result in the study: that achievement in Catholic schools is less dependent on family background than achievement in public or other private schools. Bryk, for example, questions our interpretation by arguing that Catholic schools are narrower, focusing primarily on academic preparation, while public schools have more diverse objectives and, thus, "institutions with diverse objectives produce diverse results" (p. 505). However, diverse objectives and different school programs should not be coincidental with family background. Moreover, this presumed focus on academic preparation is exactly the argument that Bryk and others have used to explain why Catholic and other private schools show higher achievement for comparable students than do public schools. But here, the non-Catholic private schools and public schools are described as having diverse objectives. This is a classification for convenience to fit the desired result; otherwise, the high dependence of achievement on family background in the non-Catholic private schools is inexplicable.

But leaving aside the non-Catholic private schools, what about Bryk's alternative explanation of the lesser dependence of achievement on family background in Catholic schools? If that explanation is correct, then the result should disappear, as Bryk suggests, when the student's program is taken into account. Within an academic program or within a general program, family background should make no more difference in achievement in public schools than in Catholic schools. On the other hand, if we are correct, if the public schools have diverged, with schools serving students from higher-status backgrounds generating higher achievement than those serving students from lower-status backgrounds, the differences should remain: achievement in public schools should be more dependent on background, even controlling for the student's program.

The latter is what results when the student's program is statistically controlled. Controlling on the 17 background characteristics and on program in school shows differences, as reported in Table 1, between students with high- and low-parent education, between white and blacks, and between Anglos and Hispanics. There are 18 comparisons between the public and Catholic schools, and in all of these the difference in achievement by family background is less in Catholic schools than in public schools.

Although this analysis was done by merely statistically controlling for the effect of school program, it is possible to carry out an analysis separately for students in academic and general programs. That analysis, not reported here, shows that the public/Catholic difference holds separately for both the academic and general programs, but is particularly pronounced for the general programs.[9]

The Segregative Impact of Private Education
Braddock and Bryk take issue with our conclusions on the segregative impact of private schools. Braddock contends that our effort to arrive at a summary statement of the pri-

[9] We want to express our gratitude to Peter Mueser for his insightful criticisms of and suggestions for our cognitive achievement analyses.

TABLE 1
Differences in Student Predicted Achievement[a]

Difference in Achievement by:	Reading[b] Sophomores Pub.	Cath.	Seniors Pub.	Cath.	Vocabulary Sophomores Pub.	Cath.	Seniors Pub.	Cath.	Mathematics Sophomores Pub.	Cath.	Seniors Pub.	Cath.
Parental Education:												
College-High School	.57	.48	.43	.15	.74	.55	.63	.39	1.10	.42	1.04	.59
	(.038)	(.105)	(.041)	(.115)	(.035)	(.098)	(.038)	(.099)	(.073)	(.192)	(.078)	(.210)
White-Black	.91	.34	1.12	.56	.85	.84	1.08	.75	2.21	1.44	2.51	1.67
	(.036)	(.158)	(.042)	(.173)	(.034)	(.148)	(.039)	(.149)	(.070)	(.289)	(.080)	(.316)
Anglo-Hispanic	.68	.38	1.05	.44	.52	.36	.77	.49 ·	1.55	1.35	1.89	1.39
	(.045)	(.136)	(.054)	(.153)	(.042)	(.127)	(.049)	(.131)	(.086)	(.248)	(.101)	(.279)

[a]The variables included in the models are described in Footnote 3. The standardization is carried out according to the methods outlined in Footnote 7, with the following modifications: The means for the average public school sophomore for parental education, race, and ethnicity were replaced with specific levels corresponding to those indicated by the row labels.

[b]Numbers in parentheses indicate standard errors of differences. Standard errors for the differences are obtained by pooling the standard errors for the predicted achievement of each subpopulation involved in a given comparison. In the case of the white, black, and Hispanic estimated achievement levels, this reduces to simply obtaining the standard errors for the black and Hispanic regression coefficients, since whites are the reference category. In the case of students with different levels of parental education, the covariance of regression coefficients matrix is premultiplied by the transpose of the vector of family background composition values (set to the averages for public school sophomores, except for the predetermined values of parental education); this product is post-multiplied by the vector of background values.

vate sector's contribution to the segregation of black and white secondary-level students is deceptive, combining as it does the separate issues of access to sectors and segregation within them. We appreciate this reiteration of the importance of the within- and between-sector segregation, for it is a distinction our study goes to great lengths to make clear, but one which has been misunderstood by some critics (see Page & Keith, 1981).

Braddock argues that the important segregation issue with respect to private education is the between-sector segregation; that is, the issue of minority and low-income student access to private education. We agree, but we do not support the a priori reasoning which Braddock uses to reach this conclusion. Rather, access is the main issue precisely because we have empirically shown that within-sector segregation of racial, ethnic, and income groups is less a problem in the private sector than in the public sector.

Granted the significance of examining both the extent of between- and within-sector segregation, it is important to assess the private sector's overall contributions to the total segregation found across U.S. high schools. We have two countervailing results: black and lower-income students are underrepresented in private education, but those black and lower-income students who are in the private sector tend to be in relatively less segregated schools than similar students in the public schools. To assess the impact of private education as a whole on the total segregation, we asked whether the overall segregation in the United States would be lower if private school students were redistributed into the public schools along the same lines that public school students are presently. Our analysis indicates that if there were no private sector, the degree of segregation of blacks and whites among schools would be almost identical to what presently exists.

This is not a trivial finding. However, it is very general as it pertains to the structure of education in the United States as a whole, and as such obscures important exceptions that may be found on regional, state, and local levels. Tables 2 and 3 represent a step toward qualifying the general finding along these lines. Table 2 shows that the between-sector segregation of blacks and whites varies substantially across the four major regions of the country. Between-sector segregation is particularly high in the South, where the proportion of the total student body that is black is .229, while the proportion of the private-sector enrollment that is black is only .045. Table 3 gives the measures of within-sector segregation of blacks and whites by region.[10] A comparison of the private and

TABLE 2

Percentage Distribution of Whites, Blacks, and Hispanics in Public and Private Schools by Region[a]: Spring 1980

	Regional Total	Public	Private Total	Catholic	Other Private
East					
Number (000s)	1,539.7	1,319.3	220.3	152.8	67.5
Percent	100.0	100.0	100.0	100.0	100.0
White	80.9	79.4	90.2	88.0	95.3
Black	11.4	12.5	4.5	6.0	1.2
Hispanic	5.1	5.4	3.2	4.3	1.0
Other	2.7	2.8	2.0	1.8	2.5
South					
Number (000s)	2,118.3	1,958.0	160.3	77.5	82.8
Percent	100.0	100.0	100.0	100.0	100.0
White	66.8	65.2	86.4	79.7	92.7
Black	22.9	24.4	4.5	6.0	3.1
Hispanic	7.9	8.1	6.3	10.8	2.1
Other	2.3	2.3	2.7	3.3	2.1
Midwest-North					
Number (000s)	1,899.3	1,726.1	173.1	152.2	20.9
Percent	100.0	100.0	100.0	100.0	100.0
White	86.9	86.8	88.1	87.4	93.4
Black	7.5	7.7	5.1	5.1	4.5
Hispanic	3.7	3.6	4.9	5.4	1.4
Other	1.9	1.9	1.9	2.1	0.8
West					
Number (000s)	1,195.9	1,097.4	98.5	44.8	53.7
Percent	100.0	100.0	100.0	100.0	100.0
White	72.4	72.3	73.5	72.0	74.8
Black	5.1	5.1	5.0	5.4	4.6
Hispanic	12.9	12.7	14.6	16.1	13.4
Other	9.7	9.9	6.9	6.5	7.2

Note. Totals may not add to 100 due to rounding.

[a]The four U.S. Bureau of the Census regions used here are: (1) "East": New England and Middle Atlantic; (2) "South": South Atlantic, East South Central and West South Central; (3) "Midwest-North": East North Central and West North Central; and (4) "West": Mountain and Pacific.

[10] The segregation measures employed here are the same as those used in *Public and Private Schools*. The Appendix to the study describes the method of calculation. Our reliance on this particular index has been criticized in other forums on the grounds that other measures might yield different results. Further analysis, to be included in the final report, indicates that all of the other measures commonly employed in analyses of segregation — the dissimilarity index, the Gini coefficient, and the information theoretic index — give essentially the same results as those given by the index we employ.

public indices of segregation in each of the regions in Table 3 shows that the internal segregation in each region is less in the private sector than in the public sector — even in the Midwest and West, where the proportions of blacks in each sector are about the same.

TABLE 3
Indices of Segregation for Blacks and Whites Within Public and Private School Sectors by Region: Spring 1980

Measure	U.S. and Regional Totals	Public	Total	Private	
				Catholic	Other Private
Overall National—R_{bw}	.49	.49	.29	.31	.21
East—R_{bw}	.52	.54	.22	.22	.03
South—R_{bw}	.36	.37	.24	.24	.19
Midwest/North—R_{bw}	.62	.64	.39	.42	.07
West—R_{bw}	.43	.44	.37	.46	.29

Note. R_{bw} = the degree to which blacks and whites are segregated, ranging from 0 = no segregation to 1 = complete segregation.

In order to examine the problem of the overall contribution of private schools to the total racial segregation in the various regions, the index of segregation for the public sector in each region is compared with the index for each region as a whole. In the South, enrollment in the private sector slightly increases the overall segregation of blacks and whites (from .37 to .38); enrollment in the private sector in the East, Midwest, and West slightly decreases the overall black-white segregation. The analysis of within-sector segregation across the four regions shows that the pattern for the country as a whole is generally found across regions as well. This conclusion gives additional weight to the main point of our original analysis of private-sector student composition: with respect to black enrollment, the issue is access.

As a first step toward identifying the causes of black underenrollment in private education, we examined three hypotheses. The first hypothesis proposed that private schools tend to be located in communities where the proportions of the school-age black populations are lower; and that residential segregation may create lower access for blacks to private education. Our analysis showed that this factor is not an important one (pp. 31-35).

The second hypothesis, that the lower incomes of blacks are responsible for their lower private-sector representation, is supported for the Catholic sector. (We discussed the technical aspects of this analysis previously.) The difference between the proportions of blacks and whites at each income level ranges from 2 to 3 percent, which contrasts with a difference of 4.2 percent when income is not taken into account (pp. 36-38).

The third hypothesis proposed that blacks are underenrolled in the private sector because these schools are predominantly organized by religious communities in which blacks have traditionally had low membership. The data only allow us to examine this hypothesis with regard to the Catholic sector. We find that black students and white students who indicate that their religious background is Catholic are equally likely to be in Catholic schools, and that non-Catholic blacks are slightly more likely to be in Catholic schools than are non-Catholic whites. When we control for income and religious background, we find that at most income levels black Catholics are more likely to be enrolled in parochial schools than white Catholics, and that black non-Catholics are also more likely to enroll than white non-Catholics.

The findings in regard to these latter two hypotheses suggest that blacks are no less interested in the alternative that Catholic schools represent than whites. Nonetheless, the substantive limitations of this crosstabular analysis are apparent, since there are certainly other factors affecting the probability of Catholic school enrollment which, if left uncontrolled, presumably bias the estimates we make. Furthermore, the relatively large standard errors for the estimated black enrollment rates at higher income levels – particularly when stratifying by religious background – must be kept in mind.

In light of these problems, we have taken some preliminary steps toward addressing the issue more rigorously. As part of the analysis of selectivity bias discussed above in regard to cognitive outcomes, we estimated a probit model for determinants of private sector enrollment. The model gives the effects of 17 background variables – including race, income, and religious background – on the probability of private school enrollment. The results (not presented here) strongly confirm the patterns discovered in the crosstabular analysis: When the other variables are held constant, the dummy variable for race shows that blacks are substantially (14 percent) more likely to enroll in private schools than whites, and the difference is statistically significant. The probit model also shows that income still exerts a powerful influence on private school enrollment when the controls are applied.[11]

What should be said about the problem of black access to private education in light of these findings? We conclude that the lower income of blacks restricts their access to private education, particularly to Catholic education. Many critics see things otherwise, arguing in effect that nothing can be said. Bryk follows this course, apparently led there by the standard errors of the proportions of blacks at higher income levels. In drawing our conclusions we are positively impressed by the consistency of the results, and negatively by the lack of any reasonable substantive alternative to the interpretation we have set forth.

Other critics, apparently reluctant to acknowledge the possibility that many blacks and low-income families are interested in an alternative to what is currently available for them, see the economic constraint as an immutable barrier that is part of the essence of private education. This position is quite consistent with the view held by many producers of education for minorities and low-income students: that is, that only they can or will meet the "special needs" of these students. Defense of the public schools in the name of equal opportunity often amounts to little more than a defense of the producers of education for the poor rather than the interests of the consumers, the poor themselves. It is as if an economist would defend shops in the ghetto against competition on the grounds that the competition would hurt ghetto businesses, without pointing out

---

[11] In addition to those mentioned, the variables in the model include parental education, parental expectations, household possessions, and region of the country (northeast versus other). If the black and white means for the variables included in the model are substituted into the equation, but blacks are given the average white income, the estimated percentage of blacks enrolled in private schools increases by 1.5 percent, to about 4.4 percent.

that their potential loss of business would occur through expanded opportunity for their customers. Some of the concern for interests of public schools with a captive audience in low-income neighborhoods might well be reserved for the interests of low-income public school students, who constitute that captive audience.

Possible Inferences about the Effect of Policy Changes

The broader question of the study's relevance to public policy involving private schools is raised by Finn, Murnane, Heyns, and Guthrie and Zusman. Finn argues that it is relevant to policy while the others argue that it is irrelevant. Murnane and Guthrie and Zusman ignore our investigation of academic demands and discipline that differentiate private from public schools and make a difference in achievement even within public schools. Their arguments that the differences between public and private schools make it impossible for any policy implications to be drawn sound like the statements of public educators, bemoaning the many constraints that preclude higher student achievement. Finn, writing that he has long since wearied of such complaints, discusses the implications of the study for school policy by showing these arguments exactly for what they are arguments for inaction, arguments to preserve the status quo.

It is useful to specify a conception of the ways schools affect achievement that arises from our analysis along with one that is suggested by our critics. This should clarify the issues and suggest the relevance of our study for possible policy changes. Figure 1 describes a general model into which these varying conceptions fall.

The focus is school policies, where they come from and how they affect student achievement. School policies, such as level of homework, curriculum, and disciplinary practices, indirectly affect a student's achievement by influencing that student's behavior (see path 10). This is the most straightforward path. In addition, those policies directly affect student's achievement (illustrated by path 11) and include such factors as teachers' skill or commitment. Our study suggests that school policies vary between sectors, as well as within sectors (particularly in the public and non-Catholic private sector), and are indeed related to student achievement.

There is, however, another path through which school type and school policies can affect achievement: through the background and behavior of other students (see sequence 4 7 12 13 and 4 6 9 12 13). With a given level of tuition, coupled with a given income distribution, and specific policies of student selection, the school type "determines" the distribution of other students in the school. These background variables greatly affect the other students' behavior in the school (path 7), and may directly affect school policies (path 6), which in turn affect student behavior (paths 9 and 10). Other students' behavior can affect a given student's achievement in either of two ways: through their direct effect on that student's behavior (for example, a hard-working and committed student body will ordinarily generate commitment among its incoming members); or through school policies. A disobedient or truant student population can impede academic and disciplinary policies to the point that the demands are relaxed and the policies accommodated to the students' behavior. This is one aspect of the change that many schools underwent during the student revolt of the late sixties and early seventies.

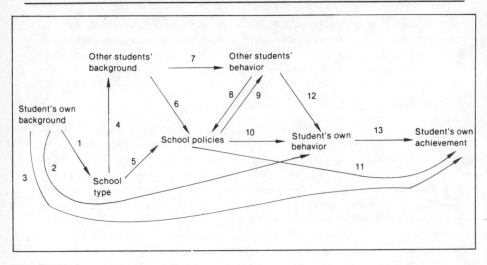

FIGURE 1
General Model for Achievement

It is the alternative path, from school type to other students' background (path 4) that is responsible for Murnane's and Guthrie and Zusman's doubt about the continued efficacy of private schools if their use were made available to students now unable to attend them. In part, what is at issue in disagreements about the effects on achievement of making private schools available to a broader range of students lies in implicit beliefs about the relative importance of paths 4, 6, 7, 8, and 12 compared to 5, 9, 10, and 11. If the principal effect of the school type on achievement is through the sequence 4-7-12-13, or 4-7-8-10-12-13, or 4-6-10-13, then such broadening of availability would have little impact on achievement because the policy change would disrupt path 4. If a large component of the effect is through paths 5, 9, 10, and 11, then such increased access to private education should not dilute the school's impact on achievement. Furthermore, if the effects are through 9, 10, and 11, then *any* change that resulted in the appropriate changes in school policies, whether or not it had anything to do with private schools, would be effective in increasing achievement. Thus, where such things as curriculum and disciplinary policies have effects on student behavior and achievement that are independent of school type and student background, then we can institute changes in any school that would affect achievement. It is for this reason that the results in the last portion of our study (section 6.3, pp. 197-223) are as relevant to public schools as they are to private schools.

Two other doubts expressed by Heyns, Murnane, and Guthrie and Zusman concern the effect of any governmental policy that facilitates private schooling on path 5. The first doubt is whether the newly created private schools would have policies similar to existing private schools. A second question is what the effect of government regulations would be on private schools' policies if they received a public subsidy.

These are important questions. They are hardly questions with which to fault the study. They illustrate, however, a point we made earlier. Policy research does not provide an authoritative and judicious answer for policymakers; rather, it shows that certain arguments are not tenable, and raises the policy discourse to a higher level, to focus on issues that are closer to the core of the desired outcomes. The result is that policy, when it is made, is more likely to be effective.

Is This the Way Policy Research Should Be Done?

One issue that occupies the attention of most of the reviewers has nothing to do with technical questions of the analysis, nor with substantive issues concerning policy related to public and private schools. It has to do with the question of the proper role and character of research related to social policy.

First, one point should be clarified. The study was not, as Murnane and Bryk suppose, designed to be especially relevant to tuition tax credit legislation. When *Public and Private Schools* was planned in early 1980, and written in August 1980, no such legislation was evident. At that time, there were two broad policy directions — one toward facilitating private schooling, exemplified by proposals for vouchers at the state level, and the other toward restricting private schooling, exemplified by a recent IRS proposal to remove tax exemption from private schools that did not meet a racial-balance criterion.[12] It was in the broad context of addressing the issue of policy direction that this research study was designed, not in the narrow context of addressing the issue of particular legislation. As Heyns's review implies, general purpose survey data can seldom be used to examine the effects of particular legislation; rather one should begin with the specific details of the proposed law and work outward from there.

But once it is clear what the study is and is not, there is still substantial disagreement about the appropriateness of this type of study as policy research. Bryk characterizes it as a policy argument, contrasting it to disciplined inquiry, which he holds up as the ideal mode of social research. The grounds on which he distinguishes the study from disciplined inquiry are principally its failure to present full information on errors: sampling errors, nonsampling errors, reliability and validity of tests, and errors of measurement associated with each survey question. In the final report, additional material on sampling and nonsampling errors will be included; and in the meantime, the interested researcher is free to obtain this information from the authors and to carry out analysis with the public-use files.

The matter of disciplined inquiry raised by Bryk is more complex, however, than one of including or failing to include information on sources of error. Presumably, Bryk is referring to some aspect of our research beyond inclusion of information about errors. It can perhaps be best examined by looking at the character of research papers in any social science discipline.

The term "hypothesis testing" is often used in social science research, but the image it evokes is quite misleading — for that imagery, like the phrases used by Bryk to describe

[12] See in particular "Tax Exempt Status of Private Schools," Hearings Before the Subcommittee on Oversight of the House Committee on Ways and Means for information on the IRS proposal (Note 1). Voucher proposals have been proposed in California, and may be considered by referendum there in the next year.

disciplined inquiry, presents the researcher as a passive judge, weighing evidence and coming up with an authoritative judgment. Instead, such research is characterized by the discovery of a consistent set of findings or relationships in the data, using statistical tests as contraints. The appropriate imagery is one of an active search, with the investigator pursuing various possible paths, abandoning those that evidence shows to be incorrect, and making a case for the one consistent with the evidence. In this search, statistical tests are used as constraints, as reins to keep the developing concepts consistent with reality itself. Such reins are necessary because of the psychological fact that an investigator presses to develop as consistent a conception of reality as possible, and to make the case for this conception as strong as possible.

Even with such constraints, it is never assumed in disciplinary research that the investigator who pursues such a path and develops an internally consistent conception of reality will have imposed all the possible constraints and therefore have arrived at an uncontestable conception of reality. Competition within the discipline performs the service, which the original investigator is in a poor position to perform, of casting a jaundiced eye at the results and discovering all the ways in which they might be incorrect. These become starting points for investigations of possible alternative conceptions of reality; but until one of those alternative conceptions is developed and proves more consistent with the evidence from reality, the original conception stands.

Now let us move from disciplinary research to policy-related research. Those engaging in policy research are no more passive judges than those engaged in disciplinary research. They, too, will engage in an active search for an internally consistent conception of reality that is consistent with the research results. There is, however, an important difference.

In policy-related research there are various interests and values, and a given conception of reality will be more favorable to certain interests and values than to others. In this setting, a new ad hominem question arises when deciding how minutely to scrutinize the consistency of the conception of reality with the evidence: Did this particular conception of reality just happen to favor a given interest, or did the investigators begin with the aim of developing a conception that favored a particular interest? One cannot take the authors' declarations on this, since they may be self-serving. In the case of *Public and Private Schools*, external evidence based on the authors' backgrounds is mixed. On the one side: Coleman has in various writings expressed himself in favor of greater parental choice in education, and even in favor of vouchers which would aid the private sector. His children, although they all attended public schools, nevertheless ended up graduating from private high schools. On the other side: All three authors attended only public schools through high school. The study's results are most favorable to Catholic schools, yet none of the authors is Catholic and none has any special ties to Catholic schools, nor has any of them shown a special affinity to Catholic schools in earlier work.

Although such ad hominem questions are necessary, it is neither correct nor fair to prejudge the motivational origins of the results, as Bryk does, labelling the research as policy argument and stating that "the evidence is assembled to support a particular policy recommendation" (p. 507). Such an evaluation arises from an incorrect image of disciplinary research, against which the policy research is measured — research carried out by passive judges weighing evidence and arriving at authoritative judgments rather than an active search for an internally consistent conception of reality. If one recognizes instead that policy research, as well as disciplinary research, consists instead of an active search for an internally consistent conception of reality, constrained by evidence and scientific method, then it should not be surprising that the conception of reality which emerges from the study coincides with one or another interest. For neither we, nor other policy researchers, are judges issuing authoritative judgments. In this case, as with other policy research and research in the discipline, the conception of reality we arrived at will stand until another is shown to be more consistent with the evidence. It is not sufficient to show reporting deficiencies, nor to speculate about possible selection bias, as many of the critics, including Bryk, have done. It is necessary to present a conception of reality that is more consistent with the evidence and that conflicts with the one we present.

Murnane's comments regarding how policy research should be done extend beyond this study, to the 1966 report, *Equality of Educational Opportunity* (Coleman, Campbell, Hobson, McPartland, Mood, Weinfeld, & York). Paralleling a number of commentators' (including his own) statements that the descriptive material of *Public and Private Schools* is valuable while the analysis is not, Murnane writes that the same is true for the 1966 report. But in doing this, he and other commentators confound two elements: the actual analysis presented in the 1966 report and the use that was made of the analysis in policy debates. Murnane says the "report came to be associated with the conclusions that schools don't matter much, and that busing to achieve racial balance is the most effective way to improve the education of minority group children" (p. 484). The statement is true, but this is a statement about the use of the report, not the analysis it contained. The analysis could be and was used to provide support for those arguments; but the analysis itself in the report came to no such conclusions. He goes on to say that "it took several years of reanalysis and discussion, however, to clarify what *Equality of Educational Opportunity* [EEO] (Coleman et al., 1966) could and could not tell us. In the interim, the Coleman Report figured prominently and inappropriately in the acrimonious and painful discussions about educational policy" (p. 484).

This statement seems to imply that the reanalyses upset the original analysis. They did not; what happened was that the courts finally realized that evidence, strong or weak, about the consequences of desegregation was not relevant to the constitutional question of equal protection. But this says nothing about the analytical result in the report that was for a time used in desegregation conflicts — black students achieve more highly in school settings with high proportions of middle-class students. In fact, Murnane later in his review affirms such a result in arguing that selection (which private schools can use) is an instrinsic part of the educational program provided by private schools.

On the "schools don't matter much" argument, the issue was more complex. The 1966 report began to clear away the widespread conventional wisdom of the time, that traditional measures of school resources, mostly associated with increased expenditures, would bring about increased achievement.[13] The 1966 report, and many others since then, showed that this was simply not correct. Only recently, in subsequent work, including that of Murnane and Phillips (1981) and the *Public and Private Schools* study,

---

[13] Hanushek's work (Note 2) is a recent contribution. He reviews the results of a large number of studies demonstrating that traditional measures of school input resources show little relationship with achievement measures.

has quantitative analysis started to show what kinds of elements in school functioning do bring about increased achievement. Clearing away the old conventional wisdom was an important precursor to that work.

Murnane raises a deeper issue about policy-relevant research. In what sense (other than the courts' inappropriate use in school desegregation cases based on the 14th Amendment during the period from about 1968-1971) was the use of the EEO report in social policy discussion inappropriate? There is a school of thought which subscribes to the notion that policy research is useful and appropriate only when it can provide prescriptions to a set of policymakers. The implication is that there are no conflicting interests, or if there are, good policy research will provide information that eliminates such conflicts by pointing out the correct policy. But educational policy is very different: there is no set of policymakers; there are numerous conflicting interests; and the appropriate role of policy research is to inform the various interest groups.

Better policy as a consequence of policy research is then the result of interested individuals being better informed when pressing their case. The result of policy research will not be to eliminate conflicts among differing interests, but to raise the content level — perhaps at the same time strengthening the arguments of some interests and weakening the arguments of others. An example is provided by the responses to *Public and Private Schools*. Old arguments against the Catholic schools were that they were too rigidly disciplinarian and provided inferior education. In the presence of this study, these arguments may no longer carry weight. Much more sophisticated arguments, such as those Murnane presents, must now be introduced. As a result, the policy discussion about public and private schools — and about policies within the public schools themselves — will be carried out at a higher level.

U.S. Secondary Education in the 1980s

We mentioned near the beginning of this response that it is important to view the results of this study in the larger context of changes in secondary education in the United States. Guthrie and Zusman raise two relevant issues: the first is raised in answering the question of why public school policy cannot profit from the private school example, and the second in answering the question of why the qualities found in private school education could not survive legislation that would provide public support.

Their first point is that private schools, composed of students whose parents have chosen to send them to that school, have a consistency of purpose and consensus of values about the importance of their educational task. If, as Guthrie and Zusman imply, the differences in achievement between public and private schools arise simply because of the different structural constraints under which they operate, then the question arises immediately: Why did not the public schools always produce lower achievement than the Catholic schools? Despite their initial comment about conventional wisdom, the conventional wisdom twenty years ago went in the reverse direction: Catholic schools were seen by most persons to be inferior to public schools. Their current superiority appears to be a recent phenomenon, though there is no systematic evidence on the point. If, as seems likely, there has been a change in their relative capacity to generate achievement, this throws doubt on the immutability of the differences due to the various constraints under which they function. In both aspects discussed by Guthrie and Zusman — value consensus and government constraints — public schools are currently at a greater disadvantage vis-á-vis private schools than they were twenty years ago.

Their second point is more obvious: government regulations concerning the organization of schools have in some cases impeded the educational task of the schools. Would some form of public subsidy to private schools lead to equally debilitating constraints? Guthrie and Zusman assume it would; but they cite no convincing evidence. If this is a central question about the consequences of giving public support for private schools, then it should be the focus of research. But the question should not be used to dismiss the policy, and an answer should not be assumed without evidence.

It is less evident that Guthrie and Zusman's first point, on the absence of parental consensus in the average public school, represents a change compared to twenty years ago. Yet it is here that the change is probably most extensive and most important for secondary education. It was true then as now that parents had little choice about where to send their children to public school, except by moving their residence. But in the intervening period, there has come to be an extraordinary change in one important area: the consensus among parents about maintaining authority over and responsibility for their adolescent children's activities. That consensus, once quite strong, is no longer present. One result at the extreme is high school youth living outside their parents' household or the household of any parent figure. Another result with extreme consequence for the functioning of schools is the willingness of some parents to go to court to support their child's right to contravene the rules of the school. The legal result has been the substitution of due process and "children's rights" in schools for the earlier principle of in loco parentis under which schools had operated. The functional result for many high schools has been an inability to exercise effective authority in the absence of a new parental mandate of some sort.

These two changes taken together, both of which have affected public schools far more than private schools, may have reduced the effectiveness of secondary education in the United States. As youth become less and less subject to adult authority, we can expect that the decline in effectiveness will continue. In such a context, the issue of public schools versus private schools will pale in significance beside the question of how youth can be kept in school at all — or if not that, how youth can be brought toward adulthood in an environment less predatory than that of the full adult world. Although that situation is not yet upon us, it is wise to ask what kinds of institutions are most viable as educational environments for youth.

One answer may lie in providing parents with a greater range of choices of institutional settings for their adolescent children. An avenue of choice that will be taken by many is toward a setting (which we may call a "school" for convenience, though the term may be too narrow) in which there is a consensus of values or interests — in some cases religiously based — among the parents and between the parents and staff. We see value communities forming already as settings for children and youth: free schools, basic-education schools, conservative Christian schools, Nation of Islam schools, and Jewish schools. Within the public sector we see the growth of magnet schools, where interests are shared, and of parent-school contracts, where values are agreed upon. It seems likely that these schools, even those with certain parochialisms, are more capable of demanding from youth the kinds of effort and internal discipline that are conducive to psychological and cognitive growth than are schools whose student bodies are formed by administrative assignments. When a broad and general interest by parents in maintaining authority over their children through the end of schooling can be assumed, the parochialism and potential devisiveness of such value communities may outweigh their virtues. But in the emerging social context within which young people are coming into adulthood, these virtues seem particularly important. To return to the results of the current research which show greater discipline, greater academic demands, and greater achievement in the private schools, it is these virtues that we have outlined which, we believe, are responsible for these results.

Reference Notes

1. 96th Cong., 1st Sess., pt. 1 (1979).
2. Hanushek, E. A. *Throwing money at schools* (Public Policy Analysis Discussion Paper No. 8004). University of Rochester, 1981.

References

Alexander, K. L., Cook, M., & McDill, E. C. Curricular tracking and educational stratification: Some further evidence. *American Sociological Review*, 1978, **43**, 47-66.

Coleman, J., Campbell, E., Hobson, C., McPartland, J., Mood, A., Weinfeld, F., & York, R. *Equality of educational opportunity.* Washington, D.C.: U. S. Government Printing Office, 1966.

Coleman, J., Hoffer, T., & Kilgore, S. *High school achievement: Public, Catholic, and other private schools compared.* New York: Basic Books, in press.

Heckman, J. J. Sample bias as a specification error. *Econometrica*, 1979, **47**, 153-162.

Murnane, R. J., & Phillips, B. R. What do effective teachers of inner-city children have in common? *Social Science Research*, 1981, **10**, 83-100.

Page, E. B., & Keith, T. Z. Effects of U.S. private schools: A technical analysis of two recent claims. *Educational Researcher*, 1981, **10**, 7-17.

25

An Evaluation of the Costs of Computer-Assisted Instruction

Henry M. Levin and Louis Woo

The purpose of this paper is to estimate the costs and cost feasibility of utilizing computer-assisted instruction (CAI) for compensatory education. Cost data were collected from an experiment on the effectiveness of CAI that had been established in Los Angeles and sponsored by the National Institute of Education. Based upon the resource ingredients approach to measuring costs, it was found that up to three daily 10-minute sessions of drill and practice could be provided for each disadvantaged child within the 1977-1978 allocation of funds from Title I of the Elementary and Secondary Education Act of 1965. If the computer system were shared between two schools, the higher costs would permit only two daily sessions.

Costs were also estimated for a more advanced CAI system, and somewhat surprisingly the costs were in the same range. This finding reflects the very heavy costs of "software" that do not seem to decline with more advanced technologies. Also, it is possible that the latter technology will be found to be more effective at the same cost level. However, because comparative effectiveness data between the CAI approach and other instructional strategies are not readily available, such cost-effectiveness comparisons will have to be deferred until some future date.

Various educational technologies such as educational radio, educational television, and computer-assisted instruction (CAI) have been proposed in recent years as partial solutions to both the problems of rising educational costs and the failure of the educational system

The authors are respectively Director and Research Assistant, Institute for Research on Educational Finance and Governance, Stanford University.

This analysis was prepared under a contract to Educational Testing Service as a part of a project financed by the National Institute of Education. The authors wish to thank Roberta Woodson, Warren Juhnke, Dick Lubin, and other personnel of the Los Angeles Unified School District and personnel of Computer Curriculum Corporation for assistance. Dean Jamison provided the authors with a critical reading of the paper, and the authors wish to express appreciation for his comments. [Manuscript received September 26, 1979; revision accepted for publication December 14, 1979.]

to impart basic skills to disadvantaged youngsters. The logic of the cost-saving aspects of educational technologies is conditioned heavily upon the assumption that the high labor costs of education can be reduced by substituting relatively lower cost capital inputs without sacrificing educational results. The view that certain educational technologies can improve the quality of educational results for disadvantaged youngsters is premised on the fact that such approaches as CAI can be individualized to take account of the particular strengths and deficiencies of the learner.

These assumptions about the comparative advantages of replacing some portion of traditional classroom instruction with a more capital-intensive educational technology would seem especially pertinent to the case of CAI. Recent technological breakthroughs in computers, particularly the advent of minicomputers and inexpensive memory devices, have both expanded the capability and flexibility of computers with respect to their instructional applications and reduced their costs considerably. Also, CAI permits a large variety of methods for individualizing instruction according to the actual performance of the learner. For example, a computer-based curriculum can be designed to provide automatically additional problems in any area in which a student is not performing according to some preset standard, or it can be arranged in particular sequences of instructional tasks that emphasize a student's special instructional needs.

Despite the promise of educational technology in improving educational outcomes and reducing costs, there is little supporting evidence of a rigorous nature for either the relative costs or educational results.[1] In response to this evaluative deficiency, the National Institute of Education decided to undertake an experimental study of CAI in order to evaluate its effects on the improvement of reading, language skills, and arithmetic operations of elementary school children. The experiment was initiated in the fall of 1976 on the basis of a research design that was prepared by the Educational Testing Service (ETS) and implemented in the Los Angeles Unified School District (LAUSD). Known as the ETS/LAUSD Study on Computer-Assisted Instruction and Compensatory Education, the study was intended to ascertain the effects of a particular computer-based instructional system and curriculum on student test scores in three subject areas as well as the costs for replicating this particular system.

---

1. The best studies in this area are Jamison et al. (1976 and 1970) with respect to CAI. However, cost effectiveness analyses of other technologies can be found in *Instructional Science* (1975). See Carnoy and Levin (1975) for a critique of the methodologies of these studies.

With respect to educational effectiveness, the research design was constructed in order to ascertain the effects on test scores in reading, arithmetic, and language arts of the "drill and practice" curriculum of the Computer Curriculum Corporation (CCC) among students at different elementary grade levels. The evaluation was arranged to determine the effects of 10-minute daily sessions of CAI on student achievement. Comparisons of test results for disadvantaged students are being made according to the number of daily sessions of CAI, the subjects in which CAI sessions were given, and the number of years in which students received CAI. The studies of effectiveness are intended to reveal the educational impact of this particular CAI approach across subject areas, grade levels, amounts of exposure, and different types of students (race, sex, ethnicity, socioeconomic status, and so on).[2]

The evaluation of the effectiveness of this CAI approach does not address the issue of costs. Given its focus on the educational needs of disadvantaged students, two questions arise pertaining to costs. The first question is based upon the assumption that funding for special educational services for disadvantaged students is derived primarily from special categorical aid for that purpose, such as that received under Title I of the Elementary and Secondary Education Act of 1965. Therefore, it is important to know if CAI can be provided within the budget that is available for these compensatory educational services for disadvantaged youngsters. Second, it is important to know if the CAI approach can improve the educational proficiencies of disadvantaged students at costs that are similar to or less than those associated with other instructional alternatives.

The first issue is one of cost feasibility. If the costs of this CAI approach exceed the funds available for instructional purposes for disadvantaged youngsters, it will not be within the boundaries of feasibility. The second issue is one of cost effectiveness. Even if CAI can be provided within the present budgets for compensatory education, it should be adopted only if it provides better results relative to its costs than do existing alternatives.

Cost feasibility can be examined by evaluating the costs of CAI and ascertaining whether it is within the budgetary allocations provided for compensatory education by Title I of the Elementary Secondary Education Act of 1965 or by various state and local compensatory programs. Cost effectiveness comparisons can be made only by comparing both the results and the costs of the CAI approach with the results and costs of other instructional alternatives.

---

2. Preliminary findings are reported in Holland, Jamison and Ragosta (1980).

Although this study can establish the CAI costs, it is not designed to pursue its effects. However, the overall CAI experiment on which this study is based will provide rather sophisticated estimates of test score results associated with student exposure to different amounts of CAI in different subjects. Accordingly, the costs that are estimated in this study can be combined with the experimental effects of CAI for cost effectiveness comparisons with other instructional approaches.

In this paper we will estimate the replication costs of the CAI approach used in the ETS/LAUSD experiment, that is; the cost of replicating that system in other school settings. In doing this we will limit those costs only to ones that are associated with the delivery of CAI while omitting costs that are tied uniquely to the experimental status of the present system. That is, we are concerned with the costs of introducing this particular CAI approach into other schools outside of the present experimental situation. At the same time, we are concerned with modifications of the experimental CAI that might affect costs. In particular, there exists a later version of the present computer that is more advanced. The cost implications of the newer computer will be examined after exploring the costs of replicating the present experimental approach.

The organization of this paper will be as follows. First, a brief description will be given of the present CAI system and its configuration in the ETS/LAUSD schools. Second, a short presentation will be made of the costing methodology that will be used in this study. Third, cost estimates for replicating the present CAI system will be made. Fourth, the cost feasibility of adopting this system of CAI for compensatory education will be evaluated as well as the cost implications of a more advanced system.

THE SYSTEM OF COMPUTER-
ASSISTED INSTRUCTION

The purpose of this section is to provide a brief summary of the implementation of computer-assisted instruction in the ETS/LAUSD study. This description is of special importance because each CAI approach and installation is associated with different resource costs and effects. The ETS/LAUSD experiment is based upon the use of a particular computer system and curriculum that have been utilized in a specific way. Therefore it is important to provide some description of the system and its application. It is equally important to bear in mind that the evaluation of this particular CAI approach with respect to costs or educational effects cannot necessarily be generalized to other CAI approaches. Rather, all results will be limited to the specific CAI application that is being evaluated.

The heart of the ETS/LAUSD instructional approach is the use of the A-16 computer for providing drill and practice instruction for the students. Each student is seated at a terminal that consists of a keyboard reasonably similar to that of a typewriter and a cathode ray tube (CRT) that is similar to a television screen. Each A-16 can be used to service up to 32 terminals simultaneously. The A-16 contains curricula for all elementary grades for each of the three subject areas: mathematics, reading, and language arts. Each session lasts for 10 minutes, although some students may be assigned to undertake more than one session per day.

Each student signs in at his or her terminal and begins the session where he or she had left off in the previous session. A problem is displayed on the CRT, typically in a multiple-choice or a "fill in the blank" format. For example, the student might be given a problem in arithmetic operations such as vertical addition or subtraction, and he or she must type in the solution. Or, the student might be asked to fill in the correct form of a verb in a sentence. If the answer is correct, an asterisk is displayed on the CRT; if it is incorrect, the student is so informed. In either case, a new problem is displayed. When a student achieves adequate proficiencies on a particular part of the curriculum—as evidenced by a high enough proportion of correct answers—the system provides problems of the same type at a higher level of difficulty. The curriculum is not designed to introduce new material as much as it is to provide an opportunity to practice concepts that have already been taught.

There are two principal personnel who assist the students in working with the CAI system. A *coordinator* is responsible for the entire operation in a particular school including the scheduling of students; the provision of summaries of progress for each class to the classroom teachers (available from a printer that is attached to the A-16); the security and condition of the equipment (such as ensuring that the equipment is working properly and calling maintenance personnel when necessary); and the overall supervision of the students in working at the terminals. The coordinator is assisted by a *teaching aide* who monitors the students and answers their questions or assists them when they seem to be having difficulties.

The ETS/LAUSD experiment was based upon results from four experimental schools and two comparison ones that did not receive CAI. Two of the four experimental schools were large enough to utilize an A-16 with a full complement of 32 terminals. The other two schools had smaller student populations, so they shared an A-16 through the use of telephone lines and special equipment (multiplexer and modems). Each of these schools had 16 terminals installed so that the shared A-16 was also attached to a total of 32 terminals. The CAI rooms had to be modified to accommodate the special configuration of equipment as well as to assure security and an appropriate climate of temperature and humidity for maintaining the computer.

COSTING METHODOLOGY

The concept of costs typically tends to be confusing to evaluators. Often the tendency is to review budgets to estimate the costs of a particular project. But the costs that one finds in a budget or accounting statement are often in error or are misleading for a number of reasons. First, budgets typically show estimated costs rather than actual ones. To the degree that there are discrepancies between the real costs and the estimated ones, budgetary costs will not be accurate. Second, budgetary costs often provide costs of resources that will be used over different time periods. For example, although salaries in a given year will cover the labor services during that period, a piece of equipment may be utilized for many years. Yet the cost will be assigned only to the year in which the equipment was purchased, whereas it should be divided over the entire period of use on an annualized basis. Third, costs of contributed inputs are not included in budgets, confusing the question of what are the true costs of a project with the question of who paid the costs. Finally, some budgetary costs are distorted because they represent special purchases or transactions that do not reflect the true market values of the transactions.

A more appropriate method for estimating costs is to use the ingredients method.[3] This method is based upon the assumption that whenever resources that have alternative uses are allocated to a particular activity, those resources have a cost to society. The cost is equivalent to the value of the resources in their most productive application. The most typical way of estimating these costs is to use the market value of the resource. Further, in order to obtain annual

---

3. Virtually all the issues discussed here are reviewed methodologically in Levin (1975). The best application of costing methodologies to instructional technologies is Jamison et al. (1978).

costs of an alternative, the costs of various ingredients that are utilized over more than one year are "annualized" in order to charge
to each year only the costs for that period (rather than assigning the
entire cost to the year of the purchase). Because there are sources
that can be used to evaluate the techniques of cost analysis within
this framework, we will not discuss these techniques in detail here.[4]

The following steps are necessary for estimating costs, using the
ingredients approach.

1   List all ingredients or resources required for implementing
    the instruction.
2   Estimate the costs of each ingredient on the basis of ac-
    tual costs or estimated market values.
3   Convert costs into the appropriate categories for analysis
    such as annualized costs, average costs, or marginal costs.

In this particular case we wish to estimate the costs for replicating
the ETS/LAUSD system of CAI in other educational settings, and we
wish to evaluate costs under different organizational arrangements.

CAI Ingredients and Their Costs

Before enumerating the various ingredients of the CAI system and
their costs, it is useful to mention the bases on which ingredients
might be classified as well as the sources of the cost information. The
classification of ingredients can be done in any way that is functional
to the questions that will be raised. For example, one can classify
ingredients under personnel, facilities, equipment, and miscellaneous
categories. Or one can set out categories of ingredients that represent
fixed investments as well as those that represent recurrent cost items.
The main criteria are that all ingredients are accounted for in the
classification approach, and that the ultimate categories are useful
for analytical purposes.

The derivation of cost information for the various ingredients will
be done in a number of ways. Where budgetary and accounting information are appropriate they will be used. Where such cost data are
inappropriate or misleading, other methods of obtaining costs will be
utilized. In all cases the sources of the cost information will be specified as well as the methods of cost estimation. In this way the reader
can ascertain how the costs were derived; it is also possible to modify

---

4. Ibid. This paper will not include student time as a resource because it is difficult to place
a value on this dimension. However, alternative instructional strategies with mostly different
demands on student time should take this component into account.

the assumptions on cost estimation to determine the sensitivity of costs to different premises.

COST ESTIMATES

For purposes of cost estimation, the ingredients of the CAI approach will be divided into six categories: (1) Facilities and Equipment; (2) Training; (3) Personnel; (4) Curriculum Rental; (5) Maintenance; and (6) Miscellaneous Factors. Each of these will be evaluated, in turn, and they will be combined in analyzing the overall costs of CAI.

1. Facilities and Equipment

Any CAI approach has the obvious requirement of the equipment needed as well as the facilities needed to provide CAI. In the case of the Los Angeles experiment, the equipment for a school using a single A-16 computer, 32 terminals, and a printer is estimated at about $121,000. The complete breakdown for each type of equipment is shown in Table 1. That table also presents the estimates of facility costs. These include the cost of construction of a normal

TABLE 1.   FACILITIES AND EQUIPMENT, 1977-1978.

Facilities		
Cost of construction of a CAI room[a]	$ 50,000	
Renovation cost[b]	18,500	
		$ 68,500
Equipment[c]		
One A-16 computer system	$ 68,120	
installation	3,000	
32 Hazeltine Modular I terminals at $1,440/ea	46,080	
delivery at $63/ea	2,016	
One Hazeltine Thermal Printer	1,950	
delivery	23	
		$121,189
Total		$189,689

a. It was reported from the Educational Housing Branch in Los Angeles that to replace space in which the CAI experiments are housed in the 1979 construction market would cost approximately $50,000 per room.

b. The renovation costs include counters, intrusion alarm, carpentry, paint, electrical work, window grilling, air conditioning, and the labor involved.

c. These costs are derived directly from the CCC contract.

instructional classroom as well as the renovations that must be made to accommodate CAI.[5] Renovation costs include special carpentry work, protective devices, electrical work unique to the CAI installation, and air conditioning. In 1977-1978 the facilities costs were estimated to be about $68,500, and the total value of the equipment and facilities was assessed at almost $190,000 per school.

However, we are not concerned with the total costs of these ingredients as much as we are with their annualized costs. That is, a classroom is assumed to have a life of 25 years, so that only about 1/25 of the cost should be allocated to a particular annual period.[6] The renovations are assumed to have a life span of 10 years, and the equipment is estimated to have a life span of 6 years.[7] In each case we must use a standard approach to convert the overall costs into annualized ones, where the annualized cost represents the depreciation and interest costs foregone on the investment for each year. The annualized cost will depend on three factors: (a) the overall investment cost; (b) the life of the facilities or equipment or the amortization period; and (c) the rate of interest on the investment that is foregone.[8]

Table 2 shows the annualized values of facilities and equipment costs with the specific assumptions about the amortization period and three different interest rates. The 1979 rate of interest on U.S. treasury bonds of about 10 percent seems to be a reasonable figure for calculating foregone interest on the investment. On that basis the annualized cost of facilities is about $8,524 and that of equipment is about $27,873. Thus the estimated cost of facilities and equipment is about $36,397 per year.

2. Training

Training costs are composed of two types: direct and indirect. The direct costs are the most obvious ones, consisting of such items as sal-

---

5. As school enrollments decline, it is common for some observers to question whether any cost should be attached to newly available classrooms that are no longer needed to service regular enrollments. However, such facilities are not costless as long as they have alternative uses. In fact, there are a large number of alternative uses as evidenced by the expansion of special education programs, rental of rooms to other public agencies, or the closing of schools and their rental or sale.

6. The useful life of school facilities is taken from estimates by LAUSD administrators.

7. CCC staff gave us a figure of 6-10 years depending on level of utilization and assessments of technical obsolescence. We have used the 6-year figure because of the very intense level of utilization of the equipment. However, extending the estimated life to 10 years would have the effect of reducing the overall instructional costs by no more than 2-3 percent.

8. See Levin (1975) and Jamison et al. (1978).

TABLE 2.   ANNUALIZATION OF FACILITIES AND EQUIPMENT COSTS, 1977–1978.

Cost Categories	Amortization Period (years)	Cost	Annualized Cost		
			0%	10%	15%
Facility					
Construction of a CAI room	25	$ 50,000	$ 2,000	$ 5,508	$ 7,750
Renovation	10	18,500	1,850	3,016	3,682
Facility subtotal		$ 68,500	$ 3,850	$ 8,524	$11,432
Equipment[a]					
Equipment subtotal	6	$121,189	$20,198	$27,873	$31,994
Total			$24,048	$36,397	$43,426

a. Refer to Table 1 for the details. The amortization period for all computer-related equipment is assumed to be 6 years.

aries of instructors and costs of materials. The indirect costs refer to the value of the time of the trainees. In the case of the ETS/LAUSD project, the direct costs of training were included in the costs of equipment by CCC. However, the indirect ones had to be borne separately. According to the experience of CCC personnel, it is usually sufficient to provide workshops of 1.5 days for coordinators and 0.5 day for teachers. The cost for each teacher and coordinator will vary according to experience and training and the salary levels in the particular school district. However, in Los Angeles it appeared in 1977–1978 that salaries and fringe benefits averaged about $20,000 for a school year that was not more than 200 days. This suggests that a pay rate of about $100 per day is an appropriate basis for calculating costs of the time required by teachers and coordinators to obtain training. For 40 teachers to an elementary school, the indirect costs of teacher training are about $2,000 for a half-day workshop and about $150 for a 1.5-day workshop for the coordinator. Thus, the total estimated indirect costs of training are about $2,150.

One question that arises is how this figure translates into an annualized cost. It is unlikely that training costs of this magnitude would be required for each year, for the carryover of trained teachers and coordinators from year to year would be rather high. Yet any turnover of teachers will require some training to take place each year, even if it is merely the coordinator taking the teacher away from his or her classroom duties for half a day for instruction. For example, with a turnover rate of 10 percent per year, about 4 new teachers would have to be trained each year at a cost of about $200. In fact, after the first year this would be the only cost of training as well as the interest foregone on investments for training in previous years. If we use those two components to estimate costs, the total indirect training costs would be 10 percent of the previous investment in training per year plus the costs of training new teachers. On the average, 10 percent of the training investment over a 6-year period would be about $250 and the indirect cost of training 4 new teachers a year would be about $200 for a total of $450 a year. Whatever the assumptions are about the costs of this component, the overall cost implications are so small that they will have little impact on the total cost calculations.

3. Personnel

Personnel ingredients for the CAI demonstration include administrative resources, the CAI coordinator, two teaching aides, and substitutes to cover the absences of the coordinator, as shown in Table 3.

TABLE 3. ANNUAL PERSONNEL COSTS, 1977-1978.

Administration	$ 1,965
CAI coordinator	22,500
Fringe benefits on above	
at 16.7%	4,086
Two teaching aides	5,220
Substitutes	780
Total	$ 34,551

The function of the administrative personnel is to negotiate the contracts with the companies that maintain the equipment, to arrange payments, and to provide general financial and logistical administration of the project. The annual personnel costs for this function in 1977-1978 were estimated at $1,965 on the basis of previous experience of the Los Angeles schools with these types of projects.

The CAI coordinator is responsible for the overall functioning of CAI including scheduling and coordination of instruction, reports to teachers on student progress, and monitoring of equipment functioning and maintenance. Especially important is the latter function, because equipment failures result in the loss of instructional sessions. Accordingly, the coordinator must be aware of problems and the methods of getting them solved by the appropriate maintenance personnel. Further, the coordinator must work closely with classroom teachers to integrate the drill and practice sessions of CAI with classroom work.

In the ETS/LAUSD case, the coordinators were so carefully chosen and so well trained that they needed little administrative supervision from the school principal or other school administrative personnel. Whether this high level of initiative and independence can be maintained in a replication is problematic. However, based upon the success of coordinator autonomy in ETS/LAUSD, we have not indicated any supervision in the cost estimates. The cost of the coordinators can be determined directly by calculating salaries and fringe benefits. The salary component was estimated at $22,500 and the fringe benefits for that portion of the administrative costs and the coordinator were $4,086. Fringe benefits do not apply to the other personnel categories because of their part-time nature.

Teaching aides monitor the performance of students and assist them in understanding the CAI problems and in solving them. Essentially they wander among the students, looking for situations in which assistance or supervision is needed. Their rate of pay in 1977-1978 was $4.35 per hour, and it takes two teaching aides working about 600 hours each school year to assist in a CAI room with 32 terminals. This particular arrangement has been considered highly satisfactory by the Los Angeles coordinators. The total cost per CAI room of the two aides is about $5,220 a year.

The final personnel cost is related to the need for substitute teachers to undertake the coordination functions if the regular coordinator is ill. Under the Los Angeles arrangements, a teacher or coordinator can receive up to 12 days a year in paid sick leave. Therefore, provision for up to 12 days of substitute teaching at about $65 a day would cost about $780 per year. Based on these amounts, the personnel costs per year for 1977-1978 totaled about $34,551.

4. Curriculum Rental

The curricula that are used for the CAI approach are rented from CCC, the company that provided the A-16 system. The rental covers the cost of using the three sets of subject curricula in mathematics, reading, and language arts. The cost of the rental is set at $204 a year for each of the 32 terminals in a CAI room, for an annual total of $6,528.

5. Maintenance

The provision for maintenance of the equipment is arranged through contracts with firms that specialize in such care. Although some of the maintenance is routine and periodic, a major requirement is services of an emergency nature to repair malfunctions. The annual cost of maintaining the A-16 computer in 1977-1978 was $6,120 a year; each of the 32 terminals has a maintenance cost of $300 a year, or $9,600 for all terminals in a CAI room; and the thermal printer has a maintenance cost of $360 a year. The total cost of maintenance is about $16,080 a year.

6. Miscellaneous Factors

Miscellaneous cost factors include insurance, supplies, and the costs of energy and routine maintenance of the classroom. The appropriate insurance costs are those that are incurred directly from the CAI facility and equipment, including the additional insurance costs for theft, fire, and liability. Of these components, it appears that liability insurance is largely unaffected, and the impact on fire insurance costs is not readily ascertainable. However, the additional theft insurance for the equipment was estimated by the Los Angeles school authorities at about $3,000 a year for the computer, 32 terminals, and printer. The use of only the theft component may understate slightly the true insurance costs by omitting the fire component. However, the overall omission is likely to have a relatively small effect on total costs, for insurance represents a very small relative cost item.

Supplies, energy, and routine maintenance of the classroom contain many items. Supplies typically include pencils, paper, books, and paper for the printer. Energy and telephone costs and facility maintenance refer to the telephone in each classroom that is necessary for rapid access to maintenance personnel and CCC in case of breakdowns; normal heating, lighting, and power for the equipment; and routine cleaning and maintenance of the classroom. Taken together, these are estimated at about $3,000 per year. Again, even substantial changes in this amount (for example, 50 percent) would have little effect on overall costs per student session because of the relatively small magnitude of costs for the category. Each classroom is capable of providing a daily session on an annual basis for over 700 students, so an error of $1,500 is only about $2.00 per session.

Summary of Annualized Costs

The annualized costs in 1977-1978 for a 32-terminal classroom utilizing the CCC A-16 system can be summarized in the following tabulation.

Facilities and equipment	$36,397
Personnel	34,551
Training	450
Curriculum rental	6,528
Maintenance	16,080
Miscellaneous	6,000
Total	$100,006

It appears that in 1977-1978 it cost about $100,000 a year to provide a classroom, personnel, and equipment for servicing 32 terminals with this particular approach to CAI.

Average Cost per Session

It is important to know the cost per session on an annual basis for each student. That is, what is the cost for providing one daily session of 10 minutes of drill and practice for a full school year to each student? The reason that this particular cost figure is important is that it would enable us to ascertain the cost feasibility of this approach to CAI as a method of providing compensatory education to disadvantaged youngsters by comparing the amount per session with the average amount of compensatory funds provided by the federal government under Title I of the Elementary and Secondary Education Act of 1965.

The cost per session depends on the number of daily sessions that can be provided by the CAI system on an annual basis. This depends not only on the length of the session but also on the organizational capacity and time required to process each group of student users. That is, there must be time between the end of one 10-minute session and the beginning of the next for one group of students to sign off the system and return to class, while a new group arrives, is seated, and signs in. Finally, the number of sessions will also depend upon the overall reliability of the equipment and its operability during school hours.

In theory, the system could be used for up to 6.5 hours a day during regular school hours, if sessions began at 8:30 A.M. and proceeded to 3:00 P.M. with no interruptions for lunch. In practice, this would be difficult to do organizationally, for time is needed both at the beginning and at the end of the day to accomplish record-keeping and other instructional tasks associated with CAI. Further, it would be difficult to coordinate classes around the lunch period, and a relief coordinator would be needed during that period. With respect to the number of sessions per hour, even 5 sessions of 10 minutes each provide only about 2-minute transition periods. Accordingly, there are clear limits on the numbers of sessions that can be accommodated. Based upon the actual records for the ETS/LAUSD system, it appeared that the range varied from 21 sessions to 25 sessions per day, with a median of about 23 sessions. On the basis of these experiences, we can estimate the cost per daily session per student for a school year.

Number of Sessions per Day		Annual Cost per Daily Session
Per Terminal	For 32 Terminals	
21	672	$148.80
23	736	135.90
25	800	125.00

Depending on the number of sessions per day for each terminal, a configuration using the A-16 and 32 terminals in a single classroom can accommodate from 672 to 800 sessions a day. Assuming that the most probable estimate is the median of 23 sessions a day per terminal, 736 sessions can be provided. By dividing the number of sessions by the $100,000 estimated annual total cost for this CAI configuration, it appears that the annual costs for a daily session of 10 minutes can vary from about $125 to almost $150 per year for one daily session of CAI. The estimate for 23 sessions a day at $135 is probably the most reasonable one.

Cost Estimate for the Shared System

Before comparing that cost with the level of funding available for compensatory education, it is important to estimate the annual cost per daily session when two schools share an A-16 system. This situation presents itself when there is not an adequate student enrollment base in a particular school to accommodate about 700 daily sessions. It can also be evident in situations where only a particular grade level utilizes CAI. Of course, by providing multiple daily sessions (for example, two sessions a day), an A-16 can be utilized to full capacity by even 350-400 students. However, in the Los Angeles situation, the design of the CAI experiment meant that in two participating schools there were not adequate students assigned to CAI to fully utilize a 32-terminal system in each school. This situation provides us with the opportunity to ascertain the costs of a shared CAI computer.

The basic configuration for the shared system was that the A-16 computer and 16 terminals were placed in one school, and the other 16 terminals were placed in a "sister" school. The terminals were connected to the first school through a leased telephone line, and additional equipment was required in order to operate the sharing arrangement. Table 4 shows the additional costs incurred for a shared A-16 system. With the shared arrangement, two classrooms must be utilized for the terminals rather than one classroom. Based upon the costs for a classroom and required renovations that were presented in Table 2 and replicated in Table 4, the total cost of additional facilities for the shared arrangement would be $68,500, which would be about $8,524 on an annualized basis.

The additional equipment (two modems and two multiplexers) and their installation have a cost of almost $12,500, which translates into an annualized cost of about $2,866. Taken together the additional outlay for the shared facilities and equipment is almost $81,000, which translates into an annualized cost (using a 10 percent interest rate on the undepreciated portion) of $11,390. With respect to personnel for the shared arrangement, we assume that the administrative costs for making financial arrangements and monitoring contracts is roughly equivalent to the single-school approach. However, an additional coordinator is needed for the classroom in the shared configuration, and additional provision for substitutes is necessary.

TABLE 4. ADDITIONAL COSTS INCURRED FOR SHARED A-16 SYSTEM, 1977-1978.

Cost Categories	Amortization Period (years)	Cost	Annualized Cost 10%
Facility			
Construction of a CAI room	25	$ 50,000	$ 5,508
Renovation	10	18,500	3,016
Subtotal		$ 68,500	$ 8,524
Equipment			
Two modems	6	$ 4,710	$
Two multiplexers	6	7,550	
Installation	6	200	
		12,460	2,866
Total		$ 80,960	$ 11,390
Personnel			
One coordinator			22,500
Fringe benefits on above at 16.7%			3,758
Substitutes			390
Subtotal		$ 80,960	$ 26,648
Maintenance			
Printer			$ 360
Miscellaneous			$ 3,000
Grand Total		$ 80,960	$ 41,398

Note: It is assumed that the system is shared by two schools in the same local telephone area. If schools are at a greater distance, the miscellaneou⌐ cost category will increase according to the increase in telephone charges.

These are estimated to cost about $26,648 per year. The training cost for the additional coordinator is so small that it is inconsequential (about $150 for the 1.5 day of salary) and will not be included in the total.

Additional costs of maintenance seem to affect only the additional printer at $360 a year; the modems and multiplexers are maintained on the basic CCC contract so their costs cannot be easily broken out. Miscellaneous costs include the telephone line between schools, routine maintenance of the facilities, lighting, heating, electric power, and supplies. These are estimated at about $3,000 per year, and insurance costs are not affected by distributing the terminals between the two schools.

When these additional costs of the shared arrangements are totaled, about $41,400 is added to the total cost in comparison with the single-classroom, 32-terminal A-16 approach. Again, assuming 23 daily sessions per terminal and a total cost of about $141,000 per year for the shared system, the annual cost per daily session of CAI instruction is about $192. In other words, the shared system increases the cost per session by about 40 percent or $56.

COST FEASIBILITY

Are these costs high or low? That depends on what the costs are buying in terms of educational services and effectiveness in relation to what spending those funds on alternatives might produce. Such cost effectiveness comparisons are absolutely essential in using cost information to ascertain whether a particular educational technology or other instructional approach is a good investment. However, we lack both the cost of other alternatives and effectiveness data on CAI versus other alternatives for this study. Some of those data will be forthcoming at the completion of the CAI experiment and can be drawn upon for cost effectiveness comparisons at that time.

The purpose of cost feasibility analysis is much more modest. It simply asks if the costs of the instructional approach can be accommodated within the limits of the budget assigned for such purposes. In order to answer that question, we will compare the costs of CAI with the level of funding provided for compensatory education by Title I of the Elementary and Secondary Education Act of 1965. That is, presumably the CAI system that is being evaluated is addressed primarily to drill and practice for remediation.

In fiscal year 1977, Title I had appropriations of about $2 billion for about 5 million youngsters. This means that on the average about

$400 was provided for each of the students covered by the program. But not all of this amount was allocated to classroom instruction. Some was expended on such items as administration, health, diagnostic, and nutrition services. However, let us assume that about $400 per pupil represents an upper limit for compensatory education in the classroom. Using this as a basis for cost feasibility, $400 would cover about three daily sessions of CAI at $136 per session with 32 terminals to a classroom, or two sessions at $192 under the shared arrangement. This means that all three curricula could be provided under the lower cost configuration, or two could be provided under the higher cost one. It also means that two curricula, for example reading and mathematics, could be provided under the lower cost option, while allowing the remaining $128 per student to be used for other purposes. On this basis, one would conclude that the CAI approach that has been evaluated meets a general cost feasibility test. That is, it is feasible to consider this approach within the constraints of existing provisions for compensatory education.

COSTS OF A MORE ADVANCED SYSTEM

One of the major questions that arises in evaluating the costs of a changing technology is the direction and magnitude of future costs based upon more advanced approaches. This is particularly important in any strategy based upon computers because the technology of minicomputers and memory devices has been developing at a rapid pace with drastic reductions in the cost of any given capability. The longer run situation would thus suggest that at least the cost of equipment at a given performance level would decline, and it is important to ascertain the impact of these potential equipment cost declines on the overall costs of CAI.

However, before examining some evidence on this question, it is important to point out a phenomenon that is typically overlooked in predicting cost changes of technological innovation. The annualized costs of all computer equipment, including the terminals, represented only about 28 percent of total annualized costs, as evidenced by comparing the costs of $27,873 in Table 2 with the total costs of $100,000 for a 32-terminal classroom. This means that even a rather drastic reduction in the 28 percent of the cost accounted for by equipment will amount to a much smaller reduction in the total cost. For example, if the cost of equipment declined by one-third, total costs would decline by less than 10 percent. At the same time, the costs of personnel, maintenance, construction, and other personnel intensive categories are rising rapidly, at least partially offsetting the potential declines in the cost of computer hardware. Accordingly, it is important to recognize that there will be inherent limits to cost reduction for CAI, even with rapid technological improvements in hardware.

In the particular case of the A-16 system, we were fortunate in that CCC had developed a more advanced CAI approach during the implementation phase of the ETS/LAUSD experiment. The more advanced computer is the CCC-17, which can drive about 96 terminals rather than the 32 terminals to which the A-16 is limited. CCC also claims that the 17 is more flexible and productive than the A-16 for a number of reasons. First, it uses special terminals provided by CCC that permit more flexible design and format of curricula as well as a wider variety of interactive feedback responses between the pupil and the computer. Second, the central processing unit has greater capacity for storing additional curricula and can process curricula of a wider variety than the A-16. For these reasons the CCC-17 may also be more effective for each session than the A-16, although that is ultimately an empirical issue rather than a theoretical one. CCC has provided the CCC-17 for one classroom for the final year of the ETS/LAUSD experiment, hence some empirical data should be forthcoming on this issue.

However, the purpose of this investigation is to ascertain the cost per session of the newer technology. Because the CCC-17 represents a larger system capable of supporting 96 terminals, we will estimate the costs of using a single CCC-17 for providing CAI to three classrooms of 32 terminals. This will enable us ultimately to compare the costs of the CCC-17 for 96 terminals with that of the A-16 on a 32-terminal classroom basis.

Table 5 shows the estimated total and annualized costs of both the facilities and equipment for the CCC-17 configuration. The cost of the facilities component is identical to that shown in Table 2 except that it is based upon three classrooms rather than one classroom. (Of course we will evaluate the costs per session based upon the larger number of terminals serviced by the CCC-17 to make the cost estimates comparable on a student session basis.) The equipment costs include the CCC-17 system, 96 terminals, a cluster controller for every 32 terminals that provides power to the terminals and that routes information between the computer and terminals, a printer for each school, modems for remote schools, and tables for each CAI room. All cost figures are taken from published documents furnished by the marketing office of CCC and dated April 17, 1978. Total facilities and equipment costs are $534,114 or about $101,128 in

TABLE 5. ANNUALIZED COST FOR THREE SCHOOLS SHARING THE CCC–17 SYSTEM, 1977–1978.

Cost Categories	Amortization Period (years)	Cost	Annualized Cost		
			0%	10%	15%
Facilities					
Construction of CAI room	25	$150,000	$ 6,000	$ 16,500	$ 23,250
Renovations	10	55,000	5,550	9,047	11,045
Subtotal		$205,500	$ 11,550	$ 25,547	$ 34,295
Equipment					
Computer-related equipment (includes terminals)	6	$314,814			
Installation	6	13,800			
Subtotal		$328,614	$ 54,769	$ 75,581	$ 86,754
Total facilities and equipment		$534,114	$ 66,319	$101,128	$121,049

TABLE 6. ANNUAL COSTS OF PERSONNEL, TRAINING,
CURRICULUM RENTAL, MAINTENANCE, AND
MISCELLANEOUS COMPONENTS OF THE CCC-17.

Personnel		
Administration	$ 5,895	
Coordinators	67,500	
Fringe benefits on above		
at 16.7%	12,257	
TAs	15,660	
Substitutes	2,340	
Subtotal		$103,652
Training (indirect costs)		$ 1,350
Curriculum rental		20,857
Maintenance		42,072
Miscellaneous		18,000
Total		$185,931

annualized costs when the interest rate on the undepreciated investment is 10 percent.

Personnel costs and the indirect costs of training were calculated
in the same manner for the CCC-17 configuration as for the A-16
except that they are shown for three classrooms. These and other
costs are reflected in Table 6. Curriculum rental was estimated by
CCC at $20,857 and maintenance at $42,072. The miscellaneous
costs are also similar to those calculated for the A-16. The total
of all of these components is $181,931 and when the annualized
costs of the equipment and facilities of $101,128 are added, the total
annualized cost of the CCC-17 in 1977-1978 was estimated to be
$287,059. In order to find the average cost per session, we need only
divide this annual cost by the number of daily sessions provided on
an annual basis. This is shown under different assumptions about the
number of daily sessions provided:

Number of Sessions per Day		*Annual Cost per Daily Session*
Per Terminal	*Per 96 Terminals*	
21	2,016	$142.30
23	2,208	130.00
25	2,400	119.60

Based upon the median number of 23 daily sessions, the average cost per session for the CCC-17 is estimated to be about $130 in comparison with about $136 for the A-16.[9]

This suggests that the CCC-17 has a cost that is about 5 percent lower per CAI session than the A-16. This represents a rather small difference, especially because it assumes that the CCC-17 is utilized to capacity. One of the advantages of the smaller scale of the A-16 is that it provides somewhat more flexibility. Because it can be utilized in multiples of 32 terminals, there is likely to be less of a problem in underutilization than a system that must be implemented in multiples of 96 terminals. Because of the high fixed costs of these types of systems, underutilization hardly reduces total costs at all. This means that one must divide relatively irreducible total costs over fewer sessions, with a marked rise in cost per session. For that reason, the 5 percent reduction in cost per session under assumptions of full utilization would deteriorate rather quickly if the CCC-17 could not be fully utilized at a scale of 96 terminals.

One other point that ought to be emphasized is that of the total annual cost of $287,000 for the CCC-17, only about $76,000 is accounted for by the cost of the computer hardware. This means that almost three-quarters of the cost is allocable to factors that are not ostensibly affected by improvements in computer technology, thus limiting the cost savings obtainable by technological advances in the CAI system. In fact, as a general rule, virtually all technologically based instructional systems will show that only about one-quarter to one-third of the costs are associated with their hardware. This means that drastic reductions in the costs of such hardware may have only nominal effects on overall costs of the instructional strategy. Further, to the degree that the decrease in even those costs is associated with a larger scale of operation, even these cost reductions may not be realized unless the system can be utilized to full capacity.

It should be noted that according to CCC, the CCC-17 is educationally superior to the A-16. Admittedly the cost per session is not as important as the cost per unit of educational effectiveness. Thus, even if the costs of the CCC-17 are comparable to those of

9. Jamison et al. (1970) suggest that at that time a cost of $50 per session was attainable on an earlier CCC system. That estimate seems overly optimistic; even when adjusted for inflation it is about half of our estimates. Most of the difference appears to arise from the fact that coordinators were not used in the configuration that they describe as well as the assumption that the utilization rate would be 25 sessions daily. They do not mention the number of minutes per session. Early "drill and practice" curricula utilized 7-minute sessions, and they may be assuming these shorter sessions.

the A-16, a superior level of effectiveness may still make it a better investment. However, without data on the relative effectiveness of the two systems, it is impossible to evaluate this claim.

SUMMARY

The purpose of this paper was to estimate both costs and cost feasibility of utilizing a particular CAI approach for compensatory educational purposes. The particular approach that was chosen is the CCC A-16 and its implementation for a four-year experiment on the effectiveness of CAI that had been established in the Los Angeles Unified School District. Based upon the ingredients approach to cost analysis, it was found that up to three sessions of drill and practice of 10 minutes duration could be provided for each disadvantaged child at the 1977-1978 level of Title I expenditures. This means that three different subjects could be provided, or that multiple sessions in one or two subjects could be offered, for each child. As such, it appears that the instructional strategy is cost feasible within present provisions for compensatory education. Utilizing the A-16 between two schools would increase costs rather substantially, but two sessions of CAI would still be feasible within 1977-1978 compensatory educational allocations.

Costs were also estimated for the more advanced CCC-17 computer system, and somewhat surprisingly the costs were in the same range as those of the A-16. In part, this finding reflects the very heavy software component of CAI approaches, and, in part, it may reflect the possibility that the CCC-17 is more effective than the A-16 (even though the costs are quite similar). It is clear that a more exhaustive analysis of the merits of different CAI approaches, as well as a comparison between them and other instructional strategies, will require effectiveness data as well as cost estimates. Some of these should be forthcoming from the ETS/LAUSD experiment, and it is hoped that a cost effectiveness comparison can be made at some future date.

REFERENCES

Carnoy, M., and H. Levin/1975
EVALUATION OF EDUCATIONAL MEDIA: SOME ISSUES. *Instructional Science* 4: 385-406.

Holland, Paul, Dean Jamison, and Marge Ragosta/1980
COMPUTER-ASSISTED INSTRUCTION: A LONGITUDINAL STUDY. Paper presented at the Meeting of the American Education Research Association (April).

Instructional Science/1975
Vol. 4.

Jamison, D., J.D. Fletcher, P. Suppes, and R.C. Atkinson/1976
COST AND PERFORMANCE OF COMPUTER-ASSISTED INSTRUCTION FOR EDUCATION OF DISADVANTAGED CHILDREN. In *Education as an Industry*, edited by J. Froomkin, D. Jamison, and R. Radner. Chapter 5. National Bureau of Economic Research, Universities—National Bureau Conference Series no. 28. Cambridge, MA: Ballinger.

Jamison, D., S. Klees, and S. Wells/1978
THE COSTS OF EDUCATIONAL MEDIA. Beverly Hills, CA: Sage Publications.

Jamison, D., P. Suppes, and C. Butler/1970
ESTIMATED COSTS OF COMPUTER-ASSISTED INSTRUCTION FOR COMPENSATORY EDUCATION IN URBAN AREAS. *Instructional Technology* 10: 49-57.

Levin, H.M./1975
COST-EFFECTIVENESS ANALYSIS IN EVALUATION RESEARCH. In *Handbook of Evaluation Research*, edited by M. Guttentag and E. Struening, Vol. 2, pp. 89-122. Beverly Hills, CA: Sage Publications.

26

Program Evaluation of a Special Education
Day School for Conduct Problem Adolescents

Charles A. Maher

A procedure for program evaluation of a special education day school is described, and empirical evidence of its application in a school for conduct problem adolescents is reported. Use of the procedure enables a program evaluator to: (a) identify the priority evaluation information needs of a school principal and school staff, (b) involve those persons in evaluation design and implementation, and (c) determine the utility of the evaluation for program decision-making purposes.

Although the importance of special education program evaluation has been discussed in the literature (see, e.g., Dunst, 1979; Maher, 1979a), applications of practical program evaluation procedures seldom have been reported. This is especially the case when the concern is for evaluation of organizational units such as special education day schools (Kennedy, 1978). This paper describes a procedure for program evaluation of a special education day school for conduct problem adolescents, and provides empirical evidence of its application in that context.

EVALUATON PROCEDURE AND EVALUATION CONTEXT

The evaluation procedure to be described is based upon a conception of program evaluation as a process whereby information is obtained so that judgments (decisions) can be made about the worth of various aspects of a program (Maher & Kratochwill, in press). Moreover, the procedure rests on a belief that program evaluation is useful only to the extent that the evaluation information needs of program decision makers are identified, and to the degree that these persons are involved in designing an evaluation that addresses the identified needs (Maher, in press). Thus, given this conceptual framework, the procedure consists of four steps: (1) Identification of Evaluation Information Needs, (2) Design and Implementation of the Evaluation, (3) Analysis and Dissemination of Evaluation Information, and (4) Evaluation of the Usefulness of the Evaluation.

The context for application of the program evaluation procedure was the Northover Cooperative School, a public special education school in central New Jersey, which provided special education and related services to approximately 45 adolescents. Although administratively classified as emotionally disturbed and socially maladjusted, the pupils manifested conduct problems such as truancy, absenteeism, fighting with peers and teachers, disruptive classroom behavior, and refusal to complete class assignments. All pupils were of at least average intelligence and were considered by their respective school districts as not able to profit from placement in a regular public high school. The present placements were considered as the least restrictive environments for the pupils, as noted in their individualized education programs (IEPs). A full-time staff of seven, including a principal, three teachers, and three teacher aides, provided special education services. In addition, they were supported by specialists, consisting of a part-time school psychologist, a school nurse, and several student teachers. The school operated on a broad-based behavioral philosophy with 12 Educational Programs comprising the school

From Charles A. Maher, "Program Evaluation of a Special Education Day School for Conduct Problem Adolescents," 18(2) *Psychology in the Schools* 211-217 (April 1981). Copyright 1981 by Charles A. Maher. Reprinted by permission.

curriculum. These programs were: (a) academic subject programs of Mathematics, Language Arts, Science, Reading, and Social Studies; (b) special subject programs of Art, Music, and Physical Education; and (c) life skills programs of Employment Training, Social Education, Work Study, and Group Counseling.

In the remainder of the paper, each step of the evaluation procedure will be discussed, as applied in the above evaluation context.

IDENTIFICATION OF EVALUATION INFORMATION NEEDS

The program evaluation was undertaken by the author (evaluator) at the request of the principal and professional staff of the school. These program decision makers indicated a general need to know how effective their school was in terms of individual pupils and in terms of the 12 Educational Programs. By means of a series of structured interviews and small group meetings with principal, teachers, and specialists, the evaluator identified three specific evaluation information needs that were agreed upon by these groups as priority needs. First, the principal and executive board desired substantive data regarding the overall effectiveness of the Programs provided in the school. Second, the staff desired information that would help pinpoint strengths and weaknesses of these programs, including information about the social validity of the programs as perceived by the pupils. Third, since the school initially had been designed to facilitate the educational planning process by means of individual goal setting and concretizing educational outcome expectations for each pupil, the principal and staff wanted information about the extent to which that purpose was being fulfilled. These three evaluation information needs served to focus the manner in which the evaluation was designed and implemented.

DESIGN AND IMPLEMENTATION OF THE EVALUATION

In order to design an evaluation that addressed the three evaluation information needs, as well as to ensure its implementation, a Program Evaluation Committee was formed at the beginning of the school year by the evaluator. The Committee consisted of the evaluator, who served as chairperson, an academic classroom teacher, a special subject teacher, a life skills teacher, and the school psychologist.

The evaluation was conducted during September through June of the school year. Forty-five pupils, or nearly 95% of the entire pupil population, were included as data sources for the evaluation. The few pupils not included in the evaluation transferred prior to its completion.

The evaluation activities to be implemented were described by the Committee in a written evaluation plan that was agreed to by the principal and executive board of the school. The evaluation was designed so that evaluation information could be gathered, analyzed, and reported about two aspects of the school: Individual Pupil Functioning and Program Functioning. Goal Attainment Scaling and a Program Satisfaction Questionnaire were the two primary evaluation methods used. Each method is described below.

Goal Attainment Scaling

Goal Attainment Scaling (GAS) is a method, initially developed to evaluate programs in community mental health centers (Kiresuk & Sherman, 1968), but recently applied to evaluation of public school programs (Maher, 1979b). The GAS method is flexible, in that it can be used to assess goal attainment of individual pupils and programs that serve groups of pupils, such as the 12 Educational Programs of the Northover Cooperative School.

In using the GAS method, both for individual pupil goal attainment and for program-level goal attainment, a Goal Attainment Follow-Up Guide was constructed by the appropriate teacher. Table 1 is an example of a completed Goal Attainment Follow-Up Guide for a pupil enrolled in the school's Social Education Program.

TABLE 1

*An Example of a Completed Individual-level Goal Attainment
Follow-up Guide for a Pupil enrolled in the Social Education Program
(all goals were weighted equally)*

Goal Attainment Scale Categories	Improved School Attendance	Improved Classroom Productivity	Improved School Socialization
Best anticipated success (+2)	100% daily attendance	90-100% completion of academic classroom assignments in all academic classes	0-1 disciplinary referrals to vice-principal
More than anticipated success (+1)	90-100% daily attendance*	80-90% completion of academic classroom assignments	2-4 disciplinary referrals to vice-principal*
Expected level of success (0)	80-90% daily attendance (based on school attendance records)	70-80% completion of academic classroom assignments (based on teacher record books)*	5-6 disciplinary referrals to vice-principal (based on office records)
Less than expected success (-1)	60-80% daily attendance √	50-70% completion of academic classroom assignments	7-10 disciplinary referrals to vice-principal
Most unfavorable outcome thought likely (-2)	Less than 60% daily attendance	Less than 50% completion of academic classroom assignments √	More than 10 disciplinary referrals to vice-principal √

Date of program implementation: October 15; date of program evaluation: May 15.
Goal Attainment Score at Oct. 15 = 30.8; Goal Attainment Score at May 15 = 61.2; Goal Attainment Change Score = 30.4.

√ = level of pupil attainment at program implementation.
* = level of pupil attainment at program evaluation.

In construction of a Guide, individual pupil goals or program goals were placed on the guide and expanded into Goal Attainment Scales that included, for one or more goal, a range of three to five scales that indicated the most to the least favorable outcomes thought likely to occur for a specified time interval (e.g., school year). By means of interviews, observations, and reviews of records conducted by independent raters, a rating was made as to what level of outcome had been realized both prior to program implementation, and at time of program evaluation (see Table 1).

Based upon the ratings, Goal Attainment Scores were determined prior to and following a program, and a Goal Attainment Change Score was calculated. These scores were determined using a computational formula created by Kiresuk and Sherman (1968), which includes a procedure for weighting the relative importance of each goal when more than one goal is set. Conceptually, the Goal Attainment Score is a global index of the degree to which outcome expectations have been realized. Using Kiresuk and Sherman's formula, for each goal that is set, a score of 50 indicates that the short-term goal (expected outcome level) has been achieved; a score of 40 indicates less than expected attainment; 30 much less than expected outcome; 70 indicates that the long-term goal was achieved; 60 indicates intermediate level of attainment between the short- and long-term goal. More detailed information about the use of goal attainment scaling can be found in Kiresuk and Sherman (1968), Kiresuk (1978), and Maher (1979b).

Although not visually portrayed, due to space limitations, program-level goals also were placed on Goal Attainment Follow-Up Guides by the appropriate teacher or specialist in a manner similar to that of Table 1. For example: for the program goal of "Improved School Attendance" for the Social Education Program, the "expected level of success (0)" was described as: "75-80% of all pupils enrolled would attain their expected level of individual goal attainment." The "most unfavorable outcome thought likely (−2)" was: "Less than 50% of all pupil enrollees would attain their expected level of individual goal attainment." The "best anticipated success (+2)" was: "90-100% of all pupil enrollees would attain their expected level of individual goal attainment."

Prior to the start of the school year, the evaluator, as specified in the evaluation plan, undertook the task of training the staff to construct Goal Attainment Follow-Up Guides for individual pupils and programs, based upon a manual developed by Garwick (1976). Training occurred by means of five, two-hour workshop sessions, not discussed here due to space limitations.

Program Satisfaction Questionnnaire

A Program Satisfaction Questionnaire (PSQ) was administered to each pupil enrolled in each of the 12 Educational Programs during May of the school year. On the PSQ, pupils provided a rating of the helpfulness of each program by means of a five-point scale: (5) extremely helpful (4) very helpful, (3) helpful, (2) somewhat helpful, (1) not helpful. Also, information on the strengths and weaknesses of each program was obtained by means of open-ended questions included as part of the PSQ (copy of the PSQ is available on request from author).

Data Collection Procedures and Measurement Reliability

Standardized Goal Attainment Follow-Up Scores and Goal Attainment Change Scores were obtained for each pupil and for each program at the beginning and at the end of the school year. In this evaluation, all scores were based on equally weighted scales. Mean Goal Attainment Scores were calculated for the pupils. Also, Goal Attainment and Goal Attainment Change Scores based on program goals were obtained. For individual-level and program-level Follow-Up Guides, degree of goal attainment was assessed by two trained independent raters (doctoral school psychology students). Interrater agreement was assessed by the evaluator by comparing the frequency of rater agreements over frequency of agreements and disagreements multiplied times 100 for each Guide. For the individual-level Guides, interrater agreement was 95% at the beginning and 94% at the end of the year. For the program-level Guides, interrater agreement was 94% and 96% at the beginning and end of the year, respectively. From the PSQs, the mean rating of "helpfulness" for the 5-point question was calculated for each of the 12 Educational Programs.

ANALYSIS AND DISSEMINATION OF EVALUATION INFORMATION

Following data analysis, the procedures of which were specified in the evaluation plan, the evaluation information was disseminated in three ways by the Committee. First, an executive summary report was provided to the principal and executive board, that consisted of a digest version of the evaluation information obtained. Second, a more detailed report was provided to school staff, that consisted of a narrative description of the results, graphical and tabular presentation of data, and evaluation conclusions. Third, an "Evaluation Forum" was held at which evaluator, principal, and staff discussed the evaluation, considered questions and issues raised from reading the evaluation reports, and delineated tentative recommendations for program development and improvement. Evaluation results are briefly summarized below for illustrative purposes. A more detailed report can be obtained from the author.

Evaluation at the Individual Pupil Level

The mean number of individual pupil goals set for each individual pupil goal attainment follow-up guide was 3.78. Across all pupil follow-up guides, the mean Goal Attainment Score at the beginning of the school year was 35.20, the mean Goal Attainment Score at the end of the school year was 45.21, and the Goal Attainment Change Score was 10.01 ($p < .05$). Also, of the 45 pupils, 24 (53%) either met or exceeded the individual goals established for them. In terms of Goal Attainment Change Scores, 23 pupils revealed changes in scores in a positive direction, 13 showed no change, while 9 had negative change scores. These findings suggest that, in general, pupils attained or very nearly attained their expected level of educational outcomes.

Evaluation at the Program Level

On the basis of program-level Goal Attainment Scores (not reported here) and the PSQ "helpfulness" question (5-point scale), it was possible to identify overall strengths and weaknesses of the 12 Educational Programs of the Northover Cooperative School. In this regard, the evaluation plan called for examination of relationships between pupil satisfaction ratings of the helpfulness of the 12 Programs, and the program-level Goal Attainment Follow-Up Scores and program-level Goal Attainment Change Scores of each Program. Thus, the 12 Programs were ranked from high to low in terms of the pupil ratings and the program-level Follow-Up and Change Scores, with correlations between these sets of ranks being explored using the Spearman-rho formula. In this regard, it was determined that there was a correlation of .74 ($p < .01$) between program-level Follow-Up Scores and pupil ratings. Three examples illustrate the kinds of results obtained: The Employment Training Program, while being ranked first on the basis of Follow-Up Score, had a pupil rating rank of 4.5. The Reading Program had a Follow-Up Score rank of 2 and a pupil rank scaling of 1. The Group Counseling Program ranked last (12th) on both Follow-Up Score and pupil ratings. With regard to program-level Change Scores and pupil ratings, a correlation of .36 was obtained, which did not reach significance at the .05 level. Also, in terms of the open-ended questions on the PSQ, those programs that were higher in program-level goal attainment also had more responses that indicated pupil satisfaction with the following areas: (a) clarity of class expectations in terms of grading, (b) consistency of the teacher in dealing with behavioral management problems in the classroom, (c) diversity of instructional experiences provided by the teacher, and (d) willingness of the teacher or specialist to understand the pupil's problem.

Discussion of Evaluation Results

Evaluation results suggested that, from both staff and pupils' point of view, educational progress had been made during the school year. Also, the data obtained revealed those programs that appeared to be contributing most to the educational progress of pupils. For example, it was found that the Employment Training, Mathematics, and Reading programs demonstrated the most appreciable overall impact on pupils. Also important, however, was the fact that the school staff succeeded in facilitating individual pupil goal setting and in encouraging the formation of overall goals for educational programs. In this regard, the staff was generally pleased with the benefits derived from Goal Attainment Scaling. They reported that they were able to discuss the progress of pupils in an orderly way by using the pupil Goal Attainment Follow-Up Guides that were at their disposal. They indicated that the approach focused their programming activities in an instructionally relevant way.

The correlation between program-level Goal Attainment Follow-Up Scores and pupil ratings was significant ($r = .74$, $p < .01$). However, the correlation between program-level Goal Attainment Change Scores and pupil ratings ($r = .36$) failed to reach significance at the .05 level. One inference that can be made is that, as an index of program efficacy, Follow-Up Scores were more valid than Change Scores. A more conservative point of view, however, suggests that Change Scores did not demonstrate sufficient validity to be used even as a measure of program success. However, it must be remembered that correlations were obtained between program-level scores and pupil ratings. Also, it should be noted that while the correspondence between program-level Goal Attainment Change Scores and pupil ratings was not statistically significant, a positive trend was apparent. Thus, it is possible that if there had been a larger sample size and if individual pupils' scores as well as program-level scores had been utilized, significant correlations between Change Scores and relevant criteria could have been attained. This kind of calculation was not undertaken, nor were individual pupils' Goal Attainment Scores and other independent criteria of educational progress (e.g., standardized achievement test data) calculated in the present evaluation. This was due to limitations of available data and the consensus of the Committee to keep the evaluation within manageable proportions during the first year that such an approach was implemented in the school.

EVALUATION OF THE USEFULNESS OF THE EVALUATION

Following the dissemination of evaluation information, two meetings were held between the evaluator and the principal and staff of the school to assess the utility of the evaluation. Feedback suggested that the evaluation information gathered and reported satisfied the evaluation information needs of these program decision makers. In particular, staff commented that they appreciated the objective view of program efficacy the evaluation provided, as well as the acquisition of helpful educational program-planning and evaluation skills in the form of the Goal Attainment Scaling. Moreover, the information derived from the evaluation was publicly acknowledged by the school's executive board as being used in their decision to expand the size and scope of the school during the ensuing school year. Also, the evaluation procedure has been made a routine part of the school's operational procedure.

REFERENCES

DUNST, C.   Program evaluation and the Education for All Handicapped Children Act. *Exceptional Children*, 1979, *46*, 24-31.

GARWICK, G.   *Guide to goals*. Minneapolis, MN: Program Evaluation Resource Center, 1976.

KENNEDY, M. M.   Developing an evaluation plan for Public Law 94-142. *New Directions for Special Education*, 1978, *1*, 19-38.

KIRESUK, T. J.   Goal attainment scaling. In C. C. Attkisson, R. Hargreaves, J. Sorenson, & J. M. Horowitz (Eds.), *Evaluation of human resource programs*. New York: Academic Press, 1978.

KIRESUK, T. J., & SHERMAN, R. E.   Goal attainment scaling: A general method for evaluating community mental health programs. *Community Mental Health Journal*, 1968, *4*, 443-453.

MAHER, C. A.   The school psychologist and special education program evaluation: Contributions and considerations. *Psychology in the Schools*, 1979, *16*, 240-245. (a)

MAHER, C. A.   Guidelines for planning and evaluating school psychology service delivery systems. *Journal of School Psychology*, 1979, *17*, 203-212. (b)

MAHER, C. A.   Program evaluation for school psychologists. In T. R. Kratochwill (Ed.), *Advances in school psychology, Vol. 1*. Hillsdale, NJ: Lawrence Erlbaum, in press.

MAHER, C. A., & KRATOCHWILL, T. R.   Principles and procedures of program evaluation: An overview. *School Psychology Monograph*, in press.

27

Local Uses of Title I Evaluations

Jane L. David

Statement of the Problem

Title I of the Elementary and Secondary Education Act of 1965 (ESEA) was the first major social legislation to require program evaluation. The original requirement for Title I evaluations and its subsequent elaboration in the 1974 and 1978 Amendments to the Act have resulted in a variety of interpretations of the purposes of the evaluations and several Federal strategies for their conduct. Since 1965, the Federal strategies for Title I evaluation adopted by the United States Office of Education (USOE) emphasize Federal information needs. By contrast, the recent legislative history of ESEA reflects a strong and growing interest in the provision of evaluation information which is also useful for program improvement at the local level. The extent to which Title I evaluations have met Federal information needs has been studied, but there has been little attention paid to the impact of Federally mandated evaluations at the local level. This study was designed to investigate whether the same evaluation system can serve both local and Federal needs through an examination of local uses of Title I evaluation.

Objectives

This study was designed to answer two major questions: Do local staff use Title I

The study on which this article is based was conducted by the author at SRI International for the Office of the Assistant Secretary for Planning and Evaluation, DHEW.

evaluation results and, if so, in what ways? What factors explain the use or lack of use of the evaluation results? Specifically, the study investigated how local Title I staff and parents use their Title I evaluation, what information they use in judging the effectiveness of their program, and how they make decisions about changing the program. The objective was to produce a report to document (1) the uses of Title I evaluations by local staff and parents, (2) the other types of information used by local staff and parents in judging and in improving their program, and (3) the implications of these findings for the current Federal Title I evaluation strategy.

Methodology

The primary sample consists of 15 Title I districts in six states. The districts were selected among those reputed to have an above-average emphasis on or concern with evaluation. The identification of such districts was based on recommendations of USOE staff, Technical Assistance Center directors, and state Title I directors. Although the sample is not nationally representative, choosing districts especially concerned with evaluation ensures that the findings are based on situations with the greatest potential for use of evaluations. In addition, the sample was augmented by field notes from another 15 districts collected in a concurrent USOE-funded study that involved interviews concerning evaluation in Title I districts.

The data collection consisted of face-to-face interviews with Title I administrators, principals of Title I schools, Title I teaching staff, and parents of Title I students. Copies of evaluation reports and other related documents were also obtained. One or two interviewers visited each district for 1 to 2 days. The interviews were structured to the extent that the same topics were pursued in each interview, but the emphasis on each topic and the specific questions were tailored to each situation and respondent.

The analysis consisted of drawing a tentative set of generalizations from several readings of the field notes. For each generalization, the notes were gone through carefully, and evidence was extracted in support of and opposed to the generalizations. After refining the general statements to be reported, quotations illustrating each point were pulled from the notes. From these lists, examples were selected for inclusion in the report, thus ensuring that the quotations reported in the text are indeed representative of the responses.

Major Findings

I found that the main part of the district Title I evaluation report for all the Local Education Agencies (LEA's) visited consists of posttest or gain scores reported for each project on standardized achievement tests. A few evaluations included additional information, such as the results of questionnaires given to staff and parents soliciting their opinions of the project. On the whole, however, program evaluation is synonymous with standardized achievement test scores. Accordingly, the findings presented throughout often indicate uses of and attitudes toward standardized achievement tests rather than the evaluation report per se.

The findings are organized under three general questions: How is the Title I evaluation used in general? How is the evaluation used in judging the Title I program? How is the evaluation used for program improvement?

How is Title I Evaluation Used?

There is little doubt that the primary function the evaluations serve is to meet

the state- and Federal-reporting requirements of Title I. Districts employ standardized tests because they are the simplest way of meeting the Federal mandate as interpreted by their state. LEA's are totally accustomed to the fact that receiving Federal money has a number of strings attached to it, of which the evaluation requirement is merely one. For example:

> This district will accept all strings that go with the Federal money. Richer ones might not but we need the money. (Director)[1]

Therefore, with the exception of staff concerns with the time devoted to testing and the reporting burden, evaluation is usually perceived as just one of the many hoops to go through in order to receive the funds.

> We go along with externally imposed regulations as long as they do not impose an overwhelming burden. When they are burdensome, we will exercise our own judgment about what is legitimate and not go down without a fight. (Evaluator)

> Evaluation is not a burden; it is an unnecessary but required evil. It does little harm but is of no particular use. (Teacher)

So long as the burden is not undue and some local autonomy is preserved in designing their program, most local staff responsible for conducting the evaluation are concerned primarily with meeting the legal requirements:

> Testing is an economical and straightforward way of complying with the regulations; we send the data in and then go about our business. We're not going to lose any sleep over whether or not the results show effectiveness. (Evaluator)

Providing data to meet evaluation requirements is an accepted fact of life. Title I staff also believe that the Federal Government has a right to request the data because they are footing the bill. Moreover, many but not all Title I staff

---

[1] Throughout the text, the type of respondent is identified in parentheses. All directors, administrators, evaluators, teachers, and parents are part of Title I. Principals are all in Title I schools and non-Title I administrators are all superintendents.

think that there is a real need for the data at higher levels (i.e., district, state, or Federal). One district director described the perceptions of his staff in the following way:

> Teachers feel that all this data collection goes on because the state needs it or more generally the government needs it and they are sympathetic with their need for knowing what happens with their money. But outside of this necessity, they see little purpose. (Director)

In the context of the new USOE evaluation models, the district evaluator said:

> I can see the Federal and state need to demonstrate bang for the buck but cannot see why they avoid educators in coming up with guidelines. (Evaluator)

The second primary use of evaluation results is to *provide feedback*. Feedback in this context connotes simply communicating evaluation results to program staff and parents. Theoretically, this is the area that provides the greatest potential for use of evaluation in making judgments and decisions about programs leading to improvements. As one district administrator stated:

> If the test data are not useful to the principals, they aren't useful at all. (Administrator)

All districts provide some type of feedback, but the type of information fed back varies enormously. At a minimum, feedback consists of sending the evaluation report to the Parent Advisory Council (PAC) and the principals of Title I schools. This situation is the one least likely to lead to any utilization (or even understanding) of the information. Principals rarely look at the report under these conditions, and teachers often do not see it. Most districts, however, provide school-by-school results, and sometimes class-level results, which are transmitted to the appropriate individuals.

Sometimes this information is quite comprehensive. For example, in one district, each Title I school receives a 15-page mimeographed document containing graphs of the relationship between school level poverty indices and achievement (with the particular school's code circled), detailed test score results for the school (by subtest and skill area), with national percentiles, and a comparison with the previous year's data for that school. It also contains other descriptive data on school and community characteristics such as mobility, enrollment, and income. The introduction to the report reads:

> The purpose of this report is to share information about students in Title I schools in _____. It is intended that the report be seen not as an evaluation report but as a collection of information that will help administrators, teachers and parents plan even stronger programs for the children in these schools.

This district was extraordinary in the efforts put forth by the evaluation staff to make evaluation part of the program-planning effort. They go to considerable effort to present the information for each school clearly and to explain the findings in person to teachers, parents and the principal. In this district, as well as others, it was stated that feedback that included personal explanations by evaluation staff was much more likely to be understood and to make an impression on the school staff; and, hence, have the potential to be utilized. In another district, the director said:

> Principals won't make any use of evaluation results if you just send data—you need to go talk with them about it. (Director)

In sum, the provision of feedback, particularly when explained in person, provides what may be a necessary but not sufficient condition for utilization of the evaluation information.

Although the primary local uses of evaluation are to meet requirements and to provide feedback, other uses are not precluded. The third major use falls under the category of gross or *rough indications of program effectiveness*. This category differs from the previous ones in that it occurs at the individual rather than the system level. The use of evaluation as a gross index of program accomplishments takes several forms, the most common of which is use of evaluation to confirm one's existing beliefs about a program. For example:

I look at test scores mainly to confirm my own impression. If they differ, my impression counts. (Teacher)

A related use of evaluations under this category is that of giving a rough index of program success, but not as a guide to action. For example:

Tests can only be interpreted as a rough guide. (Principal)

Also related to this category is the use of evaluation as a public relations document:

I want information to justify expansion of the program. I'm not interested in information showing students are behind national norms. (Superintendent)

To illustrate another form of public relations, in one district the evaluator explicitly pointed out the need to use the evaluation report as a way of educating the district administration and board to have realistic expectations about the effectiveness of their Title I program. Similarly, in another district the reading program director described the situation in which a school wanted to withdraw from participation in Title I:

They claimed that Title I was associated with a decline in test scores. We were able to pull out the evaluation report and demonstrate that this was not true. (Administrator)

In another district, the superintendent stated:

Day-to-day problems don't show up in the evaluation. Subjective feedback is often more useful in daily operation of the program. The other stuff is what you impress people with. (Superintendent)

These common uses of evaluation—as a source of confirmation of existing beliefs, as an indicator of success, and as a public relations document—share an important characteristic: They are triggered only by positive results. Thus, the evaluation report as an end in itself (apart from meeting requirements) is seen as useful only when the results are positive. When the results are negative, the evaluation is discounted for any number of reasons. (Elaboration of these reasons is contained in the following section.) Thus, it is often

the case that negative findings, rather than being taken as informative about the program, are viewed as an annoyance which must be explained away:

One year the scores for second grade were low. We looked for the reason by talking with the teachers to see if the skills tested matched the curriculum and if the students' scores matched the teachers' judgment. From this, we concluded that the test was invalid. (Evaluator)

In another district, the district staff were all extremely upset over results that showed negative Normal Curve Equivalent (NCE) growth.

We are having the TAC [Technical Assistance Center] reanalyze our data looking for floor effects. We know instructional growth is taking place. The negative results hurt us in several ways. First, Congress is always talking about the possibility of tying funds to gains and, second, we get a bad reputation. Poor results limit our ability to share information about the program and lead to low morale. (Director)

And in another district, one school had very low scores:

We discovered that there had been an influx of Vietnamese students into the school. In another school with low scores we found that there were a number of students who were near EMR [educable mentally retarded]. (Director)

However, not all evaluations with negative findings are ignored. There are a few instances in which they are taken as a gross indicator of a weakness, but this occurs primarily in the context of needs assessment. Although the same set of standardized scores, or at least the same type, are used for both needs assessment and evaluation, they are far more likely to be seen as useful and acted on when they are viewed as needs assessment data as opposed to evaluative data.

Ironically, there is almost unanimous agreement that standardized tests (especially when combined with teacher judgment)[2] form a good basis for selecting

---

[2] Two districts were exceptions. One felt strongly that teacher judgment should not be included and another based selection exclusively on teacher judgment.

students for the programs. Although this use does not relate specifically to evaluation, it is mentioned here because it is a widely approved "good" use of standardized tests in a world in which they are usually criticized severely.

In summary, the primary local uses of Title I evaluations are to meet legal requirements, to provide feedback, and to provide gross indicators of program effectiveness. Title I evaluations do not seem to serve, as primary purposes, either as a basis on which to judge the program or as a guide to program improvement. Because direct inquiries about uses of evaluation results did not reveal use in program planning and improvement, we pursued the issue in greater depth by asking respondents how they judge the programs and how decisions about programs are made.

How is Evaluation Used in Judging Programs?

Everyone involved in a Title I program makes judgments about its effectiveness. From asking respondents how they would demonstrate that their programs were successful and how they would make judgments about other programs, it is possible to deduce why evaluation plays such a limited role in these judgments. There are three classes of reasons limiting the impact of evaluation on judgments of program success: The data they provide are not considered as persuasive as other sources of information; the analyses ignore important mediating variables; and the evaluations do not measure important goals.

When local staff weigh standardized test results against other sources of information in judging the success of their program, the *other sources of information carry more weight* in most situations. Conflicting information from standardized tests and sources such as criterion or other skills-related tests and personal judgment (gleaned from observation, intuition, or some combination) are inevitably resolved in favor of the other sources.

Some examples follow:

> Individual diagnostic tools provide the basis for my judgment of program

success; not the standardized tests. (Principal)

> The CTBS [Comprehensive Test of Basic Skills] tells us by grade where the school is the weakest. We also use our curriculum tests. The results don't always match; then we go with the curriculum tests because they are more immediate and frequent. (Teacher)

> I would trust my own opinion over a test score. (Teacher)

In general, as one director put it:

> People use evaluation to support their beliefs but will not change their beliefs on disconfirming evaluation evidence. (Director)

Two findings connect this last point to the fact that negative standardized test results are usually ignored. First, school staff (and generally all Title I staff and parents) are happy with their programs. Second, evaluation results are looked at primarily with an eye toward confirming beliefs. Together, then, positive results serve to reinforce existing positive feelings toward the program but negative results are ignored and, if necessary, explained away as inappropriate. When the results are negative, it does not seem to be the case that staff already knew there was a problem; in fact, the case is usually that the problem perceived is not with the program but with the tests.

The above examples illustrate the ease with which tests are discounted when test results are incompatible with existing beliefs about program effectiveness. The widely publicized methodological critiques of standardized tests facilitate this process in that people who are displeased with test results can quickly call to mind "scientific" reasons for rejecting the tests. As one administrator stated:

> If the standardized test scores are negative, it's okay because everyone buys the argument that they can be discredited. (Administrator)

And if the problem is not with the tests, it is with the testing conditions:

> If my judgment and the test scores tell different stories, I believe my judgment and look for explanations such as problems in giving the test or how the child felt. (Principal)

Or. there is a problem with the analysis, as described below.

A frequent explanation for ignoring standardized test results in judging programs is that the scores are not meaningful because *the results have not considered important background characteristics* of schools or children. Explanations of this type usually arise in the context of negative or low test results and potential comparisons with other schools or programs. For example:

> The evaluation should have more information on the characteristics of the kids because there can be big differences between schools in socioeconomic status and mobility and other things you can't measure readily. (Teacher)

> Each school in the district has different objectives. So a good school may be ranked lowest because it has harder objectives. (Parent)

> The school's drop in ranking can be explained by several factors not having to do with the program. You need to take into account the students' IQs, the number of students per staff, and the amount of instructional time per student. And some schools exclude students with low IQ's when it comes to testing while others include them. (Principal)

> There is great difficulty in using the same tests even if restricted to programs with the same goals because of differences in populations. For example, the bottom kids in this state are not as low as the bottom kids in New Jersey. (Evaluator)

Finally, in judging their program's effectiveness, staff and parents look to information that assesses what they believe to be the most important goals of the program, usually in addition to, but occasionally instead of, achievement. Evaluation results are usually found lacking because *important goals are not measured.*

> We would like to see all kinds of alternative goals given equal place: parent involvement, student self-concept, attendance rates, library records and student enthusiasm. (Administrator)

> Test scores on the CTBS don't say very much about whether the program was successful. Test scores are less important than growth in the affective areas. (Teacher)

> Evaluation data do not show what is effective. Teacher-pupil relationships and the quality of the teacher are what make the biggest difference. (Director)

A related concern vis-a-vis goals is that emphasis of achievement tests has narrowed the focus of Title I:

> Title I was first a poverty program; now it is entirely achievement—all activities are now instructional, as a result, in part, of using standardized tests; also because achievement tests are used as allocators at the school level. (Evaluator)

> I would like to do more than reading and math but you can't measure them so the state won't allow it. (Principal)

> We are suspicious of all hard data and see Title I shifting to reflect an obsession with testable outcomes. (Administrator)

In summary, there are multiple reasons for the minimal use of evaluations in judging program effectiveness. Generally, the reasons that are stated reflect preferences for measures of achievement other than standardized tests, a fear of misleading comparisons, and the view that programs have multiple goals.

Because one purpose of this study is to provide a starting point for considering how evaluations might be made more useful, it is helpful to report the types of information that respondents cite when asked about program effectiveness. I consider both what information respondents claim they use and what other types of information they say they would like in three areas: information related to cognitive growth, growth in noncognitive areas, and outcomes in areas not related to the child. The responses described under these topics were elicited primarily by asking questions such as: How would you convince me your program is a success? If you were choosing a new program, what would you consider?

Most respondents are concerned with growth in *cognitive areas,* usually reading and math. Thus the tendency not to cite evaluation data as a source for program judgements is more a reflection of the perceived limitations of standardized tests than of the domain being assessed. Respondents, particularly teachers, are more likely to cite specific measures of skills as better indicators of growth than standardized achievement tests, but just as frequently they cite their own observations and experiences. Hence:

> If I were to judge a program, I would first look at the written goals of the program and then at the specific goals for each child. I would want to see pre- and posttest scores on individual skills rather than standardized achievement tests. (Teacher)

> I judge the program on the basis of my own experience. And I would back this up with the opinions of teachers and parents when the students get to the higher grades. (Principal)

Staff also prefer to base their judgments on relative rather than absolute (external) standards; that is, they want to assess progress individually as compared to where the child started:

> What matters is how far students have come, not whether they're at grade level. (Teacher)

> I would judge students' gains by where they started and the amount of instruction they received. (Administrator)

Parents, understandably, rely primarily on observation of their own child. For example:

> I know whether my child can read by observing him. I have seen increases in the number of books he brings home, and the amount of time he spends reading and this is evidence to me that the program is helping my child. (Parent)

Additionally, staff frequently expressed an interest in basing judgments on the long-term impact of the program—information rarely contained in evaluation reports. For example:

> I would like to know how the students do in ninth grade as judged by their teachers. Are the gains sticking? Will they graduate? Are they interested in school? (Principal)

As some of the above quotations indicate, staff and parents are also interested in noncognitive child outcomes, although it is generally agreed that there are few, if any, good noncognitive measures. Usually staff and parents cite their own observations or those of others. Some examples are:

> To convince someone the program was good, I would use the Reading Inventory Test of Skills, even though it is not normed. Also, I would use observation of students' motivations to see changes in personality and attitude. (Administrator)

> To see if the program was effective, I would look at four things: how well the students were doing in other classes, especially in areas that first caused them to come to the reading lab, pre- and posttest scores on the ICRT, teacher reports, and the students' attitudes to the programs. (Teacher)

> The program is successful if students get attached to their teacher, if they want to go to the program. You also know something special is going on if students not in the program want to join it. Parents get a sense of the program and communicate it to their children too. (Principal)

> The program is effective if children know what they are doing. (Teacher)

Generally then, school staff express interest in areas such as student attitude and self-concept, although formal measures are rarely cited as information sources for these areas.

In addition to judging program effectiveness on the basis of information about the participants, either cognitive or noncognitive, some staff expressed interest in the effect of the program on groups other than children. Some examples are:

> There are lots of ways of telling if the program is effective. Test scores are one. Others are the working relationships, the atmosphere and community attitudes toward the program; perhaps the last is most important. The community lets you know if anything is wrong. (Principal)

> Yes, the program is a success because the parents and the kids think it is help-

ful and the teachers are enthusiastic. (Administrator)

After initial resistance, the staff has become supportive and you can tell it [the program] is a success when teachers say good things about the kids. (Principal)

Overall, although most staff are concerned primarily with the program's impact on children, there is interest in knowing the impact of the program on the community, parents, and staff itself. As with noncognitive outcomes, however, little mention was made of formal ways of measuring these areas of interest.

How is Evaluation Used for Program Improvement?

A determination of the utility of evaluation results in program improvement must recognize two features of school districts. The first is that local districts have several levels of people involved in Title I, each with different information needs and decision-making authority. Administrators are concerned with the program as a whole; principals are concerned with their schools, teachers with their classes, and parents with their children. Although their information needs are not necessarily mutually exclusive, they often differ substantially. The second is that Title I programs are, by and large, remarkably stable. At least five of the 15 districts stated this explicity. For example:

There really isn't much program planning going on any longer. It's more a matter of continuing to operate the way they have been doing. (Director)

Major changes in the program are never made. (Teacher)

There have been no basic changes in Title I. The goals and methods are largely unchanged. (Director)

From the small number of examples cited when respondents were asked about program changes, it is clear that they are limited in all districts. Therefore, it should be kept in mind that the universe in which to find connections between program changes and evaluation is quite restricted.

Evaluations are rarely considered in the context of program improvement. One reason is that "evaluation" tends to be interpreted as a basis for someone else to judge the effectiveness of the program. Thus, "evaluation" is often associated with *accountability* rather than with information for identifying strengths and weaknesses of the program. Ironically, when test scores are referred to as "needs assessment," the reaction to them can be quite different.

A second reason is simply that evaluations are seen as *irrelevant* to program decisions. This finding is in part an inference based on staff comments concerning the overriding importance of other factors (e.g., administrative, budgetary, and political). Other indications that evaluations are viewed as irrelevant include distrust of evaluation in general and the practical constraint of timing. For example:

I doubt that testing provides the kind of information on which to base decisions. Title I was designed to let locals define needs. Local philosophies and priorities should shape the program. (Director)

Implying that the whole notion of evaluation is irrelevant, another director said:

How can you evaluate when kids are starting at different places and developing at different rates? Means don't mean anything. (Director)

Finally, if the evaluation results are not available when decisions are made, they are irrelevant. In all districts there is a delay between data collection and reporting of results. Usually the evaluation is based on a spring test administration and the results are not reported until the following fall. This means, first, that program planning for the next year has already occurred, often during the spring even prior to the administration of the posttest. Second, at the teacher level, the students who were evaluated are no longer with the same teacher. Although, theoretically, data one year out of date are not totally useless, some staff suggested that this timing did preclude utilization. Some examples are:

Evaluation reports cannot be included

in planning because plans must be submitted to the state before evaluation is available. Planning must be done at the busiest time of the year. (Evaluator)

Data from the previous spring are too late to be of use, except to purchase materials.

The only way we were able to determine any connections between evaluation and program decisions was to work backwards from program decisions previously made. We asked what changes had been made in the program and then asked why the noted changes, if any, were made. From the field notes for each of the original 15 districts, I extracted every example of a connection between a program decision and some kind of information (defined broadly). There were approximately 35 such illustrations in total. The examples should be interpreted in the light of how they were collected; to wit, we took all responses at face value. We attempted neither to trace program decisions to a primary source nor to resolve conflicting explanations from different respondents in the same district. Because no program change stems from a single cause, and perceptions of causes often differ, such a task would have been impossible within this study. For example, in one district, parents were convinced that they had been responsible for the introduction of a math component; administrators, on the other hand, felt that the program had been initiated because they perceived the need and funds were available.

About one-quarter of the illustrations cited *evaluation or test scores* as contributing to a change in the program. Two examples are:

From the survey information in the evaluation, I saw that some teachers in the school weren't as well informed about the Title I program as they should be so I made it a point to work with them more. (Teacher)

I circle the high and low posttest scores and meet with the teachers on weaknesses to consider for next year's class. (Administrator)

Several examples in this category suggested less than a compelling connection

between the test scores and the change initiated (or the change was described in such vague terms that the connection was difficult to determine). Some examples are:

I took heed to the low scores in comprehension and did some inservice. (Principal)

I look at the class results to see if anything is out of phase. I found some had dropped in math and diagnosed the problem as three different approaches being used schoolwide. So I picked the one most widely used and stopped the rest. (Principal)

We stopped serving 3-year-olds because they scored too high at the end of the year to be eligible as 4-year-olds. (Director)

These examples suggest that changes associated with test scores tend to be minor (excepting the last), and that the vagueness of the changes perhaps reflects the state-of-the-art in the field of education—limited clear remedies even when a weakness has been identified.

Another quarter of all the illustrations cited *fiscal and political considerations* as the most important factors in motivating change. Three examples are:

The math program came about because we had carryover funds accumulating and felt a need for a math program. (Principal)

Aides cost more each year so we have to eliminate some. (Principal)

The math program was started because the state suggested it. (Director)

I suspect that budgetary and political considerations are even more influential than the total number of illustrations suggests but would tend to be mentioned less often, particularly in the context of an interview directed at local utilization of evaluation.

The largest category of illustrations (over one-third) cited *subjective information.* Most of these illustrations suggest that changes were based primarily on staff observation of the program. Some examples are:

I will expand the content area of the reading lab to science because of the success I have had using social studies materials, because science is interesting to the students, and because I hope to help them improve their work in other classes. (Teacher)

We use informal evaluation (teacher experience) to modify the curriculum and use trial and error to find the right activities. The big decisions (e.g., dropping kindergarten, food, etc.) are political and administrative. If hard data are available and on the right side, things are easier to sell. (Director)

Changes are often based on questionnaires filled out by teachers and principals and on my observation. (Administrator)

Several examples in this category indicate a major concern with program manageability and teaching philosophy. Some examples are:

We chose a new reading series because we felt we needed a less individualized approach and more direct contact. So we had the faculty evaluate several and also visited other schools to look at it and the scores. The faculty liked it because it gave introductions to stories and had built-in testing. (Principal)

We chose a new math program because the existing curriculum wasn't unified. We wanted the same program in kindergarten through sixth grade. Thus we looked at materials. Second, we looked at whether it would be effective. We did this by involving the whole staff, recommendations from the district, and we knew we wanted one that didn't rely heavily on reading and that had built-in tests. (Teacher)

Finally, there were three examples that suggested use of evaluative information, but not that information reported formally in the evaluation. The three examples are:

One school claimed that their self-concept program was great so I measured it and found no gains. This got them to think more about what they were doing and what they expected. (Evaluator)

We have made a major change based on 3 years of files from problem-solving sessions with teachers. We reduced record keeping and increased small group

activities. We also changed class size based on teachers' recommendations and changed materials distribution and space based on their recommendations. (Administrator)

I got interested in unobtrusive measures to assess library use. I got a librarian to cooperate and had him checking to see if Title I kids were reading as much. They were but it tended to be the easier books. So the librarian ordered more easy books that would be of interest to the older kids—stuff that would not embarrass them. (Evaluator)

In summary, there are so few examples altogether of connections between program changes and information that it is risky to generalize from them. The fact that so few exist, especially examples in which evaluation was used, is by far the most important finding.

Interpretation of the Findings

The stated reasons for not using evaluations tend to focus on the characteristics of the information in the evaluation. Standardized achievement test scores, the backbone of Title I evaluations, are viewed as inadequate at best for program judgments and planning. Reasons expressed for this view range from the limitations of these tests in measuring the attainment of specific skills to the omission of measures of other outcomes considered important, such as children's attitudes and parental involvement. These stated reasons imply that if the type of evaluative information reported were changed, use of the information would increase. However, a close reading of all the statements of the respondents suggests otherwise. The statements in toto suggest that there are constraints on evaluation use imposed by the context and structure of the programs, as well as unstated explanations for not using evaluation results, both of which must be addressed directly if use of evaluation in program planning is to increase. Merely changing the type of information reported is insufficient in itself.

The Context of Title I Programs

Two constraints on the use of evaluations posed by characteristics of the program and its evaluation were mentioned above. First, programs tend to be quite stable, thus limiting the universe in which changes are likely to be made, whether based on evaluations or not. Second, the timing of the evaluation can, by itself, restrict its potential utility by not meshing with the timing of program planning. Because evaluation results are generally reported after the planning has occurred, their use is at best limited to that of year-old data.

Several other constraints imposed by the structure of programs were observed, if not stated directly by respondents. Perhaps most important is the fact that, in almost every district, there is little connection between program staff and evaluation staff. This is a function of the administrative structure of the program in almost every district. The person or persons responsible for the administration and the content of the program are not those who are responsible for the design and conduct of the evaluation. Additionally, the evaluator, particularly when he/she is external to the program staff, reports only to the Title I director and is usually completely isolated from the program. As one evaluator stated:

> I don't know whether the test scores are useful as a basis for making changes in the program because I don't deal with the content of the program. (Evaluator)

Similarly, an external evaluator expressed distance from the program by saying:

> I am not involved with the program or process evaluation. My main audience is the education department of the district and the state. (Evaluator)

There were two districts in which this gap was bridged, but not without considerable effort on the part of an administrator in one and the evaluator in the other.

Another difficulty posed by the system is that a Title I program contains multiple potential audiences for evaluation, each of which has different information needs. Title I evaluation is frequently discussed in terms of meeting Federal, state, and local needs; often overlooked in this context, however, is the fact that each LEA is a complex organization itself, with several levels from the director to curriculum supervisors or other intermediate administrators to principals and teachers, as well as parents.

Finally, there is a general constraint on using evaluation that stems not from the specific context of each district but from the state-of-the-art in educational treatments. Ideally, evaluation is expected to provide evidence on the strengths and weaknesses of programs that can in turn guide planners on directions in which their programs can be improved. This ideal presupposes, however, that if a weakness is identified, there are one or more potential remedies available. The limited knowledge on what constitutes a successful strategy in educational treatments, therefore, limits the extent to which evaluation can be fully utilized, both from the lack of proven alternatives and from the feelings of frustration that this lack produces. This is not meant to imply that there is a magic solution just around the corner, but rather that education is a difficult if not impossible area in which to apply fully a rational model of evaluation as a guide to decision making.

The constraints of the system are not necessarily permanent fixtures, but they do characterize the current state of affairs in the districts visited, and, I suspect, in most others. As such, they not only limit uses of evaluation directly, but also strongly affect how individuals in the system perceive evaluation. The isolation of the evaluator from the program, the relative stability of programs, and the timing of evaluations together contribute to a climate that is not conducive to viewing evaluation as a potentially constructive tool. This climate provides an important perspective for understanding why individuals in the system view evaluation as they do. This view, gleaned from looking beyond what respondents said, is described next.

Underlying Attitudes Toward Evaluation

Two facts about the state of mind of local staff suggest strongly that, regardless of the type or quality of the evaluation data, the data are not likely to be favorably received and, hence, not used. The first is the narrow and usually negative way in which evaluation is perceived and the second is the strong motivation of individuals to protect their basic beliefs.

Put in the simplest terms by one evaluator: "Evaluation is a dirty word." In general, evaluation is viewed as a set of procedures designed to provide one's superiors with information on which to judge the program's success, on the basis of criteria defined by the superiors. Evaluation is therefore more likely to be associated with the threat of accountability to someone else than with its potential as a useful source of information for one's self. To the extent that the evaluation questions and criteria for success are imposed externally and that the evaluation is conducted primarily to meet externally imposed requirements, this negative view of evaluation is reinforced by actual experience. Furthermore, its threatening nature is exacerbated by the psychological distance between evaluation and program staff. As long as evaluation is viewed in this narrow and essentially threatening way, it is doubtful that the information it contains will be used, regardless of its characteristics.

The second state of mind can be characterized as the "true believer" syndrome. It is common knowledge that an individual deeply committed to a particular belief is not likely to change that belief merely because "objective" evidence against the belief is presented. Politics and religion abound with relevant examples. This is not to imply that local Title I staff and parents are akin to religious zealots, but they are by and large strongly committed to their programs. When people invest their time and energy in a cause they view as worthy, they will seek out and readily accept evidence that their work has not been in vain. Likewise, they will ignore or explain away information that suggests they have failed. Title I staff, particularly those involved daily in implementing the program, often invest considerable energy in their work because they view it as important and worthwhile. Therefore, it is not surprising that they interpret evaluation results selectively, accepting the positive and rejecting the negative. As one director said,

"We are successful even if we can't show it on paper."

Conclusion

From this analysis, I conclude that changing the type or quality of information contained in the evaluations will not, by itself, affect the level of evaluation utilization. But simply changing the nature of the information is the focal point of the USOE evaluation models and the primary role of the TAC's, which is to assist in the implementation of the models. The models address only the "symptoms," that is, technical weaknesses of the outcome measures and procedures for data collection and analysis. I suggest that this approach, and any approach that focuses exclusively on the information contained in the evaluations, cannot by itself significantly affect local use of evaluation. Instead, changes in the evaluation system designed to increase local utilization must address the underlying reasons for lack of use, including individual attitudes and beliefs about the program and evaluation. At the same time, such a system must address those elements of the context amenable to change that reinforce existing negative views toward evaluation.

Tackling the area of attitude change is obviously far more challenging than merely changing the test or metric, but it is not beyond reach. The fact that there are even a few instances of evaluation use in program decisions suggests that increased use of evaluation is possible. This fact, together with an understanding of the impediments to use of data, point to some promising directions for the shaping of a Federal strategy that can increase local use of evaluation.

Implications for Policy

Of the two current Federal strategies for Title I evaluation, an independent national study and the three-tiered reporting scheme, only the latter has the potential to encourage local use of evaluation. Because independent national studies are generally agreed to be the best source for providing evidence of the national impact of Title I, it should be possible to emphasize local use of evaluation in the three-tiered reporting system without sacrificing a source for national impact data. Therefore, the implications discussed below take the form of recommendations for changing the emphasis of the three-tiered reporting system to one that encourages local use of the evaluation data.

First of all, any strategy designed to increase local use of evaluation must be grounded in a Federal commitment to this goal—a commitment that must be understood and shared by the states and communicated clearly to local districts. As long as districts collect data primarily or exclusively for state and Federal use, they are unlikely to change their views toward evaluation. This suggests, at the least, that deadlines for evaluation reporting should be coordinated with the local planning cycle.

Second, districts need assistance in increasing communication and cooperation between program staff and evaluation staff. Our visits suggest that the provision of feedback can be used as one way to facilitate understanding between program and evaluation staff. However, the information fed back must be designed in a way that makes it clearly understandable to staff and parents and must address the different needs of different levels within a district. For example, a curriculum supervisor overseeing a program in six schools views the program from a different perspective and has information needs different from those of a classroom teacher. Additionally, the findings suggest that results should be presented in person if they are to be clearly understood and, hence, utilized by staff.

Finally, Title I staff and parents need assistance in developing an understanding of the constructive role which evaluation can play and in acquiring certain types of nontechnical evaluation skills. Incorporating evaluation information into planning and decision making is not an automatic process, yet it is one in which local staff have received little if any training. In particular, they need assistance in learning how to ask their own evaluation questions. If the primary purpose of evaluation remains that of answering questions imposed externally, the evaluation will continue to be potentially more threatening than helpful. If, on the other hand, the evaluation responds to questions about program effectiveness that the staff have expressed interest in, the potential for using the results should increase dramatically. Until Title I staff and parents come to see Title I as a program to be improved continually based in part on evaluation, the evaluation results, even if technically sound, will fall on deaf ears.

Author

JANE L. DAVID, President, Bay Area Research Group, 385 Sherman Ave., Suite 3, Palo Alto, CA 94306. *Specializations:* Policy research and Evaluation.

28

The Validity of the Title I Evaluation and Reporting System

Robert L. Linn, Stephen B. Dunbar, Delwyn L. Harnisch, and C. Nicholas Hastings

Based on results of tests administered to 298,833 third-grade students in the fall of 1979 and again in the spring of 1980, the estimated gain in reading achievement due to Title I participation for the nation as a whole is 7.3 NCEs. The corresponding gain in mathematics achievement for 2464 fourth-grade Title I participants in the State of Kentucky was 9.4, while 36 second graders in reading project number 0115A showed a gain in reading achievement of 12.1 NCEs. These are but three among thousands of numbers produced by the Title I Evaluation and Reporting System, TIERS. These numbers are purported to answer the question: "How much more did students learn by participating in the Title I project than they would have learned without it?" (Tallmadge & Wood, 1976, p. 2). The purpose of this chapter is to evaluate the trustworthiness of the answers to this basic question derived from TIERS.

The focus of this chapter is on the technical adequacy of TIERS. The guiding question for our analysis is: "How valid are the estimates of the impact of Title I on student achievement that are derived from TIERS?" This seemingly straightforward question has many facets and is subject to several interpretations. For example, the system is designed to provide information about the impact of Title I at the local, state, and national levels. The importance of factors that affect the validity of estimates and the conclusions that are based on them may differ substantially at different levels of aggregation.

Questions of validity may be interpreted narrowly (e.g., Are the scores reported for a particular test accurate?) or broadly (e.g., Is Title I effective in improving the achievement of participating students?). Although the broader questions are generally more difficult to answer and require more interpretation, they are also more important and will guide much of our discussion.

Authors' Note: This report was prepared pursuant to the U.S. Department of Education contract 300-82-0009. It does not, however, necessarily reflect the views of that agency. We thank Leigh Burstein and Richard Jaeger for their advice on the project and critique of drafts. We also thank the many people involved with Title I evaluations at local or state levels, at Technical Assistance Centers, and at RMC Research Corporation who provided us with information and advice.

From Robert L. Linn, Stephen B. Dunbar, Delwyn L. Harnisch, and C. Nicholas Hastings, "The Validity of the Title I Evaluation and Reporting System," original manuscript.

ESTIMATED PROJECT IMPACT

TIERS is designed to provide information on several aspects of Title I projects. A good deal of the information is decriptive in nature. For example, TIERS provides data on the number of students participating in Title I projects, on the extent of parental involvement in school advisory councils, on Title I staff, and the on the type of services provided to participating students. The primary focus, however, is on student achievement in the basic skills, reading, language arts, and mathematics. Estimates of impact on student achievement are obtained at the project level, which might, for example, involve a half-dozen students who are pulled out of their regular classes for three or four hours a week and given special instruction in reading by a Title I teacher. On the other hand, a "project" may have several hundred participating students who receive instruction from dozens of different teachers at a variety of school buildings within a district. Thus, the term "project" has rather diverse meanings.

Data from individual projects are reported to an LEA which, in turn, analyzes, summarizes, and reports them to the SEA. Additional analyses and summarizations occur at the state level in preparing the State Title I Report and in transmitting the information to the federal level. The estimated gains in achievement listed in the opening paragraph of this chapter are three of thousands of estimates that result from this process.

What does it mean to say that third-grade Title I participants gained 7.3 NCEs from fall to spring? This is an overall estimate of the typical or average impact of Title I, which is obtained by comparing the achievement test results that are actually obtained in the spring with the "no-project expectations." The latter value is based on the performance of the participants when tested in the fall in comparison to normative data reported by publishers of standardized tests. A value of zero is intended to be indicative of no positive impact of Title I beyond what would have resulted without it. Any positive number is supposed to indicate a beneficial effect of participation in Title I.

The estimated gains are reported using a scale called Normal Curve Equivalents, or NCEs. This scale ranges from 1 to 99 and is based on normative data provided by test publishers. NCEs and percentile ranks have the same numerical value at 1, 50, and 99. They differ at intermediate values but there is a unique percentile rank associated with each NCE. For example, an NCE of 10 corresponds to a percentile rank of 23. In other words, 23% of the norm group score below an NCE of 10.

The gain of 7.3 NCEs may be made more concrete by reference to the actual fall and spring results. In the fall, the mean reading achievement of third-grade Title I participants was 28.6 NCEs and by spring it was 35.9 for a gain of 7.3. In more familiar terms, the average Title I third-grade student scored higher than only 15.5% of all third graders in the test publishers' normative samples when tested in the fall, but when retested in the spring the average Title I student scored higher than 25.1% of all such students.[1] In the absence of Title I, it is assumed that the standing of participants would have remained constant relative to the national norm.

The gain of 7.3 NCEs (or from the 15th to the 25th percentile) sounds good, but there are many questions that need answers before it can be accepted. This is clearly recognized in the Education Department Annual Evaluation Report from which the number was obtained. In that report it is noted that the results "must be viewed with great caution, since these data: (1) are based on scores aggregated across many different tests, of varying quality and appropriateness, and administered under locally controlled conditions; (2) in some situations were obtained in States or district implementing new evaluation procedures for the first time; and (3) in some situations quality control procedures may not have been adequately implemented" (Annual Evaluation Report on Education Programs, 1982, p. 30). The remainder of this chapter is devoted to evaluating the seriousness of these and other threats to the validity of the estimates of impact and to suggesting, where possible, ways of alleviating problems.

VALIDITY OF THE ESTIMATES

There are numerous factors, some already mentioned, that may affect the validity of the estimates of impact on student achievement. Questions may be asked about comparability of results based on the use of different evaluation models, of different testing patterns, and of different tests. Testing conditions, sample attrition, and quality control are but a few of the technical issues that are of potential concern. Moreover, the tenability of the basic assumptions used to derive the "no-project expectation," which is the fundamental benchmark for any of the estimates, is subject to serious question. We have attempted to deal with the most cricitical concerns in as nontechnical a way as possible. More technical discussion, where necessary, has been reserved for a separate report.

Three basic models were developed and refined by RMC Research Corporation for inclusion in TIERS. Variations are allowed in each of the models and, with appropriate approval, however, there is only Model A, the norm-referenced model, since use of the other recommended models, or of approved exceptions, is extremely rare, accounting for only about 1% of the project evaluations. Consequently, we have focused almost exclusively on Model A.[2] In discussing Model A and its implementation, we focus on the cumulative effects of statistical artifacts, unrepresentative norms, conversion errors, student selection, test administration procedures, attrition, and practice effects on the validity of estimates derived from TIERS.

MODEL A

Test publisher norms provide the basis for the "no-project expectation" in Model A. It is simply assumed that, in the absence of participation in a Title I project, participants would maintain, on the average, a constant position relative to the norm. For example, if on the average, participants scored higher before the project than 20% of the nation's students in the same grade and at the same time of year, then they would be expected to score higher than 20% of all students following the project. Since students in the norm group improve their skills and score higher at the time of the second test than at the time of the first test, the project participants would have to get more answers right at the time of the second testing in order to maintain a constant percentile rank. To show a positive estimated impact, the Title I group would have to gain faster than the norm.

The assumption of constant relative standing in the absence of a project, commonly called the "equipercentile assumption," has been questioned by a number of authors. The assumption has been challenged because it is inconsistent with established statistical theory,[3] because the target group in Title I evaluations may not be well represented in the norm group, and because the norms are obtained under testing conditions that may differ from those used in the Title I evaluation.

Statistical Artifacts

The models developed by RMC Research Corporation were designed to minimize a statistical artifact, known as the regression effect, that is frequently a serious problem in evaluation studies. If properly implemented, Model A procedures clearly reduce the bias in estimates of project impact due to the regression effect. A careful analysis shows, however, that the regression effect is reduced but not completely eliminated by use of Model A. In other words, based on statistical theory, there are reasons to expect the estimated gains produced by Model A to be somewhat too large (see Glass, 1978, or Linn, 1980, for discussions of these reasons).

Research conducted primarily by staff of the RMC Research Corporation (see, for example, A.O.H. Roberts, 1980b; Tallmadge, in press; and Wood, 1980) has convincingly shown that, although there is a bias in the estimates of gain in the direction that is predicted from statistical theory, the bias is not large. As summarized by Tallmadge (in press), "The bias appears to be positive and on the order of 1 NCE when typical Title I groups are examined." In other words, the estimated gain is artificially inflated due to a statistical artifact by about 1 NCE. An adjustment for this small, but systematic, bias in the estimated gain would be simple and possibly worthwhile. As will be seen, however, it is not the most serious threat to validity.

Relevance and Quality of Norms

The validity of the TIERS results depends on the quality of normative data and the comparability of the testing for normative and for Title I evaluation purposes. For an evaluation, only students who are tested before and after (the pretest and the posttest) are included in the estimate of the impact of a Title I project. Publishers' norms relevant for the pretest and for the posttest, however, typically include students who are tested one time but not the other. In the case of a spring-to-spring testing pattern, the norms are based on entirely different students. For a fall-to-spring testing pattern the norms are usually based on a mixture of students tested on both occasions and tested on only one of them. Seventy percent of the school districts included in the fall norms of one test publisher, for example, also participated in the spring norming. Another publisher had all the districts participate on both occasions. A third publisher reported overlap of about 20% of the students.

Results for students tested both in the fall and in the spring (longitudinal norms) are somewhat different than those for all students tested on either occasion (cross-sectional norms). Results reported by Kaskowitz and Norwood (1977) for one major test publisher suggest that the practice of comparing the longitudinal data required for Title I evaluation to cross sectional norms provided by a test publisher results in a small positive bias of roughly 1 NCE on the average. Although this result is based on only one test and must be viewed with some caution, it still suggests that the use of cross-sectional norms causes a small bias due to statistical regression discussed above. These biases work to inflate the estimated gains and the effects can be expected to be cumulative. Together they may mean that the gains are overstated by roughly 2 NCEs.

In addition to the question of appropriateness of cross-sectional norms for longitudinal evaluation data, questions have been raised about the relevance and representativeness of the norms. Test publishers must rely on voluntary cooperation of school districts to collect normative data. Districts are scientifically selected by publishers to yield norms that are representative of the nation as a whole. But, many of the selected districts decline to participate. Indeed, according to Baglin (1981), invited districts are more apt to refuse than to agree to participate. Consequently, the "purportedly random 'national' norming sample are not at all random. . . . In other words, each test is normed on a nonrepresentative, nonrandom cross section of the population" (Baglin, 1981), p. 105). Not only are participation rates low, but they have apparently declined substantially from what they were in the past.

The impact of lack of representativeness of publisher norms on the validity of TIERS is problematic. Representativeness would clearly be crucial if the focus in TIERS were on the students' level of achievement at one point in time. The focus in TIERS, however, is on gains relative to the norm rather than on assessing achievement status, and even nonrepresentative norms may provide a useful benchmark for this purpose. On the other hand, it is true that different normative samples can produce different estimates of NCE gains from a given set of test results (see, for example, S. J. Roberts, 1980). What remains unclear is whether the differences due to nonrepresentativeness are consistent across publishers and, if so, whether the bias this introduces inflates or deflates the estimates of gain. Thus, lack of representativeness increases uncertainty regarding validity but does not necessarily bias the estimates.

Conversion Errors

In order to obtain NCE scores, tests must first be scored by counting the number of correct answers. The result is known as a "raw score," which must be transformed to NCEs by use of normative tables provided by publishers. Often the conversion is a two-step process. Raw scores are entered into a table to find a corresponding percentile rank and percentile ranks are then converted to NCEs by another table look-up.

States and districts vary in the degree to which this conversion process is automated. In some instances all of the conversion is done by machine. In other instances, Title I teachers or other local staff score the tests and convert the raw scores to percentile ranks. The final conversion to NCEs is then done more centrally at the district or state level.

A certain amount of human error in recording scores and converting raw scores to percentiles is bound to occur. Studies (e.g., Elman, 1981; Finley, 1979) provide evidence that it is indeed the case that project level report forms contain a substantial number of errors of various kinds. Moreover, Elman's results indicate that conversion errors inflate the estimated gains much more frequently than they deflate them, creating a positive bias somewhat larger than 1 NCE. Again, this bias is in the same direction, toward inflated gains, as the two previously identified biases.

Cumulatively, the three systematic sources of bias considered so far amount to roughly 3 NCEs. The third source of bias only applies to districts and states relying on manual conversion of scores at the local level, however. Uniform adoption of currently available computer-based conversion systems could effectively remove this source of bias.

Student Selection

In the majority of the project evaluations for TIERS, a "pretest" is administered in the fall and is used to derive the "no-project expectation" against which the "posttest" scores obtained the following spring are judged to determine gain. The standard version of Model A, which is used in almost all cases to estimate the gains, requires that "pretest scores . . . play *no* part in the selection process because this will introduce a bias" (Tallmadge & Wood, 1981, p. 29, emphasis in the original). The developers of Model A had sound statistical reasons for the above requirement and the statement that student selection on the pretest will create bias is quite right.[4] If this model requirement is violated, the estimated gains are artificially inflated. The magnitude of the bias depends on the use of the pretest scores for selection, but the direction of the bias is once again toward an overstatement of gains.

Cautions against the use of the pretest for selection of project participants may have been relatively effective in preventing a major bias due to this misapplication of the model. Based on interviews conducted, however, we concluded that some subtle violations of the stricture against *any* use of pretest scores occur. Intending to comply with the guidelines, students may be selected for the Title I project prior to administration of the pretest. This may be done appropriately using previous test results, teacher judgments, or a combination of the two. So far, so good, but then the pretest is administered and a few of the selected students do better on it than had been expected. It seems intuitively reasonable to use this new information and reverse the initial decision for those students and, indeed, such selection out of Title I on the basis of pretest scores does occur.

Although using pretest scores in this way may be educationally sound, it introduces a bias that tends to make the estimated gains too large. In the words of one of the evaluators we interviewed, there is a "selection-evaluation dilemma." The goal of doing the best possible job of selecting students from an educational point of view may sometimes conflict with what is needed for the most valid evaluation.

We do not have, from available studies, a good basis for estimating the extent of the problem caused by partial selection on the pretest. However, it is one more source of bias in the direction of inflating gain estimates, and while the bias due to this source may be small, it adds to the cumulative bias in the direction of overestimating the impact of Title I.

Attrition by "Graduation"

Students who change schools between the time of the pretest and the posttest are not included in the estimation of gains. As stated in the section on norms, the loss of these students tends to introduce a positive bias in the estimates. However, students who are taken out of the Title I project may also be lost for purposes of the evaluation. If students are taken out of the Title I project because of their high achievement, but not included in the test results, then the gains for the project would be understated. It is important that test results for such midyear "graduates" of the project be obtained and included in the estimates. We lack evidence regarding the extent to which this is done. It could be a source of negative bias in contrast to all the other biases so far identified.

Administration Conditions

When tests are normed they are generally administered to intact classrooms and there is little riding on the outcome for teachers or students. In Title I evaluations on the other hand, the tests are often administered to small groups, e.g., to a group of students who have been removed from their regular classrooms for special instruction by a Title I teacher. There is also a reason to want test scores to be higher in the spring than in the fall. One need not invoke a conspiracy theory or accuse teachers of intentionally cheating by altering time limits or giving answers to students to conclude that administrative conditions tend to favor positive results. Such flagrant practices may occur but we suspect that they are extremely rare, causing no serious distortion of the overall results.

More subtle variations in test administration conditions are apt to be more common and we believe these variations contribute some unknown amount to the cumulative positive bias. One of the people we interviewed, a person with considerable experience with testing and program evaluation, told of an experience he had when working on a testing program where a test administrator complained that the time limits for the test were too stringent leading to failures to complete the test and lower scores. The "problem" disappeared when the students were warned before the test that they would have a limited amount of time and the time remaining was periodically posted at the front of the room during the test. Such "minor" variations in administration conditions or the presence or absence of pep talks stressing the importance of an exam can affect the results. When there is pressure to achieve a particular result, higher spring than fall scores, the effect, even with the best of intentions is apt to be in the direction of producing the desired result. Studies in other contexts of experimenter bias (e.g., Rosenthal, 1966) support this general conclusion.

Administration Dates

The rules for implementing Model A call for the administration of tests within two weeks of the test publisher's norming date. This rule is intended to reduce bias in the estimates caused by using norms obtained at one time of the school year as the benchmark for judging test results of a test administered at a different time of year. By administering the pretest two weeks before the fall norming date and the posttest two weeks after the spring testing date, however, it is still possible to have four more weeks of instruction for project participants between test administrations than was available between normative dates. Following the above testing pattern would tend to inflate the estimates of gain. Recognizing this potential, some states have added a requirement that the deviations of test administration dates from the norming dates in the fall and spring be considered together so that the difference in the fall-to-spring interval is no more than fourteen days. Such a requirement is potentially useful for reducing the bias. As is discussed below, however, the bigger need is to switch from the predominant fall-to-spring testing cycle to an annual testing cycle.

Practice Effects, Teaching to the Test, and Learning

Evidence provided by A.O.H. Roberts (1980a) based on a careful review of the literature is quite consistent and supports several conclusions regarding practice effects, "test-wiseness," and the effects of coaching students for tests.

(1) Practice at taking tests tends to yield score increases at all grade levels.
(2) The gains are larger at the early grades, especially grades 1 and 2 and kindergarten, than at the later grades.
(3) Multiple test exposures yield additional, but rapidly diminishing, returns.
(4) Coaching or explicit instruction in test-taking skills can have sizable effects, sometimes on the order of magnitude of 5 NCEs.

(5) Test publisher norms reflect increasing test-wiseness of students, but cannot compensate for variations in the typical frequencies with which students are tested.

It is important, albeit often very difficult, to distinguish between test-specific learning and learning that is more generalizable, with test performance being just one of a variety of possible indicators. The common concern of a Title I project presumably is not with test performance, per se, but only inasuch as the performance is indicative of the students' skills, knowledge, and understanding. The dilemma for evaluators and for those who would rely upon test results produced in an evaluation was well summarized almost 20 years ago by Cronbach (1963), who argued that:

> The demand that tests be closely matched to the aims of a course reflects awareness that examinations of the usual sort "determine what is taught." If questions are known in advance, students give more attention to learning their answers than to learning other aspects of the course. This is not necessarily detrimental. Whenever it is critically important to master certain content, the knowledge that it will be tested produces a desirable concentration of effort. On the other hand, learning the answer to a set of questions is by no means the same as acquiring understanding of whatever topic that question represents (p. 681).

One of the features of TIERS has the potential of being both a strength and a weakness in regard to the dilemma articulated by Cronbach. The flexibility in the choice of a test that is built into TIERS enables districts to select a test that is judged to be most appropriate for the particular program. The *User's Guide* stresses the importance of selecting an appropriate test, noting that "the content of the test must match the content of the instructional program being evaluated" (Tallmadge & Wood, 1981, p. 74). This is sensible advice, because it is clear that "the content of the achievement test used to evaluate a program is critical to the resulting estimate of its effectiveness" (Jaeger, 1981, p. 6), but several questions need consideration in interpreting the results. For example:

- If the content of the test and the instruction is better matched in the project evaluation than in the test publishers' norming studies, do the norms provide a fair comparison?
- Are the results generalizable, or are the students "learning the answers" to a specific set of questions rather than "acquiring understanding"?

These are important questions, but they are not ones that have been addressed by the host of studies of the technical quality of TIERS that have been undertaken. Hence, we lack a solid basis for estimating the effects of test-specific instruction on the estimation and interpretation of project impact. Indirect evidence from several sources, however, suggests that some inflation of gains is to be expected as the result of learning that is specific to the text.

In addition, apparently trivial changes in the way a question is asked can influence results. Whether additional problems are presented horizontally or vertically, for example, influences scores. More importantly, the scores are affected by the match between the way the problems are presented in the instructional materials and on the test (Alderman, Swinton, & Braswell, 1979; Glass, 1978). Other researchers (e.g., Leinhardt & Seewald, 1981) have reinforced the belief that the match between what is taught and what is tested is vitally important. There is also evidence that superficially similar tests vary greatly in the specifics of content coverage (e.g., Hoepfner, 1978). Careful selection of the test and/or the instructional materials to enhance the match provides a project with a net advantage in comparison to the norms against which the gains are judged but leaves doubts about the effectiveness of the project in terms of generalizations beyond the specific test (see House, 1979, pp. 409-411).

Limitations of the Mean

The entire focus of TIERS is on the average gain. While this focus is understandable, changes in means cannot be expected to tell the whole story. An average gain of five points, for example, could result from all participants gaining a low while the initially lowest-scoring participants gain essentially nothing, or from a variety of other patterns. Hence, it would be desirable to have information not only about the changes in the means, but about the changes in the proportion of participants scoring below specified NCE scores. The latter information could be useful in judging how effective Title I is at raising the floor of the achievement distribution.

CUMULATIVE EFFECTS

A number of threats to the validity of the TIERS estimates of impact have been briefly reviewed. In some instances (e.g., attrition or the lack of representativeness in the norms), threats increase uncertainty regarding the interpretation of the results but do not necessarily bias the estimated gains in one direction or the other. This is also true of a variety of other threats to validity (e.g., floor or ceiling effects caused by tests that are too hard or too easy, and errors in test equating) that were not discussed due to space limitations.[5] In mose cases, however, each threat to validity was found to lead to a small but systematic bias that causes the impact of the program to be overestimated. No single source of bias was large enough, by itself, to invalidate the results. But, the effects are cumulative and in the same direction. Together, they probably account for most of the relatively large estimated gains obtained for the bulk of the 1979-1980 results, which were based on a fall-to-spring testing pattern.

This conclusion is consistent not only with the above analysis of individual threats to validity of the estimates, but with other sources of evidence that support the conclusion that the effect of Title I on student achievement is positive, but quite small—much smaller than the fall-to-spring results would suggest.

Two major national studies, the "Compensatory Reading Study" (Trismen, Waller, & Wilder, 1975), and the "Sustaining Effects Study" (e.g., Wang, Bear,

Conklin, & Hoepfner, 1981), support the conclusion that compensatory education services provided through Title I result in small increases in student achievement in reading and/or mathematics. The order of magnitude of the effect is closer to 1 or 2 NCEs in these studies than to the 6 to 9 NCEs estimated from TIERS for the fall-to-spring testing pattern. In other words, rather than estimating that Title I services move a typical third grader from the 16th to the 25th percentile nationally between fall and the following spring, as would follow from TIERS, the gain is more nearly from the 16th to the 17th or 18th percentile.

Corroborative evidence that the fall-to-spring TIERS estimates are artificially large is provided by other data from TIERS itself. Although fall and spring testing is the predominant pattern, used for roughly three-fourths of the students, there is still a sizable number of students (roughly 100,000 per grade in grades 2 thru 6), who are tested on an annual testing cycle. As can be seen in Figure 1, the annual testing cycle results yield estimated gains that are considerably smaller than those obtained from fall to spring. The annual testing cycle results are also much more consistent with previous findings from national studies.

The dashed lines in Figure 1 connect the pretest and posttest averages of students tested on an annual basis (usually spring of one year to spring of the next year). The solid lines show the corresponding results for participants tested on a fall-to-spring testing cycle. The typical gain for the annual testing cycle is approximately 2 NCEs compared to between 6 and 9 for the fall-to-spring cycle.

Based on the above analyses, we conclude that the difference in the two results is due to biases in the fall-to-spring estimates. Several of the sources of bias that we have reviewed affect only the fall-to-spring results or are apt to have a larger effect on those results than on results for an annual testing cycle. In an annual testing cycle, one year's posttest may be the next year's pretest. Thus, actions that artificially inflate the scores to yield higher gains for one year lead to a higher starting position and thereby lower gains for the next year.

Even the estimates based on an annual testing cycle are apt to have a small positive bias since some of the factors leading to bias exist for either testing cycle. For example, spring-to-spring results still are subject to small biases due to statistical regression and the use of cross-sectional norms to judge longitudinal data. Hence, an estimated impact of two NCEs is apt to be, if anything, slightly on the high side.[6]

PROJECT-LEVEL INFORMATION

TIERS was developed in response to a congressional mandate. Hence, it is not at all surprising that the creation of nationally aggregated results was the primary focus in its development and in many of the studies of the technical quality of TIERS. The system is also intended, however, to serve local and state evaluation needs and, through the activities of the Technical Assistance Centers, considerable effort has gone into improving the quality of state- and local-level evaluations.

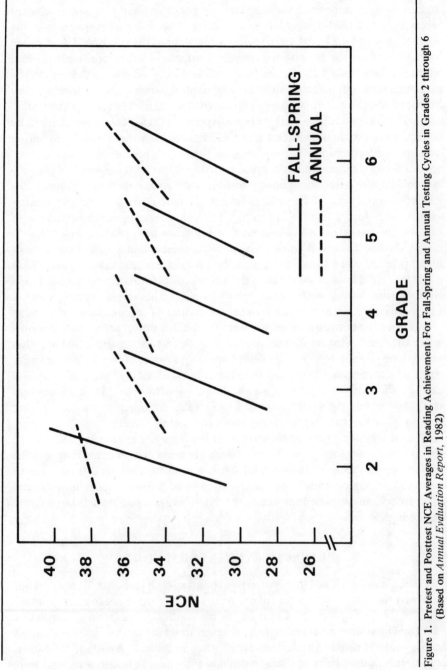

Figure 1. Pretest and Posttest NCE Averages in Reading Achievement For Fall-Spring and Annual Testing Cycles in Grades 2 through 6 (Based on *Annual Evaluation Report*, 1982)

Although efforts to improve the quality of state and local level evaluations of Title I have probably had many effects,[7] it is not our purpose to try to assess them. Our focus is much narrower. We want to know how trustworthy the estimates of project impact are and how they should be interpreted.

A great deal of aggregation has already taken place in producing state-level estimates of gains. The threats to the validity of the state-level estimates and the pitfalls in inferring that they are the result of Title I are much the same at the state and national levels. The threats to validity are also present with the results at the local level. In addition, the local-level results, especially at the level of the individual project, have the uncertainties caused by the limited number of observations.

Small sample sizes lead to large variability in estimates of gain. This is a well-established statistical principle and has been well documented in the context of TIERS by Horst (1981). For a second grade-project with 10 students, Horst estimated that a gain (or loss) anywhere between -13 and +13 NCEs could readily be attributed to a variety of factors other than the project, such as school and teacher characteristics, local testing practices, and the vagaries of chance. For larger projects, the band of uncertainty gets narrower, but is still substantial. The band is also somewhat smaller in higher grades than in the early grades. For example, with 50 participants Horst's estimated and of uncertainty is from -11 to +11 at grade 2 and from -7 to +7 at grade 5.

Even the latter interval of -7 to +7 is large, meaning, for example, that a project of 50 fifth-grade students who began the year with an average pretest score at the 25th percentile nationally (a gain of 6 NCEs) may not have had a positive effect. Such a gain might easily have resulted from the variety of nonproject factors considered by Horst. Furthermore, the majority of the projects have considerably fewer than 50 students. Slightly more than half (51.3%) of the 7608 second-grade projects reporting relatively complete data in 1979-1980 had their achievement gains estimated on fewer than 10 students. For these projects, even a gain from the 25th percentile to the 45th percentile is not compelling evidence that the project has had a positive effect since gains (or losses) of this size are not unusual for groups of 10 or fewer second-grade students where no project exists. "The fundamental problem facing local evaluators who wish to measure achievement gains of project students via a norm-referenced model is the large amount of variance inherent in the gains of *non-project* students" (Horst, 1981, p. 27).

CONCLUSIONS

(1) The predominant pattern of testing project participants in the fall to establish a benchmark against which spring test results are compared to estimate gains is subject to many sources of bias. Although no single source of bias is large enough to invalidate the results, they tend to push the results in the same

direction and the cumulative effect is large enough to make the estimated gains overstate the amount of impact by a substantial margin.

(2) An annual testing cycle produces results that are less subject to bias than those obtained from a fall-spring testing cycle. Even the gains estimated from an annual testing cycle still have a small positive bias, but it is apt to be only about 1 or possibly 2 NCEs. An annual testing cycle would substantially reduce the testing burden for Title I students as well. Title I students on a fall-spring testing cycle sometimes are required to take three standardized tests in a single school year: one as part of a regular district-wide testing program, which may be also used in selecting students for Title I projects, a pretest in the fall, and a posttest in the spring. The latter two are given solely for the purposes of TIERS. Use of an annual testing cycle could reduce the number of tests from three to one by making use of the existing district-wide testing. The same test could serve as the posttest for the previous year as well as the selection and pretest for the following year. Such use of a single test for all three purposes is made possible by the variation of Model A described in the 1981 *User's Guide* (Tallmadge & Wood, 1981, pp. 31-35). Use of this approach would not eliminate the bias inherent in the fall-spring test cycle but would even reduce the already relatively small bias in the standard version of Model A with an annual testing cycle.

(3) Models B and C and the non-normed variation of Model A suffer severely from either technical inadequacies, practical limitations, or both. Coupled with the rarity with which the variations are used, it is doubtful that the models are worth retaining except, possibly, for reasons of conveying a sense of flexibility and to accommodate a small number of districts.

(4) The uncertainties inherent in the estimated gains at the local project level, which typically have fewer than 30 students and about half the time have fewer than 10 students, make it pointless to expect "precise measures of *small* impacts based on a single fall-to-spring test cycle" (Horst, 1981, p. 37). On the basis of data from a single year they can only be expected to reliably detect exceptionally large effects. The local-level estimates of project impact should be accompanied by an indication of the degree of the estimates. This might take the form of stating estimates as a range of values rather than a single number which gives the misleading appearance of precision. Once-a-year estimates of performance level are apt to be more trustworthy and more useful than the estimated gains for small districts.

NOTES

1 The 15.5% and 25.1% are derived from the fact that an NCE of 28.6 equals a percentile rank of 15.5 and an NCE of 35.9 equals a percentile rank of 25.1.

2. Although Tallmadge and Wood (1976) stated a preference for Models B and C over Model A, a subsequent research (e.g., Stewart, 1980; Tallmadge & Wood, 1981) led to a reassessment of Model C, which was found to produce erratic and biased estimates. Model B was used in only about one-

tenth of one percent of the projects in 1970-1980 and when used, practical compromises required to implement it largely, if not entirely, eliminate the advantages of Model B (see Tallmadge, in press).

3. A well-known, albeit frequently misunderstood, statistical phenomenon known as "the regression effect" would lead to an expectation that is contrary to the equipercentile assumption.

4. There is a variation of Model A in which selection of program participants is based on the pretest. This variation has much to recommend it and will be discussed later. This variation has not been used much, if at all, to date and requires special analytical procedures, however.

5. These issues are discussed in a variety of technical reports that are available through the Title I Evaluation Clearinghouse located at the American Institute for Research, Palo Alto, California.

6. Even for the annual testing cycle, the starting performance in each grade is always below the ending performance of the previous grade. While this would seem to suggest that the gains are artificial and there is no real impact, the estimates are based on different groups of students and fewer students participate in higher grades. Thus, the overall trend may paint an overly pessimistic picture.

7. Several of the people we talked to were of the opinion that TIERS-related activities had greatly improved the understanding of tests and their use in evaluation at the state and local levels.

REFERENCES

Alderman, D. L., Swinton, S. S., & Braswell, J. S. Assessing basic arithmetic skills and understanding across curricula: Computer-assisted instruction and compensatory education. *Journal of Children's Mathematical Behavior*, 1979, *2*, 3-28.

Annual evaluation report on education programs. Washington DC: U.S. Office of Education, 1982.

Baglin, R. F. Does "nationally" normed really mean nationally? *Journal of Educational Measurement*, 1981, *18*, 97-108.

Cronbach, L. J. Course improvement through evaluation. *Teachers College Record*, 1963, *64*, 672-683.

Elman, A. *Quality control in Title I: Manual versus computer conversions of test scores*. Palo Alto, CA: American Institute for Research, May, 1981.

Finley, C. J. *What can state education agencies do to improve upon the quality of data collected from local education agencies*? Paper presented at the Annual Meeting of the American Educational Research Association, San Francisco, April, 1979.

Glass, G.V. *Regression effect*. Unpublished memorandum, March 8, 1978.

Hoepfner, R. Achievement test selection for program evaluation. In M. J. Wargo & D. R. Green (Eds.) *Achievement testing of disadvantaged and minority students for educational program evaluation*. Monterey, CA: CTB/McGraw-Hill, 1978

Horst, D. P. *Title I Evaluation and Report System: Examination of the models at the project level*. Mountain View, CA: RMC Research Corporation, March, 1981.

House, E. H. A review of reports from the National Institute of Education on the Compensatory Education Study (6 vols.). (A review of *Proceedings of the National Academy of Education* [Vol. 6].) Washington, DC: National Academy of Education, 1979.

Jaeger, R. M. *On the use of standardized achievement tests in follow through program evaluation*. (Technical Report, National Institute of Education contract No. NIE-P-80-0179.) Greensboro, NC: Center for Educational Research and Evaluation, University of North Carolina at Greensboro, January, 1981.

Kaskowitz, D. H., & Norwood, C. R. *A study of the norm-referenced procedure for evaluation project effectiveness as applied in the evaluation of project information packages*. Menlo Park, CA: Stanford Research Institute, January, 1977.

Leinhart, G., & Seewald, A. M. Overlap: What's tested, what's taught? *Journal of Educational Measurement*, 1981, *18*, 85-96.

Linn, R. L. Discussion: Regression toward the mean and the interval between test administrations. In G. Echternacht (Ed.), *New directions for testing and measurement*. 1980, *8*, 83-89.

Roberts, A.O.H. *Practice effect of test-wiseness.* Mountain View, CA: RMC Research Corporation, July, 1980.(a)

Roberts, A.O.H. Regression toward the mean and the regression-effect bias. In G. Echternacht (Ed.), *New Directions in Testing and Measurement.* 1980, *8,* 59-82.(b)

Roberts, S. J. *Differences in NCE gain estimates resulting from the use of local norms versus national norms.* Mountain View, CA: RMC Research Corporation, September, 1980.

Rosenthal, R. *Experimenter effects in behavioral research.* New York: Meredith, 1966.

Stewart, B. I. *The regression model in Title I evaluation.* Mountain View, CA: RMC Research Corporation, August, 1980.

Tallmadge, G. K. An empirical assessment of norm-referenced evaluation methodology. *Journal of Educational Measurement,* in press.

Tallmadge, G. K., & Wood, C. T. *User's Guide: ESEA Title I evaluation and reporting system.* Mountain View, CA: RMC Research Corporation, October, 1976.

Tallmadge, G. K., & Wood, C. T. *User's Guide: ESEA Title I evaluation and reporting system.* Mountain View, CA: RMC Research Corporation, 1981.

Trismen, D. A., Waller, M. I., & Wilder, G. *A descriptive and analytic study of compensatory reading programs.* (Final Report, Volume I, Contract No. DEG-0-71-3715.) Princeton, NJ: Educational Testing Service, 1975.

Wang, M., Bear, M. B., Conklin, J. E., & Hoepfner, R. *Compensatory services and educational development in the school year.* (Technical Report No. 10 from the study of Sustaining Effects of Compensatory Education on Basic Skills.) Santa Monica, CA: System Development Corporation, 1981.

Wood, C. T. *The adequacy of the equipercentile assumption in the Norm-Referenced Evaluation Model.* Mountain View, CA: RMC Research Corporation, July, 1980.

V

HEALTH

Evaluation in the health professions has increased sharply in the last decade. The articles chosen for this publication represent the diversity of methods and objects of evaluation that characterize the growth of health care and health program evaluation. Often, the assumptions, approaches, and conclusions reached in these evaluation studies raise as many questions as they provide answers.

The first article in this section, "Problems in Retrospectively Evaluating a Large-Scale Health Intervention Program," describes in detail some practical limits to health program evaluation, specifically, the evaluation associated with the Newark Childhood Lead Screening Program. In spite of the foreshadowing about "problems" in the title, one finds the revelations about the evaluation study refreshing.

The authors describe both a process and a product evaluation. The process analysis focused on three questions: How efficient were the test procedures used as a screening tools? To what extent were children with previously unrecognized undue lead absorption identified and followed? To what extent were screening results used to abate households with lead-based paint? The product analysis was used to assess impact on a grander scale, i.e., "If preventive educational efforts and environmental repairs are effective, then the incidence of undue lead absorption in the target population should diminish over time, provided that the population tested is reasonably stable, reliable measures of incidence are available, and the testing procedures are comparable over the period of observation."

Throughout the article, the authors lament their inability to "control" the evaluation in terms of research design, reliability and validity of testing instruments, and the objectives, scope, and population served. They find it difficult to evaluate after the fact. The interest in "designing experiments" as a model for evaluation is a persistent one in social program evaluation—it is based on the concern to determine "once and for all" the effects of an intervention. However, one might question the possibility of doing so in large-scale health programs, and more importantly, the desirability of manipulating the circumstances within which health programs operate for the sake of evaluation.

The next article, "An Evaluation of the Nutrition Education and Training Program: Findings from Nebraska," describes an evaluation designed as a classic randomized experiment. The evaluation "focused on assessing how well the program was implemented and the impact it had on children's nutrition-related knowledge, attitudes, preferences, and habits." The study included one pretest measure among students in treatment and control schools and two posttests. Analysis of covariance was the method of analysis. In order to couch the findings in educational theory, the authors describe a hypothetical causal chain of change. Simply put, nutrition-related knowledge leads to changes in attitudes that cause changed food preferences and finally, altered food-related behaviors. Their findings did not support the ordered chain theory.

This attempt at theory building suggests another problem of program evaluation. As an applied methodology, should program evaluations engage in "theory building," particularly when evaluations are conducted in so many particular contexts? In this example the goal is not to extend cognitive theory in any formal way, but its introduction raises questions about the purpose and scope of program evaluation.

The third article in this section, "The Geriatric Long-Stay Hospital Patient: A Canadian Case Study," represents a different approach than that advocated in the previous article. Through the case study reporting, the authors strive to tell a story of a nagging problem in hospital and long-term care facility coordination— the use of acute beds by the elderly in Manitoba. The reader soon learns that in spite of major initiatives between 1972 and 1976, such as construction of additional long-term treatment beds, expansion of home care resources, and extension of insurance coverage, the transfers of elderly from acute hospital beds to long-term care facilities took longer in 1976 than in 1972. This "foreshadowing" sets the stage for an analysis of problems and administrative choices that remain unresolved at the article's end, though the authors endorse one policy choice over others. Still, the reader begins to understand, through the descriptive use of case study methods, the strengths and weaknesses of the major health-planning initiatives.

There are problems when the authors move from description to analysis (an inevitable problem perhaps in case study methodology). The problems lie in the assumptions the authors make about what constitutes evidence of "back-ups" in the use of acute beds. The authors dismiss the possible contributing factors of general aging in the population or an increase in certain types of illnesses, and conclude that the transfer (coordination) process is the major contributing factor. This poses a problem in that the reader must accept their conclusions since the reader lacks sufficient information to reach an independent conclusion. This problem of dependence on the author as interpreter is often an argument against the value of evaluation findings, particularly those derived from case study approaches.

The next article, "Analysis of Interrupted Time Series Mortality Trends: An Example to Evaluate Regionalized Perinatal Care," outlines in detail the underlying assumptions and possible applications of "segmented or piecewise regression" to analyze historical trends in local and state perinatal postneonatal mortality trends in North Carolina. Application is made to trends (1948-1974) prior to implementation of a Regonalized Perinatal Care program. Comparable trend data are collected from a "control" region. These baseline data are to be used to estimate future trends. However, the program's impact will not be assessed until after 1981 data have been collected. This regression method permits an evaluator to study, *indirectly,* the effects of the program. It removes the need for collecting primary data by using statistics available from birth and death statistics. However, it nevertheless depends on the quality of the vital statistics.

The fifth article, "Quality Assessment by Process and Outcome Methods: Evaluation of Emergency Room Care of Asthmatic Adults," is an effort to correlate a normative, process audit with outcome criteria in an attempt to study the process of health care—in this case, the assessment of emergency room care of asthmatic adults in both a voluntary and a municipal hospital. Weighted assessment criteria in the process audit were selected from other protocols and the asthma literature and subjected to professional peer review for modification prior to use. Outcome was measured by 24-hour and 7-day follow-up telephone and personal interviews.

Although the authors find a positive and a statistically significant correlation between process and 24-hour outcome, they note that the nature of the criteria and their weighting determines the shape of the curve. No firm conclusion can be drawn. This article reveals the dilemma of normative versus clinical assessments of treatment and outcome in health care. One can potentially learn "more" (as suggested by the authors) about the quality of care—i.e., nurses roles, patterns of care in institutions—through the normative audit, but the need for clinical outcome measures, the patient's health as a result of treatment, still dictates the bottom line in much health care evaluation.

The final article in this section, "Mental Health Service Policy and Program Evaluation: Living in Sin?" is an investigation of the relationship between policymaking and evaluation and the need for independence between the two. The authors are particularly concerned that "the critical objectivity important for program evaluation may be incompatible with commitment to program support functions." The authors investigate this concern by reviewing "proper and improper relationships" between program evaluation and policymaking by illustrating examples of the policy and evaluation relationship in the history of the Community Health Centers Program and by discussing the advantages of performance contracting as outlined by Rossi in a three-step strategy for evaluating human services.

This article raises an issue that appears throughout this publication as to the goals of evaluation—is it to monitor service *processes*? To determine client/ patient/subject *outcomes*? Or both? In this case, the authors report the view of experts that "client outcome was not yet a feasible criterion for use in a (mental health program) performance-based accountability system." The authors' conclusions are to proceed with performance measures of service processes to prevent the corruption of system goals by the personal goals of staff and to ensure accountability of intended goals. It becomes apparent that a systems analysis model is the favored choice of the authors.

29

Problems in Retrospectively Evaluating a Large-Scale Health Intervention Program

Marvin A. Lavenhar, Douglas O. Gause,
James Foster, and Donald B. Louria

ABSTRACT: Some of the major problems encountered in retrospectively evaluating the effectiveness of ongoing community intervention programs, and some approaches to their solution, are illustrated through a detailed description of the methods employed to assess the performance of the Newark Childhood Lead Screening and Control Program between 1970 and 1976. A process analysis, along with a limited product analysis, provided some basis for judging the effectiveness of the intervention program, despite the absence of an a priori research design, the changing characteristics of the population screened, and the limitations to the measurements used to assess the impact of the program.

    Even though rigorous scientific control is often unattainable when evaluating community programs, some level of critical assessment of programs is needed to determine whether or not they merit continuing public support.

The need for unbiased, objective evaluation of community intervention programs in the health field has long been recognized but is still too infrequently practiced. Few programs are designed with an effective built-in evaluation component, making it difficult to measure their impact. Although well-designed evaluation strategies are often difficult to implement, the problems of evaluating large-scale interventions without an a priori evaluation plan are even more formidable. However, the growing demand for more effective performance in the face of limited financial resources has created considerable pressure for effective evaluation of new and continuing health programs.

The Newark Childhood Lead Screening Program is a typical example of a large-scale community effort that began as a crisis intervention program

At the time of this study, the authors were with the Department of Preventive Medicine and Community Health at the College of Medicine and Dentistry of New Jersey, New Jersey Medical School, Newark, New Jersey 07103. Dr. Lavenhar is now Professor and Director of the Division of Biostatistics, Mr. Foster, Clinical Instructor, and Dr. Louria, Professor and Chairman of the Department. Dr. Gause was an Instructor in the Department and is currently affiliated with Ciba-Geigy Pharmaceutical Co., Summit, N.J.

    The authors gratefully acknowledge the extensive programming and data processing support provided by Thomas Forker, M.D., and Martin Feuerman, M.A.

    A condensed version of this paper was presented at the annual meeting of the American Public Health Association, Washington, D.C., October 31, 1977.

From Marvin A. Lavenhar, Douglas O. Gause, James Foster, and Donald B. Louria, "Problems in Retrospectively Evaluating a Large-Scale Health Intervention Program," 6(3) *Journal of Community Health* 164-180 (Spring 1981). Copyright 1981 by Human Sciences Press. Reprinted by permission.

with no built-in evaluation mechanism. The following describes some of the multiple pitfalls encountered in attempting a retrospective evaluation of the impact of this changing program. The experiences drawn from the evaluation effort in Newark will be used as a basis for presenting a working example of a practical approach to evaluating a program, given a wide range of constraints.

DEFINING THE PROBLEM

The vast majority of dwelling units in Newark, New Jersey, are deteriorating; more than two thirds of the occupied housing were built prior to 1940, when most paint was lead based.[1] Although Newark has long provided a high-risk environment for the ingestion of lead-based paint chips and plaster by children, the severity of the lead hazard was not fully recognized until 1969, when three childhood deaths were attributed to lead poisoning.

The Department of Preventive Medicine & Community Health of The College of Medicine and Dentistry of New Jersey, New Jersey Medical School (NJMS), promptly initiated a lead screening program, employing urine analysis for detection of aminolevulinic acid (ALA).

PROGRAM DEVELOPMENT

In mid-1970, assessment of the initial phase of lead screening in Newark revealed that screening involved too few children (approximately 2,000 were tested), the ALA screening test was unreliable, and medical and environmental follow-up of children suspected of lead poisoning was inadequate.[2] As a result, a mass screening program was implemented that relied on blood lead levels. Children with screening levels equal to or greater than 40 μg. per 100 ml. whole blood were referred to follow-up testing and evaluation.

In 1971 Lead Poison Control Program, established within the Newark Division of Health of the Department of Health and Welfare, was charged with inspecting the dwellings of children who had blood lead levels equal to or greater than 50 μg./100 ml. In 1972 a municipal lead poisoning ordinance was passed in Newark requiring landlords to abate lead paint violations.

In October 1972, Newark began receiving federal support under the Lead Based Paint Poisoning Prevention Act. The reorganized Newark Childhood Lead Poisoning Prevention and Control Program expanded its neighborhood screening, focusing upon a target population of approximately 29,000 children between one and six years of age residing in the most dilapidated central city areas.

Blood lead testing was initially done by a macro analysis that required a minimum sample of 5 ml. obtained by venipuncture. Mass screening was given an impetus in 1972 with the introduction of a micromethod technique requiring only 0.1 ml. of blood, obtained by sticking the fingertip and spotting the blood on filter paper. This led to a dramatic increase in the number of Newark children screened in 1973 and 1974.

In 1975, the Center for Disease Control, which had assumed responsibility for administering the federal program, defined a blood lead level of 30 µg. per 100 ml. as requiring evaluation and follow-up. The reduction of the positive level from 40 to 30 micrograms more than doubled the number of children requiring follow-up. Late in 1975, a change in the method of collecting blood specimens, from filter paper to capillary tube, and the addition of an erythrocyte protoporphyrin (EP) test, reduced the likelihood of contamination and the necessity for obtaining a second blood sample to confirm the initially high results.

The major components of the Newark Childhood Lead Poisoning Prevention and Control Program were: 1) screening and referral, 2) laboratory analysis, 3) Central Lead Registry, 4) hazard reduction, 5) medical therapy and follow-up, and 6) health education.

Since the initial federal grant, federal, state, and local support has approached a total of $4 million. Between 1970 and 1976, more than 50,000 Newark children were tested, more than 15,000 were tested on two or more occasions, and the total number of tests performed exceeded 91,000.

PREVIOUS PROGRAM ASSESSMENTS

The spontaneous mobilization of Newark's childhood lead poisoning control program, initially understaffed and underfinanced, precluded any consideration of a built-in evaluation mechanism. The program staff was hard-pressed to maintain a manually operated Central Lead Registry for Newark children containing the results of all blood lead analyses. With the advent of federal funding, support was available for the Central Lead Registry staff, but no provision was made for comprehensive program assessment. Evaluation at the national level was limited to collecting program statistics describing the distribution of lead screening results and summarizing the number of children with positive screening tests who were followed and treated.

Subsequent assessments of the Newark Lead Program focused on mortality trends and upon patterns of hospitalization of children with acute lead poisoning.[3,4] These studies, based on hospital records, revealed that no deaths were attributed to childhood lead poisoning since the onset of the intervention program and that progress was being made in reducing the severe clinical manisfestations of childhood lead poisoning in Newark. Registry data were utilized in a three-year study of blood lead levels among five-year-old Newark school children, which found a significant decrease in the rate of undue lead absorption over the study period.[5]

In 1977, the principal author (M.A.L.) was charged with the responsibility of retrospectively evaluating the impact of the Newark lead program since its onset in 1970. The following is an anatomy of the evaluation effort, with emphasis on some of the major obstacles encountered and approaches taken to circumvent them.

NATURAL HISTORY OF LEAD POISONING

The first step in formulating appropriate questions to be answered by a retrospective evaluation of the Newark Lead Program was to gain an understanding of the natural history of lead toxicity in children.

It has long been recognized that a child with a confirmed blood lead level of 60 μg. per 100 ml. or greater is subject to a high risk of central nervous system damage. In fact, traditionally, pediatricians have not become overly concerned until levels of blood reach 60–80μg., the contention being that at levels below this no disability exists or results. In recent years this threshold view of lead toxicity has been under attack. Even though there has been no consistent, unequivocal evidence demonstrating the relationship of lower blood lead levels with pathologic effects, the results of several investigations suggest that relatively small elevations of blood lead in asymptomatic children may result in subsequent significant deficits in intellectual or behavioral development.[6-11]

When the lead control program began in Newark, staff pediatricians considered a blood lead level of 40 μg./100 ml. in young children to be an undue absorption level requiring close surveillance. In 1976, the Committee on Toxicology of The National Research Council concluded that the first metabolic effects in children become evident when the blood lead concentration exceeds 30 μg. per 100 ml.[12] It was therefore postulated that the adverse effects of lead absorption are likely to be positively and continuously associated with blood lead levels with three critical points at 30 μg. (first metabolic effects), 40 μg. (undue absorption), and 60 μg. (high risk of severe CNS damage).

REQUIREMENTS FOR A SUCCESSFUL SCREENING PROGRAM

A preliminary review of the development of the Newark Lead Screening Program indicated that the following prerequisites for a successful early case-finding program, as outlined by Hutchinson,[13] were fulfilled:
1. An effective therapy was available to treat lead-poisoned children (chelation), and preventive education and abatement of homes with lead-based paint could be employed to prevent acute lead poisoning in children with slightly elevated blood lead levels.
2. A diagnostic test was available that was capable of detecting lead toxicity at an asymptomatic stage, before its usual time of diagnosis.

3. There were one or more critical points in the natural history of the condition.
4. The critical points occurred after the time when diagnosis first became possible and before the time when diagnosis was usually made in the community.
5. The earlier the condition was detected, the greater the likelihood of achieving maximum benefits.

PROGRAM OBJECTIVES

The overall objective of any disease intervention program is to alter favorably the natural course of a disease or condition.

Initially, the Newark program was primarily concerned with identifying and bringing to immediate medical attention all children with excessively high ($\geqslant 60$ μg./ml.) blood lead levels to reduce the severe clinical manifestations of childhood lead poisoning. Previous assessments indicated that the program was successful in meeting this objective. [3,4]

Subsequently, the program expanded in scope, following children with undue lead absorption levels ($\geqslant 40\mu$g./100 ml.) in an effort to prevent acute lead poisoning and to reduce the risk of future deficits in growth and development.

EVALUATION OBJECTIVES

This evaluation effort was started on the premise that the impact of the program should be judged not only on its record of reducing the serious medical consequences of lead poisoning (tertiary prevention) but also on its achievements both in early recognition and management of asymptomatic children with elevated lead levels before they reached acute stages (secondary prevention) and in reducing the incidence of undue lead absorption (primary prevention).

Although the program initially concentrated its screening efforts on a high-risk population of 29,000 children between the ages of one and six residing in the "lead belt" area of central Newark, services were by no means limited to this target area. Therefore, the retrospective evaluation defined the population at risk to include all Newark children in this age group who lived in old deteriorating housing.

EVALUATION DATA

Between 1970 and 1976 blood samples were drawn from Newark children for lead testing at various health department sites, at local hospitals and community health centers, and by private physicians. Virtually all blood lead specimens were analyzed at either the NJMS Environmental Toxicology Laboratory in Newark or at the State Health Department Laboratory in Trenton by atomic absorption spectrophotometry. The test results were reported to the submitting source, to the Newark Department of Health and Welfare and to the NJMS Central Lead Registry.

Data accompanying each blood sample included the name, address, date of birth, ethnic group, and sex of the child, and the mother's name, the date the specimen was collected, the submitting source, and the reason for testing.

At the Central Lead Registry, the basic data on each form were reviewed for completeness and a unit case numbering system was maintained for record linkage purposes. A manually operated filing system was initially instituted. As the volume of lead testing increased in 1973, a computerized system was implemented. All test data, retroactive to 1970, were transferred onto tabulation cards, edited by means of computer programs, and stored on magnetic tape files. These files contain the results of virtually all lead tests performed on Newark children between 1970 and 1976. The subset of the test data on more than 45,000 asymptomatic children who were screened for elevated blood levels during this time period provided the basis for the retrospective evaluation.

EVALUATION MODEL

To evaluate the performance of the Newark Lead Screening Program, both process and product analyses were performed. Process analysis focused upon secondary prevention by assessing the screening program yield (i.e., the extent to which children with previously unrecognized undue lead absorption were identified and brought to treatment as a result of the screening). The yield depends upon several measurable components, including the validity and reliability of the screening tests, the prevalence of the unrecognized condition in the population, the magnitude of the screening effort, and the effectiveness of the mechanism for follow-up of positive screening results. Product analyses centered upon the examination of trends in screening results. Product analyses centered upon the examination of trends in screening levels of undue lead absorption over the study period (1970–1976) to assess the program's achievements in primary prevention.

Process Analysis

The process analysis of the lead screening program addressed the following three questions:

1. How efficient were the test procedures used as screening tools?

2. To what extent were children with previously unrecognized undue lead absorption identified and followed?
3. To what extent were screening results used to abate households with lead-based paint?

Evaluation of Screening Tests

When a new screening test is developed, it usually is validated in small-scale pilot studies. The assumption is then made that validation of a test in these small-scale studies automatically validates the usage of the test in a broad-scale program. However, to determine the practical applicability of a given test, it should be validated in the program setting with respect to its appropriateness, its acceptability to patients, its effectiveness, and its efficiency. Aside from the laboratory proficiency tests mandated by the federal funding agency, there was little evidence of any attempt to validate the performance of the lead screening tests employed in the Newark program.

A valid screening test is one that consistently provides a good preliminary indication of which individuals have a given disorder and which do not. The validity of a test is often defined by its sensitivity and specificity.[14] Sensitivity measures the ability of a test to give a positive finding when the individual has a given disorder. Specificity measures the ability of the test to give a negative finding when the individual does not have the given disorder. Measures of sensitivity and specificity are determined by examining the extent to which screening results agree with those derived by a more definitive test.

Table 1 shows the distribution of Newark screening blood lead levels by method and year. From 1973 to 1976 the microscale method of blood lead screening was employed in the vast majority of tests. To estimate the sensitivity and specificity of this screening method, a series of 88 blood samples analyzed in 1972 by both the micro and macro methods were reexamined. The macro method was assumed to be the more definitive test, and a positive test was defined as one that results in a blood lead level equal to or greater than 40 μg. per 100 ml. Cross-tabulations of the test results (Table 2A) to the 1972 distribution of macro test results in a hypothetical sample of 1,000 tests (Table 2B) were used to estimate the sensitivity of the microscale screening method to be 71.4% and 88.4% respectively. That is, almost three of ten children with elevated lead levels were likely to have been undetected (false negatives) by the micro test, and approximately one of nine children with nonelevated lead levels would have been incorrectly labeled as positives (false positives) by this screening procedure.

Another useful measure of the efficacy of a screening test is its predictive value—the likelihood that the subject yielding a positive test actually has the disorder and the likelihood that a subject with a negative test does not have the disorder.[15]

r

TABLE 1
Screening Blood Lead Levels by Method and Year

Method/Lead Level (µg./100 ml.)	1970 (%)	1971 (%)	1972 (%)	1973 (%)	1974 (%)	1975 (%)	1976 (%)	Total (%)
Macromethod								
1-29	41.7	59.0	53.1	58.3	59.0	72.4	68.6	58.8
30-39	29.8	25.8	28.6	26.5	26.2	19.2	20.4	25.6
40-49	16.4	10.3	11.9	10.0	10.1	5.8	7.9	10.3
50-59	6.4	3.4	4.3	3.5	3.2	2.0	2.1	3.5
60-79	3.2	1.1	1.5	1.4	1.2	0.5	0.9	1.3
80 +	2.6	0.4	0.5	0.3	0.3	0.2	0.1	0.5
40 +	28.5	15.2	18.3	15.2	14.8	8.4	11.0	15.6
Total screened	1,202	5,568	5,895	3,707	3,934	2,811	2,143	25,260
Micromethod								
1-29			58.1	31.7	40.2	53.5	66.0	44.0
30-39			25.5	46.6	39.5	33.5	26.3	38.2
40-49			9.9	14.7	11.5	7.9	4.7	10.9
50-59			4.0	4.9	5.7	3.4	1.8	4.6
60-79			2.4	1.9	2.6	1.4	0.9	2.0
80 +			0.1	0.3	0.4	0.1	0.2	0.3
40 +			16.4	21.9	20.3	13.0	10.7	17.8
Total screened	0	0	959	5,443	7,785	3,639	2,211	20,037

The estimation of the predictive value of a screening test requires that the sensitivity and specificity of the test and the prevalence of the disorder in the population are known or can be estimated. With an assumed sensitivity of 71.4%, a specificity of 88.4% and a population prevalence (blood lead level $\geq$ 40) of 18.2%, the predictive value of a positive microscale test in a hypothetical population of 1,000 children based on the 88 1972 samples was estimated to be 57.8%; the predictive value of a negative test was estimated to be 93.3%; (Table 2B). In other words, if the assumed levels were close to the true levels, then more than 40% of the children with positive tests would not have elevated blood levels and approximately 7% of the children with negative tests would have undetected elevated levels. Since paired macro and micro test results were not available during the latter part of the study period, it is not known whether the sensitivity, specificity, and predictive values changed in subsequent years.

The reproducibility of the blood lead screening procedures was also assessed by comparing the results of two consecutive tests repeated on the same child within a two-month interval. The proportion of positive macro tests following a negative micro test ranged from 0 to 14% during the study period. The proportion of positive macro tests following a positive micro test ranged from 29% to 43%. A comparison of the positive results of two consecutive macro tests on the same child within a two-month period also revealed substantial discrepancies. The proportion of positive macro screening tests that were confirmed by repeat macro tests varied by year from 50% to 68%. Therefore, it is apparent that the reproducibility of the screening tests not only depends on variation inherent in the methods of analysis but also is subject to variations over time.

TABLE 2
Comparison of Micro and Macro Blood Lead Test Results
1972

A. 88 Blood Samples

Macro Results (µg./100ml.)	Micro Results <40	(µg./100ml.) ≥40	Total	False Pos. %	False Neg. %
<30	5	0	5	0	
30-39	16	8	24	33.3	
40-49	13	22	35		37.1
50-59	3	13	16		18.8
≥60	0	8	8		0
	37	51	88		

B. Hypothetical Sample of 1000 Blood Lead Screening Tests

Macro Results (µg./100ml.)	1972 (%)	Sample n = 1000	Estimated Micro Results (µg./100ml.) <40	≥40
<30	53.2	532	532	0
30-39	28.6	286	191	95
<40	81.8	818	723	95
40-49	11.9	119	44	75
50-59	4.3	43	8	35
≥60	2.0	20	0	20
≥40	18.2	182	52	130
Total	100.0	1000	775	225

Micro (µg./100ml.)

Macro (µg./100ml.)		≥40	<40	Total
	≥40	130	52	182
	<40	95	723	818
	Total	225	775	1000

% Sensitivity = (130/182) × 100 = 71.4
% Specificity = (723/818) × 100 = 88.4
Predicitive Value (+) = (130/225) × 100 = 57.8
Predictive Value (-) = (723/775) × 100 = 93.3

Magnitude of the Screening Effort

Between 1970 and 1976, the Newark Childhood Lead Screening Program succeeded in testing more than 45,000 children between the ages of one and six (Table 1). The screening effort reached a peak in 1974, when close to 12,000 children were tested for the first time. The proportion of children screened during the study period with positive test results (≥ 40 µg.) was 15.6% when samples were analyzed by the macro technique and 17.8% when the micro method was used. All told, approximately 7,400 children had positive tests when screened for the first time.

Confirmation of Positive Screen Tests

Table 3 shows the extent to which children with positive (≥ 40 μg./100 ml.) blood lead screening tests were given repeat or confirmatory tests for each study year. Approximately one of four children with elevated screening blood lead levels in 1970 were subsequently retested. In almost all cases, the interval of time between the first and second tests exceeded two months. The rate at which confirmatory tests were performed increased to over 60% in 1971 and 1972 but then decreased during the peak screening years of 1973 and 1974. Substantial progress was not made until 1976, when more than one half of the children with elevated blood lead screening tests were concurrently given confirmatory erythrocyte protoporphyrin (EP) tests. In 1976, 83% of the children with initially elevated blood lead levels were retested, either by an EP test on the same specimen or by a repeat blood lead test. For the most part, children with excessively high blood levels (60 + μg.) were more likely to be retested than those with moderately elevated levels, and the trend was toward reducing the interval of time between the first two tests in those cases where a confirmatory test was made. However, prior to 1976 at least 30% of the children who had screening tests yielding lead levels of 60 μg. or more were not retested each year, and the majority of the confirmatory tests were performed more than two months after the highly elevated screening test.

The proportion of positive confirmation tests was positively associated with the initial blood lead level and negatively associated with the interval of time between the first two tests (Table 3).

Continuity of Care

Examination of the long-term follow-up of children with confirmed positive blood lead levels provides an indication of the continuity of care. Between 1971 and 1975, only 35% of the confirmed positive children (those with two consecutive blood lead levels $\geq 40\mu$g./100ml. within two months) were tested more than six months after the initial screening test. In approximately one half of the cases in which a retest was performed at least six months after discovery, blood lead levels were still elevated. Long-range follow-up was best among 1972 confirmed positives (57%), but fell off thereafter.

Abatement of Lead-Based Paint

The records of the Lead Poison Control Program of the Newark Department of Health and Welfare indicate that, during the period from 1971 to 1976, a total of 4,380 dwelling units were inspected, 3,443 (79%) were found to have lead based paint, and, of those, 2,224 (65%) units were abated.

It is difficult to determine the number of household units in Newark that are in need of abatement. In 1970, there were approximately 48,000 housing units built prior to 1940 that were occupied by households of two or

TABLE 3
Repeat Testing of Children with Positive Lead Screening Tests
1970-1976

Test		1970	1971	1972	1973	1974	1975	1976	Total
Initial test 40-49 μg./100ml.	(No.)	197	570	798	1173	1298	453	274	4763
Repeat test (≤2 mos.)	(No.)	1	54	135	195	168	82	64	699
Repeat test (>2 mos.)	(No.)	53	291	368	454	303	112	19	1600
Total repeat tests	(%)	27.4	60.5	63.0	55.3	36.3	46.6	79.9	51.5
Positive tests (≤2 mos.)	(%)	100.0	59.3	46.7	44.6	48.2	51.5	50.5	48.8
Positive tests (>2 mos.)	(%)	30.2	43.3	34.5	36.1	29.0	41.1	52.6	36.1
Total positive tests	(No.)	17	158	190	251	169	97	111	993
Initial test 50-59 μg./100ml.	(No.)	77	191	291	397	572	180	85	1793
Repeat test (≤2 mos.)	(No.)	0	31	62	81	94	38	24	330
Repeat test (>2 mos.)	(No.)	17	101	137	156	190	40	6	647
Total repeat tests	(%)	22.1	69.1	68.4	59.7	49.6	47.2	85.9	57.3
Positive tests (≤2 mos.)	(%)	-	67.7	53.2	60.5	62.8	48.9	53.7	57.9
Positive tests (>2 mos.)	(%)	47.1	75.2	56.9	52.6	51.1	45.0	50.0	56.0
Total positive tests	(No.)	8	97	111	131	156	40	39	582
Initial test>60μg./100ml.	(No.)	69	86	146	180	293	76	48	898
Repeat test (≤2 mos.)	(No.)	0	7	20	44	42	15	10	138
Repeat test (>2 mos.)	(No.)	16	53	81	72	94	19	5	340
Total repeat tests	(%)	23.2	69.8	69.2	64.4	46.4	51.3	91.7	57.0
Positive tests (≤2 mos.)	(%)	-	85.7	55.0	65.9	45.2	55.0	74.4	61.0
Positive tests (>2 mos.)	(%)	43.8	62.3	63.0	72.2	57.4	57.9	80.0	62.4
Total positive tests	(No.)	7	39	62	81	73	22	33	317
Initial tests≥40 μg./100ml.	(No.)	343	847	1235	1750	2163	709	407	7454
Repeat test (≤2 mos.)	(No.)	1	92	217	320	304	135	98	1167
Repeat test (>2 mos.)	(No.)	86	445	586	682	587	171	30	2587
Total repeat tests	(%)	25.4	63.4	65.0	57.3	41.2	47.2	82.6	53.5
Positive tests (≤2 mos.)	(%)	100.0	64.1	49.3	51.6	52.3	51.2	54.2	52.8
Positive tests (>2 mos.)	(%)	36.0	52.8	43.7	43.7	40.7	43.9	56.7	44.5
Total positive tests	(No.)	32	294	363	463	398	159	183	1892

more persons.[1] Since about one of four Newark families includes at least one child under six years of age, there are potentially some 12,000 Newark dwelling units requiring environmental abatement.

Product Analysis

Evaluation of the program impact on primary prevention, by means of product analysis, proved to be a much more difficult task than the process analysis previously described. If preventive educational efforts and environmental repairs are effective, then the incidence of undue lead absorption in the target population should diminish over time, providing that the population tested is reasonably stable, reliable measures of incidence are available, and the testing procedures are comparable over the period of observation. Unfortunately, these conditions are seldom met in community lead screening programs, prompting Guinee to conclude that comparisons of lead level statistics from year to year yield epidemiologic patterns that differ more in definition than in substance.[16]

The distribution of the Newark screening tests over the study period varied with respect to the age and ethnicity of the children tested and also with respect to method of testing and the season of the year in which tests were conducted. All of these factors were highly associated with screening test results. As previously noted, micro tests generally yielded higher proportions of elevated blood levels than did macro tests. In the population tested, blood lead levels tended to be highest among black children, among children two–three years of age, and among those tested in June, July, or August. In evaluating incidence trends, stratification of the data could control for these known differences in the test characteristics over time. However, in the absence of random selection, other unknown or unmeasurable factors may have affected the test results. In fact, if early screening efforts were directed at "high-risk" neighborhoods and later efforts focused upon "low-risk" neighborhoods, this could create the spurious impression that incidence rates declined. However, examination of incidence trends within fairly homogeneous neighborhoods revealed patterns that were similar to those observed for the entire study sample.

Inasmuch as a new screening program will initially detect new and old cases, and subsequently identify mainly new cases, a decline in the case-finding rate in the first few years of a program would not necessarily indicate a true reduction in the incidence rate. Therefore the analysis of incidence trends was confined to children between one and two years of age when first screened. These children were just entering the "at risk" pool each year and cases detected at this age level were most likely to be new cases.

The annual blood lead level screening rates reported for black children between one and two years of age are provided by method of analysis and season of the year in Table 4. Hispanic and other white children were excluded because of insufficient numbers. The chi-square procedure outlined by Everitt for analyzing trends in proportions was applied.[17] The test results shown in Table 4 reveal that, although the overall chi-square tests for differences in proportions was significant only for macro testing and not for micro testing, the more sensitive chi-square test designed to detect a decreasing trend in these proportions was significant at least at the 0.05 level in each analysis. Furthermore, the chi-square test for departures from a linear trend indicated that the decreasing trend was linear for micro tests and nonlinear for macro tests. These findings suggest that there was a significant decrease in case finding over the study period in the one–two age group. The decrease was fairly constant (linear) for microscale testing, but was represented by a sharp drop in 1975 for macroscale testing.

TABLE 4
Elevated Blood Lead Level Screening Rates by Type of Test and
Season of the Year, Black Children, Age 12-23 months, 1971-1976

Test	Season		1971	1972	1973	1974	1975	1976	X_1^2	X_2^2	X_T^2
Macro	Fall-	n	237	402	425	353	258	276	8.67	11.07	19.7
	Winter	%pos.	14.0	19.2	12.9	14.7	7.8	11.2	**	*	**
Macro	Spring-	n	285	733	417	400	306	206	15.35	10.35	25.7
	Summer	%pos.	20.4	24.6	17.5	21.0	15.3	11.2	***	*	***
Micro	Fall-	n		53	220	262	115	72	5.38	1.81	7.1
	Winter	%pos.		20.8	25.4	21.0	16.5	12.5	*		
Micro	Spring-	n			292	450	154	103	4.90	2.77	7.6
	Summer	%pos.			27.1	29.3	24.0	16.5	*		

X_1^2 Tests for a linear tread (1 d.f.).
X_2^2 Tests for departures from a linear trend (k-2 d.f.).
X_T^2 Is the overall test for differences in k proportions (k-1 d.f.).
*   Significant at the 0.05 level.
**   Significant at the 0.01 level.
***   Significant at the 0.001 level.

DISCUSSION

A detailed description of the steps taken to assess the performance of the Newark Childhood Lead Screening Program between 1970 and 1976 illustrates some of the major problems encountered when attempting to evaluate a large-scale community intervention program retrospectively. The absence of a predetermined research design, the changing characteristics of the population tested, and the limitations to the measurements used to ascertain the impact of the program provided formidable obstacles to definitive evaluation. Nevertheless, a process analysis, along with a limited product analysis, provided some basis for judging the effectiveness of the intervention program.

A successful screening program depends, to a large extent, on the availability of effective screening tools. Examination of the sensitivity, specificity, predictive value, and reproducibility of the major screening procedure raised some serious questions regarding the reliability and validity of the test results. One of the main questions raised is whether or not lead screening tests are measuring what they are purported to measure. Blood lead tests monitor current lead absorption, providing an indication of the amount of recent exposure and not the cumulative effect of that exposure. This may at least partially explain why they are not reproducible within a short period of time. The statistical phenomenon of regression to the mean may also be a major determinant of blood lead level change. [18]

Recently, tests measuring erythrocyte protoporphyrin (EP) and zinc protoporphyrin (ZP) levels have been promoted to identify lead toxicity, on the grounds that they are reasonably stable from day to day and that they may also better reflect the total body burden of lead than blood levels do.[11,19] However, the micromethod procedure for blood lead analysis and the protoporphyrin tests tend to produce false positive results. The former is highly vulnerable to lead contamination, and the latter can produce positive results in the presence of iron deficiency, sickle cell anemia, and chronic infection.[20] A cause of greater concern is that both of these procedures may be seriously lacking in sensitivity as well as specificity. The sensitivity of the micro blood lead test was estimated to be 71% in 1972. The sensitivity of the EP test, based on examination of 931 blood samples tested by both the macroscale and EP methods in 1976, was estimated to be 77.3%. These findings suggest that approximately one of four children with elevated blood lead levels would have been undetected by either screening method at selected time periods. These limitations to the efficiency of the available lead testing procedures raise serious questions regarding the effectiveness of ongoing screening programs.

Between 1970 and 1976, the Newark Childhood Lead Screening Program reached more than 45,000 asymptomatic children between the ages of one and six, of whom approximately 7,400 had positive test results for undue lead absorption ($\geq$ 40 μg/100 ml.). Since the objective of any screening program is the early detection of diseases whose treatment is easier or more effective when identified early, these programs have a responsibility to provide follow-up and long-term care, if necessary, to those who volunteer to be screened and are found to be positive at the initial screening test. The process analysis of the Newark program identified many gaps in following children with positive screening levels.

Confirmatory tests of positive screening tests were infrequent or delayed prior to the introduction of the EP test in 1976. Moreover, efforts in secondary prevention were consistently inadequate. Between 1971 and 1975 only one out of every three children with confirmed positive lead tests was followed by the program for at least six months. Effective medical follow-up is seldom achieved in large city screening programs. In New York City, only one of four children with blood lead levels of 50 μg or higher received repeat tests,[21] and only 36% of the lead poisoned children ($\geq$ 60 μg./100 ml.) residing in the highest incidence areas were retested six months after the initial diagnosis.[22]

Despite the evidence pointing to serious deficiencies in following Newark children with undue lead absorption, previous studies have shown that the severe clinical manifestations of childhood lead poisoning have been reduced in Newark.[3,4] This apparently paradoxical situation may be explained by the fact that, with increasing public and professional awareness, lead poisoned children who are symptomatic or have excessively elevated blood lead levels are most likely to receive early medical attention and follow-up, thereby averting the more serious nervous system sequellae. However, the incidence of acute lead poisoning does not necessarily reflect the potential dangers of undue lead absorption, since asymptomatic children with slightly elevated blood lead levels are likely to be at risk of long-term deficits in growth and development.[6-11]

The limitations in the research design and data base suggest that caution must be exercised in interpreting the results of any analysis of trends in the distribution of blood lead levels in the study sample. A limited assessment of the impact of the program, focusing on black children tested between one and two years of age, resulted in a statistically significant decrease in case finding over the study period. These findings are in agreement with the results of a previous three-year study of lead levels among five-year-old Newark school children.[5] While it appears that some progress has been made in reducing undue lead absorption in Newark children, the lead levels measured in the study sample in 1976 were still alarmingly high. If in fact a blood lead concentration of 30 μg. per 100 ml. places a child at risk of subsequent defects in development, then, according to the more conservative macro test results, almost one of three children screened in 1976 would fall into the "at risk" category.

Considering the increasingly intensive screening and medical and environmental follow-up effort that has been made in recent years, why hasn't there been more of an impact upon the blood lead levels among Newark children? According to program statistics, more than 2,000 household units have been abated since 1971 in addition to the substantial amount of deteriorated housing that has been demolished in Newark's urban renewal program. However, Foster and co-workers investigated the housing conditions of a sample of Newark children with blood lead levels over 50 μg. per 100 ml. and concluded that only one quarter of the units had been properly abated and one quarter had not been investigated at all by health authorities.[23] Abatement of dwellings with lead-based paint in Newark, as well as in other urban areas, has long been hampered by inadequate law enforcement and by limited resources and personnel. Furthermore, although a computerized data collection and retrieval system was belatedly established in Newark for the purpose of monitoring lead test results, the potential of this system for identifying delinquencies in medical and environmental follow-up was never fully realized because of inadequate lines of communication between the Registry and follow-up personnel.

What lessons can be learned from the Newark evaluation effort? Clearly, most of the major drawbacks to effective scientific evaluation were present, including: 1. absence of a built-in evaluation mechanism at the onset; 2. changes in the objectives, scope, testing methods, and population served during the observation period; 3. absence of the key elements in experimental research: random selection of subjects and appropriate control groups; 4. use of testing instruments of questionable validity and reliability; and 5. inadequate provision for continuous, timely feedback of evaluation results. These limitations are serious deterrents to assessments aimed at measuring program success by means of *direct* indexes of the desired change. Therefore, caution must be exercised in evaluating the impact of the Newark lead program on trends in children's blood lead levels. Without appropriate controls, one can only speculate as to what extent desired changes would have taken place without a structured community intervention program. Without an appropriate research design, the impact of individual program components is also a matter of speculation. Although it is usually most desirable to examine *direct* measures of program success, when administrative considerations preclude such an approach much can still be learned from focusing on *indirect* measures reflecting assumed changed brought about by the program. Thus, an examination of the process of medical and environmental follow-up employed in the Newark Lead Program disclosed many gaps in following children with elevated screening blood lead levels.

Although the costs of health intervention programs have increased dramatically, there is often little scientific evidence to demonstrate their efficacy. Unfortunately, in the community setting it is frequently difficult, if not impossible, to attain the level of control required for true scientific experimentation. However, if administrative or ethical considerations preclude the imposition of rigid control over the many potentially influential variables, some level of control can often be achieved through the use of quasi-experimental research designs. Even observational or pre-experimental studies can yield useful information by identifying program strengths and weaknesses.

Even though true scientific research may not be attainable, an evaluation component should be an integral part of every community intervention program. Moreover, evaluation should be viewed as a continuous circular process providing immediate and useful feedback to program administrators. In the face of increasing costs and limited resources, critical assessment of ongoing programs is needed to determine whether or not they merit continuing public support.

REFERENCES

1. Bureau of the Census: Census of Housing: 1970, Metropolitan Housing Characteristics, Final Report HC(2)-150 Newark, NJ, SMSA, Washington, DC, Government Printing Office, 1972.
2. Browder AA: Lead poisoning in Newark. *J Med Soc NJ* **69**: 101–106, 1972.
3. Browder A, Joselow M, Louria DB, et al: Evaluation of screening program for childhood lead poisoning by analysis of hospital admissions. *Am J Public Health* **64**:914–915, 1974.
4. Schneider J: Impact of lead screening on hospitalization for plumbism. Presented at the annual meeting of the American Public Health Association, Miami Beach, Florida, October 21, 1976.
5. Gause D, Chase W, Foster J, et al: Reduction in lead levels among children in Newark. *J Med Soc NJ* **74**:958–960, 1977.
6. Perrino I, Ernhart CB: The relation of subclinical lead level to cognitive and perceptual performance in black pre schoolers. *J Learning Disab* **7**:616–620, 1974.
7. De La Burde B, Choate MS: Early asymptomatic lead exposure and development at school age. *J Pediatr* **87**:638–642, 1975.
8. Landrigan PJ, Whitworth RH, Baloh RW: Neuropsychological dysfunction in children with chronic low-level lead absorption. *Lancet* **1**:708–712, 1975.
9. Piomelli S, Seaman C, Zullow D, et al: Metabolic evidence of lead toxicity in "normal" urban children. *Clin Res* **25**:459A, 1977.
10. Needleman HL, Gunnoe C, Leviton A, et al: Deficits in psychological and classroom performance of children with elevated dentine lead levels. *N Engl J Med* **300**:689–695, 1979.
11. Repko JD, Corum CR: Critical review and evaluation of the neurological and behavioral sequelae of inorganic lead absorption. *CRC Crit Rev Toxicol* **6**:135–187, 1979.
12. National Research Council, Committee on Toxicology, Assembly of Life Sciences: Recommendations for the prevention of lead poisoning in children. *Nutr Rev* **34**:321–327, 1976.
13. Hutchinson GB: Evaluation of preventive services. *J Chron Dis* **11**:497–508, 1960.
14. Friedman GD: *Primer of Epidemiology*. New York, McGraw-Hill, 1974. P. 213.
15. Vecchio TJ: Predictive value of a single diagnostic test in unselected populations. *N Engl J Med* **274**: 1171–1173, 1966.

16. Guinee VF: Lead poisoning in New York City. *Trans N Y Acad Sci* 33:529-545, 1971.
17. Everitt BS: *The Analysis of Contingency Tables.* New York, John Wiley & Sons, 1977. P. 51.
18. McCusker J: Longitudinal changes in blood lead level in children and their relationship to season, age, and exposure to paint or plaster. *Am J Public Health* 69:348-352, 1979.
19. Lin-Fu JS: Lead poisoning in children—What price shall we pay? *Child Today* 8:9-13, 36, 1979.
20. Pincus D, Saccar CV: Lead poisoning. *Am Fam Physician* 19:120-124, 1979.
21. Guinee VF: Lead poisoning. *Am J Med* 52:283-288, 1972.
22. Eidsvold G, Mustalish A, Novick LF: The New York City Department of Health; Lessons in a lead poisoning control program. *Am J Public Health* 64:956-962, 1974.
23. Foster JD, Lauria DB, Stinson L: Influence of documented lead poisoning on environmental modification programs in Newark, New Jersey. *Arch Env Health* 34:368-371, 1979.

30

An Evaluation of the Nutrition Education and Training Program
Findings from Nebraska

Robert G. St. Pierre, Thomas D. Cook, and Roger B. Straw

This article summarizes methods and findings from a classical randomized experiment used to evaluate the Nutrition Education and Training (NET) Program that was developed and implemented in Nebraska. The evaluation focused on assessing how well the program was implemented and the impact it had on children's nutrition-related knowledge, attitudes, preferences, and habits. Data were collected from over 2300 children in 96 classrooms distributed across grades 1-6 in 20 schools spanning the state of Nebraska. The 20 participating schools were selected from 98 volunteers and were assigned to treatment or control status using a modified random assignment procedure that resulted in equivalent pretest means on outcome measures. Pretest data and two waves of posttest data were collected. The evaluation found strong positive effects in all grades on several measures of nutrition knowledge, positive effects on reported food preference, and willingness to select new foods in the school lunch line in grades 1-3, positive effects on willingness to taste previously rejected foods in grades 4-6, and no consistent effects on food attitudes, reported food habits, or plate waste.

This article summarizes methods and findings from a classical randomized experiment used to evaluate the Nutrition Education and Training (NET) program that was developed and implemented in Nebraska using funds provided by the U.S. Department of Agriculture. NET was established in 1977 by PL 95-166, an amendment to the 1966 Child Nutrition Act. Its legislated purpose is "to encourage effective dissemination of scientifically valid information to children participating in or eligible to participate in school lunch and related child nutrition programs." NET funds of approximately $25 million in federal fiscal years 1978 and 1979, $20 million in 1980, and $15 million in 1981 were distributed through state education agencies to local schools and districts for use in training

Authors' Note: The research reported herein was performed pursuant to Contract No. 53-3198-9-38 with the U.S. Department of Agriculture, Food and Nutrition Service, Office of Policy, Planning and Evaluation. Points of view or opinions do not represent official U.S. Department of Agriculture position or policy. Readers wishing to know more about this study should see St. Pierre, Glotzer, Cook and Straw (1981). We wish to express our thanks to Dr. Thomas Ferb of Abt Associates Inc. who directed the early stages of this evaluation, to Drs. Jack Radzikowski and Victor Rezmovic of USDA/OPPE who provided ongoing guidance, and to members of the Nebraska State Department of Education including Ms. Glenda Uhrmacher, Dr. Ray Steinert, and Ms. Jaime Ruud who helped implement the evaluation.

teachers and school food service personnel, and in conducting nutrition education activities that draw upon school food service facilities as well as classroom resources.

Each participating state education agency hired an NET coordinator to conduct a needs assessment and to develop a model for implementing nutrition education activities at the local level. Some states developed a centralized model in which "packaged" curricula were to be used in all participating school districts in the state. Other states opted for a decentralized model by setting broad guidelines for the use of NET funds and for providing training and resources, but giving local projects the responsibility for deciding exactly which nutrition education activities to implement. Still other states implemented a regional model where nutrition information and training was provided to local projects by multiple resource centers.

Because of widespread interest in nutrition education at the federal, state, and local levels, the Office of Policy, Planning and Evaluation in the Food and Nutrition Service of the U.S. Department of Agriculture contracted with Abt Associates, Inc. to conduct a national evaluation of the NET program (St. Pierre, 1981). One of the objectives of that study was to identify exemplary state-level models of nutrition education funded by NET and to evaluate their effectiveness. The strategy of limiting the evaluation to potentially successful models was employed in order to demonstrate what NET could accomplish under the best of circumstances, to maximize the chances of detecting positive effects, and to minimize the changes of "washing out" positive effects by averaging them with negative ones. If no positive effects are found under these conditions it is safe to say that the program will not be successful under less favorable circumstances. On the other hand, finding that a program demonstrates success when well implemented enables policymakers and program practitioners to concentrate on improving the program, on ensuring faithful implementation, or on disseminating the tested successful versions.

The Nebraska program was selected for study because it is nationally recognized, was nominated by regional and national FNS staff as well as other nutrition education professionals, and has an approach to nutrition education that involves the three major target groups of the NET legislation: teachers, food service personnel, and children. It also had some preliminary evidence of effectiveness and is being adopted in seven other states, and the Nebraska State Department of Education was eager to help plan and participate in the evaluation.

THE NEBRASKA NET PROGRAM

The Nebraska NET program is centrally administered with all participating school districts implementing the same curriculum, known as "Experience Nutrition," which was developed through joint efforts of the Nebraska State Department of Education, *experience education*, and the Swanson Center for Nutrition,

Inc. The curriculum consists of eleven prepared packages of instruction for grades K to 6. Each package includes 12 to 20 class hours of instruction and, in varying degrees, all involve food service personnel, teachers, and students in one or several activities within packages. The "Making Meals at Schools" curriculum package focuses on acquainting students with food service personnel and on developing positive attitudes about school lunch. The "Fruits" and "Vegetables" packages aim at increasing student familiarity with a wide variety of fruits and vegetables. "Snacks" is intended to help students select snacks that are beneficial nutritionally and "Breakfast" suggests new ways of thinking about breakfast food. "Great School Menus" aims to provide knowledge and understanding of food service responsibilities and the benefits of school lunch. "Physical Fitness" emphasizes exercise along with a good diet, and "Key Nutrients" makes use of lab work to explain the properties of nutrients. "Food Habits" encourages students to think about the origin of their and others' food patterns. "Food Advertising" raises student consciousness about food buying patterns. Finally, "Food Safety" focuses on both food preservation and safe-keeping as well as the issues of additives.

DESCRIPTION OF THE EVALUATION

The evaluation assessed the Nebraska NET program in terms of how well it was *implemented* and the results it had upon children's *knowledge* of nutrition, upon their *attitudes* and *preferences* in the nutrition domain, and upon their reported and observed behavioral nutrition *habits*. The major questions addressed in the evaluation were: (1) To what extent was the Nebraska NET program implemented in the participating schools? (2) What are the short-term consequences of the Nebraska NET program as it influences nutrition-related knowledge, attitudes, preferences, and habits? (3) What are the likely long-term consequences of the Nebraska NET program?

The Evaluation Design

An evaluation design was implemented that, at the level of schools, is close to the ideal of a randomized experiment. The opportunity for a randomized evaluation was created by the facts that the NET program was being implemented widely in Nebraska for the first time, that there were many schools that wanted to participate, and that Nebraska officials were willing to cooperate with the evaluation.

Data were collected from over 2300 children in 96 classrooms distributed across grades 1-6 in 20 schools spanning the state of Nebraska (Table 1). The participating schools were randomly selected from 98 volunteers for NET and were assigned to treatment (13 schools) or control (7 schools) status using a modified random assignment procedure,[1] with the understanding that control schools would be guaranteed participation in the evaluation; however, in some

TABLE 1   Sample Size by Grade and Treatment Group

Grade	NET	Non-NET
1	439	176
2	326	43
3	174	91
Total	939 children in 35 classes	310 children in 13 classes
4	437	97
5	171	125
6	104	168
Total	712 children in 30 classes	390 children in 18 classes
Grand Total	1651 children in 65 classes	700 children in 31 classes

instances classes were selected only at particular grade levels. All children in any selected class were included in the evaluation.

The NET sample was approximately twice the size of the non-NET sample, and provided a sufficiently large number of classrooms to allow stratification after the fact in the event that implementation of NET varied greatly. This sampling strategy, which was intended to ensure that we could examine the effects of well-implemented classrooms, is consistent with our initial strategy of sampling exemplary state-level programs—we wanted to give NET a chance to show that it could work.

Table 2 summarizes the evaluation design and shows that a battery of measures was given to children on three occasions: the full battery was administered to the full sample as a pretest in February 1980 and again as a posttest in May 1980; a 50% subsample of NET and non-NET children were followed-up in December 1980 with a subset of the measurement battery.

Thus, the pretest/posttest time period was ten weeks; the pretest/follow-up time period was ten months. Questionnaires were mailed to teachers and food service managers in May and December 1980 to obtain self-reports of the degree to which they implemented the curriculum.

Nebraska program developers held a one-day training session for teachers in NET schools the week before program implementation was scheduled to start. The emphasis in this session was on using the curricular materials to illustrate the mechanics of coordinating classroom and lunchroom activities, to discuss teaching strategies, and to convey a limited number of key nutrition concepts.

Because the pre/post data collection had to be completed in spring 1980, the evaluation was limited to an assessment of the effects of three curriculum packages in grades 1-3 and three others in grades 4-6. Teachers were asked to

TABLE 2   Summary of Evaluation Design

		February 1980		May 1980		December 1980
T	R	Pre	NET	Post$_1$	"NET"	Post$_2$
C	R	Pre	–	Post$_1$	"NET"	Post$_2$

T	= treatment schools.
C	= control schools.
R	= random assignment of schools to treatment/control status.
Pre	= administration of pretest measurement battery.
NET	= implementation of the treatment.
"NET"	= partial and inconsistent implementation of the treatment.
Post$_1$	= administration of posttest measurement battery.
Post$_2$	= administration of follow-up measurement battery (excluded behavior measures).

"concentrate" delivery of these packages into the ten-week pre/post time span. Therefore, we evaluated a subset of the Experience Nutrition curriculum packages (6 out of 11) in a cross-sectional rather than longitudinal fashion. That is, two parallel studies were conducted—one assessing the impact of the Making Meals at School, Fruits, and Vegetables packages on children in grades 1-3, and another assessing the impact of the Great School Menus, Key Nutrients, and Physical Fitness packages on children in grades 4-6.

Measurement

This study was seen by the client, Nebraska personnel, and the evaluation team as primarily an evaluation of program impact rather than a study of the causal relationships among various outcomes. Still, it was necessary to give some consideration to the planned causal processes of the program in order to decide what to measure.

The Nebraska NET program intends to change children's nutrition-related knowledge, attitudes, and behavior via a curriculum-oriented, hands-on approach. A model of the causal change hoped for through the Nebraska NET program posits that training of teachers and food service personnel, accompanied by a prepared set of classroom and cafeteria curriculum packages should lead to the delivery of classroom and cafeteria lessons. Further, specific changes should occur in the cafeteria. Implementation of the curriculum in the classroom and cafeteria, along with a host of external factors, are hypothesized to impact on children's nutrition-related attitudes, beliefs, values, knowledge, and dietary habits/behavior. However, the causal relationships among these variables are unclear. Changes in attitudes, knowledge, and behavior, once they occur, are presumed to lead to improved dietary behavior, then to improved nutritional status, and finally to improved health status.

This chain of events is such that changes in early or "proximal" outcomes (e.g., delivery and receipt of classroom instruction) will lead to changes in later or "distal" outcomes (e.g., improved health status). Though the causal relationships among program outcomes such as nutrition knowledge, attitudes, preferences, and habits are unclear, a cognitive theory of the causal relationship between education and health status posits that children first need to learn new information, which will then affect their beliefs and feelings about nutrition related behaviors, which in turn will affect the nutritional behaviors in question (Zeitlan and Formacion, 1981; Stanfield, 1976).

This cognitive model has served as the basis for many nutrition education programs; however, Harman (1977) notes that the hypothesized causal chain from increased knowledge to modified attitudes to improved behaviors is naive. Models other than the cognitively oriented one reviewed above exist and have been used as the basis for preparing programs. For example, Kotler and Zaltman (1977) review the effectiveness of using the mass media for consumer advertising and Kelman (1974) discusses the interactions between attitudes and behavior based on the theory of cognitive dissonance.

In spite of the range of available theories, Zeitlan and Formacion (1981), believe that thinking in terms of knowledge, attitude, and behavior change "is necessary for evaluating the effectiveness of education programs but is insufficient for program planning purposes" (p. 38). Most of the available theories call for measurement of roughly the same set of concepts, even though different relationships among the concepts are hypothesized.

Because of the limited time available for the Nebraska evaluation we concentrated on measuring children's knowledge, attitudes, food preferences, and eating behavior. An outcome such as improved nutritional status was not included both because of its distal nature and because of the limited scope of the evaluation. That is, while improved nutritional status and health are the most distal outcomes of NET, we doubt whether a NET program would affect such variables, particularly over the short time period of this planned research.

The measurement battery was developed by constructing some new instruments, using some that had been developed in Nebraska specifically for the purpose of evaluating the Experience Nutrition curriculum, and using "standardized" measures of nutrition knowledge. Because of time pressures the measurement battery was developed quickly without vigorous pilot-testing. We therefore subjected the pretest data to a thorough psychometric analysis in order to delete poor items and construct reliable scales to use as outcomes measures. This process produced measures representing each content domain at each grade level. Table 3 lists the measures used in the evaluation, the number of items in each measure, and gives the reliability by grade level.

In addition to paper and pencil measures of nutrition-related knowledge and attitudes, the evaluation included two assessments of food-related behavior. In grades 1-3 children were surveyed to determine the frequency with which they ate each of several fruits and vegetables. Based on this information a decision-making situation was set up in which children were given a choice in the school lunch line between familiar and unfamiliar fruits and between familiar and unfamiliar vegetables. The Nebraska program developers hypothesized that

TABLE 3   Summary of Measures and Results from the Nebraska Evaluation by Content Domain, Measure and Grade Level

				Grades 1-3								
Content Domain	Measure*	Measure** Developer	Number of Items	Reliability*** by Grade			Pre/Post**** Effects by Grade			Pre/Post**** Effects Across Grades	Follow-up**** Effects Across Grades
				1	2	3	1	2	3		
Nutrition Knowledge	Knowledge of Breakfast Foods	Nebr.	6	.73	.70	.70	+	0	+	+	+
	Knowledge of Foods that Grow Underground	Nebr.	4	.39	.43	:04	+	+	0	+	+
	General Nutrition Knowledge	D.C.	19	NA	NA	.59	NA	NA	0	0	+
Food Attitude	Food Attitudes	AAI	10	.70	.74	.63	0	0	0	0	−
Food Preference	Vegetable Preference	AAI	8	.77	.68	.74	0	+	+	+	0
	Willingness to Select New Fruits	Nebr.	NA	NA	NA	NA	NA	+	NA	+	NA
	Willingness to Select New Vegetables	Nebr.	NA	NA	NA	NA	NA	NA	NA	+	NA
Food Habits	"Good" Consumption Habits	AAI	4	.57	.40	.46	0	0	0	0	0
	"Bad" Consumption Habits	AAI	4	.58	.65	.58	0	0	0	0	0
	Willingness to Taste New Foods	AAI	NA	NA	NA	NA	NA	NA	NA	0	NA
	Plate Waste	AAI	NA	NA	NA	NA	NA	NA	NA	0	NA

Category	Measure	Developer									
Nutrition Knowledge	Great School Menus	Nebr.	10	.53	.56	.49	+	+	+	+	0
	Relation of Energy to Calories	Nebr.	6	.32	.45	.33	+	+	+	+	+
	Energy Balance Knowledge	Nebr.	3	.28	.20	.33	+	+	0	+	0
	Digestive System Knowledge	Nebr.	7	.65	.70	.52	+	+	0	+	+
	What Nutrients Does Food Supply?	Nebr.	6	.45	.39	.57	+	0	+	+	+
	Recognition of Nutrients	Nebr.	5	.58	.50	.76	+	+	+	+	+
	General Nutrition Knowledge	PD&E	25	.56	.65	.77	+	+	+	+	0
Food Attitude	Food Consumption Attitudes	AAI	8	.52	.54	.54	0	0	+	0	0
	School Lunch Attitudes	AAI	7	.76	.77	.80	0	0	0	0	-
	Breakfast Foods Attitudes	AAI	5	.75	.78	.74	+	-	-	0	0
Food Preference	Fruit Preference	AAI	4	.58	.61	.54	+	+	0	+	0
	Vegetable Preference	AAI	10	.78	.77	.66	0	0	0	0	0
Food Habits	School Lunch Habits	AAI	4	.61	.71	.74	0	0	0	0	-
	"Good" Consumption Habits	AAI	2	.60	.49	.65	0	0	0	0	0
	"Bad" Consumption Habits	AAI	4	.57	.59	.48	0	0	0	0	0
	Active Habits	Nebr.	8	.62	.64	.56	0	0	0	0	0
	Inactive Habits	Nebr.	6	.51	.44	.45	0	0	0	0	0
	"Good" Consumption Habits	PD&E	6	.49	.42	.48	0	0	0	0	0
	"Bad" Consumption Habits	PD&E	7	.54	.54	.44	0	0	0	0	0
	Willingness to Taste New Foods	AAI	NA	NA	NA	NA	NA	NA	NA	+	NA
	Plate Waste	AAI	NA	NA	NA	NA	NA	NA	NA	0	NA

* These measures were derived via a psychometric analysis of several curriculum-specific and off-the-shelf nutrition education tests.

** Developer of test from which this specific measure was derived. Nebr. = Nebraska, D. C.= National Dairy Council, AAI = Abt Associates Inc., PD&E = Planning, Development and Evaluation Associates.

*** Cronbach's alpha.

**** + signifies a statistically significant effect (p < .05) favoring the treatment group.
− signifies a statistically significant effect (p < .05) favoring the control group.
0 signifies a null or non-significant effect.
NA signifies that a grade level estimate could not be made.

NET children would be willing to experiment with new foods and would select the unfamiliar fruits and vegetables more often than non-NET children.

A second behavioral assessment, amount of waste of each food item in the school lunch, was made in grades 1-6. Because of the expense and logistical difficulties involved, plate waste data were collected according to a quasi-experimental design that involved subsampling approximately 500 children in three NET and two non-NET schools that volunteered for the study. Plate waste data were gathered for four days at pretest and again at posttest. The same menus were served on the same days at both test points, and measurements were made of the amount of each food item remaining for each child. Two measures of waste were examined: (1) total waste and waste by food group as percentages of average serving sizes, and (2) the proportion of children who ate none of a given food at pretest but who at least tested that food at posttest. In this area the Nebraska program developers noted that while overall waste reduction was not a goal of their program, NET children should be more willing to try previously rejected foods than their non-NET peers.

Analysis

The primary analytic technique used to assess the impact of the Nebraska NET program was the analysis of covariance. Analyses were performed within grades and across grades (for grades 1-3 and for grades 4-6). Further, analyses were conducted using both children and classrooms as the unit of analysis. As can be seen in the results section, the unit is of little consequence to the overall findings because in nearly all cases the same pattern of statistically reliable results emerges, whatever the unit. Finally, separate analyses were performed for each dependent variable. The analytic model used for each outcome variable in the cross-grades analyses had a single covariate (pretest score), two stratification factors (grade and sex), and a treatment contrast (NET versus non-NET). The within-grade model was identical except that sex was the only stratifier.

An analysis of pretest scores for NET and non-NET children revealed minimal differences, reinforcing our confidence that the randomized design lead to essentially equivalent treatment and control groups. The strength of this design is that it rules out a host of hypotheses that otherwise would compete with the treatment as possible causes of observed effects (e.g., preexisting treatment/control group differences). Further, the design permits replication across three grades, two units of analysis, and many measures. This explicit strategy of replication serves, in many cases, to render a number of otherwise plausible alternative hypotheses implausible and permits us to look for patterns of effects instead of relying solely on the statistical reliability of a single analysis.

RESULTS

The discussion of evaluation results presented here includes findings about (1) program implementation, (2) program impact on measures of nutrition-related

TABLE 4   Summary of Pre/Post Results by Content Domain and Grade Level

Content Domain	Grades 1-3	Grades 4-6
Nutrition Knowledge		
(Curriculum-Specific)	Positive Effects	Positive Effects
(General Knowledge)	No Effects	Positive Effects
Food Attitude	No Effects	No Effects
Food Preference		
(Reported Preference)	Positive Effects	Mixed Effects
(Willingness to Select New Foods)	Positive Effects	N.A.
Food Habits/Behavior		
(Reported Habits)	No Effects	No Effects
(Willingness to Taste New Foods)	No Effects	Positive Effects
(Plate Waste)	No Effects	No Effects

knowledge, attitudes preferences, and habits, and (3) the results of a follow-up study.

Implementation of the Program

Teachers and food service personnel did, in fact, implement the Experience Nutrition curriculum packages. In order to accommodate the evaluation, delivery of the packages had to be "concentrated" into a ten-week span. In spite of this, the average classroom teacher implemented close to eighty percent of the scheduled class-level activities, and the average school food service director implemented close to sixty percent of the scheduled school-level activities. Comments supplied by classroom teachers suggest that they may well have, without our knowledge, implemented portions of the school-level packages that were intended to be taught by food service personnel, and so the estimates of school-level implementation are likely to be lower bounds on the real values. The Experience Nutrition program developers do not specify any particular sequence or timing for implementation, preferring that teachers use the curriculum packages to fit their needs. Thus, the amount of activities covered in the ten-week span allowed a fair test of the treatment.

Impact of the Program

The Experience Nutrition curriculum had positive effects on children in some areas and no effects in others. Table 4 presents a summary of results by content domain and grade level, while Table 3 presents more detailed information.

Effects on knowledge. The strongest and most positive finding is that of positive treatment effects on nutrition knowledge. These effects are compelling as they hold across grades and across different measures of knowledge. Further, they are stable when either children or classrooms are used as the unit of analysis. The positive knowledge effects are clearest in grades 4-6 where statistically significant effects are exhibited on all seven different knowledge measures (e.g., recognition of nutrients, knowledge of the digestive system, relation of energy to calories, knowledge of what food supplies). Perhaps most impressive is the fact that the knowledge gains produced on the six measures, which were developed specifically to assess the effects of the Experience Nutrition curriculum in grades 4-6, are replicated in statistical significance and in magnitude by gains on a "standardized" test (the Nutrition Education Assessment Series) developed by Planning, Development and Evaluation associates to measure a broader spectrum of nutrition knowledge. Clearly, "teaching the test" is easier than producing knowledge gains that transfer to a more general, but still heavily overlapping, measure of knowledge.

In grades 1-3, positive effects on nutrition knowledge exist but are not quite as clear as those in grades 4-6. The major difference is that in grades 1-3 positive knowledge effects are found on curriculum-specific measures (e.g., knowledge of breakfast foods, knowledge of foods that grow underground), but not on the more general measure of nutrition knowledge derived from the Nutrition Achievement Test (developed by the National Dairy Council), which was not targeted to the Nebraska curriculum.

In addition to the finding of statistically significant effects on nutrition knowledge, it is important to note that the effects are large in an absolute sense. The adjusted treatment/control group differences on the nine knowledge measures that exhibit significant effects range from .23 to .82 standard deviations. This compares favorably with other field studies in education where effects of .25 standard deviations are often regarded as large. Thus, the effects on knowledge are statistically significant and importantly large. There is also evidence that for many knowledge measures a higher level of implementation is associated with larger effects. That is, children who were taught more, learned more.

Effects on food attitudes. The curriculum did not significantly alter attitudes about food in any consistent manner. In grades 1-3 no significant effects were found in any grade. For grades 4-6 some positive effects were found with respect to attitudes toward food consumption and attitudes toward breakfast; however, these were inconsistent and varied by grade.

Effects on food preference. There is strong evidence of positive effects on food preference in grades 1-3. First, the Experience Nutrition curriculum influenced children's self-reported preference for vegetables. As was the case for knowledge, the findings are enhanced by the fact that classrooms where the curriculum package dealing with vegetables was best implemented showed more pronounced changes in reported preferences.

Second, and more importantly, positive effects were noted in grades 1-3 on a behavioral measure—increased willingness to select unfamiliar vegetables. That is, when given a choice in the school lunch line between an unfamiliar and a familiar vegetable, NET children were more likely to select the unfamiliar one than their non-NET counterparts. The evidence for effects on preference for fruits is not so consistent, but what there is suggests that the program may well have led children to select unfamiliar fruits when offered a choice in their school lunch.

In grades 4-6 the effects on food preferences are mixed. No effects are evident with respect to self-reported preferences for vegetables, and the positive results for fruits are inconsistent across grades and are not replicated when classes are used as the unit of analysis. Behavioral data on food selection were not collected in grades 4-6.

Effects on reported food habits. There were no positive or negative effects on reported food habits either in grades 1-3 or 4-6. Measures of "good" and "bad" consumption habits, school lunch habits, and active and inactive habits all showed no effect. If the program did, in fact, have an impact on reported food habits we are fairly sure it would have been detected by at least one of these measures.

Effects on behavioral food habits. Data on changes in eating patterns gathered via measurement of plate waste support the hypothesis that the Nebraska NET program had an impact on children's willingness to sample previously untasted foods. That is, after participation in the program NET children were more willing to taste foods that they did not eat before the program than were non-NET children. However, when the data are broken down by grade it is apparent that the entire treatment effect occurs in grades 4-6; there are no treatment/control group differences in grades 1-3. This is contrary to expectations since the Nebraska curriculum emphasizes experimenting with foods in grades 1-3 and knowledge gains in grades 4-6.

The data on amount of food wasted indicate that no treatment-related changes occurred either across or within food groups. There are some pre/post changes in consumption for individual foods within individual schools, but these changes are inconsistent and weak. It is reasonable to conclude that the Nebraska NET program had no consistent effect on the amount of food wasted by participating children during the school lunch period. This does not preclude the possibility of changes occurring in the home or in other food-related situations.

Because this part of the evaluation used a quasi-experimental design, findings regarding food consumption (positive effects in terms of encouraging NET children to sample previously rejected foods and no effects on total consumption cannot be given the same weight as the other findings on nutrition knowledge, attitudes, preference, and reported food habits. Even so, it should be recognized that the results conform to the pattern of effects hoped for by the Nebraska program developers who state (a) that their program encourages experimentation with different foods and teaches children to be willing to taste unfamiliar food items, but (b) that they place no value on the amount of food consumed. We have seen that the effects are at variance with expectations in one respect, because children in grades 1-3 show no change in terms of willingness to taste previously rejected foods while children in grades 4-6 show substantial change, and speculate that this pattern of effects may be reflective of a need for the provision of nutrition knowledge before behavior change can be expected.

Follow-up results. In order to investigate whether the positive effects on nutrition knowledge and food preference reported above are enhanced, sustained, or whether they decay over time, and in order to see whether effects on food attitudes and reported food habits can be detected over a longer period of time, follow-up data were collected almost a year after pretesting. As promised, treatment and control classrooms were given the option of using Experience Nutrition materials during the period between posttesting (May 1980) and follow-up testing (December 1980). Very few classrooms did so; however, many teachers reported plans to use the curriculum packages in the spring.

The follow-up data reveal that positive knowledge effects were maintained in all grades, although effects were not quite as strong as the follow-up as at the posttest (see Table 3). The positive effects on food preferences that were seen in grades 1-3 were not detected at the follow-up, leading us to conclude that these effects decayed when the program was withdrawn. Finally, there was no evidence of "delayed" or "sleeper" effects for food attitudes or reported food habits—no effects were found in these domains either in the main evaluation or in the follow-up.

CONCLUSIONS

With the pattern of effects we have found in mind, two issues need to be considered including (1) the degree to which we believe that the Nebraska program rather than some other influence was responsible for the results, and (2) the degree to which the results of this study say something about the effectiveness of the Experience Nutrition curriculum outside of Nebraska and the effectiveness of the national NET program.

We are quite confident that the treatment, rather than some extraneous factor, caused the effects reported here. An examination of plausible rival hypotheses (e.g., unreliability of measures, treatment diffusion, competing treatments, teacher administration of tests, differential attrition) uncovered little to dispel this notion (St. Pierre, Glotzer, Cook, and Straw, 1981). Further, consideration of whether this evaluation might have overestimated or underestimated the true treatment effects leads us to conclude that our findings may well represent lower bounds. It is possible that children exposed to more of the Experience Nutrition packages, over a longer time span, and measured with improved instrumentation, would exhibit larger gains than those shown in this study.

Three other studies yield additional information on the effects of the Nebraska NET program and allow us to broaden our perspective. First, Majure (1980) reported results from a quasi-experimental evaluation of Nebraska's Experience Nutrition materials in eight states and metropolitan areas. Findings of this study indicated significant positive treatment effects on several measures including breakfast variety, breakfast tradition, key nutrients, food safety, food advertising, and physical fitness.

In a second, related study, the Swanson Center for Nutrition (1979) reported the results of a field test of the Experience Nutrition materials in three Nebraska school districts. The data from many measures show pre-posttest gains, and the report concludes that the program had positive effects on children's behavior (selection of foods not previously eaten) and nutrition-related knowledge. No effects were found on attitudes. It is difficult to know whether this interpretation is valid, since the study did not employ a comparison group.

Finally, Crosby and Grossbart (1980) mailed questionnaires to the parents of children who participated in the present evaluation of the Experience Nutrition program. Parents reported positive program effects such as NET children being more likely than their non-NET counterparts to know about nutrition and about different foods, to ask for meal items and snacks learned about in school, and to believe that a balanced diet is important. Parents also reported considerable parent-child interaction over the program. The study is flawed by a rather low 44% response rate that could well have biased the results in favor of NET.

To sum up, these three studies find generally positive effects of the Experience Nutrition curriculum. Though the methodological flaws of the studies would render them unconvincing if taken alone, they corroborate the findings and increase our confidence in the present evaluation.

The evidence should therefore be regarded as showing that NET can work; that a well-developed, centrally administered, curriculum-oriented nutrition education program can have positive effects on children's knowledge and behaviors. However, it cannot tell us whether the Experience Nutrition curriculum will work as well in other locations, nor can it tell us about the success of other NET models.

DISCUSSION OF RESULTS

The pre/post findings from this evaluation have implications for the cognitive theory outlined earlier that underlies education programs having the long-run goal of impacting children's behaviors.[2] These include, for example, most nutrition and health education programs, safety training programs, and so on. To begin, we will restate the simple causal chain outlined earlier in which changes in nutrition-related knowledge lead to changes in attitudes, which in turn cause changes in food preferences, which finally lead to altered food-related behaviors.

The first piece of evidence for or against the utility of this model stems from an examination of the place of attitudes. The evaluation found positive effects on nutrition-related knowledge that is presumed to be causally prior to attitudes, as well as positive effects on food preference and food-related behaviors that are presumed to follow from attitude change. Since these effects are found in the absence of altered attitudes it is not at all clear that attitudes play an important part in the hypothesized causal change (assuming that attitudes have been measured validly in this study).

The second point to be made requires us to consider the causal chain that remains when attitudes are dropped: knowledge-preferences-behavior change. Examining the results from grades 1-3 offers a theoretical puzzle since there are positive effects on knowledge and on food preferences, but no evidence of effects on food-related behaviors, the final variable in the chain. Yet, at grades 1-3 the Nebraska curriculum is expressly oriented to behavior change.

Why, when the curriculum stresses behavior change and when we have positive effects on the two presumably causally prior variables, do we not observe changes in behavior? Several reasons can be advanced. For example, the changes in knowledge or food preference might not be large enough to lead to behavior change. Remember that at grades 1-3, knowledge change was detected on curriculum-specific tests but not on more general measures. Alternatively, it may be that for children in grades 1-3 altered knowledge and changed food preferences are not sufficient to affect behavior. Perhaps at these grades we need to affect other variables not included in our simple causal chain, e.g., parental food habits or the presentation of food in the school lunchroom. Finally, behaviors may have been altered but we failed to measure them. For example, behaviors at home might have changed whereas we observed behaviors only in the school lunch line.

The third point we will make deals with children in grades 4-6. Returning to the knowledge-preference-behavior causal chain, we have the following set of findings: large positive effects on knowledge and behaviors, but no changes on food preferences. The picture is complicated because the measurement of food preferences at grades 4-6 was less comprehensive than at grades 1-3. That is, we measured self-reported preference for vegetables and fruits, but did not obtain measures of willingness to select unfamiliar fruits or vegetables in the school lunch line. Therefore, one explanation for the absence of changes in food preferences is that they occurred but we failed to measure them. In this case the three-step causal chain is complete. If we assume the opposite, that there were no changes in food preference, then the data suggest that at grades 4-6 it is possible to leap from knowledge to behavior change without altering either attitudes or preferences.

In closing, it should be reiterated that this evaluation was not set up as a theory-testing study, and that the preceding discussion presents indirectly obtained evidence on the causal processes underlying a cognitive theory of behavior change. Though the data are generally consonant with this theory there are other theories that could also hold.

NOTES

1. The first 20 applicants for the Nebraska NET program had been guaranteed access to the program by state department officials. Hence, the three schools randomly selected from the first 20 of

the 98 applicants were all assigned to the treatment group. The remainder of the assignment process was random.

2. It was not possible to include a dicussion of the implications of follow-up results as behavioral measures were not made at the follow-up.

REFERENCES

Crosby, L., and S. Grossbart (October 1980) "Memorandum to Glenda Uhrmacher." Lincoln: University of Nebraska, College of Business Administration.

Harman, D. (1977) "Nutrition education: an analytic description of current practice." Cambridge, MA: Harvard Institute for International Development. (unpublished)

Kelman, H. C. (1974) "Attitudes are alive and well and gainfully employed in the sphere of action." *American Psychologist* (29, 5: 317.

Kotler, P. and G. Zaltman (1977) "Social marketing: an approach to planned social change." *Journal of Marketing* 35 (July: 3-12.

Majure, W. (Spring 1980) Evaluation report: Eight-state consortium. Red Oak, IA: *Experience Education.*

St. Pierre, R. G. (1981) *An Evaluation of the Nutrition Education and Training Program: Project Summary.* Cambridge, MA: Abt Associates, Inc.

———Glotzer, J., Cook, T., and Straw, R. (1981) *An Evaluation of the Nutrition Education and Training Program: Nebraska's Experience Nutrition Curriculum.* Cambridge, MA: Abt Associates, Inc.

Stanfield, J. P. (1976) "Nutrition education in the context of early childhood malnutrition in low resource communities." *Proceedings of the Nutrition Society* 35: 131.

Swanson Center for Nutrition (July 1979) *Nutrition Education Field Test Evaluation Report.* Omaha, NE: Swanson Center for Nutrition.

Zeitlan, M. F., and C. S. Formacion (1981) *Nutrition Education in Developing Countries: Study II, Nutrition Education.* Cambridge, MA: Oelgeschlager, Gunn, and Hain.

31

The Geriatric Long-Stay Hospital Patient
A Canadian Case Study

Evelyn Shapiro and Noralou P. Roos

Abstract. This article examines the use of acute beds by the elderly in Manitoba over the five-year period, 1972–1976. The analysis reveals that transfers of long-stay (greater than 90 day) elderly to long-term care facilities took longer in 1976 than in 1972 despite major provincial initiatives which included construction of additional long-term treatment beds, expansion of home care resources, and extension of universal insurance coverage to long-term institutional and home care.

Analyses of means to reduce long hospital stays prior to transfer suggests that building more long-term beds may be the least desirable policy alternative.

Across North America concern has been expressed about the so-called "back-up" of geriatric patients in acute hospitals, focusing on those who have recovered from the acute stage of illness, but for whom prompt transfer is not made to rehabilitation facilities, chronic care institutions or home care programs. This concern has been heightened by the anticipated growth in the absolute number of the elderly and their increasing proportion of the total population.

The growing number of in-hospital patient surveys designed to identify beds occupied by persons no longer requiring hospital care attests to a rising preoccupation with the appropriate use of hospital beds. Such beds are not available for new admissions (entry to them is said to be blocked) and the elderly patients in these beds are usually persons whose needs might better be met elsewhere. The report of a Committee established by the Hospital Council of Metro Toronto[1] documented the problems associated with discharging long-stay patients from hospitals. It ascribed blocking of acute beds to lack of coordination between acute and long-term care institutions, limitations of home care policies, inadequate dis-

This research was supported by Grant Number 607-1157-46 Research Programs Directorate, Health and Welfare Canada and a Career Scientist Award 607-1001-22 to the second author. The authors are indebted to members of the Manitoba Health Services Commission who helped make the research possible, particularly Reg Edwards, Fred Toll, and former member, Steve Kavanagh.

charge planning, and shortage of long-term care beds. A "spot check" of 50 New York City hospitals found ten percent of the beds occupied by "holdover patients," those for whom acute care was not needed, but for whom long-term facilities were not available.[2]

Bed-blocking is perceived as a problem by medical practitioners, hospital administrators, government and the public at large. Physicians find their ability to admit new patients restricted.[3] These restrictions limit their capacity to respond to the needs of patients requiring hospitalization and their own fees-for-service.

Pressure from their medical staffs for more rapid access to beds and their own identification as providers of acute care lead hospital administrators to become active participants in the search for solutions to this problem despite their awareness that cost savings might be obtained by "staffing down" to care for long-term patients who require fewer high cost services than the acutely ill.

Whether told directly by their physicians or informed by the media that new admissions have been delayed because long-stay patients cannot be discharged, individuals awaiting entry to hospitals and the public at large perceive bed-blocking as a real or potential threat to their own health.

Governments in both Canada and the United States perceive acute care bed-blocking without hospital staff adjustments as inimical to their interests in containing health care costs. They are also under pressure from physicians, hospitals, and the public to find solutions to the problem.

While all the above-mentioned constituencies have legitimate interests in unclogging hospital beds, long-stay patients, usually the elderly, and their relatives are often the "victims" of the current situation. Negative attitudes of hospital personnel towards these patients[4] often result in further damage to their already fragile self-esteem. Visiting relatives may be pressed by hospital staff to remove the patient from the facility. Some relatives respond by ceasing to visit patients, leaving them lonely and isolated. Mental deterioration and additional medical complications also occur when these "unwanted" patients remain in hospitals.[5] Furthermore, Hart[6] and others have noted a disturbing trend to discourage emergency admissions of the elderly for fear that they may subsequently be difficult to discharge. Bed-blocking clearly has both economic and human costs.

The solutions recommended to alleviate geriatric bed-blocking differ, depending upon the perspective of the author. They include: (1) new building programs to accommodate the rehabilitative and custodial needs of the geriatric population; (2) implementation or expansion of home care programs;[7] (3) a better health care system to ensure progressive patient care and prompt transfer of patients to the appropriate level of care;[8] and

(4) reallocation of existing beds from acute to rehabilitation or chronic care.[9]

Over the 1972–1976 period, several of these proposed solutions were introduced into Manitoba. By 1975, the province was acknowledged to have most of the components deemed essential for serving the health needs of the elderly.[10] However, by the end of 1976 concern with a geriatric back-up in acute beds had not abated.

This article will first describe the major changes in Manitoba which might have been expected to affect geriatric acute-care bed utilization. The actual changes in utilization will then be described using claims data generated by the provincial health insurance program.[11] These data present a unique opportunity to assess the impact of program and policy changes on acute care bed utilization.

Long-term care for the elderly in Manitoba

Manitoba, one of ten Canadian provinces, is located in the center of Canada. Approximately 55 percent of the just over one million Manitobans live in the City of Winnipeg; the remainder live in small cities (population under 50,000), towns, villages and rural areas. Seventy-two percent of physicians, and 57 percent of hospital beds are concentrated in Winnipeg, the provincial capitol and site of the medical school. This analysis will focus on developments in Winnipeg, since its health care resources, and therefore the impact of the new policies, were different there than in rural Manitoba.[12]

In 1976, Manitoba had approximately 5.5 acute beds/1,000 population—slightly more than the U.S. average of approximately 5 beds/1,000.[13] Between 1972 and 1976 the percentage of elderly 65 years or older in the province increased from 9.5 percent to 10.1 percent of the total population. During that time, Winnipeg sustained a small loss of approximately 100 of 3,300 acute beds (three percent). During this period the occupancy rate in Winnipeg hospitals dropped slightly but stayed in the range of 80–85 percent. Hospital care, including institutional restorative treatment and medical services, was fully covered by public insurance introduced in 1958 and 1969 respectively. Insurance is universal, with neither usage limits nor usage fees.

During the period under review, there was a major expansion of long-term rehabilitation beds in Winnipeg. In 1974, 188 such beds were added, doubling the previous supply available to the elderly.[14] Both the existing and new rehabilitation units in Winnipeg determine their own criteria for admission. Between 1972 and 1976 Winnipeg experienced a net loss of 123 nursing home beds out of approximately 4,000.[15] Thus, by 1976 Winnipeg had 68 beds per thousand residents age 65 and over. Put another way, by 1976, 6.5 percent of Manitoba's elderly (65 and over) lived in nursing homes compared with approximately five percent of U.S. elderly.[16] A major change affecting Winnipeg geriatric patients was the curtailment of long-term psychiatric care at the nearby provincial mental hospital, where occupancy was reduced from 536 to 340 and new geriatric admissions were actively discouraged.

In July 1973 nursing home care became publicly insured with admission based on assessed need for placement, rather than on ability to pay. A modest per diem charge (from $4.50 to $6.50/day) to the resident was included. Such a usage charge does not characterize the hospital nor the long-term rehabilitation system. While placement was confined to those meeting predefined criteria, each nursing home retained the right to determine whom it would admit from among its referrals and individuals retained the right to specify their institution of choice. Data gathered since the introduction of insurance coverage indicate that the average length of stay in nursing homes has increased, making somewhat fewer existing beds available each year for new admissions.

In September 1974 home care was publicly insured with access based on professionally-assessed need. Prior to this time, the budgets of all Winnipeg hospitals included funds to provide some home care services to discharged patients. The long-term ill and disabled living in the community could also receive some home care services if they qualified for social assistance. With insurance, all existing home care programs were integrated into one system. Services were also expanded in Winnipeg to more fully meet the needs of persons requiring long-term care. Home care provided basic, supportive, and remedial services (such as homemaking and nursing) at home to all persons assessed as requiring services, as long as the cost per person did not exceed the cost of equivalent institutional care required.

The agency assessing need for home care also assessed need for nursing home placement. However, persons able to manage on home care could still choose nursing home placement if they met the eligibility criteria for institutional admission and if, as indicated above, the nursing homes agreed to their admission.

To summarize, then, over the period from 1972 to 1976 important organizational and financial changes in Manitoba should have affected the use of acute beds by geriatric patients. Rehabilitation beds were built, home care programs were expanded, and access to all alternative services was based on assessed need, not ability to pay. Health planners have long viewed such developments as methods for reducing geriatric demand for acute hospital beds.[17]

However, in 1976 press reports still highlighted the problem of geriatric long-stay patients who unnecessarily occupied acute hospital beds. Research was undertaken to try to determine what happened to geriatric utilization in Winnipeg over the five-year period, 1972–1976.

What happened to the elderly's acute hospital usage and why?

From 1972–1976, the elderly's use of acute hospitals increased, despite the fact that the province's overall usage of acute hospitals fell by eleven percent.

In 1972 those age 65 and over averaged 5.39 hospital days per thousand compared to 5.56 days per thousand in 1976 (an increase of three percent). Since the number of elderly admissions to acute hospitals declined slightly, this increase was produced by longer stays for those admitted. (Average length of stay increased from 15.2 days in 1972 to 16.9 days in 1976 for those 65 and older.) The largest increases (fifteen percent) occurred in acute stays of very elderly patients (those 75 and over), precisely that group whose stays the additional long-term beds, home care services, and nursing home insurance would be expected to affect most.

Elsewhere the investigation of this apparent dilemma is reported in some detail.[18] This analysis focuses on isolating the factors which contributed to the increasing backup of geriatric patients in acute beds. Our conclusions are summarized below.

The elderly's increased usage of acute hospitals was not due to the general aging of the population, nor more importantly, to a large increase in the very elderly (those 85 and older), who are the highest users of acute hospital days. The analysis was standardized for age, and the proportion of elderly 85 and older increased no more rapidly over this five-year period than did Manitoba's population as a whole.

An increase in certain types of illnesses or multiple pathologies (a changing case-mix) among the hospitalized elderly was ruled out as an explanation for longer hospital stays. A Laspeyres-type case-mix index[19] was used to determine how much of the increased length-of-stay was due to change in case-mix between 1972 and 1976, and how much was due to increased stays for the same type of case. No change was found in case-mix over the five-year period. However, by 1976 those patients aged 76 and older were staying in hospitals much longer for any given condition than they would have in 1972. Longer stays of the younger elderly (65 to 75 years) were also not explained by a changed case-mix.

An attempt was also made to determine whether longer stays were caused by a change in treatment modes or by more short term in-hospital rehabilitation of elderly patients. If longer stays had been influenced by these factors, this would have reflected an increase in short to medium-length stays (under 90 days), rather than in very long stays. However, further analysis eliminated this explanation. The average length of under 90-day-stays actually dropped by one day over the five-year period for each of four elderly age groups examined. However, the average length of the over 90-day-stay increased sharply, with the largest increases occurring in very elderly patients' stays.

One can not conclude that increased hospital usage by elderly patients is simply an example of Roemer's Law,[20] i.e., that usage expands to fill the beds available. Over this entire period Winnipeg hospitals operated with high occupancy rates (80 percent or higher) while rural hospitals were relatively "empty" (with occupancy averaging 65 percent). Despite this difference, Winnipeg elderly patients had longer hospital stays and bigger increases in their lengths-of-stays than did elderly patients in rural hospitals.

The analysis concluded that the major factor contributing to the elderly's longer stays in acute hospitals was the transfer process. During this period there was a marked increase in the length of acute stays associated with a transfer to alternate treatment or care facilities. Table 1 reports average length-of-stay in acute hospitals over the five year period, according to the place to which patients were transferred from such hospitals.

The average time required to transfer a patient home increased slightly in Winnipeg (from 14.8 to 15.9 days). It may not be surprising that lengths of hospital stay prior to discharge home did not fall. Home care was available to Winnipeg hospital patients throughout the whole period.

In Winnipeg, despite the substantial increase in long-term rehabilitation beds in 1974, the average length of acute stays prior to transfer to such units also increased approximately four days between 1972 and 1976.

Table 1. The Elderly Patient's Average Length-of-stay in Winnipeg Acute Hospitals According to Transfer Site

Year of Discharge	Home*	Long-Term Rehabilitation	Nursing Home
1972	14.6	38.7	–
1973	14.8	43.8	34.3
1974	15.5	47.2**	53.2
1975	15.8	42.2	67.0
1976	15.9	42.4	71.2

* Includes individuals who died in hospitals and in 1972 and the first half of 1973, patients who were discharged to nursing homes.
** Based on 378 cases. All other cell sizes are larger.

However, the real back-up of geriatric patients occurred among those patients awaiting transfer to nursing homes. With a relatively constant supply of beds, the average acute stay doubled, from 34.3 days in 1973 to 71.2 days in 1976.[21]

Complexities associated with rating and funding of all institutional beds, changes in budget allocations from year to year, and other changes already referred to during this period, make it difficult to categorically assign specific causes to the elderly's increased length of hospital stay. Nevertheless, the results suggest that, despite provision of alternatives to acute care and removal of financial barriers to their use, long hospital stays were disproportionately associated with transfer problems. Why have the additional rehabilitation beds not decreased in-hospital waiting time and why has a constant nursing home bed supply resulted in increased waiting time in Winnipeg?

Why are there transfer problems?

Long-term rehabilitation units. Prompt transfer to rehabilitation units is critical if chances for improved physical functioning of the elderly are to be maximized. However, there is a conflict between an extended treatment unit's objectives and the hospital's desire to empty "misused" beds. Due to its control over admissions and its ability to select those with a high potential for successful care from both hospitals and the community, there is no assurance that an increase in the number of extended treatment beds in a facility will help speed up the transfer of long-stay hospital patients. For example, during 1975 and 1976, occupancy of the new Winnipeg rehabilitation unit was deliberately kept down if "suitable" patients were not identified.[22] Furthermore, although the number of patients accommodated in extended treatment beds increased substantially over this period, (from 726 to 1,305), the number of transfers from acute hospitals increased only slightly (from 611 to 732).

While the increase in the number of geriatricians in Winnipeg and the publicity surrounding the opening of new, long-term rehabilitation beds may have generated an increase in referrals for this service, this increased demand may only have provided a larger pool of persons from which these units could select patients.

The conclusion that even more rehabilitation beds are the solution must also be tempered by the fact that Manitoba had 13.1 beds[23] (of all types) per 1,000 population (of all ages in 1976), a figure higher than those of Alberta or Ontario, two of Canada's richest provinces. Significantly, Manitoba had more beds for higher level nursing home and rehabilitative care than did these two provinces. If Manitoba has too few rehabilitation beds, then North American standards in general must be too low.

Nursing homes. Although a timely transfer to nursing homes may not be as critical for patients' health status as transfer to rehabilitation, such transfers are critical if acute beds are to be freed. Three factors may help to explain why acute stays in Winnipeg hospitals increased markedly for patients awaiting transfer to nursing homes:

1. Patients could insist on remaining in a hospital until a nursing home of their choice was available. Although their choices were based usually on cultural, ethnic or geographic factors, a minority had economic reasons as well. By staying in a hospital, they avoided the per diem charge associated with nursing home residency.[24]
2. Nursing homes retained control over their own admissions and could also refuse to admit eligible persons or keep them waiting for a long time. People who were "different," particularly those who had behavior problems, were sometimes difficult or impossible to place. Closure of a substantial number of chronic-care psychiatric beds and a policy of discouraging psychogeriatric admissions to the remainder aggravated the problem. While only thirteen percent of the over 90-day-stay patients had psychiatric disorders in 1976, patients with such disorders were almost twice as likely to have extraordinarily long stays—one year or more—as were patients without such problems.
3. Specific payment rates assigned for each level of care produced incentives for nursing homes to give preference to admitting persons needing the lightest amount of care in the level for which they were assessed.[25]

With a slight decrease in the number of nursing home beds becoming available each month for new occupants in 1975 and 1976 and with the number of applicants remaining relatively stable,[26] these nursing homes also had more persons from which to choose their admissions.

In summary, inter-institutional transfer problems for long-stay hospital patients may not be solved by providing new resources as long as: (1) each facility to which these patients are referred retains the right to determine its own admissions criteria; and (2) there continues to be no coordination between a region's acute facilities, long-term institutions and home care services. Faced with more patients seeking admission, long-term rehabilitation facilities are likely to be more selective in choosing those who maximize their potential for fulfilling their perceived mission. Similarly, long-term care institutions are likely to select those they regard as most adaptable to their own environment and who will require the least amount of the level of service they contracted to deliver.

Policy alternatives. At present, there appears to be no combination of alternative care programs or "magic number" of rehabilitation or nursing home beds which can guarantee a substantial decrease in length of acute hospital stays for geriatric patients. The usual alternative to such back-ups is to build more beds of all types. Implementing such policy without taking account of the root causes of transfer problems will lead to a large and continuing commitment to long-term bed construction. However, the Manitoba experience suggests that a policy of just adding resources does not speed up the transfer of in-hospital patients to alternate care or treatment facilities.

Another alternative would require changes in the placement process. Rehabilitation and nursing home units could be required to accept patients according to the priority determined by a central screening and placement process. As an additional step, patients might be required to accept the first available placement pending transfer to a nursing home of their choice when the bed becomes available.

The advantage of establishing a mechanism for central assessment and placement would be its ability to ensure the transfer of an especially vulnerable segment of the population to the specific type of care most suited to each individual's needs as their needs change. If its assessment and placement functions were provided by the same community agency responsible for assessment and coordination of home care services, such a policy would have the effect of formalizing a health care system for the long-term ill, thereby enabling persons to be transferred to the lowest cost services most suited to their needs. However, as the Manitoba example also illustrates, a central assessment and placement process which does not include the right to decide who will be admitted and when individuals will be transferred is unlikely to alleviate the conditions leading to bed-blocking.

On the other hand, the loss of autonomy in determining their own admissions would likely encounter opposition from the affected institutions. Opposition could also be anticipated from patients disturbed at no longer being able to choose nursing homes in line with their ethnic, linguistic, and cultural needs even if placements elsewhere were only temporary.

Still another alternative is to do nothing. This would have the effect of reducing the number of acute beds but would do little to reduce costs unless the staffing patterns of wards accommodating long-term care patients were changed to reflect their differing needs. Furthermore, it would do little to improve the attitudes of hospital staff towards these patients and their families. Complaints and pressure for a solution from physicians could be expected to continue. However, doing nothing would serve to redistribute health dollars somewhat towards geriatric patients, a policy which Britain is pursuing through a painful resource redistribution program.[27]

A fourth alternative would be to formally redesignate some acute beds in hospitals as long-term beds. One Canadian province has decreed that at least ten percent of acute-care beds in all hospitals are to be reallocated to long-term care. Assuming a 310-day bed year, it would take 304 of Winnipeg's 3,300 acute beds to serve the long-stay (over 90 days) geriatric patient. While the afore-mentioned provincial edict applied to acute-care facilities with a relatively high bed-occupancy rate, New Jersey health officials recently recommended a somewhat similar solution by seeking federal approval to convert vacant hospital beds to nursing home units.[28] British authorities have also recommended a national formula for the redistribution of acute beds to long-term care.[29]

In such an arrangement, hospitals would staff light care units specifically for use by chronically-ill elderly patients. The kind of person who would be employed therein is likely to be more receptive to the type of work required for these patients than is the staff accustomed to an acute care setting. Furthermore, the cost of caring for the long-stay patient is considerably less than that for the acutely-ill patient. While hospitals generally do not have the same potential as do some nursing homes for providing a "homelike" residential and social environment, they have a greater capacity to provide rehabilitative treatment and follow-up care.

Redesignating beds, however, would also be likely to encounter resistance from physicians except in areas where there are more acute beds than physicians consider necessary. Hospitals would also be opposed if it meant a cut in their budgets. Also, bed-blocking could still occur if hospitals' long-term beds, once filled, were not emptied at some later date. Perhaps the potentially most serious disadvantage of this solution is that, unless it also included a central assessment and placement process, patients or their families would be encouraged to seek entry to the hospital as a way of gaining access to long-term beds.

Conclusion

While uneven development of health care resources throughout a province or state may require construction of long-term beds in some areas and use of some acute beds for long-term care in others, building more beds appears to be the least desirable option to reduce bed-blocking. Doing nothing may be the easiest option to adopt, but its social and economic costs must be acknowledged. Formally redistributing and reshuffling acute beds for long-term use would lower hospital costs, but, without an independent mechanism to determine admission priorities to the long-term beds, might favor admissions from hospital patients over community applicants. Setting up a central community-based agency for assessing need, for coordinating home care services, and for admitting persons on a priority-of-need basis to long-term treatment or care facilities may appear to be the most appropriate solution. However, it may be considered by some the most drastic because it interferes with the traditional, well-entrenched practice of institutions selecting their own admissions and of individuals selecting their own locus of care. However, such an agency could be instrumental in: (1) coordinating components of the health care system to meet the changing needs of a vulnerable segment of the population effectively and economically; and (2) maintaining an ongoing information system useful to regional resource planners. Including representation from the institutional sector in the placement decision making process and making genuine attempts to satisfy the ethnic and cultural, as well as physical, needs of persons requiring admission to long-term care facilities might increase the acceptability of this alternative to both health care providers and consumers.

Implementing one or a combination of these alternatives to building more long-term beds will be difficult. Formidable territorial, professional, and political obstacles stand in the way of an easy solution. Nevertheless, the rising cost of institutional care and a growing elderly population may make the development of a comprehensive policy package inevitable.

Notes

1. The Hospital Council of Metropolitan Toronto, *Report of the Committee on Extended Care Placement* (Toronto: The Hospital Council of Metropolitan Toronto, 1974).
2. R. I. Glass et al., "The 4 Score: An Index for Predicting a Patient's Non-Medical Hospital Days," *American Journal of Public Health* 67 (August 1977): 751–55.
3. C. McArdle, J. C. Wylie and W. D. Alexander, "Geriatric Patients in an Acute Medical Ward," *British Medical Journal* 4 (December 1975): 568–69.
4. V. W. Marshall, S. French and A. S. MacPherson, "Aged Former Patients: Dimensions of Health and Health Care." Paper presented at the Educational Meetings of the Canadian Association of Gerontology, Vancouver, B.C., November 1976.
5. C. McArdle, J. C. Wylie and W. D. Alexander, "Geriatric Patients in an Acute Medical Ward."
6. C. Hart, "Geriatric Patients in Acute Medical Wards," *British Medical Journal* 5 (January 1976): 41.
7. L. J. Shuman et al., "Reimbursement Alternatives for Home Health Care," *Inquiry* 13 (September 1976): 277–87; and V. A. Portnoi, "Sounding Board," *The New England Journal of Medicine* 300 (June 14, 1979): 1387–90.
8. W. G. Weissert, "Cost of Adult Day Care: A Comparison to Nursing Homes," *Inquiry* 15 (March 1978): 10–19; and Break D. Skelton, "The Future of Health Care for the Elderly," *Journal of the Geriatrics Society* 25 (January 1977): 39–46.
9. Department of Health and Social Security, *Priorities for Health and Personal Social Services in England: A Consultative Document* (London: Stationery Office, 1976a); and Marc Lalonde, "A New Perspective on the Health of Canadians: A Working Document," Department of Health and Welfare (Ottawa: Queen's Printer, 1974).

10. H. P. Hepworth, "Personal Social Services in Canada: A Review," *The Canadian Council on Social Development* 6 (Ottawa, Queen's Printer, 1975).
11. N. P. Roos, P. D. Henteleff and L. L. Roos, Jr., "A New Audit Procedure Applied to an Old Question: Is the Frequency of T & A Justified?" *Medical Care* 15 (January 1977): 1–18; and L. L. Roos et al., "Using Administrative Data Banks for Research and Evaluations," *Evaluation Quarterly* 3 (May 1979): 236–55.
12. E. Shapiro, N. P. Roos and S. Kavanagh, "Long-term Patients in Acute Care Beds: Is There a Cure?" *The Gerontologist* 20 (June 1980): 342–49.
13. National Center for Health Statistics, *Health Resources Statistics: 1976–77*, DHEW Pub. no. (PHS) 79-1509 (Washington, D.C.: U.S. Government Printing Office, 1979); and Manitoba Health Services Commission, *Annual Statistics 1976* (Manitoba: Queen's Printer, 1976), pp. 8–9.
14. 530 beds were officially listed in 1972 as extended treatment beds but only 140-80 of these beds provided long-term restorative treatment. The remainder were extended care beds.
15. While new homes were opened in Winnipeg, older substandard homes were closed.
16. R. L. Kane and R. A. Kane, "Care of the Aged: Old Problems in Need of New Solutions," *Science* 200 (March 1978): 913–19.
17. Nova Scotia Council of Health Background Papers, *Halifax, Communications and Information Centre*, 2 (Halifax: Province of Nova Scotia, 1972); and J. D. Restuccia and D. C. Holloway, "Barriers to Appropriate Utilization of an Acute Facility," *Medical Care* 14 (July 1976): 559–73.
18. Shapiro, Roos and Kavanagh, "Long-term Patients in Acute Care Beds."
19. Rafferty has measured variations in case proportions over time with a Laspeyres-type case-mix index. This index produces a theoretical overall mean stay that would have prevailed in 1976 if the lengths-of-stay for various types of conditions in 1976 had been the same as in 1972, but uses the actual case type proportions that existed in 1976. For example, an $I_{Case\ Mix}$ Index of 105 indicates that the overall mean stay was five percent higher in 1976 than in 1972 purely on the basis of changes that occurred in proportions of case types. A length-of-stay index was constructed to measure the independent effect of variations in individual lengths-of-stay on the 1976 mean stay. See J. Rafferty, "Enfranchisement and Rationing: Effects of Medicare on Discretionary Hospital Use," *Health Services Research* 10 (Spring, 1976): 51–52.
20. M. Roemer, "Bed Supply and Hospital Utilization: A National Experiment," *Hospitals* 35 (November 1961): 36–42.
21. The Nursing Home Insurance Program began July 1, 1973. While patients were admitted to nursing homes from acute hospitals prior to this date, no records of such transfer are available through the claims system and therefore such patients would appear in the pre-July 1973 data as discharged home.
22. L. L. Roos, "Final Report for the Evaluation of the Extended Care Unit." Report submitted to the Manitoba Health Services Commission (1978).
23. This figure includes all beds from hostels to acute care.
24. As of 1978 in-hospital patients awaiting transfer to nursing homes are also required to pay the per diem charge while in the hospital.
25. This effect has been noted in Monroe County, New York; see L. C. Price et al., "Second Year Evaluation of the Monroe County Long Term Care Program, Inc." Report prepared for the New York State Department of Social Services and the Health Care Financing Administration (December 1979). W. J. Scanlon, after reviewing U.S. studies of nursing home utilization patterns, suggests that the for-profit status homes may discriminate against the most severely impaired, precisely those with the most pressing needs. See W. J. Scanlon, "Nursing Home Utilization Patterns: Implications for Policy," *Journal of Health Politics, Policy and Law* 4 (Winter, 1980): 619-41.
26. The advent of nursing home insurance in 1973 initiated an increase in the number of Winnipeg applicants, but these numbers decreased by one-third shortly after the expansion of home care services and remained stable (with minor fluctuations) during 1975 and 1976.

27. Department of Health and Social Security, *Priorities for Health and Personal Social Services in England: A Consultative Document*.
28. *HMO and Health Services Report* (Arlington, N.J.: Gerard Associates, Inc., 1978).
29. Department of Health and Social Security, *Priorities for Health and Personal Social Services in England*.

32

Analysis of Interrupted Time Series Mortality Trends

An Example to Evaluate Regionalized Perinatal Care

Dennis Gillings, Diane Makuc, and Earl Siegel

Abstract: Interrupted time series designs are frequently employed to evaluate program impact. Analysis strategies to determine if shifts have occurred are not well known. The case where statistical fluctuations (errors) may be assumed independent is considered, and a segmented regression methodology presented. The method discussed is applied to the assessment of changes in local and state perinatal postneonatal mortality to identify historical trends and will be used to evaluate the impact of the North Carolina Regionalized Perinatal Care Program when seven years of post-program mortality data become available. The perinatal program region is contrasted with a control region to provide a basis for interpretation of differences noted.

Relevant segmented regression models provided good fits to the data and highlighted mortality trends over the last 30 years. Considerable racial differences in these trends were identified, particularly for postneonatal mortality. Segmented regression is considered relevant for the analysis of interrupted time series designs in other applications when errors can be taken to be independent. Thus, the methodology may be regarded as a general statistical tool for evaluation purposes. (*Am J Public Health* 1981; 71:38–46.)

Introduction

Interrupted time series designs occur frequently in evaluation studies since it is then possible to carry out an evaluation by taking advantage of naturally occurring situations or situations in which the evaluator has minimal control. Campbell and Stanley[1] refer to this type of design as a time series design and they proceed to consider a refinement, the multiple time series design, that also employs a control group. Ideally, the intervention is sudden, as otherwise the impact may be dissipated over a period of time, but no other restrictions are necessary. As we shall show, even the requirement of "suddenness" can be dropped because the method of analysis proposed is able to detect a sharp and immediate impact as well as slower changes that occur over time.

It is preferable to employ a control group so that a frame of reference for the interpretation of observed changes is available. The methodologic problem is the possibility that some other event (perhaps unrecognized) is responsible for observed changes rather than the innovation. The decrease in road traffic fatalities during 1956 in Connecticut following

a 1955 speeding crackdown[2,3] illustrates that sounder conclusions can be drawn if an entire time series together with a control is analyzed. There was an immediate reduction in traffic fatalities after the December 1955 crackdown but this reduction followed a substantial increase during 1955 and was of similar magnitude to previous decreases for which there was no particular explanation. In other words, the inherent instability of the time series was such that a drop for just one year was inadequate to justify program impact. However, analysis of an entire series helps the evaluator to assess changes in context and reject one year movements that may be spurious. Further, a control provides a baseline so that changes that could be due to the innovation can be distinguished from those resulting from other naturally occurring phenomena. Unfortunately, regression towards the mean may still provide an alternative, plausible explanation of program impact as it did for the Connecticut data.

The method of analysis proposed here is called segmented regression[4,5] or piecewise regression.[6] Use of the technique as an evaluation tool is illustrated through an application to assess historical trends in perinatal and postneonatal mortality. In connection with this historical review, a proposal to evaluate a Regionalized Perinatal Care (RPC) program in North Carolina using mortality and morbidity as outcomes is discussed. The definitive analysis for this mortality assessment will be undertaken when seven years of post-program data are available at the end of 1981.

A review of perinatal care literature shows the well known decline in perinatal mortality in the United States since 1965, but dramatic racial and geographic differences among mortality rates continue to exist.[7,8] In an effort to decrease these differences and further reduce mortality, RPC programs have become widespread. These programs

Address reprint requests to Dennis Gillings, PhD, Associate Professor, Department of Biostatistics, School of Public Health 201H, University of North Carolina, Chapel Hill, NC 27514. Dr. Makuc is now Statistician, Office of Deputy Assistant Secretary for Planning and Evaluation/Health, Dept. of HHS, Washington, DC. This research was done while Dr. Makuc was a doctoral student at the University of North Carolina. Dr. Siegel is Professor, Department of Maternal and Child Health, School of Public Health, University of North Carolina, Chapel Hill. This paper, submitted to the Journal January 16, 1980, was revised and accepted for publication August 25, 1980.

From Dennis Gillings, Diane Makuc, and Earl Siegel, "Analysis of Interrupted Time Series Mortality Trends: An Example to Evaluate Regionalized Perinatal Care," 71(1) *American Journal of Public Health* 38-46 (January 1981). Copyright 1981 by the American Public Health Association. Reprinted by permission.

seek to identify high risk pregnancies and newborn infants in order to obtain consultation and referral services from district (level II) and regional (level III) hospitals. Other aspects of RPC include the provision of transportation, continuing education for physicians, nurses, and other health professionals, and nutritional and social counseling during the prenatal period. These services increase costs, making it advisable to evaluate the effectiveness of regionalization. Although evaluations of RPC programs were known to be planned or in progress in at least 26 states as of 1974, there has been little published information to date.[9] Some evidence of a positive association between RPC and declining perinatal mortality was reported by the Perinatal Mortality Committee of the Province of Quebec over the time period 1967 to 1974.[10, 11]

In 1975 an RPC program was started in five rural counties in southeastern North Carolina and, from its inception, a comprehensive program evaluation has been implemented. Key to the evaluation is comparison of the five-county study region in which the program has been implemented with a three-county control region that does not have the direct benefit of regionalization. The control region was chosen on the basis of its similarity to the study region with respect to demographic, socioeconomic, and perinatal statistics as well as availability of health care facilities and local referral patterns. Details of North Carolina's program and the strategy for its evaluation have been described previously.[9, 12] The overall research design includes an evaluation of the following outcomes: perinatal and postneonatal mortality, maternal and newborn morbidity, infant developmental status, and maternal infant attachment at one year.

Objectives

The major objective of this paper is to present a segmented regression methodology to analyze interrupted time series designs, common in many evaluations today, and illustrate its use through a statistical assessment of perinatal and postneonatal mortality. An essential feature of the analysis will be to identify changes in time trends and test for differences between time trends in the study and control regions that were identified for the North Carolina RPC program evaluation. The second objective is to describe concisely perinatal and postneonatal mortality trends in the study and control regions from 1948 to 1974, the period prior to RPC program funding. The purpose of looking at an extended baseline period is to gain insights regarding reasonable expectations of future trends. It is also of interest to examine the past comparability of study and control regions, although differences prior to the late 1960s would not be expected to invalidate the evaluation design.

Sources of Data

In contrast to other aspects of the overall evaluation of the RPC program, the impact on mortality can be studied without collecting primary data by using vital statistics from

birth and death certificates. Fetal, neonatal, perinatal, postneonatal, and infant mortality rates for study and control regions were calculated by combining data from appropriate counties.[*] It is recognized that there could be differences in the quality of reporting vital statistics data between the two regions. No comprehensive assessment of the accuracy of the vital statistics data used has been undertaken although a thorough review of relevant issues was published recently in the *American Journal of Public Health*.[13, 14, 15]

Methodology

As mentioned in the introduction, the study design for the RPC mortality evaluation may be described as an interrupted time series design with a control group. The interruption is introduction of the perinatal program in the study region. The analytical method needs to be able to detect shifts or changes in trends and then test for differences between study and control changes. A suitable model that adequately describes trends in perinatal mortality from 1948 to 1974 was developed by examining yearly plots of perinatal mortality rates for the study and control regions (Figure 1, left side). The yearly plot for the study region suggests a downward trend in mortality between 1948 and the mid-1950s followed by a leveling off until the mid-1960s, and finally, another decreasing trend from the mid-1960s to 1974. In order to describe these trends in a more exact manner, it was felt desirable to fit a trend line to the yearly perinatal mortality rates. If a reasonable fit to the points was obtained, then trends could be described by a smooth line, eliminating the random variation observed in the jagged plot of Figure 1.

One method of fitting a line to these points is least squares as used in regression analysis. A curve with nonlinear terms could be used, but such a model would be difficult to interpret and not appropriate for identifying shifts due to the "interruption" of regionalization. An alternative approach which also uses least squares is segmented or piecewise regression.[4, 6] This method is appropriate when the response variable (perinatal mortality) has a linear trend over a certain range of the independent variable (time), followed by another linear trend over a succeeding range. Each time period having a separate linear trend is called a segment, and the years which divide segments are known as join points. When the number of segments and their join points are unknown, they may be estimated using relatively complex methodolo-

---

[*] The definitions of mortality rates conform with those used by the North Carolina vital statistics system: 1) *fetal* (stillbirths of 20 weeks or more gestation per 1000 live births plus fetal deaths); 2) *neonatal* (deaths less than 28 days after birth per 1000 live births); 3) *perinatal* (fetal plus neonatal deaths per 1000 live births plus fetal deaths); 4) *postneonatal* (deaths between 28 days and 364 days after birth per 1000 live births minus neonatal deaths). A 1971 North Carolina law modified the interpretation of a fetal death, since after 1971 therapeutic abortions were no longer considered to be fetal deaths. An example of the law's impact was observed in 1973 when approximately 400 fetal deaths of 20 or more weeks gestation were reported as therapeutic abortions. No information is available regarding whether the impact of the law change was equal in both regions.

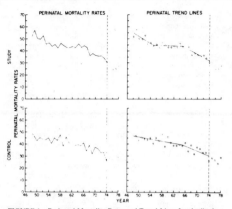

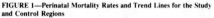

FIGURE 1—Perinatal Mortality Rates and Trend Lines for the Study and Control Regions

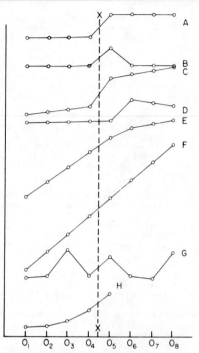

FIGURE 2—Some Possible Outcome Patterns from the Introduction of an Experimental Variable at Point X into a Time Series of Measurements, O_1-O_8. (Except for D the O_4-O_5 gain is the same for all time series, while the legitimacy of inferring an effect varies widely, being strongest in A and B, and totally unjustified in F, G, and H.)

SOURCE: Campbell DT and Stanley JC: Experimental and Quasi-Experimental Designs for Research, Chicago: Rand McNally College Publishing Company, 1966. Copyright 1963 American Educational Research Association, Washington, DC.

gy.[16,17] The choice of the join points 1955 and 1965 is subjective but is further supported by sensitivity analyses which indicate that if a preceding or following year was chosen, the trend lines would be unchanged except for shifts in the join points by one year.

Campbell and Stanley[1] identify eight patterns of time series data that may result from a program interruption. These are reproduced in Figure 2. A key consideration is the assumption of independent error terms discussed below. If errors can be considered independent, then segmented regression is appropriate for all cases except B and H. Case B represents a temporary effect and could be detected by fitting a regression line to O_1, O_2, O_3, O_4, O_6, O_7, and O_8, i.e., all points except where the temporary impact is supposed to occur. Then a 95 per cent confidence interval for O_5 may be derived from the regression equation and the observed O_5 value compared to this confidence interval. If it is outside the confidence range, then a significant effect can be inferred.

Case H would require a polynomial or other type of regression model, as a linear trend is not appropriate. Usually, situations like H may be identified by inspection or prior knowledge. Further attention to this is given below where a segmented model is compared to polynomial models. The remaining cases (A, C, D, E, F, G) could be handled by segmented regression, although the appropriate join point must be chosen for D if the impact is to be assessed with a powerful statistical procedure.

Details of the proposed segmented regression analysis for perinatal mortality trends are given as Model 1 in Appendix I. The methodology is identical to ordinary least squares regression, with the response variable perinatal mortality. The following four characteristics or parameters are estimated using this procedure:

β_0, the intercept for segment 1 or mean perinatal mortality in 1948;

β_1, the slope for segment 1 or linear trend in perinatal mortality between 1948 and 1955;

β_2, the difference in slopes or linear trends in perinatal mortality between segment 1 (1948–1955) and segment 2 (1956–1965); and

β_3, the difference in slopes or linear trends in perinatal mortality between segment 2 (1956–1965) and segment 3 (1966–1974).

If the same linear trend continues from the first segment to the second segment, then $\beta_2 = 0$. Similarly, if the same linear trend continues from the second to the third segment, then $\beta_3 = 0$. If we assume that perinatal mortality rates are normally distributed, then we can test the hypotheses $\beta_2 = 0$ and $\beta_3 = 0$ by means of standard procedures in regression.

In addition to changes in slope at the join points, it is also possible for discontinuities in the trend line to occur. This could be due to an event which causes a sudden increase or decrease in mortality with either a continuation of the slope at its previous level or a change in the slope. For example, the introduction of a program designed to decrease perinatal mortality might cause a sudden reduction in mortality rather than a gradual shift through a change in trend. To allow for changes of this sort, the model can contain additional parameters to estimate jumps in the trend line at one or more of the join points. Each additional parameter measures the discontinuity between two adjacent time segments or the difference in mean perinatal mortality for the two estimated trend lines at the join point. As before, we can test whether each of these parameters is significantly different from zero to determine whether a discontinuity at each join point exists.

In applying this methodology to perinatal mortality trends, discontinuity parameters were not included at the join points 1955 and 1965 because there was no reason to expect a sudden shift in mortality at these particular years. However, when extending the model to a fourth time period (1975-1981) to evaluate the impact of regionalization, the addition of a discontinuity parameter between time segments three and four would be appropriate. Model II of Appendix I gives the details of this extension which has two additional parameters, one to estimate discontinuity between trend lines in 1975, and the second to estimate the difference in linear trends between time periods three and four. The program's impact on perinatal mortality will be evaluated by testing whether each of the parameters is equal to zero in the study region, and also testing whether these estimates are equal to corresponding measures for the control region.

It has been suggested that the logarithm of perinatal mortality rates follows a normal distribution more closely than the actual mortality rates.[7] For this reason, the analysis was carried out twice, once using the observed mortality rates and a second time transforming the rates to logarithms. The same parameters were found to be significant in both analyses, and the residual plots were essentially identical. Therefore, to facilitate interpretation, all results will be presented using observed mortality rates rather than logarithms. It should also be noted that the tests of significance used in regression are not invalidated by mild departures from normality.

A critical assumption of the segmented regression methodology is variance homogeneity. Observed mortality may be represented by a binomial distribution, where p is the true underlying probability of death and n the number of live births (live births + fetal deaths in the case of fetal or perinatal mortality). Then np is the expected number of deaths. In practice r, the observed number of deaths, will not equal np due to chance fluctuations. These chance fluctuations correspond to the variances of interest when fitting the segmented regression model. It is required that these variances be the same from year to year (homogeneity of variance assumption) in order that the underlying theoretical assumptions be satisfied.

From year to year n will change by small amounts and p

may change as well. The variance of r will depend on both n and p. Clearly, then, the variances will vary from year to year and so will not be genuinely homogeneous. If there is considerable heterogeneity, weighted least squares procedures should be employed to fit the segmented regression instead of ordinary least squares. Alternatively, some other transformations may be tried such as the square root or arcsin to help stabilize variances. In the present example, plots of residuals showed that variance heterogeneity was only minimal. All of the above alternatives (weighted least squares, square root transformation with ordinary least squares and arcsin transformation with ordinary least squares) were tried but the results changed hardly at all. So the ordinary least squares procedure without a transformation is reported here. In practice this is also the analysis that is most well-known and is a little easier to carry out.

Assumption of Independent Error Terms

It is a moot point whether successive mortality rates are statistically "independent". Clearly, the mortality rates from year to year are linked insofar as they follow a trend and relate to a reasonably constant population in the short term. In this sense the rates from year to year are mathematically dependent. However, regression requires that the "random errors" associated with these rates be independent, not the rates themselves. The random errors are really fluctuations in number of deaths due to instability when small mortality rates are applied to small or moderate numbers of births. By and large, births from one year to the next will be to different mothers, and so there should be little direct carryover of mortality from year to year because of the same mothers giving birth. The Connecticut data concerning the speeding crackdown were analyzed under the assumption of correlated errors of measurement,[1] but those data related to many similar driving patterns by the same drivers in the same cars from one year to the next; so in that case, carryover causing correlated errors of measurement should be substantial, and the method of Box and Tiao[18] should be used. However, the perinatal data show no evidence of violating the assumption of independent error terms,** hence a simple model of segmented regression is appropriate.

Perinatal and Postneonatal Mortality Trends

The segmented regression methodology has been applied separately to all races combined and race specific***

** The Durbin-Watson test assumes a first-order autoregressive error model, and tests the null hypothesis that the autocorrelation parameter is zero. For the mortality data being analyzed, this hypothesis was not rejected and, thus, there is no direct evidence that the independence assumption needed for segmented regression is violated.

*** The term "race specific" throughout this paper is not quite accurate because Blacks and Indians are combined to form one group. This may obscure more detailed race specific differences. However, it was necessary to combine Blacks and Indians in this manner because the numbers of births to Indians were too small in the control region to allow separate analysis.

TABLE 1—Live Births, Perinatal Deaths, and Perinatal Mortality per 1,000 at Risk

	1948	1955	1965	1974
Study Region				
Live Births	6,594	6,893	4,639	4,307
Perinatal Deaths	353	308	204	132
Perinatal Mortality per 1000 at Risk	52.0	43.7	43.0	30.1
Control Region				
Live Births	4,344	4,708	3,895	3,310
Perinatal Deaths	223	195	154	88
Perinatal Mortality per 1000 at Risk	50.0	40.5	38.7	26.2
North Carolina				
Live Births	108,834	115,197	97,656	84,246
Perinatal Deaths	5,148	4,608	3,673	2,389
Perinatal Mortality per 1000 at Risk	46.2	39.2	37.0	28.0

perinatal mortality rates in the five-county study region, the three-county control region, and the state of North Carolina. Similarly, trend lines have been fitted to fetal, neonatal, and postneonatal mortality rates. In each case, a parameter indicating a shift in trend was kept in the model if it was significantly different from zero at $\alpha = .10$. Otherwise the successive shift parameters were not included, leaving the trend line smooth for the adjacent segments.

Table 1 presents the number of live births, perinatal deaths, and perinatal mortality per 1,000 at risk for the study and control regions and North Carolina for years 1948, 1955, 1965, and 1974, selected for illustrative purposes. The perinatal mortality rates reflect the proposed three segment model in that there are relatively large decreases in perinatal mortality from 1948 to 1955 and 1965 to 1974 but virtually no decrease from 1955 to 1965. At each of the selected years, perinatal mortality is slightly higher in the study region than the control, and at each of the first three time points both areas have higher perinatal mortality rates than the state as a whole.

Most critical to the evaluation of the RPC program is a comparison of perinatal mortality trends in the study and control region as shown in the right hand plots of Figure 1. For the study region, there is a significant linear decrease in perinatal mortality between 1948 and 1955 followed by a period of no change in mortality between 1956 and 1965, and finally another significant linear decrease between 1966 and 1974. For the control region, we see a somewhat different picture. The same downward slope continues over the period 1948 to 1965, indicating that there were no significant changes in linear trend between the first two time segments. This is followed by a change in slope between the second and third segments, with perinatal mortality decreasing more sharply than in segments one and two. A comparison of the two types of plots shown in Figure 1 illustrates the clarification to be gained by fitting the segmented trend lines rather than merely plotting the mortality rates.

It was previously mentioned that an alternative to the segmented regression approach would be to fit a nonlinear

curve to the data. A comparison of the proportion of variation explained (R^2) by each approach using the perinatal mortality rates for the study and control regions shown in Figure 1 yields the following results:

	R^2 for Study Region	R^2 for Control Region
Segmented regression	.91	.77
Polynomial regression		
linear	.82	.73
linear + quadratic	.82	.76
linear + quadratic + cubic	.89	.78
best model using backward elimination algorithm	.89	.77 (quadratic + cubic)

For the study region the same number of parameters are used in the segmented model as in the cubic model, and segmented regression explains a greater proportion of variation in the data. For the control region, the same fit to the data is obtained by applying backward elimination to the cubic model. However, the segmented model is much easier to interpret. The meanings of the quadratic and cubic terms are not readily apparent, particularly when it is ambiguous whether a quadratic or cubic model is more appropriate. However, the curves themselves (cubic or quadratic) are quite different as regards shape. In general, there would be no consistency between models fitted to differernt situations unless one decided arbitrarily that, say, a quadratic was preferred. As regards how well the model fitted, on some occasions it might be a cubic and on others a quadratic model. Then, it would not be clear how to make sensible comparisons between different situations.

The comparability of study and control regions was further investigated using tests of statistical significance as described in Appendix I, Model III. Null hypotheses of no difference in linear trends between the two regions were tested. During the first and second time periods, trends in the study

TABLE 2—Per Cent Nonwhite Live Births and Perinatal Mortality per 1,000 at Risk by Race

	1948	1955	1965	1974
Study Region				
Per Cent Nonwhite Births	55.3	60.4	59.0	61.8
White Perinatal Mortality	43.1	36.8	31.6	24.1
Nonwhite Perinatal Mortality	59.0	48.2	50.8	33.8
Control Region				
Per Cent Nonwhite Births	46.4	48.1	42.5	44.0
White Perinatal Mortality	40.5	35.0	26.1	18.4
Nonwhite Perinatal Mortality	60.9	46.4	55.4	35.8
North Carolina				
Per Cent Nonwhite Births	31.9	33.3	32.1	31.3
White Perinatal Mortality	37.9	31.2	29.7	23.4
Nonwhite Perinatal Mortality	63.6	55.0	52.2	38.0

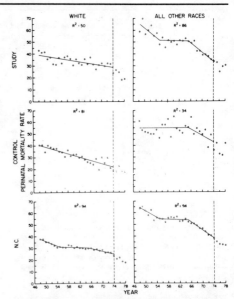

FIGURE 3—Study and Control Region and North Carolina Perinatal Mortality Trends for Whites and All Other Races

and control regions were significantly different (p .05), but there was no statistically significant difference in the more recent time period from 1966 to 1974. This supports the assumption of similarity of study and control regions during the period directly preceding program implementation. The same approach used to test differences in trends between the study and control regions prior to regionalization will also be used for evaluation of program impact during the period 1975 to 1981. The details of this extension of the model and hypotheses of interest are given in Appendix I, Model III.

Trend lines for the two components of perinatal mortality, fetal and neonatal mortality, were also fitted separately for the study and control regions. Since the results were similar to perinatal trends, particularly in the case of fetal mortality, they are not presented here.

It is well known that perinatal mortality rates differ by race with Blacks having higher mortality than Whites. For this reason, the segmented regression analysis was also carried out separately for Whites and Other Races. The racial composition of live births in the study and control regions and North Carolina is shown in Table 2, along with perinatal mortality by race. The study region has had a lower proportion of White births than the control, primarily due to a large American Indian population. In 1974, the study region had 25 per cent Indian births and 37 per cent Black births. There has been a decrease over time in both White and nonwhite perinatal mortality with the exception of the year 1965 when mortality for Blacks and Indians increased slightly.

Figure 3 presents "race specific" perinatal mortality trend lines. White trends are similar in the study and control regions, and trends for Other Races in the study region are the same shape as overall trends seen in Figure 1. However, the control region's trend line for Blacks and Others indicates that the segmented regression model is not appropriate in this case. Only 34 per cent of variation in mortality rates is explained by the trend line. Although the observed rates follow a smooth line from 1949 to 1953, in general the data points fluctuate too much from year to year for a trend to emerge clearly. This is at least partially due to small numbers since less than one-half of the births in the control region are Black.

Perinatal mortality rates for the years 1975, 1976, 1977, and 1978 have also been plotted in Figure 3. These are the only data presently available for the time period after the introduction of RPC. It is too early to apply the segmented regression methodology to determine trends for post-1974 data. At present, there is no clear evidence of any shifts in mortality rates.

The focus of the program evaluation is on the perinatal period, but it is also important to examine postneonatal trends to ensure that a decrease in perinatal mortality has not been accompanied by an increase in postneonatal mortality. Such an increase could indicate a postponement of death rather than its prevention. Figure 4 presents "race specific" postneonatal mortality trends for the study and control regions. The most striking aspect of these trends is the tremendous difference between Whites and Other Races. An adequate fit to the data is obtained in all four cases. The study and control regions have had similar trends in postneonatal mortality for Whites and Others with the study region having somewhat higher mortality rates. Prior to 1965, White postneonatal mortality decreased at a constant slope and then plateaued with a slight tendency to increase. However, this upward slope appears to have leveled off for the years 1975–1978. Prior to 1965, postneonatal mortality for Blacks and Others was strikingly higher than White mortality and fluc-

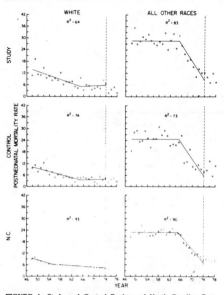

FIGURE 4—Study and Control Region and North Carolina Postneonatal Mortality Trends for Whites and All Other Races

tuated from year to year with no consistent trend. From 1966 to 1974, there was a sharp downward slope in mortality for Blacks and Others so that racial differences have narrowed considerably in recent years.

Figures 3 and 4 also present "race specific" perinatal and postneonatal trend lines for North Carolina. The North Carolina perinatal mortality trends closely resemble those for the study region as do the postneonatal trends for Blacks and Others. One difference that is observed for White postneonatal mortality is that the North Carolina rates do not show the slight tendency to increase after 1965 that was seen in the study and control regions.

Discussion

The analysis of time series designs can be awkward as it is not straightforward to distinguish discontinuities in trend lines from yearly fluctuations that typically occur. However, segmented regression seems to be a natural approach to this methodological problem in the case where the error terms for successive years may be assumed to be independent, since it is designed specifically to deal with situations that involve discontinuities or sharp changes. Segmented regression, as applied here, assumes a linear trend for each successive section. Whereas the assumption of linearity may be un-

warranted over a long interval, usually for the short haul it will serve as a good approximation to most real life situations. A comforting bonus is that linear approximations are easy to understand and the appropriate methodology relatively trivial to apply when modern computer packages are employed.[19] No statistical theory other than regression is required. The North Carolina perinatal and postneonatal data had only a small amount of variance heterogeneity and so ordinary least squares was applied. If variances are definitely heterogeneous, weighted least squares should be employed, where the weights are the inverse of the variances at each time point.

In the present example, the fitting of linear segments to data extending back to 1948 provides an historical review of the nature of previous shifts in trends. This has important implications to the ongoing RPC evaluation in North Carolina. The interpretation of, say, a significantly superior improvement regarding the reduction of perinatal mortality in the study region may be a less than convincing demonstration of the impact of regionalization if there were previous situations, without compelling explanations, where changes, in either direction and of similar magnitude, had taken place. Further, an historical comparison of study with control provides a thorough summary of the degree of similarity of perinatal and postneonatal mortality rates between the two regions. It is important for the control to be judged similar since then there is a valid basis for the assessment of program impact via a comparative analysis. North Carolina as a whole serves as an indirect control in that it identifies broader trends that have been taking place. Note that both pilot and control regional trends are contributing, albeit a small amount, to the overall state trends.

The study region was chosen partly because it had relatively high perinatal mortality, and so it is possible that regression toward the mean might operate to confuse the interpretation of results. However, the indicators of program impact used here are changes in trend as well as sudden shifts. It is unlikely that regression toward the mean will change trends to any large extent although such effects could influence the presence or size of sudden shifts. In any event, regression towards the mean would be as likely to occur in the control as the study region, and so this phenomenon is not regarded as a problem of any consequence for the analysis presented here.

It is well known that birthweight is the most powerful predictor of neonatal and perinatal mortality with the highest rates observed for low birthweight infants (≤ 2500 grams).[20, 21] A decrease in perinatal mortality should be accompanied by changes in birthweight distribution and/or weight-specific mortality rates. Evidence to date suggests that reductions in perinatal mortality have been primarily due to mortality decreases among low birthweight infants, rather than shifts in birthweight distributions, and that this decline is at least partially explained by advances in perinatal medicine such as neonatal intensive care units.[22] Future work on the evaluation of RPC in North Carolina will examine birthweight specific changes in perinatal mortality and changes in birthweight distributions using vital statistics data.

REFERENCES

1. Campbell DT and Stanley JC: Experimental and Quasi-experimental Designs for Research. Chicago: Rand McNally College Publishing Co., 1966.
2. Campbell DT and Ross HL: The Connecticut crackdown on speeding: Time-series data in quasi-experimental analysis. Law and Society Review 1968; 3:33-53.
3. Glass GV: Analysis of data on the Connecticut speeding crackdown as a time-series quasi-experiment. Law and Society Review 1968; 3:55-76.
4. Monti K, Koch GG, Sawyer J: An application of segmented linear regression models to the analysis of data from a cross-sectional growth experiment. Institute of Statistics Mimeo Series #1200. Chapel Hill: University of North Carolina, 1978.
5. Freeman JL and Koch GG: Linear segmented analysis: Statistical methodology for analyzing frequency tables pertaining to the relationship between unwanted pregnancies and media-time factors. Appendix C IN: The Media and Family Planning. Udry JR et al. Cambridge, MA: Ballinger Publishing Co., 1974.
6. Neter J and Wasserman W: Applied Linear Statistical Models. Homewood, IL: Richard D. Irwin Inc, 1974.
7. Kleinman J, Feldman JJ, Mugge R: Geographic variations in infant mortality. Pub Hlth Rep 1976; 91:423-479.
8. Garfinkel J, Chabot MJ, Pratt MW: Infant, Maternal, and Childhood Mortality in the U.S. 1968-1973. DHEW Publication No. (HSA) 75-5013. US Govt Printing Office, Washington, DC, 1975.
9. Berger GS, Gillings DB, Siegel, E: The evaluation of regionalized perinatal health care programs. Am J Obstet Gynec 1976; 125:924-932.
10. Quebec Perinatal Committee: Perinatal Intensive Care after Integration of Obstetrical Services in Quebec. Quebec: Ministry of Social Affairs, July 1973.
11. Usher RH: Changing mortality rates with perinatal intensive care and regionalization. Seminars in Perinatology 1977; 1:309-319.
12. Siegel E, Gillings DB, Guild P, et al: Planning and evaluation of regionalized perinatal care: A rural example. Seminars in Perinatology 1977; 1:283-301.
13. Frost F and Shy KK: Racial differences between linked birth and infant death records in Washington state. Am J Public Health 1980; 70:974-976.
14. McCarthy BJ, Terry J, Rochat RW, Quave S and Tyler CW Jr: The underregistration of neonatal deaths: Georgia 1974-77. Am J Public Health 1980; 70:977-982.
15. David RJ: The quality and completeness of birthweight and gestational age data in computerized birth files. Am J Public Health 1980; 70:964-973.
16. Hudson DJ: Fitting segmented curves whose join points have to be estimated. JASA 1966; 61:1097-1129.
17. Gallant AR and Fuller WA: Fitting segmented polynomial regression models whose join points have to be estimated. JASA 1973; 68:144-147.
18. Box GEP and Tiao GC: A change in level of a non-stationary time-series. Biometrika 1965; 52:181-192.
19. SAS User's Guide. Raleigh, NC: SAS Institute Inc, 1979.
20. Abernathy JR, Greenberg BG, Donnelly JR: Application of discriminant functions in perinatal death and survival. Am J Obstet Gynec 1967; 95:860-867.
21. Kessner DM, Singer J, Hark CE, et al: Infant death: An analysis by maternal risk and health care. Washington, DC: National Academy of Sciences, 1973.
22. Kleinman JC, et al: A comparison of 1960 and 1973-1974 early neonatal mortality in selected states. Am J Epidemiol 1978; 108:454-469.

ACKNOWLEDGMENTS

This work was supported by Contract No. 6100505, North Carolina Department of Human Resources, Division of Health Services and by Maternal and Child Health (Social Security Act, Title V) Grant No. MC-R-370424-01-0.

The authors gratefully acknowledge the support of Charles J. Rothwell, MS, Head, Public Health Statistics and Health Services Systems Branches, and Richard R. Nugent, MD, Lead Consultant, Perinatal Care Program, North Carolina Department of Human Resources. From the Evaluation Team, Mary Donelan, MPH, provided invaluable assistance with data management and Priscilla Guild, MSPH, contributed to design of the overall evaluation.

APPENDIX
Segmented Regression Models

Model I

The segmented regression model for mortality trends between 1948 and 1974 with join points at 1955 and 1965 can be specified as follows:

$$E(y) = \beta_0 + \beta_1 x_1 + \beta_2(x_1 - 7)x_2 + \beta_3(x_1 - 17)x_3$$

where y is the dependent variable, and x_1, $(x_1 - 7)x_2$, and $(x_1 - 17)x_3$ are the three independent variables of interest. In particular,

$$y = \text{yearly perinatal mortality rate}$$

$$x_1 = \text{year} - 48$$

$$x_2 = \begin{cases} 1 \text{ if year} > 55 \\ 0 \text{ if year} \leq 55 \end{cases}$$

$$x_3 = \begin{cases} 1 \text{ if year} > 65 \\ 0 \text{ if year} \leq 65 \end{cases}$$

β_0, β_1, β_2, β_3 are parameters to be estimated and represent respectively the intercept term and coefficients for the independent variables. The model is fitted in the normal manner for multiple regression where there are several independent variables. The fact that two of the independent variables are composites of other variables, i.e., $(x_1 - 7)x_2$ and $(x_1 - 17)x_3$ presents no problem. The composite variables are computed and handled like any other single variable. Once the variables have been defined, the model is fitted easily using PROC GLM in SAS.[19]

Model II

The evaluation of RPC requires the extension of Model I to a fourth time segment, 1975-1981. Two additional parameters are needed, one to estimate discontinuity in trend between segments three and four, and a second to estimate change in slope between segments three and four. The model is specified as follows:

$$E(y) = \beta_0 + \beta_1 x_1 + \beta_2(x_1 - 7)x_2 + \beta_3(x_1 - 17)x_3 + \beta_4(x_1 - 26)x_4 + \beta_5 x_5$$

where the definitions for Model I still apply and

$$x_4 = \begin{vmatrix} 1 \text{ if year} >74 \\ 0 \text{ if year} \leq 74 \end{vmatrix}$$

β_4 and β_5 are additional parameters to be estimated.

Model III

Model II has been used to estimate trends for each region separately. An extension of this model allows tests of significance regarding the equality of trends in the study and control regions as follows:

$$E(y) = z_1\{\beta_{01} + \beta_{11}x_1 + \beta_{21}(x_1 - 7)x_2 \\ + \beta_{31}(x_1 - 17)x_3 + \beta_{41}(x_1 - 26)x_4 + \beta_{51}x_4\} + \\ z_2\{\beta_{02} + \beta_{12}x_1 + \beta_{22}(x_1 - 7)x_2 + \\ \beta_{32}(x_1 - 17)x_3 + \beta_{42}(x_1 - 26)x_4 + \beta_{52}x_4\}$$

where

y = yearly perinatal mortality rate for the study and control regions

$$z_1 = \begin{vmatrix} 1 \text{ for study region} \\ 0 \text{ for control region} \end{vmatrix}$$

$$z_2 = \begin{vmatrix} 1 \text{ for control region} \\ 0 \text{ for study region} \end{vmatrix}$$

x_1, x_2, x_3, x_4 are defined as before

$\beta_{01}, \beta_{11}, \ldots, \beta_{52}$ are parameters to be estimated.

The following hypotheses can be tested:

H_0	Interpretation
	The study and control regions are equal with respect to:
$\beta_{01} = \beta_{02}$	perinatal mortality in 1948
$\beta_{11} = \beta_{12}$	linear trend between 1948 and 1955
$(\beta_{11} + \beta_{21}) = (\beta_{12} + \beta_{22})$	linear trend between 1956 and 1965
$(\beta_{11} + \beta_{21} + \beta_{31}) = (\beta_{12} + \beta_{22} + \beta_{32})$	linear trend between 1966 and 1974
$\beta_{21} = \beta_{22}$	change in linear trend between time periods one and two
$\beta_{31} = \beta_{32}$	change in linear trend between time periods two and three.

Hypotheses of interest for the program evaluation are:

H_0	Interpretation
$(\beta_{11} + \beta_{21} + \beta_{31} + \beta_{41}) = (\beta_{12} + \beta_{22} + \beta_{32} + \beta_{42})$	The study and control regions have equal linear trend between 1975 and 1980.
$\beta_{41} = \beta_{42}$	Change in linear trend between time periods three and four are equal for study and control regions.
$\beta_{51} = \beta_{52}$	There are equal discontinuities in the trend lines for the study and control regions in 1975.

33

Quality Assessment by Process and Outcome Methods
Evaluation of Emergency Room Care of Asthmatic Adults

Susan Mates and Victor W. Sidel

Abstract: Weighted process criteria based on chart review and weighted outcome criteria based on telephone interview were used to assess the quality of care for adult patients with asthma in the emergency rooms of a municipal and a voluntary hospital which share medical personnel. Process scores were highly correlated with 24-hour outcome scores at both hospitals but not with 7-day outcome scores. Our findings suggest that appropriate weighted process and outcome criteria are valid and useful methods for quality assessment, and underline the importance of choice of an appropriate "time window" for assessment of outcome. In addition, these assessment methods provide important "feedback" information for those providing care in the emergency room. (*Am J Public Health* 1981;71:687–693)

Several studies published in the past few years have shown little or no correlation between medical care process and patient outcome.[1-3] These findings have been used to cast doubt on current techniques for assessment of quality of care and, even more importantly, on the efficacy of medical care itself. Failure to demonstrate a correlation between process and outcome in these studies could be based in part on the failure to choose appropriate criteria for measurement; a more appropriate choice of criteria might have led to high positive correlation of process and outcome.

We have previously studied the process and outcome of care for adult women with symptoms of urinary tract infection (UTI) in the emergency rooms of a municipal hospital and of its affiliated voluntary hospital.[4] The method used for process assessment, the "Physician Performance Index" (PPI) was originally developed by Lyons and Paine;[5] in our adaptation, branch points were incorporated in order to approximate clinical decision-making more closely. This method is an example of a "normative" audit using "explicit criteria";[6] such audits are being increasingly used both to study and to control the process of care. Process assessments have been criticized as being based largely on "conventional wisdom" rather than on empirical evidence of their relevance to clinical outcome. Our study (of UTI), however, demonstrated that process scores obtained by our normative, explicit method were significantly correlated with outcome (as we measured it) at each hospital, the correlation being one of the highest reported in the literature of this field.[4]

From the Departments of Medicine and Social Medicine, Montefiore Hospital and Medical Center, Albert Einstein College of Medicine, Bronx, NY, and the Division of General Medicine, Department of Medicine, Columbia-Presbyterian Medical Center, New York, NY. Address reprint requests to Victor W. Sidel, MD, Chairperson, Department of Social Medicine, Montefiore Hospital, Albert Einstein College of Medicine, 111 E 210th St., Bronx, NY 10467. Dr. Mates is with the Department of Medicine, Montefiore Hospital and Albert Einstein College of Medicine.
Editor's Note: See also related editorial, p. 681, this issue.

Another criticism of methods using normative, explicit criteria to evaluate the quality of medical care has been that these methods are useful for only a small number of diseases such as UTI. Such diseases are selected for the relative concreteness with which their care can be evaluated rather than the frequency or severity of the disease in a patient population. Ideally, a methodology for assessment of process or outcome of care should be adaptable to the care of patients with any disease requiring study; methodology should not dictate the choice of patients and/or diseases to be studied.

Asthma is an example of a common problem for the emergency room physician that has not often been used as a basis for the explicit evaluation of quality of care because of difficulty in defining and weighting process and outcome criteria. In order to refine the methods that we used previously and to validate their applicability to a commonly-seen illness, we have applied them to the assessment of emergency room care of asthmatic adults, in a voluntary and a municipal hospital.

Materials and Methods

Setting and Patient Selection

The same voluntary hospital was used in our previous study and for this study; it is located in the north Bronx and largely serves a lower-middle income, ethnically-mixed population, 20 per cent of whom are over age 65. The municipal hospital used in the previous study has since been closed; most of its medical staff have been shifted to a new municipal hospital abutting the voluntary hospital, with which it is still closely affiliated. Although the two hospitals are adjoining, each hospital maintains its own emergency room. The municipal hospital serves a population with a greater percentage of patients who are younger, Medicaid-eligible, Black, and Hispanic than does the voluntary hospital. The two hospitals share the same house staff: junior and senior residents, who provide most of the care and work on alternate days in each emergency room. In addition, the supervising medical staff is in part shared between the two emergency rooms. The major staffing difference is that interns (PGY-1's) are used in the municipal hospital emergency room while a larger number of attending physicians are used in the voluntary hospital.

The emergency room records of all patients aged 19 to 55 presenting to the emergency room of either hospital during the same one-month period (January 1978) were reviewed. Patients with a diagnosis of "chronic obstructive pulmonary disease" were excluded. The records of all other patients with an emergency room diagnosis of "asthma" were abstracted and used to evaluate process of care and to locate the patient for the interview about outcome.

Assessment of Medical Care Process

The weighted assessment criteria used for evaluation of the emergency room treatment of asthmatic adults are displayed in the Appendix. They are based upon six protocols for examination and treatment of asthmatic adults obtained from major teaching hospitals, and on relevant asthma literature.* Weighting of each criterion was based on the frequency of its appearance in the protocols (for history and follow-up criteria) or on the recommendations in the articles reviewed (for physical examination and treatment criteria). Our draft criteria lists, with weightings and specific criteria appropriate to the evaluation and treatment of the specific problems presented by individual patients, were submitted to four experts in the treatment of pulmonary illness and to one expert in the field of evaluation of quality of ambulatory care; the suggestions made by these experts were pooled and appropriate modifications made in the criteria and in their weighting. This method is closely related to Williamson's method of obtaining expert consensual criteria[7-9] rather than the usual local normative criteria and has parallels with Mushlin's work in patient surveys.[10] The resulting weighted assessment criteria sets were the Physician Performance Index (PPI) for Asthma. These criteria sets were used for the evaluation of process.

Assessment of Medical Care Outcome

The set of criteria used for outcome assessment at 24 hours and at seven days after the emergency room visit are displayed in the Appendix. The questionnaire was administered through a telephone call to the patient or, if the patient had been hospitalized, through a bedside interview.

Results

A total of 177 patient-visits were reviewed, 99 at the voluntary hospital emergency room and 78 at the municipal hospital emergency room.** There was a significantly higher

percentage of women patients at the municipal hospital, but patient ages, ethnicity, severity of attack, and the percentage hospitalized from the emergency room were not significantly different.

A total of 90 24-Hour Outcome Scores (51 per cent of the total sample) and a total of 86 7-Day Outcome Scores (49 per cent of the total sample) were obtained: of those patients reached at 24 hours, two in each hospital were unreachable at seven days. A difference in the outcome questionnaire completion rate between the two hospitals (57 per cent at the voluntary hospital: 41 per cent at the municipal) is accounted for by the greater percentage of voluntary hospital emergency room visits in which the patient was hospitalized. At neither the municipal nor the voluntary hospital did the interviewed and non-interviewed population differ significantly in distribution by sex, mean age or age distribution, or in the distribution or mean of the PPI.

The mean PPI for all patient visits to both hospitals was 50.0, with a range of 18 – 85.25 (Table 1). Mean scores at the two hospitals differed significantly, reflecting lower scores for females and non-hospitalized cases in the voluntary hospital. The mean PPI for patient visits which resulted in hospitalization was significantly greater than that for the non-hospitalized, largely because of findings in the voluntary hospital.

Differences in PPI between hospitals were accounted for by differences in the use of laboratory tests, specifically, the determination of expiratory peak flow, which was performed in 67 per cent of the municipal hospital visits and in only 24 per cent of the voluntary hospital visits. When determination of peak flow was eliminated as a criterion in the index, there were no significant differences between the mean process scores at the two hospitals.

The mean 24-Hour Outcome Scores were significantly better at the voluntary hospital than at the municipal hospital for both hospitalized and non-hospitalized patients, but statistically significant only among the hospitalized group. Table 1 displays these data and other breakdowns by sex, age, and hospitalization.

The scattergram of 24-Hour Outcome Score plotted against Physician Performance Index is shown in Figure 1. The Figure also shows the best-fit linear regression fitted to the points by the least-squares method for the municipal hospital and the voluntary hospital separately. The correlation coefficient for the PPI and 24-Hour Outcome Scores for all patients, shown in Table 2, was 0.350 (p < .005). The correlation coefficient for each hospital separately is considerably higher than for all patients combined (0.441 and 0.517 for the municipal and voluntary hospital respectively).

For the 7-Day Outcome Score, the correlation between process and outcome is also positive, but extremely weak and not statistically significant. The 24-Hour and the 7-Day Outcome Scores were, however, highly correlated (.381, p < .001 for the two hospitals combined).

---

*The protocols and literature citations are available from the authors.

**The 99 patient-visits at the voluntary hospital were made by 69 different patients; the 78 at the municipal hospital by 54 different patients.

TABLE 1—Mean Process and Outcome Scores

Outcome Scores	Municipal Hospital	Voluntary Hospital	All Patient Visits
Physician Performance Index			
All Patients	53.7 (78)*	47.1 (99)*	50.0 (177)
Female Patients	54.9 (68)*	45.6 (62)*	50.4 (130)
Male Patients	45.7 (10)**	49.6 (37)	48.8 (47)
Non-Hospitalized Patients	53.2 (71)*	43.2 (81)*	48.1 (152)
Hospitalized Patients	59.0 (7)	64.3 (18)**	62.0 (25)**
24-Hour Outcome Scores			
All Patients	7.3 (33)*	8.1 (57)*	7.8 (90)
Female Patients	7.2 (30)*	8.1 (33)*	7.6 (63)
Male Patients	8.3 (3)	8.2 (24)	8.2 (27)
Patients Aged 19–35	7.5 (18)	7.8 (45)	7.7 (63)
Patients Aged 36–55	7.3 (15)*	9.1 (12)*‡	8.1 (27)
Non-Hospitalized Patients	7.3 (28)	7.7 (42)	7.5 (70)
Hospitalized Patients	7.2 (5)*	9.1 (15)*‡	8.7 (20)**
7-Day Outcome Scores			
All Patients	7.3 (31)	7.4 (55)	7.4 (86)
Non-Hospitalized Patients	7.2 (28)	7.0 (45)	7.1 (73)
Hospitalized Patients	8.0 (3)	9.2 (10)**	8.9 (13)**

Numbers in parentheses are the number of visits on which the mean is based.
*Difference between the mean scores at the two hospitals statistically significant at the 5% level or less.
**Difference between the mean scores within the hospital statistically significant at the 5% level or less.

Discussion

A positive correlation, and a highly significant correlation coefficient, between the PPI and the 24-Hour Outcome Score were found for the emergency room treatment of patients with asthma. As expected, the correlation between the process scores and the outcome scores was much stronger for 24-Hour Outcome than for 7-Day Outcome. The correlation coefficients found for urinary tract infection in our earlier study, with outcome measured seven days after the emergency room visit, were much closer to those found for 24-Hour Outcome for asthma than to 7-Day Outcome for asthma (Table 2). This difference appears to reflect the difference in natural history of the two diseases: with appropriate emergency room therapy, patients with asthma should feel significantly better within 24 hours, whereas the relationship of treatment for urinary tract infection to symptom resolution is less immediate. The contrast indicates the importance of selecting the appropriate "time window" for outcome measurements.[11]

TABLE 2—Correlation Coefficients: Relationship of Process to Outcome

	Municipal Hospital	Voluntary Hospital	Both Hospitals
Asthma			
24-Hour Outcome Score	.441* (33)	.517** (57)	.350* (90)
7-Day Outcome Score	.022 (31)	.190 (55)	.117 (86)
Urinary Tract Infection	.407* (96)	.342* (73)	.379* (169)

Numbers in parentheses are the data pairs on which the coefficient is based.
*Correlation significantly different from chance association at the 5% level.
**Correlation significantly different from chance association at the 1% level.

It should be noted that because of the difficulty in obtaining outcome scores for every patient, the correlations reflect only about half of the original sample. Even though the interviewed and non-interviewed populations did not differ in any of the characteristics we were able to measure, the correlations for the total sample may differ from those of the interviewed sample.

When the PPIs for asthma and UTI are stratified and plotted against the mean outcome scores corresponding to each group (Figure 2), the mean 24-Hour Outcome Scores are seen to increase with each increment in process score. For any given process score, the outcome score (at seven days) for urinary tract infection is lower than the outcome score (at 24 hours) for asthma.

While the nature of the criteria and their weighting determine the shape of the curve and no firm conclusion can

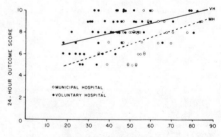

PHYSICIAN PERFORMANCE INDEX

FIGURE 1—Correlation between 24-Hour Outcome Score and Physician Performance Index for Emergency Room Care of Adult Patients with Asthma (The lines were fitted by the least-squares method).

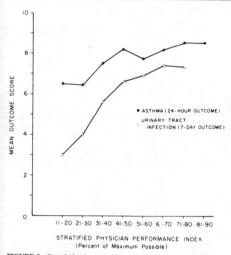

FIGURE 2—Correlation between Mean Outcome Scores and Stratified, Normalized Physician Performance Indices for Asthma (24-Hour Outcome) and for Urinary Tract Infection (7-Day Outcome)

therefore be drawn from these studies alone, it is of interest that the plot for asthma suggests linearity while that for urinary tract infection suggests possible nonlinearity. Insofar as the relationship between process and outcome for UTI depart from linearity, it would suggest smaller marginal outcome returns for increments of process at higher process scores.

Process scores at the municipal hospital when compared to those at the voluntary hospital were better both for asthma and for UTI, although the difference was statistically significant only for asthma. In both studies, the difference was largely accounted for by the more consistent performance of appropriate laboratory tests at the municipal hospital than at the voluntary. Since the same group of house officers served both hospitals, the explanation may lie in structural differences between the two institutions. At the municipal hospital, there was easier access to the peak flow meter and more consistent use of a treatment protocol for asthma.

Mean 24-Hour Outcome scores were higher at the voluntary hospital than at the municipal despite the fact that the process scores were lower. There are several possible explanations for this paradoxical finding. One is that patients using the municipal hospital have other problems which interfere with maximization of outcome; another is that their range of perception of satisfaction with care may be at a generally lower level than at the voluntary hospital. Such an explanation is not consistent with the findings in our previous study, in which patients treated for UTI at the municipal hospital reported significantly higher outcome scores even

though the process scores at the municipal hospital were not significantly higher.

Another explanation for the paradox is that, although some aspects of history (e.g., previous steroid use) and some laboratory tests (e.g., peak expiratory flow) were more consistently recorded at the municipal hospital, this information did not appear to have been integrated into the treatment plan. For example, although poor peak respiratory flow on presentation to the emergency room and lack of adequate improvement in peak flow in the first half-hour after treatment have been discussed in the recent literature[12] as criteria for *rapid* hospitalization, these criteria were infrequently used at either hospital. We were unable to test for significant difference in outcome score between "appropriate" and "inappropriate" use of the data obtained from peak flow measurement, hence were unable to demonstrate any impact on the treatment that the patient received. This is a general problem with the use of history-taking, physical examination, or laboratory examination protocols as compared with treatment protocols. Health care providers must not only be educated into *obtaining* information but also in the appropriate clinical *application* of that information.

Another possible explanation for the paradox may lie in nursing staff differences between the two hospitals. It is our impression, although we have no objective data to substantiate it, that better nursing care may be an important factor in the better outcomes at the voluntary hospital. It would not be surprising for this difference to be seen in the outcome of the care of patients with asthma but not in the outcome of patients with UTI.

The study of process and outcome of care can provide structured information about the natural history of common diseases as well as "feedback" information about the results of medical interventions assumed to be useful but in fact never critically studied. Such data can also contribute to knowledge of patterns of care in a specific institution. For example, during the course of this study it was noted that the pattern of treatment with steroids in the emergency room might require change in order to improve patient outcome. Of the ten patients who were not hospitalized but treated with steroids in the emergency room, three were *not* given steroids to take at home in tapering doses; two of these three returned to the emergency room the next day with asthma. Only one of the seven who *were* given steroids to take home came back the next day, and the remainder came back no sooner than five days later. Not only can this "outcome" information be given to the physicians concerned, but it can be incorporated in subsequent process criteria as an important variable in the treatment of asthma.

REFERENCES

1. Nobrega FT, Morrow GW, Smoldt RK, *et al*: Quality assessment in hypertension: analysis of process and outcome methods. N Engl J Med 1977;296:145-148.
2. McAuliffe WE: Studies of process-outcome correlation in medical care evaluations: a critique. Med Care 1978: 16:907-930.
3. Hulka BS, Romm FJ, Parkerson GR. *et al*: Peer review in ambulatory care: use of explicit criteria and implicit judgments. Med Care (Supplement) 1979:17:1-73.

4. Rubenstein L, Mates S, Sidel VW: Quality of care assessment by process and outcome scoring: use of weighted algorithmic assessment criteria for evaluation of emergency room care of women with symptoms of urinary tract infection. Ann Intern Med 1977;86:617-625.

5. Lyons TF, Payne BC: The quality of physicians' health care performance. JAMA 1974;227:925-928.

6. Donabedian A: The quality of medical care. Science 1979; 200:856-64.

7. Williamson JW: Assessing and Improving Health Care Outcomes. Cambridge, MA: Ballinger Publishing Co., 1978.

8. Williamson JW, Braswell HR, et al: Priority setting in quality assurance: reliability of staff judgments in medical institutions. Med Care 1978;16:931-940.

9. Williamson JW, Braswell HR, et al: Validity of medical staff judgments in establishing quality assurance priorities. Med Care 1979;17:331-346.

10. Mushlin AI, Appel FA: Testing an outcome-based quality assurance strategy in primary care. Med Care (Supplement) 1980;18:1-100.

11. Brook RH, Davies-Avery A, Greenfield S. et al: Assessing the quality of medical care using outcome measures: an overview of the method. Med Care (Supplement) 1977;15:1-165.

12. Banner AS, Ranchhodial SS, Addington WW: Rapid prediction of need for hospitalization in acute asthma. JAMA 1976;235: 1337-1338.

ACKNOWLEDGMENTS

This work was supported in part by the General Research Support Grant at Montefiore Hospital. The authors thank Susan Lindheim of the Albert Einstein College of Medicine, Class of 1981, for her assistance in the outcome interviews; Avedis Donabedian, Lewis Goldfrank, Stephan Kamholtz, Thomas F. Lyons, David McConnel, Kathleen Morton, Lloyd Novick, Lisa Rubenstein, Michael Stewart, Earl B. Weiss, and M. Henry Williams for their suggestions after review of the protocol and/or the manuscript; Herbert Levine, Montefiore Hospital Department of Biostatistics, for assistance in data processing; and Jean Nardelli, Eve Teitelbaum, and Edythe Weber for administrative support.

APPENDIX

TABLE A-1—Weighted Criteria for Calculation of the Physician Performance Index

Criteria	"Moderate" Episodes		"Severe" Episodes	
	Weighting	Total	Weighting	Total
History				
Was there evidence of inquiry about:				
Medication history	3.0		1.0	
Number of recent attacks	2.25		.75	
Sputum production, color, quantity	2.25		.75	
Presence of cough	1.5		.5	
Allergies	1.5		.5	
Recent upper respiratory infection	.75		.25	
Severity of current attack vs previous attacks	.75		.25	
Effectiveness of prior treatment	.75		.25	
Recent fever	.75		.25	
Age of onset	.75		.25	
Duration of current attack	.75		.25	
Cardiac history	.75		.25	
Emphysema/bronchitis history	.75		.25	
Total possible history score		16.5		5.5
Physical examination				
Was there evidence of examination of:				
Vital signs	3.0		1.0	
Lungs (wheezing)	3.0		1.0	
Air exchange or breath sounds	3.0		1.0	
Thoracic excursion	.75		.25	
Cardiac examination	.75		.25	
Clinical impression of "general distress"	.75		.25	
Mental status	.75		.25	
Cyanosis	.75		.25	
Pulses paradoxus	.75		.25	
Total possible physical examination score		13.5		4.5

(Table continued on next page)

TABLE A-1—(Continued) Weighted Criteria for Calculation of the Physician Performance Index

Criteria	"Moderate" Episodes		"Severe" Episodes	
	Weighting	Total	Weighting	Total
Laboratory				
Was there performance of:				
Peak flow	20		**	
Arterial blood gas	not required*		8	
Electrocardiogram	not required*		8	
Chest x-ray	not required*		8	
White blood count	not required*		4	
Electrolytes	not required*		2	
Total possible laboratory score		20.0		30.0
Treatment				
Was there administration of:				
Hydration (oral or parenteral)	5		10	
Epinephrine 0.3-0.5cc 8c.q 20 min × 2-3	5		10	
or				
Terbutaline 0.25g q 30 min × 2				
IV aminophyllin 5.6 mg/kg over 20 minutes	5		10	
then 0.9 mg/kg/hr (or as appro-				
priate for liver function)				
Corticosteroids (in steroid dependent	5		10	
asthmatics or if no improvement in				
2-8 hours) with K+ replacement				
Inhaled bronchodilator (isoetharine,	5		10	
metaproterenol, isoproterenol, or				
phenylephrine)				
Cardiac monitoring during treatment	not required		5	
O₂ via mask or cannula	5		5	
Total possible treatment score		30.0		60.0
Follow-Up				
Were arrangements recorded?		20.0		0.0***
Total possible Physician Performance Index		100.0		100.0

A "severe" episode was defined as one in which any one of the following findings on physical or laboratory examination was present: 1) central cyanosis; 2) disturbed mental status; 3) extreme fatigue; 4) hypotension; 5) cardiac arrhythmia; 6) arterial blood $pO_2 < 50$ and $pCO_2 > 35$ on room air; 7) arterial blood pH<7.30; or 8) peak expiratory flow <60L/min without at least 20% improvement after six hours.

* Required in "moderate" asthmatic when there was evidence of certain associated diseases or fever, cardiac irregularity, or failure to improve with parenteral therapy.

** Patients with "severe" asthma were often too short of breath to perform the peak flow maneuver in the emergency room.

*** Fifty points were to be subtracted if patients with severe asthma were not admitted to the hospital. This did not occur in our sample.

(Appendix continued on next page)

TABLE A-2—Weighted Criteria for Calculation of the 24-Hour Outcome Score

Criteria	Weighting		Total Possible Points
1. Are you satisfied?			
System satisfaction (complaints about waiting time, pharmacy, and so forth)	Satisfied	2	
	Somewhat	1	
	Unsatisfied	0	2
Nonsystem satisfaction (complaints about physician encounter)	Satisfied	2	
	Somewhat	1	
	Unsatisfied	0	2
2. Do you feel better?			
Feels completely better		3	
Feels better but still has symptoms of asthma		2	
Does not feel better but no longer symptoms of asthma		1	
Does not feel better		0	3
3. What do you know?			
Could repeat medicine name and dosage and reported taking it		1	
Did not understand medicine or did not take it		0	1
Understood diagnosis		1	
Did not understand diagnosis		0	l
Could repeat follow-up instructions and reported keeping following appointment		1	
Could not repeat instructions or did not keep appointment		0	1
Total possible outcome score			10

TABLE A-3—Weighted Criteria for Calculation of the 7-Day Outcome Score

Criteria	Weighting	Total Possible Points
1. Do you feel better?		
Feels completely better	3	
Feels better but still has symptoms of asthma	2	
Does not feel better but no longer symptoms of asthma	1	
Does not feel better	0	3
2. What do you know?		
Could repeat medicine name and dosage and reported taking it	1	
Did not understand medicine or did not take it	0	1
Understood diagnosis	1	
Did not understand diagnosis	0	1
Could repeat follow-up instructions and reported keeping following appointment	1	
Could not repeat instructions or did not keep appointment	0	1
3. How soon did you return to the emergency room for asthma?		
Returned within 1 day	0	
Returned in 2 days	1	
Returned in 3–5 days	2	
Returned in 5–7 days	3	
Did not return within 1 week	4	4
Total possible outcome score		10

34

Mental Health Service Policy and Program Evaluation
Living in Sin?

Charles Windle and Steven S. Sharfstein

Program evaluation requires some independence from policy and program imple-mentation. This need is illustrated in two manners: the limited extent and indirect paths by which federal evaluations of the Community Mental Health Centers (CMHC) Program had impact; and experience with mandated evaluation in local CMHCs. Rossi's three-step evaluation strategy, augmented by a performance measurement system for external monitoring, may reduce some of the impro-prieties in the relationship of programs and their evaluations.

Mental health services receive a large public subsidy. Two-thirds of all support for such services derive from the taxpayer. The "taxpayer revolt" takes many forms, not the least of which is demand to demonstrate cost-effectiveness, productivity, and accountability. Elected and appointed government officials are charged with "oversight" and requirements for program evaluation are built into law. Like the Ten Commandments, the potential for disobedience runs high as expectations run higher than human capacity or realistic technology. Yet payment for services rests on the demonstration of impact. "Sin" therefore is part of the "system," as natural as adultery due to the sanctity of the family.

The nature and intimacy of the relationships of program evaluation and management and how sinful—or how exploitative their relationship is—are of continued interest to those concerned about the effective use of this form of applied research, e.g.

Charles Windle is Program Evaluation Specialist, National Institute of Mental Health; Steven Sharfstein is Director, Division of Mental Health Service Program, National Institute of Mental Health. The views are the authors' and not necessarily those of the National Institute of Mental Health.

From Charles Windle and Steven S. Sharfstein, "Mental Health Service Policy and Program Evalua-tion: Living in Sin?" 1(1) *Health Policy Quarterly* 73-90 (Spring 1981). Copyright 1981 by Human Sciences Press. Reprinted by permission.

program evaluators and government agencies seeking non-coercive and inexpensive ways to improve services. Marriage seems an appropriate analogue, reflecting a love-hate ambivalence, complementarity of roles, and a question of the degree to which intimacy or businesslike contracts should govern the relationship.

This paper will address three issues. First, we will consider some general characteristics of an appropriate relationship between program evaluation and policymaking. Second, we will illustrate some of these characteristics in the history of the Community Mental Health Centers Program. Third, we will consider how Rossi's (1978) three-step strategy for evaluating human services can reduce some of the improprieties in the relationship of programs and their evaluations.

PROPER AND IMPROPER RELATIONSHIPS

Program evaluation is an overhead function of knowledge generation and use attached to programs in order to improve their effectiveness. There can be two types of problems in the functioning of program evaluation: (1) program evaluation may not improve the program's effectiveness, or only do so at inordinate cost, or (2) the benefits to the program may occur through procedures other than those represented as taking place. Either of these kinds of problems may occur due to undeveloped technology or technical incompetence. The task of assessing the impact of complex social problems as quickly as is necessary for managers to make decisions, doing this task at a modest cost, and achieving information which gives clear guidance to program staff on how they can function more effectively, is a huge order. It is not surprising if modestly funded program evaluation efforts fail to produce highly accurate and usable information. Further, there is often role-blurring in staff assignments within organizations, especially small ones. Staff members may be assigned several jobs, some of which may conflict logically. Thus, the function of program evaluation may be difficult to partition off from the functions of program management, public relations, and policy implementation, even though the critical objectivity important for program evaluation may be incompatible with commitment to program support functions.

There is yet another class of reasons why program evaluation may be ineffective or misrepresent itself, one which incites moral indignation. This class can go under the label of corruption (Rose-Ackerman, 1978) for it involves the displacement of public or program interests by personal gain for the program staff. Recognition of the extent of this problem within federal social service programs is evident in federal activities to counter it (Office of the Inspector General, 1979). Mental health services have this problem (Towery & Sharfstein, 1978). Program evaluation is especially vulnerable to charges of moral impropriety since (1) it often serves in a critical capacity in relation to other programs, thus begging for their revenge, and (2) its primary defining feature is idealized: "truth," i.e., accuracy and as much objectivity as possible in describing the program's functioning. The primary sin of which program evaluation is accused is that it has sold its integrity, like a prostitute, to the program which employs it, serving to advocate the program by selective presentation of information or a deliberate focus on topics where the program looks good. The most heinous form of this sell-out is when the program evaluator is aware of the misrepresentation and actually goes so far as to distort information. The crime is viewed as less severe when the evaluator is less aware of the distortions (Keith-Spiegel, 1977). The moral charge also shifts as power is seen to reside with the program staff, who can legitimately give priority to program maintenance and support over full public disclosure of the nature of their programs, rather than with the program evaluator responsible for accuracy in representation. Reasons why the evaluator should represent and stand up for truthfulness in reporting relate to the guild interest of researchers in knowledge production which is threatened by abuse of this function in program evaluation (Windle, 1976), and the responsibility to the public which care providers, especially those supported by public funds, have (Krause & Howard, 1976).

A more subtle form of this same sin is for the evaluator to be duped into playing a program-supportive role when the most benefit to the public will come from focusing on improvements in the program. Thus, Carter (1971) argues that evaluation studies tend to play a "latent, conservative function" because managers resist negative findings. Managers use results selectively, acting mainly on those which support their original expectations. Knowledge of this preference by managers leads their subordinates to present results selectively to please them. When results are adapted to be consistent with program desires "... evaluation studies may simply become a ritualistic ceremony to reinforce the image that top management actively supports scientific evaluations" (p. 122).

When program evaluation operates in a distorted fashion to aid the program, the sin may be considered one of collusion. There are also sins of abuse or exploitation. A program exploits program evaluation when managers have no intent to use the program evaluation results, but install the evaluation process in order to deceive the public or third party funders that this process is in operation to improve the program or to assure the quality of services or management. One may question whether it is a "sin" to follow this ritual when the program is required by law to do so as one condition for funding. Those who believe that program evaluation does no good but believe the funding of services performs a needed function for the public will feel the immorality is in the imposed requirement rather than in program attempts to fake compliance. In fact, of course, managers do not adopt an intention to ignore all evaluation study results. Their use of results depends upon the nature of the results and the relationship of the results to program assumptions (Weiss & Bucuvalas, Note 1). Managers' sins toward program evaluation are primarily indirect, resulting from paying more attention to other functions than is compatible with adequate attention to program evaluation.

Program managers may also exploit program evaluation by using it for taking actions against individual staff members (Silverman, Beech & Fiester, 1976). If program evaluation is to maintain its credibility it should be distinct from personnel evaluation. This also means that program evaluation should not be used as a vehicle for rewarding program staff, even though such use may lead the rewarded staff to think more highly of program evaluation. These uses tend to distort the accuracy of the evaluation contents and thus undermine the program evaluation function and the potentiality for this function to improve programs in the long run.

Exploitation of the program by the program evaluation occurs when the evaluator has an intention other than helping the program or improving the program's services to the public. The most frequent of these conflicting intentions is personal use of the evaluator's position to do research which will not improve the program directly, but only very indirectly by improving knowledge in general, but will improve the evaluator's status specifically. While trying to improve scientific knowledge is good for mankind in general, the individual facility is not usually adequately funded to support the evaluator in this endeavor. The evaluator's judgment of the propriety of working for generalizable knowledge rather than program-specific knowledge is likely to be biased by the evaluator's greater personal benefits from contributions which are regarded as of general scientific value. Another form of exploitation is where the evaluator has pre-set judgments of inadequacies in the program which he intends to extirpate through exposes. While the evaluator may think these corrective actions are for the good of the public, they may not be for the good of the program or the program staff, and the program evaluator is likely to be guilty of deceit in his contract with the program. Most persons who have had a rigorous training in research methodology and acquaintance with the mental health literature will develop pre-judgments about the efficacy of some program practices and an intention to correct public misimpressions, even at a cost to practitioners deeply wedded to these practices, psychologically and financially. Thus it is likely that evaluators will develop antagonism toward some program staff values and those who are identified with them. How explicit, unmodifiable, and ruthless judgments against current program practices are, and how ethical versus non-ethical evaluator actions can be distinguished, are debatable.

The above types of problems in the independent contribution of program evaluation to program operations seem to result from lack of both clarity in and power to support a program evaluation role of generator of accurate information, a role which needs to be distinct from program and policy implementation. This separation would prevent the abuse of the program evaluation function by programs. Clarification and strength for the program evaluator probably depend upon establishing professional groups which support program evaluation, and winning public acceptance for these groups.

PROGRAM EVALUATION IN THE EVOLUTION OF COMMUNITY MENTAL HEALTH SERVICES IN THE 1960's AND 1970's

Historical Overview

Over the past two decades what has been called the "third" revolution in mental health occurred. In broad terms it had the following stages:

1. Increasing dissatisfaction with the state mental hospital system.
2. Development of a plan for community mental health services in the form of the CMHC Act.
3. Implementation of this Act.

4. Observations of inadequacies in the implementation of the Act (1969-1975).
5. Attempts to solve the observed problems by passing a "perfect" and comprehensive law (the CMHC Amendments of 1975).
6. Development of a more flexible, but targeted service systems act, initiated by the President's Commission on Mental Health (1978), massaged by the administration to take the form of a proposed Mental Health Systems Act and submitted in May 1979 (as this report is being written) for Congressional hearings.

In the above chronology, formal studies and evaluation took place in the series of Presidential Commission studies which initiated the CMHC Act, the evaluation studies which led to the comprehensive CMHC Amendments of 1975 (Windle, Bass & Taube, 1974; Chu & Trotter, 1974; U.S. General Accounting Office, 1974) and the Presidents Commission Report which spurred development of the Mental Health Systems Act. Both of the Presidential Commissions involved formal studies, but these were as much political processes and value expressions as scholarly analyses. The federal evaluation studies in the early 1970's were designed to be more "objective," but they too accepted particular assumptions about the CMHC Program as a framework within which the evaluations were done.

Observations on the Role of Program Evaluation

1. A basis for humility. A view of the past history of community mental health services makes clear that program evaluation has played only a minor role in the major modifications in services. Schorr (1971) proposed a

> theory of randomness concerning the movement of social policy...the nation does not move from...experience to correcting errors, or from systematic evidence to programs based on that evidence....although needs produce solutions, the correspondence is very far from point to point, and some needs are never noticed....Of course social policy does not develop randomly from a political point of view, but responds to the desires of the electorate as these are expressed during the political process....Although governments are permitted considerable flexibility within the broad issues to which electorates pay attention, they have not used this latitude to be more systematic than the electorate. (p. 155-6)

Schorr suggests that this randomness is due to the influence of public values of "greed for money and status and the right of the powerful to the spoils," "our resolutely pragmatic approach to government" which protects our values from searching examination, and limitations in the practice of social science, "which is a mirror image of the larger situation, despite the fact that its traditions demand it be quite different."

The major recent modifications in mental health services, then, have stemmed from a broad social consensus in the western world that those afflicted with social problems should not be removed from society and put in total institutions for treatment, but rather should be allowed to remain part of their communities and be treated with recognition of their civil rights. Certainly the development of psychotropic drugs facilitated this trend. A Community Mental Health Centers Program was one manifestation of it. The more recent attempts to modify the CMHC Program seem influenced by the changing economic climate and a reaction to a general disappointment with the social services programs of the 1960's (Aaron, 1977). Program evaluation then does not seem to have entered importantly into the process of policymaking.

2. The contribution of federal evaluations of the CMHC Program. On the other hand once the program is implemented in response to a policy (stemming from societal pressures), program evaluation may play some role in revision of the policy and details within the program. This seems to have happened in the CMHC Program in the mid 1970's.

The CMHC Program can lay some claim to being the most widely studied program in the world. Although it began without program evaluation being a required service for individual CMHCs and without any special evaluation activities planned by the National Institute of Mental Health (NIMH), the federal agency charged with responsibility for implementing the program, both of these conditions were imposed. The first was the authorization in the CMHC Amendments of 1969 that the Secretary be able to spend up to one percent of program funds for evaluating the CMHC Program. In implementing this mandate NIMH conducted through contracts from 1969 to 1977 about 50 studies for a cost of about $4 million. These studies were initiated by examining the extent and conditions under which centers were achieving the process goals of the CMHC Program. Since the CMHC Program was conceived of as a "bold new" set of processes by which to achieve the same ultimate goals of better mental health and less mental illness that prior programs had been designed to serve, a focus on the extent to which the new processes were actually being carried out was felt initially to be the most practical way to evaluate the program (Feldman & Windle, 1973). In general these studies showed that centers were making progress, but that there was still some gap between the ideal and centers' achievements on most of these process goals (Windle, Bass & Taube, 1974). The information from these government funded studies had its greatest impact through being cited by other reviews of the program in reports which were widely publicized or given directly to Congress (Chu & Trotter, 1974; U.S. General Accounting Office, 1974). Some of NIMH's evaluation studies were also used directly by Congress in contending with the Nixon-Ford Administration concerning whether the CMHC Program should continue to be funded (Stockdill & Sharfstein, 1976). The U.S. General Accounting Office (1974) in its appraisal of the CMHC Program judged that there was need for increased attention to management of the program by the federal government and CMHCs. These judgements were reflected in the provisions of the CMHC Amendments of 1975 which attempted to dictate solutions to short-falls in the centers by legal requirements and also by making available technical assistance funds to help the centers in their management and by specifying that all centers had to conduct three types of program evaluation activities: self-evaluation covering specified issues, involvement of catchment area residents in reviewing center statistics, and quality assurance (Windle & Ochberg, 1975).

3. *Experience with mandated local CMHC evaluation.* Under contract with NIMH, the Philadelphia Health Management Corporation examined what evaluation was being done by a stratified sample of nine centers, and how useful or harmful the program evaluation requirements of P.L. 94-63 are to the evaluation efforts of the centers (Flaherty & Olsen, 1978). Most centers had done studies on most of the required topics, sometimes spending extensive effort. Centers varied widely in the topics they emphasized. Topics also differed in how often they were studied, the effort involved, the reasons they were done and their judged usefulness. Cost and patterns of use were viewed as most useful; centers did them to meet their needs for information. Other topics such as acceptability and inappropriate institutionalization were studied more often to comply with external requirements. Centers reported that their evaluation studies of program impact and acceptability of services were more likely to involve "extensive" levels of effort than evaluations of other topics. It is worth noting that both this study of centers' activities in 1978 and an analysis of centers' activities in 1973 (Majchrzak & Windle, 1980) suggested that evaluations of client outcome are of low utility relative to their expense.

Centers expressed little interest in citizen involvement in evaluation. They interpreted that the requirement for citizen review could be satisfied by involving the center's board in reviewing the evaluation report. In addition there seemed a common misconception that the required annual evaluation report is for federal consumption, and not for use by the center or to inform the public. This report was usually judged by center staff to be of little use to the center, and it was seldom non-technical, brief, and educational enough to be useful to lay citizens.

When center staff and boards were asked what program evaluation requirements they recommended, the most popular choices were to (a) maintain the present guidelines with more clarification, technical assistance, and responsive monitoring or (b) require a "core" of accountability data (e.g., use of services and costs) plus the center's annual choice of a given number of other studies. Evaluators, administrators, and fiscal managers preferred the former, while clinicians and "citizen" board members preferred the latter. Least desired was elimination of the program evaluation requirements. Thus local agencies recognize the need for a government standard-setting role.

While local agencies use discretion in their compliance with requirements, they also comply uncritically and inappropriately to some requirements, resulting in expenditure of scarce center resources on underutilized evaluation. Government, therefore, should apply requirements cautiously—preferably after field tests. This plea for legislators to be experiment-minded is not new. Perhaps the lesson for evaluators is to try to foresee and set up tests of program options before legislation is passed, rather than wait until legislators decide what laws they favor. We often talk about feeding evaluation into planning. We should talk more about feeding planning into evaluation.

4. The next generation evaluation approach: Performance measures. Rivlin (1971), viewing our ignorance of the comparative costs and benefits of social programs, advocated that programs be designed so that we can learn from them. This would require longitudinal "natural" experiments and systematic experimentation with planned variations. Both of these approaches require better measures of effectiveness and publicized results of the tests of effectiveness. Wholey (1979) has carried further this argument of the need to specify program performance measures by urging that exploratory evaluations or evaluability assessments precede more formal study. This preparatory study phase would assure that programs have clear measurable goals which evaluation studies can use as criteria, or would establish such goals when they are lacking.

A similar appreciation of the need for measures of program performance has sprung from concern about program accountability. National disappointment with social programs of the 1960's and the fiscal pressures on government from inflation have caused federal emphasis on cost containment, efficiency, and prevention of fraud, abuse, and waste. The President's Commission on Mental Health (1978) recommended that performance contracting be used, especially in relation to the states:

> An adequate, humane system of mental health care cannot exist until the special needs of Americans with long-term and severe mental disabilities are met, and until Federal, State, and local government share the responsibility for meeting this goal. (p. 22).
>
> ...there is a need to define clearly the roles and responsibilities assumed by the individual States and the Federal Government. This can be done if the States describe the approach they intend to take to meet the national goals, and if the Federal Government negotiates contracts with each State to provide the resources necessary to achieve these goals.
>
> In addition, the contract can provide a mechanism for consolidating Federal funds which States currently receive for services to persons with chronic mental illness and for augmenting those funds with new money. These contracts should be *performance contracts* (emphasis added). A State which met the terms of the contract would continue to receive money. A State which did not would have its funds withdrawn. The Commission therefore recommends that:...The Department of Health, Education, and Welfare develop a model for performance contracts in order that national goals for phasing down State hospitals, upgrading the quality of care in those that remain, and improving aftercare services can be achieved in a mutually agreed upon manner. (p. 23)

The PCMH described performance contracts as

> A way to clearly define mutual expectations, responsibilities, and commitments. Both parties spell out what they intend to accomplish, how it will be done, at what pace, and at what cost. After goals have been mutually agreed upon, variations in means and mechanisms to achieve these goals are allowed for, but end points remain constant.

Interestingly, the PCMH did not suggest application of this approach to service agencies, and did not mention this approach in sections on planning, information and data gathering, and quality assurance and program evaluation (pp. 26-27). Further clarification of the intent of performance contracts is contained in the Report of the Task Panel on State Mental Health Issues submitted to the PCMH on February 15, 1978, (PCMH, Vol. IV). This Task Panel described existing funding mechanisms as fostering an unequal "parent-child" relationship, perpetuating "confusion and mistrust."

To create equal partners, recognizing that all three levels of government are involved in planning, providing, and monitoring these services, the Task Panel proposed that

> A new intergovernmental relationship be established built upon performance contracts. Annual performance contracts should be developed between Federal and State governments and [between] State and local governments, providing equal partners with ongoing mechanisms for defining functions and responsibilities, establishing time lines, and guaranteeing accountability in delivery [of] services to [the] mentally disabled. With such contractual arrangements, the three levels of government can be involved in setting the performance standards and criteria against which they will be evaluated. The setting of these standards will assure responsiveness to differing needs and characteristics. Such a contractual system will obviate the need for prescriptive regulation and bureaucratic redtape in favor of needs assessment, performance standards, and outcome measurements. (PCMH Report, 1978 Vol. IV, pp. 1994-5)

Federal responsibilities under performance contracts would include a commitment of dollar allotments consistent with the national plan and priorities, technical assistance, quality assurance, and other obligations. The work plan for the States would include both qualitative and quantitative expectations, and the means by which those expectations (objectives and priorities) are to be achieved. "Contract monitoring, then, would take the form of reviewing compliance with work plans for meeting performance objectives" (p. 1997).

The Mental Health Systems Act (*Public Law 96-398*) prepared by the Carter Administration to implement the concepts of the Presidents' commission and passed in 1980 contains provisions which could lead to a performance measurement accountability system.

Part C—Performance
Performance Contracts

Sec. 315. No payment may be made under any grant or contract made or entered into under title II or this title unless the Secretary has entered into a contract with the entity to which the grant has been made or with which the contract has been entered into specifying the following with respect to the performance of the activities for which the grant or contract was made or entered into:

(1) A schedule for the performance of such activities.

(2) The standards by which the performance of such activities by the entity will be monitored and evaluated, the incentives which will be provided the entity to meet such standards, and the role of the Secretary and of consumers and representatives of communities affected by such activities in such monitoring and evaluation.

Performance Standards

Sec. 316. (a) The Secretary shall prescribe standard measures of performance designed to test the quality and extent of performance by the recipients of grants and contracts under title II and this title and the extent to which such performance has helped to achieve the national or other objectives for which the grants or contracts were made or entered into.

(b) In determining whether or not to approve an application for a grant or contract under title II or this title, the Secretary shall consider the performance by the applicant under any prior grant or contract under title II or this title as measured under subsection (a).

On the other hand, "any recipient of a grant or contract . . . may use a portion of that grant or contract for evaluation of the project or activity involved" and the secretary may use up to 1% of appropriations directly "or through contracts with State mental health authorities or other entities, to monitor activities of the recipients of grants and contracts . . ." (Sec 317).

On the other hand, grant applicants can use portions of their grant to evaluate their own projects or activities and the secretary of DHEW can use appropriations "for reviewing performance by recipients of grants . . . to determine the extent to which they have complied with the requirements . . . and the extent to which they have advanced the national or other objectives for which the grants were made." (Sec. 624)

Earlier versions of this proposed Act were clearer about the intent to establish a performance measurement accountability system. One such draft stated that:

The Secretary shall develop a *standard set of performance measures* for each major state and local activity authorized in this Act. Measures shall address: (1) quantity, quality, availability, and cost of services, (2) staff productivity, (3) treatment outcome and changes in client statistics, and (4) management capacity. (An attachment suggested 37 measures for state systems and community systems.)

Each State and locality in its award application *shall specify objectives to be achieved during the award year for each type of activity,* the specific measures to be used for these objectives and an initial set of baseline data for those measures.

State and local grantees may select particular objectives best suited to their situation, but measures of these objectives shall be uniform and selected from the list provided by the Secretary.

Final selection of objectives shall-be negotiated as jointly agreed upon by HEW and the awardee. The Secretary will consider the degree of achievement in making renewal awards.

Federal monitoring shall focus on review of performance measures and management improvement.

The retreat from specificity from the earlier drafts to the final proposal seems unfortunate from the viewpoint of clarity, but may be helpful in avoiding premature commitment to specifics which have not been thought through.

Details would be more appropriate in regulations and guidelines to be prepared by the Secretary of DHEW. Among the issues which must be resolved to achieve specificity are: (1) the extent to which there should be standardization of performance measures, (2) the extent to which and means by which the government should set standards of quality on these measures, (3) how various criteria can be aggregated into program oversight decisions of approval, disapproval, or conditional approval, (4) what means should be used to make and verify the accuracy of performance measurements, and (5) how to monitor constructively the benefits and costs of a performance measurement approach to accountability.

The effort to base a mental health system on performance measures is an attempt to use a different approach than traditionally used to improve the system. Performance measures have a special potential to correct the normal perversions of a system in which system goals get replaced by personal goals of staff, leading to confusion about what the "real" goals are. Performance measures demand specification of publicly supportable program purposes, which then limits slippage toward personal staff goals.

IMPROVING EVALUATION BY ALLOCATING RESPONSIBILITIES

Rossi (1978) has noted that human services are especially difficult to evaluate because the underlying theories are often deficient, and service delivery is "highly operator-dependent and hence often radically transformed in delivery in ways that tend to negate the intended treatment effects" (p. 573). He proposed that we can best identify program problems by a progression of evaluation activities: (1) testing the underlying theory, (2) testing the ability of any system to deliver the proposed services, and (3) assessing whether the proposed services are actually delivered. These three activities differ in research methods (Rossi, 1978), the scope and timing of their application (from entire national programs before program enactment to individual agencies' services after enactment), and the agencies which bear most responsibility to conduct them. These variations are shown in Table 1.

Williams and Elmore (1976) argue that the third of these levels, implementation, is "the most crucial barrier to improving the quality of social programs" (p. xi). Two of the major themes in analyses of implementation failures are the weak linkages between policy and operations, causing slippage from enunciated policy, and reluctance to assume responsibility.

Federal evaluation of mental health service programs has focussed mainly on the third of Rossi's evaluation levels, assessing the services delivered. The National Institute of Mental Health has put most energy into three approaches: (1) national level special studies of the achievement of program process goals, (2) encouragement of local agency self-evaluation, and (3) an oversight function which combines technical assistance, site visit compliance monitoring and much local autonomy in a way which leads most centers to attribute most responsibility for changes to their own efforts rather than to federal or state government pressure (Yeshiva University, 1979).

The testing of theory, Rossi's first phrase, is provided for through research grants. The results of such grants and other

Table 1

A model phased program evaluation strateqy

Evaluation stage	Preferred timing	Preferred auspice	Preferred methods	Major study variables
Theory testing	Pre-program	Large government research funds	Experimental and controlled research	Service processes related to client and community outcome
Feasibility testing	Pre-program	Large government "research" funds	Field testing	Service processes and costs
Implementation testing:				
1. National	Post-program	Large government "evaluation" funds	External monitoring and self-evaluation	Service processes and costs
2. Local	Post-program	Local agencies and communities (from "service" funds)	External monitoring and self-evaluation	Service processes and costs

research are presumed to enter into and shape the thinking of Presidential Commissions and legislatures which initiate new programs. This presumption is often unmet, since legislatures are not known for accurate reflections of the state of scientific knowledge. Weak as this link is, it is stronger than the next—feasibility testing of programs. Often new legislative proposals are supported by descriptions of model programs which may have been funded as "demonstration" programs, but these demonstrations are often heavily funded, are unusual in the personal involvement of the staff in the innovation, and are seldom assessed rigorously.

The advocacy by DHEW of program performance assessments is now causing a rethinking of NIMH's evaluation strategy to give more attention to: (1) the purpose of accountability to others rather than program self-improvement, (2) data generation in standardized forms which permit comparisons, and (3) specification of program objectives in measurable terms. An early attempt to prepare for possible implementation of a program performance measurement system in the proposed Mental Health Systems Act supports the necessity to subdivide evaluation into phases. In June 1979 experts in client outcome measurement and state management information systems for mental health services were assembled for a three day meeting to consider the state of the art in client outcome measurement and, among other topics, recommend steps for program performance measurement. The majority view was that client outcome was not yet a feasible criterion for use in a performance-based accountability system. There was agreement that this was a desirable long-run goal, requiring methodological research. It was also suggested that the use of service process measures of performance requires research to validate the relationship between service processes and client and community outcome. This is the type of research, which fits into Rossi's first stage, should be funded through the federal research programs, and should precede legislation funding and mandating certain service processes such as continuity of care, needs assessment to identify the underserved, and community participation. When such processes are validated they could be used as criteria for both performance-based monitoring, and self-improvement evaluation within service agencies.

CONCLUSION

The public often assumes that professions which claim to have special knowledge about some domain will put this knowledge to use in their personal lives. There is irony in sickly physicians, indigent investment advisors, accountants who can't balance their checking accounts, lawmen who break the law, and divorced marriage counselors. Some of us within professions recognize the extent to which our knowledge is merely theoretical, and the size of the gap between abstract knowledge and its application. Further, the technological capabilities of most professions are much less than professionals care to make evident to the public. However, there is a moral obligation for professions to themselves apply what they advocate for others.

Mental health professionals bear a special, heavy burden from public expectations, since the clinical arena in which they profess expertise is huge in scope and includes the "human factor" other professionals use to excuse their own deviation from their preaching. Thus there is some legitimacy to expecting that program evaluation within mental health service organizations would follow principles which facilitate rather than threaten the personal and organizational mental health of the program evaluated.

At least two dimensions of mental health ideology might be expected: (1) humanistic values which give priority to the well-being of both clients and staff of programs (e.g., American Psychological Association, 1977; Weber & McCall, 1978) and (2) the social science and psychiatric technology employed in the implementation of humane goals (American Psychological Association, 1977). The humanistic values should be expressed in both the methods and substance of program evaluation. Its manifestation in methods includes recognition of the human rights of clients and staff from whom information is sought.

Writers on program evaluation have pointed out that the prospect of evaluation engenders fear and distrust within organizations (Wildavksy, 1972), that this procedure has a large potential for being used punitively and coercively by program managers (Silverman, Beech & Fiester, 1976), that is can be corrupted into a "game" by staff administrators played against the public (Boen, 1975; Etzioni, 1974) and how its ultimate use may be to conserve a status quo in which power and benefits are disproportionately retained by providers at the expense of the public and potential consumers (Carter, 1971). Humanistic values would lead to safeguards to substitute personal growth of staff and rewards for productive behavior in place of adverse actions or additional unappreciated work, and would direct the uses of evaluation information into long-run benefits for the public.

Performance measurement accountability systems have a considerable potential for reducing the discretion of care providers to underserve the public. Since statements of program intentions are most notable for their virtuousness in benefitting the public, if this virtuousness can be captured by clear specification and systematized measurement of achievements, programs will be influenced to conform to their rhetoric more closely. Further, when the government establishes a specific accountability system to apply to the agencies it funds, the government itself is forced into being more accountable for the entire program. First, to establish specific criteria for measuring performance the government has to commit itself on program goals and values, and on the program assumptions of what services produce what results through what mechanisms. This specificity also allows others to question the program. Second, with specific criteria to use in monitoring, the government's own oversight efforts can be assessed more easily and meaningfully by Congress and the public.

REFERENCE NOTE

1.   Weiss, C.H., & Bucuvalas, M.J. *Truth tests and utility tests: Decision makers' frames of reference for social science research.* Unpublished manuscript, Center for Social Services, Columbia University.

REFERENCES

Aaron, H. Remarks. Evaluation Research Society National Conference. Washington, D.C., October 1977.
American Psychological Association. Ethical Standards of Psychologists. January 1977.
Boen, J.R. Will evaluation outgrow the game stage? *Evaluation,* 1975, *2,* (2), 9-10.
Carter, R.K. Clients' resistance to negative findings and the latent conservative function of evaluation studies. *American Sociologist,* 1971, *6,* 118-124.
Chu, F.D., & Trotter, S. *The madness establishment.* New York: Grossman, 1974.
Etzioni, A. Alternative conceptions of accountability. *Hospital Progress,* 1974, *55,* June 34-39; July 56-59.
Feldman, S., & Windle, C. The NIMH approach to evaluating the Community Mental Health Centers Program. *Health Services Reports,* 1973, *88,* 174-180.
Flaherty, E.W., & Olsen, K. Assessment of the utility of federally required program evaluation in community mental health centers. Report to the National Institute of Mental Health by the Philadelphia Health Management Corporation on Contract No. 278-77-0067, December 1978.
Keith-Spiegel, P. Violation of ethical principles due to ignorance or poor professional judgment versus willful disregard. *Professional Psychology,* 1977, *8,* 288-296.
Krause, M.S., & Howard, K.I. Program evaluation in the public interest: A new research methodology. *Community Mental Health Journal,* 1976, *12,* 291-300.
Majchrzak, A., & Windle, C. Patterns of program evaluation in community mental health centers. *Evaluation Quarterly,* 1980, *4,* 677-691.
Office of Inspector General. *Annual Report, January 1, 1978-December 31, 1978.* United States Department of Health, Education and Welfare, March 1979.

President's Commission on Mental Health, *Final Report and Task Panel Reports*. Washington, D.C.: U.S. Government Printing Office, 1978.

Rivlin, A.M. *Systematic thinking for social action.* Washington, D.C.: Brookings Institute, 1971.

Rose-Ackerman, S. *Corruption: A study in political economy.* New York: Academic Press, 1978.

Rossi, P.H. Issues in the evaluation of human services delivery. *Evaluation Quarterly*, 1978, 2, 573-599.

Schorr, A.L. Public policy and public interest. In I.L. Horowitz (Ed.), *The use and abuse of social science,* New Brunswick, N.J.: Transaction Books, 1971, 155-169.

Silverman, W.H., Beech, R.P., & Fiester, A.R. Community psychologist as researcher: Hidden and unhidden agenda. *Professional Psychology*, 1976, 7, 141-146.

Stockdill, S.W., & Sharfstein, S.S. The politics of program evaluation: The mental health experience. *Hospital and Community Psychiatry*, 1976, 27, 650-653.

Towery, O.B., & Sharfstein, S.S. Fraud and abuse in psychiatric practice. *American Journal of Psychiatry*, 1978, 135, 92-94.

U.S. General Accounting Office. *Need for more effective management of community mental health centers program.* Report to Congress. Washington, D.C.: U.S. Government Printing Office, 1974.

Weber, G.H., & McCall, G.J. (Eds.) *Social scientists as advocates: Views from the applied disciplines.* Beverly Hills: Sage, 1978.

Wholey, J.S. *Evaluation: Promise and performance.* Washington, D.C.: The Urban Institute, 1979.

Wildavsky, A. The self-evaluating organization. *Public Administration Review*, 1972, 32, 509-520.

Williams, W., & Elmore, R.F. (Eds.) *Social program implementation.* New York: Academic Press, 1976.

Windle, C. A crisis for program evaluation: An embarrassment of opportunity. *Rhode Island Medical Journal*, 1976, 59, 503-4, 510-16.

Windle, C., Bass, R.D., & Taube, C.A. PR aside: Initial results from NIMH's service program evaluation studies. *American Journal of Community Psychology*, 1974, 2, 311-327.

Windle, C., & Ochberg, F.M. Enhancing program evaluation in the Community Mental Health Centers Program. *Evaluation*, 1975, 2, (2), 31-36, 103-104.

Yeshiva University. *Impact of oversight activities on community mental health centers.* Report to the National Institute of Mental Health on Contract No. 278-77-0075(MH). February 1979.

VI

COMMUNITY AND SOCIAL

The evaluation of social and community programs constitutes a major portion of current evaluation work. The following articles describe such evaluations and illustrate the issues and techniques that arise in the conduct of assessments of social programs.

Hendricks, in the first article, describes an approach that he calls service delivery assessment. Programs under the auspices of the U.S. Department of Health and Human Services are evaluated by this approach, which relies more on observation and discussion and less on the traditional social science model. Service delivery assessment focuses on an evaluation of the delivery of services at particular sites. The intent is to take advantage of a diversity of perspectives and issues in order to report useful information directly to the secretary and other department officials. This evaluation of federally funded programs is unique in that decision makers need not depend on abstracted, quantitative data to make management decisions. The decision-making function is presumably more reality-based by this procedure, which communicates a qualitative perspective of the delivery of health care, social services, an educational services. Hendricks describes in some detail what constitutes service delivery assessment and the benefits of such an evaluation approach.

The evaluation of youth employment programs is placed in a larger policy context in the second of these articles. Fuller reviews five causal models (functionalist, socialization, psychosocial, subcultural, and community development) that underlie youth employment and educational programs. He illustrates that different variables are relevant for determining the effectiveness of a program, depending on the model that is implicit in a particular program. Fuller suggests that explicating the models that guide the development and implementation of youth employment programs is necessary if one wants to understand the relative effectiveness of program models as well as alternative models. In so doing, the evaluation not only addresses the site-specific issues, but also addresses the centralized policy questions, both of which Fuller sees as important. To conclude his argument, Fuller discusses the "workplace versus in-school training" issue and how evaluation can work to delineate which mode of learning is most efficacious for inner-city youth in search of productive roles.

The next two articles look specifically at the role of citizens as information sources in evaluating social programs. Dinkel et al. discuss the participation of citizens in the evaluation of CMHC programs as a neglected potential. Evaluations of CMHCs have largely reflected professional concerns with the technical aspects of treatment to the exclusion of what might be valued by the public. The authors describe seven roles that citizens can assume in an evaluation. These range from the passive role of subject to the most active role of citizen as evaluator. Although citizen participation in evaluating CMHCs has been infrequent, the authors outline several examples which illustrate that such a tactic can lead to useful and relevant information for the improvement of CMHC services.

Stipak's article discusses more specifically the involvement of clients or recipients of services in evaluating programs. With caution he suggests a consumer perspective of program evaluation. Stipak sees the development of social indicator research and primarily the use of survey techniques as one way to obtain assessments from clients. In the author's view client evaluation can be a major contribution to program evaluation but only under certain conditions and usually such data require careful statistical analysis. Stipak discusses several types of performance measures that are client derived, the potential biases of using client evaluations, and procedures for analysis. The discussion is concluded by six rules that should guide the use of client evaluations in the larger context of program evaluation.

Frankfather presents a case study of a private social service agency with emphasis on the development of a specific demonstration project. In a philanthropic organization such as the one discussed in this article, many concerns other than the provision of needed services become relevant. Frankfather documents the development of the Older Adult Community Service Program as a result of what he calls welfare entrepreneurialism. Although the demonstration project has vague goals, a questionable purpose, and unclear impact, the survival and expansion of social programs is achieved. Pleasing the trustees and donors of the organization becomes at least as important as satisfying the service needs of clients. As a result, the quality of programs and service delivery suffers at the expense of expansion in services for political and economic reasons. Frankfather concludes that the credibility of social programs and evaluation efforts will be threatened by political rather than methodological obstacles. He suggests greater autonomy for evaluators as a check on entrepreneurialism.

Wells's case study of a cooperative farm in the Salinas Valley of California emphasizes the need for evaluation that focuses on more than the traditional judgment of program output in relation to program goals. The Cooperativa Central is successful or unsuccessful depending on the perspectives from which the program is viewed, a fact that may be overlooked if only outcome measures are used. For example, the traditional business model that favors an assessment of profits and level of economic self-sufficiency would find the success record of the co-op disappointing. On the other hand, members of the cooperative have a much broader view of significant accomplishments (e.g., stability of residence, control over work environment, and so on) and therefore see the farm as successful. Rather than advocating only one perspective, Wells points out the advantage of and necessity for including qualitative measures of success that will be sensitive to unintended and unanticipated program consequences. A collaborative approach to evaluation is encouraged to take account of multiple goals, perspectives, and assessments of success.

35

Service Delivery Assessment
Qualitative Evaluations at the Cabinet Level

Michael Hendricks

For the past three years, an unusual group of federal employees has been walking the field with migrant farmworkers, observing tenants' meetings in public housing projects, riding along with meals-on-wheels volunteers and crisis intervention teams, and following legal proceedings in both courtrooms and judges' chambers. These unlikely bureaucrats, members of the Office of Service Delivery Assessment (SDA) in the U.S. Department of Health and Human Services (HHS, formerly the Department of Health, Education, and Welfare, HEW), have made countless visits to nursing homes, Social Security offices, community mental health centers, hospitals, Indian reservations, boarding homes, senior centers, kidney dialysis units, daycare centers, rural health clinics, and other sites at which HHS-funded services are provided for clients.

The author wishes to thank Sue Clain, Dennis Coughlin, Richard David, Milton Fick, Ted Koontz, Mike Mangano, Alan Meyer, Jack Molnar, Bill Moran, Sylvia Rivers, Nick Smith, Jan Tebbutt, and Charles Windle for their helpful comments on an earlier version of this chapter.

Reprinted with permission of the author and publisher. Hendricks, M., "Service Delivery Assessment: Qualitative Evaluations at the Cabinet Level." In N. L. Smith (Ed.) *New Directions for Program Evaluation: Federal Efforts to Develop New Evaluation Methods*, no. 12. San Francisco: Jossey-Bass, 1981.

These site visits and the accompanying discussions with clients, front-line service providers, local administrators, program officials at the local, state, and federal levels, and many others knowledgeable about service delivery are not part of any audit, investigation, research study, compliance review, monitoring exercise, or traditional program evaluation. Instead, they represent an innovative approach to program evaluation—an approach that relies less on the social science model and more on the open-ended, flexible observations and discussions familiar to sociologists, anthropologists, and investigative journalists. After four years of operation, this approach, unique in the federal bureaucracy, provides regular reports and briefings to the Secretary and other top HHS officials.

Service Delivery Assessment was established in January 1977, when Joseph A. Califano, Jr., was appointed Secretary of HEW. Califano had been Lyndon Johnson's domestic advisor and was therefore quite familiar with the decision-making processes used by cabinet members. Califano felt that the Secretary of a department as large as HEW had information needs that could not be satisfied by the traditional systems. He, like Peter Drucker, saw that the chief executive of a major organization could easily become isolated and insulated from the front-line activities of the organization. "When top management has to depend totally on abstractions, such as formal reports, figures, and quantitative data, rather than be able to see, know, and understand the business, its reality, its people, its environment, its customers, its technology, then a business has become too complex to be manageable. A business is manageable only if top management is capable of testing against concrete reality the measurements and information it receives—that is, its abstract figures, data, and reports" (Drucker, 1973, p. 681).

Califano resolved not to be insulated from conditions and activities at the local level, so with then Inspector General Thomas D. Morris, he sketched requirements for the SDA function. First, this new system was intended not to replace the traditional information systems but to supplement them with information from the "client's end of the pipeline." Second, only in-house federal employees were to conduct SDAs; outside contractors were not to be used. Further, only a small staff (currently three professionals) were to manage the SDA function from Washington; the bulk of SDA employees (currently fifty professionals) were to be located in the ten regional offices around the country. Third, SDA was to study a wide variety of topics relating to health care, social services, income maintenance, and (in those days) education. Fourth, SDAs were to be completed very quickly, typically within three to five months after the assignment.

Finally, and perhaps most important, SDA was required to focus on the delivery of HHS-funded services, not on such other aspects as management objectives or long-range effects. The latter concerns were judged the proper domain of evaluability assessment, traditional evaluation, or research studies. "I mandated the development of Service Delivery Assessment (SDA) because I believe that our offices need continuing, rapid access to information about how HEW programs function from many perspectives at the local level" (Califano, 1978). Thus, SDAs are mainly focused on the input, process, and output of service programs.

In emphasizing service delivery, SDA embodies a concern of many evaluators: "the critical feature of human services is that they are highly operator-dependent and difficult to standardize. Hence, it is always problematic whether a treatment is being delivered as designed, whether the mode of delivery is adding some unintended treatment to the basic one, and finally whether a treatment can be delivered in a reasonable way at all by the typical human services organization" (Rossi, 1978, p. 596; Freeman, 1980). Rossi (1978) identifies eight different ways in which service delivery systems can fail: no services are delivered, agencies "cream" the most treatable clients and do not serve the most needy, the method of service delivery dilutes or negates the services, services vary in uncontrolled ways from site to site or even within sites, only a "ritual" compliance with delivery procedures occurs, services are too sophisticated for clients, clients are too heterogeneous for a single service, and clients reject services completely or in part. The purpose of SDA was to assess these and other possible weaknesses in service delivery programs.

Assignment by the Secretary

One noteworth aspect of the SDA process is the personal involvement of the Secretary of HHS. Through all four years of its operation, every SDA project has been personally selected and assigned by the current Secretary. This top-level assignment of projects contrasts with other evaluation activities in HHS, and it can occur in two different ways.

First, the Inspector General, who manages the SDA process for the Secretary and who possesses functional management authority over all SDA staff, prepares an annual workplan for the Secretary's review and approval. After soliciting proposed topics from all Assistant Secretaries, Commissioners, and Principal Regional Officials, the Inspector General forwards approximately twenty topics to the Secretary for consideration. Rather than automatically approving these suggestions, the Secretary typically selects between ten and twelve from this list and adds an additional five to seven topics not originally suggested by the Inspector General. These fifteen to nineteen projects then comprise the annual SDA workplan for the fiscal year.

However, the SDA process is designed to respond to the Secretary's changing or emerging needs, and high-priority studies can be initiated at any time via a second, informal assignment process. For example, the Secretary has requested the Inspector General to conduct quick studies of the arrival of Indochinese refugees and the first implementation of the low-income energy assistance program. In both instances, SDA teams were at local sites when problems first began to appear, and they were able to suggest specific remedies for the program to consider. Such "emergency" studies can be completed within ninety days of assignment.

The Secretary's reason for assigning an SDA varies. Some programs are suspected of having operational problems that may be correctable with close examination. Others may be experiencing or planning major changes that will affect operations at the local level. Expiring or proposed legislation can prompt an SDA assignment, and some programs have high visibility in the department, Congress, or among citizens. Some programs warrant special attention because of their size or complexity, and still others simply attract the personal interest of a Secretary.

For whatever reasons, the SDA workload has expanded during each year of its operation. In the first year (1978), seven SDAs were assigned and completed. Following this successful trial year, the number of assignments jumped to fifteen. In 1980, Secretary Harris assigned seventeen topics to SDA: civil rights enforcement, toll-free telephone lines to Medicare Part B beneficiaries, restricted patient admittance to nursing homes, low-income energy assistance, community health centers, availability of physician services to Medicaid beneficiaries, end-stage renal disease, health systems agencies, Title XX services, National Health Service Corps, HHS services to public housing residents, Medicare physician assignment, child abuse, Indochinese refugees, daycare linkages with health care and social services, nutrition services for the elderly, and developmental disabilities.

Preassessment

Once the Secretary has determined the SDA workplan, the Inspector General assigns each project to a "lead" regional office. SDA is a highly decentralized function, with a staff of three professionals in Washington, D.C., to manage SDA on a day-to-day basis. The remainder of SDA staff—approximately fifty professionals—are distributed among the department's ten regional offices. (Regional offices are located in Boston, New York, Philadelphia, Atlanta, Chicago, Dallas, Kansas City, Denver, San Francisco, and Seattle.) While this decentralization parallels the SDA philosophy of remaining close to actual service delivery, it probably results more from the availability of these regional staff, who were planning and evaluation specialists under a former administration.

The first task for the lead region, and for the three to four "support" regions assigned to assist it in all phases of the project, is to conduct a preassessment aimed at understanding the reality of local conditions and reaching an understanding of the important issues to pursue during the study. The former goal is important, since "knowledge of how the actual activities are being carried out is needed to determine what can be measured, what those measurements would be, how much they would cost, where they would be obtained, and how reliable and valid they would be in describing a program's activities, processes, outcomes, impacts, and effectiveness" (U.S. General Accounting Office, 1977, p. 4). SDA considers this a critical aspect of the project's development, and it probably devotes more resources to determining possible respondents, possible contact settings, and required methods than most evaluations do. Several site visits are conducted immediately after assignment to allow SDA staff members to get their feet wet, and these site visits are explicitly patterned after the open-ended approach favored in Scriven's (1972) goal-free evaluation (see also Harrington and Sanders, 1979). Visits are also made to program officials at both the state and federal levels to obtain their perspectives on services and activities. Finally, a brief literature review of major studies is conducted.

The second goal of preassessment, reaching a consensus on the issues to pursue, is even more important. The Secretary's mandate for the study can either be very specific about the issues to be explored or it can be quite vague and general. In the second case, the lead region is responsible for defining the issues and scope of the study. The initial site visits, discussions with state and federal officials, literature review, and previous experience help its staff in this process. However, since SDA serves the Secretary and top department officials, much effort is spent contacting those closest to the Secretary for their views on the particular topic being assessed. Such persons include special assistants, policy coordinators in the Executive Secretariat, the Deputy Undersecretary, the Undersecretary, or even the Secretary. "In order to have data used in the way we prefer, then we need to assure that the evaluation is oriented toward specific questions which are of interest to the manager and which are program-related" (Cox, 1977, p. 505; Rossi and McLaughlin, 1979; U.S. General Accounting Office, 1976).

In addition to their use in clarifying the issues to examine, pre-assessment discussions with top department officials also help in determining the types of information needed by the Secretary. Does the Secretary need a representative snapshot of reality that describes local conditions, clients, and operations as a context for understanding how services are actually delivered? Does the Secretary need an early warning of potential or emerging problems that could develop into major headaches unless corrected? Does the Secretary need an objective view of issues about which there are differing opinions within the department? Or does the Secretary need an analysis of best operating practices, which can then be transferred to other delivery sites? SDAs have provided these and other types of findings to fill specific needs of the Secretary.

Designing the SDA

After finishing preassessment, the lead region has sufficient understanding of both the operations at the local level and the issues at the national level to design the full-scale SDA. At this point, SDA departs radically from the traditional social science model of evaluation. For a variety of reasons, an SDA project includes no control groups, no single treatment that can be identified and isolated, no pretests, no control over client condition, and little quantitative measurement. Instead, SDA has borrowed methods from a variety of disciplines, including investigative journalism (Guba, 1978), "particularly responsive evaluation" (Stake, 1975), sociology, anthropology, and policy analysis, which allow a subjective, open-ended examination of processes and outcomes in a complex, dynamic situation.

The primary technique for gathering SDA information is one-to-one personal discussion with a wide variety of respondents at the local level. The variety of perspectives, a key feature of SDA, is essential to. gaining a full picture of service delivery. Assessment of clients' perspectives of service delivery is surprisingly rare among federal evaluation efforts; in fact, some claim that SDA may be the only federal mechanism for providing regular client input into the top decision-making process of a department.

However, since SDA staff have learned that clients often respond favorably to services regardless of their actual quality (a fact also noted by Scheirer, 1978), information is also sought from others close to the delivery process. "Focusing on the different perspectives among different groups seems to be our best technique for exposing cultural bias. Clients describe a service agency differently from agency workers or administrators, . . . and their views are important for the total assessment of a program" (Cochran, 1978). One excellent example of the diversity of perspectives that SDA seeks is contained in a study on domestic violence, which sent teams to hospitals, shelters for battered women, private homes, police stations, jails, judges' chambers, community centers, city service agencies, schools, township government offices, and on routine cruises with crisis intervention teams.

A second technique for gathering SDA data is to observe local conditions and activities. In the study of migrant farmworkers, for example, much was learned by observing the living conditions and interactions between migrants and health and social service officials. SDA teams sometimes attend already scheduled meetings. Observation of local school board meetings taught SDA staff much about the allocations being made for education for handicapped children. Sometimes, staff also examine documents that are available at sites. In an assessment of Social Security services to the public, examination of letters from SSA officers verified the complexity of terms and processes that had been mentioned by clients. Still another technique for gathering information lies in retrieving data collected at the local level that, for one reason or another, are not forwarded regularly to state and federal program managers. Often, these local data can indicate the accuracy or inaccuracy of data upon which decisions are being made at higher levels.

In addition to specifying the types of respondents and the methods to be used in gathering information, the SDA design outlines such things as the sites to be visited. Unlike many evaluations, SDA does not require random-sampling procedures to select sites. Instead, each SDA samples only those sites that fulfill its particular needs. For example, an SDA that aims to describe the average service delivery site would deliberately exclude sites known to be very poorly managed, very well managed, very new, very turbulent, or atypical in other ways. The typical SDA only visits between fifteen and thirty local sites, so an SDA looking for the average site cannot afford to visit sites that deviate much from the norm. However, an SDA focused on best practices or on service problems might wish to exclude average sites and look instead at sites suspected of being deviant.

Staff

As mentioned earlier, SDA employs no outside contractors; all stages of the SDA process are conducted by employees of the Department of Health and Human Services. Fortunately, these SDA staff are highly talented and dedicated professionals, for the SDA task is a difficult one. Staff need public policy skills in order to refine the issues of importance to the Secretary in a constantly changing national environment; they need political and social skills in order to gain access to local projects without the oversight of federal, state, or local program officials; and they need technical skills in order to design ways of guiding open-ended discussions without losing flexibility, record pertinent information from lengthy conversations, and analyze findings.

Of course, SDA shares the need for highly skilled staff with all evaluation efforts. However, qualitative evaluations like the SDA process are highly dependent on the information gathered from complex interactions with respondents and situations, and they require a greater level of staff input than evaluation efforts do. Qualitative evaluations produce no findings that are not filtered through the eyes and ears of evaluators before they are recorded. "Human observers are the best instruments we have for many evaluation issues" (Stake, 1975, p. 16; Brickell, 1976). Unfortunately, not all instruments, human or otherwise, are created equal.

An SDA attempts to maximize staff abilities through two methods. First, all staff assigned to an SDA complete a training session prior to site visits. This session which may be held in a central location with all project staff who usually number between ten and fifteen, or separately in each regional office, usually lasts between two and three days and covers such diverse topics as the purpose of the SDA, background on relevant programs, issues being assessed, design of the SDA, settings and respondents likely to be encountered, and analysis and reporting plans, and it provides practice with instruments necessary for recording observations or discussions. Given the variety of this information and the short time for training, it is inevitable that SDA staff must sometimes rely on past knowledge and expertise while on site.

However, not all members of SDA teams share the same knowledge and expertise. Since there are only fifty SDA staff in the ten regional offices, SDA teams are often augmented with temporary staff from various federal programs and staff offices. Sometimes, these staff have never participated in an SDA, or they have never visted a local site to determine the state of service delivery. Training is even more vital for these non-SDA staff, although there are acknowledged limits to the ability to train qualitative evaluators (Scriven, 1975).

Thus, the second way in which SDA maximizes staff abilities is careful selection. Increasingly, SDA relies on full-time SDA staff for most, if not all, of its activities. While early SDAs involved between sixteen and twenty-four team members, recent studies have used fewer team members, almost all of whom have been full-time SDA staff. In recent studies, some lead regions have conducted SDAs with between three to five SDA staff from their own immediate offices. This approach ensures that staff are highly knowledgeable and highly experienced, but suffers from the disadvantage of excessive travel demands and the danger of too narrow a perspective on the issues of interest. However, SDA staff generally agree that, whenever feasible, it is probably a wise decision to rely more on SDA team members than on others.

Conducting Site Visits

As noted earlier, perhaps the single most distinctive feature of SDA is the emphasis on site visits to actual service delivery locations. Unlike evaluations that rely on existing data, mailed questionnaires, or site visits by other (typically contracted) analysts, SDA sends its own staff to gather information that will later be reported to the Secretary. As former Undersecretary Hale Champion remarked while discussing Service Delivery Assessment, "You've got to go out and look at how actual individual people are affected" (Demkovich, 1979, p. 1000).

A typical SDA involves visits to between fifteen and thirty sites across the nation, with a team of two or three staff spending three or four days at each site. Given the average of five discussions per day per team member, each site visit can yield between thirty and sixty discussions. As a result of logistics and other duties, the number of discussions yielded by a typical site visit is closer to the lower number. Given an average of twenty sites, most SDAs produce approximately 600 discussions with a variety of respondents.

This variety of respondents embodies the first of two objectives for an SDA site visit: comprehensiveness of perspectives. Team members deliberately seek out all viewpoints on the program and services being assessed, so that no single perspective dominates the findings. This requirement to uncover differing viewpoints almost automatically precludes the use of randomized selection procedures, another way in which SDA differs from traditional evaluations. While some respondents can be identified in advance and by random selection procedures, others can be discovered only on site or by referral from another respondent. Since the referral is to a specific individual, it is difficult to see how random selection procedures could be applied. Instead, such techniques as haphazard, quota, and judgment sampling are employed (Demaline and Quinn, 1979).

For example, an SDA team assessing health maintenance organizations (HMOs) can identify all HMOs receiving federal funds and use stratified random sampling to choose the HMOs that team members will visit. However, since each HMO employs only one executive director, sampling of these persons is not possible. It is true that staff of each HMO can be selected randomly, either by simple random or by cluster sampling, but leaders of a rival health group probably cannot. Also, it is difficult to apply random procedures in selecting among the few officials responsible for monitoring a particular HMO. Thus, while SDAs can use a combination of random and nonrandom selection procedures, most respondents are selected by nonrandom methods.

The second objective for an SDA site visit is flexibility in pursuing information. While the preassessment process has provided the lead region with a set of issues that appear to be relevant for service delivery, the SDA process explicitly recognizes the possibility that issues of equal or greater importance may surface from site visit discussions and observations. "Responsive evaluation procedures allow the evaluator to respond to emerging issues as well as to preconceived issues" (Stake, 1975, p. 15). It is in this area of flexibility that the parallel between an SDA team member and an investigative journalist is most pronounced. Once on site, all SDA team members, especially the more skilled SDA staff, become very investigative and pursue unexpected information vigorously.

A second, recent attempt at maintaining responsiveness to emerging issues alternates site visits with analysis in each regional office. After the first week of visits, team members often can suggest interesting leads for all regional staffs to pursue. By holding a national conference call before teams make the second set of visits, the lead region can elicit the unexpected issues and investigate them systematically in subsequent discussions and observations. Both strategies allow SDA to obtain the type of serendipitous information that does not appear regularly in normal department information systems.

Analysis

The intensive, comprehensive, and flexible efforts during site visits typically yield between 400 and 600 discussions that involve a wide variety of respondents and cover a wide variety of issues. Such rich data are beneficial in highlighting emerging issues, effective local practices, national consistencies and regional variations, and the viewpoints of respondents most knowledgeable about local reality. Perhaps of even greater benefit is their propensity to illustrate the critical intervening variables that make or break service delivery but often escape notice in less intensive evaluations (Hendricks, 1980).

However, such a wealth of information is a mixed blessing, for it is sometimes extremely difficult to analyze properly. Unlike more traditional evaluations that use fairly standard analysis procedures, qualitative analysis of information has no established guidelines. Most disciplines that employ qualitative analysis recognize the process as one of consensus building by iterative steps of gathering information, checking for patterns and trends, and seeking new information to verify or refute preliminary hunches (see Guba, 1978, for a discussion of such procedures used by journalists as "circling," "shuffling," and "filling.")

The SDA process uses three separate techniques in its attempts to reach a consensus. The logic is that three different techniques, each with its own strengths and weaknesses, can illustrate consistencies and deviations better than one technique used alone. Such "triangulation" is intended to shape and refine the perspectives and knowledge of the lead region staff who must declare and present the SDA findings.

First, each region involved in site visits completes a site or regional report, using a format developed by the lead region. Generally, these reports follow the outline of the issues to be addressed, but they also contain room for unexpected information or comments from team members. Second, each discussion is typically recorded using some type of discussion guide prepared by the lead region to ensure that important issues are discussed and that relevant information is captured. These guides are photocopied and forwarded to the lead region for further analysis. Depending on the SDA and the preferences of the lead region, this analysis can range from a thorough reading of all guides to a computer analysis of coded responses. The quantified findings are then used in conjunction with the regional and site reports — as a supplement, not as a substitute.

The third, and perhaps most important, analysis technique is a two-to-three day debriefing session involving all lead region staff and the leaders of teams from other regions. At this session, the lead region discusses each issue and solicits views from every team leader. Consensus or differences are noted, findings are ranked in order of importance, the report is outlined, and some tentative suggestions for change may be drafted. SDA studies differ from many evaluations in that the debriefing sessions are generally afforded more weight in establishing the studies' findings than written reports from the field or quantified results from individual discussions.

The findings that result from an SDA are of three kinds: description of local conditions and activities, comparison of services against one or several standards, and interpretation of the findings from the lead region's perspective. The description of local conditions and activities is important, since the SDA process has been intended to serve as the eyes and ears of the Secretary since the outset. In fact, one of the motives for establishing SDA in the first place was to supplement the Secretary's ability to visit delivery sites. It has been a continuing value of SDA to increase the understanding of local reality among top-level department officials.

However, the simple description of service delivery is not sufficient, since information must be placed in context to be meaningful. Accordingly, SDA makes appropriate comparisons between the services being assessed and selected standards. These standards can include the hypothetical performance of ideal services, the original aims of legislation or regulations, other services to similar clients, past service delivery, or service delivery under ideal conditions. As is true with most other aspects of SDA, the appropriate standard for comparison depends on the unique topic and objective of the individual SDA.

After describing the services and comparing them to appropriate standards, the SDA team adds its own interpretation to the findings. While the Secreatary and other top officials may disagree with these interpretations, it is important, for both the immediate and long-term viability of SDA, that this information be provided. Interpretations can identify strengths and weaknesses of service delivery, barriers to better performance, best operating practices, relationships between findings (particularly notions about causes and consequences), and issues that bear further analysis. While it is difficult to document how such interpretations are reached in general, SDA teams have found it helpful to shift back and forth between individual findings and a larger perspective while analyzing the study findings.

Reporting Findings

Once the analysis has been completed, the findings are presented to the Secretary in two forms. The first reporting mechanism is a short written report, typically between fifteen and twenty pages in length, with perhaps three to six pages of appendixes. Drafts of this report are reviewed by a variety of persons within the department, including SDA staff, officials from the program being assessed, policy coordinators in the Office of the Secretary, planners and evaluators, and others knowledgeable about the issues of interest. Following the revisions prompted by reviewers' comments, the report is forwarded to the Secretary. Since reports are kept short and understandable (Staats, 1980), the Secretary reads almost every one.

The second reporting mechanism is an oral briefing, usually involving a twenty-minute presentation and forty minutes of questions and answers. This briefing, which generally involves between eight and ten well-prepared charts and handouts, is first presented to key staff from the program and the Office of the Secretary. This trial run provides an opportunity to identify missing information that must be obtained, prepare for likely questions, and polish the presentation style of lead region staff.

The final briefing is for the Secretary, although key staff from both the program and the Office of the Secretary also attend, depending on the topic being presented. Due to the history of Secretary-level support for SDA, these briefings typically attract the highest echelons of the department. For example, a recent briefing on restricted patient admittance to nursing homes included the Secretary; Undersecretary; both Deputy Undersecretaries; the Assistant Secretaries for Planning and Evaluation, Legislation, and Management and Budget; the General Counsel; the Director of the Office for Civil Rights; the administrators of the Social Security Administration, Public Health Service, Health Care Financing Administration, and Office for Human Development Services; and the heads of the programs being assessed. Since top-level managers often do their most important communicating orally (Cox, 1977), these briefings for the Secretary allow SDA to present its findings in the most effective and personal manner possible.

Impact

It is a well-known fact among evaluators that public policy decisions are made incrementally and that no single set of findings can hope to influence major decisions by itself. "Research impacts in ripples, not waves" (Patton, 1978; Cox, 1977). The experience of Service Delivery Assessment is no different, and thus it is difficult to cite specific examples of immediate use of SDA findings to alter programs. Instead, SDA is used like all other evaluation data: It provides one set of information that is combined with many other sets of information to create an overall framework for viewing a program or services.

Even so, there are several ways in which SDA findings have

affected HHS programs. First, some changes have occurred as a result of SDA reports and briefings. Often, the Secretary ends an SDA briefing with assignments to various agency administrators and program heads. Usually, these assignments involve preparing an action plan for providing further analyses, but sometimes they serve to change programmatic directions. For example, following the SDA briefing on Indochinese refugees, the Secretary adopted the primary recommendation and doubled the current allocation for English language training. On another occasion, the Secretary halted a planned national strategy and ordered demonstration projects suggested by the SDA team.

A second way in which SDA has had impact is better informing the Secretary and other top department officials about service delivery at the local level. In speeches and memoranda, by personally assigning the SDA workplan, by reading reports, and by continuing to schedule SDA briefings, the Secretary has affirmed the value of SDA in fulfilling this informative role. While this top-level support is important for any evaluation system, it is especially critical for a system like SDA, which must gain and maintain the attention of high-level officials for the study to be completed.

Third, key staff within the Office of the Secretary use SDAs in better fulfilling their own roles. Policy coordinators in the Executive Secretariat, who are responsible for preparing and reviewing briefing materials for the Secretary, routinely use SDA reports to supplement materials sent to the Secretary. For example, staff from planning and evaluation units consulted an SDA on the first year of the low-income energy assistance program when drafting regulations for the second year of operation, and staff from the Office for Civil Rights have taken an increasing interest in SDA findings that illustrate inequities in service availability at the local level.

Fourth, program officials themselves use SDA reports the better to manage their own operations. In one instance, a new program within the department used a recent SDA on that program, along with two other documents, as an overview and introduction to the program for incoming staff. Illustrating the adage that "imitation is the sincerest form of flattery," the Office of Human Development Services initiated a process known as Delivery Level Assessments to provide the same type of client-level information obtained from SDAs. Unfortunately, budget restrictions have severely curtailed the efforts of this new unit (Zimlich, 1979).

Others outside the department are also imitating the SDA approach. Most notably, the Education Department (ED) has created within the Office of the Assistant Secretary for Evaluation and Program Management a Service Delivery Assessment function modeled on the function in HHS. While the future of this unit is in doubt, since the Education Department may undergo major revisions, the first product of this ED unit was an influential study of bilingual education at the local level.

Finally, Congress has become aware of SDA and has used reports on more than one occasion. Twice, SDA findings have been cited on the floor of the House and Senate as evidence that services are needed at the local level. On another occasion, oversight hearings were held by a Senate subcommittee responsible for the services addressed by one SDA report. More recently, the General Accounting Office's new Institute for Program Evaluation has begun to examine the SDA function and its applicability to the GAO and other federal agencies.

Conclusion

On the basis of this description of the Service Delivery Assessment process, what generalizations can we draw regarding qualitative evaluations? One lesson must be that qualitative evaluations, when measured against the traditional criteria of methodological rigor, possess weaknesses that will invite criticism from quantitative evaluators. Since qualitative evaluators are a minority among federal evaluators (and probably among state and local evaluators as well), such criticism will have to be accepted or combated.

Sampling of both sites and respondents is one ground for criticism: The lack of random selection procedures can be argued to imply a lack of representativeness of findings. To the extent that random sampling is possible, this criticism is valid; it can be avoided by employing sophisticated sampling procedures. Such randomization can prevent SDA team members from being steered toward particular sites or respondents by their own biases or by others'. It is no less inexcusable for qualitative evaluators than for quantitative evaluators to forego careful selection of sites and respondents simply from lack of effort.

However, random sampling is not possible for many aspects of qualitative evaluation. The necessity of including or excluding certain sites or respondents with specific traits, the difficulty in obtaining information on the subtle local differences that affect service delivery, and the flexibility needed to pursue referrals all prohibit randomized procedures. Since the only alternative to nonrandom selection in these areas is to exclude this valuable information from the study, qualitative evaluators employ much purposive sampling.

Staffing for site visits is also a concern, since all qualitative information is first assessed by field staff before it is recorded for later analysis. Of course, any research process involves some intermediate steps between direct client responses and data analysis, but qualitative evaluations rely heavily on the judgments and talents of field staff. Many SDA team members, especially full-time SDA staff, are well trained and experienced in observations and discussions. These staff are the backbone of the SDA process and perform the bulk of field efforts, especially in tasks that are particularly difficult or sensitive.

However, others, albeit in decreasing proportion, take part in SDA field work and contribute information for analysis, and their contributions are less consistent. Indeed, their lack of familiarity with either the substance or the process of site visits is responsible for their diminished involvement in SDAs. To the extent possible, other qualitative efforts might consider limiting field staff to persons with known competence in the required duties. It is our experience that training, especially the short-term training required for a short-term project, is often not sufficient to ensure high-level performance from new personnel.

A related weakness, yet also a strength, of qualitative evaluation is the open-ended nature of the information-gathering process. Unlike predetermined evaluations that use standardized instruments or measures, qualitative evaluations are designed to pursue unexpected information as it appears. SDA uses several techniques to achieve this goal, including minimally structured discussion guides and repeated instructions to team members to remain flexible. The resulting information often supplies some of SDA's more interesting findings. However, this flexibility yields nonuniform information from team members, since not all field staff have pursued or probed the same issues with the same respondents. Nor have all field staff followed the same order or techniques for eliciting information. It can be hoped that as a result of the numerous team members involved in a project, the hundreds of discussions, the several methods of analysis, and the final distillation by the lead region, these differences in information-gathering techniques will be diluted. Yet the dilemma remains, and qualitative evaluators need better techniques for eliciting fairly uniform types of information in a decidedly nonuniform process.

Analysis of information from site visits also poses problems. Given the nonuniformity of information, how can findings be distilled? Three separate techniques used in SDAs have been described in this chapter, and it has been suggested that triangulation of methods helps to compensate for the idiosyncracies of any one approach. Yet there remain the problems of weighting information from different sources, conducting content analyses on records of varying depth, and blending information gleaned from discussions, observations, document analyses, and other methods. Currently, the analysis of qualitative evaluation is at least as much art as it is science, and methods remain undeveloped. It is perhaps this area that offers the most potential for major contributions in qualitative evaluation.

Yet, in spite of these areas of concern, SDA illustrates that qualitative evaluation can become an accepted contributor to the decision-making process. The reason for such acceptance is quite simple: SDAs are useful to top officials in planning, managing, and evaluating department programs. "To meet standards of utility, evaluation reports must be informative to practitioners and must make a desirable impact on their work" (Stufflebeam, 1974, p. 7). SDAs make this desirable impact because they meet Stufflebeam's six criteria for evaluation effectiveness: relevance, importance, scope, credibility, timeliness, and pervasiveness.

Service Delivery Assessments are useful because they are relevant to the needs of decision makers. Too often, evaluation projects are viewed by program managers as of more interest to researchers than to those who must wrestle with the problems of service delivery on a day-to-day basis (Pratt, 1980). Given this perception, it is not surprising that managers pay little attention to either the needs or the findings of many evaluators.

SDA adopts a different approach, preferring to consider itself a tool that aids top management to address issues of interest. Throughout the development of issues, conduct of site visits, drafting of reports and briefings, and presentation of findings, SDA staff and program staff work closely to ensure that program concerns are addressed. This does not imply that the objectivity of SDA staff is compromised, since it is possible to work closely yet to maintain an independence from program pressures.

SDAs are also important, since they respond to the Secretary's current needs and receive the attention of the highest officials of the department. Thus, they receive the full cooperation and resources that are needed to complete them. A common complaint about evaluation efforts is that the important issues are not examined. SDA, and other evaluations that aim to be useful, must make special efforts to avoid this mistake.

The scope of an SDA is important, since some important issues may be addressed while others may not. To be useful, an evaluation must address all issues of interest. SDA, through the extensive preassessment efforts as well as the regular review by program staff and experts, remains open to new issues as they arise. Often, the site visits suggest new issues to consider, and sometimes these new issues are unknown to program staff. A useful evaluation system is sufficiently flexible to incorporate new issues as they arise.

Like all evaluations, an SDA must be credible to be useful. While this credibility implies respect for the methods and procedures used in the study, it also requires a respect for the evaluator as an individual or group (Singer, 1979). SDA has the dual advantage of operating for the Secretary and of being managed by the Inspector General, neither of whom can afford to condone efforts that are less than fully objective. Even so, many suspicious program managers have changed their opinions of Service Delivery Assessments only through personal experience, and to that extent an impeccable track record is essential for any evaluator.

One of the most useful traits of an SDA is that it is timely. "If a decision must be made by a certain date and the information is late, the data will have little value. . . . However, most decision makers do not have the time or the resources for extended studies" (Staats, 1980, p. 20). Stufflebeam says that this "is perhaps the most critical of the utility criteria. This is because the best of information is useless if it is provided too late to serve its purpose" (1974, p. 9). Clearly, an evaluation must be completed in time to assist the decision makers. However, this timeliness implies an almost inevitable trade-off with methodological rigor. Each step of an evaluation requires time, and usually the more time, the better. Certainly, SDA staff would prefer to have more time for preassessment, design, training, site visits, and analysis. Yet, if the alternative to coping with time pressures is to miss the deadline for being useful, SDA clearly prefers to provide its best information on time. Unfortunately, at least from a policy perspective, not all evaluation efforts make this decision.

The final criterion for useful evaluation is that it be pervasive. This means that the findings are disseminated to all involved parties in an understandable form. The personal involvement of the Secretary and the Inspector General ensures that SDA findings reach the necessary individuals within HHS. This type of support should be the aim of all evaluations. Yet, the SDA staff themselves have a major responsibility to ensure that the findings are presented clearly and concisely (Nathan, 1979). The emphasis on short and readable documents and briefings helps SDA to disseminate its findings, and the personal briefing with the Secretary resolves any misunderstandings that may occur.

In summary, Service Delivery Assessment has become a useful

evaluation tool largely because it satisfies several important criteria for effectiveness. It allows the managers of diverse, complex service programs to remain informed about and responsive to the realities existing at the "client's end of the pipeline." Equally important, it provides this grassroots perspective quickly enough to affect upcoming decisions. As the field of program evaluation turns from exclusive reliance on experimental methods (Smith, 1978), Service Delivery Assessment provides one example of an innovative approach. It can be hoped that other examples will soon emerge and that the combined lessons of SDA and these other models will enable the entire field of evaluation to advance.

References

Brickell, H. M. *Needed: Instruments as Good as Our Eyes.* Kalamazoo: Evaluation Center, College of Education, Western Michigan University, 1976.

Califano, J. A., Jr. "Service Delivery Assessment." Memorandum to Heads of Principal Operating Components, Washington, D.C., March 6, 1978.

Cochran, N. "Cognitive Processes, Social Mores, and the Accumulation of Data: Program Evaluation and the Status Quo." *Evaluation Quarterly*, 1978, *2* (2), 343–358.

Cox, G. B. "Managerial Style: Implications for the Utilization of Program Evaluation Information." *Evaluation Quarterly*, 1977, *1* (3), 499–508.

Demaline, R. E., and Quinn, D. W. *Hints for Planning and Conducting a Survey and a Bibliography of Survey Methods.* Kalamazoo: Evaluation Center, College of Education, Western Michigan University, 1979.

Demkovich, L. E. "The Rewards and Frustrations of the Federal Bureaucracy: An Interview with Hale Champion." *National Journal*, June 16, 1979, pp. 998–1000.

Drucker, P. F. *Management: Tasks, Responsibilities, Practices.* New York: Harper & Row, 1973.

U.S. General Accounting Office. "Evaluation and Analysis to Support Decisionmaking." Washington, D.C.: U.S. General Accounting Office, 1976.

U.S. General Accounting Office. "Finding out How Programs Are Working: Suggestions for Congressional Oversight." Washington, D.C.: U.S. General Accounting Office, 1977.

Freeman, H. "Future Developments in Evaluation Research." In C. Abt (Ed.), *Problems in American Social Policy Research.* Cambridge, Mass.: Abt Books, 1980.

Guba, E. G. *Metaphor Adaptation Report: Investigative Journalism.* Paper and Report Series No. 4. Portland, Ore.: Research on Evaluation Program, Northwest Regional Educational Laboratory, 1978.

Harrington, P. J., and Sanders, J. R. *Guidelines for Goal-Free Evaluation.* Kalamazoo: Evaluation Center, College of Education, Western Michigan University, 1979.

Hendricks, M. "A New Approach to Program Evaluation at HEW." In C. Abt (Ed.), *Problems in American Social Policy Research.* Cambridge, Mass.: Abt Books, 1980.

Nathan, R. "Ten Rigorous Rules for Relevant Research." In C. Abt (Ed.), *Costs and Benefits of Applied Social Research.* Cambridge, Mass.: Council for Applied Social Research, 1979.

Patton, M. Q. *Utilization-Focused Evaluation.* Beverly Hills, Calif.: Sage, 1978.

Pratt, J. "State-Level Impacts of Social Policy Research." In C. Abt (Ed.), *Problems in American Social Policy Research.* Cambridge, Mass.: Abt Books, 1980.

Rossi, P. H. "Issues in the Evaluation of Human Services Delivery." *Evaluation Quarterly,* 1978, *2* (4), 573–599.

Rossi, R. J., and McLaughlin, D. H. "Establishing Evaluation Objectives." *Evaluation Quarterly,* 1979, *3* (3), 331–346.

Scheirer, M. A. "Program Participants' Positive Perceptions: Psychological Conflict of Interest in Social Program Evaluation." *Evaluation Quarterly,* 1978, *2* (1), 53–70.

Scriven, M. "Pros and Cons About Goal-Free Evalution." *Evaluation Comment,* 1972, *3* (4), 1–4.

Scriven, M. *Evaluation Bias and Its Control.* Kalamazoo: Evaluation Center, College of Education, Western Michigan University, 1975.

Singer, J. W. "When the Evaluators Are Evaluated, the GAO Often Gets Low Marks." *National Journal,* November 10, 1979, pp. 1889–1892.

Smith, N. L. *The Development of New Evaluation Methodologies.* Paper and Report Series No. 6. Portland, Ore.: Research on Evaluation Program, Northwest Regional Educational Laboratory, 1978.

Staats, E. B. "Why Isn't Policy Research Utilized More by Decision Makers?" In C. Abt (Ed.), *Problems in American Social Policy Research.* Cambridge, Mass.: Abt Books, 1980.

Stake, R. E. *Program Evaluation: Particularly Responsive Evaluation.* Kalamazoo: Evaluation Center, College of Education, Western Michigan University, 1975.

Stufflebeam, D. L. *Meta-Evaluation.* Kalamazoo: Evaluation Center, College of Education, Western Michigan University, 1974.

Zimlich, N. "HDS Delivery Level Assessments for FY 1980." Memorandum to Regional HDS Administrators, Seattle, Wash., August 23, 1979.

Michael Hendricks is assistant director for policy coordination, Office of Service Delivery Assessment, U.S. Department of Health and Human Services. His academic training includes postdoctoral study in methodology and evaluation research at Northwestern University.

36

Educational Evaluation and
Shifting Youth Policy

Bruce Fuller

Social programs, including interventions helping disadvantaged youth, offer implicit models regarding what behavioral changes will cause various social and economic outcomes. Responding, in part, to the work of evaluators, federal and state youth policies advance different intervention models. This article reviews five causal metaphors running throughout youth employment and education programs: (1) The functionalist economic model, arguing that increased skills will improve youth employment; (2) the institutional socialization model, suggesting that earlier entrance to the "adult work world" will ease youth "transition"; (3) a psychosocial view of youth development, emphasizing the individual's sense of social efficacy in learning and work situations; (4) the subcultural model, pointing to the importance of local opportunity structures and social norms functional within specific subcultural conditions; and (5) a self-determined community development vision, urging local economic growth in disadvantaged areas. Evaluation evidence, increasingly abundant, should begin to look across these models to improve program strategies. A review of such research for youth employment efforts is included. When feasible, evaluation sponsors and evaluators should explicitly articulate programs' causal models to nurture broader theoretical understandings and minimize being overly confined within the immediate program model one is evaluating.

*E*clipsing modest state and federal augmentations to school-based programs in recent years, the federal youth employment initiative has grown dramatically. In 1977, a decade after James Coleman sparked skepticism over schools' influence on ameliorating social inequality, a $1.5 billion youth employment bill was signed by President

AUTHOR'S NOTE: *The author would like to thank Steve Weiner, University of California at Berkeley School of Public Policy, and Mike Kirst, Stanford University School of Education, for their support. This work was also aided by Sanford Dornbusch, Boys Town Center for Youth Development, and the Institute on Finance and Governance of Education, Stanford University.*

From Bruce Fuller, "Educational Evaluation and Shifting Youth Policy," 5(2) *Evaluation Review* 167-188 (April 1981). Copyright 1981 by Sage Publications, Inc.

Carter. Youth development policy continues to be shifting from exclusively school issues to a broader spectrum of questions regarding job creation and workplace-based learning for disadvantaged youth.[1]

This article suggests that if educational researchers and evaluators are to contribute to the burgeoning field of education and work, alternative assumptions regarding human development must be understood. Employment and educational policies have developed independently. Only in the past 15 years have federal programs addressed youth unemployment, usually distant from local and state supported school-based programs. Yet, as the fields of youth employment and formal schooling blend together (particularly in trying to serve out-of-school innercity youth), each could gain much from the other. If employment program designers listen to what educational evaluators are discovering about effective learning environments, much progress may occur. We must build common understandings of our theoretical assumptions and share knowledge gained from evaluation efforts.

As educational evaluators grow increasingly sensitive to the policy context's influence on program evaluation (Weiner et al., 1978; Weiss, 1972), several aspects of this movement in federal youth policy are especially important. First, this shift away from exclusively school-based programs, in part, responds to program evaluation findings over the past decade. Assessments of classroom vocational education programs, for example, yield rather consistent evidence of ineffectiveness in matching youth with actual jobs (Carnegie Council, 1979). In response, youth programs increasingly emphasize job creation and integration of workplace-based learning with classroom instruction. Similarly, community-based participation in program development seems more effective than programs centrally prescribed by government "experts" (Berman and McLaughlin, 1975). Federal policy acknowledges this evaluation finding by encouraging learning options delivered by community agencies. This is particularly important in reaching the one-third of innercity youth who never finish high school.

Second, the rise of youth programs focusing more on work and less on school illustrates the importance of understanding alternative definitions of what "the social problem" actually is. Evaluators often argue that effects of categorical programs are lost within the more pervasive and enduring influence of the social environment. To the extent a theoretical model of youth development guides federal policy, a greater emphasis on addressing structural labor market conditions is now emerging through job creation and distribution strategies. This shift away from only supporting schools as the instrumental agent creates a provocative dialectic from which new understandings of the problem may emerge. This more structural approach also accommodates critics of categorical educational programs which fail to address the economic environment surrounding schools. Minimally, this debate broadens questions related to what specific skills best empower disadvantaged youth and communities to improve their quality of life, and through which social interactions these competencies are most effectively learned.

Most often, evaluators are required to accept program outcome indicators prescribed (or hoped for) by program administrators. In exploring alternative ways of seeing the youth unemployment problem, this article attempts to demonstrate how different theoretical models of the problem suggest different variables which the evaluator might examine within these formally prescribed program outcomes. Ideally, educational evaluations help refine theoretical understandings regarding youth development beyond meeting immediate information needs of the evaluator's client.

Third, responding to progress in the evaluation field and fiscal conservatism among the American people, recent youth programs are making some progress within a "knowledge development strategy," to more carefully structure program models which yield clearer evaluation information. While this creates tension with the stronger emphasis on grass roots program development, nurturing endless varieties of demonstration programs increasingly appears to be an unwise political approach as government resources reach a plateau.

As differentiated categorical programs and locally varied projects reflect diverse assumptions about human learning and antecedents to labor market success, evaluators must recognize alternative ways of defining the problem. From child care to vocational training, programs are founded upon diverse, often implicit assumptions about the goals of, and preferred settings for, education. This article's first section elaborates different ways of seeing the youth unemployment problem. Contrasting program models and assessment methods flow from each. The article's second section explores how program evaluations in the employment field influence youth development policy. Finally, a brief glance is taken at the broader question of how what we have learned might generally enhance social reform.

WAYS OF SEEING "THE YOUTH PROBLEM"[2]

The perceptual lens through which we view the youth problem enormously influences the character of policy action and evaluation strategy. For example, the emphasis on skill training during the 1960s stemmed from an assumption by Great Society architects that general economic growth would provide sufficient labor market demand and opportunities for as many unemployed youth as could gain prerequisite skills. Since then, we have realized that labor demand growth in the 1960s was atypical and occurred disproportionately in white-collar jobs. Improved knowledge has grown more sensitive to labor market conditions, moving beyond the bias of simply "treating" the unemployed. As this article explores, social psychological factors may also be critical, usually ignored by economists seeking quick material outcomes (job placements). The quality of early jobs may determine the youth's basic feelings about work. Interpersonal skills and one's self-concept may be more important in determining labor market success than manual dexterity. Improved understandings of effective learning environments (Baker, 1978; Brookover, 1977; Cohen et al., 1976) have not generally been applied to employment programs.

Subcultural differences and personal values notwithstanding, we generally assume social interaction contributes to one's quality of life. If the interaction involves productive work, so much the better. Quality of life seems to rest on social experiences, psychological health, and material security. Therefore, the apparent isolation and idleness of innercity youth is viewed as a problem.[3] Beyond these abstractions, how the problem and corresponding antecedent causes are defined varies enormously. Certain explanatory models hold considerable currency. These five viewpoints are interrelated; evidence questioning one model often prompts a new view of the problem and ways of building social programs.

The five models discussed offer understandings of how human skills relate to labor market experience, how individual employers behave, and how the economies of local communities operate. Each model also emphasizes different learning and skill areas, and implicit philosophical values regarding probable and desired directions of economic and social change.

The *functionalist economic model* argues that modern industrial nations require a highly skilled work force. Human capitalists suggest that if only the unemployed would learn technical job skills, unemployment would diminish. This model places major responsibility on youth to learn manual skills and assumes a major role for formal schooling.

The task is to enable disadvantaged youth to adapt to the mainstream economy within the primary labor market.

However, while skill shortages may occur in early stages of industrial development and at times appear in certain growth sectors today, most entry level jobs require minimal manual skills. The growth in service occupations emphasizes the importance of communication skills and attitudes over technical manual competencies. The human capital model only vaguely distinguishes which cognitive and social competencies are needed across occupations versus knowledge necessary for particular jobs (Thurow, 1970). The human capital viewpoint also responds largely to employers' interests. Human capital is viewed as another input to the production function. Maximizing productive efficiency is the goal.

Bowles and Gintis (1976) argue that the human capital viewpoint has been incorrectly, though subtly, accepted by many educators. This critique suggests that while we pursue liberal educational goals—self-direction, informed criticism, and liberation—for the middle-class college student, job programs concentrate on socializing innercity youth to accept passive roles in authoritarian workplaces.

The conventional economic model does possess explanatory value. However, it also ignores qualitative aspects of working. For example, O'Toole (1977) argues that anxiety and disruption suffered by the working poor stem more from the poor quality of jobs than unemployment. This is a critical question as youth employment programs strive to place youth in entry level jobs, assuming that any work will have positive motivational and social effects.

Similar to schools, youth employment programs seem to be wandering in cross-currents of social values. Shifts in social values already influence young workers and potentially affect youth employment programs. There are egalitarian challenges to hierarchical workplaces; demystification of authority in schools, families, churches, and workplaces has increased since the mid-1960s (Yankelovich, 1974). While middle-class youth reject authoritarian workplaces, job programs often assume disadvantaged youth should respond differently, more passively. Is it realistic to expect innercity youth to find personal and social meaning in work which the society increasingly questions?

The rational decision-making emphasis of labor economics has improved labor supply and demand data. When thoughtfully utilized by local employment and schooling agencies, work and training decisions of unemployed youth can be aided enormously. However, Bullock's (1973) pioneering work emphasizes the importance of informal information channels in learning about jobs. Ogbu (1974), in an ethnographic study, agrees with Bullock that relatives and friends are primary sources of job information, not formal agents such as counselors or employment services. Informal innercity networks additionally communicate that schooling does not always deliver the promised social and financial rewards. In contrast, rationalist federal efforts in career education usually assume that formal organizations are important sources of labor market information for all social classes and that the data have meaning to youth when communicated (Grubb and Lazerson, 1975).

These trends suggest that youth programs might reasonably choose to present alternative images of workplace realities—for these realities are changing. Bowers (1977) points out that schools tend to objectify the world, painting deterministic views of social relations. Yet socialization that obscures the "human authorship of culture" clearly diminishes a youth's sense of power in affecting one's own life. Teaching innercity youths that they can restructure a boring job or become managers may be unrealistic. However, presenting a single deterministic view of work life and economic reality seems equally detrimental.

The *institutional socialization model* argues that youth remain in school too long, resulting in a rough transition between school and work. Knowledge relating to productive interaction is not gained until after leaving high school. This separation of school and work decreases knowledge about the labor market and job-related skills. The school-based developmental path has become so normative that anyone diverging from it becomes deviant. The predominance of schooling has raised employers' credentialing requirements, adding rigidity to the schooling process.

Coleman's (1973) work is grounded in this framework, arguing that integration of school and work opportunities would result in more balanced adolescent development. Earlier and more extensive work experience would enable easier crossing of a critical threshold into the "adult world of work" and pursuit of a career. Work experience provides improved adaptation to adult life—toward which social goals (consumption, leisure, family) is not explicitly considered. This model tends to view all work as meaningful and educational. A linear view of youth-to-adult development is also assumed; adult values are good, youth values and behaviors are less desirable. Placing less emphasis on differentiated skills imparted by schools, this model suggests that earlier mingling in the adult world will enhance social integration.

Several concepts of the economic and institutional socialization models are often integrated into a viewpoint which emphasizes youth development. This confounded framework, while deemphasizing labor market structure, offers no real departure. The new synthesis does, however, prompt a distinct *psychosocial model* of youth development. The following discussion first pulls out pertinent pieces of the economic and institutional socialization models, then outlines the emergent psychosocial framework.

By defining "the youth problem" as joblessness, the meaning of development is often narrowed by policy makers to consider those processes or individual characteristics important in obtaining a job. Two schools of thought define this spectrum. Many argue that all youth initially explore the work world in an informal way, first to make money and later to examine different occupations. The task in helping disadvantaged youth, therefore, is to offer general work experience opportunities and to encourage more work through formal schools (Spring, n.d.). Socialization to, and familiarity with, work habits and social norms is the short-run goal. In the 1978-79 fiscal year, just over $3 billion, or 26% of CETA expenditures, supported general work experience programs, largely concentrated on youth aged 14-18.

At the opposite end of the spectrum, the argument is made that youth need specific marketable skills, obtained through formal classroom or on-the-job training (OJT). In the 1978-79 fiscal year, over $2.1 billion, or 18% of CETA dollars nationally, were spent on training programs. Of these funds, two-thirds will be spent on formal classroom instruction. Less than 6% of all CETA expenditures will support worksite-based (OJT) training.[4]

Both the work experience and skill training viewpoints reflect a human capital perspective: The quality of life for youth will improve if basic cognitive and specific manual skills are provided and youth are moved into the labor market.

Alternative concepts of youth development suggest different priorities in designing policy and programs. Considerable theoretical and empirical research suggests a stronger emphasis on developing a sense of social competence and self-esteem (Lambert et al., 1978). Such growth may occur through a decentering process where one is able to view oneself through others' perspectives. Researchers looking at development of innercity youth emphasize the importance of feeling strong about one's cultural background and potential, balanced with awareness and critical assessment of others' viewpoints (Banks and Grambs, 1972; Steinfield, 1975; Yankelovich, 1978).

Whether CETA youth programs nurture such feelings of self-determination is unclear. The problem obviously lies in the structure of many workplaces—which no government program alone can realistically influence. However, after failing according to the norms of school achievement, placing an out-of-school youth in a boring job within a hierarchical work organization may be counterproductive to long run development. Urging youth back into formal classroom instruction may also be unwise. Bachman's (1971) longitudinal research reveals that dropout rates are twice as high for youth with low self-esteem and negative affective states, including feeling distant from the social community. Also, Greenberg (1978) reports that self-esteem may actually rise after youth leave school.

CETA youth efforts may yield clearer understandings on how to address this central area of development. For example, the Department of Labor (DOL) is supporting a network of youth enterprises through Youthwork and the Corporation for Youth Enterprise, two nonprofit organizations. These projects involve youth in the management and operation of small-scale businesses, such as recycling centers, auto repair shops, or crafts production. This approach emphasizes development of self-efficacy by involving youth in all levels of a productive enterprise, and by providing more individualized apprenticeship experiences in small business settings (Rist et al., 1979).

Recent efforts of educational evaluators are yielding clearer understanding of the concept of social competence and efficacy and their central importance. For example, Brookover (1977) found that "students' sense of academic futility" explained 48% of the variance in student achievement among Michigan elementary schools. Efficacy, or futility, was an equally strong predictor of achievement in black schools as in white schools. The efficacy concept combines situational and interactive emphases of sociological evaluation approaches with psychological understandings of self-concept.

Unfortunately, youth policy often views schooling as either instrumental to labor market success or possessing unworkable developmental goals for innercity youth. Under the former assumption, dropouts are urged to quickly obtain a high school diploma and/or skills training. However, the economic yield on either a diploma or classroom vocational training is questionable (Yankelovich, 1979). Assuming that schools' goals are inappropriate, federal policies often shift toward quick job placement for innercity youth. Indeed, many youth, having mostly experienced failure in school, prefer to find jobs and earn money.

Yet the process through which one feels efficacious within a social setting, either school or workplace, is equally important. The extent to which a youth attributes success to one's own effort will likely influence achievement, whether in school or at work (Dweck, 1976). However, continued failure in conventional high schools will not likely build a sense of efficacy, and entry level jobs may intensify a feeling of social powerlessness. Policy makers too often view school as instrumental to economic success or romanticize about the value of work, minimizing careful understanding of social interactions within these environments. Educational evaluators could play a vital role here in assessing the implict learning content of work, particularly in terms of learned powerlessness.

The *subcultural model* looks directly at differences in social patterns between the mainstream middle-class and unemployed lower-class. This framework at times corresponds to secondary labor market theory. A sociological explanation is used, suggesting that as innercity youth fail according to the school's achievement norms and adults fail in terms of employers' criteria, youth values and motivation will functionally adapt. Forms of achievement are subsequently redefined, and subcultural values emerge. Where youth and adults fail in school or work, adaptive ways of coping, including alternative achievement norms, inevitably develop.

The subcultural model is useful in exposing the unintended paternalistic quality of some social program approaches. "Compensatory programs" since the 1960s often assumed deprivation or inferiority within lower social class communities. This viewpoint assumes great homogeneity among innercity families. The subcultural framework suggests that where social groups exist separate from the white middle-class, different subcultural values and social ways will emerge or simply continue from past ethnic histories (Valentine, 1968; Leacock, 1971).

While social reformers have, more recently, recognized the heterogeneity and strengths among *and* within subcultures, the assumption remains strong that The American Dream is sought by all. The image of black activists opposing school busing vividly draws the issue: Do assimilationist goals diminish a sense of community within American subcultures? The central tenet of opportunity programs is, after all, to equalize chances for winning a uniform, competitive social race (Moynihan, 1969).

Most research assumes consensus over the value of academic achievement and work experience for innercity youth. This obviously is the purpose of schools, and we know much about measuring academic competencies. However, unless dominant economic and social roles change for low-status parents, academic and work-related competencies may hold little relevance for their youth. Local subcultural employment and opportunity structures largely determine available social roles and associated interpersonal and technical competencies (Ogbu, 1979). Academic skills will have little utility unless these skills instrumentally enhance social and job opportunities. While innercity parents may value skills obtained in schools, unless youth experience adults utilizing and benefitting from these competencies, internal school sanctions and norms may have short-lived effects.

Undoubtedly, white America's level of material comfort is desirable in the eyes of the poor. Resources from middle-America via social programs and private sector investment will help. However, as some minority communities seek to determine their own futures, enhancing subcultural values and identity, indigenous sources of development will play a strong role. A *self-determined community development model* may move beyond the subcultural framework in redefining which program outcomes are most important to assess and how such outcomes should be evaluated.

The community development conceptualization values subcultural and ethnic pluralism. However, rising energy costs and resulting structural economic changes broaden this model's applicability to understanding decentralized organizations and means of production (Stavrianos, 1976). This model fundamentally provides an alternative understanding of the youth unemployment problem. Indeed, the community development theme significantly influenced Great Society architects in the early 1960s. Community action agencies played a pivotal role locally in the War on Poverty. Indeed, current successors to the Office of Economic Opportunity, the Community Services Administration and the Economic Development Administration, continue to support local Community Development Corporations. Yet, since the first days of OEO, major expansions occurred mostly in individual categorical programs. A more holistic self-determined approach to community development is difficult when each program must be applied for individually, within different regulations, and accountable to various federal bureaucracies (Kramer, 1969).[5]

Furthermore, private capital and economic activity remain limited in innercities. Sundquist (1978) recently proposed corporate tax credits for businesses that locate in impoverished urban and rural areas. Similarly, federal urban development proposals often seek stronger direct lending and loan guarantees to encourage innercity investment.

Social and structural notions of self-determined community development parallel psychological research. Bruner (1971: 30) summarizes this theme in speaking of subsistence cultures:

It may be that a collective, rather than an individual, value orientation develops where the individual lacks power over the physical world. Lacking personal power he has no notion of personal importance. In terms of his cognitive categories he will be less likely to set himself apart from others and the physical world. He will be less self-conscious at the same time that he places less value upon himself.

Program evaluation often becomes so focused on outcomes to meet accountability demands that underlying processes by which outcomes are reached or not attained remain hidden. For example, a student's sense of efficacy seems very much related to cognitive achievement. This association may operate independently of social class and school input variables (including school expenditures and teacher experience). Yet, if evaluation sponsors constantly respond only to immediate outcomes, efficacy-building processes will not be understood. Individual efficacy and community building may be key determinants of youth employment program success. However, reporting the number of job placements as the performance criterion will not approach these more subtle processes. The resulting message heard by local program operators is that evaluation is a centralized tool for judging failures, not for enabling improvement of programs.

REVIEW OF EMPLOYMENT PROGRAM EVALUATIONS

PHILOSOPHY AND USES OF PROGRAM EVALUATION

The current skepticism of government highlights the need to understand the impact of social programs. However, evaluators are usually called in after programs have been funded, minimizing careful evaluation of different models. Planned variation strategies, involving the evaluator up front in designing programs, have highlighted the difficulties in carefully structuring programs to ensure variation in only those variables of interest. Also, planned variation studies which are national in scope, including several local sites, are very difficult to manage and ensure common local program structures, processes, and conditions over time (House et al., 1978).

The alternative "experimental" strategy is to legislate a variety of demonstration programs. In the early 1960s, demonstration programs were assumed to be potentially effective program models. The initial local projects were intended to demonstrate their broad importance. The Great Society architects would then go back to the Congress for national funding. With slightly more humility, demonstration programs as used in recent federal youth legislation justify funding diverse programs. The diversity was initially prompted by various instincts among individual members and staff of the Congress and Administration officials about which program models would work best. Broader support of the legislation was constructed by funding several separate programs.

In considering how program evaluation may be used in refining programs, three additional issues must be recognized. First, most information gathering often tries to better describe program activity. Pressures for accountability require extensive descriptive data: How are dollars spent? For what services? Who is being served? At what cost? This basic information is also internally necessary to refine programs. For example, basic knowledge is available regarding characteristics of CETA participants and costs of different CETA services (Congressional Budget Office, 1978). Such monitoring information has enormous political value in demonstrating compliance with legislative intent and management competence. However, from the local program viewpoint, this summative information is often of little use in a formative way, in improving one's program.

Policy concerns usually determine which evaluation questions are asked. So, for example, evaluators ask whether in-school vocational training programs increase participant earnings. A national evaluation may yield one answer. However, a summative evaluation will not identify which factors contribute to the success of particularly high quality programs, or why ineffective programs failed (Smith and Bissell, 1970). This information is less important to budget planners—but critical to those trying to improve programs. We become so concerned with the centralized policy question of whether social interventions make a difference, we ignore the micro issues related to why specific local projects succeed.

Where the evaluator aids local community administrators and program staff in looking at alternative ways of approaching outcomes, the evaluator becomes a resource, not a burden. This involves qualitative interaction with program staff, and may result in a questioning of how program outcomes are conventionally defined. Questions of whether the evaluation is conducted externally from the program, accepts predetermined performance criteria, and relies on quantifiable outcome data are value issues which must be addressed by evaluators and sponsors. They revolve around whose decisions are of highest priority and how serious one is about improving, versus simply judging, programs (Baker et al., 1978; Stone, 1978; Dressel, 1976).

Second, fragmentation of social programs has resulted in an organizational segmentation of expected outcomes and performance criteria. For example, internal evaluations of vocational education programs often focus on describing student characteristics and instructional services. Little attention is directed at subsequent labor market experience: Did the skill training assist in getting a job? On the other hand, employment program evaluations focus heavily on whether participants obtained jobs. The social processes utilized in pursuing educational outcomes are less valued.

Weiner et al. (1978) suggest changes in how different evaluation strategies might help remedy these problems. Evaluators could be given greater freedom to interact with program clients and organized constituencies supporting the programs. Where evaluators remain distant from the local service delivery process and the political process determining future fundings and program regulations, their findings will have minimal influence. Even when the funding agency agrees with the evaluator on a recommended program change, program constituencies may stifle attempts at administrative or legislative changes suggested by the evaluation. Evaluations might also relate to broad problem areas, across programs. For example, looking at several programs involved with innercity youth may yield very different action agendas than looking at several programs individually. This approach would enable aggregation of knowledge regarding a problem area rather than a growing pile of segmented program evaluations.

PROGRAM EVALUATIONS

After 15 years of evaluating employment programs, knowledge about program effectiveness suggests tentative directions—or at least points to how fundamental questions can be better understood. However, national evaluations rarely identify specific successful program models or techniques. In particular, participant and organizational learning objectives, content, and outcomes are rarely discussed. This review focuses on evidence regarding the relative influence of workplace versus in-school job skills training on economic outcomes (employment and wage rates).

On-the-job Training. Workplace instruction generally increases posttraining earnings by at least 20 to 30% more than school-based training (Congressional Budget Office, 1978). Early experience with OJT also indicates higher postprogram employment rates. More recent evaluations reach similar conclusions, highlighting association between positive labor market experience with length of participation in the program (Perry et al., 1975).

The ongoing national longitudinal study of CETA participants reveals significantly more positive impact of OJT programs compared to classroom training, adult work experience, and public service employment. This research reports a 42% increase in earnings for OJT participants between one year prior to entry and three months after completing training (Westat, 1978). Initial experience also indicates strong earnings and employment gains where OJT programs work with a limited number of employers in training skilled workers (Department of Labor, 1973). Importantly, OJT programs are consistently less costly than in-school training. Private businesses may be covering costs beyond the training subsidy supported by CETA.

Problems do exist with these generally optimistic findings. OJT experiences with youth are limited. Early success with OJT may be due to higher skill levels among OJT entrants compared to classroom training participants. OJT participants generally earned higher wages before entering the program. Thus, positive impacts on youth with lower skills at entry may be less. Most OJT jobs appear to be in large businesses. This offers advantages in terms of job security and advancement. However, the learning content of these jobs may be stifling for youth.

In-School Vocational Training. CETA funded skills training differs from school-based vocational education primarily in terms of organization and accountability. Vocational education programs usually exist within high schools or community colleges. Some school districts also support independent job skill centers. CETA-funded institutional training is often delivered through skill centers, including Job Corps centers (Levitan and Johnston, 1975). Such centers and school-based vocational programs must demonstrate job placement rates to justify funding. School-based vocational education programs receive state (and some federal) funding regardless of placement success.

Evidence on the impact of school-based vocational education programs is very discouraging. After reviewing over 50 vocational education evaluations, Reubens (1974) reports: (1) Enrollment in many high school vocational programs so far exceeds actual job openings that serious oversupply problems are averted only by high dropout rates and selection of jobs unrelated to students' training. (2) Many vocational graduates enter unskilled or semiskilled jobs requiring little or no prior training. (3) Many occupations require only a short two- to four-week job training period, and this is necessary regardless of prior vocational instruction. As few as 20% of all first jobs obtained by youth require any formal vocational education. (4) Where earning gains for vocational graduates do appear, they disappear in the long run. (5) Longitudinal research shows no significant improvement in employment rates of vocational graduates compared to other youth with similar socioeconomic characteristics. (6) Dropout rates for vocational programs are higher than other high school programs, even when controlling for students' academic achievement and socioeconomic characteristics. This finding is particularly distressing given the faith held by many vocational educators and youth program administrators that vocational training will attract innercity youth to remain in, or return to, school. (7) Vocational educators' concern with improving job skills (labor supply) results in ignoring actual characteristics of labor market demand.

Wilms (1974) extensively studied the impact of various vocational programs offering training in higher-skilled (accountants, computer programmers, electronic technicians) versus lower-skilled (secretaries, cosmotologists, dental assistants) occupations. Both public and private proprietary vocational programs were included. Only 20% of the participants in high-skill vocational programs obtained training-related jobs. Initial earnings, however, did not exceed wages of graduates taking jobs unrelated to their training. These benefits may be positive for those youth previously unemployed. Affect on self-efficacy in choosing a training program and obtaining subsequent employment may also be positive. The inefficiency of high-skill training programs is distressing, as is the fact that proprietary schools often provide low-skill training programs at one-third the cost and in less time than comparable public school programs. With the exception of skill training in high labor areas where classroom instruction is particularly efficient (for example, clerical or nursing), limited effects of traditional vocational education are confirmed by more recent research (Carnegie Council, 1979; Grasso and Shea, 1979).

Work Experience. Some evidence exists that inclusion of work experience opportunities may improve the impact of in-school vocational programs. While Neighborhood Youth Corps (NYC) programs do not increase high school persistence rates, "impact on earnings is significant" (Congressional Budget Office, 1978). Interestingly, Egloff (1970) reports no school-related effects but argues that NYC programs provide self-perceptions of success and self-esteem gains. The program also appears to be most successful in small towns and rural areas—suggesting a possible research direction for looking at influential social environmental factors (General Accounting Office, 1979).

Beyond individual program impact, Levin (1977) questions whether cognitive skill gains among the unemployed actually influence economic outcomes. Only slight relationships have been found between test scores and reading levels with earning levels (for innercity youth). Thus, school-related gains may influence economic labor market outcomes only after early labor market experience among disadvantaged youth. Earlier work experience and formal instruction later in life may be more effective for innercity youth who are turned off by schools.

Research is scarce on how local programs influence noneconomic youth development outcomes. In reviewing 200 program evaluations, Perry (Shea, 1977) found only 17 that explore outcomes other than employment and earning rates, such as work attitudes, social interaction, and personal health. Bridging better understandings of noneconomic outcomes and effective development with local program experience and methods may, however, yield powerful results. One evaluation of early (1964-65) MDTA training participants found generally positive feelings toward the training experience, and found little general association between internal work values and self-concept with post-training earnings. However, among hard-core disadvantaged participants, feelings of self-efficacy and ability to influence one's environment were related to earnings. This research also suggests that programs focus less on treating the *internal* values and possessed skills of disadvantaged youth and emphasize development of self-efficacy through *interactive* experiences of success within a work or other social environment (Gurin, 1970). Evaluation of another work experience program for high school dropouts found a significant drop in youth-perceived powerlessness (National Office for Social Responsibility, 1977). Independent evaluations report on the apparent importance of peer support in workplaces and in other program activities (Manpower Demonstration Research Corporation, 1976). These studies provide an initial framework for future research, including looking into how workplace characteristics may be related to social development.

SUGGESTED DIRECTIONS

First, design of youth employment programs should flow from improved summative and formative evaluation information. The most valued information among youth program people, prescribed from Washington policy makers and often internalized by neighborhood activists, describes program expenditures, participant job placement rates, and starting wages. These summative data are obviously important. However, this essay has hopefully demonstrated the power of (a) how we perceive the problem, and (b) knowledge regarding relative effectiveness of different program models. Until policy and local discussions involve these knowledge areas, computerized collection of administrative information may please the Congress and minimize ripoffs, but public and private sector efforts will creatively improve very slowly.

Second, improving our knowledge of relative program effectiveness must be an explicit outcome of program implementation. The Department of Labor's "knowledge development" strategy provides an optimistic sign. Hopefully, DOL's segmented evaluations of the several YEDPA programs will balance (1) assessment of relative program effectiveness utilizing common performance criteria with (2) sensitivity to unconventional criteria and differences in goals and characteristics between programs. This task is very difficult. Knowledge development objectives are barely articulated at state and local CETA levels. Economic criteria continue to be relied upon.

Sensitivity to, and understanding of, social psychological development of youth is allegedly the business of schools. However, disadvantaged youth have largely left schools. We hold only primitive understandings of how to integrate workplace experiences with formal learning goals. Nor do we understand how social processes nurtured or ignored by educational and employment programs, such as efficacy-building, might improve program outcomes as evidence suggests in school-based programs.

Third, we should carefully examine new human development strategies. The marked success of on-the-job training for adults, in contrast to school-based vocational training, suggests that workplace training should be expanded for disadvantaged youth. Let us systematically determine where training is more effective—workplace versus school—for which jobs. Just because schools are seen through white middle-class eyes as the primary youth agency may not always be a sufficient reason to fund programs through schools. For example, CETA ironically supports school-based work experience programs to encourage youth to spend more time out of school, working. Community-based organizations may perform this task more effectively at considerably less cost.

We should not become blindly romantic about the world of work. Many jobs facing innercity youth are boring and degrading; learning content is rich—in dissuading youth from ever working again. Employers may rarely seek to improve communication and social skills. Schools should perhaps focus on these learning areas. A distinct identity and purpose for the school is critical. Millions of dollars are pumped into schools to prepare youth for, and encourage, working—rather than simply placing youth in workplaces or creating more jobs. Many disadvantaged youth do not view schools as the best place to be, why should program designers? The effect will likely be rising credentialism, not real learning. Schools could effectively complement on-the-job and apprenticeship training by focusing on development of communication and interpersonal competencies.

Finally, we might more often view youth unemployment as part of a broader community development task. At both the social and individual level, self-efficacy and competence in influencing one's social environment seem critical. Schools could play a critical role; they are locally-based and respond to considerable community participation. Similarly, community-based small businesses may offer better work experiences in encouraging community responsibility and cohesion.

Where schools are bureaucratically impervious to community influence, community-based organizations may undertake learning goals related to community development. Rather than only bolstering conventional learning objectives of schools, CETA youth programs could enormously improve community-based learning toward community and individual self-determination. However, this will be unlikely as long as CETA agencies see the problem through the traditional economic model and are encouraged to seek only quick, entry-level job placements.

Somehow we must delineate which learning is most important to empower an innercity youth to achieve a productive role. This learning will be meaningful only if the youth's perceptions and feelings are recognized. Then, the most effective learning environments must be provided. This may be a workplace, classroom, or less formal setting. Finally, society must deliver on its promise that learning and self-development pay off in terms of social experience and material security. This pay-off can best be provided through private action by employers and individual citizens. Public agencies can help; yet social programs will not succeed as long as private individual action fails to share social opportunities and material affluence.

NOTES

1. The Carter Administration proposed in early 1980 a $2 billion expansion of youth programs. Half of these funds would expand Title I (Elementary and Secondary Education Act) related efforts for in-school disadvantaged youth. The second billion would flow through the existing CETA system, targeted for out-of-school youth. The expansion, however, has been postponed indefinitely while the Congress attempts to balance the federal budget.

2. This framework for contrasting varied explanations of a social issue is suggested by Tyack (1976).

3. In December 1977, 38% of all nonwhite youth, aged 16-24, were unemployed and looking for work. Many more had simply given up looking, left the labor market, and were therefore not included in the statistic (Congressional Budget Office, 1978). The youth unemployment problem is related to the economy's general health. However, unemployment of innercity minority youth actually increased slightly during the economic recovery period between 1975 and December 1977, while overall youth unemployment dropped from 16.1 to 12.3%. In 1969, when adult unemployment equalled only 2.8%, black teenage unemployment was at 21.3% (Bullock, 1973). Recent increases in youth employment among whites have not been shared by minority out-of-school youth (Young, 1978). Some claim the youth unemployment problem will go away once the baby-boom bulge passes. Since the late 1950s, the proportion of the working age population (16-64) did increase from 20 to 27%. Yet this passing bulge only accounts for 4% of overall youth unemployment, and only a slightly higher part of much higher nonwhite youth joblessness.

4. The bulk of CETA funds (53%) now go to more direct job-creating public service employment programs, equalling over $6.2 billion this year (Congressional Budget Office, 1978). Reagan Administration cutbacks may affect this picture.

5. Local school site councils, involving teachers, parents, students, and administrators in collective governance, offer one form of legislating a more participatory decision process. Such local councils, first required in ESEA Title I, are included in recent youth employment legislation. The National Labor Relations Act is an early ancestor of federal actions which realign social participation patterns.

REFERENCES

ALKIN, M. C. (1972) "Evaluation theory development," in C. H. Weiss (ed.) Evaluating Action Programs. Boston: Allyn & Bacon.

ALLMAN, T. D. (1978) "The urban crisis leaves town." Harper's (December).

BACHMAN, J. (1971) Youth in Transition. Ann Arbor: University of Michigan.

BAKER, E. L. (1978) "Evaluation dimensions for program development and improvement," in S. B. Anderson (ed.) Exploring Purposes and Dimensions. San Francisco: Jossey-Bass.

——— J. L. HERMAN, and J. P. YEH (1978) Evaluation of the Longitudinal Effects of the Early Childhood Education Program. Los Angeles: University of California.

BANKS, J. A. and J. D. GRAMBS (1972) Black Self-Concept. New York: McGraw-Hill.
BERMAN, P. and M. McLAUGHLIN (1975) Federal Programs Supporting Educational Change. Volume IV: The Findings in Review. Santa Monica: Rand Corporation.
BOWERS, C. A. (1977) "Cultural literacy in developed countries." Prospects, UNESCO 7 (3)
BOWLES, S. and H. GINTIS (1976) Schooling in Capitalist America. New York: Basic Books.
BROOKOVER, W. (1977) Schools Can Make a Difference. East Lansing: Michigan State University.
BRUNER (1971) The Relevance of Education. Cambridge: Harvard Univ. Press.
BULLOCK, P. (1973) Aspiration Versus Opportunity: "Careers" in the Innercity. Ann Arbor: Wayne State University Institute of Labor and Industrial Relations.
Carnegie Council on Policy Studies in Higher Education (1979) Giving Youth a Better Chance. San Francisco: Jossey-Bass.
COHEN, E. G. et al. (1976) "Center for interracial cooperation: a field experiment." Sociology of Education (January).
COLEMAN, J. (1973) Youth: Transition to Adulthood. Washington, DC: President's Science Advisory Committee.
Commission of Inquiry Into Poverty (1978) School Community and Work: Urban and Rural Aspects. Canberra: Australian Government Publishing Service.
Congressional Budget Office (1978) Youth Unemployment: The Outlook and Some Policy Strategies. Washington, DC: U.S. Government Printing Office.
DAANE, C. et al. (1969) Developing Group Counseling Models for the Neighborhood Youth Corps. Tempe: Arizona State University.
Department of Labor (1973) A Model for Training the Disadvantaged: TAT at Oak Ridge, TN. Manpower Research Monograph 29. Washington, DC: Author.
DEUTERMANN, W. V. and S. C. BROWN (1978) "Voluntary part-time workers: a growing part of the labor force." Monthly Labor Review, Department of Labor, Washington, DC (June).
DRESSEL P. L. (1976) Handbook of Academic Evaluation. San Francisco: Jossey-Bass.
DWECK, D. S. (1976) "Children's interpretation of evaluative feedback: the effect of social cues on learned helplessness." Merrill-Palmer Q. 22 (2).
EGLOFF, M. (1970) The Neighborhood Youth Corps: A Review of Research. Manpower Research Monograph 13. Washington, DC: Department of Labor.
General Accounting Office (1979) More Effective Management Is Needed To Improve the Quality of the Summer Youth Employment Program. Washington, DC: Author.
GINZBERG, E. (1980) "Youth unemployment." Scientific Amer. (May).
GOODWIN, L. (1972) Do the Poor Want to Work? A Social Psychological Study of Work Orientations. Washington, DC: The Brookings Institution.
GRASSO, J. and J. SHEA (1979) Vocational Education and Training: Impact on Youth. Berkeley: Carnegie Council on Policy Studies in Higher Education.
GREENBERG, D. F. (1978) "Delinquency and the age structure of society," in A. Pearl et al. (eds.) Valuing Youth. Davis, CA: Dialogue Press.
GRUBB, W. N. and M. LAZERSON (1975) "Rally 'round the workplace: continuities and fallacies in career education." Harvard Educ. Rev. (November).
GURIN, G. (1970) A National Attitude Study of Trainees in MDTA Institutional Programs. Ann Arbor: University of Michigan Institute for Social Research, Survey Research Center.
HOUSE, E., G. GLASS, L. McLEAN, and D. WALKER (1978) "No simple answer: critique of the follow through evaluation." Harvard Educ. Rev. 48, 2.

KRAMER, R. M. (1969) Participation of the Poor. Englewood Cliffs, NJ: Prentice-Hall.
LAMBERT, B. G. et al. (1978) Adolescence: Transition from Childhood to Maturity. Monterey, CA: Brooks-Cole.
LEACOCK, E. (1971) The Culture of Poverty: A Critique. New York: Simon & Schuster.
LEVIN, H. M. (1977) "A decade of policy developments in improving education and training for low-income populations," in R. H. Haveman (ed.) A Decade of Federal Antipoverty Programs. New York: Academic.
LEVITAN, S. A. and B. H. JOHNSTON (1975) The Job Corps: A Social Experiment that Works. Baltimore: Johns Hopkins Univ. Press.
MANGUM, G. L. and S. F. SENINGER (1977) Coming of Age in the Ghetto: The Dilemma of Ghetto Youth Unemployment. Salt Lake City: University of Utah.
Manpower Demonstration Research Corporation (1976) First Annual Report on the National Supported Work Demonstration, 1976. Washington, DC: Author.
MOYNIHAN, D. P. (1969) Maximum Feasible Misunderstanding. New York: Macmillan.
National Office for Social Responsibility (1977) An Approach to Integrated Programming. Arlington, VA: Author.
National Office for Social Responsibility (1977) An Approach to Integrated Programming. Arlington, VA: Author.
National Planning Association (1974) An Evaluation of the Economic Project of the Public Employment Program, Vol. I. Washington, DC: Author.
OGBU, J. (1979) "Social stratification and the socialization of competence." Anthropology and Education Q. (Spring).
———— (1974) The Next Generation. New York: Academic.
O'TOOLE, J. (1977) Work, Learning, and the American Future. San Francisco: Jossey-Bass.
PERRY, C. et al. (1975) The Impact of Government Manpower Programs. Philadelphia: Univ. of Pennsylvania Press.
QUINN, R. P. et al. (1970) Turnover and Training: A Social Psychological Study of Disadvantaged Workers. Ann Arbor: University of Michigan Institute for Social Research, Survey Research Center.
RENTZ, C. C. and R. R. RENTZ (1978) Evaluating Federally Sponsored Programs. San Francisco: Jossey-Bass.
REUBENS, B. G. (1974) "Vocational education for all in high school?" in J. O'Toole (ed.) Work and the Quality of Life: Resource Papers for "Work in America." Cambridge: MIT Press.
RIST, R. et al. (1979) Education and Employment Training: The Views of Youth. Youthwork National Policy Study. Ithaca: Cornell University.
ROGERS, C. (1976) On Personal Power. New York: Delacorte Press.
SHEA, J. (1977) "Education and employment: knowledge for action." Council for Policy Studies in Higher Education. (unpublished)
SMITH, M. S. and J. S. BISSELL (1970) "Report analysis: the impact of Head Start." Harvard Educ. Rev. (February)
SPRING, W. J. (n.d.) Youth Unemployment, Bridge Jobs, and National Policy. Washington, DC: U.S. Government Printing Office.
STAVRIANOS, L. S. (1976) The Promise of the Coming Dark Age. San Francisco: Freeman.
STEINFIELD, G. J. (1975) "Piaget's concept of decentering in relation to family process and therapy," in G. I. Lubin et al. (eds.) Piagetian Theory and the Helping Professions. Los Angeles: University of Southern California.

STONE, J. S. (1978) "e-VALUE-ation," in S. B. Anderson (ed.) Exploring Purposes and Dimensions. San Francisco: Jossey-Bass.

SUNDQUIST, J. L. (1978) "Needed: a national growth policy." Bull. of The Brookings Institution, Washington, DC (Winter-Spring).

THUROW, L. C. (1970) Investment in Human Capital. Belmont, CA: Wadsworth.

TYACK, D. (1976) "Ways of seeing: an essay on the history of compulsory schooling." Harvard Educ. Rev. 46, 3.

VALENTINE, C. A. (1968) Culture and Poverty. Chicago: Univ. of Chicago Press.

WALTHER, R. H. (1976) Analysis and Synthesis of Department of Labor Experience in Youth Transition to Work Programs. Alexandria, VA: Manpower Research Projects.

WEINTER, S. S., D. P. RUBIN, and T. P. SACHSE (1978) "Pathology in institution structures for evaluation and a possible cure." Stanford University Evaluation Consortium. (unpublished)

WEISS, C. H. (1972) Evaluating Social Action Programs: Readings in Social Action and Education. Boston: Allyn & Bacon.

WESTAT (1978) Post-Program Experience. Continuous Longitudinal Manpower Survey. Washington, DC: Department of Labor.

WILMS, W. W. (1974) Public and Proprietary Vocational Training: A Study of Effectiveness. Lexington, MA: D. C. Heath.

WOLMAN, J. et al. (1972) A Comparative Study of Proprietary and Nonproprietary Vocational Training Programs. Final Report, Vol. I. Palo Alto: American Institutes for Research.

YANKELOVICH, D. (1979) "Who gets ahead in America." Psychology Today (July).

——— (1978) "The new psychological contracts at work." Psychology Today (May).

——— (1974) The New Morality. New York: McGraw-Hill.

Bruce Fuller is a former staff consultant to the California Legislature's subcommittee on postsecondary education, and is now studying youth development at Stanford University's School of Education.

37

Citizen Participation in Community Mental Health Center Program Evaluation
A Neglected Potential

Nancy R. Dinkel, Joan Wagner Zinober,
and Eugenie Walsh Flaherty

ABSTRACT: *A rationale for involving citizens in CMHC planning and evalua-tion is presented from three perspectives: (1) values, (2) responsiveness to the community, and (3) utilization of evaluative findings. Current practices in citizen involvement in CMHC evaluation are reviewed and several examples are given. Seven roles citizens can play in CMHC evaluation are described. Data indicating that citizens can provide useful, relevant information and recommendations which can lead to positive changes in the CMHC are offered. The paper concludes that citizen participation in CMHC evaluation occurs infrequently and presents suggestions as to how this situation can be remedied.*

In 1975 the Ninety-fourth Congress mandated a number of requirements concerning community mental health center (CMHC) program evaluation. Among the requirements was that centers should review with residents of the catchment area the center's statistics and other information to "assure that (the community mental health center's) services are responsive to the needs of the residents of the catchment area" [P.L. 94-63, Section 206 (c)(a)(B)].

This requirement (and others which are not addressed here) resulted from problems observed in the centers' programs up to that time. A U.S. Government Accounting Office study (1974) criticized NIMH and centers for in-adequate identification of local mental health needs and low citizen involve-ment in center planning and operations.

Requiring citizens to become involved in evaluation presented a tremen-dous challenge to CMHC staff and to community residents. This paper gives an overview of the current status of the practice of citizen involvement in CMHC evaluation, takes a critical look at the level of current practice, and makes suggestions for improving the "state of the art."

Much of the material in this paper is based on the work of NIMH Contract No. MH 278-77-0067, Eugenie Walsh Flaherty, Principal Investigator, and NIMH Grant number MH 28784, Joan Wagner Zinober, Principal Investigator.

GOALS AND THEORY

It is important to note that program evaluation (1) involves values, (2) should result in making services more responsive to the community, and (3) is intended to be used to improve services. Citizens can contribute to each of these aspects of evaluation.

Values

There is an imbalance in power and information between providers and consumers in the mental health system in this country. This is reflected by the dominance of professionals in all decisions about services (Alford, 1975; Chu & Trotter, 1974; Olander & Lindhoff, 1975). Although taxpayers and local communities pay the bill for CMHCs, the main control of the CMHC is in the hands of the professionals (Nassi, 1978).

The balance in power is a concern because there is empirical evidence that health professionals and citizens often have different and sometimes conflicting views on many of the issues surrounding mental health services such as the criteria for assessing appropriate treatment and acceptable outcomes of treatment (Ellsworth, 1977; Hornstra et al., 1972; Skodol et al., 1980; Swanson et al., 1974).

Professional values tend to reflect the more technical aspects of treatment. This bias is a logical influence of the professional's training and circumstances. It has been argued that professionals also are likely to advocate more extensive treatment for both the protection and the benefit of the professional (Illich, 1976; Muller, 1972). This underscores the need to include citizens in the CMHC program evaluation.

Responsiveness to Community

Clearly, in order to balance the self-interest and technical bias of professionals and make evaluation more objective and responsive to the community, a continuing dialogue between citizens and professionals is essential (MacMurray et al., 1976). Most professionals to some extent are influenced by self-interests which lead them to advocate those programs which employ them and services they enjoy providing. Most evaluations of CMHC programs are conducted by evaluators who are employed either directly or indirectly by the programs they evaluate, thereby creating a conflict of interest. Peters et al. (1979), referring to citizens who have not used the CMHC services, point out, "the citizens' major strength is their freedom from personal commitment to a particular agency or to a particular form of treatment. This freedom allows them to question, without defensiveness, the way in which things have been done in the past." Although citizens have a point of view, it is likely to be very different from the provider point of view.

Dialogue between professionals and citizens has been hampered by the pervasive view that providers are better judges of the needs of individual clients and the community than are citizens in general or consumers in particular. This attitude is particularly prevalent in mental health where clients are characterized as being incapable of knowing what they need or want (Chu & Trotter, 1974). There is growing evidence, however, that consumers can give responsible and useful input to CMHCs (Morrison & Gaviria, 1979).

Furthermore as MacMurray et al., (1976) point out, "Citizens have the *right* to be involved in the decision making for several reasons: (1) because they support the services with their tax dollars, (2) because they are recipients of the care, and (3) because in the particular case of the Community Mental Health Centers' Program, federal legislation mandates citizen participation."

Aiken and Hage (1968) found that innovativeness of an institution is associated with the openness of its boundaries and its linkages to external influences. To have citizens participate in a joint effort in evaluating CMHC services is an important means of establishing this type of openness.

Use of Evaluative Findings

There are at least three models of the way program evaluation information can be used: (1) for accountability, (2) for advocacy, and (3) for amelioration. These are seldom used in pure form but rather in combinations (Windle & Neigher, 1978). Citizens can play an important part in encouraging the use of evaluation information in each of these ways.

The *Accountability Model* implies that a program should be evaluated by the public which supports it so that wiser decisions about support can be made. This public involvement also helps to motivate advocates to greater support and staff to greater efficiency and public service by their awareness that their activities are being monitored. When community mental health centers present their evaluation information to the community through radio, newspapers, open forums, etc., a measure of accountability is accomplished. More active involvement on the citizens' part only increases the effects of accountability.

The *Advocacy Model* assumes that programs are competing for resources and that information is one of the tools for the competition. As has been pointed out, it is in their own self-interest for evaluators to serve as program advocates. Logically, the Advocacy Model includes a "counter advocacy" role (Windle & Neigher, 1978) in which the evaluator tries to reform or eliminate a program. This is seen when the evaluator is employed by an outside organization. Citizens involved in evaluation have "counter-advocate" credibility since they do not necessarily need to advocate for services through self-interest (Peters et al., 1979).

The *Amelioration Model* assumes that managers will use better information to guide their decisions and that program staff want to improve their programs on the basis of the feedback evaluation can provide. However, evaluation findings seem to be used by administrators to increase financial and community support, and in the management of subordinates more frequently than for changing programs to increase effectiveness (Carter, 1971; Gurel, 1975; Windle and Volkman, 1973).

It is reasonable to expect that if evaluative findings become the subject of public debate, administrators will be more likely to use program evaluation to improve programs. Windle (1979), has gathered empirical evidence that having the public involved in evaluation or aware of evaluative findings does, in fact, increase the likelihood that the findings will be used. Also, citizens have demonstrated (Morrison & Gaviria, 1979; Zinober et al., 1980) that they can give relevant, important input for program improvement.

Gordon and Marquis (1966) have concluded from their studies that research conducted in applied settings is more likely to be implemented than purely academic research. Encouraging cooperative efforts at evaluation between nonprofessionals and professionals will necessarily increase the applied nature of evaluation and research thus increasing the likelihood the information will be used.

The rationale for involving citizens in community mental health center evaluation is compelling. The following section reviews the evidence of the extent to which citizens are currently involved in CMHC evaluation.

CURRENT PRACTICE IN CITIZEN REVIEW OF CMHC EVALUATION

In interviews at nine centers, Flaherty and Olsen (1978) found that while there was relatively substantial compliance with other requirements for self-evaluation and quality assurance, compliance with the particular requirement to involve community residents was very low. Landsberg and Neigher (1978) in a survey of CMHCs in DHHS Region II found that only 4 percent of the centers had held an open forum for citizens.

Community mental health centers are monitored by periodic site visits to the centers to assess areas of strengths and weaknesses. These annual site team visits are done by the ten DHHS regional Offices. A 1974 estimate of the types of persons participating in this evaluation revealed that not more than approximately 4 percent of the team are lay citizens or their representatives such as politicians or health service agencies (Premo, 1980). It appears that there is a limited amount of citizen and consumer participation in CMHC evaluation.

There are, however, some examples of citizen involvement. The roles citizens can play in the evaluative endeavor represent a broad range of activities from a more passive recipient of evaluation information to the active conduct of evaluation studies. These roles can be presented in seven major categories of activities listed here in order of degree of citizen control.

— Citizens as subjects (community or client surveys)
— Citizens receive evaluation information through the media or at open forums
— Citizens act as a liaison between the community and the agency
— Citizens review program goals
— Citizens review evaluation findings
— Citizens help plan agency evaluation
— Citizens conduct evaluation independently or with the agency

The locus of the impetus for citizen involvement might be citizen-initiated or agency-initiated. Citizen-initiated involvement could come from citizen groups, media representatives, consumer protection groups, mental health associations, etc. Agency-initiated involvement would include cases for which the impetus would come from within the mental health agency itself.

The following is a description of several examples of citizen involvement. These cases illustrate a diversity of citizen roles in evaluation and stem from different auspices. The first case is an example of citizen *review* of evaluation findings. The impetus for these groups came from within the centers.

Florida Consortium

The Florida Consortium Project organized 17 groups of citizens and worked with them in reviewing evaluation findings in seven mental health agencies. This process consisted of recruiting a group of citizens who were not employed by the center and were selected as representatives of the community according to a predetermined plan. These citizens attended a limited series of structured meetings during which they reviewed CMHC evaluative findings, gathered pertinent information, and made recommendations to the facilities' governing boards. Some of these groups were homogeneous with respect to type of citizen (e.g., all former clients, all referral agents, all high risk citizens). Some groups were heterogeneous (a mix of citizens designed to represent parts of the community that were related to the specific issue at hand). The responsibility for guiding the citizen review process was varied in the research project. In some groups the responsibility rested with the center evaluator, in some with the governing board, and in some with the citizen groups themselves. An analysis of the effects of this project indicates that the citizens gave useful input that resulted in changes in the service agencies.

The 277 recommendations made by the citizen groups in this project reflected various concerns. Some requested physical changes such as redesigning the waiting room to provide a feeling of privacy and confidentiality. Other recommendations called for increased public relations such as more media coverage, and the use of brochures. A third type of recommendation called for administrative changes such as adjusting fee schedules, more training for governing board members, reassigning staff, and billing for "no shows." Other recommendations suggested changes in services primarily in the direction of expanding existing services or adding new services. Seventy-one percent of the 277 changes recommended were adopted totally or to some extent by the centers.

The next several cases are all examples of citizens engaged in the actual evaluation exercise. The first case (Lancaster County) describes citizens conducting evaluation projects under the guidance of the governing board. In Contra Costa County groups of advisory board members are performing the evaluations. In the Mid-Missouri example although the project was initiated by NIMH, citizens evaluated programs independent of staff direction and planning. The Mental Health Associations' site visit teams in Metropolitan Atlanta and Dade County and San Francisco are citizen initiated, independent evaluations of a range of mental health services.

Lancaster County

Since 1974 the Lancaster County Mental Health, Retardation, Drug, and Alcohol Program in Lancaster, Pennsylvania, has been conducting citizen evaluation. Expanding their already active board participation, this process has involved over 175 citizens each of whom has contributed over 50 hours to the evaluation project. The Lancaster project recruited citizens by means of a media campaign and letters to businesses, civic and volunteer organizations. The two, 13 member review teams were comprised of consumers, business persons, attorneys, counselors, clerks, homemakers, and educators. These teams were given regulatory authority and the responsibility for implementing two evaluation methods. The board had endorsed the use of Program Analysis of Service Systems (PASS) and Funding Determination (FUNDET) (Wolfensberger & Glenn, 1975) as the primary evaluation tools. PASS is a system for evaluating the extent to which the principle of normalization is carried out in mental health programs. A criterion reference scale, FUNDET is a mechanism for assessing how well programs are meeting standards and guidelines for funding. The citizen teams conducted the evaluations by using these methods, and made comments and recommendations based on their findings.

The effects of the process used at Lancaster are reported (Bonfield et al., 1978) as broadening the center's base of community understanding and support, creating a training ground for prospective, well-informed board members, and yielding a service delivery system that is responsive to the needs of its citizens. For example, the physical facility which housed one inpatient psychiatric unit was expanded and changed considerably on the basis of the, recommendations of a citizen team. The team made recommendations that took into account factors such as room temperatures, interior decor (lighting, furniture, and color scheme) and the separation of spaces for different functions.

Contra Costa County

In Contra Costa County, California, teams of Community Mental Health Services Advisory Board members have evaluated community service facilities (Morentz, 1979). These citizens include a variety of professionals and volunteers and have evaluated a broad scope of issues. Findings are based on a consensus of impressions of the evaluating team and data from questionnaires and interviews with clients and agency staff. These evaluations are judged to have had direct impact on the programs studied and as a consequence have motivated other programs to improve evaluations for accountability. An example of this citizen involvement is the evaluation of a private nonprofit day treatment facility for disturbed children. The team reviewed agency records, interviewed parents, staff, and other agencies. Based on the problems revealed, the team suggested extensive changes. Most of the activities of this particular program were terminated. This action motivated other programs to spend more resources in developing evaluation methods to demonstrate the quality of their work. Volunteers from the advisory board see their future evaluation function as that of reviewing the self-evaluations of programs.

The Mid-Missouri Mental Health Center Evaluation

This case is one in which a seven member team of citizens collected and analyzed data on admissions and discharges by interviewing center staff and staff at other local agencies which provided follow-up care. The project was funded by NIMH as part of a research project on citizen evaluation. The citizens involved were identified by the board of directors of the local county association for mental health and the citizen advisory board of the mental health center. The interviews were done by the team members and a final report was written and completed 13 months from the beginning of the project. This model gave consumers evaluation and/or research decision–making power formally reserved as inherent to the role of the provider. Hessler and Walters (1976) concluded that having citizens do CMHC evaluation is possible and does have advantages. These citizens were provided technical assistance although they had control over the research decision making. Hessler and Walters further conclude that the citizens need to understand methods in evaluation and develop skills in data analysis techniques so their potential may not be limited.

Mental Health Association Citizen Evaluation

The Mental Health Association (MHA) has initiated citizen evaluation of mental health services. An example of this is the Metropolitan Atlanta Chapter of MHA-sponsored site visits of community mental health centers. Twelve teams of four to six citizens evaluated 12 CMHCs in the seven county catchment area. After spending a day and a half at training sessions, each team interviewed the staff, volunteers and clients in one CMHC. They developed reports and made recommendations to the director and the governing board of the center. The Dade County Chapter of the MHA enlists a cross section of 15–18 lay citizens to do site visits and evaluate a segment of the mental health delivery system each year. In 1979, this Blue Ribbon Jury, as it is called, evaluated nursing homes and adult congregate living facilities. Preston Garrison (1980) of the Florida Division of the MHA stated that the Metropolitan Atlanta evaluations were positively received and "some" recommendations were incorporated by the centers. The recommendations from the Dade County team were referenced in current state legislation on nursing homes.

Critical Evaluation of Current Practice and Suggestions for Improvement

The infrequency of citizen participation in CMHC evaluation appears due to a lack of motivation for such participation by either the citizens or the center staff. Certainly part of this reluctance is the natural desire of the staff to retain control and a lack of experience with, and understanding of, the role which board members and citizens might play in evaluation, or of the activities they might perform. The wide range of roles suggested for citizen participation in evaluation reflects the ambiguity that exists in this area. Some of these suggested roles for citizens are:

(1) To provide a structured channel for suggestions and complaints from consumers and citizens in the community to the CMHC staff (Bertelsen & Harris, 1973; Hagedorn et al., 1976; Weiss et al., 1977).

(2) To assess community needs (Krause & Brill, 1971; Weiss et al., 1977).

(3) To conduct evaluation independently or in collaboration with staff (Hammer, 1976; MacMurray et al., 1976).

(4) To define topics for evaluation study by the center (Hagedorn et al., 1976).

(5) To review and plan evaluation studies together with staff (Hester, 1977).

This ambiguity in the citizen's role has been attributed to federal policies and practices in citizen participation which are "erratic, piecemeal, misunderstood, and possibly not really cared about" (Mogulof, 1974). Mogulof believes there are three basic roles for citizen participation and that federal policies are unclear about the specific role to be adopted by various federal programs. These roles are *Advisory, Adversary/Control,* and *Coalition.* Part of this confusion is due to the fact that the natural evolution from one role to another is not understood.

The Advisory role is the role most favored by existing federal policies. Mogulof believes that the Advisory role, which provides little decision making power for citizens, is only a transition role and evolves toward Adversary/Control or Coalition. If the Advisory role does not move toward a Coalition where decision making is shared by citizens and agency, Mogulof believes that the Adversary/Control arrangement is inevitable and the two groups (citizens and agency) become polarized. One group, either citizens or agency has real control while the other group becomes adversarial to gain influence. In an Adversary/Control arrangement there is a struggle for control between citizens and staff and the separation between the two groups becomes institutionalized and immutable. Mogulof states that the Coalition is the most desirable role because the presence of the citizens in the Coalition means better representation for the community. This is true only if the citizens involved are representative of the community.

Ambiguity about an appropriate role for citizen involvement is not the only impediment to citizen evaluation (Flaherty & Windle, 1979). Other barriers are:

(1) Board members are resistant to community citizens other than themselves being involved because they see their own function as representing those citizens (Flaherty & Olsen, 1978).

(2) Center staff resist sharing power with citizens. Not only is sharing power difficult and time-consuming, but it creates an uncertain and threatening situation for professionals accustomed to paternalistic practitioner–client relationships (Flaherty & Olsen, 1978).

(3) There are few incentives for citizens to be involved in evaluation and they are often unaware of the opportunities for them to participate or of the influence they have (Weiss et al., 1977; Thomson, 1973).

(4) Citizens lack knowledge about the center and evaluation techniques (Borus & Klerman, 1976; Thomson, 1973; Weiss et al., 1977).

(5) The lack of back-up resources to support citizens limits their ability to work independently or follow-up on their decisions (Weiss et al., 1977).

(6) There is a lack of knowledge of demonstrated procedures for accomplishing citizen review (Flaherty & Olsen), 1978).

Suggestions for Improvement

In a survey of nine mental health centers, Flaherty and Olsen (1978), asked their respondents to suggest ways current practice of citizen involvement in evaluation could be improved. The suggestions made were directed both to National Institute of Mental Health and to local centers. Actions recommended on the basis of this survey by Flaherty and Olsen for NIMH are:

The specific goals of citizen involvement in evaluation should be clarified. This clarification would facilitate the development of specific mechanisms by which centers might achieve these goals.

A definition of what is meant by representative citizens should be developed. The different citizen constituencies include present and past clients of the center, C&E recipients, elected local officials, distinct ethnic and demographic groups, and social services agency representatives. What combinations of these would make up a representative group of citizens?

The purposes of the Annual Evaluation Report should be clarified by federal legislation and guidelines. If intended for the public, rather than federal officials, it should be written to be understandable to lay citizens. It should be disseminated through channels to reach the public.

NIMH should spell out proper channels for disseminating the Annual Evaluation Report to those who should receive the information.

To improve citizen involvement, boards should be informed of existing data about the center's operation which are available on an annual basis.

Technical assistance to citizens could be done by increasing the dissemination of already available materials to organizations such as the Mental Health Association, the National Council of Community Mental Health Centers, citizen representative boards, and local citizens' organizations.

Actions recommended for the local centers include:

Centers can also be involved with technical assistance to citizens. This assistance should be tailored to the specific needs and abilities of local citizen groups, avoiding procedures which demand much time and sophisticated reading skills. This training could include films, on-site consultation, and simply written illustrated materials directed towards citizens of a wide range of educational and cultural backgrounds.

To circumvent the problem of limited resources, Yin et al., (1973) recommend that a fixed budget be made available to the citizen board. Some centers have elected to assign a staff member, full or part-time to the citizen group.

To expedite the technical assistance to centers and citizens who need information on strategies for citizen involvement in CMHC evaluation, several books have recently been published for use by CMHC staff and by citizens. One of these manuals, *Citizen Roles in Community Mental Health Center Evaluation: A Guide for Citizens* by Peters et al., 1979, was prepared under contract support from NIMH and is especially helpful as a resource for lay citizens. The book *Citizen Evaluation of Mental Health Services: An Action Approach to Accountability* by MacMurray et al., 1976, was designed under an NIMH grant to assist citizen groups in performing program evaluation. The National Association for Mental Health has written a *Site Visitation Handbook* which is available from the National Association for Mental Health, Inc., 1800 North Kent Street, Arlington, Virginia 22209. *A Citizens' Manual for Evaluating Mental Health Services* by the Mental Health Association of Alameda County is a useful guide for lay citizen groups interested in evaluating public mental health services. The Florida Consortium Project, as part of its NIMH grant obligations, is developing a manual outlining the method of citizen involvement used in their study. This manual will give step by step information on:

how to decide what type of citizens to include in the groups

how to recruit citizens

what information to present citizens and how to present it

fhow to conduct review meetings efficiently

group processes and how they can be improved

how to advocate for citizens ideas with agency staff and governing board.

The particular process developed by the Consortium is called the Citizen Review Group (CRG), and provides a mechanism for adapting the process to a particular center. At a beginning stage the CRG process can be under the control of the center staff, thus making the initial commitment of the center staff to citizen review easier. One variation of this process is for the board to take the responsibility. As Mogulof (1974) pointed out, this role should evolve to gradually allow the citizens more responsibility. Ultimately external groups could take on the main responsibility to guide citizen review of evaluation. The use of this CRG method for citizen review of evaluation can help to relieve such problems as: (1) lack of knowledge of a specific strategy for citizen involvement, (2) staff and board resistance to citizen involvement, and (3) confusion over the role citizens should play in CMHC evaluation.

In conclusion, it must be recognized that although there are compelling reasons for involving the community in CMHC evaluation, to date there have been few examples of such activity. Because the idea of citizens in evaluation represents a change of some magnitude in both the thinking of CMHC staff and board members, as well as the organization of center evaluation activities, this is not an easy step to take. We have presented several roles through which the community can participate in the evaluation of mental health and suggestions of ways both the National Institute of Mental Health and local CMHCs can improve the current practice of community involvement in evaluation.

It is hoped that this information will augment the amount of community involvement in evaluation since it has been shown that citizens can provide useful information, perspectives, and recommendations that, when implemented, can increase a CMHC's responsiveness to its community.

REFERENCES

Aiken, M., & Hage, J. Organizational interdependence and interorganizational structure. *American Sociological Review*, December 1968, *33*(6), 912-930.

Alford, R. R. *Health care politics: Ideological and interest group barriers to reform.* Chicago: University of Chicago Press, 1975.

Bertelsen, K., & Harris, M. R. Citizen participation in the development of a community mental health center. *Hospital and Community Psychiatry*, 1973, 4(3), 533–556.

Bonfield, M. B., Olds, M. L., Shreve, B. W., Smith, M., & Schoenberger, V. E. *Citizen evaluation with program analysis of service systems.* Lancaster County Office of Mental Health/Mental Retardation, 1978.

Borus, J. F., & Klerman, G. L. Consumer-professional collaboration for evaluation in neighborhood mental health programs. *Hospital and Community Psychiatry*, 1976, 27(6), 401–404.

Carter, R. K. Clients' resistance to negative findings and the latent conservative function of evaluation studies. *The American Sociologist Journal*, 1971, 6(2), 118–124.

Chu, F. B., & Trotter, S. *The madness establishment.* New York: Grossman, 1974.

Ellsworth, R. B. *Utilizing consumer input in evaluating mental health services.* Paper presented to the Conference on Impact of Program Evaluation on Mental Health Care, Loyola University, Chicago, Illinois, 1977.

Flaherty, E., & Olsen, K. *An assessment of the utility of federally Required Program Evaluation in Community Mental Health Centers.* Philadelphia Health Management Corporation, 1978. [NIMH Contract No. 278-77-0067 (MH)]

Flaherty, E., & Windle, C. D. *Lessons learned from past federal evaluation policy for community mental health centers: Framework for a new policy.* Unpublished manuscript. Philadelphia Health Management Corporation, 1979.

Garrison, P. Executive Director, Florida Division of the Mental Health Association, 132 East Colonial Drive, Orlando, Florida 32801. Personal Communication, July, 1980.

Gordon, G., & Marquis, S. Freedom, visibility of consequences, and scientific innovation. *American Journal of Sociology*, September 1966, 72(2), 195–202.

Gurel, L. The human side of evaluating human services programs. In M. Guttentag & E. Struening (Eds.), *Handbook of evaluation research* (Vol. 2). Beverly Hills, California: Sage Publications, 1975.

Hagedorn, H. J., Beck, K. J., Neubert, S. F., & Werlin, S. H. *A Working Manual of Simple Program Evaluation Techniques for Community Mental Health Centers.* (DHEW Publication (ADM) 76-404). Washington, D.C.: U. S. Government Printing Office, 1976.

Hammer, R. J. Working with community groups. In R. Hammer, G. Landsberg, & W. Neigher, (Eds.), *Program evaluation in community mental health centers.* Brooklyn, New York: Maimonides CMHC, February 1976.

Hessler, R. M., & Walters, M. J. Consumer evaluation research: Implications for methodology, social policy, and the role of the sociologist. *The Sociological Quarterly*, Winter 1976, 17, 74–89.

Hester, P. Evaluation and accountability in a parent-implemented early intervention service. *Community Mental Health Journal*, 1977, 13(3), 261–267.

Hornstra, R. K., Lubin, B., Lewis, R. V., & Willis, B. S. Worlds apart: Patients and Professionals. *Archives of General Psychiatry*, October 1972, 27, 553–557.

Illich, I. *Medical nemesis: The expropriation of health.* New York: Random House, 1976.

Krause, R., & Brill, M. *National Institute of Mental Health Planning Aid Kit.* National Institute of Mental Health, January 1971.

Landsberg, G., Hammer, R., & Neigher, W. *Analyzing the evaluation activities in CMHCs in NIMH Region II.* Paper presented at the 1978 Annual Meeting of the National Council of CMHCs, Kansas City, Missouri. February, 1978.

MacMurray, V. D., Cunningham, P. H., Cater, P. B., Swenson, N., & Bellins, S. S. *Citizen evaluation of mental health services: An action approach to accountability.* New York: Human Sciences Press, Behavioral Publicaiton, Inc., 1976.

Mogulof, M. B. Advocates for themselves: Citizen participation in federally supported community organizations. *Community Mental Health Journal*, 1974, 10(1), 66–77.

Morentz, P. E. A citizen-conducted evaluation of acceptability: The Ronoh School evaluation committee. In G. Landsberg, W. D. Neigher, R. J. Hammer, C. Windle, & J. R. Woy (Eds.), *Evaluation in practice: A sourcebook of program evaluation studies from mental health care systems in the United States.* (DHEW Publication No. (ADM) 80-763). Washington, D.C.: U. S. Government Printing Office, 1979.

Morrison, J. K., & Gaviria, B. The role of the client-consumer in the delivery of psychiatric services. In J. K. Morrison (Ed.), *A consumer approach to community psychology.* Chicago: Nelson-Hall, 1979.

Muller, C. The over medicated society: Forces in the market place for medical care. *Science*, May 5, 1972, *176*, 488-492.

Nassi, A. J. Community control or control of the community? The case of the community mental health center. *Journal of Community Psychology*, 1978, *6*, 3-15.

Olander, F., & Lindhoff, H. Consumer action research: A review of the consumerism literature and suggestions for new directions in research. *Social Science Information*, 1975, *14*, 147-184.

Peters, S., Lichtman, S. A., & Windle, C. *Citizen roles in community mental health center evaluation: A guide for citizens.* (DHEW Publication No. (ADM) 79-789). Washington, D.C.: U. S. Government Printing Office, 1979.

Premo, F. Personal Communication, April 1980.

Skodol, A. E., Plutchik, R., & Karasu, T. B. Expectations of hospital treatment: Conflicting views of patients and staff. *The Journal of Nervous and Mental Disease*, 1980, *168*(2), 70-74.

Swanson, R. M., Wilson, N. Z., Ellis, R. H., & Mumpower, J. *Dimensions of mental health treatment goals: A tri-informant conception.* Fort Logan Mental Health Center, 1974. (Unpublished Manuscript)

Thomson, R. The why's and why not's of consumer participation. *Community Mental Health Journal*, 1973, *9*(2), 143-150.

U.S. General Accounting Office. *Need for more effective management of community mental health center programs.* Washington, D.C., August, 1974.

Weiss, C., Monroe, J., Bray, C., David, H., & Hunt, B. Evaluation by citizens. In R. Coursey (Ed.), *Program evaluation for mental health.* New York: Grune & Stratton, 1977.

Windle, C. The citizen as part of the management process. In H. C. Schulberg, & Jerrell, J. M. (Eds.), *The evaluator and management.* Beverly Hills, California: Sage Publications, 1979.

Windle, D., & Neigher, W. Ethical problems in program evaluation: Advice for trapped evaluators. *Evaluation and Program Planning*, 1978, *1*(2), 97-107.

Windle, C., & Volkman, E. M. Evaluation in the center's program. *Evaluation and Change*, 1973, *1*(2), 69-70.

Wolfensberger, W., & Glenn, L. *PASS: A method for the quantitative evaluation of human services.* Field manual 3rd. edition. National Institute of Mental Retardation, Toronto, Canada, 1975.

Yin, R. K., Lucas, W. A., Stanton, P. L., & Spindler, J. A. *Citizen organizations: Increasing client control over serices* Santa Monica, California: The Rand Corporation, 1973. (NTIS No. PB 240 456).

Zinober, J. W., Dinkel, N. R., Landsberg, G., & Windle, C. Another role for citizens: Three variations of citizen evaluation review. *Community Mental Health Journal*, 16(4), 1980.

38

Using Clients to Evaluate Programs

Brian Stipak

Abstract—Client surveys can provide valuable information for monitoring and evaluating public programs. However, the widespread use of measures of clients' satisfaction and of clients' subjective evaluations, without an appreciation of the complications of interpretation and analysis, will set back rather than advance the methodology of program evaluation. This paper examines the important issues concerning the use of client-derived information in program monitoring and evaluation, and critically reviews existing research and current practices. Finally, the paper offers a number of recommendations, including six general rules for using client evaluation and satisfaction ratings.

USING CLIENTS TO EVALUATE PROGRAMS

PROGRAM evaluation is increasingly turning to the clients of public programs for measures of program performance. A growing concern with public sector efficiency has helped foster a consumer perspective, in which citizens are seen not merely as passive recipients of agency services provided according to professional standards, but rather as discriminating consumers who make the final evaluation of program effectiveness. Whereas official records were once viewed as the only source of 'objective' information, program professionals are now recognized as having their own self-interest and biases, which are reflected in agency records. According to this new perspective, clients can therefore provide more valid and less biased information than official records for evaluating public programs.†

Complementing the growth of a consumer perspective in program evaluation, social indicator research (e.g. [1, 2]) has developed measures of people's satisfaction and assessments of their lives to augment traditional economic indicators. This approach arises from a desire to change from an overriding concern with economic prosperity to a greater concern with sense of well-being. Since this approach considers quality of life as ultimately a subjective experience, it attempts to directly measure the subjective dimensions of life quality, rather than relying on typically available objective measures. Analogously, this approach suggests that program evaluators should measure the satisfaction and assessments of program clients, and not just rely on so-called objective data generated by program professionals.

These arguments for using clients to evaluate public programs require close scrutiny. As this paper will show, client evaluations can contribute to program evaluation only under some conditions, and even then usually require careful statistical analysis. The widespread use of client evaluations in evaluation research, without an appreciation of the complications of interpretation and analysis, will set back rather than advance the methodology of program evaluation. This paper will examine the most important issues concerning the use of client-derived performance measures in evaluation research. The paper's scope does not include measuring citizens' preferences for use in policy making, but rather is limited to using client-derived information for measuring program performance or effectiveness. However, the scope does encompass not only clients of human service and social welfare programs, but also clients receiving benefits from services provided by any public agency. For example, citizens living in a municipality are clients, as the term is used in this paper, of all city departments that provide municipal services to the general public.

---

† See Bush and Gordon (1978, pp. 767–776 [3]) for arguments why client-derived information may be more valid and less biased than information derived from agency records.

TYPES OF CLIENT-DERIVED PERFORMANCE MEASURES

Several types of client-derived information can be used for measuring program performance or effectiveness. Performance measures can be objective or subjective. Some subjective measures are intrinsically important measures of outcomes and others are not. Among subjective measures that are not intrinsically important, a useful distinction is between general vs specific client evaluations. The following sections will examine each of these distinctions.

Objective vs subjective measures

Considerable confusion surrounds the distinction between objective and subjective measures. Nunnally (1975, pp. 107–109 [4]) identifies four different reasons client evaluations of programs have been called subjective:

(1) lack of observable evidence to verify the client's stated evaluation
(2) difficulty in instructing clients how to give an evaluation on a rating scale
(3) instability of client evaluations over time and across clients
(4) artificial influences on how clients make evaluative ratings.

Reason (3) concerns reliability, and reasons (2) and (4) concern possible threats to the validity of measurement. Since problems of reliability and validity plague all performance measures, reasons (2–4) do not clearly differentiate subjective from objective measures. Reason (1), however, concerns an important and useful distinction for evaluation research. A client's evaluation of a program on a rating scale, or a client's expressed satisfaction with a service, measures a psychological characteristic not easily verified by observable evidence. Although clients' expressed evaluations can sometimes be partially verified by observations of clients' behavior (Bush and Gordon, 1978, p. 768 [3]), a client's expressed evaluation or satisfaction reflects an internal psychological state of the client that only the client can know directly.

Much valuable information that evaluators might obtain through client interviews is objective, not subjective. For example, the Health Interview Survey, a continuing national sample survey conducted by the U.S. Census Bureau, collects data on illness, injuries and other health topics. Since other people besides the respondent (i.e. a family member) might also have directly observed whether the respondent suffered from a particular illness or injury, these data are intrinsically objective, even for a respondent for whom no one is available to verify the information, and even for a respondent who supplies false information. Thus, objective data are not errorless data. Both objective data and subjective data can suffer from lack of reliability as well as validity. However, subjective measures involve special problems of interpretation and analysis in program evaluation, as will be discussed later.

Crime victimization surveys illustrate well the potential value of client interviews for obtaining objective data useful to program evaluation. Schneider (1976, pp. 136–137 [5]) reports that after an anti-burglary program was implemented in Portland, official crime statistics showed an increase in the burglary rate. In contrast, crime victimization surveys conducted before and after the implementation of the program revealed a decrease in the burglary rate, but combined with an increased willingness of victims to report burglaries to the police, resulting in an erroneous increase of the official burglary rate. Thus, without the victimization surveys evaluators may incorrectly have concluded that an effective program was ineffective.

Objective data obtained through client interviews, like data from agency records, also contain measurement error. Whether client interviews or agency records provide more reliable or valid objective data depends on the measurement errors inherent in each type. Client interviews are often done for only a sample of clients, resulting in sampling error and loss of reliability. Although agency records may be complete in the sense that all interactions with clients are recorded, the agency may have contact with only a subset of the potential clients, which may threaten the validity of the data for making inferences to the larger client population. In the case of crime statistics, victimization surveys suffer from sampling error, whereas official records suffer from under-reporting. Thus, the choice between client interviews and agency records as a source of objective data about a total client population may sometimes involve a trade-off between reliability and validity.

Of course, client-derived objective data also can suffer from threats to validity. For example, Schneider (1975, pp. 13–14 [6]) hypothesizes that poor interviewing technique will cause crime victimization surveys to underestimate victimization rates and overestimate the proportion of crimes reported. To minimize these threats to validity, the interviewer must probe to make the respondent remember minor crimes that are more likely to go unreported. On the other hand, Levine (1976, pp. 311–325 [7]) argues that crime victimization surveys may overestimate crime rates because of lying, interviewer biases, memory failures about when crimes occurred, coding unreliability and mistaken interpretations of non-criminal incidents as crimes.

Since crime victimization surveys typically yield estimated crime rates 1.5 to 5 times larger than official rates (National Advisory Commission on Criminal Justice Standards and Goals, 1973, p. 199 [8]), serious biases must exist in one or both measures. This discrepancy is typically ascribed entirely to under-reporting biases in official crime rates. If a program analyst is willing to assume that the discrepancy between the survey results and the agency records is due largely to biases in the official records, then the analyst can compare victimization survey rates to official rates to compute ratios for estimating true crime rates from reported rates. Expensive victimization surveys need only be done occasionally, to ensure that the ratios have not changed greatly, and crime rates based on agency records can be inflated by the calculated ratios to estimate true rates. As this example shows, objective data derived from client interviews can usefully augment objective data from official records.

Intrinsically important vs not intrinsically important subjective measures

An often over-looked but critical distinction is between subjective measures that are intrinsically important, vs measures that are important only because of a presumed relationship with other variables. For example, contrast citizens' fear of crime with citizens' evaluative ratings of police services. Fear of crime and consequent feelings of insecurity decrease people's sense of well-being and enjoyment of life. In contrast, citizens' expressed evaluations of police services have no compelling *a priori* meaning; rather, interpretation must proceed from assumptions about the determinants of the expressed evaluations. For example, if the expressed evaluations reflect experience with and perceptions of services the police have provided, then the evaluations are a subjective measure of police performance. On the other hand, if expressed evaluations primarily reflect the feelings toward governmental authority found among different demographic groups, then the expressed evaluations are a measure of evaluative predisposition towards government. Clients' expressed evaluations of governmental programs differ therefore, from intrinsically important subjective measures of psychological states that contribute directly to people's quality of life, such as fear of crime, feelings of insecurity, general sense of well-being, sense of personal competence and feelings of stress and anxiety.

Since clients' expressed evaluations of governmental services have no clear *a priori* meaning or intrinsic importance, their appropriate use in program evaluation is debatable. Stipak [9] views client evaluations as performance measures only if they reflect some characteristics of the services actually provided, and emphasizes the need to establish a linkage between subjective evaluations and objective service characteristics before using client evaluations for measuring performance. Another perspective (e.g. Shin [10]) accepts on the basis of face validity that client evaluations and expressed satisfaction measure some aspect of the quality of service actually provided.

Both perspectives concerning the interpretation and use of client evaluations have disadvantages. The first perspective (Stipak [9]) suffers from the problem that client evaluations may be responses to subtle aspects of objective service performance not easily identified or measured. That perspective therefore biases program evaluators towards discarding client evaluations as irrelevant. However, the second approach probably suffers from more severe problems. Public opinion research has found that citizens will readily express political opinions, despite knowing little about government or public affairs.† Similarly, clients may quite willingly provide evaluations of programs on the basis of little experience or knowledge. Client evaluations could therefore be meaningless, artificial creations of the interview process. Alternatively, expressed client evaluations could reflect real client attitudes that result from general feelings about government and public authority, from attitudes prevalent among client reference groups or subcultures, or from other causes irrelevant to the clients' experiences with the program being evaluated. The less contact the client has with the service agency, the more likely expressed evaluations will be meaningless. Thus, the conservative approach to interpreting client evaluations goes beyond face validity and examines the relationship of expressed evaluations to other performance measures and to service characteristics.

General vs specific client evaluations

Another important distinction concerns the specificity of the client's evaluation. For example, contrast the following two items from a client questionnaire used for monitoring mental health services (Urban Institute, 1978, p. A–3 [14]):

In an overall sense, how satisfied are you with the service you received?
Very satisfied, mostly satisfied, indifferent or mildly dissatisfied, quite satisfied.
Were the receptionist and clerical staff at the Center courteous and helpful?
Not at all, not much, somewhat, very much.

To cite another example, an Urban Institute report concerning municipal service evaluation recommends monitoring the percentage of households rating neighborhood park and recreation facilities as satisfactory, as well as specific evaluations concerning the condition of recreation equipment and the hours the facilities are available (Hatry *et al.*, 1977, p. 42 [15]). Thus, expressed client evaluations and satisfaction can range in specificity from evaluations of very explicit service characteristics to very general, global assessments.

Specific evaluations are probably less often meaningless creations of the interview process, since specific item referents are more likely to evoke responses based on the client's actual experience with the service agency or perceptions of service characteristics. Not surprisingly, specific subjective measures usually have higher reliability than global measures (Campbell *et al.*, 1976, p. 480 [1]). Skogan (1975, p. 58 [16]) criticizes the practical value of general evaluations for administrators, arguing that "general evaluations do not tell administrators what actions to take in the face of low ratings," and that "public officials need direct measures of those specific activities that are amenable to administrative manipulation." In a similar manner, Stipak (1979a, p. 51 [9]) argues that vague satisfaction and evaluation items confound in one indicator different aspects of service performance that should be measured separately. However, other researchers (Campbell *et al.*, 1976, p. 493 [1]) view global subjective measures as necessary expedients for requiring people to mentally summarize many specific factors. Evaluators can construct alternative general evaluation measures by combining a number of specific evaluation items, but this approach also suffers from problems (see Gutek, 1978, p. 52 [17]). Overall, evaluators can probably feel more confident of the reliability of specific client evaluations, compared to more general or global evaluations.

POSITIVE BIAS OF CLIENT EVALUATIONS

A problem in using clients to evaluate programs stems from the tendency of clients to provide highly favorable evaluations of all programs. Katz *et al.* (1975, p. 64 [18]) found

---

† Converse (1975, pp. 79–83 [11]) discusses information levels and opinion formation in the general public, and Stipak (1977, pp. 50–51 [12]) discusses processes of local political attitude formation in the absence of strong perceptions. For a discussion of meaningless responses to attitude items see Converse [13].

that about two-thirds of the clients of different governmental service agencies rated their satisfaction with the way the agency handled their problem as very satisfied or fairly well satisfied, compared to only about one-third answering somewhat dissatisfied or very dissatisfied. Across all services, 43% replied very satisfied, compared to only 14% replying very dissatisfied. As Campbell (1969, p. 426 [19]) has commented, voluntary and solicited testimonials from program participants provide an excellent source of favorable evaluations. Moreover, clients appear to express favorable evaluations and high levels of satisfaction regardless of program effectiveness. Scheirer (1978, p. 56 [20]) reviews a number of evaluation studies that found favorable client evaluations for programs that were not effective in achieving program goals. Perhaps the best example concerns the gastric freezing procedure for treating stomach ulcers (see Scheirer, 1978, pp. 53–54 [20]). By 1964, about 10,000 patients a year received this treatment and studies found that as many as 70% of the patients reported complete remission. Finally, in 1969 a large-scale, rigorous evaluation of the treatment was completed which showed that the treatment had no effect.

Other evidence also indicates there is a positive bias in people's subjective evaluations. Campbell et al. (1976, p. 99 [1]) found high levels of expressed satisfaction for a variety of different life domains. Only a small minority of the respondents admitted dissatisfaction or unhappiness, a finding Campbell et al. (1976, p. 99 [1]) point out agrees with the general finding from psychological research that subjects tend to use the positive side of rating scales more than the negative side. Another general research finding that shows a positive bias in people's subjective evaluations is the evidence (see Gutek, 1978, pp. 49–50 [17]) that people tend to evaluate more favorably their own lives and experiences, including experiences with governmental agencies, than the lives and experiences of other people. Similarly, Fowler (1974, pp. 149, 153 [21]) found that people think there is less crime in their own neighborhoods than other neighborhoods. In reviewing the extensive literature of job satisfaction, Taylor (1977, pp. 243–245 [22]) concludes that measured job satisfaction remains inexplicably high and that satisfaction levels do not vary with evidence of worker discontent such as absenteeism, strikes, or plant sabotage.

Why should subjective evaluations, in particular client evaluations of governmental programs, be so positively biased? Scheirer (1978, pp. 58–60 [20]) shows that social psychological theory would predict a positive evaluation bias due to several factors, including social desirability response bias, ingratiation attempts and cognitive consistency. Also, both program clients and program staff often receive a variety of benefits from participating in the program, regardless of the program's effectiveness in attaining official program goals (Scheirer, 1978, p. 59 [20]).

After reviewing the evidence and explanations for a positive bias of client evaluations, Scheirer (1978, pp. 61, 66 [20]) concludes that this bias is insidious in two ways. First, the processes creating positive evaluations are largely unconscious, and result from the client's social role. A positive bias therefore stems from more fundamental causes than gratitude, which Campbell [19] cites as the source for positive client testimonials, and will exist even when clients attempt to provide honest information for improving the program. Second, the positive evaluative bias helps to maintain ineffective programs, because of the demands and political pressure of program participants.

The positive bias of client evaluations necessitates a fundamental rule for program evaluation: Do not conclude a program is effective based only on the distribution of client responses on an evaluation or satisfaction rating scale.† A majority of clients will almost always choose a positive or satisfied response category. Evaluators should expect a majority of positive or satisfied responses and consider that an inconsequential finding. However, a finding of a majority of negative or dissatisfied responses indicates something unusual and provides a danger signal.

Some evidence indicates that specific evaluations exhibit less of a positive bias than

---

† However, evaluators can sometimes make inferences about program effectiveness by comparing responses for different groups, for different programs, and over time, as will be discussed later.

general evaluations. Campbell *et al.* (1976, p. 480 [1]) found less expressed satisfaction for the more specific and unambiguous life domains, compared to the more general and ambiguous. Bush and Gordon (1978, p. 777 [3]) found that clients of social welfare services provided consistently positive responses to general satisfaction questions, but were more discriminating in answering questions about specific aspects of the services. Thus, questions that refer to very specific program or service characteristics may tend to elicit a lower proportion of responses on the positive or satisfied side of the scale, compared to more general questions. Nonetheless, the evaluator does not know what biases exist for a particular evaluation or satisfaction item, or what interpretation to give different response categories. Conclusions about program effectiveness, based only on the distribution of client responses on *any* evaluation or satisfaction rating scale, are highly suspect.

CORRESPONDENCE BETWEEN CLIENT-DERIVED MEASURES AND OBJECTIVE CONDITIONS

The degree to which client-derived measures correspond to official records, to program characteristics and to the services actually provided has important implications for their use in program evaluation. This is true for client-derived objective measures, for intrinsically important subjective measures, and for client evaluations and expressed satisfaction. This section will discuss these implications, examine the findings of relevant research, and consider the importance of client expectations.

Implications for program evaluation

The implications of the correspondence between client-derived objective measures and official records was illustrated earlier, using the example of crime victimization studies. When there are no problems of validity, the choice between client-derived measures and agency records depends simply on cost and reliability—i.e. program analysts should collect those data that maximize reliability for a given cost. Thus, if crime rates estimated from victimization surveys and from official records were not biased relative to each other, program analysts should dispense with expensive victimization surveys. However, the huge discrepancies between official crime rates and victimization survey estimates reveal a problem of validity caused by under-reporting biases in official crime rates. As previously discussed, studies analyzing the correspondence between official rates and survey estimates can yield ratios for correcting the official rates. Thus, program analysts need not always resort to expensive victimization surveys to obtain valid estimates, as long as occasional studies monitor changes in the calculated ratios over time and across geographic regions. In this manner, careful analyses of the correspondence between client-derived objective measures and official records can alert evaluators to problems of validity, provide a method of correcting measurement biases and lower the costs of monitoring objective conditions and measuring performance.

The degree to which intrinsically important subjective measures correspond to objective performance and conditions determines the extent to which an agency's objective performance can change those subjective measures. Improving intrinsically important subjective measures, such as reducing fear of crime, is by definition a valuable public goal. Thus, research that establishes a correspondence between intrinsically important subjective measures and objective measures corroborates the importance of the objective measures. In fact, some objective measures, as Campbell *et al.* (1976, p. 3 [1]) argue, are important only because of an assumed relationship to the subjective experience of life. When studies fail to find a correspondence between objective agency activities and the intrinsically important subjective measures of concern, then changing those activities has no efficacy for improving those subjective measures. If no link to any normal agency activities can be identified, agencies should consider mass media campaigns and other efforts to affect directly people's subjective feelings. For example, Skogan (1977, p. 10 [23]) argues that the mass media's extensive crime coverage may heighten fear of crime, which a public information campaign could reduce by presenting more realistic information on the crime problem.

The degree to which client evaluations and satisfaction correspond to objective conditions is critical. As discussed earlier, clients' expressed evaluations and satisfaction have no clear *a priori* meaning and intrinsic importance. Client evaluations can potentially be artificial creations of the interview process, or can reflect client attitudes that result from causes irrelevant to the program being evaluated. Whether client evaluations are valid measures of agency performance depends by definition on whether those evaluations do, in fact, correspond to any activities or services the agency performs. Therefore, research findings concerning the relationship between expressed client evaluations and objective measures are critical for interpreting the meaning of client evaluations, as well as for deciding on their appropriate role in program evaluation.

A potential complication concerning the relationship between client evaluations and objective conditions arises from possible simultaneity. Regardless of whether service performance affects clients' evaluations, clients' evaluations may affect clients' cooperation with program personnel, thereby affecting program performance. For example, Stipak (1979a, p. 52 [9]) hypothesizes that widespread dissatisfaction with police services may lower cooperation with law enforcement personnel. Variations in satisfaction across geographic areas, across demographic groups, or over time may consequently affect performance of police functions. Therefore, statistical attempts to estimate the impact of objective service conditions on subjective measures are potentially subject to simultaneity bias, resulting in spurious causal inferences.†

Although possible simultaneity complicates analyses that attempt to understand the causal relationships between subjective and objective measures, simultaneity does not complicate the practical task of measuring program performance. As long as a variable empirically corresponds to activities or services the agency performs, regardless of the direction of causal influence, that variable can serve as a valid performance indicator. Thus, the possibility that client evaluations may themselves affect objective program performance actually enhances their potential value as a performance indicator, even if actual performance has no effect on client evaluations.

A different type of simultaneity can potentially occur when both objective and subjective data are obtained from program clients. For example, analyses of crime victimization surveys (e.g. Parks [24]) typically interpret victims' evaluations of the police as a function of police response time and services rendered; however, Schneider *et al.* (1978, pp. 8–9 [25]) found that victims' attitudes toward the police affected victims' reports about response time and about police activities taken at the scene. This creates a serious problem for causal analysis, since measurement error in the objective variables is correlated with the subjective variable. Thus, analyses of relationships between client-derived objective and subjective measures are especially subject to simultaneity bias, resulting in spurious causal inferences. Moreover, this type of simultaneity, unlike the type previously discussed, does not enhance the value of the subjective indicator for measuring performance.‡

Client perceptions of service conditions

How accurately do clients perceive objective conditions and the actual services governments provide? Carroll [26] studied neighborhood residents' perceptions of their local streets, and found that about 80% of the residents correctly answered whether the street surface on their block was concrete or asphalt, and that over 90% correctly answered whether the street on their block had curbs. Schneider *et al.* [25] compared

---

† For example, assume an objective measure has no effect on a subjective measure, but that the subjective measure does affect the objective measure. Estimating a single equation model that regresses the subjective measure on the objective measure would reveal a spurious effect of the objective measure.

‡ Simultaneity in this case results solely because of the subjective measure's effect on measurement error in the objective variables. In the example previously discussed, simultaneity results because of the subjective variable's effect on actual objective performance.

objective data obtained from crime victimization surveys to official police records and found a close correspondence between the survey and police report data for factual details such as age and sex of suspects, number of suspects and events that occurred during the crime. In contrast, substantial differences were found for some factual details, including the race of the suspect, whether the victim knew the suspect, actions the police took at the scene and the month when the crime occurred. These discrepancies apparently resulted largely from errors in the information provided by survey respondents, but Schneider et al. (1978, pp. 5–6 [25]) were not able to determine the reason for such errors. A study conducted in Portland examined citizen perceptions of a large-scale program for improving and adding street lights in a target area. Only one-quarter of the citizens in the target area were aware of the new lights and almost two-thirds stated that no street lights had been added or improved (Schneider, 1976, p. 147 [5]). Finally, in the Kansas City Preventive Patrol Experiment the intensity of routine preventive police patrol was varied widely across areas within the city, but no effect was found on citizens' perceptions of the time police spent on patrol (Kelling et al., 1976, p. 637 [27]).

As these research findings illustrate, client perceptions and client-derived factual information vary in how closely they correspond to objective conditions and actual service characteristics. Based on Carroll's [26] finding that citizens accurately perceive aspects of their neighborhood streets, Ostrom (1975, p. 9 [28]) concludes that citizens probably perceive fairly accurately specific attributes of other services. However, the accuracy of citizen perceptions almost certainly decreases rapidly as the objective conditions or service characteristics become less specific, less tangible and more removed from the citizens' immediate environment. Residents who accurately perceive salient physical characteristics of services on their block (e.g. type of street surface or presence of curbs) may have only vague impressions of less tangible neighborhood or community services. Clients of human service programs, social-welfare programs and other programs involving close interaction between clients and agency personnel probably have more accurate perceptions of at least some service characteristics than clients of programs involving less intense interaction between the agency and the clients.

Relationship between client evaluations and objective performance measures

A number of research studies have found almost no correspondence between subjective measures, such as client evaluations, and a variety of objective measures. Stipak's [9, 29] results showed little relationship between evaluations of local services in the Los Angeles area and different outcome, workload and input measures. According to the results of the Kansas City Preventive Patrol Experiment, large differences in the intensity of preventive police patrol have little effect on citizens' satisfaction with the police, on a variety of other attitudes toward the police, or on citizens' fear of crime (Kelling et al., 1976, pp. 631–637 [27]). Several studies have found little or no relationship between attitudes toward the police and being the victim of a crime (Ostrom et al., 1973, pp. 40–41 [30]; Smith and Hawkins, 1973, p. 140 [31]; McIntyre, 1967, p. 37 [32]). Analogous research on workers' job satisfaction has found little relationship between the level of satisfaction workers express and other measures of worker discontent such as strikes, absenteeism and plant sabotage (Taylor, 1977, p. 243 [22]).

Other research has found some correspondence, although weak, between subjective evaluations and objective measures. A program in Washington, D.C., to improve cleanliness in target neighborhoods apparently resulted in somewhat more favorable citizen evaluations of local street cleaning and alley cleaning services (Office of Policy Development and Research, 1978, pp. VI58–VI59 [33]). Schneider (1976, p. 148 [5]) found a modest relationship, within specific sub-areas in the Portland metropolitan area, between citizen evaluations of street lighting and interviewer counts of the number of street lights within sight of the respondent's household. Schuman and Grunberg (1972, pp. 376–377 [34]) examined city-level correlations between mean satisfaction with city services and objective measures such as the number of police *per capita*, the number of parks *per capita*, and the crime rate and concluded that "dissatisfaction is related at least slightly to measurable aspects of city services." Finally, Marans and Wellman (1977, pp. 89–95 [35]) compared objective measures of water quality in northern Michigan lakes to subjective evaluations of residents living along the lakes. The subjective evaluations of water quality corresponded only modestly to the objective indicators of water quality.

Yet other research has found strong relationships between subjective evaluations and objective measures. Pelissero (1978, p. 36 [36]) reported that city residents living near a park provided more positive evaluations of local park and playground facilities, compared to respondents not living near a park. According to Skogan (1977, p. 7 [23]) people who have not been victims of crimes report less fear of crime than victims. Parks (1976, pp. 97–98 [24]) found that crime victims who reported high levels of satisfaction with how the police handled their call also provided more favorable general evaluations of police services and infers that how favorably victims respond to actions taken by police at the scene affects victims' general evaluations. Fowler (1974, pp. 59, 61 [21]) rank-ordered ten cities according to property tax rates and according to the percentage of city respondents who said local taxes were too high and concluded that the similarity in the two rank-orderings is "a very good testimony to the degree to which reality is reflected in people's attitudes." Finally, Aberbach and Walker (1970, p. 530 [37]) found that black respondents from Detroit who reported having experienced more racial discrimination gave more negative evaluations of city services.

Methodological flaws are one reason why different research studies have reached different conclusions about the correspondence between subjective evaluations and objective measures. For example, Peliserro [36] concludes a strong relationship exists between citizen evaluations of city parks and whether the citizen lives near a park; in contrast, Stipak [9, 29] found no independent relationship between distance to the nearest park and citizen evaluations of parks. Pelissero's analysis, however, does not include other independent variables (e.g. demographic variables) having possible confounding effects, whereas Stipak's analysis does. Even more seriously, Pelissero's objective measure of the availability of park facilities is the respondent's own report about whether a park is nearby. This measure almost certainly suffers from the problem discussed earlier of simultaneity between client-derived objective and subjective measures. In contrast, Stipak uses a very accurate, independently obtained measure of distance to the nearest park.

Spurious inferences due to simultaneity probably account for discrepancies between the conclusions reached by other studies, besides the Pelissero and Stipak analyses. Parks [24], for example, takes issue with prior research that concludes there is little independent relationship between crime victimization and evaluations of the police. Based on the finding that victims who were highly satisfied with how the police handled their call provided more favorable general evaluations of the police, Parks infers that actions of police on the scene improve victims' evaluations and thereby suppress the overall relationship between victimization and evaluations. But simultaneity may make this inference completely spurious, since initially having more positive evaluations of the police may predispose victims to report more satisfaction with actions police take on the scene.

Spurious conclusions that strong relationships exist between subjective evaluations and objective measures can result not only from simultaneity, but also from omitted variables, measurement error and data aggregation. The problem of omitted variables mentioned earlier when comparing the Pelissero [36] and Stipak [9, 29] analyses and the possibility of non-random measurement error in client-derived objective measures, also discussed previously, provide examples of how omitted variables and measurement error may create spurious subjective–objective relationships. Aggregating survey data to the level of cities or other geographic units maximizes the likelihood of spurious inference. Schuman and Grunberg [34] and Fowler [21], for example, aggregate citizen evaluations to the city level by computing city means and examine bivariate relationships between those means and city-level objective measures. This approach fails to statistically control for other variables that may have important effects on subjective evaluations, such as demographic characteristics of the respondent. The correct approach keeps the individual respondent as the unit of analysis and appends to the individual-level data objective data from other sources, as more detailed explications of these technical issues describe.†

Another approach to studying the impact of objective performance on subjective evaluations is the so-called "most similar systems" methodology some researchers have used to compare alternative institutional arrangements for providing local services (e.g. Ostrom *et al.* [30]; Rogers and Lipsey [38]). This approach is little more than what Campbell and Stanley (1963, p. 12 [39]) call the static group comparison design, except that some effort is made to choose groups for comparison that differ as little as possible on characteristics other than the treatment variable. However, since choosing two groups that match on all characteristics deemed relevant will usually be impossible, analysts should estimate the independent group effect by regressing the individual's subjective evaluation on a dummy group variable and other relevant independent variables (e.g. demographic variables), and not just compare frequency distributions or means for the two groups. Even then, measurement error in the independent variables and possible threats to internal validity due to selection‡ can produce overestimates of the independent effect that results from the objective inter-group performance difference.

Considering all the methodological problems that can spuriously increase the strength of relationship between subjective and objective measures, the overall results of existing research show amazingly little correspondence between client evaluations and objective service performance. A possible interpretation is that past studies have used inappropriate objective measures and that strong relationships do exist between service characteristics that clients care about and client evaluations. Further research concerning relationships between subjective and objective measures should attempt to identify, if possible, objective service characteristics that do affect client evaluations. As of now, existing research suggests that client evaluations usually do not correspond strongly to actual program characteristics.

Another important and largely unanswered research question concerns what factors affect the strength of the relationship between client evaluations and actual program characteristics. Campbell *et al.* (1976, pp. 478–482 [1]) hypothesize that the degree of correspondence between objective conditions and subjective judgements increases with the specificity and clarity of the object of judgement. Similarly, the previous discussion of client perceptions hypothesized that clients perceive less accurately those services that are less specific, less tangible and more removed from the clients' immediate environment. Lacking strong perceptions of such services, clients may express evaluations less related to actual service characteristics. Thus, expressed client evaluations of human service and social welfare programs may correspond more closely to program characteristics than would, for example, citizen evaluations of municipal police services or park facilities. Also, evaluations expressed by citizens who frequently use an available service, such as municipal park and recreation facilities, probably correspond more closely to objective service characteristics than do the evaluations expressed by nonusers.

Effect of client expectations

The expectations clients have for service performance probably decrease the correspondence between client evaluations and objective conditions. Assume that a client expresses an evaluation based on both perceived program performance and on performance expectations or standards the client uses for comparison. In that case, an improvement in perceived performance will produce a more positive evaluation. However, people may accommodate themselves over time to objective conditions by adjusting their aspir-

---

† For a comprehensive discussion of these statistical problems and their solutions see Hensler and Stipak [40]. For an analysis of when researchers can compute unbiased estimates of individual-level parameters from aggregate data see Firebaugh [41].

‡ As Skogan (1975, p. 49 [16]) comments regarding Rogers and Lipsey's [38] study of the effect of small versus large police departments, the citizens in the small, independent police jurisdiction had chosen by referendum not to be serviced by the large department. Skogan (1975, p. 49 [16]) argues that "all we know is that people who were so pleased with their local services that they voted to keep them are still pleased, while those who were not, are not."

ations and expectations (Campbell *et al.*, 1976, p. 485 [1]). Thus, an improvement in perceived performance may produce a more positive evaluation in the short term, followed by an increase in performance expectations, resulting in more negative evaluations. Similarly, a decrease in perceived performance may initially produce more negative evaluations, followed by decreased expectations and improved evaluations. Therefore, if client expectations adjust in a lagged manner to program performance, client evaluations may respond to short-term changes in objective performance, but adjustments of clients' expectations will ensure that only weak long-term or cross sectional relationships exist between client evaluations and objective performance measures.

Adaptation theory based on psychophysical experiments supports this view of the role expectations have in determining objective–subjective relationships. Although physical stimuli that depart greatly from a person's adaptation level excite a strong subjective reaction, repeated stimuli change the person's adaptation level and consequently lessen the subjective reaction (Helson, 1964, p. 227 [41]). Adaptation of expectations to objective conditions may explain Campbell *et al.*'s (1976, p. 466 [1]) finding that older blacks expressed higher satisfaction with their lives than either younger blacks or older whites, despite their impoverished material circumstances. Similarly, adaptation of expectations may partially explain the finding that the job satisfaction of workers in the same types of positions generally increases with job tenure (Taylor, 1977, p. 248 [22]).

The more that clients' expectations adjust to actual performance, the more the cross sectional and long-term relationships between client evaluations and objective performance measures will be attenuated. Thus, adjustment of expectations can invalidate using client evaluations to compare programs, or to monitor the same program over time. Evaluators making such comparisons should at least recognize the possible bias towards minimizing inter-program and over-time differences. Also, very high or low initial expectations of clients may greatly depress or inflate client evaluations of new programs, before clients' expectations have had time to adjust. Gutek (1978, p. 54 [17]), for example, speculates that widespread pre-existing negative views of public service agencies may greatly inflate reported satisfaction of new clients, since clients usually receive better service than they initially expect. Thus, the potential importance of client expectations in mediating objective–subjective relationships not only complicates the comparison of client evaluations across programs and over time, but also provides another reason, in addition to the positive bias of client evaluations discussed previously, for not using the distribution of client responses on an evaluation or satisfaction rating scale to assess the effectiveness of a program.

INTERPRETING CLIENT EVALUATIONS AS A BENEFIT OR PERFORMANCE SCALE

Client evaluations could be extremely useful to evaluation research if program evaluators could interpret them as a performance measure that scales programs according to program effectiveness, i.e. according to how much clients benefit from the program. In that case, evaluators could use client evaluations for comparing the performance of different programs, as well as for comparing the performance of one program over time and across different geographic areas or demographic groups. Unfortunately, using client evaluations as a performance scale can be erroneous for numerous reasons and is reasonable only under quite restrictive assumptions.

The previous sections have already covered some of the reasons why client evaluations cannot be interpreted *a priori* as a performance scale. Client awareness of service conditions and program characteristics appears to vary greatly. Similarly, existing research has not found a close correspondence between client evaluations and the activities and services agencies perform. Also, lagged adjustment of client expectations to objective conditions may weaken long-term and cross sectional relationships between client evaluations and actual program performance.

For these reasons, the first step towards a more sophisticated interpretation of client evaluations requires recognition of the naivete of the simple consumer perspective that views client evaluations as the final judgment about program performance. Rating scales that require program clients to express an evaluation or a level of satisfaction do not necessarily measure the degree to which the actual program satisfies clients' consumption preferences. Even when expressed evaluations are linked to program performance, they probably reflect only some performance dimensions, and those only imperfectly. For example, Mechanic (1972, pp. 296–297 [42]) concludes that measures of patients' satisfaction with health services primarily reflect the personality and demeanor of the attending physician, not the physician's medical skill or the technical quality of the medical care. Patients' expressed satisfaction therefore measures limited aspects of program performance that may be unrelated to other performance aspects that the patients themselves probably consider critically important. Moreover, the physician's personality and demeanor are probably the aspects of performance least under the control of program administrators. As this example illustrates, program evaluators must recognize that client evaluations may at best tap only some aspects of program effectiveness and not necessarily those aspects most critical to program goals or most valuable for administrators to monitor.

The second step towards a more sophisticated interpretation of client evaluations requires an appreciation of the different possible types of client evaluation processes. Assuming that expressed evaluations are linked to some dimension of actual performance, they can result from several alternative processes that link expressed evaluations to perceptions of actual performance. Expressed evaluations may result from comparing the perceived effectiveness of some aspect of the program to a standard. If the standard of comparison is the ideal, best performance, which actual performance can only approach, then the client's expressed evaluation will increase monotonically with perceived effectiveness. Similarly, if the standard is an expected level, perhaps based on the client's past experience, which the client considers desirable not only to achieve but also to exceed, the client's evaluation will also increase monotonically with effectiveness. But if the standard is a specific, desired level of service, which the client considers desirable to achieve but not to exceed, the client's evaluation will not increase monotonically. For example, a specific, desired level of service could result from a rational consumer's calculation of the marginal cost and benefit of improved performance. For some clients, therefore, expressed evaluations may begin to decrease after some point with further increases in performance.

As Stipak (1979b, p. 424 [43]) points out, some clients may have complicated preferences that yield not only non-monotonic but also non-single-peaked evaluation functions, the functions that map the perceived performance dimension into the measured subjective responses. For example, some inner-city residents might desire a high level of preventive police patrol in order to minimize crime. At the same time, they might prefer a low level of patrol to an intermediate level, if they believed intermediate levels provoke more disruption than they prevent. Non-single-peakedness of the functional relationship between subjective measures and objective performance dimensions clearly increases the difficulty of analyzing subjective measures in order to provide administrators with useful information for modifying program performance.

The third step towards a more sophisticated interpretation of client evaluations requires an understanding of the issues involved in using client evaluations to compare performance for different individuals and groups. As already discussed, some evaluation processes may result in a non-monotonic relationship between evaluations and perceived effectiveness, at the level of the individual client. However, even if evaluations at the individual level are monotonic and can therefore be interpreted as a benefit scale, for several reasons monotonicity across individuals is not assured (Stipak, 1979b, p. 424 [43]). First, different individuals may base their subjective assessments on different aspects of service performance. Second, different individuals may apply different expectations or standards in evaluating program performance. Thus, even if each individual client will express more favorable evaluations the better the perceived performance,

clients expressing more favorable evaluations do not necessarily perceive better performance.

These issues concerning cross-individual comparisons of client evaluations are analogous to issues concerning utility in microeconomic theory. Whereas in microeconomic
theory a consumer's utility function ranks the desirability of alternative consumption
decisions, a client's expressed evaluation ranks the benefit of possible performance
options, assuming a monotonic evaluation function as discussed previously. However,
just as in microeconomic theory interpersonal comparisons of utility cannot be made in a
theoretically sound way, cross-individual comparisons of client evaluations encounter
problems of different expectations, standards, perceptions and evaluation processes.

Groups of clients that express higher average evaluations do not necessarily perceive
better performance, due to all of the threats to individual-level and cross-individual
monotonicity discussed above. In addition, variation in actual performance within each
group complicates what sensible interpretations program evaluators can make from
group averages or distributions on an evaluation item (Stipak, 1979b, p. 425 [43]). If
considerable variation on actual performance does exist within each group, then attempts
to rank-order groups must assume that either the shape of the distribution of the relevant
objective performance dimension is similar within each group, or that no overlap exists
between groups on the level of objective performance. Otherwise, attempts to rank-order
the groups and to infer from group averages that one group experiences higher actual
performance, are meaningless because of inter-group overlap. Finally, comparisons of
group means assumes the reasonableness of treating the evaluation item as an interval
scale.†

Because of these complications in interpreting client evaluations as a performance
scale, eventually research may completely eschew the use of clients' subjective evaluations
to measure program performance. That would be a mistake. Despite these theoretical
complications, evaluators should not discard a tool of some potential practical value for
measuring performance. Rather, evaluators must recognize what assumptions are necessary in order to consider a subjective evaluation measure an increasing monotonic function of some actual performance dimension. First, any reasonable analysis of a subjective
indicator for purposes of measuring performance requires the assumption that clients
base their responses on the same (or on empirically related) aspects of service performance, which the clients perceive fairly accurately. Second, individual-level monotonicity is
required. An assumption of cross-individual monotonicity, however, is not reasonable or
theoretically defensible—fortunately, it is unnecessary. What is necessary is an assumption that cross-individual differences are not systematically related to the client groups
being compared, but rather are random differences that do not distort the inter-group
comparisons.

To better understand the problem that cross-individual differences poses for program
evaluation, consider this problem a result of the lack of a defined scale for subjective
evaluation items. Different individuals scale the response categories to the items differently, in terms of the level of objective performance to which each category corresponds.
Thus, the observed subjective measure has an error component due to interpersonal
differences in scaling. The critical requirement for program evaluation is that this error
component be statistically independent of membership in the groups the evaluator is
comparing. In that case, lack of cross-individual comparability in scaling has no systematic effect on the relative group averages. However, if different groups tend to have
different expectations or standards for service performance, systematic effects on the
group averages can distort the rank-order of the groups on the subjective measure.

PROCEDURES FOR ANALYZING CLIENT EVALUATIONS

An obvious use of client evaluations and other subjective measures is for comparing

---

† See Hensler and Stipak [44] for a discussion of methods of estimating interval scale values for survey item
response categories. For almost all applications in program evaluation, however, it is reasonable to simply
assign rank-order numbers and treat the evaluation item as an interval variable.

programs, for comparing different client groups and for monitoring a program over time. For example, a program administrator might compare groups of clients, who had participated in a human service program for different lengths of time, in terms of their distribution of responses to an item asking for an evaluation of the services they received. Similarly, a city official might compare levels of expressed satisfaction with a municipal service in different geographic areas within a city, or a program evaluator might compare average satisfaction levels for participants in two alternative types of job training programs. The purpose of such comparisons usually is to judge relative program performance, not merely to describe expressed satisfaction. Whenever evaluators interpret client responses to an evaluation or satisfaction item as a reaction to actual program characteristics or agency services, that measure assumes the status of a performance measure, not just a measure of an internal psychological state of the client. Public officials may even proceed to reallocate program expenditures, based on comparisons between clients from different demographic groups or geographic areas (Webb and Hatry, 1973, pp. 20–22 [46]). As the previous section discussed, such comparisons require (1) client responses based on the same or empirically related performance aspects, (2) individual-level monotonicity, and (3) independence between cross-individual differences and group membership. This section will discuss analytical procedures that allow relaxing the last requirement.

Whenever cross-individual differences in scaling are related to the groups being compared, those differences will systematically distort comparisons of the group averages and distributions on the subjective measure.† For example, one group may have a disproportionate number of clients with especially high expectations for service performance and report lower satisfaction even though actual performance is higher. In order to make valid inferences in such cases about relative service performance therefore, evaluators cannot simply compare group means or distributions.

Rather than comparing group means, evaluators should use multiple regression analysis, often referred to as analysis of covariance (ANCOVA) in the evaluation research literature.‡ This technique can take into account other differences in the groups' composition, preventing those differences from distorting the comparisons of relative program performance. The basic approach involves using the client as the unit of analysis, and regressing the subjective performance measure on dummy variables distinguishing between the client groups being compared, plus variables for all other individual-level characteristics that might distort the inter-group comparisons. Stipak (1979b, pp. 430–432 [43]) presents simple simulation examples that illustrate how this method avoids erroneous conclusions arrived at by comparing group means. Although this method can potentially suffer from measurement error and other problems, as discussed later, it provides a far superior general method than direct comparison of group means for comparing client groups on an evaluation or satisfaction measure.

Evaluators using multiple regression analysis to compare client groups on a subjective measure should carefully consider what individual-level variables they need to take into account. Ideally, all differences in group composition that may create artificial differences between the groups must be accounted for by variables included in the regression equation. For example, if people of different socio-demographic characteristics tend to differ in their performance standards, in their susceptibility to some type of response set,§ or in other ways affecting the subjective measure, the evaluator should include

---

† Stipak (1979a, p. 50 [9]) demonstrates this in a more formal manner.

‡ Analysis of covariance is simply multiple regression analysis that includes both nominal-level and interval-level predictors. In the terminology of analysis of covariance a dummy variable, such as a variable indicating membership in a particular client group, is called a factor and an interval-level independent variable is called a covariate.

§ Campbell et al. (1976, p. 106 [1]) observe that comparisons of groups on a subjective indicator may lead to erroneous conclusions about group differences if group members differ in their susceptibility to a response set. For example, assume that people in one demographic group are more prone to acquiescence response set and that they perceive positive evaluations of a program as the socially desirable response. Members of that group will consequently tend to provide more positive evaluations, ceteris paribus.

variables representing those socio-demographic characteristics in the model. The evaluator can represent nominal-level client characteristics, such as race or sex, by using dummy variables. Since evidence exists that demographic characteristics such as race and age are related to client evaluations (e.g. Katz et al., 1975, pp. 78–79 [18]), the conservative analytic strategy is to include variables for any socio-demographic characteristics by which the groups differ. If client evaluations were obtained prior to clients' intimate exposure to the program being evaluated, including that measure as an independent variable may help to account for differences in initial evaluative orientations.

Although far better in general than the simple comparison of group means, multiple regression analysis does not prevent all possible distortions of relative differences between client groups. Statistical biases can result from a number of possible causes.† Explicit measures of clients' performance expectations and general evaluative tendencies are usually not available. Analysts must therefore resort to using demographic variables as proxy variables, on the assumption that those variables correlate highly with the unmeasured variables. The weaker the correlation between the proxy variables and the unmeasured variables, the greater will be the distortions in the results of the regression analysis. Analysts sometimes introduce needless measurement error by categorizing continuous variables—an unnecessary practice in regression analysis, in contrast to crosstabular (contingency table) analysis.‡ By attempting to include relevant individual-level variables and to measure those variables as accurately as possible, program evaluators can minimize distortions of the estimates, obtained through regression analysis, of the relative inter-group differences that result from differences in actual program performance.

In most cases evaluators can probably reduce bias due to measurement error and omitted variables sufficiently to justify interpreting the estimated inter-group differences as possible reflections of differences in program performance. However, some potential problems can completely invalidate such interpretations. First, if important individual-level client differences are perfectly related to the groups being compared, no statistical method can separate the group-level performance differences from the effects of the individual-level variables. For example, if all clients in one program are of a different race than clients in another program, the differences on the subjective measure due to race and to the program are perfectly confounded. The smaller the client groups, the greater must be the heterogeneity within the groups to ensure the same level of accuracy. Similarly, individual-level client differences can also be confounded with differences in actual service performance. For example, program personnel may provide better service to clients of one race than another. When evaluators use geographic service areas to group clients for analysis, differences in service performance may become confounded with other differences across geographic areas. For example, citizens living in neighborhoods with dilapidated housing may tend to generalize their dissatisfaction with housing conditions to all aspects of their local area, including local governmental services (Stipak, 1979a, p. 49 [9]). These and other problems that seriously confound effects due to program performance with effects due to other variables make it impossible to extract any performance information from the subjective measure.

SUMMARY AND RECOMMENDATIONS

Client surveys can provide valuable objective and subjective information for monitoring and evaluating public programs. Crime victimization surveys and personal health surveys illustrate well the potential for client surveys to provide otherwise unavailable objective information and to correct validity problems in objective measures based on official agency records. When client-derived objective measures correspond closely to

---

† See Hensler and Stipak [40] for a concise overview of causes of statistical bias in such analyses and for greater detail see discussions in the econometrics literature of specification error and measurement error.
‡ Crosstabular analysis tends to produce not only measurement error due to categorization, but also specification error due to omission of relevant explanatory variables, since a small number of variables can be included at one time. Therefore, program evaluators should usually avoid crosstabulation.

official records, evaluators should simply use the combination of data collection techniques that maximizes reliability for a given cost.

Client surveys can provide information about intrinsically important subjective measures, such as citizens' fear of crime. When an intrinsically important subjective measure is causally linked to a public program or governmental service, administrators can potentially use that measure as one measure of performance† and can attempt to improve that measure through changes in program operations. When no causal linkage exists, officials may have no other recourse than public information campaigns for improving intrinsically important subjective measures.

Client surveys can also obtain information on clients' subjective evaluations of the program. The sensible use of clients' subjective evaluations and expressed satisfaction for purposes of program monitoring and evaluation involves a number of considerations evaluators must keep in mind. First, program clients are strongly biased towards providing highly favorable evaluations and expressing high levels of satisfaction. Second, the accuracy of clients' perceptions decreases for programs not involving close interaction with the agency and for less tangible governmental services that are removed from the citizens' immediate environment. Third, specific evaluation items usually have higher reliability and validity than general assessments. Fourth, even if actual program performance does not affect a subjective evaluation measure, that measure may reflect citizen attitudes that may themselves affect program performance. Fifth, using client evaluations to compare performance for different client groups requires client responses based on perceptions of the same or empirically related performance aspects, monotonic client evaluation functions and either independence between cross-individual differences and group membership, or else the use of statistical techniques that remove the distortions from those differences.

The sensible use of subjective data for measuring performance also requires the availability of necessary staff and data-processing capabilities. The analysis staff should definitely have training in multivariate statistics, especially multiple regression analysis, and preferably have some background in attitude measurement and scaling as well. The importance of statistical skills is probably greater for analyzing subjective measures of performance than for analyzing client-derived objective data or data about citizen preferences. The analytical staff will require access to some data-processing support or facilities; however, the widespread availability of statistical packages and the increasing use of computers and innovation in computing technology insure that data-processing will seldom present major problems. Almost any large public agency today can easily provide the necessary staff and data-processing support. Only very small public agencies may lack staff with the required statistical training or lack access to data-processing services. Those agencies should either forgo using subjective data for measuring performance, or else obtain capable help from consultants.

Outside consultants, agency staff, or program evaluators who use subjective performance measures should write a non-technical executive summary of their findings for general distribution. However, the findings should be based on rigorous analysis, usually documented by a technical report, that observes the following general rules.

Rule 1: Do not base conclusions about program effectiveness only on the distribution of client responses on an evaluation or satisfaction rating scale. Expect a majority of positive or satisfied responses and consider that finding inconsequential. However, recognize a majority of negative or dissatisfied responses as an unusual result and perhaps a danger signal.

Rule 2: Be alert for especially high or especially low client expectations. Unusually high or low client expectations, perhaps based on past experience, can greatly inflate or depress the initial evaluations of new program clients and of clients of new programs.

Rule 3: Look out for factors that may create non-monotonic client evaluation func-

---

† Note that using intrinsically important subjective measures for evaluating program performance involves some of the same analytical complications discussed regarding subjective evaluations and expressed satisfaction.

tions. Widespread publicity about the high cost of a program may cause clients to consider relative program costs and benefits, and to provide poor evaluations despite high levels of perceived effectiveness. Sometimes clients may perceive non-monotonic relationships between desired outcomes and agency workloads.

Rule 4: Ask how actual performance varies within each of the client groups being compared. If the groups overlap considerably on objective performance, judgements about overall group differences may be meaningless.

Rule 5: Use multiple regression analysis, rather than directly comparing group means or frequency distributions, when the groups differ on demographic or other obvious individual-level characteristics. Measure these characteristics as accurately as possible and include them as independent variables. Use proxy variables for relevant unmeasured characteristics.

Rule 6: Recognize when confounded effects make it impossible to extract performance information from subjective measures. The effects of actual program performance may sometimes be inextricably confounded with the effects of client characteristics and other differences between client groups and service areas.

REFERENCES

1. Campbell A., Converse P. E. and Rodgers W. L. *The Quality of American Life*. Russell Sage, New York (1976).
2. Andrews F. M. and Withey S. B. *Social Indicators of Well-Being*. Plenum, New York (1976).
3. Bush M. and Gordon A. C. The Advantages of Client Involvement in Evaluation Research, *Evaluation Studies Review Annual*, T. D. Cook (Ed.), Sage, Beverly Hills (1978).
4. Nunnally J. C. The Study of Change in Evaluation Research: Principles Concerning Measurement, Experimental Design and Analysis, *Handbook of Evaluation Research*, E. L. Struening and M. Guttentag (Eds), Sage, Beverly Hills (1975).
5. Schneider A. L. Victimization Surveys and Criminal Justice System Evaluation, *Sample Surveys of the Victims of Crime*, W. G. Skogan (Ed.), Ballinger, Cambridge (1976).
6. Schneider A. L. *Measuring Change in the Crime Rate: Problems in the Use of Official Data and Victimization Survey Data*. Oregon Research Institute, Eugene, Oregon (1975).
7. Levine J. P. The Potential for Crime Overreporting in Criminal Victimization Surveys, *Criminology* **14**, 307–330 (1976).
8. National Advisory Commission on Criminal Justice Standards and Goals. *Criminal Justice System*. U.S. Government Printing Office, Washington (1973).
9. Stipak B. Citizen Satisfaction with Urban Services: Potential Misuse as a Performance Indicator, *Public Administration Review* **39**, 46–52 (1979). Reprinted in *Evaluation Studies Review Annual*, L. Sechrest (Ed.), Sage, Beverly Hills (1979).
10. Shin D. C. The Quality of Municipal Service: Concept, Measure and Results, *Social Indicators Research* **4**, 207–229 (1977).
11. Converse P. E. Public Opinion and Voting Behavior, *Handbook of Political Science*, F. I. Greenstein and N. W. Polsby (Eds), Addison-Wesley, Reading, MA (1975).
12. Stipak B. Attitudes and Belief Systems Concerning Urban Services, *Public Opinion Quarterly* **41**, 41–55 (1977).
13. Converse P. E. Attitudes and Non-Attitudes: Continuation of a Dialogue, *The Quantitative Analysis of Social Problems*, E. R. Tufte (Ed.), Addison-Wesley, Reading, MA (1970).
14. Urban Institute. *What Happens to the Clients? Monitoring the Outcomes of State and Local Mental Health Services, Interim Report*. Urban Institute, Washington (1978).
15. Hatry H. P., Blair L. H., Fisk D. M., Greiner J. H., Hall J. R. Jr. and Schaenman P. S. *How Effective are Your Community Services? Procedures for Monitoring the Effectiveness of Municipal Services*. Urban Institute, Washington (1977).
16. Skogan W. G. Public Policy and Public Evaluations of Criminal Justice System Performance, *Crime and Criminal Justice*, J. A. Gardiner and M. A. Mulkey (Eds), Lexington Books, Lexington, MA (1975).
17. Gutek B. A. Strategies for Studying Client Satisfaction, *Journal of Social Issues* **34**, 44–56 (1978).
18. Katz D., Gutek B. A., Kahn R. L. and Barton E. *Bureaucratic Encounters: A Pilot Study in the Evaluation of Government Services*. Institute for Social Research, Ann Arbor (1975).
19. Campbell D. T. Reforms as Experiments, *Am. Psychol.* **24**, 409–428 (1969).
20. Scheirer M. A. Program Participants' Positive Perceptions: Psychological Conflict of Interest in Program Evaluation, *Evaluation Quarterly* **2**, 53–70 (1978). Reprinted in *Evaluation Studies Review Annual*, L. Sechrest (Ed.), Sage, Beverly Hills (1979).
21. Fowler F. J. Jr. *Citizen Attitudes Toward Local Government, Services and Taxes*, Ballinger, Cambridge (1974).
22. Taylor J. C. Job Satisfaction and the Quality of Working Life; A Reassessment, *J. occup Psychol.* **50**, 243–251 (1977).
23. Skogan W. G. Public Policy and the Fear of Crime in Large American Cities, *Public Law and Public Policy*, J. A. Gardiner (Ed.), Praeger, New York, Praeger (1977).
24. Parks R. B. Police Response to Victimization: Effects on Citizen Attitudes and Perceptions, *Sample Surveys of the Victims of Crime*, W. G. Skogan (Ed.), Ballinger, Cambridge (1976).

25. Schneider A. L., Griffith W. R., Sumi D. H. and Burcart J. M. *Portland Forward Records Check of Crime Victims*, U.S. Government Printing Office, Washington (1978).
26. Carroll S. An Analysis of the Relationship Between Citizen Perceptions and Unobtrusive Measures of Street Conditions. Research report No. 10, Measures of Municipal Services: Multi-Mode Approaches Project. Workshop in Political Theory and Policy Analysis, Department of Political Science, Indiana University.
27. Kelling G. L., Pate T., Dieckman D. and Brown C. E. The Kansas City Preventive Patrol Experiment: A Summary Report, *Evaluation Studies Review Annual*, G. V. Glass (Ed.), Sage, Beverly Hills (1976).
28. Ostrom E. Multi-Mode Measures: From Potholes to Police. Paper presented at the Conference on Productivity and Program Evaluation: Challenges for the Public Service, organized by the Midwest Intergovernmental Training Committee (1975).
29. Stipak B. *Citizen Evaluations of Urban Services as Performance Indicators in Local Policy Analysis*. Ph.D. Dissertation, University of California, Los Angeles (1976).
30. Ostrom E., Baugh W. H., Guarasei R., Parks R. B. and Whitaker G. P. *Community Organization and the Provision of Police Services*. Sage, Beverly Hills (1973)
31. Smith P. E. and R. O. Hawkins. Victimization, Types of Citizen-Police Contacts and Attitudes Toward the Police, *Law and Society Review* **8**, 135–152 (1973).
32. McIntyre J. Public Attitudes Toward Crime and Law Enforcement, *The Annals* **374**, 34–46 (1967).
33. Office of Policy Development and Research. *Improving Productivity in Washington, D.C. Neighborhoods: A Case Study*. Washington: Dept. of Housing and Urban Development (1978).
34. Schuman H. and Grunberg B. Dissatisfaction with City Services: Is Race an Important Factor? *People and Politics in Urban Society*, H. Hahn (Ed.), Sage, Beverly Hills (1972).
35. Marans R. W. and Wellman J. D. *The Quality of Non-Metropolitan Living: Evaluations, Behaviors, and Expectations of Northern Michigan Residents*. Institute for Social Research, Ann Arbor (1977).
36. Pelissero J. P. *Citizen Evaluations of Community Services in Oklahoma*. Bureau of Government Research, University of Oklahoma (1978).
37. Aberbach J. S. and Walker J. L. The Attitudes of Blacks and Whites Toward City Services: Implications for Public Policy, *Financing the Metropolis: Public Policy in Urban Economics*, J. P. Crecine (Ed.), Sage, Beverly Hills (1970).
38. Rogers B. D. and McCurdy L. C. Metropolitan Reform: Citizen Evaluations of Performances in Nashville-Davidson County, Tennessee, *Publius* **4**, 19–34 (1974).
39. Campbell D. T. and Stanley J. C. *Experimental and Quasi-Experimental Designs for Research*. Rand McNally, Chicago (1963).
40. Hensler C. and Stipak B. Contextual Analysis: Problems of Statistical Inference and Their Solutions. Unpublished manuscript available from Brian Stipak, Institute of Public Administration, Pennsylvania State University, University Park, PA 16802 (1979).
41. Firebaugh G. A Rule for Inferring Individual-Level Relationships from Aggregate Data. *American Sociological Review* **43**, 557–572 (1978).
42. Helson H. *Adaptation Level Theory: An Experimental and Systematic Approach to Behavior*. Harper, New York (1964).
43. Mechanic D. *Public Expectations and Health Care*. Wiley, New York (1972).
44. Stipak B. Are there Sensible Ways to Analyze and Use Subjective Indicators of Urban Service Quality?, *Social Indicators Research* **6**, 421–439 (1979).
45. Hensler C. and Stipak B. Estimating Interval Scale Values for Survey Item Response Categories, *American Journal of Political Science* **23**, 627–649 (1979).
46. Webb K. and H. P. Hatry. *Obtaining Citizen Feedback: The Application of Citizen Surveys to Local Governments*, Urban Institute, Washington (1973).

39

Welfare Entrepreneurialism and the Politics of Innovation

Dwight L. Frankfather

Ostensibly, demonstrations are undertaken to test innovations in service delivery. In the following case study, however, a private social agency manipulates the rhetoric and appearance of innovation to satisfy entrepreneurial ambitions. Obscure service coordination mechanisms, unmeasurable objectives, high coverage/low impact services, a strong cash-flow position, and control of information prove to be successful strategies for capturing demonstration grant funds. As a result, lower-quality services and exaggerated policy implications are exchanged for organizational expansion and new prestige. A greater public demand for straightforward program evaluations could restrain welfare entrepreneurialism. At issue is the control over social programming, therefore any alterations in existing arrangements will be complex and controversial.

In the human-service domain, and among private social agencies in particular, there is an idealistic tendency to assume that clients' interests always come first or coincide with organizational interests. The welfare of the client and the interests of the organization are not always compatible, however, and compromise and conflict occur. For example, university training hospitals may neglect patients whose ailments offer little potential for educating student physicians.[1] Special education programs may be supported by local school boards only if troublesome students are isolated and controlled.[2] Mental hospitals may be more favorably disposed toward patients amenable to counseling and analytical therapies.[3] Public welfare department intake workers may alter criteria for judging applications in order to satisfy political and organizational pressures.[4] Public relations units in private social agen-

From Dwight L. Frankfather, "Welfare Entrepreneurialism and the Politics of Innovation," 55(1) *Social Service Review* 129-146 (March 1981). Copyright © 1981 by The University of Chicago Press. Reprinted by permission.

cies may function to conceal the discrepancies between client and organizational interests.[5]

Survival and expansion are organizational imperatives also found in human service agencies. In this case study of a private social agency, the Public Welfare Institute (PWI or Institute), organizational entrepreneurialism is expressed through manipulating the rhetoric of innovation and the public image of a demonstration program. The Institute and the Administration on Aging (AOA) in the Department of Health and Human Services jointly financed the Older Adult Community Service Program (OACSP). The program's central purpose was to prevent institutionalization of the community's aged by expanding and coordinating local services. The following analysis describes the use of entrepreneurial strategies which led to successful expansion but may have compromised demonstration and evaluation principles.

Data Collection and Analysis

Data were obtained primarily through participant observation and interviews. These complementary methods capture extensive detail about the actions of the participants and the social meaning they attribute to their actions.[6] The Institute's administrative memos and public documents were also a source of data. Data on the service project (OACSP) and PWI were collected for a period of ten months through most of 1976. The OACSP staff meetings and regular meetings with local providers were observed. Staff members were interviewed at least once, and the most important ones were interviewed repeatedly throughout the data collection period. Local social service professionals familiar with OACSP were interviewed, as were city officials responsible for overseeing the expenditure of public dollars. Periodic observations were made of PWI/OACSP joint activities for twelve months beyond the initial data collection period.[7] The OACSP had been in operation for three years when the study began, so data were collected from program documents which described activities prior to the time of the study.

The analysis is guided by the principles of the case study method. Data are organized to reconstruct a holistic portrait of the phenomenon under study. A broad array of data is incorporated, including relevant economic, political, psychological, and sociological factors.[8] The unit of analysis is the PWI. This paper describes and assesses the politics of innovative programming as it is practiced by an administrator in a large and prestigious philanthropic social agency.[9]

Private Philanthropy and the
Public Welfare Institute

Today the investment of philanthropic wealth in social welfare represents a small fraction of total welfare expenditures. The scale of government provision has made traditional philanthropic service functions insignificant in volume. In order to reestablish a unique welfare role, private agencies have struggled to define new domains, develop appropriate new expertise, and obtain internal organizational consensus on new directions. Anticipating the changing form and substance of social problems, foundations established at the turn of the century sought a wide latitude in making future commitments. This absence of a historical commitment to a particular substantive area has contributed to the contemporary confusion of direction.[10]

The PWI, a private social agency located in a major metropolitan region, typifies this phenomenon. The Institute had survived for decades providing casework services. Neither the importance nor superior quality of their product was challenged by trustees, administrators, or staff. Then in the early 1970s the board of the Institute "rediscovered" poverty and a plethora of social ills and concluded that casework was no longer the principal technology in the war against poverty, racism, riots, urban decay, segregation, and the abridgment of civil rights. In response, the PWI leadership redirected its resources toward the discovery of solutions to complex social problems. Programs were to focus on communities, not individuals, and "shared power" between professionals and consumers was to be the style of operation. The substance of future programs and problems was not specified. The PWI board's overriding motivation was to recapture a leadership position and to reestablish their tradition of excellence in the social welfare field. Projects that conveyed the impression of leadership and excellence were likely to win the support of the Institute's trustees regardless of the program or the problems it addressed.[11]

In 1976, PWI had an annual operating budget of $6.5 million. In the fiscal year 1975 the Institute distributed $3.9 million among eleven community programs and the service administration in the central office. In terms of the size of urban problems, that seems like a small amount of money; but compared with the resources that a small community program can marshal on its own, even a fraction of that amount is a windfall. These resources put the Institute in a commanding position among social agencies in any community which it chose to enter.

The OACSP was the largest of the Institute's eleven service projects in 1976. At the time of the study, the program employed nineteen full-time staff members in a neighborhood office and was financed by

AOA demonstration money and a PWI matching contribution. Together their resources equaled $300,000 annually at the time of the study. The OACSP also administered a $150,000 hot lunch program funded by the AOA. The program was, and is, guided by a coordination rationale. As the first OACSP newsletter stated, "The [program] concept is to enlist the total resources of the community in a coordinated effort to provide comprehensive service to older persons in the area." Four coordination task forces composed the structural base for the principal coordination activities. Local professionals from public and private social agencies, hospitals, and health centers voluntarily participated in the social service, health, education, and senior citizens' center task forces. A community board consisting primarily of task force members was to assume authority over the program during its third year of operation. In addition to the professional structure, senior citizens were invited to become members of a council and sit on any or all of the seven council subcommittees.

At the time the study was undertaken, OACSP had achieved a favored status within the Institute. One PWI service administrator had cultivated long-standing relationships with influential trustees of PWI, and together they secured a stable if not increasing share of the Institute service investments of OACSP. Unlike most other modern institutions, philanthropic organizations do not have a guiding principle or mechanism for regulating the allocation of resources. In the public domain, elected officials are held accountable for the allocation of tax dollars by means of the ballot box, and in free enterprise, competition for customers through a market mechanism imposes some discipline on the producers. But philanthropic foundations are neither profit motivated nor are they public institutions, so budget allocations are subject only to the controlling forces within them.[12] Stanton makes the point that in philanthropic organizations program survival depends on pleasing the trustees and donors, not the client.[13] Further, trustees are generally volunteer welfarists who remain unconcerned about the operation of the organization as long as the reputation for excellence is upheld. In other cases, trustees become rigid advocates of specific programs and bargain for expansion of their favorites.[14] This latter situation tended to occur at PWI.

Innovative Coordination and Services for the Elderly

From a historical perspective, "aging" was a safe field for philanthropy in the 1970s. The elderly were one of the few "problem populations" that still welcomed professionals. There was no trace of the militancy that characterized the involvement of other activist populations at the time and which was so unacceptable to private philanthropy.[15] The Institute had a tradition of providing casework services to the aged. A sympathetic constituency existed among trustees and staff. Services for the elderly were, and still are, an expanding sector of the social service industry. For PWI, this meant new opportunities to compete for influence and resources in an undeveloped domain. The Institute was thus predisposed toward aging in its search for a new direction.

In the early 1970s the AOA was advocating service coordination. Amendments to the Older Americans Act in 1973 directed newly founded area agencies to establish a comprehensive and coordinated network of services.[16] Area agencies were not empowered to provide services directly, but to plan, implement, and oversee services provided by others.[17] The strategy was ideally suited to the needs of PWI. It appeared that coordination might reinstate PWI in the vanguard of public welfare.

Late in the 1960s and early 1970s the rubric of systems analysis and operations research began to influence the definitions of service delivery problems in health and social welfare.[18] Some believed that systems analysis would be the new solution. The systems concept seemed to offer uniquely appropriate explanations of problems associated with the proliferation in the 1960s of services at the local level and the mounting confusion about the relationships among the service components. New agencies were being formed and assimilated into the community; existing agencies competed for new money and provided new services; new organizational associations formed, and old ones were renegotiated. The expansion resulted in instability in the delivery system, coupled with the growing consensus that improvements were not as helpful or as useful as originally expected.[19] Coordination appealed to professionals because it was supposed to enable clients to better "negotiate the system." It would make services generally more "accessible" and less fragmented.[20] It would overcome the lack of accountability in the referral process.[21] In an era of rising costs, coordination had political appeal. Inefficiencies in service delivery meant scarce resources were wasted. The costs of coordination at least ought to be less than costs attributed to inefficiency.

The professional staff of PWI initially embraced coordination in good faith and with confidence. Both staff and trustees, however, were impervious to criticisms of coordination which appeared in the mid-1970s. The Institute had gained prestige and recognition among professional gerontologists. Considerable federal money had been attracted to OACSP. The Institute had no incentive to scrutinize its program's tangible benefits for service recipients.

The criticism of voluntary coordination as practiced in OACSP was severe. Alfred Kahn, once an advocate of coordination, wrote about the inability of local programs to influence service delivery problems which have their roots at the state and federal level, saying that "the neighborhood service center . . . cannot adequately correct or undo program fragmentation at the federal or state level. It is an understandable strategy tied to a lost cause. The problem is not overcome by goodwill generated at meetings of equals who pledge cooperation but sacrifice nothing precious."[22] Carroll Estes, in a study of community planning of service for the aged, observed that ". . . the motive of planning task (conceptualized in broad and ambiguous terms) and the structure of the planning organizations (essentially federative) combined to prevent . . . the objective identification of gaps and needs . . . and social action."[23] In another study of federal regulation and coordination under Title III of the Older Americans Act, Marmor and Kutza anticipated the situation at PWI. They reason that ". . . coordination as a problem-solving technique is highly supported but little understood. . . . Its utility for its advocates is subtle and not openly acknowledged."[24] Other authors boldly assert that ". . . coordination means getting what you want."[25] In other words, the principal beneficiaries appear to be the professional coordinators, not the clients in whose name they operate.

The Older Adult Community Service Program

In response to publicity in the early 1970s about new directions at PWI, the Institute was approached by a citizens' committee from one of the metropolitan neighborhoods. This group had apparently been instrumental in the construction of a high-rise public housing project for the elderly and was looking for an organization to provide social services in the building. Using the Institute's resources, a PWI administrator wrote a demonstration proposal that called for a community coordination program to be implemented by this citizen group. The AOA funded the proposal and PWI paid the community's cost-sharing portion. Under the grant, the citizen group became the Older Adult Community Service Program.

The PWI administrator was the principal investigator on the project. All accounting and financial management was carried out by PWI staff. The content of future proposals was decided by the PWI administrator. Salary scales and benefit plans for employees were established under PWI policies. As a result OACSP became an extension of PWI with very little autonomy. According to OACSP administrative staff, even such small items as the telephone bills were scrutinized by the

PWI staff. The OACSP staff had to fight for the right to exercise independence in such matters as the use of a mimeograph machine to reproduce and disseminate public statements without prior PWI approval.

One of the original citizen group leaders was appointed to direct the new coordination program. She was best known for her activities in a local church and had no administrative or professional experience. She was wholly dependent upon the PWI administrator for professional direction and interpretation of the demonstration objectives. Even though the director was not well prepared to administer the program, she was an important symbolic figure, representing moral authority in the local community. It was especially useful in this politically active and service-conscious community that OACSP be associated with such an authority. A competitive spirit exists among agencies, and coordinators are frequently accused of being late arrivals who want to take charge. One OACSP administrator observed, "I said this is not the place to do coordination. It's too competitive and factional. Groups are trying to knock each other out of the park." The director's moral integrity and local identity conveyed an impression of autonomy which encouraged local service competitors to accommodate OACSP's presence. At the same time, the weakness of her leadership permitted PWI to direct the program without local staff interference.

The Institute and OACSP relied heavily upon the rhetoric of community control. The program was said to be a manifestation of the "community working together," and "a total community effort." It was claimed that the elderly themselves set the priorities. To determine their priorities, the staff informally circulated a questionnaire among senior citizen centers in the community but obtained only twenty responses the first year and thirty-seven the next. Since the program reported providing 80,000 units of service to 35,000 elderly, only one out of every 1,000 active clients was surveyed. The very low response rate reflects the small commitment by staff to systematic assessment of priorities. In theory, priorities of the elderly were also to be asserted through a "senior citizens' advisory council" and its seven committees, by the OACSP community board and its five subcommittees, by the hot lunch program community board, and by the four professional task forces for health, education, social services, and senior citizen centers. Since all nineteen components were encouraged to simultaneously set program priorities without any procedure for doing so, no orderly or organized expression of priorities could emerge. Furthermore, it is not obvious that any "community" priorities could emerge. Supposedly, demonstration program objectives were specified in the proposal. Also, the chief governing body at the local level, the OACSP Community Board, had no legal authority and did not administer any funds. The minutes of the Board of Directors meeting of January 28, 1976, stated,

"PWI still maintains fiscal and policy making control of OACSP." At every meeting the treasurer of the board reported, "I'm a treasurer without funds." With so many components and people involved in "directing" the program, the staff was left to its own interpretation of needs and priorities. In this situation, no organized community resistance for any hierarchically directed activity could emerge.

The program as defined in the demonstration proposal had no operational objectives. The following "goals" appeared in the first demonstration proposal:

Long Range	Short Range
1. Enhance physical and mental health	1. Outreach
2. Comprehensive service delivery	2. Health care
3. Develop a prototype with a broad base of community support	3. Personal and home services
4. Maintain elderly in the community	4. Counseling
	5. Consumer purchase program
	6. Group activities
	7. Safety program
	8. Tenant service program
	9. Information and referral
	10. Transportation
	11. Program for homeowners
	12. RSVP

Maintaining the elderly in the community (item 4) was the most frequently cited of these objectives and the principal justification for the program's existence. But the long list of short-range objectives legitimizes any and every kind of possible program activity. Nothing is precluded. The causal relationship, for instance, between maintaining vulnerable elderly in the community and a consumer-purchasing or group-activities program appears to be tenuous. Furthermore, the staff raised a lack of commitment to objectives to the level of high principle. Staff members explained, "We are creative, open to anything. . . . In a shifting society, you can't set priorities. Everything changes. . . . We've responded to felt need. . . ."

Even the notion of "community" had no definitional function in OACSP. For four years OACSP claimed to serve a community of 35,000 elderly. When it was learned that the area served did not include the 35,000 elderly originally estimated, the boundaries were simply redrawn to show the program serving a larger area. One day the number of clients jumped to 70,000 because the funding sources in city government complained that financial resources were overcommitted to the area. The PWI administrator reported, "We were told by the city office there was too much AOA money in the community so we had to enlarge the boundaries." The expansion occurred without prior sanction of the local governing board and without altering any program operations. Boundary definitions were determined by judgments about a politically acceptable cost-benefit ratio, with size of target population as a crude estimate of benefit.

Without competent local leadership, program boundaries, preestablished objectives, or specified operations, OACSP could assume any functions for which the PWI administrator could obtain funding. Generality and flexibility permitted the PWI administrator to cast OACSP in the framework most convenient for winning additional funding.

Contributions of the direct service capacity.—The appearance of successful coordination requires a high service volume. Through the senior citizen center, OACSP successfully attracted a large number of clients with minimal needs. Of the more than 80,000 service contacts reported by OACSP in the fiscal year 1975–76, nearly 90 percent were for meals and recreational and cultural activities. These included pool, card games, crafts, birthday parties, travelogue films, theatrical productions, videotape and slide shows, trips to museums, and so forth. Such services no doubt have attractive qualities for those who seek them out. They also have the advantage for the coordinator of being inexpensive to produce, and a high volume production can result when the unit cost is minimized. However, such services can have only a meager impact on those aged facing a serious risk of institutionalization. Therefore they are not instrumental in achieving the programs' central purpose. Most senior citizen centers serve elderly who are physically able to transport themselves, and those with serious handicapping conditions are infrequent patrons.[26] The elderly attracted to OACSP were typical of this pattern.

In sharp contrast to these activities OACSP tried for three years to establish a visiting program for the homebound. It was to be a major initiative and was more plausibly related to the program's central objective. However, the program was unable to identify people who claimed to be homebound. Social service professionals from the OACSP task forces refused to give names of their clients. An OACSP staff member explained that "only two professionals responded. They won't circulate names unless they are confident something good will be delivered." The elderly volunteer home visitors refused to go into unfamiliar neighborhoods. They were only willing to visit their friends. Eventually one elderly homebound resident was provided "information and referral." But even if contact had been made with seriously impaired individuals, there were no services to be provided.

The direct service component engaged the elderly who were least vulnerable to institutionalization, providing generally pleasant but ephemeral services. It was unable to locate or support the more seriously impaired. The OACSP demonstrated that as long as direct services were harmless and free, an adequate supply of healthy recipients could be recruited. Services that are likely to have significant impact on elderly with serious physical or mental impairments are too difficult and costly for a coordinator to produce. The coordinator thus may avoid those elderly whose serious problems may interfere with high volume numbers.

The coordinating structure.—As previously noted, four task forces comprised the coordinating structure of OACSP. It was their responsibility to implement changes in allocation, production, and distribution of services that would improve the overall delivery of care for the elderly. A coordinating structure must maintain a large membership. Voluntary member organizations, however, are likely to maintain their relationship with the coordinator only so long as their boundary control is not seriously threatened. In the first three years of the program, virtually no substantial request for professional services or finances was made of members. Even occasional attendance at meetings was not required for membership. There was no pooling of member agency money or staff lines which characterizes some coordination projects.[27] For many of the regular members, routine attendance was the upper limit of their voluntary contribution. One community service organization staff member explained, "The time of the meeting is valuable. It's worthwhile. But the added something that I should donate—time—it isn't worth it to me. We're too busy to send a worker over to help." Simply communicating in task force meetings was thought to be an achievement by itself. As the staff explained, "There are constant changes. We can't effect them, but we can disseminate knowledge about them."

The education task forces dealt primarily with recreation and entertainment for the elderly. When local junior colleges wanted to boost enrollment, they advertised and recruited through this task force. The senior citizen center task force was concerned with coordinating recreational events among the local senior citizen centers. (The one exception undertaken in the name of this task force is discussed in a later section.) The social service task force held regular meetings but carried out no sustained activity. In its most substantial undertaking during the period of observation, members agreed to collect data on hospital emergency-room use by the elderly, but a report was never written. No uniform or reliable data were collected because of a lack of provider cooperation.

The health task force undertook one of the earliest and most substantial of OACSP's coordinated service initiatives. A member hospital located a health clinic in the public housing project for the elderly. The program claimed that health services for the community's elderly had expanded. At best, however, services had been redistributed, since no new medical or nursing manpower had been added and a part-time doctor had been merely relocated. In fact, it is conceivable that the supply of services had even been reduced since elderly community residents would not patronize a health clinic located behind the locked doors of a public housing project. The need for the clinic had even been questioned by the OACSP staff, but its public relations value was considered to be significant. One OACSP administrator commented: "Some people raised questions in the early proceedings about the necessity of having another clinic with a private clinic so close. We felt an on-site health clinic would add to our appearance." Similarly, a community hospital administrator remarked that "Community Hospital had a public relations problem. We weren't doing anything in the community."

Even if there is reason to question the clinic's impact on community elderly, it was at least a coordinated, functioning service. Because no other health or social service task force activity matched the complexity of the clinic, its day-to-day operation best portrays coordination at work. A close examination of the service revealed that the elderly patients were dissatisfied with a foreign-speaking physician whom they considered rude, intolerant, and impossible to understand. In spite of numerous patient complaints registered against the physician, the hospital resisted the travails of physician censure and removal. The coordinators, although claiming to have been instrumental in establishing the clinic, refused even to discuss the issue with the hospital. Apparently, OACSP did not want to antagonize and risk losing a coordinating team member.

At the time of the study, Community Hospital was experiencing a surplus of psychiatrists, so two of the psychiatric unit staff were reassigned to the clinic. The coordinators were not enthusiastic because they felt no need for a psychiatrist, particularly one who would offer only chemotherapy. An OACSP administrator complained, "I wasn't asked if we want a psychiatrist. I was told, 'goody,' a psychiatrist is coming. We were all upset that this was going to be only a chemotherapy program. Chemotherapy is a cop-out when it comes to the elderly." Even though they objected to his services, OACSP personnel supported the psychiatrist's arrival. Expansion alone was sufficient justification. Their interests were succinctly expressed by the administrator who said, "What am I supposed to do, look a gift horse in the mouth?" After expending considerable energy in recruiting patients for whom the psychiatrist could prescribe medications, the OACSP staff failed to locate an adequate number. Then they worried about losing the service. The following dialogue, for example, occurred between two staff members:

Staff 1: We're going to lost our psychiatric service if we aren't able to provide more patients.
Staff 2: We don't want that to happen.
Staff 1: Maybe we can tickle him into some other things.
Staff 2: *It has to be a service the hospital can collect for.*

Some of the coordinators' health services were unreliable in quality and of questionable necessity. In the above example, task force members were willing to coordinate, not in spite of marginal services but because of them. The hospital needed to recover manpower costs for a psychiatric staff that generated little or no revenue. Exporting this otherwise unusable manpower was both its contribution to coordination and an attempt to locate a more viable market.

Members had other incentives to participate. The Institute had brought service money to the community, and there was always the possibility that more money would be distributed among the faithful participants. Also, participation in a coordinating mechanism has a multiplier effect on credit taking. For example, when a member hospital independently opened a geriatric clinic, OACSP claimed to have expanded its "coordinated" service network. In that way, twice as much credit was claimed for the same amount of expansion. Furthermore, other task force members were free to claim to have participated in achieving this improvement. The hospital in return obtained free advertising when the coordinators circulated news of the addition.

The Entrepreneurial Administrator

The presence of an entrepreneurial personality is important, and the PWI administrator and principal investigator on the OACSP demonstration project was an aggressive and successful entrepreneur. He explains, "My job is to be attuned to what's happening in the city and federally . . . to link trends to our projects. Six years ago I was aware of a trend at the national level towards coordination." An OACSP administrator expresses the same point differently: "He [the administrator] is on top of every funding opportunity. Any money he can find he sends our way. His is definitely not the need-priority model." The PWI administrator established a reputation as a professional capable of starting ventures and capturing resources, rather than as a person who can implement an innovation thoroughly in a way that achieves its central objectives. It was important that the administrator's professional convictions about successful coordination were vindicated by the award of federal grants. No harm to the elderly was perceived by the administrator, and his intentions were benevolent. Unfortunately, his strong convictions prohibited curiosity about the degrees of relative benefit that might result from the alternative strategies of professional competitors.

As previously noted, the PWI administrator assiduously constructed a fiction of local autonomy for OACSP. When he recruited funds, he presented himself as an objective spectator advancing the community's interests rather than his own. The prestige which PWI claimed for itself also gave the administrator a peer status with the city commissioner for the Department for Aging, who has considerable influence over AOA service funds.

On one occasion during the data collection period, the PWI administrator organized a city-wide conference on the elderly. He obtained the use of a plush downtown auditorium, invited hundreds of professionals to attend, and hired a nationally celebrated aging specialist to speak. The administrator opened the conference ceremonies by presenting a plaque to his "close friend" (the commissioner) in honor of her long service to the elderly. The classical interlocking public-private relationship was dramatically portrayed.

The PWI administrator tightly controlled all hierarchical exchanges of information. He was the sole link between the program staff and PWI and between staff and the funding agents in public office. Only the most laudatory statements were allowed to surface, and no one asked any probing questions. The city government official from the Department of Aging nominally charged with monitoring the program admitted to leaving that task entirely to the PWI administrator. The administrator had cultivated a reputation in PWI and city government as the "mastermind" of the program that "had done everything." While the city official may have been captivated by that reputation, his reluctance to monitor may also have been a tacit acknowledgment of the close liaison between his boss and the PWI administrator. The Institute's public announcements of program success were couched in research jargon in order to convey the impression of systematic documentation. For example, the program was said to be "cost-effective" and "proven cost-effective" although no cost or effectiveness study had been undertaken. Similarly, it was claimed that the health clinic "made exemplary improvements in the health of the elderly of the community." No measurement of anyone's health was ever made. Previously presented data suggest the service was of questionable quality, and at best it achieved a relocation of a very modest delivery capacity. The administrator would occasionally arrange for a group of PWI trustees to visit the OACSP offices, where the program and its clients could be displayed. The purpose of these orchestrated displays was to cultivate trustee support, not to expose the program to close scrutiny.

The Institute had a large income to devote to services. That money was used to absorb costs usually borne by a community program itself. By his estimate, the administrator controlled $100,000 per year in in-kind (accounting, public relations, pension, insurance) services provided by PWI. Private philanthropy has historically accepted government sponsorship of its programs as the ultimate success.[28] The administrator convinced the PWI board to purchase its success by supplying the cost-sharing portion of federal grants for OACSP. The administrator was also able to use PWI wealth to obtain additional federal grant money. In the first year of the program, and on the last day of the fiscal year, state officials on aging discovered an unspent $100,000. This money was offered to the PWI administrator for OACSP if he could raise the matching money the same day. A PWI commitment was obtained, and the community program doubled its budget. Obviously, few community programs could guarantee matching funds on an eight-hour notice. In effect, the administrator created a self-reinforcing spiral where private funds brought in public money which brought out more private funds.

The PWI funds were also used to conceal poor planning and to convert imminent failures into "successes." At one point the administrator required OACSP to submit a proposal to the Department of Transportation for the purchase of three vans. In two years of fund raising, the program struggled to raise, on its own, the required $4,000 matching money for equipment. At the time the contracts were to be signed, the local staff first prepared estimates of annual operational costs. The estimated $22,000 annually was obviously beyond the capacity of OACSP. The PWI administrator arranged a convenient solution: a paper charge of fifty cents per ride was assessed to each rider, and the payment was made by PWI to OACSP in the form of cash assistance for individuals. The Institute concealed its subsidy and fostered OACSP's autonomous image. Although the van program would certainly have failed without PWI providing the operating capital, OACSP claimed it to be one of its many successes.

The importance of PWI financing was most dramatically portrayed in securing OACSP's long-term survival. It was originally funded for three years. At the end of three years, the administrator was successful in obtaining a two-year extension from both PWI and AOA. In the fifth year, PWI had contributed $125,000 in matching money; at the end of the fifth year, PWI terminated its official sponsorship of the community program and OACSP supposedly became an independent agency. The following news release was issued by the PWI public relations office to the city press: "OACSP BECOMES MAJOR, INDEPENDENT INCORPORATED AGENCY. The establishment of a major new non-profit agency was hailed today by the Public Welfare Institute. OACSP, which had been sponsored by PWI . . . has now become an independent incorporated agency which is serving 20,000 senior citizens a month. 'It is unusual that a demonstration project achieves permanence,' said the president of PWI. 'The fact that OACSP has made the transition . . . represents a tremendous achievement on the part of the . . . community, and is a landmark in PWI's history.' "

How was this transition to local autonomy accomplished? First, the administrator secured permanent AOA financing for the program. Second, PWI *sponsorship* was replaced by PWI *affiliation*. The terminated $125,000 from PWI for the "sponsored agency" was replaced with a $100,000 affiliation grant. A self-described "aggressive fund raising program" to achieve independence was engineered by PWI and conducted by OACSP. Only $8,000 was raised in the local community. The proclaimed transition did not take place. In fact, the community failed to economically support OACSP; the program survived because federal and PWI financial commitments were extended. Only the public image changed.

Conclusions

Survival and expansion were obtained at the expense of service quality and programmatic discipline that are essential in a demonstration. The services sponsored by agency representatives acting as members of the coordinating structure were inexpensive and simple to produce. The OACSP attracted a large number of relatively healthy older persons to free and entertaining services. Furthermore, it demonstrated that agencies will voluntarily participate in a coordinating structure when few burdens are imposed, when inactive resources may be employed, and when public image is improved. Once local visibility was well established, the impression of massive impact was created through careful use of language and control of communication. The PWI administrator made extravagant claims of program success and appeared to offer supportive evidence using the language of research and evaluation. Program methods and objectives were articulated with such generality that they permitted any future activity and prohibited any empirical measurement of impact. At neither the federal nor city level was there any surveillance of public expenditures. Welfare entrepreneurialism is achieved through the politics of innovation when poorly defined programs, flimsy operational rationales, and products of questionable value are parlayed into the acquisition of new resources and expanded service control. Lack of a program definition, unclear logic, and inadequate management are not rare in social services,[29] and the utility of these "problems" for entrepreneurial practices should not go unnoticed.

Because the most powerful figure in the OACSP operation was outside the organizational chart, the program conveyed the impression of autonomy and independence. The location of the entrepreneurial administrator inside the PWI administration gave him unique access to substantial financial resources and political influence. The Institute's reputation and endowment was used to cultivate a personal following among public and private funding sources.

Although the program did not achieve the envisioned objectives, PWI did achieve the leadership position essential to its self-image. The administrator imaginatively combined money, rhetoric, and influence in a manner which other private welfare organizations would struggle to duplicate. The OACSP pattern was not consistent throughout the Institute. None of the other demonstration programs approached OACSP's level of public acclaim. It may be, however, that excellence in entrepreneurialism is the model for success which will wittingly or unwittingly guide future private-public sector relations in social welfare.

The conditions observed in this case study are at best undesirable from a social policy perspective. A strong case could be made that public money was misused. Some services did not even address, let alone achieve, the central purpose of maintaining elderly in the community. The significance of impact was seriously overestimated, and failures were routinely concealed. Although an independent policy analyst might be convinced by the data that public money was misused, it is unlikely that any of the principal actors in OACSP, PWI, or AOA officialdom would be similarly impressed. The OACSP frontline staff is genuinely convinced that anything they do for the aged in their community is an a priori good. There is no consideration of better or best services. The elderly who participate find the services attractive. The PWI trustees want to believe that the programs they support are successful, but their information is highly filtered by administrative staff and they do not make substantial personal commitments to close program scrutiny. Other PWI administrators are unwilling to subject OACSP to criticism which might apply equally to their own programs. Public officials are reluctant to admit that money has not been well spent or that they have been remiss in their responsibilities to monitor spending. The only potentially dissatisfied party is the seriously disabled elderly to whom the program rhetoric was chiefly addressed, but they were never participants. Therefore, there is no responsive audience for skeptical policy conclusions. The disinterested observer is likely to be without influence and the influential observer is unlikely to be objective.

When there is no independent but authoritative audience to hear uncensored program evaluations, then the increasing clamor for "accountability" in social welfare may inadvertently further entrepreneurial opportunities. Funding sources frequently require providers to evaluate their own programs. The production of supposedly scientific evidence through self-evaluation can create misplaced confidence in the integrity of the findings. It is a mistake to think that self-evaluation findings are reliable, accurate, and objective. The inherent risk is that proclaimed accountability will become a persuasive public relations gimmick, and no more. Martin Rein and Sheldon White have written that the ". . . federal administration tried to use research and evaluation as a way of wresting control from local voluntary agencies that pre-empted the social welfare field"[30] in the early days of the Poverty Program. It may be that the voluntary sector has responded to this historical threat by learning to play the innovation/evaluation game to its own advantage.

The most serious obstacles to more credible innovation and evaluation efforts will be administrative and political, not methodological. A search for administrative changes will inevitably raise questions about the control of social programming. Greater autonomy and authority for program evaluators may be a necessary check on the entrepreneurial potential inherent in the politics of innovation.

Notes

1. Alan Towbin, "Organizational Duplicity and Professional Ethics: A Tale of Two Settings," *The Helping Professions in the World of Action* (Lexington, Mass.: Lexington Books, 1973).

2. Carl Milofsky, *Special Education: A Sociological Study of California Programs* (New York: Praeger Publishers, 1976).

3. Dwight Frankfather, *The Aged in the Community: Managing Senility and Deviance* (New York: Praeger Publishers, 1977).

4. Jeffrey Manditch Prottas, *People Processing* (Lexington, Mass.: Lexington Books, 1979).

5. Esther Stanton, *Clients Come Last: Volunteers and Welfare Organizations* (Beverly Hills, Calif.: Sage Publications, 1970).

6. Jacqueline Wiseman, *Stations of the Lost: The Treatment of Skid Row Alcoholics* (Englewood Cliffs, N.J.: Prentice-Hall, Inc., 1970), pp. 269–90.

7. Twenty-one staff members in PWI and OACSP were interviewed at least once. The OACSP director and two administrators were interviewed five times. Twelve community professionals representing local public agencies (Department of Human Services, Social Security Administration), three hospitals and one neighborhood health clinic, and three private social agencies were interviewed at least once. Each of these and an additional thirty-five professionals were repeatedly observed in the committees and task forces which comprised the coordinating mechanisms of OACSP. Approximately forty such meetings were observed. As a result the most important staff and other professional participants were observed or interviewed on forty to fifty separate occasions.

8. William Goode and Paul Hatt, *Methods in Social Research* (New York: McGraw-Hill Book Co., 1950), pp. 313–40.

9. The names of the principal organizations and actors have been changed. Not all the programs at PWI were as entrepreneurial as OACSP. The tactics of the OACSP team were not endorsed by all of the staff, or even the general director. Although PWI continues to fund OACSP, there have been significant personnel changes at PWI. Fictitious names are used as a precaution against the overgeneralization of these findings to all of PWI and its present staff.

10. James Douglas and Aaron Wildavsky, "The Knowledgeable Foundation in the Era of Big Government or If Foundations Are Supposed to Do What Government Doesn't, What's Left?" in *The Future and the Past: Essay on Programs* (New York: Russell Sage Foundation, 1977), pp. 19–54.

11. The voluntary sector's preoccupation with appearance and prestige is described in great detail in Stanton and in Gertrude S. Goldberg, "New Directions for the Communi-

ty Service Society of New York: A Study of Organizational Change," *Social Service Review* 54, no. 2 (June 1980): 184–201.

12. Waldemar A. Nielsen, *The Big Foundations* (New York: Columbia University Press, 1972).

13. Stanton, pp. 15–45.

14. Goldberg, pp. 184–219.

15. Bertram Beck, "Settlements in the United States—Past and Future," *Social Work* 4 (July 1976): 268–73.

16. Robert Hudson, "Rational Planning and Organizational Perspectives: Prospects for Area Planning in Aging," *Annals* 415 (September 1974): 41–54.

17. Ibid.

18. Jane Kronick, Felice Perlmutter, and Burton Gummer, "The APWA Model for a Social Service Delivery System," *Public Welfare* 31 (Fall 1973): 47–53; James Thompson, *Organizations in Action* (New York: McGraw-Hill Book Co., 1967).

19. Robert Morris et al., "Social Service Delivery Systems: Attempts to Alter Local Patterns," mimeographed (Waltham, Mass.: Brandeis University, 1975).

20. Neil Gilbert, "Assessing Service Delivery Methods," *Welfare in Review* 10 (May/June 1972): 25–33; Michael March, "The Neighborhood Concept," *Public Welfare* 31 (April 1968): 97–111.

21. Alfred Kahn, "Service Delivery at the Neighborhood Level: Experience, Theory, and Fad," *Social Service Review* 50 (March 1976): 23–36; Stuart Kirk and James Greeley, "Denying or Delivering Services," *Social Work* 4 (July 1974): 439–47.

22. Kahn, pp. 23–36.

23. Carroll Estes, "Community Planning for the Elderly: A Study in Goal Displacement," *Journal of Gerontology* 6 (December 1974): 684–91.

24. Theodore Marmor and Elizabeth Kutza, "Analysis of Federal Regulations Related to Aging: Legislative Barriers to Coordination Under Title III," mimeographed (Chicago: University of Chicago, School of Social Service Administration, 1975).

25. Jeffrey Pressman and Aaron Wildavsky, *Implementation* (Berkeley: University of California Press, 1973).

26. Frankfather, pp. 36–38; Alice Wooster et al., *Seniors Community Outreach Program*, NTIS publication no. 242874 (Washington, D.C.: National Technical Information Service, 1972).

27. Stephen M. Davidson, "Planning and Coordinating Services in a Multi-organizational Context," *Social Service Review* 50 (March 1976): 117–34.

28. Douglas and Wildavsky, pp. 19–54.

29. Pamela Horst et al., "Program Management and the Federal Administration," *Public Administration Review* 34 (July 1974): 300–308.

30. Martin Rein and Sheldon White, "Policy Research: Belief and Doubt," *Policy Analysis* 3 (Spring 1977): 239–72.

40

Success in Whose Terms?
Evaluations of a Cooperative Farm

Miriam J. Wells

A PIVOTAL PROBLEM IN evaluation research is
that of setting criteria for assessment that reflect the full
range of program consequences. Most often evaluative criteria
are established by those outside the target population: funding
agencies, hired evaluators, program staff. Due to the biases of
and political constraints on these parties, evaluation is
customarily accomplished through the isolation of precise and
measurable goals that can provide an index to program success
(Deutscher 1977; Jones and Borgatta 1972:41; Rossi and
Williams 1972).

Scholars of evaluation are becoming increasingly aware,
however, that externally imposed standards of this sort may
limit understanding of the actual consequences of social programs. Increasing, although as yet still limited, attention is being directed to finding alternative ways to think about evaluation. One approach has been to shift the emphasis from after-
the-fact judgments of output in terms of predetermined goals,
to ongoing analysis of the processes of social change
(Allerhand 1971; Chommie and Hudson 1974; Deutscher
1973; Fry 1973; Weiss 1973). Another approach has been to increase attention to qualitative measures of performance and to
the unintended and unanticipated consequences of social programs (Brenner et al. 1978; Patton 1978; Cook and Reichardt
1979; Deutscher 1977; Hyman and Wright 1967). And a third
strategy has been to involve staff, clients, evaluators, and even
funding sources in the cooperative negotiation of reasonable
goals and methods of evaluation (Cain and Hollister 1972;
Deutscher 1977; Glennan 1972; Harper and Babigian 1971;
Weiss 1971). These innovations are particularly significant in
light of recent evidence (see Figlio 1975; Prager and Tanaka
1980) that the intended beneficiaries of social programs may
have quite different conceptions of goals, accomplishments,
and shortcomings than do evaluators and staff.

This article aims to demonstrate the importance of
qualitative indicators and multiple goals to assessors of program performance. It employs the case study of a publicly
sponsored cooperative farm to show that the goals of sponsoring agencies may mask and undervalue the accomplishments

of such projects as seen through the eyes of participants.
Moreover, these latter benefits themselves may reduce progress in areas of most import to sponsors.

The cooperative studied here and the standards applied to its
evaluation must be understood in light of the sociopolitical
context within which it originated. Since the mid-1960s, the
convergence of minority civil rights movements and the federal
War on Poverty has renewed governmental interest in agricultural cooperatives. Local-level agencies, most recently in the
form of community development corporations (Blaustein
1975; Blaustein and Faux 1972), have been mandated to channel federal funds to economic development projects such as
cooperatives. By the mid-1970s, these cooperatives were
estimated to number several thousand, with membership in ex-
cess of two million (Williams 1974:913; Finney 1975:29).
Although most publicly sponsored cooperatives were initiated
in the South in the 1960s (Williams and Biser 1972:2), a new
wave of cooperative organizing has gathered force since 1970.
During the 1970s, as many as 50 cooperative farms were
organized in California by Mexican-Americans whose sense of
the legitimacy of their claims on public resources had been
heightened by farm labor organizing. Most of the cooperatives
dissolved after the first years because of inadequate capitaliza-
tion, lack of technical assistance, insufficient scale of operation, and internal organizational problems (Wells in press).
Although only a handful of the original cooperatives remain,
organizing is again on the increase, and an estimated 15 farmworker cooperatives are now in operation in the state.

Federal sponsors' goals for these cooperatives have changed
since supportive policy was first enacted. During the mid- to
late 1960s, cooperatives were viewed as a means of minority
empowerment, in line with the prevailing rationale behind
poverty programs at that time (Kravitz 1969:55-59; Blaustein
and Faux 1972:114; Sundquist 1969:248; Moynihan 1970:81).
By the late 1960s, however, governmental concern with empowerment and broad social development had subsided and
been replaced by a more narrow emphasis on minority en-
trepreneurship (Moynihan 1970:128-66; National Advisory
Council 1973:4; Zurcher 1970:375-83). As a consequence,
public sponsors and private agencies providing supporting
funds have tended to evaluate the farmworker cooperatives as
they would a standard business enterprise, that is, in terms of
their attainment of levels of profit and economic self-
sufficiency comparable to those in the private sector. Not only
have sponsors' criteria of assessment been primarily economic,
but they have identified cooperative success with membership
continuity. From these points of view, the cooperative studied
here has had a disappointing record. It has generated income

Miriam J. Wells is Assistant Professor of Anthropology,
Department of Applied Behavioral Sciences and the
Agricultural Experiment Station, University of California,
Davis. The research project on agricultural cooperatives on
which this article is based has been funded from 1976 to 1981
by the College of Agricultural and Environmental Sciences
and the Agricultural Experiment Station of the University of
California, Davis.

Reproduced by permission of the Society for Applied Anthropology from *Human Organization*
40(3): 239-246, 1981.

at rates lower than those in private industry, and it has had considerable turnover in membership.

Cooperative members, on the other hand, have tended to take a broader view of cooperative accomplishments, emphasizing its impact on the quality of their social, political, and economic life. Moreover, aware of the improvement in their own circumstances, members have tended to evaluate the cooperative in relative terms. While concerned with absolute economic success and discouraged by the recent downturn in the profitability of their enterprise, members compare their experience in the cooperative favorably with their former situations as farmworkers and sharecroppers. The very fact that participants now view their lives as having potential for improvement has enhanced their sense of optimism and well-being.

The following discussion will describe the cooperative study and consider the cooperative's accomplishments through members' eyes in providing access to increased income, in permitting control over the work environment, and in enhancing connection to critical social groupings. It will then examine sponsors' goals and the ongoing tension between participants' and sponsors' evaluative frameworks.

The Cooperative Study

Cooperativa Central, one of the largest and most successful of the Mexican American cooperatives, began operation in 1973 with the purchase of an 88 ha strawberry ranch in the fertile Salinas Valley. The purchase was financed by a large loan from the Migrant Division of the Office of Economic Opportunity, by a matching loan from Wells Fargo Bank of San Francisco, and by a guarantee of the bank loan by a national minority business guarantor.[1] Membership was expanded from the core group of farmworker organizers by asking the sharecroppers of the purchased ranch to join. Since that time Central has become one of the major producers of strawberries in the region.

The present analysis is based primarily on in-depth interviewing and participant-observation within Cooperativa Central from 1976 to 1980.[2] In the summer of 1977, open-ended interviews concerning the impact of the cooperative on member well-being were conducted with 31 of the then 52 members of Cooperativa Central.[3] Two questions were especially important to the present discussion: (1) members were asked to spontaneously indicate and rank their most important reasons for joining and staying in the cooperative; and (2) they were asked to describe at length the aspects of the cooperative organization that contributed to their increased or diminished life satisfaction. This response usually took a comparative form: members contrasted their well-being within the cooperative with their previous situations as farm laborers and sharecroppers.

Although the randomly selected sample for these interviews represents over half the cooperative's membership, its absolute size is small, limiting the statistical inferences that may be drawn from the data. I would argue, however, that the general tendencies as well as the details of particular responses are indicative of the orientation of members within and the benefits offered by such enterprises.

Members' Economic Evaluations: Access to Increased Income

While funding sources have tended to evaluate Central as an end-product of economic development, members view the cooperative as part of a continuum, as a means to their social, political, and economic empowerment. A first dimension of their economic evaluations centers around the cooperative's impact on economic mobility. All members mention the benefit of higher income earned within the cooperative. Some also emphasize the options it opens for occupational mobility outside the cooperative.

Those who believe firmly in the ideal of group farming and in the reality of Cooperativa Central focus their economic evaluations on the higher incomes and the greater degree of economic security they have enjoyed since joining the cooperative. Of the 31 members interviewed, 12 were former farmworkers, 12 sharecroppers, 2 farm foremen, and 5 miscellaneous (construction workers, factory workers, and truck drivers). They indicated the following average estimated family incomes before joining the cooperative: $6,299 for farmworkers, $7,875 for sharecroppers, $9,500 for foremen, and $6,900 for other occupations. Interestingly, sharecroppers did not necessarily make more than farm laborers. Although three sharecroppers (9.7% of the total respondents) made between $12,000 and $16,000, as opposed to only one farmworker (3.6%), the same number of farmworkers as sharecroppers (4 or 13%) made $4,999 or less in the year before joining the cooperative. As a consequence of this range in prior incomes, not all members found the initial years of the enterprise equally satisfying. When the cooperative harvested its first crop in the summer of 1973, it returned an average of $6,397 to each member: an advance for some but a step backwards for others. By 1976, however, average payments to members excluding hired labor costs had grown to $25,300, although they dropped to about $16,000 in 1977 and ranged between $14,000 to $15,000 in 1978 and 1979.[4] These income levels were, on the whole, clearly higher than the previous incomes of member families.[5]

As an illustration of this greater influence, 90.3% of the sample had bought a new (to them) car since joining the cooperative, and almost half (45.1%) owned or were buying their own homes. While 22 or 71% reported that they had had no savings before joining the cooperative, 13 or 41.9% had been able to save since they joined.[6] Although almost 63% of the sample had had to resort to food stamps or general welfare assistance in the years before joining, none had done so subsequently. Since unemployment compensation was not available to farmworkers until 1975, members had not previously tapped such funds. However, the current heavy utilization of unemployment compensation by farm laborers between the months of November and March indicates that the obviation of such support is another measure of the economic impact of the cooperative.

Aside from its relative success in raising incomes, however, some participants are also concerned with the cooperative's impact on their future economic options. These members regard Central not as a permanent occupational niche, but as a stepping-stone to other, more desirable work. Such members generally report that they entered the cooperative for instrumental purposes or that they gradually became dissatisfied with the way Central was fulfilling its ideological promise. Membership in Central has been valuable to those who have started individual farms, have organized another cooperative with members and operating principles more to their liking, and who aspire to employment in public agencies. The cooperative facilitates movement into such occupations first by enabling members to accumulate the economic resources to support mobility: for example, the 2 members who started small farms on their own and the 12 members who left Central to form a new cooperative would have been unable to pursue such options without their savings from the cooperative. Second, Central has enabled members to establish relationships with individuals who can facilitate the transition to desired occupations. For example, the new cooperative and independent farmers were aided invaluably by their previous acquaintance with realtors, bankers, government officials, and farm advisors. Aspiring public employees made valuable contacts with potential state and federal level employers. Third, members are able to learn in the cooperative skills that are useful in their occupations-to-be. These include farm production, planning, business management, public speaking, and leadership skills.

Although Central has raised members' incomes and improved their potential for further economic mobility, this was not their sole goal when they joined the cooperative, nor does it fully account for their increased sense of well-being since joining. Joining the cooperative was a choice for members, not an entirely constrained course of action. The overwhelming majority of the sample questioned (28 or 90.3%) had other work options as sharecroppers or farm laborers when they joined. Many expected that these other positions would give them equal or greater income; only two were unemployed. Cooperative farms were a new concept in California and had not yet demonstrated their potential as a reliable form of enterprise. Many of those who joined were not confident of greater affluence in the cooperative. Although to some extent their joining indicated a willingness to gamble, this was not the whole story. For those who had a relatively comfortable standard of living before joining, strictly economic motives were even less persuasive.

Direct questioning of the Central sample indicates that the social and political benefits of the cooperative have been more important than has higher income in members' evaluations of increased well-being. Only 19.4% (6) of the sample cited higher income as the most important reason for joining and remaining in the cooperative. By contrast, 51.6% (16) cited greater independence and more control over working conditions as the major benefits of cooperative membership. In addition, 29.1% (9) cited more influence over improved relationships with their family and community as the major advantages of membership.

Members' Economic Evaluation: Control of the Work Environment

In their appreciation of increased workplace control, members emphasize farm ownership, the ability to set organizational policy and structure, increased control over the conditions of employment, and the power to shape the work process itself. The interviews revealed that, contrary to contemporary assumptions as to the unimportance of ownership to modern workers,[7] the potential for land ownership was one of the major attractions of Cooperativa Central. Members attribute this

value to the rural Mexican background of most, to the ideals of the Mexican Agrarian Reform, to the American dream of a family farm, and to the importance of land ownership in the status system of the surrounding agricultural community. They approve the elimination of what they regard as the employer "middleman," and they appreciate the ability to direct the use of common funds to such projects as emergency loans to members, social gatherings, and perhaps a day-care center.

The opportunity to set general organizational policy and structure is another aspect of control over the workplace that members value. Most importantly, this has meant the chance to determine the division of labor within the enterprise. In contrast to the hierarchical authority structures of their former work settings, Cooperativa Central has an ideally egalitarian organizational ideology and division of labor.[8] Policy decisions are reserved to the membership on the basis on one member one vote, and members perform, or are trained to perform, as many of the tasks in the cooperative as possible. While there are pressures toward increasing hierarchy, the cooperative has been remarkably successful in circulating access to positions of authority.

Greater influence over the conditions of employment is also cited frequently as a source of satisfaction. Job security, working conditions, and adequate income levels had been continuing uncertainties for sharecroppers, and even more for farm laborers. Although climate and market fluctuations affect the economic stability of Central as they do that of any farm, security of employment and good working conditions are not contingent on the whims and conflicting economic self-interest of an employer.

It is greater control over the immediate work process that draws the most emphatic appreciation from members. In this area they mention the ability to determine the pace and timing of work, to be free from external work pressure, to have liberty of physical movement, and to decide on the quality and quantity of production. Since members determine the division of labor, and since all cultural and harvest tasks in strawberry production are customarily performed by hand, members have considerable flexibility in shaping the work process. They are vehement in their denunciations of the foremen who constantly "pushed" them for higher production in their former jobs, a condition they describe as slavery. The absence of overseers is not reflected in a lax attitude toward work: quite the contrary. Members can be seen in the fields from dawn to dark, and are active in their efforts to ferret out information that will improve their performance as growers. Despite the demanding nature of work in the cooperative, daily work rhythms provide numerous opportunities for rich social interchange. From time to time small groups of members can be seen pausing for refreshments, consulting as to the causes of weak plants, sharing news of family happenings, or formulating strategy about a funding proposal to the state.

Members' Social Evaluation: Sociopolitical Linkage

At least as important as its economic accomplishments has been the impact of the cooperative on members' ability to preserve and develop satisfying relationships with their families, with an occupational community of cooperative farmers, and with the larger society and polity.

Members emphasize that Cooperativa Central was started specifically as a "business for families" and as a "community that respects the family." They regarded migrant labor as particularly damaging to the family in that it forced separation of children from their parents, encouraged delinquency among untended teenagers, and disrupted children's schooling. The cooperative not only permits year-round stability of residence, but it enables parents to play an active role in guiding their children's development in accord with Mexican family norms. Central chose to farm strawberries in part because the crop permits families to work together, a consequence of perceived social as well as economic value.' The familial group, supplemented at peak harvest by hired workers who are usually friends or relatives, is the customary work team. Members relate that the cooperative permits them to teach their children "how to work" and "prevents them from becoming bums." They appreciate the lull in strawberry production between November and February that enables them to visit relatives in Mexico. They especially value the fact that girls and women can work in the fields without being humiliated by obscene language or sexual overtures. Having suffered considerable disregard in their earlier lives and prizing personal and familial honor, members treasure the present atmosphere of respect and consideration.

In addition, members regard their children's improved life options as a major benefit of the cooperative. Almost all parents insist that their children attend school and watch their progress closely. They report that their educational and vocational aspirations for their children have risen substantially since joining the cooperative. When asked to spontaneously indicate the educational levels they hoped their children would attain, 18 or 58.1% of the sample said they wanted their sons to go to college and 12 or 38.7% wanted their daughters to. Similarly, 19 or 58.9% hoped that their sons would become professionals, and 7 or 22.6% hoped their daughters would become secretaries.[10]

On a larger scale, members mention their enhanced sense of involvement and potency within the occupational community of cooperative farmers. They identify job competition, transience, and the regulation of social interaction by overseers and machines as factors that limited their solidarity as farmworkers in the past. The cooperative represents an end to that isolation. Despite some internal strife, members voice a common belief in worker control and love of the land. The cooperative is a center of identification and belonging, as well as a place of work. Group cohesion is reinforced by informal breaks and planned leisure activities, and the chance to influence procedures and policies increases members' commitment to the farm. They believe that working together in the cooperative has made them more supportive of one another, as illustrated by members weeding the parcel of one farmer who was tending a sick relative, and donating money to another family for its son's funeral expenses.

The cooperative serves as a vehicle within which members may be able to provide for themselves many of the services they previously lacked or had to seek from public agencies. Three of these services are child care, health insurance, and a credit union. Central has investigated the possibility of establishing them within the cooperative, but the costs and regulations involved have prevented their initiation to date.

The members of Central also feel greater connection with the broader community of actual and aspiring Mexican-American cooperative farmers in California. Since they believe strongly in the role of cooperatives as vehicles of progress for Mexicans, a good portion of their time is spent in giving advice to groups interested in starting a cooperative. Most of the members participated in the co-op to co-op training program that operated out of Central between 1976 and 1979, traveling to other cooperatives to provide technical and managerial advice, and encouraging those groups to come to Central to see a successful cooperative in action.

The final sociopolitical consequence of membership has been members' increased sense of participation in the broader political process. Land ownership and longevity have raised members' self-esteem and are changing members' status in the surrounding community. Central's members believe that their farm and others like it have contributed to the nation's progress. They are proud of the fact that, unlike many persons who have been farm laborers most of their lives, they no longer need welfare aid and are stable, taxpaying citizens. Increased political involvement has been one consequence of this improved self-regard. As farmworkers and sharecroppers, members felt marginal to the political process. Migrant workers did not stay in an area long enough to know or be committed to local issues. None of the members interviewed knew their local or state representatives before joining the cooperative, and few were registered voters.

The cooperative, however, has given members valuable firsthand experience with political actors and institutions. They have met a variety of public officials in their petitions for governmental funding, have traveled to the state and national capitols to lobby for their interests, have participated in a state policy task force on the problems of small farmers and cooperatives, and have gained representation on the state Strawberry Advisory Board, the main body for industry self-governance. Members are keenly interested in improving the competitive position of Mexican-Americans in the public arena and see cooperatives as a means to that end.

From the members' points of view, then, Central has been a substantial success. Unfortunately, however, this assessment has not been shared by its sponsors.

Sponsors' Evaluations: Business Performance and Membership Continuity

Central's sponsors have tended to be unaware of or less concerned with the sociopolitical benefits that are so important to members. Although some sponsors have sought ways of assessing the social impacts of the enterprise, the general focus within the broader funding hierarchy has been on business performance. From this point of view, Central's record has not been outstanding.[11]

While Central has improved members' standards of living in relative terms, in absolute terms the enterprise has not achieved the self-reliance and profitability that would enable it to compete in the private sector. Although Central has demonstrated its independence by obtaining loans from private banks for operating expenses and land purchase, it continues to rely on various forms of government and private subsidies to support production and augment members' incomes. Central still holds the original loan from the O.E.O. and has recently received an additional ten-year loan from the Campaign for Human Development.[12] Members also sporadically receive stipends for various forms of training.

In addition, the cooperative's production has continued to lag behind that of other growers in the industry. Estimates for Central and other cooperatives in the area set their average yields at 1,000 to 1,280 crates per ha (Ekland 1980:3), in contrast to the 1,800 to 2,000 crates per ha that a central coast county farm advisor sets as the "threshold" for successful strawberry production in the region. This advisor also notes that the top three growers on the central coast harvested 3,320 crates per ha in the low-production 1979 season.[13] A more telling summary of the cooperative's production performance may be derived by comparing its dollar and kilogram per hectare yields in recent years with the statewide averages (Table 1). As the table indicates, while the quantity of berries produced has been below average for two out of the three years, their quality, as reflected in larger freezer sales and consequently lower market prices, has consistently been below the statewide average. In short, although more successful than most cooperatives in the state and offering a decided improvement in living standards from the individual members' points of view, Central has yet to achieve the economic goals set for it by sponsors.

Ironically, some of the major benefits that members reap from the cooperative have had the side-effect of reducing its actual and perceived success as a business enterprise. The apparent import of one set of such consequences is primarily a result of sponsors' narrow focus on economic performance. The other category of deleterious effects poses more serious economic costs and is less clearly counter-balanced by attendant advantages.

The impact of high turnover falls within the first category. While members appreciate Central's ability to open new economic options, sponsors have viewed the resultant high turnover as a sign of organizational instability. Although some of the turnover does result from internal factionalism, low production rates, or other member dissatisfactions, a great deal of it is due to the fact that members use the enterprise as a means of economic mobility. Sponsors are generally unaware of the motivations behind turnover, and see their goal of establishing a business for a stable group of cooperative entrepreneurs as poorly served. They are concerned about the additional expenditures of time, energy, and capital that bookkeeping and new member training require.

The members' long-term interest in building a social and political community also at times conflicts with the cooperative's short-term economic interests. The social goals of Central place special demands on collective resources in terms of expenditures for social gatherings and social services. Advising other cooperatives, organizing a statewide confederation of cooperatives, showing visiting government officials around the farm, and representing their interests in state and national arenas sometimes takes time away from crucial farm tasks. Not all such activity can be scheduled around production demands. In addition, the fact that the cooperative is perceived by many members to be morally responsible to a broader political community of cooperatives raises occasional conflicts between using resources for Central's own members, or passing them on to cooperatives that lack the necessary leverage to obtain inputs by themselves. To date, however, the economic costs of these social and political functions of the cooperative have been minimal and have been largely outweighed by their concomitant benefits.

Another category of tensions between the social goals of members and the economic profitability of the enterprise remains, however, and it is one whose elements pose significant problems for the viability of the farm. Within this category fall the conflicts between the members' goal of independence and their need for technical assistance, between the ideal of workplace democracy and the necessity of functional differentiation in jobs, and between the belief in mutual support and the need to ensure a high and substantially equal rate of contribution to the enterprise.

First, the salience to members of the ideal of independence as a founding principle of the cooperative reduces their willingness to follow the advice of hired production managers and of farm advisors and university pomologists. Since forced obedience to directives in their former occupations symbolized their lower status, members often regard production advice as the legitimate subject of a power struggle between themselves and the experts. Rather than treating this information as technical assistance that could improve their business returns, members often see it as evidence that the expert is trying to control them. This response not only arises from members' past histories of subordination but is supported by the present behavior of some experts and by the negative stereotyping of Mexican-Americans in the region. As a consequence of their anticipation of attempted domination, members often bargain with production information, adopting a course of action somewhere between what the expert advises and what they as individuals affirm. Since many procedures in strawberry farming are calculated quite precisely to produce the best possible crop, and since members are still too new as strawberry growers to profitably experiment with the less rigid procedures, this approach tends to lower levels of production.

Second, Central also experiences persisting tension between

TABLE 1. COMPARISON OF COOPERATIVE AND STATE AVERAGE PRODUCTION RECORDS, 1977-1979

	1977		1978		1979	
	Co-op	State	Co-op	State	Co-op	State
Kg per hectare	40,305	50,320	44,773	43,580	32,383	44,928
$ per hectare	25,243.89	35,681.79	26,224.23	27,535.22	23,079.92	35,468.98
Fresh	44%	65.7%	62%	74.1%	43%	68.5%
Freezer sales	56%	34.3%	38%	25.9%	57%	31.5%

Sources: (1) Processing Strawberry Advisory Board, *Manager's Annual Reports,* January 1980, Charts 2 and 3. (2) Federal-State Market New Service, *Marketing California Strawberries-1978,* Tables 10, 16. (3) Phone call to Crop Reporting Board for 1979 prices. (4) Cooperative records.

the ideal of workplace democracy and the practical need for managerial and productive efficiency. The time-consuming nature of collective decision making sometimes delays crucial production decisions. In addition, the importance to members of egalitarianism and independence creates opposition to the specialized positions necessary for efficient management. The production manager, business manager, and bookkeeper are the targets of considerable criticism. As a consequence, their tenures in office are often so short as to undermine the continuity of their function. Moreover, members' desire for equal access to all positions does not accord with their current unequal possession of the skills necessary to perform the duties of the office. Expertise in production, marketing, organizational mechanics, and bookkeeping is unevenly distributed or, in some matters, absent within the membership. The process of acquiring the necessary skills has involved errors in judgment and periods of diminished efficiency.

Third, the belief in mutual support and the primacy of bonds of friendship and kinship have hampered the development of formal or informal mechanisms for ensuring farm productivity. Members have sometimes neglected their crops while they have gone to the aid of needy relatives in the United States or Mexico. Since this sort of concern is approved by the members, they are unwilling to censure the behavior. The fact that the cooperative is viewed as a mutually supportive community also makes it difficult for members to reprimand or expel those who do not carry their share of the load. The quality and quantity of member production is in fact quite variable, placing unequal burdens on members in sustaining the cooperative and consistently diminishing the profit levels of the whole. In recent years this situation has caused some of the better producers to leave the cooperative.

In sum, although members identify significant improvements in the conditions of their lives and work, the economic and organizational performance of Cooperativa Central has encouraged a negative assessment of its present and likely future viability as a vehicle of economic development. This contradictory record suggests several directions for future evaluation and assistance.

The Cooperative as End Versus the Cooperative as Means

The sharp disparity between participants' and sponsors' evaluations of a publicly sponsored cooperative farm suggests the wisdom of more extensive examination of the goals and consequences of antipoverty programs. The statements of members as to what they have gained from Central indicate that the cooperative has not only significantly improved their economic well-being but has also accomplished some of the broader goals of citizen empowerment important at the outset of the War on Poverty. Central has raised the incomes of members and has provided them with some of the tools for further economic advancement. By consolidating their relations with other Mexican-American cooperative members and providing a means of access to political institutions, the cooperative has in a very real way improved members' capacity for civic participation. As the environment in which members spend most of their waking hours, the cooperative has enabled them to conduct their lives in accord with deeply held values of

familial solidarity, mutual support for friends and relatives, close parental guidance of children, and respect for the individual.

In a broader sense, the cooperative has also enabled members to realize in their lives a value that lies at the heart of the American normative system: that of individual progress and opportunity. As scholars of American society have pointed out (see Rainwater 1969), belief in the possibility of upward mobility and self-realization is a distinctive and dominant feature of American culture. In fact, however, achievement of this goal has been confined almost exclusively to those of middle-class status and above: to that sector of the population whose economic resources sufficiently exceed the bare minimum to make training for further mobility possible, and whose occupational starting points permit advancement (Myrdal 1969).

As indicated by the testimonies of the members of Central, exclusion from the possibility of upward mobility and self-direction is one of the most socially and personally damaging aspects of poverty. In line with the findings of some other investigations of impoverished populations (Liebow 1967; Rainwater 1969), the members of Central attribute much of their prior sense of alienation from the larger society and polity, their previous belief in the futility of education, and their problems with delinquency among their children to their lack of control over their own lives. In this sense, the cooperative addresses the issue of poverty not simply as the lack of income but more broadly as the lack of potency and choice. It provides an environment that enhances members' control over their own destinies and enables them to participate in the social and political life of the community.

In light of the fact that the lack of choice and power results in attitudes and behavior that the larger society finds socially and economically costly, and for which a variety of remedial social services has been established, the rationale for supporting such an overarching antipoverty mechanism is especially compelling. Since the need for services such as special education programs for migrant and minority children, adult literacy classes, general assistance, food stamps, public health clinics, job training programs, and unemployment insurance stems from the character of an entire living environment, not from the absence of a single resource, it makes sense to adopt remedial mechanisms that address themselves to an integrated context. The cooperative not only improves income levels but it does so in a way that does not create dependency, that preserves the work ethic, and that promotes independence.

The positive evaluation that emerges from this analysis of member perspectives indicates the danger of assessing performance solely in terms of the goals set by external observers. In this case the sponsors' standards of business performance neglected more qualitative benefits of import to participants and worthy of attention by promoters of social change. The focus on sponsors' goals also obscured an important source of information as to why those goals were not being met: that is, the additional and sometimes conflicting agendas of program participants.

It is clear that a more collaborative approach to evaluation, and a broad analysis of social change processes rather than a measurement of output in terms of predetermined standards, would have helped disclose the full array of program intentions and consequences in this situation. Economic self-sufficiency will continue to be of central interest to sponsors, given the current political climate and real limitations on public resources. As a result, collaboration between cooperatives and their evaluators will need to address the persistent barriers to profitability that arise from the multiple functions such cooperatives serve. Although the negative import of some of these obstacles disappears when their long-term economic, social, and political benefits are acknowledged, major problem areas remain. Some of these include providing cooperatives with technical advice in a way that acknowledges members' desire for respect and self-direction, reducing costly turnover in managerial personnel without undermining the cooperative goal of an egalitarian division of labor, and ensuring that collective interests are protected while maintaining a sensitivity to individual needs and social commitments. Although some of these conflicts may not be resolvable, their explicit recognition could promote a more informed assessment of adequate accomplishment and direct specific attention to diminishing undesirable outcomes.

Such an approach could increase the efficacy of and support for production cooperatives as an antipoverty mechanism. It would be overly simplistic to argue that cooperative development alone can deal with all the facets of rural poverty in America, or indeed address its causes. But cooperatives do have considerable promise in terms of generating self-esteem and individual initiative, and may in the long run prove to be more economical than more fragmented income transfers and social services.

NOTES

See Wells (in press) for a detailed discussion of the founding, internal organization, and relation with external agencies characteristic of these cooperatives.

[2] Findings have been reinforced and perspective provided by a survey of the location and structure of cooperative farms in California, as well as by numerous informal contacts with members of other cooperatives around the state. I have interviewed, spoken informally with, and participated in task forces and in conferences with a number of the public sponsors of these cooperatives.

[3] These interviews lasted from two to three hours each and were conducted alone with the interviewee in Spanish. Privacy and the assurance of anonymity reduced the possibility that responses would be shaped by fear of group censure.

[4] Payments to member families are the net amount after common expenses are deducted. Payments exclude, however, harvest- and cultivation-related costs which are borne by individual member families and are difficult to estimate. Families vary in the extent to which they hire outside labor. Since family labor is encouraged by cooperative ideology, and since observance of minimum wage levels and other labor guidelines varies, members are reluctant to state the amount paid for outside labor. In 1977, the cooperative estimated that the annual average cost of nonfamily labor for each member family was $2,500.

[5] The 1977-78 and 1978-79 seasons were difficult ones for the cooperative both because of the heavy debt load of newly purchased land and because bad weather and rising labor costs placed special strains on the still-developing productive skills of members. Members' responses to this experience indicate that while they do not judge the cooperative strictly in terms of the accomplishments of private farms, economic advancement is important to them. For some, the lower income levels have approached those of their earlier occupations; these members maintain a comparative framework in their evaluations of

the benefits of the cooperative, and they include the social and political consequences of membership in their decisions as to whether to remain or leave.

[6] Most interviewees were unwilling to reveal the amount of savings. I subsequently discovered that some who did cite an amount had not mentioned such forms of investment as land purchase. In short, I am confident of the fact of savings but unable to estimate the amount.

[7] See Wells (1981) for a more detailed discussion of the substance of these interviews and their significance for the study of workers' central life interests.

[8] These features are characteristic of cooperatives in general. See Rothschild-Whitt (1979) for a detailed discussion of the contrasts between collectivist and rational-bureaucratic organizations.

[9] Since members are self-employed, their children are not subject to minimum age legislation for child labor.

[10] Significantly, only 4 or 12.9% of those interviewed wanted their sons to succeed them as cooperative members.

[11] I do not argue that all individuals within public sponsoring agencies personally adhere to the perspective of business development. In fact, a number of them do sympathize with the broader vision of minority empowerment. However, as position holders in bureaucracies that are informed by the narrower set of goals, they are forced to justify their continued support of cooperatives in terms of quantitative measures and economic performance. A number of these individuals have sought qualitative information of the sort presented here in order to document a case for the more inclusive impacts of the cooperatives they sponsor. They have some hope that this information will enlighten the public and their governmental superiors about the accomplishments of such development projects. But they acknowledge that at this point in time they must bear the burden of establishing the legitimacy of this broader set of goals.

[12] The fact that the cooperative continues to seek loan guarantees from such federal and state agencies as Opportunity Funding Corporation and Cal Rural, which specialize in the support of minority businesses, should not be seen as evidence of distinctive dependency. Private farmers are subsidized to a comparable extent through such publicly assisted, noncommercial credit sources as Production Credit Association and Farmers' Home Administration. To date, the cooperative and others like it have been excluded from these credit sources which offer longer-term and lower-interest loans than do commercial banks. As a consequence, the cooperatives have had to turn to commercial banks for loans, most of which have required the security of a loan guarantee.

[13] Conversation with Santa Cruz County Farm Advisor Norman Welch, January 15, 1980, Davis, California.

REFERENCES CITED

Allerhand, Melvin E.
    1971 The Process Outcome Research Model: An Alternative to Evaluation Research. *In* The Organization, Management, and Tactics of Social Research. Richard O'Toole, ed. Pp. 131-51. Cambridge, Mass.: Schenkman.
Blaustein, Arthur I.
    1975 Economic Justice and Social Policy. Reporter. Pp. 9-20.
Blaustein, Arthur, and Geoffrey Faux
    1972 The Star-Spangled Hustle. New York: Doubleday.
Brenner, M. P. Marsh, and M. Brenner, eds.
    1978 The Social Context of Method. London: Croom Helm.
Cain, Glen G., and Robinson G. Hollister
    1972 The Methodology of Evaluating Social Action Programs. *In* Evaluating Social Programs: Theory, Practice, and Politics. Peter H. Rossi and Walter Williams, eds. Pp. 109-37. New York: Seminar Press.

Chommie, Peter W., and Joe Hudson
    1974 Evaluation of Outcome and Process. Social Work 19:682-87.
Cook, Thomas D., and Charles S. Reichardt
    1979 Qualitative and Quantitative Methods in Evaluation Research. Sage Research Progress Series in Evaluation, Vol. 1. Beverly Hills, California: Sage Publications.
Deutscher, Irwin
    1973 What We Say/What We Do: Sentiment and Acts. Glenview, Illinois: Scott, Foresman and Company.
    1977 Toward Avoiding the Goal Trap in Evaluation Research. In Readings in Evaluation Research. Francis Caro, ed. Pp. 221-38. New York: Russell Sage Foundation.
Ekland, Roy
    1980 Cooperative Production. Manuscript. Salinas, California: Confederación Agrícola.
Figlio, Robert
    1975 The Seriousness of Offense: An Evaluation by Offenders and Non-Offenders. Journal of Criminal Law and Criminology 66:2:189-200.
Finney, Henry C.
    1975 Problems of Local, Regional, and National Support for Rural Poor People's Cooperatives in the United States: Some Lessons from the "War on Poverty" Years, Reprint No. 142. Madison: University of Wisconsin, Institute for Research on Poverty.
Fry, Lincoln L.
    1973 Participant Observation and Program Evaluation. Journal of Health and Social Behavior 14:274-78.
Glennan, Thomas K.
    1972 Evaluating Federal Manpower Programs: Notes and Observations. In Evaluating Social Programs: Theory, Practice, and Politics. Peter Rossi and Walter Williams, eds. Pp. 187-220. New York: Seminar Press.
Harper, Dean, and Hartouton Babigian
    1971 Evaluation Research: The Consequences of Program Evaluation. Mental Hygiene 55:151-56.
Hyman, Herbert H., and Charles R. Wright
    1967 Evaluating Social Action Programs. In The Uses of Sociology. Paul F. Lazarsfeld, et al., eds. Pp. 741-82. New York: Basic Books.
Jones, Wyatt C., and Edgar F. Borgatta
    1972 Methodology of Evaluation. In Evaluation of Social Intervention. Edward J. Mullen, et al., eds. Pp. 39-54. San Francisco: Jossey-Bass.
Kravitz, Sanford
    1969 The Community Action Program: The Past, Present and Its Future? In On Fighting Poverty. J. L. Sundquist, ed. Pp. 52-69. New York: Basic Books.
Liebow, Elliot
    1967 Tally's Corner. Boston: Little, Brown.

Moynihan, Daniel P.
    1970 Maximum Feasible Misunderstanding. New York: Free Press
Myrdal, Gunnar
    1969 Challenge to Affluence: The Emergence of an "Underclass." In Structured Social Inequality. Celia S. Heller, ed. Pp. 138-43. London: Macmillan.
National Advisory Council on Economic Opportunity
    1973 Sixth Annual Report. Washington, D.C.: U.S. Government Printing Office.
Patton, M.
    1978 Utilization-Focused Evaluation. Beverly Hills, Calif.: Sage.
Prager, Edward, and Henry Tanaka
    1980 Self-Assessment: The Client's Perspective. Social Work 25:1:32-34.
Rainwater, Lee
    1969 The Problem of Lower Class Culture and Poverty War Strategy. In On Understanding Poverty. Daniel Patrick Moynihan, ed. Pp. 229-59. New York: Basic Books.
Rossi, Peter, and Walter Williams
    1972 Evaluating Social Programs: Theory, Practice, and Politics. New York: Seminar Press.
Rothschild-Whitt, Joyce
    1979 The Collectivist Organization: An Alternative to Rational-Bureaucratic Models. American Sociological Review 44:509-27.
Sundquist, James L., ed.
    1969 On Fighting Poverty. New York: Basic Books.
Weiss, Carol
    1971 Utilization of Education: Toward Comparative Study. In Readings in Evaluation Research. Frances Caro, ed. Pp. 136-42. New York: Russell Sage Foundation.
    1973 Where Politics and Evaluation Research Meet. Evaluation 1:37-45.
Wells, Miriam J.
    1981 Alienation, Work Structure and the Quality of Life: Can Cooperatives Make a Difference? Social Problems 28(5):548-62.
    in press Political Mediation and Agricultural Cooperation: Strawberry Farms in California. In Economic Development and Cultural Change. Chicago: University of Chicago Press.
Williams, Raymond, and Lloyd Biser
    1972 Analysis of Emerging Cooperatives, 1965-70. Farmers Cooperative Service Information, Bulletin, No. 85. Washington, D.C.: U.S. Department of Agriculture.
Williams, T. T.
    1974 The Role of Low-Income Rural Cooperatives in Community Development. American Journal of Agricultural Economics 56(6):913-18.
Zurcher, Louis A.
    1970 Poverty Warriors: The Human Experience of Planned Social Intervention. Austin, Texas: University of Texas Press.

VII

POLICY

The relationship between policymaking and program evaluation is, at best, blurred. Some evaluators would argue that policy is what happens after decision makers have reviewed evaluation information. Others suggest that program evaluation (or policy analysis in particular) is an a priori method, a form of analysis to decide among policy alternatives. In this section we have collected an array of articles that support one or the other of these definitions about the application of evaluation procedures to policy issues. However, the blurred nature of the relationship between policy and evaluation may lie in the assumptions evaluators hold about how to shape social information into policy directives, e.g., assumptions about the form and meaning of social data may dictate whether or not an evaluator sees policy as separate from analysis. For example, the qualities that characterize scientific and humanistic evaluations, as discussed by House in the introduction to this volume, may underlie some of the arguments presented by these authors. It seems certain that policy and evaluation are closely linked, both conceptually and in practice. The articles in this section argue that the links take differing forms.

The first article is both timely and challenging. In "Making Block Grants Accountable," Chelimsky reviews the circumstances surrounding the reduction in mandates for categorical grants, the rise of block grants, and the subsequent implications for program accountability and evaluation. The author emphasizes that there is a significant shift in policy when moving from categorical to block funding, and after outlining the arguments for and against categorical programs, she finds the block grant approach only moderately responsive as a policy alternative. Finally, she recommends a "typology of elements" that must be considered to make the block grants accountable. For example, Chelimsky is concerned that as state and local governments control block funds, some of the most needy may be ignored. Her recommendation for guarding against this potential hazard is an accountability model that is centrist in form (at the federal level) and is characterized by a standard-setting monitoring system. Although her concern for the needy under block grants is a legitimate one, opponents may question whether her preferences for accountability (so similar to the federal monitoring model used during the past fifteen years) are appropriate. Nevertheless whatever one's preferences in terms of evaluation, the challenge to monitor block grants is quite real.

The second article in this section, "Implementing Equal Education Opportunity Policy: A Comparison of the Outcomes of HEW and Justice Department

Efforts," questions the assumption that desegregation produces conditions for a viable equal opportunity policy in public schools. The title of the article suggests that the authors are concerned primarily with the success or failures of two governmental agencies charged with desegregation responsibilities, but the main arguments of the article focus on interpreting measurements of "second-generation discrimination" in schools desegregated by HEW and justice departments.

The authors use two measures of second-generation discrimination: "the level of black overrepresentation among students assigned to special education classes, and the level of black underrepresentation among faculty (in selected schools between 1968 and 1974)." The authors raise a concern about the appropriateness of these measures but argue that their use is justified on the grounds that the Office of Civil Rights uses them in compliance reviews and that the measures are frequently cited in reports that allege widespread patterns of continuing discrimination. The methods of analysis were t tests of the differences in means of (1) the ratio of the percentage of black students in special education compared to the percentage of whites and (2) the ratio of black students to black teachers compared to white students and white teachers. The findings suggest that, on the average, by 1974 black students were more likely to be placed in special education than white students. To a lesser extent, but similarly, black faculty were more likely to be underrepresented in proportion to black student enrollment than were white teachers to white students. The authors suggest this evaluation of equal opportunity policy confirms policymaker errors in assuming that desegregation could lead to reduced discrimination. "The fact that discrimination could continue was incompatible with the policy makers' definition of the problem."

The third article in this section, "Professional Models for Policy Analysis," reviews possible role models for a discipline of public policymaking. Of particular interest are the author's differentiations among types of policymaking (with different underlying assumptions about methods and purposes) and his demand for a specification of ethical standards for policy analysis. This article reinforces the view of policy analysis as method, suggesting there are "experts" with particular skills that may assist decision makers in choosing among policy alternatives. In a section on "implications" the author calls into question the problems of power and elitism when using "experts" in public policy. Recognition of these problems serves as an impetus for the discussion of ethics in the article. One of the interesting questions raised by this article is whether or not it is possible to "train" experts who can blend "the technological skills of the physical and social sciences with a sense for both humanistic goals and practical politics."

The fourth article, "Qualitative and Quantitative Information in Health Policy Decision Making," uses health policy as a backdrop for a discussion of the use of qualitative data in policymaking. The author argues that quantitative data lack the capacity to reveal the variety of meanings associated with social information. He suggests that quantitative methods may disrupt rational policymaking by making the "process more irrational, capricious and more detached from the very phenomenon under consideration." In making the case for qualitative methods, the author describes the links between qualitative methodology and certain assumptions about social meaning and compares these with other assumptions about quantitative methodology. But the author does not reject quantitative input. He argues that multiple methods are both useful and desirable in helping formulate policy decisions.

The fifth article, "Designing Health Policy Research for Utilization," offers a comprehensive discussions of ways to meet demands for useful "evaluation" (policy research) information. Solomon and Shortell echo in some ways the call for multifaceted evaluations recommended in the previous article. Specifically, they focus on the need for continuing interaction between data providers and policymakers at the levels of needs for information, research design and methodology, utilization, and dissemination. The authors note that "scientific quality should not be the principal research standard for social programs, but that policy-oriented research should be comprehensible, correct, complete, and credible to partisans *on all sides* (emphasis inserted)." This quote hints at the possibility that a policy's impact (and criteria for what constitutes impact) may be defined in different ways for different groups. It appears that the authors' framework for the observation of impact is defined by their preference for the scientifically oriented quantitative methodologies.

In the last article of this section, "Critical Theory and Public Policy," Dallmayr tackles some of the problems of assumption posed in the first paragraph of the introduction to this section. The article begins with a history of the rise of policy studies and presents a discussion of the need for a critical analysis not only of policy evaluation but of "the very meaning and status of policy." Much of the article is a discussion of the assumptions about social science, both purpose and methods, that are implied in some of the arguments in the preceding papers. Eventually, Dallmayr argues, public policy should function unfettered by instrumental action. Dallmayr suggests that *non*instrumental action is public policy unrestrained by demands for evidence of effectiveness, particularly when the demand for evidence transforms public policy into social experiments. He suggests that "non-instrumental action (in public policy) must be construed as action unconcerned with outcomes or goal attainment."

One of the hopes for this volume of evaluation studies is to highlight the persistent ambiguity of what it means to "evaluate" a program or intervention. The articles in this section on policy propose different methodologies for evaluating policies or policy alternatives and imply differing definitions about the intents, purposes, and roles of evaluation in policymaking. It appears that policies about "what's good for society" are inextricably tied to the technologies or crafts devised for "making judgments of worth."

41

Making Block Grants Accountable

Eleanor Chelimsky

The proposal by President Reagan to consolidate 84 categorical grant programs, transform them into six block grants in the areas of health, education, social services, and emergency energy aid, and simultaneously cut the overall funding for those grants in differing amounts, arises from a groundswell of public criticism of federal spending. This criticism, which had developed over a number of years, contained strong ideological and federalist components among the diversity of complaints articulated, and focused heavily on the categorical grants which have formed the backbone of federal expenditure for social programs over the years. The criticism peaked sharply in California with the Proposition 13 referendum of June 1978, and again nationally in November 1980 with the conservative success in the general elections.

The question of which sectors of the budget would be cut was never open to much doubt, given the campaign concentration on "wasteful social programs" and "inflexible categorical grants," and given also the conservative character of the new administration. Conservatives have long argued for minimum involvement of the government in the lives of citizens except in support of the social order[1] (that is, to maintain the rule of law, established institutions, a strong military defense, and the right to acquire, retain, and inherit property); and for minimum taxation to assure only those public functions which cannot be handled by the private sector. "Big" government,

AUTHOR'S NOTE: The views and opinions expressed by the author of this chapter are her own and should not be construed to be the policy or position of the General Accounting Office.

heavy taxes, and the resource redistribution favored by liberals have been seen by conservatives as harmful to the economy, destructive of the "work ethic," and generally damaging to social institutions. .

Given these views, it was perfectly predictable that the budget cuts proposed by a conservative administration should have heavily affected social programs which seek to equalize or redistribute income or other resources, rather than, say, defense programs. In addition, it was also natural that budget constraints should focus on categorical grant programs, given that these are of such relatively recent vintage, had grown so rapidly during the 1970s, and had received so much criticism from federalist, as well as conservative, perspectives.

Specific federalist criticism of categorical grant programs has been, first, that too much power is vested in the national government at the expense of states and localities; and second, that this overweening power (expressed, they feel, in red tape, overlapping jurisdictions, and uncoordinated requirements at the national level) has made it impossible for states and localities to carry out the programs effectively.

In sum, categorical grants have received criticism emanating from both ideological and federalist perspectives; however, the boundaries of the current critique of these grants extends far beyond those perspectives.

THE CURRENT CRITIQUE OF
CATEGORICAL GRANT PROGRAMS

One place where both federalist and ideological criticisms have converged is in the area of categorical program goals, many of which are likely to be unacceptable, a priori, to conservatives and to certain (states' rights) federalists. Six different kinds of goals can be distinguished:

(1) Case transfers or transfers-in-kind of collective goods (such as social or mental health services) to low income or other target population groups;

(2) The diffusion of innovations in the delivery of public services (to increase productivity via the introduction of modern information processing equipment, for example);

(3) The development of needed skills and capabilities at state and local levels, and within the labor force generally (often also called "capacity-building" or "-sharing");

(4) The dissemination of information and the attempt to influence local consumer preferences in accordance with national policy (vaccination, speed-limit, anti-alcohol or anti-smoking campaigns, for example);

(5) The improvement of the bargaining power of the poor, of minorities, and of the disadvantaged at the local level (via employment training or unemployment compensation, for example); and

(6) The removal of obstacles (usually through grants for multijurisdictional planning, or through 100 percent funding, where required) raised by jurisdictional boundaries [adapted from Schultze, 1974: 183-185].

All of these goals, however—whether or not they are acceptable to everyone— derive either from traditional kinds of collaboration which have always existed within the federal system (Elazar, 1962), or from more recent income redistribution policies begun in 1913 (made possible, in fact, by the income tax, which was a straightforwardly redistributive measure). Service programs such as Medicare and Medicaid, or Aid to Families with Dependent Children (AFDC), clearly embody and crystallize one or more of these objectives.

Despite its somewhat hallowed traditions, however, the categorical grant program as a policy mechanism is now the subject of criticism coming not only from conservatives and states' rights federalists but from every ideological direction and every level of the federal system. This was *not* the case for service programs developed under the liberal New Deal. Contemporary criticism of those programs (such as accusations of socialism, interventionism, academism, red tape, confusion and waste, on the one hand, or of irrelevance and irrationality resulting from an unwillingness to attack "the root causes" of social problems, on the other hand) had typically come either from conservatives who were politically weakened by the Great Depression, or from ephemeral, "share-the-wealth" Populists (under Huey Long) and from a small, splintered radical movement. President Roosevelt's overwhelmingly dominant liberal reform movement could thus fend off most of these accusations, although it did make some efforts to placate the Populists during their period of political ascension. Again, in the 1960s, the Kennedy/Johnson "massive innovative wave" (Sundquist with Davis, 1969: 261) would give short shrift to the complaints of conservative doubters generally, and at state and local levels in particular (Martin, 1965: 77), but did lend an ear to (domestic) radical movements which appeared to be gathering political momentum on its left.

What is different today, then, is that much of the current criticism of categorical grant programs derives from liberals who were the architects and supporters of the very programs under attack. This criticism has, of course, occurred on the basis of performance, not of ideology. But these liberals thus join the ranks of conservatives, who would normally be expected to oppose the programs on ideological grounds (although many have also voiced criticisms of program performance), and of those intergovernmental system practitioners, administrators, and legislators who have come to see in service programs a glaring exposition of the flaws in the current ability of the intergovernmental network to act effectively in response to public problems.

One of the inferences which may be drawn from the above discussion is that a problem with liberal thinking in the past may have been a failure to recognize the importance and power of the federal system framework in the implementation of categorical programs. This failure, however, appears to have been both integral to certain liberal beliefs and goals, and a predictable result of them. The liberal faith in centralization, given the conservative stance taken by many states and local governments with regard to social reform (a stance which may have closed liberal ears to any validity in their criticisms), the inability of reform governments to maintain the integrity of needed program planning, and the liberal preoccupation with national objectives which was so intense and exclusive as to divert talented liberal attention from focusing also on the means for achieving them, are all factors which impeded awareness of growing state and local criticism.

This is not, of course, to assert that failures of implementation are restricted to liberal social programs, categorical or otherwise. The mindset attending the Three Mile Island nuclear plant system design, with its inattention to the most ordinary needs of operational procedures, and the implementation-monitoring difficulties prevalent in service program activities championed by conservatives (crime control or court-delay reduction efforts, for example) illustrate adequately that implementation failures are neither a social nor a liberal nor a governmental monopoly. They are, however, of particular concern to liberals insofar as liberals have identified themselves with social reform and are hence responsible for the federal initiatives—especially categorical grant programs—implemented in pursuit of that reform.

The implementation deficits which have occurred in many programs are now well recognized by the least some liberals. In the words of Senator Levin (1979):

My fear is that the programs I so strongly support are going to be doomed—not by a flaw in intent but by a flaw in implementation.

It is not clear, however, that the failure of the categorical grant concept to integrate the federalist administrative and practitioner network—which is a major component of the "flaw in implementation"—is as well recognized or understood. Nonetheless, this failure figures prominently among performance criticisms currently leveled at categorical programs.

In addition to failures of planning, of implementation, of networking, and of evaluation, however, categorical grant programs have helped to produce an unanticipated side effect: the creation and multiplication of interest groups. This development has become the source of an important (and newer) criticism leveled at categorical grant programs: to wit, that service providers and service beneficiaries have evolved into stakeholders, that new organizational structures have been built and new political alignments or coalitions have developed because of them, and that the public, in general, is no longer well served in these circumstances. The War on Poverty, for example, supplied

Mayor John Lindsay of New York with a surrogate for the party support he lacked. (As Lindsay remarked, "The community corporations cracked up traditional systems . . . the traditional Democrats were more fearful than my crowd. I supported the Poverty Program, the black community knew I would support it . . . now I don't have to call them for payoffs. They'll support me in the fall" [Tolchin and Tolchin, 1972: 77-80].) Other city officials have used categorical programs to prevent the organizations which elected them from dissolving (as an example, Mayor Ivan Allen of Atlanta, who was elected by "an unstable coalition of blacks and businessmen," cemented that coalition "primarily through his ability to get and give federal patronage in the form of grants for the benefit of both groups" [Tolchin and Tolchin, 1972: 67].)

Not only have categorical programs influenced the development and viability of interest groups, however; interest groups have also influenced the development and viability of categorical programs. Intervention by stakeholder groups at the program planning stage may mean that legislation is postponed or never enacted, as was the case with President Kennedy's "bold new approach" to mental health centers in 1963, according to Lucy Ozarin:

> The hearings went forth, both in the Senate and in the House. The original proposal was for legislation that would provide money to build mental health centers and also staff them. Now, at that time, the American Medical Association was very much against what they called socialized medicine, and they saw the staffing provision—money to hire staff—as smacking of socialized medicine. Building was all right, however; there'd been the Hill-Burton program for years to build hospitals and health facilities. The AMA was able once again to swing enough weight, to object strongly enough, so that the final legislation which emerged in 1963 was a construction program. For two years, that's what we had [Chelimsky, 1979: 810].

Interventions by stakeholder groups at the program implementation stage have been equally powerful. If programs to increase productivity in a city agency, in the classroom, or in a police district, for example, are opposed by municipal, teacher, or police unions which can paralyze city operations with strikes, or control state legislatures with campaign funds, these programs are not likely to be either well implemented or institutionalized.

These circular interactions between categorical programs and interest groups mean that: (1) these programs (and other federal policy mechanisms) have enormous obstacles to overcome in areas where stakeholders are both opposed to the program and entrenched; (2) where programs address goals desired by powerful stakeholder groups, federal efforts will be facilitated in the Congress (and also at state and local levels, insofar as stakeholder influence is reflected in individual state and local power structures); (3)

federal agencies are stimulated to work very closely with stakeholder groups and the relevant congressional committees, thereby forming (and contributing to the multiplication of) "iron triangles";[2] and finally, (4) units of general state and local government—at least partly in reaction to these developments and relationships—now find themselves taking on (willingly or defensively) some of the characteristics of stakeholder groups. This last point is of importance because the federalist perspective of state and local units which are *also* stakeholders is likely to be different from the perspective of those which are not.

The increasing dependence of state and local governments on federal aid, along with the increase in number, strength, and scope of stakeholder groups, has now blurred earlier distinctions between governmental and lobby groups. States, cities, counties, regional councils of government, all have built staffs in Washington to try to shape the federal grant formulas to their benefit and to achieve a more dominant voice in federal policy. Almost half the states now maintain grantspersons in Washington. "to look for more federal money" for their own state (Herbers, 1978). But the dependence which such a relationship has generated was recently made clear when the states were warned by U.S. Senator Muskie about their efforts to develop a budget-balancing amendment:

> It's not a threat, but a matter of arithmetic. We could save $31 billion . . . merely by killing revenue sharing, education grants, sewerage construction and block grants [Pine, 1979].

All of these factors—the growth in numbers and influence of stakeholder groups (whether hostile or supportive); the fact that the responsibility for this growth is at least partly attributable to categorical grant programs; and the transformations which that growth appears to have engendered in the nature of governmental relationships and in the character of the programs themselves—have notably added to current criticisms of categorical programs.

In summary, ideological and federalist criticism of categorical grant programs has been joined more recently by a public critique of the stakeholder or interest group phenomenon. Beyond the predictable focus of conservative criticism on program goals, there has also been a strong conservative critique of program *performance,* involving the effects of programs and program regulations on market operations, on the economy, on personal or corporate freedom, and on the social order (impacts of public assistance on the "work ethic," for example). The criticism of interest group influence has tended to reinforce the conservative critique by bringing evidence to bear that the liberal goal of achieving social reform through innovative programs may have been transformed, at least for some programs, into the less avowable goal of achieving affluence and influence for some stakeholder groups. On the other hand, some liberal and federal system critics—while rejecting the view that program goals were wrong, illusory, or inappropriate—have now come to view many categorical programs as inadequately realized, based on the experience of program performance over the past 15 years, and have become concerned as well about the increasing development of interest groups.

The following 14 criticisms present some of the major complaints about categorical grant performance which have been most frequently heard over the last few years. Categorical grants are accused of being:

(1) *Ineffective in achieving their goals* (examples typically given here are the AFDC, job training, environment-saving or federal crime control programs which are alleged neither to have reduced dependence on public assistance, nor moved well-trained people into private sector jobs, nor reduced air, water, and noise pollution, nor made the streets safe, as they had promised, or had been expected, to do);

(2) *Inefficient in their operations,* involving both poor management and waste by agency administrators, and also abuse both by service providers and beneficiaries (examples given are the Medicaid program, where fraud is reported as considerable on the part of health care providers and where services are said to be of unacceptably quality; or the Comprehensive Employment and Training Administration program, where local control and accountability have been considered inadequate; or the AFDC program, where recipient abuse is thought to be unacceptably high);

(3) *Excessively centralized and controlled at the national level,* thereby decreasing proper and constitutional state and local political independence and decreasing as well both the likelihood of program and service appropriateness, and the quality of implementation at the local level;

(4) *Distortive of state and local priorities* in the pursuit of national priorities: that is, the criticism is that categorical grants force state and local governments to find matching money they would not otherwise have been spent without the existence of the federal funding; that they create dependence upon the national government (states and localities are often called "federal junkies" in this regard); and that their planning requirements use up many man-hours of local government time and scarce expertise;

(5) *Substantively fragmented and uncontrolled across topical areas at the national level* (both *among* and *within* agencies) due to the proliferation of similar or overlapping programs, thereby causing major problems of administration at local, state, and national levels (fragmentation, or lack of coordination *among* agencies has meant that the federal agency manager of each program may pose different and complex requirements, despite simultaneous or concurrent juris-

diction with other agencies which operate independently: a recent example involves the town of Junior, West Virginia, which has spent seven years trying to conciliate the conflicting demands of six federal agencies involved in its effort to build a sewage treatment plant [Herbers, 1979a]; fragmentation *within* federal agencies has meant that the responsible management of public programs can become extremely difficult, if not impossible, to accomplish);

(6) *Underfunded,* such that success, in terms of stated objectives, is not a realistic possibility (a basic failure of public housing, for example, is that demand vastly exceeds supply; the same is true for day care and public service jobs);

(7) *Inequitable,* when the supposed beneficiaries benefit little, if at all, versus other populations (public housing, urban renewal, and manpower or employment training programs are most often cited as examples: it is claimed that "urban-renewal programs have destroyed twice as many dwellings as they have built" [Wilcox, 1969: 282]; that they benefit developers and the affluent who move into "luxury hotels and apartments"—created with money from HUD—rather than the needy; that public housing serves the "nonthreatening" elderly—of the 3.2 million people now living in 1.2 million public housing units, 48 percent are elderly—rather than low-income, and especially minority, families; and that public employment and training programs have typically benefited populations other than the poor, as, for example, in the CETA program, where federal funds have been used [or misused] to rehire teachers, police officers, and firefighters whom municipalities could no longer afford to pay, or in earlier programs where "less than half the participants in public service jobs were economically disadvantaged" [Mayor Ernest N. Morial of New Orleans in Joint Economic Committee, 1978]); in particular, and very significantly, it is claimed that categorical grant programs have often done more to stimulate the growth of state and local bureaucracies than they have to affect substantively the social problem addressed;

(8) *Generative of decreased* (or decreasingly rising) *national economic productivity,* as a result of the induced expansion of the public sector whose contribution to economic productivity, although difficult to quantify, is typically calculated as low relative to the private sector;

(9) Productive of *overgreat expectations:* that is, the promise of equality implied by federal service programs is in fact a disservice to those they purport to serve, in that they raise hopes which cannot be fulfilled (as, for example in the effort to reduce current rates of unemployment among inner-city minority youths which far exceed those of the Great Depression; the point here is that while job skills can be taught and learned, if the real problem for these youths in getting and holding jobs in the private sector is that the economy

"doesn't really need these kids" [Sar Levitan in The Economist, 1978: 52], then the teaching and learning of these skills are futile exercises);

(10) *Value-eroding* (that is, service programs are not only productive of disappointment because of underfunding, inequitability, and illusory expectations of utopian equality, but they also tend to demean the idea of merit and of reward for merit; the pursuit of equality, in this sense, is said to have reversed the old humanist idea that justly earned rewards should not be *denied* because of race, creed, sex, or age, and converted it to one in which those rewards are claimed *because* of race, creed, sex, or age, as opposed to merit [Daniel Bell in Greider and Kotz, 1973]);

(11) *Bureaucratizing:* that is, tending to substitute compliance with bureaucratic rules and regulations for the achievement of substantive— and formally targeted—program outcomes;

(12) *Nonterminable and noncontrollable,* because of the enduring power of their constituencies, and productive of additional interest groups, either developed at state and local levels because of categorical grant funding, or constituted nationally as the result of new programs (programs for the elderly and the handicapped, for example);

(13) *Wasteful,* in terms of increasing the use of public monies for salaries and administrative expenses; and, finally,

(14) *Self-interested:* that is, categorical grants are said to enhance a tendency on the part of agencies and service-providers, themselves stakeholders, to be inward-looking, and to put their own interests ahead of those of program beneficiaries.

This synthesis of the defects ascribed to categorical grant programs, most of which have been frequently repeated in the literature of the past few years,[3] gives rise inevitably to the question: If these programs are so bad, why have they been in vogue for so long? In effect, in weighing the shift to block grants, it is also important to ask what qualities and advantages categorical grants may possess that explain their survival to date despite such a chorus of disapproval.

First, there is unquestionably the matter of *national objective,* of legislative intent. The characteristics of the current categorical grant system reflect decisions made by the Congress to serve national goals as defined by the Congress. When these grants are administered and controlled at the national level, it is possible to target very specifically the kinds of problems (such as poverty, sickness, inner-city housing deterioration) which the administration and the Congress feel must be addressed nationwide as matters of national policy and priority, as well as the kinds of populations (such as children, elderly, the mentally ill, crime victims) who have the greatest need of help, even using conservative criteria for government activity (see note 1).

Second, there is the matter of direct *accountability for federal funds*. Since categorical grants have typically been quite clear about what the national objective is, this allows various functions to occur which bring knowledge of whether the implemented program at state and local levels is faithful to the national purpose; whether the program is well implemented and well managed, according to that purpose; and whether the program made any difference. Since the basic concept is that of a contract, there is an obligation and a quid pro quo on each side. As one federal administrator has expressed it:

> A large proportion of categorical grants provide a specific sum of money, with a very high federal matching ratio (80, 90, or 100 percent) for a very particular purpose, and specify the delivery of very particular forms of collective goods. . . . [M]any of these grants are a means by which the federal government uses state and local governments (or in some cases local non-profit organizations) as agents or subcontractors to produce centrally determined amounts and kinds of collective goods, since, for a number of reasons, principally historical and political, the federal government itself virtually never delivers collective goods or services at the local level [Schultze, 1974: 182-183].

With categorical grants, therefore, there is, at least theoretically, a kind of bargain-exchange situation which specifies both expectations and willingness to perform on the part of the contracting parties. This builds in understandings of anticipated performance, measurement of that performance, and remedies for lack of performance if the need should arise. In short, categorical grants try to assure that the public gets value for its money; yet it is this very effort which has been responsible for many of the complaints leveled at categorical grants: red tape, data collection, performance forms and questionnaires to fill out, applications to file, plans to rationalize, and so on.

Third, there is the matter of *national capability and expertise*. Although there is, of course, variability in different substantive areas, the national government, its civil servants, and its research arms have a long record of capability and demonstrated technical skills in administering complex programs. Categorical grant programs have especially benefited from this institutional expertise, and, above all, from the continuity of that expertise, at the national level. Although some states and localities may have equal expertise, this is not true of all states and localities. In particular, it is difficult to compare state and local programs with national programs because most of the former are never evaluated.

Fourth, there is the matter of program *information at important decision points*. The presence of evaluation staff and evaluation mandates in national-level agencies has permitted the preparation and planned coordination of nationwide program reports for the use of executive branch and legislative branch decision makers. In this way, information about program status is generally available, and both sets of users are assured that the data developed at state and local levels can be planned for and designed in terms of their relevance to user information needs and decision-points; and that the reliability and validity of evaluative information developed at state and local levels can be checked.

Fifth, there is the matter of *program integrity*. Categorical grant managers, who are responsible at the national level to the President and the Congress, are required to monitor programs carefully to ensure ongoing knowledge of management problems. Audit staff at the national level can be held responsible under categorical grants for reporting on the maintenance of adequate accounting and inventory systems at state and local levels. This signifies a national check on whether state and local agency accounting, inventory, and unallowable expenditure problems are being identified and corrected, and on whether financial status reports, for example, are accurate.

Sixth, there is the matter of national *program standards*. The categorical grant system features a reasonable level of similarity among state or local programs. This diminishes the incentive for program clients to cross state lines to obtain better (or different) benefits, and it ensures some equality among states with regard to federal programs.

Seventh, there is the matter of *interstate control*. Categorical grant programs can assure coordination across states in topical areas such as disease or pollution, which do not respect state boundaries. Interstate tracking of "neighborhood or external effects" such as public health risks has always been a national-level responsibility, even under the most conservative criteria (see note 1).

Finally, there is the matter of topical areas involving *shared responsibility,* such as the health care or criminal justice "systems." The categorical grant system can ensure that federal monies are targeted according to need and so as to promote coordination and interdependence (when the national policy so dictates) by settling the issue of "Who gets how much" outside the framework of historical organization and power at the state level.

In summary, although categorical grants have been heavily criticized for defects of implementation, they also present major qualities which may be important to try to retain. As the shift to block grants is contemplated and debated, it is therefore useful not only to examine which of the 14 problems outlined above are likely to be improved or solved, but also, which of the 8 advantages may be degraded or lost. Some categorical programs, after all, have achieved major successes in meeting their objectives. The Food Stamp program, Head Start, Education for the Handicapped, all have done a lot of what they set out to do. The point here, however, is that the reason why their success has in fact been demonstrated through audit and evaluation is that audits and evaluations were among the conditions that recipients had to accept in order to receive their categorical grants. Eliminating these conditions, then, carries the major risk that the performance of federally funded programs will remain essentially unknown.

BLOCK GRANT PROGRAMS AS A REMEDY TO THE CRITIQUE OF CATEGORICAL GRANT PROGRAMS

In analyzing prospectively what block grants are likely to mean vis-à-vis the problems and advantages of categorical grants discussed above, it is first necessary to pinpoint what a block grant is. To say that it occupies the midpoint between the "no-strings-attached" approach of revenue sharing and the "tight national control" of categorical grants does not characterize the mechanism with much precision. Furthermore, it is not even clear that a block grant does occupy such a midpoint, given that there are so many different forms of block grants, some closer to revenue sharing, some closer to categorical grants. The focus of that "midpoint" is even harder to situate over time if the experience of the past is any guide: in effect, as problems of accountability of one sort or another have arisen in the block grants of the 1970s, a phenomenon known as "creeping categorization" has ensued as the Congress has struggled to exercise some control over the federal funds. Thus, a block grant which starts out in life as a transfer mechanism whose purpose is to increase recipient discretion over spending decisions may not, over time, end up doing so. In general, block grants can be more accurately described as occupying "a span of policy space within which shifts may occur reflecting a balance between national (state) and local program preferences and power" (Dommel, 1981:1).

The Advisory Commission on Intergovernmental Relations (ACIR) has identified five design characteristics which help to distinguish block grants from other types of federal transfer (1977: 6; emphasis added):

(1) Federal aid is authorized for a wide range of activities *within a broadly defined functional area.*
(2) Recipients have substantial discretion in identifying problems, designing programs, and allocating resources to deal with them.
(3) Administrative, fiscal reporting, planning, and other federally imposed requirements are kept to *the minimum amount necessary to ensure that national goals are being accomplished.*
(4) Federal aid is distributed on the basis of a statutory formula which results in narrowing federal administrators' discretion and providing a sense of *fiscal certainty* to recipients.

(5) Eligibility provisions are statutorily specified and favor general-purpose governmental units as recipients, and elected officials and administrative generalists as decisionmakers.

Thus, a block grant may be defined as "a program by which funds are provided to general-purpose governmental units in accordance with a statutory formula for use in a broad functional area largely at the recipient's discretion." However, it is important to note that block grants neither fail to express the national objective sought in funding a program (Reagan, 1972: 63), nor do they eliminate (a) state and local accountability for the funds received, or (b) national responsibility for the appropriate use of national revenues (Dommel, 1981: 1).

If evaluations are done so that a record of ongoing experience with block grants is developed, it should be possible to say whether the worst fears or most optimistic expectations have been realized. While it is hard to imagine that the block grants will eliminate all 14 of the problems cited in categorical funding, it is equally hard to imagine that a number of successes will not occur. However, the absence of retrospective information does not preclude prospective examination of the likely ability of block grants to cope with the problems experienced by categorical grants. To begin with, it would appear that there are three problems which the block grant can be expected to affect favorably:

(1) *Excessive centralization and control at the national level* should certainly be reduced by block grants; that is one of their major purposes. But while block grants are almost certain to address this criticism, it remains to be seen whether more local discretion will lead to better local implementation and management (see Netzer, 1974). Further, it is not clear that "excessive centralization and control" at the state level will not be substituted for that of the national level. As the U.S. General Accounting Office (GAO) has pointed out (1979: 23), "Federal formula block grants to states often are transformed into discretionary categorical grants to local governments from the state."

(2) *Fragmentation and loss of control across topical areas* are likely to be improved by the use of block grants, *but only if there is proper, continuous, and careful oversight at the national level* (see Herbers, 1979a).

(3) With regard to *overgreat expectations,* it seems that the move to block grants, especially accompanied by large budget cuts, should reduce, not raise expectations. While it is true that the reduction of social expectations may not be cost-free, it is nonetheless clear that block grants accompanied by major budget cuts are certainly a step toward such a reduction.

On the other hand, it would appear likely that some problems may get worse. In particular, both logic and experience point to two problems which have not benefited from decentralization in the past:

(4) *Inefficiency in operations* ("inefficiency" involves poor management, waste, fraud, and abuse; see item 2 in the list of categorical grant complaints) is likely to be aggravated by moving to block grants. It is true that state and local programs are sometimes well managed, sometimes not, as is the case for federal programs. Again, corruption among officials is a problem on which no level of government has a monopoly. However, the experience of both the LEAA and CETA block grant programs has been that waste, fraud, and abuse of federal dollars became so widespread, flagrant, and uncontrollable without built-in elements of accountability, that the Congress eventually voted to increase the national control over recipient discretion. It is also important to recognize that initial cost savings (such as those potentially achievable through "cutting out layers of bureaucracy") are not the only factors in efficient management. The assurance of such management (one which can control costs and allocate resources effectively over the long term) requires, among other things, good record systems, performance standards, and the ability to compare management results with those of other managements. Unfortunately, under block grants, decentralization or local autonomy has often meant notably different record systems and performance standards, with the consequent inability to know what is happening in a given management system, and to compare across managements. An illustration of the multiplicity and dissimilarity of local systems is given by the property tax which is "the only tax for which there exists more than 70,000 different legal tax rates, hundreds of thousands of distinctive effective rates—because of assessment nonuniformity—and probably, when all the overlaying local taxing units are added up, several *million* distinctive effective tax rate combinations" (Netzer, 1974: 231). In sum, the experience of the past, along with the problems of local differentiation and uncertain instruments of accountability, all suggest that block grants are more likely to exacerbate than improve inefficiency.

(5) *Inequitability* might have been expected to improve under block grants, because it seems reasonable that decentralization should help to target monies better on needy local populations; unfortunately, experience once again has shown that needy populations may not have the organization and power to wrest those monies from state and local governments where they have little or no representation, if accountability mechanisms are not present. Under revenue sharing, for example, which represents the "no-strings" extreme, civil rights violation complaints have been numerous (770 were declared as

"pending" in 1979), yet the Treasury Department, which administers revenue sharing, does not have the necessary personnel to evaluate these complaints nor to "sort out all the inequities" of which Department officials are aware. (Herbers, 1979b). Since block grants must serve whatever target populations are indicated in the law, it seems at first glance that they would have lesser problems with equity than would revenue sharing—similar problems, in fact, to those existing with categorical grants. There are, however, the additional difficulties that—given "minimal," or lessened, accountability—(1) the target populations intended and specified by the law may not actually be the ones served, and (2) without evaluation mechanisms, it may be nearly impossible to find this out. Block grants are thus likely to be more, not less, inequitable than categorical grants because of the ability of state and local bureaucracies to support their requests for funds effectively, and because of the "minimal" national accountability which has often accompanied block grants.

On four problems, uncertainty exists. Although the block grant may have some potential for impact in these areas, there are strong arguments for both positive and negative effects:

(6) The *decreased productivity* claimed for categorical grants could theoretically improve under block grants if the latter were to cause a reduction in public sector employment. However, it is not clear that this will occur for several reasons: (a) Some of the programs that are targeted for block grants have never been administered by the states and will therefore require "wholly new state bureaucracies" (Stanfield, 1981: 828). (b) The trend in federal programs has been toward increased (not decreased) bureaucracies as program control increases. Finally, (c) even "minimal" requirements for accountability at state levels will mean increased work as states take over the federal responsibilities for such things as processing local applications, grant decision-making, the checking of local financial and performance reports, or the conduct of audits and evaluations, for example.

(7) *Wastefulness* may be no better under block grants. At this time, it is not clear whether administrative expenses will in fact be lessened or not, and, as discussed above, it is certainly not likely that inefficiency, fraud and abuse will decrease under block grants.

(8) *Distortion of state and local priorities* may occur just as well under block grants as under categorical grants if national funds continue to be sought whose purposes are not state or local purposes. Certainly, the *national* objectives may be less well served if the activities chosen by states and localities for implementation under the grant are peripheral or noninstrumental to those objectives. While it is true

this would imply at least some reduction of state and local priority distortion, it would certainly increase national priority distortion in comparison with categorical grants. Whatever the outcome, it seems likely that any immediate improvement gained through block grants in adhering to state and local priorities might be bought at the risk of more fundamental long-term distortion because of "fiscal certainty," a design characteristic presented by block grants. Such fiscal certainty provided to recipients is likely to increase, rather than decrease, their dependence upon the national government and distort their priorities on a long-term basis. Block grants do not seem able, in and of themselves, to help with this problem, and they could increase it.

(9) *Noncontrollability and nonterminability of grants,* a problem due to *current* constituent power, may not continue to be the case under block grants. First, the national lobbies may not be represented in the same proportions or with the same power in the different states. Second, the block grant concept could force constituencies such as the disadvantaged and handicapped to compete with each other for federal funds. However, *other constituencies*—the traditionally strong ones in individual states—could quickly develop the same stranglehold on federal funds in block form as the national lobbies exercise on federal funds in categorical form. Also, at a higher level, if one perceives state and local governments themselves as stakeholders or constituencies, and grants are given with "fiscal certainty," then there is not likely to be much improvement in either the controllability or terminability of federal programs under the block grant mechanism.

Finally, for five of the categorical grant problems cited, the problem does not appear susceptible to being addressed via a change in the grant mechanism:

(10) The *self-interest* of agencies is a property of units at all levels of government. It would be surprising if block grants could help.

(11) *Underfunding* is a criticism which seems entirely unrelated to funding mechanisms. Block grants can neither help nor hurt.

(12) *Ineffectiveness in achieving program goals* is related to so many profound difficulties other than the intergovernmental transfer mechanism (such as the intractability of the problem addressed, the lack of understanding of the problem, the failure to pilot-test proposed program-solutions, and so on) that it would be hard to see why or how changing the mechanism could help. Block grants would seem to be neutral for this problem.

(13) *Value-erosion* is not likely to change under block grants since the same purposes or national objectives would continue to be served; only the transfer mechanism would differ.

(14) *Bureaucratization* is no better or worse in state or local agencies than at the national level. Rules, regulations, and rituals are normal aspects of agency activity. Block grants are not likely to change that.

The analysis of problems encountered in implementing a system cannot, of course, be the only focus of prospective comparison between categorical and block grants. In the previous section, eight advantages were ascribed to the categorical grant system and it is also useful to question the ability of block grants to encompass these assets while concurrently bringing a new set of strengths. The argument can be set forth as follows:

First, with regard to the *national objective,* this would still be spelled out under block grants. It might be more broadly defined, and it is certain that much more discretion would be allowed to state and local officials with regard to the choice of activities, but the fact that the national objective is explicitly specified means that national revenues *should* continue to go to national priorities, *given the presence of adequate accountability measures.* However, efforts to reverse prior "distortion of state and local priorities" may lead to some distortion of the national objective (see item 8 in the list above) and further, the fungibility resulting from the greater discretion accorded would also be expected to cause at least some leakage from the grant purpose. The difficulty involved in tracking any such leakage again points to the need for accountability in this area.

Second, the *accountability for federal funds* still exists under block grants, not only at state and local but also at national levels. However, the effort to achieve "minimal" reporting requirements may make it difficult or impossible to find out (1) whether activities are implemented which are directly relevant to achieving the national objective, and (2) whether the results of those activities reveal that they are effective and useful.

Third, the loss of *national capabilities and expertise* are likely to be sorely missed. There is much debate about the capacity of *all* states and localities to take on the new responsibilities implied in the block grant proposal. The general view, however, is unfavorable, given the concurrent budget reductions, the existing skills and expertise in some states, and the timing of the shift which is planned to occur with great rapidity. Asking for the "maximum lead time possible" in testimony before the Senate Labor and Human Resources Committee in April, North Carolina's Governor Hunt (Chairman of the National Governors' Association's Human Resources Committee) said the proposed cuts in expenditure, given the speed with which the administration wants to implement them, leaves "little doubt that the block grants proposed will result in a reduction of services" (Stanfield, 1981: 829). If this occurs, however, it will be very difficult to say which part of the reduction in services is attributable to budget cuts, and which to the state and local capacity to operate and account for complex programs.

Fourth, *decision-point information* may not be available at all under block grants. The potential loss of all information about program effectiveness appears to involve so much more important risks in terms of congressional oversight and accountability responsibilities that it appears likely the "minimal" requirements will need to focus on those, to the detriment of ordinary, generalized program status information. However, the Congress can in fact ensure that such information is both collected and made available, even under block grants.

Fifth, given past experience, it seems likely that *program integrity* would suffer under block grants unless a major effort at coordination were made by the national agency responsible (see the discussion under "inefficiency" above).

Sixth, national *program standards* or guidelines for performance would now be missing, and it is predictable that there would be considerable variability in state and local programs implemented with block grant funds, setting up incentives for "program-hopping" among some beneficiaries and reinforcing the likelihood of increased fraud and abuse.

Seventh, unless the national agency responsible in the topical program area were given the authority, it is not clear how *interstate problems* could be handled.

Finally, with regard to program areas requiring *shared responsibility*, it seems that little progress is likely to be made. The data available from the LEAA block grant program, for example, make clear that the lack of strong authority at the national level precluded any real development of integrated relationships among the police, prosecutorial, judicial, and correctional functions. In ACIR's words, (1977: 91), on reviewing the LEAA block grant experience over 8 years:

> Despite growing recognition that crime needs to be dealt with by a functionally and jurisdictionally integrated criminal justice system, the Safe Streets program has been unable to develop strong ties among its component parts.

In summary, in addressing the 14 performance problems identified here for which categorical grants are most often criticized, one may reasonably speculate that block grants are likely to be: *useful* in trying to improve three problems (those of "excessive centralization and control at the national level," "fragmentation and lack of control across topical areas," and "overgreat expectations"); *neutral* in the case of five problems (those of "ineffectiveness of achieving program goals," "underfunding," "value-erosion," "bureaucratization," and "agency self-interest"); *hurtful* with respect to two problems (those of "operational inefficiency" and "inequitability"); and *uncertain* with regard to four problems (those of "decreased productivity," "wastefulness," "distortion of state and local priorities," and "constituency uncontrollability").

Turning to the categorical grant advantages enumerated above, it appears that the only one likely to survive more or less intact is the specification of national objectives. It is uncertain what the state and local capacity will be for handling block grant responsibilities, or how and if interstate problems will be dealt with under block grants. Finally, it seems probable that program standards, decision-related information, shared responsibilities, and program integrity will all suffer notable erosion or will fail to be maintained—without special action by the Congress—under block grants.

Thus, in moving to block grants, only 3 of the 14 major problems found with categorical grant programs seem likely to improve. Past experience predicts that problems of inefficiency—including problems of integrity such as fraud and abuse—and problems of inequitability are likely to worsen notably due to the weakening of the accountability mechanisms present in categorical grant programs. It is therefore especially important to examine what can be done to improve accountability in block grant programs, without restricting unduly the increased recipient discretion, flexibility, and control they promise, as compared with categorical grant programs.

MAKING BLOCK GRANTS ACCOUNTABLE

The preceding effort to compare categorical grants and block grants in a general way suggests that there are some important problems encountered by categorical grants which either do not appear to be addressable by block grants or may well be worsened by the adoption of this mechanism. At the same time, the President and the Congress are likely to lose at least some of their ability to judge what is happening in these programs because many of the advantages of categorical grants—chief among which, surely, is the assurance of recipient and national-level accountability for federal funds—will have been lost.

If the Congress should decide to adopt the President's proposal for budget cuts coupled with the consolidation of categorical grants and their transformation into block grants, and if the rapid implementation schedule for that effort is not modified, it will probably be important to look very carefully at the accountability measures provided in the proposal and to decide whether or not they are adequate for national policy-making purposes.

Before beginning an examination of those measures, and of the various existing alternative measures which could potentially bolster their effectiveness, it may be useful to discuss the concept of accountability very briefly here, so as to be a little bit more precise about what it signifies. Accountability is, of course, defined by the dictionary as "the condition of being answerable, responsible, obliged to account for one's acts," presumably, *to someone else.* But if there *is* someone else, the accountability implies a relationship: one person is accountable to another (or to many others) with regard to something entrusted to that person's care; the "something" is, of course, taxpayers' money, the accountability is for public funds.

The accountability relationship, then, is a little like a contract, which is "a bargain or agreement voluntarily made upon good consideration between two or more persons capable of contracting to do, or forbear to do, some lawful act" (Justice v. Lang, 42 N.Y. 493, 1 Am. R. 576). Such a contractual agreement creates rights and duties on both sides (as in the accountability relationship where the person receiving funds from the public purse is answerable for those funds to the appropriating entity and—through that entity—to the public). Further, these rights and duties are legally binding; that is, they are recognized and enforced by the courts.

Accountability on the part of one party thus implies at least some measure of control on the part of the other, since the duties of one are the rights of the other. In this way, because accountability signifies accounting to someone for something, the proper receiver of that accounting must be in a position to control or ensure both its delivery and quality. Mosher (1979: 234) points out that three requirements need to be met for the accountability relationship to exist effectively. There must be:

(1) *Information* about the actions and decisions of the individuals and organizations who are held accountable (transmitted) to those who are holding them to account.... The nature and usefulness of the information provided—its honesty and accuracy, completeness, specificity, relevance, adequacy, and timeliness—have always been critical attributes of accountability.

(2) *Receivers of the information,* who are able and willing to examine it, investigate it if necessary, digest it, and report it or initiate appropriate action based on it.

(3) *Recourse* on the basis of such information, to correct deficiencies and improve performance and/or to reward honorable and effective performance or penalize dishonesty, concealment, fraud, inefficiency, or ineffectiveness.

Accountability without adequate information from the accounting party, or without adequate oversight on the part of the receiver, or without at least potential recourse to sanctions in case of problems, is merely symbolic accountability, a kind of gesture in the right direction without real significance. As Etzioni (1975: 279) phrases it:

> The hallmark of "accountability as gesture" is that that it is pure norm with little or no instrumentality attached. That is, the speaker or writer advocating accountability fails to follow up the use of the term by outlining specific arrangements.

Fortunately, the block grant mechanism (unlike revenue sharing, as discussed above) provides for real accountability, and the administration has recognized this. While the block grant programs proposed vary somewhat in their provisions, they do presently contain elements of accountability. Most frequently, these include clauses requiring reports on intended and actual use of funds and periodic financial audits, as well as prohibitions against using those funds for buying land or constructing buildings, for satisfying matching requirements of other federal programs, or in a way which discriminates on the basis of race, sex, age, or physical handicaps. Some also include "maintenance-of-effort" provisions of various sorts.

Generally, however, these elements of accountability relate almost exclusively to financial responsibility and to equitable treatment issues; they do not provide an adequate basis for judging: (a) the match of the actual programmatic focus with the legislative intent regarding the program, (b) the quality of management and implementation in the program, (c) the delivery of services in the program, or (d) the outcomes or effectiveness of the program.

It is true that the Reagan proposal represents one way of addressing some of the complaints raised against the categorical grant system; however, simplification and consolidation do not require that the issues of the fidelity of program focus or program effectiveness be disregarded. In fact, in times when budgetary constraints require the elimination or drastic reduction of numerous existing programs, means for determining the relatively less effective programs become extremely important. Further, it is clear from the "creeping categorization" experience of many block grant programs of the past not only that such accountability is possible without diminishing the special advantages of the block grant mechanism, but also that if accountability is not provided for from the beginning of the block grant legislation, then the Congress will need to move toward this effort later on, with the greater cost and loss of information that this entails.

This section therefore begins what probably should be an ongoing effort to list the various elements and tools of accountability which currently exist, with the idea that such a typology would be helpful for examining the current block grant proposal. Such elements or tools must obviously address the requirements for accountability given above:

- instruments for obtaining *information* of the relevant kind and quality;
- instruments by which *receivers* can investigate and control the information collected and/or delivered; and
- instruments for *recourse* in the event of failures of accountability.

Many questions need to be confronted in beginning to structure such a typology for use with block grants, not least of which are: Accountability to whom? Accountability by whom? Accountability for what? How much accountability?

The first question, "Accountability to whom?" is a somewhat more difficult one for block grants than for categorical grants. With the latter, it is assumed that all accountability to the public will be through the Congress. With block grants, accountability to the public takes two forms: through the Congress, with regard to the national objective, through the state legislature and/or judiciary with regard to state and local objectives.

The second question, "Accountability by whom?" is a fairly straightforward one to answer since the people who are accountable under block grants are the same ones who are accountable under categorical programs. In the words of one analyst:

> Block grants eliminate neither state and local (or recipient) accountability for the money nor federal responsibility for assuring proper use of federally collected revenues [Dommel, 1981: 1].

The third question, however, "Accountability for what?" is a vastly more complex matter which the foregoing examination was intended to address. To recapitulate the findings of the prospective analysis which has been performed here, it seems likely, under block grants, that—given the larger discretion available at state and local levels—there is some danger of *inequitability* with regard to national target populations, and some danger of *irrelevance to the national program purpose* with regard to the selected activities. It seems likely, further, that—depending on how the Congress construes "minimal" accountability—there is some danger of *lack of information* at the national level with regard to *program performance* and with regard to *program costs*. It seems likely, finally, that, given state and local government variability, given lack of uniform standards or definitions, given the difficulty of assuring formal reporting across states, and given the painful historical experience, there is danger of *increased inefficiency, waste, fraud, and abuse* in block grant programs.

Block grant programs, then, need to gear their accountability instruments to the areas where they are most likely to be vulnerable and, if this analysis is correct, "accountability for what?" should thus focus on three issues:

(1) Accountability for achieving the *national objective* in funding the program; this issue focuses on (a) whether the program has followed the legislative intent (with regard to activities and target populations, if specified, for example) and (b) whether it has proven effective in meeting the broad national objective;

(2) Accountability for achieving *state and local objectives;* given that recognition of such objectives is a major reason for adopting the block grant mechanism, this issue focuses on whether specific state and local activities are effective in meeting *their* objectives (this, of course, is a responsibility for the recipient to decide, but it is important to envisage the possibility so as not to frustrate or preclude this account-ability in the federal design of the block grant); and

(3) Accountability for *program integrity and efficiency;* this issue focuses on whether sound program management is ensuring that objectives are pursued in the least costly way and with the internal controls over eligibility and expenditure needed to prevent waste, fraud, and abuse.

With regard to the fourth question, "How much accountability?" it is clear that the Congress will want to vary accountability measures—and especially degrees of accountability within those measures—based upon its own prior-ities for a particular program, upon acceptability to the administration and to state and local governments, and upon the objectives, structure, functions, and a host of other factors in the block grant. This question, then, is one which the Congress must decide and which will need to be addressed on a case-by-case basis.

While it is thus impossible to be specific here with regard to the degrees of accountability which may need to be incorporated in particular block grant programs, and while other work currently in progress will help to characterize the needed accountability framework, it is probably not premature to sketch out some of the elements or tools of accountability which could be embodied in block grant programs, and which should respond both to accountability *requirements* (that is, information, receiver control, and recourse instru-ments) and accountability *issues* (national program intent and effectiveness; state and local objectives and effectiveness; program management efficiency and integrity).

There are many elements of accountability—and degrees of accountability within those elements—which the Congress can possibly consider in address-ing the three accountability requirements and the three "accountability for what?" issues, depending on: the substance and type of the program, the particular program history (that is, the problems and successes it has already encountered), and the congressional sense of special priorities and accountability requirements within the program.

Clearly, the Congress will feel differently about different block grants. For some, experience will have shown that the national intent and/or target population are less likely to be well served at state and local levels than for others. Certain block grants will have demonstrated a high susceptibility to fraud and abuse; others will not. Thus, elements of accountability (and degrees of accountability within those elements) need to be targeted to block grants in terms of (a) the Congress' expectations and priorities for a particular program, and (b) the ability of the elements to measure and report this information.

All elements of accountability have special characteristics and applicability. Some may have seemed ineffective in some programs but might be useful in others. Eighteen of them are presented here in the effort to begin a typology of elements which can lead to improved flexibility while maintaining needed controls in block grants.

(1) *Specification by the Congress of the National Objective Sought in Funding the Program.*

This first element is the foundation for accountability at the national level. Without specification of the national objective (and, as discussed earlier, block grants can accommodate various shades of specificity moving from extremely broad definition to relatively detailed precisions about eligible activities and populations, for example), no accountability is possible on whether implementation moves in the desired national direction (since that direction is not clearly given), or on whether the program is effective (since effectiveness is only meaningful with regard to an objective). This element addresses the first accountability issue and is a prerequisite both for the generation of information and for receiver control.

(2) *Requirement by the Congress that Decisions on the Use of Block Grant Funds be Made Through Whatever Budget Process the State or Locality Uses for Its Own Funds.*

This element, if selected, would address the second and third accountability issues and ensure that block grant funds will produce at least the same budgetary and accounting information as other state and local funds. This is a minimal level of accountability at state/local levels.

(3) *Provision by the Congress that Block Grant Funds be Disbursed Through an Auditable Accounting System.*

This element would address the second and third accountability issues and ensure the production of good expenditure information. If the system were also made subject to periodic independent audit, then that would help to fulfill the second accountability requirement, that of receiver control. Degrees of accountability can vary with the frequency and type of the audit.

(4) *Requirement by the Congress for the Submission of State Plans to the Relevant Federal Agency Detailing the State's Intended Strategies and Activities in Implementing the National Objective.*

This element seeks to address the first accountability issue and might be selected as a fairly stringent means of ensuring the survival of the national objective in the 50 state programs by obtaining state attention to that objective in the development of the plan. It produces both information and receiver control. Various degrees of accountability can be ensured here by using other accountability elements jointly with the plan (through the means of guidelines by the federal agency on project eligibility or expenditure controls, for example, or through plan review and/or approval at the federal level, or through citizen participation in the development of the plan). This element also develops information on state activities which is important for the later performance of evaluation at either recipient or national levels. However, state plans are costly to prepare, have generated major problems (in the LEAA block grant program, for example) and may not be as useful for evaluation as are individual project applications featuring an evaluation component, for example.

(5) *Requirement by the Congress for a Formal Application Process by Which Potential Recipients Explain What They Will Do With Funds Received Under the Program and Why.*

This element if chosen, would represent a fairly stringent effort to ensure (a) the understanding and acceptance of the national objective at the recipient level; (b) the development of state and federal-level information about how the national objective is being implemented and what funding decisions are being made; and (c) the state or federal ability to sanction recipient misuse of funds with regard to the recipient's own assertions of intent. Degrees of stringency in this accountabiity element can be determined through differing review and approval processes.

(6) *Provision for Citizen Participation in State and/or Local Level Planning and/or Program Review.*

This element represents one possible way of addressing the problem of inequitability in the case of a specified target population, that is, the first accountability issue. It could be chosen in an attempt to ensure that the largest number of state and local voices will be heard, and that the programs implemented at state and local levels will in fact reflect state and local priorities within the broad national objective. Degrees of accountability within this element concern the types of citizen participation employed (public hearings, advisory planning, councils, citizen review boards), and the uses to which that participation is put within the program (input to state plans, voluntary assistance in service delivery, opinion surveys). This element, however, which has been a feature of both revenue sharing and block grants, tends to generate new constituencies and special interest groups; accordingly, there have been problems at state and local agency and provider levels in dealing effectively with citizen participation as a tool for accountability.

(7) *Requirement for a Recipient Report (to the State Agency or the State Legislature or the Congress or the Federal Agency) on the Use of Funds.*
This element, which calls only for performance data and does not require assessment, can be selected for two reasons. It provides retrospective information on how the block grant funds have been expended and it addresses the first two accountability issues.

(8) *Requirement by the Congress for Monitoring of Recipient Implementation by State and/or Federal Agencies.*
This element provides for receiver control of recipient-generated information. It can be chosen to address at least partially all three accountability issues (national and recipient objectives as well as management), if that were desired. Monitoring is also useful as a prerequisite for more sophisticated information, since evaluation depends on implementation monitoring to report on effectiveness. This then is an extremely important element of accountability, because the lack of provision for any implementation monitoring would signify first, that little reliable status information on program progress could be available in a timely manner either to state agencies, executive branch agencies, state legislatures, or the Congress; and second, that each audit or evaluation performed will be more expensive in that it must first proceed to the development of information on the status of implementation. Degrees of accountability can be specified in the comprehensiveness of the monitoring information sought, in the frequency of its performance, and in the procedures for assessing the reliability of the information produced (analysis, control, on-site visits, and so forth).

(9) *Requirement by the Congress for a Recipient Performance Report on Effectiveness Based on Independent Audit and/or Evaluation.*
This element can be used to address the three accountability issues. It provides both information and receiver control to those to whom the recipient is accountable. The usefulness of the information and the degree of confidence which the receiver may place in it are both dependent, however, on the quality of that information.

(10) *Provision for Technical Assistance in Accounting and Evaluation to Recipients by Federal and/or State Agencies.*
This element can be included so that less technically advanced localities/recipients may provide higher quality information to re-

ceivers. It thus can address both the problem of inequitability (by ensuring that eligible receipients are not denied help because of inadequate "grantsmanship"), and the first and third accountability issues. Further, if evaluation and audit (which report on program quality and integrity) are to be performed, they will both need good planning, data collection, and accounting systems in place if they are to address accountability objectives. Depending on the amount of audit and evaluation information deemed necessary by the Congress in a particular program, various degrees of accountability can be developed through the use of technical assistance.

(11) *Requirement by the Congress for the Audit of Recipient or Federal Agency Program Management.*
This element can be chosen so as to address all three accountability issues. Its use would have two purposes: first, the knowledge that there is provision for audit in a program tends to deter unsound management practices; second, the audit itself provides both information and receiver control to decision makers on program costs, implementation, management, and performance. Degrees of accountability are provided via the frequency, comprehensiveness, and program level of the audit.

(12) *Requirement by the Congress for Federal Agency Performance of Program Evaluation at Recipient or National Levels on the Effectiveness of Recipient Activities.*
This element, like audit, could be selected to address all three accountability issues but is especially useful in (a) the provision of empirical evidence of program effectiveness in terms of the national objective sought; (b) the pilot testing of new programs, management systems, or technology; and (c) the synthesis of retrospective information for policy use. Again, the prospect of evaluation constitutes the program equivalent of Mencken's "still, small voice that tells us someone is watching." Thus, the knowledge of a mandate for evaluation tends to deter deviations from expected courses of action. Degrees of accountability are afforded by the frequency, scope, duration, and level of the evaluation.

(13) *Requirement for Project Reports by Local Agencies to the State.*
This element could address, on a case basis, all three accountability issues and provide detailed information from the site level on a particular project useful for both state and federal receiver control. Degrees of accountability in this element concern the subject matter of the report, its frequency, and the methods of checking on its validity.

(14) *Provision for the Issuance of Program Standards or Guidelines by Federal or State Agencies.*
This element might be used to ensure that there will be some uniformity either across state programs or across level program

within a state with regard to program substance, internal controls and sanctions to deter fraud and abuse, and program reporting. Such uniformity assists all three accountability issues by building the national and/or recipient objectives into the standards or guidelines; by helping to ensure the development of cross-site information on program substance and quality; and by reducing the likelihood of unsound management. Varying degrees of stringency can occur here based on the type and specifity of the guidelines and standards; the number, frequency, and detail of program reporting requested; and the monitoring, audit, and evaluation functions called for to check on individual program status and uniformity across sites and programs.

(15) *Requirement by the Congress for an Annual Performance Report by the State to the Executive Branch Agency.*
This element can be used to provide information on program progress for an entire state to the federal agency, thus fulfilling two accountability requirements and addressing two issues. Degrees of accountability in this element relate essentially to the subject matter of the report (this can cover a range of materials moving from a recapitulation of state plans, a description of what was implemented, an explanation of how complete the various projects were in achieving coverage of the objective, through a summary of state and local evaluation, audit, and monitoring findings, to a set of state conclusions and recommendations based on the results of funded activities and the problems encountered), and to the methods adopted by the federal agency (or the Congress) for checking or analyzing its validity.

(16) *Requirement by the Congress for an Annual Performance Report by the Executive Branch Agency to the Congress.*
This element can be selected to hold the executive branch agency accountable to the Congress in the oversight process. The performance report may involve degrees of accountability ranging from the inclusion of simple status report information for each state (establishing the degree to which the block grant activities are faithful to the national program objective) through the provision of national monitoring, auditing, and evaluation reports generating information on program effectiveness, costs, and management integrity, to the recommendation of proposed changes in substance, procedures, and funding. Stringency in this element may be increased by congressional mandates for independent audit or evaluation of the federal agency program. This element can thus fulfill two (or even three) accountability requirements, depending on whatever independent reviews are accomplished, and can address all the accountability issues.

(17) *Requirement by the Congress for a Performance Report from an Independent Agency (for example, GAO) on Recipient Activities, Covering Integrity, Efficiency, and Effectiveness.*
This element can be used to ensure a high level of accountability with regard to the first and third accountability issues, and to provide both information and receiver control.

(18) *Specification of Sanctions for Failures of Accountability at Any Level and of Rewards for Effective Performance.*
This element can be selected to deter malfeasance and to provide incentives for sound performance; it serves the recourse requirement presented earlier. As Mosher (1979: 235) states:

Among the cruder tools for enforcing accountability (historically) . . . have been death, replacement, removal, demotion, elimination or reduction of authorities or resources, and legal action, either civil or criminal or both, to redress grievances. Less extreme but still significant instruments to penalize failures in performance include reprimands, loss of repute among superiors, peers, and subordinates, social penalties on self and family, and countless others. Instrumental to all these, and increasingly potent unto itself, is simply disclosure and publication. The key to accountability is thus, quite simply, information—the openness with which an individual or agency operates and the access to information by persons outside who are in a position to do something about it, if necessary, and the ways in which relevant information is selected, processed and utilized.

To recapitulate briefly, this section has developed 18 accountability elements which range from minimal to stringent and which can be selected to assure accountability in block grants based on the degree of specificity of the national objective; and the importance attached by the Congress and the administration to the determination of whether or not it is being accomplished. As specificity and importance increase, it seems natural to move up the ladder in *stringency,* going from a self-reporting system (providing information without receiver control), through a national agency reporting system (providing two levels of information and one level of receiver control) to an independent national-level reporting system (providing two levels of information and two levels of receiver control). In the same way, within a single type of reporting system, the elements move up the ladder in *rigor,* going from monitoring through audit to evaluation at either recipient or national levels.

SUMMARY

In conclusion, then, this chapter has sought to make five points:

(1) that the criticisms leveled at categorical grants may not all be addressed by turning the programs into block grants;

(2) that some aspects of current programs—notably their equitability, efficiency, and integrity—may be worsened by the block grant mechanism's loss of uniformity, definition, reporting and coordination across state programs at the national level;

(3) that measures are needed to ensure appropriate accountability by federal, state, and local personnel for the use of federal funds based on accountability requirements for:

- relevant information,

- an entity to receive and control the information, and

- recourse in case of failure;

and based on the accountability issues of:

- the achievement of the national objective;

- the achievement of the recipient objective; and

- program integrity and efficiency.

(4) the accountability measures are consistent both with the basic concept of the block grant and with the duty of policymakers to assure the proper use of federal funds; and finally,

(5) that at least 18 elements of accountability exist which can be considered by the Congress in varying degrees of stringency, depending upon the particular program involved, the specificity of the national objective, and the congressional view of the importance of knowing whether or not that objective is being accomplished.

Accountability, of course, is not cost-free. Some constraints and restrictions on program administration are unavoidable in any effort to monitor and assess program performance. Without "strings" of some sort, there will be no valid and reliable data by which to follow program activity, and no established criteria by which to judge program results. On the other hand, there is no reason to assume that the kinds of structure and demands imposed by the present largely categorical system are the only (or best) means to assure accountability. The costs which that system imposes in administrative inflexibility and fragmentation are real. The question that needs to be posed is what sort of requirements of national, state, and local governments will provide the information and criteria necessary for accountability in a particular program with a minimum of administrative overload to state and local program administrators.

NOTES

1. Milton Friedman (1962: 22-36), for example, has distinguished four reasons for governmental action in a free society: to make rules and to serve as umpire; to prevent or counter monopoly; to overcome "neighborhood" or external effects; and to protect those who cannot protect themselves, such as the insane or children.

2. The operation of an "iron triangle" usually involves a smooth and solid relationship among an administrative federal agency, the relevant legislative committees and subcommittees, and an intercessor client group or lobby.

3. In particular, the synthesis was developed using materials from Chelimsky (1979), the proceedings of a symposium which was jointly funded by the National Institute of Education, the National Institute of Justice, and the MITRE Corporation. This symposium brought together national, state, and local government program managers with evaluators and auditors in an effort to examine federal program problems and discuss ways of addressing them.

REFERENCES

Advisory Commission on Intergovernmental Relations (1977) "Safe Streets reconsidered: the block grant experience, 1968-1975." (unpublished)
——— (1977b) "Block grants: a comparative analysis." (unpublished)
CHELIMSKY, E. (1979) Proceedings of a Symposium on the Institutionalization of Federal Programs at the Local Level. Washington, DC: MITRE Corporation.
DOMMEL, P. R. (1981) "Statement prepared for the Senate Committee on Labor and Human Resources." Washington, DC: The Brookings Institution.
The Economist (1978) "Does CETA work?" April 29: 52.
ELAZAR, D. J. (1962) The American Partnership. Chicago: University of Chicago Press.
ETZIONI, A. (1975) "Alternative conceptions of accountability: the example of health administration." Public Administration Review (May/June): 279.
FRIEDMAN, M. (1962) Capitalism and Freedom. Chicago: University of Chicago Press.
GREIDER, W. and N. KOTZ (1973) "False hopes and faulty panaceas." Washington Post, April 8.
HERBERS, J. (1979a) "Washington, an insider's game." New York Times Magazine, April 22.
——— (1979b) "End to federal revenue-sharing expected in forthcoming budget." New York Times, July 9.
——— (1978) "Deep government disunity alarms many U.S. leaders." New York Times, November 12.
Joint Economic Committee (1978) "Hearing on Structural Unemployment and Public Policy." Washington, DC: Government Printing Office.
LEVIN, C. (1979) "Keepers of the dream." Washington Post, August 2.
MARTIN, R. C. (1965) The Cities and the Federal System. New York: Atherton Press.
MOSHER, F. C. (1979) The GAO: The Quest for Accountability in the American Government. Boulder, CO: Westview Press.

NETZER, R. (1974) "Discussion of 'The Property Tax: Progressive or Regressive.' " American Economic Review (May): 231.

PINE, A. (1979) "Senator Muskie criticizes states on budget-balancing moves." Washington Post, February 14.

REAGAN, M. D. (1972) The New Federalism. New York: Oxford University Press.

SCHULTZE, C. L. (1974) "The Great Society versus the New Federalism: sorting out the social grant programs." American Economic Review (May): 183-185.

STANFIELD, R. L. (1981) "Block grants look fine to states; it's the money that's the problem." National Journal, May 9.

SUNDQUIST, J. L. with D. W. DAVIS (1969) Making Federalism Work. Washington, DC: The Brookings Institute.

TOLCHIN, M. and S. TOLCHIN (1972) To The Victor. New York: Vintage.

U.S. General Accounting Office (1979) Perspective on Intergovernmental Policy and Fiscal Relations. (GGD-79-62). Washington, DC: Government Printing Office.

WILCOX, C. (1969) Toward Social Welfare. Homewood, IL: Irwin.

42

Implementing Equal Education Opportunity Policy
A Comparison of the Outcomes of HEW and Justice Department Efforts

Joseph Stewart, Jr. and Charles S. Bullock III

This research examines the differential impact of HEW and Justice Department enforcement efforts to implement equal educational opportunity policy in four Southern states between 1968 and 1974. The evidence indicates that equal education opportunity remains an unfulfilled goal and that the patterns of deviation from the ideal are at least partially attributable to the enforcement agency. Reasons are suggested for the patterns found. Policy analysts will find clear examples of the impact of both problem definition and implementation on policy outcomes.

While Southern school desegregation efforts have succeeded to the extent that Southern students are less racially isolated than those in other parts of the country (Bullock and Rodgers, 1975), equal-education opportunity has not become a reality in the region. Given what is known about institutional racism (Knowles and Prewitt, 1969) and the attitudes of Southern educators (Rodgers and Bullock, 1976), it is not surprising that racial discrimination continues after de jure segregation disappeared. Thus Rodgers and Bullock (1972: 69) find, "In many of the schools that have been integrated in the South

AUTHORS' NOTE: *We thank James H. Kuklinski, James F. Sheffield, Gary L. Wamsley, and two anonymous reviewers for helpful comments on an earlier draft of this article.*

From Joseph Stewart, Jr. and Charles S. Bullock III, "Implementing Equal Education Opportunity Policy: A Comparison of the Outcomes of HEW and Justice Department Efforts," 12(4) *Administration & Society* 427-446 (February 1981). Copyright 1981 by Sage Publications, Inc.

the most invidious kinds of racial discrimination persist."
Various reports conclude that overt, de jure discrimination has
often been succeeded by a "second generation" of discrimination in Southern schools ("Children out of school in America,"
1974; "It's not over in the South," 1972; "The status of school
desegregation in the South, 1970"; "The student pushout,"
1973). This discrimination has been manifest in underrepresentation of black administrators and faculty and overrepresentation of black children in certain kinds of classes.

The incidence of second-generation discrimination has not,
however, been constant across either districts or time. A variable that may be related to the severity of new modes of discrimination is the agency responsible for desegregating a
district. The Departments of Justice, and Health, Education,
and Welfare worked as discrete agents in desegregating Southern schools with somewhat different consequences. In the Pratt
decisions (Adams v. Richardson, 1972; Adams v. Weinberger,
1975), the district court implied that stricter standards were
used for determining whether segregation remained in districts
that HEW had desegregated than in ones desegregated by
Justice. Giles (1975) found that districts desegregated by
Justice had desegregated less in 1968 and 1970 than districts
handled by HEW. The enforcement agency was an important
variable even after controlling for proportion black and size
of district enrollment.

The purpose of this paper is to move beyond examination
of the policy output—desegregation—and to compare the
districts desegregated by each of the enforcement agencies in
terms of the degree of second generation discrimination
found—the policy outcome.[1] Data are examined for school
districts in four Southern states—Arkansas, Georgia, Louisiana, and Texas—which had between 1% and 99% black enrollment from 1968 to 1974.[2] Based on research which assesses the
efficacy of Justice and HEW efforts, higher levels of second
generation discrimination are initially expected in districts
desegregated by Justice.

BACKGROUND AND HYPOTHESES

Over 81% of the South's biracial districts were desegregated by either HEW or the Justice Department. The typical scenario saw HEW attempt to negotiate a desegregation plan using federal fund termination as the ultimate weapon. Some districts submitted plans beginning in 1965 and kept pace with increasingly stringent HEW guidelines. Other awaited the initiation of administrative proceedings by HEW to terminate federal funds before they complied. A third set of districts waited until until HEW had terminated federal funds before desegregating.

However, even this drastic step did not raise the cost of noncompliance sufficiently for some local school officials. When HEW failed to achieve desegregation, districts were assigned to the Justice Department where remedies were pursued in the federal courts. Justice won court orders imposing specific desegregation plans. The most recalcitrant schools were desegregated when Justice resorted to an innovative, comprehensive strategy: suing the state board of education to enjoin it from providing state funds to noncompliant districts. This technique was particularly effective because most Southern school districts are financed largely with state funds. Regardless of the technique Justice employed, once it assumed jurisdiction, HEW ceased to be involved. Thus, the departments worked separately, with Justice desegregating the most recalcitrant districts.

Since districts desegregated by Justice were slower to disestablish dual school systems, and since districts with relatively high levels of segregation had less need to employ second-generation discrimination, the first hypothesis is

H1: Districts desegregated by the Justice Department will display significantly *lower* levels of second-generation discrimination at the earliest data point available (1968) than districts desegregated by HEW.

One factor lessens the likelihood of either agency effectively thwarting second-generation discrimination. Initially, both agencies mistakenly accepted the assumption that desegregation was equivalent to equal-education opportunity. For a time, desegregation was seen as an end, not a means; an outcome, not an output. Thus it was assumed in some quarters that once schools were desegregated, the objectives of HEW and Justice would be achieved.

Some federal agents responsible for achieving equal-education opportunities may have consciously opted to ignore one aspect of second-generation discrimination, the displacement of black faculty. A rationale for this strategy was that it avoided further antagonizing white parents who opposed desegregated classes and would find a black teacher even harder to accept. Another reason is offered by a Justice attorney:

> There may have been a feeling on the part of many people at HEW and Justice that there were a lot of black teachers who had been giving black kids bad educations and it wouldn't be surprising if you were going to lose a lot of these black teachers through desegregation.

As it has become clear that new guises of discrimination developed in many desegregated schools, HEW has been quicker to take corrective actions than Justice. In part this is because the agencies possess different enforcement capabilities. HEW has more personnel and they are more geographically dispersed, while Justice lawyers generally work out of Washington, D.C. Because of these features, HEW is better prepared to monitor progress. Moreover, the historically greater obstinacy of Justice districts militates against Justice combatting second-generation discrimination as effectively as HEW. Furthermore, second-generation discrimination is a subtle phenomenon which is more difficult to demonstrate and treat as an adjudicable dispute than the former dual school system. Thus, the bureaucracy may be a more appropriate "arena of conflict" for dealing with this problem than the judicial system.

While HEW's efforts have been far from comprehensive, its Office for Civil Rights has investigated a number of school districts to see if they are guilty of racial discrimination in special education, ability grouping, punishment, or personnel practices. Such monitoring has occurred for district which apply for Emergency School Aid Act (ESAA) funds. Surveys done by one of the authors with OCR staffers in 1974-1975 revealed that most of them believed that these pregrant clearances were quite useful in combatting second-generation discrimination.

In contrast, interviews conducted during the same period with lawyers of the Education Section of Justice's Civil Rights Division indicated little concern about second-generation discrimination. A few suits had been brought on behalf of black faculty in the South, but at the time of the interviews, Justice attorneys were focusing increasingly on racial inequities in schools outside the South. One attorney acknowledged that, "Once you get outside the area of student desegregation we've not done much." Because of the relative inferiority of Justice as a monitoring agent and HEW's greater concern about continuing discrimination due to its ESAA responsibilities:

H2: Districts desegregated by the Justice Department will display a significantly *greater* increase in levels of second-generation discrimination over time than districts desegregated by HEW.

CONSEQUENCES OF SECOND-GENERATION DISCRIMINATION

The existence of second-generation discrimination in desegregated Southern schools has important implications for society and for policy-making. First, a second generation of discrimination would prevent correction of the problems that desegregation was supposed to achieve—improvements in black achievement levels, self-images, career opportunities, social mobility, and educational attainment.

Second, post-desegregation discrimination violates the spirit of the law. The original intent of civil rights policy was to provide equal-education opportunity, with desegregation perceived as the obstacle to be removed. Second-generation discrimination contravenes this intent.

Third, successful contravention of the spirit of the law could undermine general respect for the law and affect the ability to achieve social change through law. Diffuse support for the legal system and the ability to achieve social change through relatively passive legal means are important contributors to regime stability.

Finally, if bureaucratic agencies do not meet the challenge of continuing efforts to achieve equal-education opportunity, victims of second-generation discrimination will be limited to pursuing remedies through private suits. Some cases have already appeared (e.g., Hobson v. Hansen, 1967; Larry P. v. Riles, 1972). As was seen in the desegregation effort, there may be negative consequences when courts must assume most of the responsibility for policy innovation (Rodgers and Bullock, 1972: 74). This branch, when acting alone or in advance of the other branches of government, finds policy implementation extremely difficult and risks loss of support for its decisions in other areas. Moreover, when private litigants bear the brunt of policy innovation, change tends to be halting, uneven, and to benefit primarily those able to afford attorneys and long delays (Bullock and Rodgers, 1975).

MANIFESTATIONS OF SECOND-GENERATION DISCRIMINATION

Two measures of second-generation discrimination are used: the level of black overrepresentation among students assigned to special education classes, and the level of black underrepresentation among faculty.[3]

SPECIAL EDUCATION

Assignment of students to classes for the educable mentally retarded (EMR) is a means of handling "problem" students and offers a tool of discrimination which may be couched in "educational" terms. If blacks are disproportionately assigned to EMR classes, then regular classes will have fewer blacks, the result being higher levels of racial isolation. The consequences of discriminatory tracking are pointed up in a 1970 report which asserted that 35% of the remaining high school segregation in the South and 60% of the remaining elementary school segregation was the product of ability tests which were usually instituted at the time of desegregation ("The status of school desegregation in the South," 1970: 35). (The coincidence of using test scores for class assignment and desegregation raises suspicions about the intent of the testing.) A Washington-based children's advocacy group estimated that at least 32,381 more black students were in EMR classes in 1973 in five Southern states than one would expect, given the ratio of black to white enrollments (Children out of school, 1974: 5).

Black overrepresentation persists despite HEW guidelines prohibiting practices, including testing, which promote racial isolation and requiring that racially identifiable special-education programs be shown to be educationally necessary and educationally successful; i.e., students must perform better than they would if they were left in regular classrooms. Such classes must have special curricula and be taught by specially trained teachers. Observers and participants suggest that these standards are often not met. To cite some examples, predominantly black special-education classes in Greenville, Mississippi, were larger than predominantly white "smart sections." In the same locale, a student misassigned to a special-education class required several months of intensive work, once the mistake was discovered, to regain the level of performance found in regular classes. Faculty and counselors in Florence, South Carolina, opined that the negative psychological effects and self-fulfilling prophecies of special-education teachers negated the theoretical benefits of special education ("It's not over in the South," 1972: 111).

Many educators believe that ability grouping or tracking, of which EMR classes are one type, reinforces class distinctions which are correlated with racial distinctions (Clark, 1964; Rist, 1970; Weber and Pearl, 1966). Tracking negatively reinforces those who have a history of failure and promotes attitudes and behavior which contribute to further failure by those who know that they have been branded as "slow learners" (Clark, 1965; McCullough, 1974; Stein, 1971).

Moreover, the tests used to track black students are frequently attacked for having middle class, white bias (Kirp and Yudof, 1974; 668). Some argue that present procedures are inadequate and measure the effects of previous discrimination (Clement et al., 1976).

In determining eligibility for ESAA grants, HEW's Office for Civil Rights considers enrollment in special-education classes. Eligibility requires that black enrollment in special-education classes not exceed the proportion black in the system by 20 percentage points.

OCR's enforcement efforts have received some support from the courts beginning with Hobson v. Hansen (1967). Later a Louisiana federal district court held ability grouping invalid when the program's initiation coincided with desegregation (Moses v. Washington Paris School Board, 1971). A federal district court in California held that a school district violated the equal-protection clause when blacks constituted 28.5% of the district's enrollment but 66.0% of all students in EMR classes (Larry P. v. Riles, 1972). The Fifth Circuit prohibited a school district from using ability grouping in previously segregated schools until time has erased the effects of earlier discrimination (McNeal v. Tate County Board of Education, 1975).[4]

FACULTY DISCRIMINATION

As dual school systems were dismantled, hundreds of black teachers were dismissed and demoted. A 1970 report ("Status of school desegregation") found that of 467 districts surveyed, "34 districts had dismissed black teachers, and 103 had demoted black teachers." The National Education Association concluded that "what is happening . . . is not *integration*; rather it is *disintegration*—the near total disintegration of black authority in every aspect of the system of public education" ("Pushout report," 1970: 6).

Dismissals are, of course, the most extreme means of discrimination. Common explanations were that: (1) with the elimination of the dual school system there was less demand for teachers; (2) those dismissed had done poorly on the National Teachers Examination, or (3) firings were for "incompetency," "lack of qualifications," or "improper credentials." These latter reasons were often patently discriminatory since the same teachers had taught in black schools for years without these deficiencies being discovered ("The status of school desegregation in the South," 1970: 75, 85-88).

Not only were blacks being dismissed, but blacks were not being hired to fill new positions (It's not over in the South, 1972: 84-95). The result of such practices was an estimated net decline of 526 black teachers in Georgia and 519 in Louisiana in the immediate wake of desegregation (Brown, 1971). Rodgers and Bullock (1976: 115) found evidence of underrepresentation of black faculty in the 31 districts they studied.

As early as 1966, the courts held that nondiscrimination was required among faculty and staff (U.S. v. Jefferson County Board of Education, 1966). The courts have further decided that existing patterns of black faculty dismissal "cast the burden of proof on school boards to show that failure to rehire was for nondiscriminatory reasons, and require that such proof be clear and convincing, before the failure to reemploy may be upheld" (Williams v. Kimbrough, 1969). HEW supported that ruling with its own regulation (Office for Civil Rights, 1968) and in reviewing ESAA grant applications.

MEASUREMENT AND METHODOLOGY

The measures of equal treatment used here are based on the assumption that blacks should be represented in special-education classes and faculty employment at about the same rate as their proportion in a system's student population. For special education the measure is the ratio of the percentage of blacks in special education to the percentage of whites in the system who are in special education. In definitional formula form, this is (Formula 1)

$$\frac{b/Bs}{w/Ws}$$

where b is the number of blacks in special education classes, Bs, the number of blacks in the school system w, the number of whites in special education classes, and Ws, the number of whites in the school system.

The assumption is that blacks and whites, regardless of their representation in the school system, should be placed in special education classes at the same rates.[5] That is, if 6% of the blacks within the system are assigned to special education, 6% of the whites should be also. Hence, 1.0 on this measure indicates equality, and values greater than 1.0 suggest evidence of discrimination against blacks, with the implication becoming stronger when scores are high.

This measure is, however, inappropriate for measuring faculty discrimination. There is no categorization of faculty for which data are available which has the same implications as categories for students do. Black faculty are employed, or they are not. The general assumption is that black faculty should be represented in the system in a proportion equal to the proportion black in the student population. Therefore, if black teachers are employed proportional to black enrollment, the ratio of black students to black teachers should equal the ratio of white students to white teachers. This measure is represented by the following definitional formula: (Formula 2)

$$\frac{Bs/Bt}{Ws/Wt}$$

where Bs is the number of black students in the school system,
   Bt, the number of black teachers in the school system,
   Ws, the number of white students in the school system, and
   Wt, the number of white teachers in the school system.

A score greater than 1.0 indicates underrepresentation of black faculty and possible discrimination.

The data for the computation of these measures are taken from forms filed with HEW by school systems. Some gaps exist because of failure to file loss of records, differences in federal sampling frames, or absence of a special-education program.

The method of testing the hypotheses is to use t-tests of the difference in means for the two sets of districts. The means of each group are used to establish the direction of the difference. Thus, if the first hypothesis is to be confirmed, a significance level of .05 or less should be found, and the 1968 means for districts desegregated by the Justice Department should be lower than the means for districts desegregated by HEW. If the second hypothesis is to be confirmed, the means of the two types of districts will have converged by 1974, and the significant difference will disappear. Or the significant difference may reappear in the opposite direction (i.e., a .05 level of

TABLE 1

Means for School Districts Desegregated by HEW and
the Justice Department, Special Education and Faculty
Discrimination Indices, 1968-1974

	1968	1969	1970	1971	1972	1973	1974
Special Education							
HEW Districts, $\overline{X}$	3.29	3.31	4.22	4.32	4.33	4.06	4.75
	(171)	(163)	(264)	(268)	(260)	(337)	(298)
Justice Districts, $\overline{X}$	2.09	2.17	2.79	4.56	4.49	5.09	5.74
	(27)	(33)	(67)	(85)	(88)	(100)	(101)
t - probabilities	.001	.001	.000	.285	.335	.004[a]	.011[a]
Faculty							
HEW Districts, $\overline{X}$	1.99	2.37	2.41	2.55	2.31	2.79	2.48
	(426)	(304)	(501)	(350)	(379)	(298)	(161)
Justice Districts, $\overline{X}$	1.25	1.33	1.72	2.01	2.00	2.13	2.22
	(74)	(62)	(117)	(106)	(113)	(102)	(103)
t - probabilities	.000	.000	.000	.000	.001	.000	.047

NOTE: Number of cases in parentheses.
a. HEW districts have significantly less evidence of discrimination than do Justice districts.

significance may be attained with the means for HEW districts being lower than the means for Justice districts).

THE FINDINGS

Table 1 presents t-probabilities on the differences in discrimination-index scores between districts desegregated by HEW and Justice. For special education, as hypothesized, Justice districts had significantly less evidence of discrimination from 1968 through 1970 than did HEW districts. For faculty, Justice districts were significantly less discriminatory than HEW districts for the entire period. Thus the data support the first hypothesis, i.e., there is less evidence of discrimination in Justice districts in 1968.

Figures 1 and 2 present the trends in mean discrimination index scores for special education and faculty, respectively, for 1968 to 1974. In the four states studied, the indication of discriminatory policy has become markedly stronger in special education, where the means in 1974 were 4.75 in HEW districts and 5.74 in Justice districts. This means that in the average district, black students were more than 4.5 times as likely to be placed in special-education classes than were whites. While the rise in the discrimination index has been less dramatic for the faculty data, it has nonetheless increased in both Justice and HEW districts. By 1974, the mean in HEW districts was approximately 2.5, indicating that, on average, the pupil to teacher ratio among blacks is 2.5 times as great as among whites. In Justice-desegregated schools black teachers were not as severely underrepresented, with the mean being 2.22. Thus blacks are overrepresented in special-education classes but underrepresented on faculties. Conditions worsened between 1968 and 1974 in both HEW and Justice districts.

Examination of the means and the t-tests sheds light on the second hypothesis. For special education, the significant difference disappears for 1971 and 1972, but after 1973 discrimination is significantly more prevalent in Justice than HEW districts. In terms of proportional growth, the mean 1974 special education score for Justice districts is 175% higher than the 1968 score; the mean 1974 HEW score is only 44% higher. Thus, the second hypothesis is clearly supported for special education.

Data on faculty discrimination show that the significant difference found in 1968 persists through 1974. Justice Department districts continue to be less discriminatory than HEW districts, although the gap narrows between 1968 and 1974. The mean Justice score in 1974 is 78% higher than the 1968 score; the comparable figure for HEW districts is only 25%. Thus, the differential rates of increase for faculty discrimination converge, although means in HEW districts remain significantly higher.

In summary, districts desegregated under the aegis of the Justice Department were significantly less discriminatory in 1968 than those desegregated by HEW. In the subsequent years, however, Justice-desegregated districts have evinced increasing discrimination at a higher rate than have HEW districts. In special-education classes, Justice districts are now significantly more discriminatory. For faculty, the differential

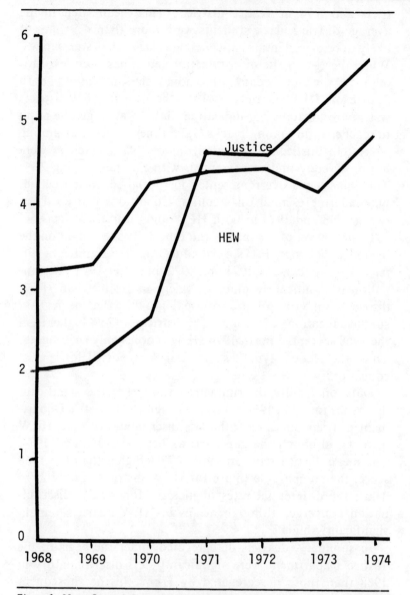

Figure 1: Mean Second Generation Discrimination Index Score for Sepcial Education, by Year and Enforcement Agency

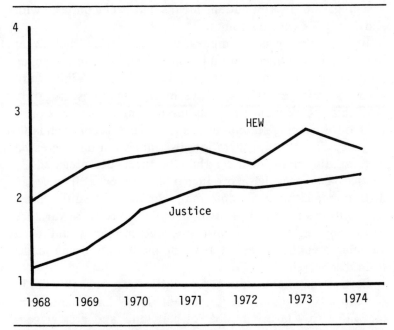

Figure 2: **Mean Second Generation Discrimination Index Score for Faculty, by Year and Enforcement Agency**

rates of change have brought the two categories closer, but without eliminating the significant difference.

IMPLICATIONS

The evidence of second-generation discrimination at the levels found here has grave implications for public policy-making. Second-generation discrimination has come in the wake of a policy nominally aimed at achieving equal-education opportunity. The fact that discrimination could continue in desegregated schools was incompatible with the policy makers' definition of the problem. Thus, a misconception of the policy problem seriously affected the subsequent steps of implementation and evaluation.[6] By accepting desegregation as synonymous with equal-education opportunity, policy makers were unprepared to combat the emergence of post-desegregation discrimination. Means had been confused with ends; outputs with outcomes.

Beyond these general implications, this article shows that the enforcement agency is an important variable in the policy outcome of second-generation discrimination. While both agencies were generally effective in achieving desegregation (and this achievement was truly monumental), neither can be lauded for curbing second-generation. HEW is commendable only because second-generation discrimination has increased less rapidly in its districts than in those desegregated by Justice. This may be a product of continued differences in district recalcitrance in addition to administrative differences. (Separation of continued district recalcitrance from variance caused by different administrative techniques would be a valuable breakthrough, but as yet no method for doing so has been discovered.)

Part of the explanation for the differences probably lies in the capacity to monitor enforcement. HEW has clear advantages due to a larger number of personnel and greater geographic distribution of its staff. While it is apparent that HEW's Office for Civil Rights has not been adequately staffed or funded for the effort needed to fully combat second-generation discrimination, the Justice Department is in even worse shape.

Another part of the explanation lies in relative will to monitor. Queries of key Justice Department personnel (conducted by the authors in 1974-1975) concerning monitoring were met as if the interview were being conducted in a foreign language. Until Adams v. Richardson (1972), HEW rarely monitored Justice districts. Even second-generation discrimination in Justice districts comes under HEW scrutiny only when a district requests ESAA money or a complaint about district practices is registered with OCR. In HEW districts, some attention may be paid to the problems of continuing discrimination even if the district is being reviewed primarily for some other reason.[7]

It appears that monitoring is necessary if not sufficient to ensure compliance with social-policy innovations (see Bullock and Rodgers, 1975). A lack of monitoring will result in the institutional subversion of policy goals, particularly if those goals are as ill defined as in this case.

Finally, the rise in discrimination is less pronounced against faculty than it is against students in special education. This suggests that administrative enforcement may be easier when the potential victims are adults who are likely to be aware of their rights. Blacks assigned to special-education classes may be less able to enlist help to pursue their rights, since they often must rely on their parents or outside activists to lodge complaints. Also, it may be easier to detect discriminatory personnel practices than inequities in special-education placements. The latter are usually couched in terms of helping students—only probing below the surface will determine whether the program pays educational dividends or is simply a subtle tactic to promote racial isolation.

This article provides insights on how not to maximize the effectiveness of social policy. There should be a broad, uncompromising definition of both the problem and the policy objective with vigorous enforcement and continued monitoring to ensure compliance. While this may seem unrealistic, the results are unlikely to be more disappointing then those obtained by present practices. Because equal-education opportunity was initially defined simply as desegregation, many are deluded into believing that it now exists, when it actually remains an unfulfilled goal. When policy deals with a symptom rather than the disease, other symptoms will have to be treated in the future. Until this lesson is learned, social policy change in the United States will remain an expensive and often frustrating proposition.

NOTES

1. The distinction between output—"what a government does"—and outcome— "the consquences for society, intended or unintended, that flow from action or inaction by government," is particularly important in this context. For a pellucid statement of this difference, see Anderson (1979: 5).

2. We have excluded northern and western Texas districts for two reasons: these districts are administered separately by HEW, and they have low black enrollments. Equal educational opportunity issues in these districts tend to be cast in terms of Chicano discrimination, which is beyond the scope of this article. For southern and eastern Texas and for the other three states we have included all biracial districts which were desegregated through HEW or Justice efforts for which data are available.

There are variations in the number of districts per year because some districts failed to return the survey forms distributed by federal authorities or filled incorrectly. Another cause for changes in the number of cases is that HEW and the Equal Employment Opportunities Commission—the agencies which collected the raw data analyzed here—have used differing criteria over the years in determining which districts to survey. When HEW gathered faculty data (1968-1972) it surveyed more districts than did EEOC (1973-1974). The increase in the number of districts for which special education data are available results from a growth in the number of districts having these programs. The big jump in special education programs in 1970 coincides with the implementation of final desegregation plans in many southern school systems. The juncture of these events supports our contention that many systems inaugurated special education not so much to enhance the education of the participants as to maintain racial isolation in officially desegregated schools.

It is not feasible to include a control group of districts not subject to either HEW or Justice. There are too few districts in these states which desegregated as a result of some other force, i.e., as a result of suits filed by private plaintiffs. All districts in the four states studied desegregated as a result of one of the following: HEW efforts, Justice suits, or private plaintiff suits.

3. The validity of using these measures for inferences about discriminatory intent may be legitimately questioned. However, their use here is appropriate on two grounds: (1) these are measures used by OCR in compliance reviews, and (2) these are measures frequently cited in the anecdotal reports that allege widespread patterns of continuing discrimination. Undoubtably, these measures incorporate the effects of forces other than discrimination, intentional or unintentional. It has already been noted that Justice Department districts were harder to desegregate than HEW districts. Examination of variables beyond the scope of this study (e.g., socioeconomic or educational variables) or use of more elaborate measures might shed more light on the general phenomenon. But, this does not lessen the utility of these measures for our evaluation of enforcement agencies using their own criteria.

4. This series of cases shows that, while courts have confronted questions about the legality of special-education programs, the impetus for these reviews has been suits by private plaintiffs, rather than by the Justice Department.

5. This method has been used by the Office for Civil Rights. See "Pushout report: user's guide," OCR internal document. Of course, this assumption may be contaminated by variance in the distribution of past educational opportunity along racial lines. However, the evidence (see note 2) suggests that racial discrimination, not compensatory treatment, is often experienced by blacks in newly desegregated schools.

6. For an explication of the sequential model of policy-making, see Anderson (1979).

7. Because of rigid timetables for responding to complaints imposed as part of Adams v. Califano (1977) and because of a lack of staff, OCR personnel are now less able to look broadly into discrimination in districts where they become involved than previously.

CASES

ADAMS v. CALIFANO (1977) 430 F. Supp. 118.
ADAMS v. RICHARDSON (1972) 351 F. Supp. 636.
ADAMS v. WEINBERGER (1975) 391 F. Supp. 269.
BROWN v. BOARD OF EDUCATION OF TOPEKA (1954-1955) 347 U.S. 483; 349 U.S. 294.
HOBSON v. HANSEN (1967) 269 F. Supp. 401.
LARRY P. v. RILES (1972) 343 F. Supp. 1306.
McNEAL v. TATE COUNTY BOARD OF EDUCATION (1975) 508 F. 2d 1917.
MOSES v. WASHINGTON PARISH SCHOOL BOARD (1971) 330 F. Supp. 1340.
U.S. v. JEFFERSON COUNTY BOARD OF EDUCATION (1966) 372 F. 2d 836.
WILLIAMS v. KIMBROUGH (1969) 295 F. Supp. 585.

REFERENCES

ANDERSON, J. E. (1979) Public Policy-Making. New York: Holt, Rinehart & Winston.
BROWN, J. (1971) "State school suit hits black ousters." Atlanta J. (March 18): 1, 15.
BULLOCK, C. S., III (1976) "Compliance with school desegregation laws: financial inducements and policy performance." Presented to the annual meeting of the American Political Science Association, Chicago, September 2-5.
——— and H. R. RODGERS, Jr. (1975) Racial Equality in America: In Search of an Unfulfilled Goal. Santa Monica, CA: Goodyear.
"Children out of school in America" (1974) Children's Defense Fund of the Washington Research Project, Inc.
CLARK, K. B. (1965) Dark Ghetto: Dilemmas of Social Power. New York: Harper & Row.
——— (1964) "Clash of cultures in the classroom," pp. 18-25 in M. Weinberg (ed.) Integrated Education—Learning Together. Chicago: Integrated Education Association.
CLEMENT, D. C., M. EISENHART, and J. W. WOOD (1976) "School desegregation and educational inequality: trends in the literature, 1960-1975," in The Desegregation Literature: A Critical Appraisal. Washington, DC: National Institute of Education.
GILES, M. W. (1975) "H.E.W. versus the federal courts: a comparison of school desegregation enforcement." Amer. Politics Q. 3 (January): 81-90.
GOLDBERG, M. S., A. H. PASSOW, and J. JUSTMAN (1966) The Effects of Ability Grouping. New York: Teachers College Press.
"It's not over in the South: school desegregation in forty-three Southern cities eighteen years after Brown" (1972) Alabama Council on Human Relations; American Friends Service Committee; Delta Ministry of the National Council of Churches; NAACP Legal Defense and Educational Fund, Inc.; Southern Regional Council; and Washington Research Project.
KIRP, D. L. and M. G. YUDOF (1974) Educational Policy and the Law: Cases and Materials. Berkeley, CA: McCutchan.

KNOWLES, L. and K. PREWITT [eds.] (1969) Institutional Racism in America. Englewood Cliffs, NJ: Prentice-Hall.

McCULLOUGH, T. (1974) "Urban education: 'it's no big thing.'" Urban Education 9: 117-135.

MERCER, J. R. (1974) "A policy statement of assessment procedures and the rights of children." Harvard Educ. Rev. 44, 1: 125-141.

"Pushout report: user's guide" (1970) O.C.R. internal document. Report of NEA Task Force III, School Desegregation: Louisiana and Mississippi, November.

Office for Civil Rights (1968) Policies on Elementary and Secondary School Compliance with Title VI of the Civil Rights Act of 1964. Washington, DC: Government Printing Office.

RIST, R. C. (1970) "Student social class and teacher expectations: the self-fulfilling prophecy in ghetto education." Harvard Educ. Rev. 40: 416-451.

RODGERS, H. R., Jr. and C. S. BULLOCK, III (1976) Coercion to Compliance: Or How Great Expectations in Washington Are Actually Realized at the Local Level, This Being the Saga of School Desegregation in the South as Told by Two Sympathetic Observers—Lessons on Getting Things Done. Lexington, MA: D. C. Heath.

——— (1972) Law and Social Change: Civil Rights Laws and Their Consequences. New York: McGraw-Hill.

"The status of school desegregation in the South, 1970" (1970) American Friends Service Committee; Delta Ministry of the National Council of Churches; Lawyers Committee for Civil Rights Under Law; Lawyers Constitutional Defense Committee; NAACP Legal Defense and Educational Fund, Inc.; and Washington Research Project.

STEIN, A. (1971) "Strategies for failure." Harvard Educ. Rev. 41: 158-204.

"The student pushout: victims of continued resistance to desegregation" (1973) Southern Regional Council and Robert F. Kennedy Memorial.

WEBER, G. and A. PEARL (1966) "Two views concerning ability grouping." Southern Education Report 2, 5: 2-8.

Joseph Stewart, Jr. is Assistant Professor of Political Science at the University of New Orleans where he teaches public administration, public policy and black politics. His research in the area of civil rights policy has appeared in the Journal of Politics, Integrated Education, *and* Policy Studies Journal.

Charles S. Bullock III is Professor of Political Science and Research Fellow with the Institute for Behavioral Research at the University of Georgia. His teaching and research specialties are public policy and legislative politics. He has authored, co-authored, or co-edited six books and articles in the American Political Science Review, Journal of Politics, American Journal of Political Science, Social Science Quarterly, *and other journals.*

43

Professional Models for Policy Analysis

John L. Foster

*A number of proposals for improvement of public policy-making call for the develop-
ment of a professional group which blends technological skills, humanistic goals, and a
sense for practical politics. This article suggests that several very different professional
roles may be appropriate to different public policy areas. These differing roles suggest
varying degrees of professional power over policy-making, different professional
ethical standards, and lead to questions of the feasibility of developing a single profession to encompass all of policy analysis.*

Many recent proposals for greater rationality in public policy-
making require development of an expert group which blends
the technological skills of the physical and social sciences with
a sense for both humanistic goals and practical politics.[1] This
article is a discussion of possible role models for such a policy-
oriented profession. It will outline several of the major issues in
the professionalization literature and subsequent models for
policy analysis. It will also examine a few apparent prescriptive
and descriptive consequences of each model.

There are a range of definitions of professionalism ranging
from the virtually all inclusive "one who is paid to do some-

AUTHOR'S NOTE: *This is a revised version of a paper originally presented at the
Southern Political Science Association Meeting, November, 1978. I would like to extend particular thanks to John Baker, Gary Brooks, Thomas Henderson, John S.
Jackson, Karen Lewis, Ron Mason, and Steve Wasby for comments and assistance
with this article.*

From John L. Foster, "Professional Models for Policy Analysis," 12(4) *Administration & Society*
379-397 (February 1981). Copyright 1981 by Sage Publications, Inc.

thing" to the much more restrictive "community without physical locus," which is common in the sociological literature, and appears most useful for this article (see Goode, 1957). According to Wilensky (1964), these professional communities are granted exclusive jurisdiction over an area of knowledge by clients who are in need of services based upon this knowledge, but who are not able to master the material themselves. Consequently, any group which seeks professional status must convince potential clients that the group: (1) has mastered a body of knowledge necessary to perform services for a client which the client cannot perform effectively or efficiently for himself, and (2) can be trusted to perform these services in the best interest of a client and refrain from the inevitable opportunities to exploit client vulnerability.[2] It is not possible to become a *true* profession by simply establishing a central organization, setting licensing standards and titles, or devising a formal code of ethics if these two critical steps have not been completed. In return, professions are normally relatively well paid and allowed to regulate themselves, as well as being accorded a high level of autonomy from supervision and personal prestige which is uncommon among the various occupational groups.

Thus it appears that if an established policy analysis profession (not occupational group) is to develop in the future, it will be necessary to devise a role model which appears plausible in light of public perceptions of the existing knowledge base. Policy-analysis professionalization is likely to be more successful if it is based upon an accurate perception of the state of the art than if it is developed around implausible claims to precise technology. In this regard, it is interesting to note that true professionalism does not seem restricted to the hard sciences or the more precise bodies of knowledge. The clergy, the military, law, and architecture are well established as professions even though they are not built on knowledge bases as precise as medicine and engineering. The key, as Wilensky (1964: 148) observes, seems to be the existence of a knowledge base which is neither "too familiar to everyone" nor "so narrow and precise that it can be quickly learned."

The knowledge base for public policy is extremely varied. Hence any discussion of possible policy-analysis role models (including such related questions as the profession's power, ethical standards, and developmental strategies) needs to be prefaced with consideration of this knowledge-base variation. James Thompson's (1967: ch. 7) classification, which was originally developed for organizations, suggests four ideal, or pure type categories for the public policy-analysis knowledge base. The four cells are based upon two variables: (1) clarity and certainty of existing expert causal knowledge in the field, and (2) client certainty or agreement on policy goals.[3] Each of these dimensions is a continuous variable, but collapsing them into a dichotomy simplifies discussion and creates the following figure.

The knowledge base of public policy appears to range across these four cells. Furthermore, the previous discussion of the importance of a knowledge base to professionalization suggests that appropriate professional role models ought to vary with the nature of the knowledge base. We shall now turn to a more detailed description of each cell, which will suggest a role analogy with an established profession, and discuss some existing policy analysis work which seems to fit the conditions in that cell.

CELL 1

Cell 1 is characterized by single client goals (or clear priorities) and relatively clear causal knowledge. In such instances, clients normally hire a professional to apply the existing technology to achieve their specified goal, and are relatively certain the desired results will follow. These conditions produce the least client involvement. It is entirely appropriate, when these cell 1 conditions are met, for the client to allow the professional to make all instrumental decisions, and to follow the professional's instructions carefully.

These conditions are met reasonably well in routine medical work and suggest the applicability of the general medical role

	Existing Expert Causal Knowledge	
	Certain	Uncertain
Single, or Clear Priorities	1	3
Multiple, or Unclear Priorities	2	4

Client Goals

Figure 1: Typology of Professional Role Models for Policy Analysis

model to policy areas which actually fit this cell. Of course, some nonroutine medical cases do not meet these cell 1 conditions and place great strains on the role model which normally governs the doctor-patient relationship. Causal knowledge on new or complex diseases such as cancer is viewed as quite uncertain; this can threaten the dominant role of the physician. Similarly, situations such as euthanasia cases do not present the single-goal situation which normally exists in medical work. This creates serious questions about the propriety of the normal professional dominance of the client by the professional.

Probably only a few public policy situations do, or will ever, meet these cell 1 conditions. Perhaps the case of the recent aerosol spray can discoveries and subsequent banning fits. The case in the policy literature which seems to come closest to these conditions is Jones's (1974) discussion of air pollution policy making during 1969-1970. Jones notes (1974: 453) that the period was characterized by "an unambiguous call for action" to "clean up the air" even though this call was made in general rather than technical or specific language. He also observes that there was a great deal of uncertainty about auto makers' ability to meet specific standards. Nevertheless, much of the knowledge base concerning air pollution is a matter of hard technology and an area in which causal knowledge, though imperfect, is a great deal clearer than in policy areas such as welfare and education. Also, Jones notes that the auto industry, and others who would be expected to oppose tighter clean air standards, did not (for a variety of reasons) mobilize conflicting experts to challenge the causal assumptions of the environmental experts. Hence the illusion of greater certainty likely prevailed.

Jones does not discuss the role of congressional and interest group expert staff in his article. However, the previous discussion suggests that the air pollution policy-making process at that time would be heavily expert dominated. That is, staff should have a relatively free hand in formulating recommendations, and their proposals should tend to be rubber stamped by the political process once available. However, air pollution policy-making does not seem to be treated as a cell 1 model now. Sufficient challenges to both the causal knowledge and the clarity of priorities have been raised by opponents of the tough policies to force professionals in the area to adopt a different role model.

CELL 2

Cell 2 contains a variation on the previous discussion in that it covers situations with relatively clear causal knowledge but much less agreement on appropriate goals. In these instances, clients may hire professionals to apply the existing knowledge to lay out a set of options and consequences for the client's consideration. Another possibility is to hire a professional analyst but not give particularly clear instructions about what the professional is to achieve.

A wide range of results can follow, which may, or may not, clarify decision-making. Option development and analysis can enable clients to clarify goals and develop clearer priorities or convince them to resign themselves to dealing with conflicting, uncertain goals. On the other hand, it may create frustrated clients who will seek a new analyst, or allow an incumbent analyst to inject his own goals into the client's uncertainty.[4]

Some routine work of several professions appears to fit this description. Oftentimes engineering work consists of applying the theoretical knowledge of several physical sciences to develop ill-defined projects. Some other forms of engineering work essentially involve a professional-client consulting process during which the expert presents a series of options and estimates of costs and benefits drawn from the technology of the field. Architects' professional activities, and the early *descriptions* of the city manager's role (which were based upon the politics-administration dichotomy) also seem to fit cell 2 reasonably well.[5]

A number of public policy projects involving the more developed facets of technology probably fall into this cell. Public construction projects such as bridges, dams, and buildings, as well as the development of weapons, information retrieval systems, accounting, and basic administrative procedures involve a fairly well developed, routine technology. At the same time, some clients may not have resolved questions such as the appropriate location of a construction project, desirability of a weapons system (particularly in peacetime) or the "human" costs of greater reliance on computerized technology.

The Brookings Institution analysis of the impact of the Community Development Block Grant dual formula in 1978 appears to represent much of the work fitting this cell.[6] The client (Congress via the Department of Housing and Urban Development) commissioned Brookings to determine the relative beneficiaries of the existing and proposed alternate CDBG allocation formulas. The study results, which indicated the sun belt city bias in the original formula was moderated by the alternate formula, were heavily used during the congressional consideration of the CDBG program. The final legislation established a dual formula and permitted cities to utilize the more favorable of the two.

CELL 3

Cell 3 is characterized by single or relatively clear priorities among client goals and great uncertainty about the basic causal knowledge in the field. An advocate model of professionalism seems appropriate for situations which fit this combination. That is, professional analysts are hired to make the best possible case, from existing knowledge, for the client's goals. Consequently, the analyst provides a source of ammunition and legitimacy to be used by a client operating in the political sphere.[7]

The legal profession comes closest to this model. Lawyers are hired to provide the best possible defense of client goals which are usually already established and known. The ethics of the profession do not condone outright fraud or blatant misrepresentation, but lawyers essentially are evaluated on the quality of causal argument they can provide a client within areas of uncertainty and are not expected to emphasize information unfavorable to a client. This is justified by the assumption that "truth," or at least desirable decisions, will emerge from the competition of clients with conflicting interests hiring advocates to make best possible cases to a third party.

Wildavsky's classic article (1969: esp. 197-198) seems to suggest an advocate model for professional policy analysts. Wildavsky notes a number of problems with the exhaustive PPBS style of policy making (expense, time, value incomparability, political obstacles to implementation, and so on) and suggests a style of analysis be developed which strives towards "a higher quality debate and perhaps eventually public choice among better known alternatives (1969: 190).

A great number of policy situations are likely to fit these cell 3 combinations. Furthermore, much of the existing policy analysis work seems in keeping with making the "best possible case" for a client or using any available policy impact information for "ammunition and legitimacy" tendencies which fall into this cell. Horowitz and Katz's (1975: 128-133) description of the Warren Court's use of sociological data supporting its decision in the Brown v. Board of Education case is one instance of the analysis for advocacy style.[8] The Nixon Administration's use of preliminary results from the New Jersey Negative Income Tax experiment to support the Family

Assistance Plan which was then pending in Congress is another example.[9]

CELL 4

The last cell contains policy situations in which clients are either uncertain about their goals or have a number of conflicting (and likely mutually exclusive) goals, and knowledge in the field is not sufficiently developed to suggest how goals could be achieved if there were agreement on them. In such cases, sponsors and analysts essentially are fishing for some information to justify some action. Cell 4 analysts are not likely to produce coherent sets of policy recommendations, and the client-analyst relationship is likely to become strained and frustrated if either party expects clear policy guidance to develop. In cell 4 cases, an academic role seems most appropriate for the professional analyst. The analyst can suggest organizing concepts, speculate on possible causal links, discuss goal priorities, and generally attempt to convince the client that a cell 4 combination exists in which it is not particularly appropriate to speak of rational decision-making.[10]

Some of the best-known studies of education and welfare policy seem to fit these cell 4 conditions. The Coleman (1966) and Jencks (1972) reports on general education, the Ohio University/Westinghouse study on Project Headstart (1969), and the New Jersey Negative Income Tax experiment (see Pechman and Timpane, 1975), have generally concluded that much of the existing conventional wisdom on causal impacts in these fields was inaccurate or inadequate, and that many professed goals are probably mutually exclusive.[11] Doubtless, these findings have not been particularly satisfying to practitioners in the field who are forced to make daily policy decisions and would prefer to have some semblance of rational justification for their actions. It should also be noted that the bulk of education and welfare evaluation work probably falls into cell 3.[12] That is, it is essentially advocacy-type work done on a grant or contract which attempts to make the best possible case for a client who needs to justify an existing program or argue in favor of a specific new alternative (Williams and Evans, 1969).

IMPLICATIONS

The distinctions between these four role models appear to have some major implications for questions such as the actual and appropriate power, ethical standards, and feasibility of a policy analysis profession. However, it is important to emphasize before discussing these implications, that both the client goal agreement and certainty of expert causal knowledge dimensions are stated in actual rather than perceived terms in this article. This raises a series of interesting questions about the consequences of misperceptions or ineptitude. If clients misperceive their degree of goal clarity or retain an analyst whose knowledge is well short of prevailing standards, they are likely to apply a professional-client role model which is inappropriate to the true situation.

Furthermore, the determination of actual goal or causal knowledge clarity is a complicated, dynamic process involving client, analyst and myriad other parties. For example, the clarity of actual causal knowledge in a field is affected by the amount of time, money, and talent devoted to research, as well as the innate complexity of the material. Consequently, the knowledge base, and appropriate professional role model, can shift over time. There may also be strong incentives for analysts to attempt to portray their causal knowledge as stronger than it actually is in an attempt to shift from a cell 3 or 4 style to cell 1 or 2, respectively. Such attempts would not alter the "true" appropriate role model, but could lead to serious misapplications which may actually damage the analyst's case for professional stature over time (see Wilensky, 1964).

There are obviously a great number of additional questions in this vein, but they warrant comment well beyond the scope of this article. We shall instead turn to some general implications of the simple four-celled model.

POWER OF THE ANALYSTS

One interesting question which has been broached in several sources is how much difference the various analytical and rational decision techniques make in policy-making, or how much power the various analysts actually have. Policy analysts often feel frustrated and impotent after their recommendations are ignored, and it is not difficult to find a number of studies which only occupy shelf space.[13] At the same time, theories exist which suggest heavy dominance of the policy process by experts, policy analysis organizations, and the interlocking elites who direct them.[14]

The resolution of this question obviously requires systematic study and will involve many of the methodological questions that exist in the community power literature.[15] What is power? How can a definition be operationalized? How does one collect the appropriate data? Presumably the investigation of the power of the analysts will also involve the old debates on the reputational approach versus the decisional approach, elite models versus pluralist models, and a number of hybrids in between.

It is not my purpose to delve far into these issues at this point. Nevertheless, the discussion in this article suggests that any investigation of the power of the analysts should consider policy area as a variable. It would appear that analysts working in policy areas with client agreement on goals and relatively precise technology (the cell 1 conditions) are likely to have much more direct impact on the policy process than those working in areas with the opposite conditions (e.g., the cell 4 circumstances). At the same time, it does seem important to follow the Weiss (1977) suggestions and look for the general, diffuse type of long-term influence on policy-making which may occur under the cell 4 conditions. The Coleman and Jencks reports, and a number of well known Presidential commissions may not have had a direct, immediate impact on policy, but may still yield a significant long-term impact on a particular policy area through concept definition, or even through the destruction of much of the incorrect existing knowledge.[16] Any power-of-the-experts studies which fail to account for these differences between cells would seem to be committing the "blind men and the elephant" fallacy.

NORMATIVE QUESTIONS

A closely related question deals with how much power a policy analysis profession should have.[17] Much of the present discussion of this question seems to assume (at least implicitly) a version of the cell 1 medical style of professional analysis. This role model essentially is an expertise-based form of elite rule which probably has its ancestry in Plato's "philosopher king." It is interesting to note, however, that this style of analyst direction of the policy process is consistent with the goal and causal conditions outlined in that cell. If goals actually are clear and a professional group does possess a clear body of knowledge on how to achieve those goals, it seems reasonable to turn the policy process over to them. To do otherwise is analagous to ignoring a doctor's advice during an appendicitis attack.[19]

Nevertheless, few present theorists would argue that many public policy situations really fit the cell 1 conditions. Hence it follows that this analyst-domination form of professional role would not normatively be appropriate very often. This observation, of course, leads to the question of who decides whether or not cell 1 conditions actually exist in a particular case.

The cell 2 and cell 3 engineering and advocate models, respectively, are much less elite-rule forms. In fact, they fit rather well with the competing-elites theme of pluralist thought.[19] The advocate model fits pluralist politics particularly well, as it outlines a process of conflicting groups hiring competing analysts as an additional weapon in the bargaining and compromising process. Furthermore, the cells 2 and 3 assumptions of value conflict or multiple goals and uncertainty on causal knowledge are quite consistent with the assumptions underlying the pluralist and incremental descriptions of the policy proess (see Braybrooke and Lindblom, 1963; Lindblom, 1968).

Wildavsky (1969), who is at least implicitly assuming that cell 3 conditions dominate the American policy process, argues that the advocate style of policy analysis is both the most feasible and the most desirable, as it might improve the level of policy debate in the political processes. This argument is consistent with a portion of this article, but several qualifications should be added. First, some policy problems do not fit cell 3, in which case the conflicting-advocates style would not seem appropriate. Second, even though the advocate style of policy analysis may be most feasible, since established groups constantly look for additional sources of ammunition, it is not likely to disturb the existing incremental patterns of bargaining very much. Groups which are already well represented in the policy process are the most likely candidates to support policy analysis advocates. Groups which are not sufficiently organized or financed to be well represented now are unlikely to be able to afford the analyst/advocates, who will not be inexpensive.

The cell 4 conditions of no goal agreement and low knowledge of causal relationships do not raise questions of an analyst-dominated policy process. In fact, they suggest that rational policy-making methods will have the least impact on policy-making and the "muddle through" procedures are apt to dominate. The extreme nonrational processes are understandably quite distasteful to many and have given impetus to the movements which push for policy analysis, PPBS, zero-based budgeting, sunset laws, and the collection of other devices intended to bring more rationality to policy-making. The major argument of this article is that such attempts are doomed to failure (at least in the short term) if applied to genuine cell 4 conditions. Some forms of basic research may prove to have some indirect impact on cell 4 policies over time. But it is most reasonable to apply the short-term rational decision devices to policy situations which fall into some other cell.

PROFESSIONAL ETHICS

This four-celled model also seems to have implications for the question of appropriate ethics for a policy analysis profession. Once again, it seems that appropriate ethical standards vary with the nature of the policy and professional role model adopted.

The cell 1 medical and cell 4 academic models may present the fewest ethical dilemmas since "unrestricted pursuit of truth" can be held as a general ideal. Analysts operating in accord with the cell 1 model may have reservations about their degree of dominance, particularly in democratic societies, and those operating under cell 4 conditions are apt to feel great frustration. But neither style of professionalism is apt to compromise the well-accepted "search for truth" ideal excessively.

The cell 2 engineering style and cell 3 advocate models seem to present rather different dilemmas. The obligation of the engineering role essentially is to provide a client with technological knowledge but not usurp the final policy decision. This circumstance may create great temptation for professionals to mix personal goals with technical advice. In other instances it may produce the "hired gun" or "mercenary" style of professionalism which is most dramatically illustrated in the military field and can occur in a range of scientific and engineering areas. Professionals in these areas can still presumably refuse services to clients whose motives they mistrust; nevertheless, doubts about purposes employers may find for one's technological skills probably never completely disappear.[20]

The advocate model may create even more dilemmas in determining professional ethical standards. The basic task of a professional advocate is to use his expertise to make the strongest case possible for a client. This overriding goal can often lead to deemphasizing contradictory information or alternate formulations. An advocacy profession, of course, can adopt ethical constraints against outright altering of information, or even against withholding certain types of conclusive unfavorable evidence.[21] However, gray areas are quite likely and, at the very least, an advocacy profession is apt to accord a higher priority to service to a client than to unrestricted search for truth. This can cause great dilemmas for those raised in the western scientific traditions.

FEASIBILITY

This leads to the last area of discussion—the feasibility of a profession built upon multiple role models. The major generalization of this article, of course, is that different policy problems seem to call for varying styles of policy analysis. Furthermore, policy analysis actually seems to be developing along different lines. At the same time, the earlier review of professionalization literature suggested that the critical step in making a profession acceptable was convincing the public that the profession was based upon an exclusive knowledge base, and that the public was best served by allowing the profession to exert relatively unchallenged jurisdiction within that area.

The critical question thus seems to be whether a profession can develop around extremely varied knowledge bases. The nature of public policy seems irrevocably varied, and it would seem the utmost folly to ignore this in developing a profession. One solution would be to focus professional policy analysis on one type of policy and ignore the other types. Still, this would seem to sacrifice much of the potential of the field. The other solution is to develop and try to market an explicit multiple role model profession.

Such a profession would be different from existing professions.[22] Essentially it would be a loose confederation of sub-professions developed around the different types of public policy. The subtypes would have varying degrees of technological skills, differing amounts of political power, alternate codes of ethics, and probably great discrepancy in salaries. This would undoubtedly place heavy strains on a central professional organization and perhaps create great difficulty in gaining public acceptance. However, what is the alternative to explicit recognition of this diversity? It is quite likely that attempts to ignore or obscure the differences in public policy and consequent appropriate role models will be, at best, futile and, at worst, counterproductive.

NOTES

1. Perhaps the most detailed statements of this position are in the works of Dror (1967, 1968, 1971). A sample of other discussions of professional policy analysis development are Bell (1967), Campbell's (1969) suggestions for treating social reforms as social experiments, Horowitz and Katz (1975) and MacRae (1975).

2. Wilensky (1964: 138) notes that "Any occupation wishing to exercise professional authority must find a technical base for it, assert an exclusive jurisdiction, link both skill and jurisdiction to standards of training, and convince the public its services are uniquely trustworthy." Goode (1957: 194) notes two keys to a group's professional status are that "its members share values in common," and that "its role definitions vis-à-vis both members and nonmembers are agreed upon and are the same for all members" (italics in original).

3. Both variables are defined as present objective conditions for purposes of this discussion. I will discuss change and misperceptions in the "implications" section. I am indebted to Thomas Henderson for suggesting the applicability of Thompson's model to this area. A similar organizational typology is described in Perrow (1967). The decision typology in Braybrooke and Lindblom (1963: ch. 4) is based upon degree of understanding and magnitude of change. This classification is probably better known than Thompson's, but does not seem as useful for this topic.

4. There is a great deal of diversity within this cell and it certainly can make a great deal of difference whether goal conflicts are eventually resolved by client or analyst, or are ignored. A number of the policy-sciences models in the literature seem to be based, at least implicitly, on these cell 2 conditions and resemble this engineering model. For example, see Dror (1971), particularly the "code of ethics" material on p. 119; and Macrae (1975).

5. Very few local government scholars would argue that many present city managers actually follow this role exclusively. In reality, city management is probably a blend of the cell 2 engineering style and the cell 3 advocate model, depending upon the policy area of concern. Another group which seems to be generally modeled on the engineering style, but resembles the advocate model more in application, is the President's Council of Economic Advisors (see Horowitz and Katz, 1975: 75-77).

6. The detailed Brookings results were described in a "not for citation" interim report released in 1978, but were summarized in Stanfield (1977). My colleague, John S. Jackson, who served as a Brookings associate during this period, suggested the example to me.

7. This cell 3 model is a somewhat more systematic version of "partisan analysis" described by Lindblom (1968: 65). This style of analysis requires substantive expertise

in addition to advocacy skills, but the causal knowledge of experts in these areas is weaker than in the cell 1 topics.

8. I do not wish to imply that the research projects cited in this section were intentionally designed to produce a desired result. The advocacy style can entail interpreting basic descriptive research to support a particular position. However, some intentional manipulation undoubtedly occurs. Edwards and Sharkansky (1978: 129) note that the "common expression at the Defense Intelligence Agency is that it exists to provide justification for what operations (the action arm of the military) wants to do," and Jones (1977: 177) observes that "one might do well to assume that evaluation is primarily an exercise in justification."

9. See Dye (1975: 339-340). A more detailed description of the political environment of the New Jersey Negative Income Tax Experiment is in Pechman and Timpane (1975).

10. In fact, it is not reasonable to apply normal standards of success to cell 4 evaluations. A more reasonable test is whether we know something more about the policy area after the research than we did before. The Caplan (1977) and Weiss (1977) descriptions of an "enlightenment" effect of policy analysis fit these cell 4 characteristics quite well. Campbell's (1969) "reforms as experiments" and experimenting society ideas also seem to fit.

11. An interesting discussion of the political environment surrounding the Headstart evaluation is Williams and Evans (1969).

12. I am inclined to place the major world modeling simulation projects into the cell 4 academic model. See Meadows et al. (1972) and Mesarovic and Pestel (1974). However, this classification depends upon the relationship between the investigators and the sponsoring Club of Rome. Clearly the causal knowledge in this field is uncertain which dictates either a cell 3 or cell 4 classification. The questions critical to final classification are to what degree the client's (i.e., the Club of Rome) goals are clear or specified, and whether the author's recommendations are in accord with the goals.

13. See Weiss (1970: 57-68; 1972: chs. 2, 6) and Meltsner (1972) for a discussion of political considerations which restrict the impact of rational analysis and suggestions for counteracting these considerations. Many of the suggestions essentially are tips on how to correctly "read the nature" (i.e., the Thompson dimensions) of the policy area of concern.

14. Dye (1978) documents the elite credentials of the directors of the Council on Foreign Relations, Brookings Institution, and Committee for Economic Development, and then asserts that such organizations set the agenda for the "proximate policy makers."

15. Friedman (1971) presents an interesting discussion of the political power of established professions.

16. Perhaps the major contribution of Coleman, Jencks, and other studies of education was to create an awareness of the inappropriateness of the cell 2 engineering model for education by creating grave doubts about the accuracy of existing causal knowledge in the field. Another example of an even more diffuse cell 4 impact on policy making is the Horowitz and Katz (1975: 94-102) description of the role of game theory concepts and vocabulary on foreign policy decisions such as the Cuban Missile Crisis.

17. For some varied treatments of this issue see Dror (1971: 137-142), Gross (1970), Horowitz and Katz (1975: chs. 8, 9), and Weiner and Wildavsky (1978).

18. The present population and energy policy areas seem to present very clear examples of these dilemmas. Some knowledge exists which suggests that present policies (or the lack of them) may threaten the long-term survival of mankind, but that several "moderate sacrifice options" followed now may reduce the long-term danger a great deal. However, the "moderate sacrifice options" may not survive the conventional political processes.

19. They also fit the Etzioni (1967) mixed scanning model well.

20. See the suggestions for a code of ethics in Dror (1971: 119). Dror essentially outlines an engineering model style of ethics which places a heavy burden on analysts to screen client goals and not deliver technical skills to those who may not use them properly. Dror has no sympathy with the best possible case for a client advocacy style. Adams (1975) outlines a series of political and ethical dilemmas which followed the CIA's systematic attempts to ignore Adams's Viet Cong troop strength estimates.

21. The CBS news broadcast "The Politics of Cancer" (shown July, 1976) alleged that some laboratories stopped animal tests of suspected carcinogens after 78 weeks, knowing that 80 weeks are required to develop that particular type of cancer. Presumably this would not be ethical even in an advocacy-model environment.

22. Even university teaching and research does not seem so varied. Scholars are at least loosely united by the goal of search for truth.

REFERENCES

ADAMS, S. (1975) "Vietnam coverup: playing war with numbers." Harpers 250: 41-44, 62-63.

BELL, D. (1967) "Notes on the post industrial society, parts I and II." Public Interest 6: 24-35; 7: 102-118.

BRAYBROOKE, D. and C. E. LINDBLOM (1963) A Strategy of Decision: Policy Evaluation as a Social Process. New York: Free Press.

CAMPBELL, D. T. (1969) "Reforms as experiments." American Psychologist 24: 409-429.

CAPLAN, N. (1977) "Social research and national policy," pp. 66-75 in S. Nagel (ed.) Policy Studies Review Annual Vol. 1. Beverly Hills: Sage.

COLEMAN, J. S. (1966) Equality of Educational Opportunity. Washington, DC: Government Printing Office.

DROR, Y. (1971) Design for Policy Sciences. New York: Elsevier North-Holland.

——— (1968) Public Policy Making Reexamined. Scranton, PA: Chandler.

——— (1967) "Policy analysis: a new professional role in government service." Public Administration Rev. 27: 197-203.

DYE, T. R. (1978) "Oligarchic tendencies in national policy making: the role of private policy planning organizations." J. of Politics 40: 309-331.

——— (1975) Understanding Public Policy. Englewood Cliffs, NJ: Prentice-Hall.

EDWARDS, G. C. and I. SHARKANSKY (1978) The Policy Predicament: Making and Implementing Public Policy. San Francisco: Freeman.

ETZIONI, A. (1967) "Mixed scanning: a third approach to decision making." Public Administration Rev. 27: 385-392.

FRIEDMAN, R. S. (1971) Professionalism, Expertise and Policy Making. New York: General Learning Press monograph.

GOODE, W. J. (1957) "Community within a community: the professions." Amer. Soc. Rev. 70: 194-200.

GROSS, B. (1970) "Friendly facism: a model for America." Social Policy 1: 44-52.

HOROWITZ, I. L. and J. E. KATZ (1975) Social Science and Public Policy in the United States. New York: Praeger.

JENCKS, C. (1972) Inequality: A Reassessment of the Effects of Family and Schooling in America. New York: Basic Books.

JONES, C. O. (1977) An Introduction to the Study of Public Policy. Belmont, CA: Wadsworth.

――― (1974) "Speculative augmentation in federal air pollution policy making." J. of Politics 36: 438-464.

LINDBLOM, C. E. (1968) The Policy Making Process. Englewood Cliffs, NJ: Prentice-Hall.

MacRAE, D., Jr. (1975) "Policy analysis as an applied social science discipline." Administration and Society 6: 363-388.

MEADOWS, D. H., D. L. MEADOWS, J. RANDERS, and W. W. BEHRENS III (1972) The Limits to Growth. New York: Universe.

MESAROVIC, M. and E. PESTEL (1974) Mankind at the Turning Point. New York: Elsevier North-Holland.

MELTSNER, A. J. (1972) "Political feasibility and policy analysis." Public Administration Rev. 32: 859-867.

Ohio University-Westinghouse Learning Corporation (1969) "The impact of project Headstart: an evaluation of the affects of Headstart on children's cognitive and affective development." Report to the Office of Economic Opportunity pursuant to contract B89-4536.

PECHMAN, J. A. and P. M. TIMPANE (1975) Work Incentives and Income Guarantees. Washington, DC: Brookings.

PERROW, C. (1967) "A framework for the comparative analysis of organizations." Amer. Soc. Rev. 32: 194-208.

STANFIELD, R. L. (1977) "Government seeks the right formula for community development funds." National J. 9, 7: 237-243.

THOMPSON, J. D. (1967) Organizations in Action. New York: McGraw-Hill.

WEINER, S. and A. WILDAVSKY (1978) "The prophylactic Presidency." Public Interest 52: 3-19.

WEISS, C. H. (1977) "Research for policy's sake: the enlightenment function of social research." Policy Analysis 3: 531-545.

――― (1972) Evaluation Research: Methods for Assessing Program Effectiveness. Englewood Cliffs, NJ: Prentice-Hall.

――― (1970) "The politicization of evaluation research." J. of Social Issues 26: 57-68.

WILDAVSKY, A. (1969) "Rescuing policy analysis from PPBS." Public Administration Rev. 29: 189-202.

WILLIAMS, W. and J. W. EVANS (1969) "The politics of evaluation: the case of Headstart." Annals 385: 118-132.

WILENSKY, H. L. (1964) "The professionalism of everyone?" Amer. J. of Sociology 70: 137-158.

John L. Foster is Associate Professor of Political Science and Director of the Master of Public Affairs Program at Southern Illinois University at Carbondale. He is the coauthor of two role playing simulations, National Policy Game *and* Urban Policy Game, *and has written research articles on innovation, bureaucratic attitudes, and the impact of educational simulations.*

44

Qualitative and Quantitative Information in Health Policy Decision Making

William J. Filstead

The meaning of information is not self evident. Rather, its meaning is created through a social process by which values, different perspectives, and the socio-political context shape the credibility and significance of the information. This paper will argue that the natural science model of evaluation research provides one type of information which creates a range of distortions that have an effect on health policy making processes. Qualitative methods are proposed as a way of minimizing the distortion created through the quantification of data.

> When the ratio of what is known to what needs to be known approaches zero, we tend to invent 'knowledge' and assume that we understand more than we actually do.
>
> (Rosenhan, 1972)

This quote was made in the context of trying to understand how psychiatric labels are applied to individuals. It has, however, ramifications far beyond that context. While some may construe this remark as representing a rather cynical perspective, I suggest that it nevertheless accurately characterizes the situations typically faced by policymakers. That is, the need to decide upon a policy or course of action when the information that is needed to make such a decision is either unavailable or at best sketchy. The reasons behind this state of affairs are many and complex. In this paper, it will be argued that the "natural science model" of evaluation research, which has become a primary resource to policymakers, is one of the major contributors to this "invention of knowledge." Furthermore, it will be argued that policy decisions made as a result of such data are probably ineffectual because

---

Requests for reprints should be sent to Dr. Filstead, the Department of Psychiatry and Behavioral Sciences at Northwestern University, Chicago, IL 60611.

they are based on a myopic conception of the very social intervention they are attempting to make decisions about.

The Social Nature of Information

One critical component of the decision making process is information. It, along with other factors such as the political climate, the "urgency" of the decision, the short and long range consequences (real or imagined), the historical context, as well as the "ramifications" of a given decision or policy, etc., all play strategic roles in shaping decisions and the policies such decisions dictate.

Information is an illusive construct. It has many sources, i.e., intuition, experience, an accumulated body of knowledge, research, etc. Information just does not exist of and by itself — it is created through a social process by which values, the "meaning" of data, and the sociopolitical context shape the creditability and significance of the information. Furthermore, the various concerns and/or questions which give rise to a need for information shape the processes and procedures that are applied to gather it. It seems clear that the need for information is not independent of the assumptions and concerns which gave rise to it. This fact needs to be clearly recognized by policymakers.

In health care, as well as other areas of society (education, law, housing, etc.), great currency is given to the use of the scientific method in generating a type of information that will facilitate policy decisions (Rivlin, 1971; Riecken & Borouch, 1975). An assumption has been made that the use of the scientific method will yield the best possible policy-relevant data (Gross, 1967; Hauser, 1975; Sheldon & Parke, 1975). Quantifying information gives it an aura of authenticity regardless of its validity.

> With the rise in literacy and the phenomenal growth of communication, the printed word was replaced by a numbers mystique. Our search for scientific rationality and factual evidence led to an irrational reverence for an authority of numbers which was seldom challenged. Quantification became fashionable because counting was comfortable and predictability was 'scientific'. Numbers seemed to be so tangible, so undeniable. (Siedman, 1977, p. 415)

More and more social problems are being quantified in order to facilitate efforts to understand the impact of intervention programs to alleviate them, their cost effectiveness, and in general, clarify the responsibility and accountability of those charged with directing such programs against criteria or standards which are operationally defined as indicators of the program's effectiveness (Attkisson, Hargreaves, Horowitz & Sorsensen, 1978; Parke & Sheldon, 1973). Given this perceived need, evaluation research, based upon the natural science model, has been deemed the most rigorous and effective way to enhance the quality and confidence in the policy decisions that are made (Wholey, 1970; Bernstein & Freeman, 1975).

The pre-eminence of this scientific rationality based on the natural science model is no longer unquestioned. The payoff of quantitative program evaluations to program administrators and bureaucrats has been far less than expected. Administrators and policymakers had expected these types of evaluations to identify "why programs did or did not accomplish their objectives," "who gets better," "what elements of the program need to be modified," etc. These expectations have not been generally met. The "Great Society Programs" and their spinoffs were created in an era when their need and impact were assumed and unquestioned. In the late 60s and early 70s, a political climate was created in which these programs, although thought to be effective, had to have empirical evidence to substantiate their continued support. The option of being committed to finding out the relative impact of variations in the intervention strategy was not available (Campbell, 1969, 1971). The tools of the scientific method plus its principles of rigor, objectivity, definitiveness, etc., represented a needed commodity to bureaucrats and policymakers. The quantitative model achieved a level of pre-eminence relative to other competing ways of assessing a program's impact. It was looked upon as *the* only way to definitively know the impact of an intervention program. In essence, it became identified as the "only available route to cumulative progress" (Campbell & Stanley, 1966, p.3). Given this climate, it is little wonder why such an allegiance to this model—almost fanatical in nature—has developed.

In recent years, publications have appeared that question the appropriateness of the "natural science model" of evaluation, the type of information it yields, and its relevancy for deciding social policy (Stake, 1976; Parlett & Hamilton, 1976; Patton, 1978; Britain, 1978; Campbell, 1978; and Filstead, 1978, 1979). The questioning of the natural science model for program evaluation by both evaluators and policymakers is most intensive. Efforts have been concentrated on developing alternative evaluation models or models that incorporate multiple methods and a variety of data collection procedures for enhancing the credibility of such research (Etzione, 1960; Suchman, 1970; Smith & Brock, 1970; Wilson, 1977; Kourilsky; 1973, Krause & Howard, 1976). The work by Schulberg and Baker (1975) and Baker (1973) is representative of efforts aimed at using a social systems framework to enhance the effectiveness and sophistication of evaluation designs by emphasizing the necessity of multiple methods and different types of data in the evaluation of intervention programs. In short, these, as well as other writers, place an emphasis on an approach to evaluation research which captures the essences and processes associated with the social intervention. This style of evaluation is referred to as qualitative analysis. In the discussion that follows, the nature of qualitative analysis will be outlined, after which its applicability to policy analysis will be discussed.

What are Qualitative Methods?

Qualitative methods mean far more than specific data collecting techniques. It is more appropriately thought of as a paradigm. That is, a set of interrelated assumptions about the social world which provide a philosophical and conceptual framework for the organized study of that world (Kuhn, 1970). Qualitative methods start with the premise that social life is a shared creativity of individuals. It is this sharedness which produces a reality perceived to be objective, extant, and knowable to all participants in social interaction. Social meaning and social order are shaped and created by individuals in the course of social interaction. It is this meaning system of social life which forms the common schemes of references for individuals.

Given this emphasis on the meaning of events to the individual who experiences, interprets, and reacts to them, the basic starting point for a qualitative analysis in conceptualizing the social world is to develop concepts and theories that are grounded in the data, i.e., concepts and theories that are derived from the data and then illustrated by characteristic examples of the data (Glaser & Strauss, 1976; Glaser, 1978). These "first order concepts" as Schutz (1967) called them, are essential to the development of second order concepts, that is, concepts which emerge from the scientific discipline that is attempting to explain a phenomenon.

> Any scientific understanding of human action, at whatever level of ordering or generality, must begin with and be built upon an understanding of the everyday life of the members performing those actions. To fail to see this and to act in accord with it is to commit what we might call the fallacy of abstractionism, that is, the fallacy of believing that you can know in a more abstract form what you do not know in a particular form. (Douglas, 1970, p. 11)

Basic data collecting activities such as participant observation, unstructured interviewing, observations, diaries, etc., are employed to tap this "meaning" dimension of social life. It is precisely this focus on the social meanings and the insistence on the fact that these meanings can only be examined in the context of individuals interacting that distinguishes this paradigm from the natural science model of inquiry. Frederick Erickson (1977) has clearly stated why qualitative social scientists have doubts about any framework for knowing which does not have these aforementioned assumptions as guiding principles:

> Researchers of the Malinowski tradition in anthropology (and 'fieldwork sociologists,' 'symbolic interactionists,' and more recently 'ethnomethodologists,' in sociology) have been concerned with *social fact* as *social action;* with *social meanings* as residing in and constituted by people's *doing* in everyday life. These meanings are most often discovered through fieldwork by hanging around and watching people carefully and asking them why they do what they do, sometimes asking them as they are in the midst of their doing. Because of this orientation toward social as embedded in the concrete, particular doings of people — doings that include people's intentions and points of view — qualitative researchers are reluctant to see attributes of doing abstracted from the scene of social action and counted out of context. (p.58)

The data collecting strategies of the qualitative paradigm are directed at describing and understanding the holistic nature of the social world from the perspectives of the social actors. However, these descriptions are much more than *just* descriptions. They are presentations of the social meanings of social facts in functional terms that have relevance to an emergent theory of the phenomenon under study:

> ...What qualitative research does best and most essentially is to describe key incidents in functionally relevant descriptive terms and place them in some relation to the wider social context, using the key incident as a concrete instance of the workings of abstract principals of social organization. (Erickson, 1977, p. 61)

In essence, the quantitative paradigm, because of the assumptions it makes about social life and the approach it takes toward comprehending social life, has been unable to provide the context within which to "make sense," "understand," and therefore arrive at the *meaning(s)* of the interactions and processes it has been examining. *One cannot infer the meaning of an event from data that does not have this dimension of information.* Unfortunately, this has been the cardinal error of the quantitative paradigm. A characterization of social life devoid of the subjective meaning of these events to the participants does violence to the image of man which portrays him as not only a reactor but a creator of his world.

Floyd Matson (1966) has commented on this fragmented conceptualization of human interaction:

The historic reliance of the social sciences upon root metaphors and routine methods appropriated from classical mechanics has eclipsed the ancestral liberal version of 'the whole man, man in person' (to use Lewis Mumford's phrase)—and has given us instead a radically broken self-image. (pp. V-V1)

Policymakers need to realize that information gathered via the natural science model has a sense of detachment to it. That is, efforts in the name of science are carried out to shape the information into its most objective, value-free form. It is believed that such processes gain an aura of objectivity and therefore credibility for the impressions and/or conclusions that are made. In fact, the opposite is more likely.

We have been encouraged to believe that quantification is impersonal and objective and, therefore, more reliable than qualitative methodology which takes into consideration such relatively intangible factors as values. But while qualitative analysis has been dismissed as too difficult, too intangible, and too subjective, few have questioned the inherent subjectivity of quantification which requires 'selection' of parameters and baseline data, the interpretation of findings, and the selection of facts and evidence. There is much to be gained by destroying the myth of objectivity since subjectivity is always integrally involved—but disavowed. . .

The canard that 'objective' is good and 'subjective' is bad denies the fundamental worthiness of human endeavor—of creativity, imagination, ingenuity, and spontaneity. Qualitative analysis restores the legitimacy of subjectivity, and—even more important—gives it visibility and weight so that decisions and actions can be more accurately assessed. (Siedman, 1977, p. 415)

Since policymakers are often faced with the responsibility of charting the course of action an intervention program will take, they, as well as others, are interested in what events "cause" what results. It is precisely this "causal-problem-solving" posture that fundamentally differentiates each paradigm, the natural science model and qualitative analysis, in their ability to articulate the relationships among events. Evaluators who employ this causal-problem-solving model in studying a social intervention program adhere to the following type of thinking which Patton (1975) described in an educational research context:

Treatments in educational research are usually some type of new hardware, or specific curriculum innovation, variation in class size, or some specific type of teaching style. One of the main problems in experimental educational research is clear specification of what the treatment actually is, which infers controlling all other possible causal variables and the corresponding problem of multiple treatment interference and interactive effects. It is the constraints posed by controlling the specific treatment under study that necessitates simplifying and breaking down the totality of reality into small component parts. A great deal of the scientific enterprise revolves around this process of simplifying the complexity of reality. (p.29)

It is precisely this fragmentation or compartmentalized style of evaluation which qualitatively oriented evaluators argue leads to distortions of reality and, as a consequence, necessitates a holistic or contextual model of evaluation (e.g. Britain, 1978; Weiss & Rein, 1972).

Focusing on a narrow set of variables necessarily sets up a filtering screen between the researcher and the phenomena he is attempting to comprehend. Such barriers, from the vantage point of those employing a holistic analysis, inhibit and thwart the observer from an understanding of what is unique as well as what is generalizable from the data, and from perceiving the processes involved in contrast to simply the outcomes. (Rist, 1977, p.47)

Even among those individuals who have been prominently identified with the quantitative scientific model of evaluation, there are clear indications that such a framework has, especially by itself, less relevance to effective evaluation efforts. For example, Campbell (1978, p. 200) has stated that: "If qualitative and quantitative evaluations were to be organized on the same programs, I would expect them to agree. If they did not, I feel we should regard it possible that the quantitative was the one in error." In a similar vein, Cronbach (1975) offers a telling commentary on how the means of the scientific method have become ends in themselves.

The time has come to exorcise the null hypothesis. We cannot afford to pour costly data down the drain whenever effects present in a sample 'fail to reach significance.' ...Let the author file descriptive information, at least in an archive, instead of reporting only those selected differences and correlations that are nominally 'greater than chance.' Descriptions encourage us to think constructively about results from quasi-replications, whereas the dichotomy significant/non-significant implies only a hopeless inconsistency. The canon of parsimony, misinterpreted, has lead to the habit of accepting Type II errors at every turn, for the sake of holding Type I errors in check. There are more things in heaven and earth than are dreamt of in our hypotheses, and our observations should be open to them. (p.127)

In short, an increasing number of the users of program evaluation data such as policymakers, administrators, etc., as well as those who design and carry out such activities, are questioning the appropriateness of the natural science model of program evaluation. Following from these observations, the data derived from such evaluations provides a selected view of the social processes under consideration. What policymakers need to recognize is that these data (social indicators, social statistics, quality of life measures, etc.) are value laden. It's a debatable question as to whether or not such data tap the values that are of central importance to the policymakers' considerations.

The Role of Qualitative Methods in Policymaking

In a recent publication on strategies for policy analysis, a five part structural framework was proposed as a mechanism for responding to complex policy issues (Stokey & Zeckhauser, 1978). This framework will serve as a model through which the use of qualitative methods would effectively respond to the issues addressed by such an analytic scheme.

1. Establishing the Context. What is the underlying problem that must be dealt with? What specific objectives are to be pursued in confronting this problem?
2. Laying Out the Alternatives. What are the alternative courses of action? What are the consequences of each of the alternative actions? What techniques are relevant for predicting these consequences? If outcomes are uncertain, what is the estimated likelihood of each?
3. Predicting the Consequences. What are the consequences of each of the alternative actions? What techniques are relevant for predicting these consequences? If outcomes are uncertain, what is the estimated likelihood of each?
4. Valuing the Outcome. By what criteria should we measure success in pursuing each objective? Recognizing that inevitably some alternatives will be superior with respect to certain objectives and inferior with respect to others, how should different combinations of valued objectives be compared with one another?
5. Making a Choice. Drawing all aspects of the analysis together, what is the prefered course of action?

Many social intervention programs in the health care field are broad in scope, complex in structure, and multifacted in nature, i.e., reimbursement models for health care, efficacy of different cancer treatments, utilization of health care services, etc. Furthermore, some of these programs have been implemented in diverse settings with varying organization arrangements. In such a situation, it is hard to understand how quantitative measures (regardless of the number employed, although in most cases there are only one to a few process or outcome measures) can tap the interwoven complexity that surrounds the concrete daily reality of such interventions. Qualitative methods would allow one to capture the holistic quality of such contexts and provide a portrayal of the interplay among different features within the environments, the perceptions of the various publics to such ongoings, and the actions/reactions such occurrences have on those affected by the intervention. Essentially, one of the clear mandates that the preceding structural model for policy analysis would require, is an examination of the basic program processes that are associated with the intervention in a manner that provides an understanding of this experience in terms of measures that have contextual meaning. Therefore, basic ethnographic questions of "who does what, where, and why" form the basis of the inquiries.

The evaluation process should try and tap the perspectives of at least four key publics associated with the intervention: the funder, the administrator, the providers, and the receivers with respect to how they perceive the intervention program. In this manner, the policymakers can cut across the perspectives and needs of these groups when considering the alternatives, consequences, outcomes, and the ultimate course of action dictated by the policy. Qualitative analyses provide a "feel for the information" in a manner that is "undeniable" (Smith, 1974) resulting in not only a holistic conception of the intervention, but a particularistic understanding of the details and nuances of the social intervention that makes for a powerful description in a narrative form of the social realities engendered by the intervention. Such data should facilitate a policymaker's understanding of the intervention, its consequences, and the outcomes of various courses of action. In fact, these very questions can be addressed as part of the analysis so as to limit the amount of "armchair theorizing/speculation" that often accompany policymaking activities.

One would suspect that an effective policymaking process requires, among other things: (1) believability in the data (validity), (2) usability of information (data is in a meaningful and understandable form, so that it addresses the "need to know" questions raised in the first place), (3) that it is timely (information is available so that it can be brought to bear on the decision making process), (4) insight into "alternative considerations" are possible, (5) a contextual understanding of the intervention is obtained, and (6) the political climate (in its broadest sense) within which these policies will be formulated and implemented is identified. The majority of the evaluations of large scale medical interventions do not meet such criteria. In fact, as a beginning, it would be very important to undertake case studies of these and other such social interventions in order to gain insight into the process and dynamics discussed above.

Presently most evaluations in the health care field, as well as other fields (although education may be an exception), are single focus in design and do not encompass looking at alternatives. Efforts such as computer modeling or simulation gaming tend to have an "other world" quality which may not accurately portray the everyday realities of the social situations under investigation. Health care evaluations often have social indicators, e.g., mortality or morbidity rates, cost/benefit ratios, etc., which are identified as the operational definition of key criterion measures of program effectiveness. Reliance on such measures underestimates or, more correctly, ignores the second-order consequences, particularly negative in nature, for such indicators when used as the sole or primary factor for decision making (Gordon, Krause & Cochran, 1977; Cochran, 1978). This process has been identified by Campbell as the "pessimistic law."

The more any quantitative social indicator is used for social decision making, the more subject it will be to corruption pressures and the more apt it will be to distort and corrupt the social process it is intended to monitor. (1975, p. 35, emphasis in the original)

Consequently such key health policy relevant indicators as: bed occupancy rates of hospital beds per population density, morbidity and mortality rates, "conquering disease" rates, cost-benifit ratios of financial reimbursement schemes, efficacy of different structurally organized health care models, etc., may be subjected to this law. Assuming the face validity of this law, it would be important to try and assess the extent to which this law is operative in the key social indicators that are routinely employed in health policy decision making. In essence, policies may be made in part on the basis of the meta-data that is gathered through the natural science model. Meta-data is "data" so far removed from the social reality it proports to represent, that in fact it is more a creation of the scientist or data-gatherer than the social phenomenon it is supposed to represent.

Before suggesting some guidelines for interfacing qualitative analysis in the process of making public policy, let me briefly clarify my position on qualitative and quantitative methods. Qualitative methods represent a legitimate research style. These methods, in their own right, can adequately evaluate an intervention program and provide the necessary data to facilitate the decision making process. They can even address the issue of causation. It is my perspective that great advantages can be obtained in creatively combining qualitative and quantitative methods in evaluation research. Such combinations would greatly enhance the process of developing and the subsequent impact of public policies. What is inappropriate is to cast either method in an inferior position vis à vis the other. Neither one has the corner on the "correct answers," although the quantitative method has gained a currency and credibility from its promoters and advocates that often borders on fanaticism.

I have chosen to emphasize the advantages of qualitative analysis over the quantitative or natural science model because the former approach is not generally recognized or acknowledged as a viable style of science, whereas the latter has already attained an unquestioned position of eminence. This imbalance needs to be corrected.

> The very dominance of one paradigm (the hypotheticodeductive, natural science model) and the subordination of the second (the alternative holistic-inductive paradigm) demonstrates that it is more important to attack this imbalance than to maintain neutrality. My concern here is twofold: first, the practitioners and adherents of the dominant paradigm show little awareness of the existence of an alternative paradigm; and secondly, that practitioners of the dominant paradigm seem to be insensitive to the degree to which their methodology is based upon a relatively narrow philosophical, ideological, and epistemological view of the world. (Patton, 1978, p. 210)

Each method reflects a stance toward the social world which embodies a unique perspective. However, it is my contention that subscribing to the quantitative paradigm promotes an illusory conception of the world whose essential characteristic is a naivete about the very phenomena it attempts to explain. It is incomprehensible that the role of meaning can be so blatantly ignored and summarily dismissed by the quantitative paradigm as being either unimportant or not requiring much effort beyond the paper and pencil tests employed to measure it.

Therefore, based upon the preceding discussion, the following guidelines are offered as suggestions for enhancing the results of policy decision through use of qualitative methods:

1. That a broad base of input (from multiple publics) into the design of evaluations aimed at assessing social interventions be developed with the emphasis placed upon the meanings and implications of the intervention program and the relevancy of the criteria standards by which it will be assessed.
2. That this initial base of input be tapped throughout the course of the project.
3. That a natural history, a diary, of the intervention be maintained by at least the project director and hopefully a representative of each interested public so as to document the reasons associated with decisions made during the course of the project.
4. That multiple methods or "data triangulation" (Denzin, 1970) be employed as the methodological strategy in trying to evaluate the meaning and significance of data from different sources.

In essence, the more one has multiple impact measures qualitatively understood and linked to quantitative measures from the key publics to the evaluation, as well as from the perspectives of the policymakers, the greater the probability one has for understanding the context and outcome of the intervention program in a way which will enhance the policymaking process.

Clearly, the health policy decision making process, and the policymaking process in general, which relies on data gathered through the natural science model of evaluation, has a fatal flaw which jeopardizes the relevance and appropriateness of the courses of action suggested by such policies. The flaw is a lack of understanding of the meaning of such information. The act of quantifying information in the hopes of facilitating a more rational course of action relative to policy decision may in fact work in a reverse manner. Such action may make the policymaking process more irrational, capricious, and more detached from the very phenomenon under consideration. Qualitative analysis can act as a mechanism for correcting this distortion.

The message of this paper is simple though perhaps controversial: health policymakers will continue to be preoccupied with questions of "how many," "how much," "at what costs," but the question of "why" appears to have been lost. The answer to why is simply not numbers, but the qualitative meanings of these figures. Until the question of "why" becomes more prominent in the policymaking process and answers can be provided which are based upon a contextual understanding of their phenomenological bases, data policy decision will continue to be impotent in terms of recommending effective courses of action vis à vis various social interventions.

REFERENCES

Attkisson, C., Hargreaves, W., Horowitz, M. & Sorensen, J. *Evaluation of human service programs.* New York: Academic Press, 1978.

Baker, F. (Ed.) *Organizational systems: General systems approaches to complex organizations.* Homewood, Illinois: R.D. Erwin Publishers, 1973.

Bernstein, I., & Freeman, H. *Academic and entrepreneurial research: Consequences of diversity in federal evaluation studies.* New York: Russell Sage, 1975.

Britain, G. Experimental and contextual models of program evaluation. *Evaluation and Program Planning,* 1978, *1*, 229-234.

Campbell, D. Reforms as experiments. *American Psychologist,* 1969, *24*, 409-429.

Campbell, D. Methods for the experimenting society. Paper presented at the American Psychological Association, Washington, D.C., 1971.

Campbell, D. Assessing the impact of planned social change. In G.M. Lyons (Ed.) *Social research and public policies.* Hanover, New Hampshire: Public Affairs Center, Dartmouth College, 1975.

Campbell, D. Qualitative knowing in action research. In M. Brenner, et al., (Eds.), *The social context of method.* London: Groom Helm Ltd., 1978.

Campbell, D. & Stanley, J. *Experimental and quasi-experimental designs for research.* Chicago: Rand McNally, 1966.

Cochran, N. On the limiting properties of social indicators. *Evaluation and Program Planning,* 1979, *2*, 1-3.

Cronbach, L. Beyond the two disciplines of scientific psychology. *American Psychologist,* 1975, *30*, 116-127.

Denzin, N. *The research act.* Chicago: Aldine Publishing Company, 1970.

Douglas, J. *Understanding everyday life.* Chicago: Aldine Publishing Company, 1970.

Erickson, F. Some approaches to inquiry in school-community ethnography. *Anthropology and Education Quarterly,* 1977, *8*, 58-69.

Etzioni, A. Two approaches to organizational analysis: A critique and suggestion. *Administrative Science Quarterly,* 1960, *5*, 257-278.

Filstead, W. Qualitative methods: A needed perspective in evaluation research. In T. Cooke & C. Reichardt (Eds.), *Qualitative and quantitative methods in evaluation research.* Beverly Hills: Sage Publications, 1979.

Filstead, W. Qualitative methods and program evaluation: Some thoughts and suggestions. Presented at the Evaluation Research Society's Meeting, Washington, D.C., November 2, 1978.

Glaser, B. *Theoretical sensitivity.* Mill Valley, California: The Sociology Press, 1978.

Glaser, B., & Strauss, A. *The discovery of grounded theory.* Chicago: Aldine Publishing Company, 1967.

Gordon, A., Krause, M., & Cochran, N. Unintended consequences of using social indicators. Grant proposal, mimeograph, Department of Sociology, Northwestern University, Evanston, Illinois, 1977.

Gross, B. *Annals of the American Academy of Political and Social Sciences,* (2 volumes), 371 and 373, 1967.

Hauser, P. *Social statistics in use.* New York: Russell Sage Foundation, 1975.

Kourilsky, M. An adversary model for educational evaluation. *Education Comment,* 1973, *3*, 3-6.

Krause, M., & Howard, K. Program evaluation in the public interest: A new research methodology. *Community Mental Health Journal,* 1976, *12*, 291-300.

Kuhn, T. *The structure of scientific revolution.* (2nd ed.) Chicago: University of Chicago Press, 1970.

Matson, F. *The broken image,* Garden City: Anchor Books, 1966.

Parke, R., & Shelden, E. Social statistics for public policy. *Proceedings of the American Statistical Association,* 1973, 105-112.

Parlett, M., & Hamilton, D. Evaluation as illumination: A new approach to the study of innovatory programs. In G. Glass (Eds.), *Evaluation studies review annual,* (Vol. I). Beverly Hills: Sage Publications, 1976.

Patton, M. *Alternative evaluation research paradigm.* Grand Forks: University of North Dakota Press, 1975.

Patton, M. *Utilization-focused education.* Beverly Hills: Sage Publications, 1978.

Riecken, H., & Borouch, R. *Social experimentation: A method for planning and evaluating social intervention.* New York: Academic Press, 1975.

Rist, R. On the relations among educational research paradigms: From disdain to detente. *Anthropology and Education Quarterly,* 1977, *8,* 42-49.

Rivlin, A. *Systematic thinking for social action.* Washington, D.C.: The Brookings Institute, 1971.

Rosenhan, D. On being sane in insane places. *Science,* 1972, *179,* 250-258.

Schulberg, H. & Baker, F. *The Mental Hospital and Human Services.* New York: Behavioral Publications, 1975.

Schutz, A. *The phenomenology of the social world.* Evanston: Northwestern University press, 1967.

Sheldon, E., & Parke, R. Social indicators. *Science,* 1975, *188,* 693-699.

Siedman, E. Why not qualitative analysis? *Public Management Forum,* 1977, July/August, 415-417.

Smith, L. An aesthetic education workshop for administrators: Some implications for a theory of case studies. AERA Conference, Chicago, Illinois, 1974.

Smith, L., & Brock, J. Go buy go! Methodological issues in classroom observational research. *Occasional Paper Series:* #5, St. Ann, Missouri: Central Midwestern Regional Educational Laboratory, Inc., 1970.

Stake, R. Case study method in social inquiry. Mimeograph, University of Illinois, Chicago Circle, Department of Education, 1976.

Stokey, E., & Zeckhauser, R. *A primer for policy analysis.* New York: W.W. Norton & Company, 1978.

Suchman, E. Action for what? Critique of evaluation research. In R. O'Toole (Ed.), *The organization management and tactics of social research.* Cambridge: Schenman Publishing Company, 1970.

Weiss, R., & Rein, M. The evaluation of broad aim programs: Difficulties in experimental design and alternatives. In C. Weiss (Ed.), *Evaluating action programs.* Boston: Allyn & Bacon, 1972.

Wholey, J., Scanlon, J., Duffy, H., Fukumotu, J. & Vogt, L. *Federal Evaluation Policy: Analyzing the Effects of Public Programs.* Washington, D.C.: The Urban Institute, 1970.

Wilson, S. Explorations of the usefulness of case study evaluations. *Evaluation Quarterly, 3,* 446-459, 1979.

Wilson, S. The use of ethnographic techniques in educational research. *Review of Educational Research,* 1977, *47,* 245-265.

45

Designing Health Policy Research for Utilization

Marian A. Solomon and Stephen M. Shortell

Given our severely limited resources, effective public policies are critical. While research cannot insure the success of policy, it can minimize failure by providing a rational decision making framework. The conduct of high quality research is not sufficient in itself to insure the utilization; the policy researcher has the responsibility for facilitating its utilization. Even under the most ideal conditions, utilization and impact is influenced by many factors including the style by which it is communicated, political and organizational factors, the availability of the research in a time frame consistent with the decision making process, and the client commitment to the research. The usefulness of policy research can be expanded both by developing studies that directly address information needs of policymakers and having appropriate dissemination plans.

POLICY RESEARCH AND UTILIZATION

In undertaking social research procedures for social planning, the policy researcher assumes a concurrent responsibility for the utilization of the research product. The conduct of high quality research is not sufficient in itself to insure its utilization (Weiss & Bucuvalas, 1980); the problems which hamper utilization are not technical (Halperin, 1978). Factors which affect utilization include the mechanism by which the policy research is communicated to the policymakers (Caplan, 1978; Lynn, 1978), the extent to which

An earlier version of this paper was entitled: Health Policy Research and Analysis: A Selective Review and Suggestions for Improving the Art, presented at the Health Policy Seminar at the American Sociological Association Annual Meeting, August 1980. Marian A. Solomon is Project Director, Innovations in Health Care Management at the Lutheran Hospital Society of Southern California. Stephen M. Shortell is Professor and Chairman in the Department of Health Services, School of Public Health and Community Medicine, University of Washington, Seattle. Requests for reprints should be sent to Dr. Solomon, The Lutheran Hospital Society, Research and Development Dept., 1423 S. Grand Avenue, Los Angeles, CA 90015.

the information needs are addressed (Boruch & Cordray, 1980), the availability and accessibility of the research (Leviton & Hughes, 1979), organizational factors (Cronbach, et al., 1980), and policymaker commitment to the research activity (Wholey, 1979). It is the responsibility of the policy researcher to expand the potential of health policy research which is addressed here.

Health policy research in the ideal provides a rational basis for decision making about the delivery of health services. It focuses on specific issues or problems about which decision makers can exercise choices. Policy research in our discussion subsumes policy analysis; we include as part of policy research both original investigations and "secondary analyses," i.e., compilations and syntheses of existing research findings and the opinions and judgments of "experts." The intent of both activities is to establish options and the associated advantages and disadvantages for the decision maker.

Policy researchers necessarily are concerned about the utilization of their work by those who make policy. Researchers, perhaps too often and too quickly, become discouraged when there is no immediate response to the information they provide, although an expectation of immediate utilization is politically naive (Gilbert, Light, & Mosteller, 1977). Andringa's (1978a) analysis of eleven variables shaping national legislation named information from Congressional hearings as the seventh most influential factor; the General Accounting Office reports and assessments as eighth; policy research studies as ninth; and program evaluation studies as eleventh. Further, evidence suggests that research which supports existing program activities and interventions is more likely to be accepted than a single study, no matter how compelling the research evidence (Weiss, 1980).

In addition, a range of organizational studies demonstrates that many factors militate against the rapid adoption of innovations, even those that are demonstrated to be particularly beneficial. As pointed out in a report on evaluation utilization in the Department of Health, Education and Welfare (Note 1), the decentralized and diverse organizational structure for evaluation and the complex policy and program management structure create many opportunities for the linkages between policy research, evaluation activities, and program changes to break down. High quality research often is ignored because either policymakers do not understand the nature and process of the research, or the policy researchers do not understand the dynamics of decision making, of which policy research is only one source of information.

THE MULTIPLE MEANINGS OF UTILIZATION

There is an emerging field of concern about the dissemination and utilization of research. (At this point it is important to emphasize one caveat. A systematic review of the literature points to an emphasis on the concern with dissemination of evaluation studies rather than on social policy research. To some extent we may be accused of overgeneralizing). Included are debates about the manner in which utilization should be assessed (Caplan, 1977). Some policy researchers (Elisburg, 1977; Hutt, 1978) measure the utility of research by the direct employment of the research by policymakers. On the other hand, those who view utilization as a process that emphasizes diffusion of findings in a variety of subtle and indirect ways into policy thinking and actions find only limited evidence that the policy research contributes to a specific decision (Weiss, 1978a). Rich (1978) distinguishes "instrumental" (the ability to document information use) from "conceptual" utilization (more general influence on a policymaker's thinking) and distinguishes between long-term and short-term utilization (Rich, 1978). Alkin, Daillak, and White (1979) emphasize the longitudinal nature of the influence on policy and program decisions.

Policymakers have their own set of standards regarding the relevance of a particular piece of policy research or analysis (Wolanin, 1978). Cronbach et al. (1980) emphasized that scientific quality should not be the principal research standard for social programs, but that policy-oriented research should be comprehensible, correct, complete, and credible to partisans on all sides. Acceptance or rejection of research findings is influenced by multiple factors, including personal characteristics of policymakers and their training, information needs and, frequently, different priorities, concerns, and potential personal rewards from acting on the information. Further, findings generated by research and analysis are only one of many competing informational inputs into the policymaking process, which also includes "facts" and opinions generated by lobbyists, the public media, and other interested parties, and which must be judged in the light of immediate political priorities (Brandl, 1978). Knorr (1978) describes the type of utilization as decision-preparing utilization in contrast to the decision-constituting role of social science knowledge. Further, policy decisions must be considered in the context of resource allocation tradeoffs involving other programs and policies. This is the "problem-setting" function described by Rein and Schon (1978).

Weiss (1978b) describes a number of ways in which research and analysis can feed into the development of public policy. Several of Weiss' models are particularly relevant to the health policy field. For example, the knowledge-driven model refers to the use of existing research when applicable to a given issue. This model fits biomedical and technological advances relatively well, in which the development of new drugs, machines, and techniques provide impetuses for the development of public policy governing the use of such innovations. Another illustration is the interactive model which assumes that research and analysis are part of a complex process in which decision makers rely on their own experience and instinct and that of their colleagues. The lengthy history of the National Health Services Corps legislation and its modifications illustrates the competing influence of politically-based views and findings from the research community. A third one of considerable relevance is Weiss' conceptualization model. Under it, researchers and policymakers engage in mutual education and subsequently identify the immediate and long-term implications of a given issue. For example, in the health insurance debates, the multiplicity of research efforts, including a major longitudinal experiment conducted by Rand, became a part of conversations, memos, and staff papers. The inability of policy research to quickly provide answers to the issues when the interests of policymakers had peaked was apparent in the debates about government sponsored universal medical converage.

At first glance, health policy research reflects its influence by resource decisions reallocating program priorities within the budget, modifying expenditure amounts and by the elimination of programs and policies. But, policy research is influential in a number of less tangible and measurable ways as well, including identifying issues and formulating problems, developing parts of policies, focusing on implementation and evaluation issues, and feeding information into the policymaking process (National Research Council, 1979). A number of research studies demonstrate the difficulty in identifying direct effects of social research on policymaking (Cronbach et al., 1980). The study of utilization is plagued with problems in its quantifications and establishing a base rate for measuring the impact of such research.

FACTORS AFFECTING UTILIZATION

Four factors appear to be influential in the utilization of policy research. As the following discussion illustrates, utilization may be enhanced or impaired by the style in which results are communicated, the structure of both the decision making and implementation organizations, the availability and accessibility of results, and the client commitment to the research.

Communication Style

Part of the skill needed by the policy researcher is an understanding of and an accommodation to the decision maker's cognitive style. Lynn (1980) emphasizes that there is no point in presenting a complex piece of analysis to a politician who cannot or will not consume the material as presented; the researcher must determine how he can usefully educate someone whose method of being educated is quite different. Rich's (1979a) research indicates that the transfer of public policy research to the decision arena involves elements of communication that differ markedly from academic research in style of presentation and in the conduits for transmission of findings. He found that the form in which the information is received, is a critical factor in utilization, with informal mechanisms being the most effective.

It is important to identify the individuals to whom the product might be useful, such as key administrators, program managers, legislators, interest groups, recipients, etc., and to target the reports to that audience (Kiresuek et al., 1981). Technical material must be appropriate for the level of analytical sophistication of the users (Halperin, 1978). The degree of sophistication of the audience and the potential use of the research provide guidance for selecting degree of rigor, the methodology, and the level of confidence necessary for the findings.

Dissemination means, such as journals and professional meetings, are not appropriate to facilitate the utilization of policy research by policymakers. Not only does the time-lag associated with publication interfere with the time-relevancy of a study, but the style and approach of academic writing is foreign to the world of decision makers. The policymaker audience requires an immediate analysis once its information needs are identified: it must be timely, be based upon current information, and consider all issues pertinent to the particular needs of particular consumers. At the same time, the information to be disseminated must be appropriately packaged. The efficiency of the communication links determines whether the relevant research reaches the person with the problem (Weiss, 1978a).

Utilization of policy analysis is not only related to timely production of reports, but to the development of a strategy geared to reaching the maximum number of decision makers at various government levels to whom they might be potentially useful (Freeman & Solomon, 1979). A 1977 GAO study was designed to determine if results from program evaluations sponsored by the Law Enforcement Administration were available in time to be used by state policymakers. Only 5 percent of officials with major responsibilities for criminal justice, state budget directors, legislators, and representatives of state executive-branch agencies, and the Governor's office felt that the studies were available in time to be of use all of the time; 15 percent said they were available most of the time; and 35 percent indicated that they did not receive evaluation information from either the federal or state government.

Organizational Factors

The flow of policy is the result of many forces created by a large number of interacting individuals (National Research Council, 1979). Political and organizational realities determine the impact of public policy research (Weiss, 1977; Cronbach et al., 1980). Anyone concerned with the utilization of research must understand the complexities of the bureaucracies and their functioning (Hargrove, 1975; Mann & Likert, 1977). The diffuse organizational stucture as well as the frequent reorganizations in the Cabinet, Executive office of the President, the major agencies confuse staff/line relations and areas of responsibility (Gideonse, 1980).

Although many discussions of research utilization focus on the effect of individuals as determinants, the organizational environment in which a decision maker or manager operates is a significant intervening variable (Majchrzak & Windle, 1980; Stevens & Tornatzky, 1980). As Williams (1971) illustrates, status within an organization does not independently result in power; an individual's responsibility and authority, the ability of the individual to operate in a bureaucratic environment, and his formal ties to power either within an agency or above it are also components of power.

A given government agency may not have the authority to implement policy research recommendations (Weiss, 1878a); the lack of authority of a single agency or individual is a major factor in the low utilization level of research results (Halperin, 1980). The competition among agencies for money, power, and turf may mean that a specific program has limited interest outside of that agency unless the competing agencies can use the results of policy research to demonstrate that its approaches to achieving specified goals is more effective, cheaper, or otherwise advantageous (Attkisson & Broskowski, 1978). The constraints imposed by conflicting program goals and the competition between agencies for control of a program are important factors in the formulation of the research problem.

Several structural characteristics of an organization have implications for the potential utilization of research results:

1. Advocacy Function — the extent to which an organization sees the research as an opportunity to promote its program interests rather than an unbiased discussion of facts (Levine, 1981).
2. Readiness to Accept Change — organizational readiness to adopt, assimilate, or carry out something different from standard practice (Glaser, 1978; Kiresuek et al., 1981).
3. Intramural Analysis Capabilites — the organizational support of staff with responsibility to provide information directly to decision makers or managers (Andringa, 1978b; Attkisson, Brown & Hargreaves, 1978; Caro, 1977).
4. Oversight Responsibilities — the role of the agency in examining the implementation of government regulations as well as the efficiency of program management (Audits and Social Experiments, 1978).
5. Dissemination Practices — the access of the general public to reports, research results or internal documents (Levine, 1981).
6. Stability of Staff — the frequency of turnover in agency leadership as well as other professional employees with responsibility for program administration and management (Patton, 1978).
7. Support for Using Research Information: personal, institutional, and financial motivations and organizational encouragement for using research (Alkin, Daillak, & White, 1979; Wolanin, 1978; Bushnell & O'Brien, 1979).

Although the role of an organization in encouraging the utilization of research (or erecting barriers) is becoming acknowledged in the literature, there are few methodologies which actually assess an organization's readiness to adopt, assimilate, or carry out something different from standard practice (Glaser,

1978). One of these models, AVICTORY, has been supported by the National Institute of Mental Health. The initials in the acronym represent eight determinants of organizational change. *Ability* is described as the willingness to commit resources and the availability of skilled manpower to execute the evaluation. *Values* include the acceptance of evaluation efforts by both administrators and their staff as well as an organizational history of responsiveness to change. *Information* refers to the availability of an accessibility to data on program functioning. *Circumstances* involve those aspects of the organizational setting which influence the quality of the relationship of the program and its clients. *Timing* is the coordination of program evaluation with organizational activities. *Obligation* is the perceived need to evaluate and take some corrective action. *Resistance* refers to the feared negative consequences resulting from the evaluation. Finally, *Yield* is the expected rewards thought to result from adopting evaluation. The analysis is recorded on a questionnaire. The scores on each of these scales are obtained though organizational analysis. Subscales have been developed which allow a further breakdown. Kiresuek and associates (1981) report that although the ability of the AVICTORY model to predict adoption of a specific evaluation is still undetermined, feedback from users suggests that it does provide useful descriptive information.

Availability and Accessibility of Information

Utilization of policy research is dependent on its availability and accessibility in relation to the need for that type of information. Policies change so rapidly that the research may become quickly outdated (Falcone & Jaeger, 1976). Policy research has shunned the "creative" role and the intellectual rewards associated with academic research for the more practical reward of producing an analysis that ultimately has influence on the design of policies and programs. Wolanin (1978) notes that the time constraints in policymaking settings are not conducive to careful analysis and systematic use of information. As a result, a decision may be to waive analytical complexity in view of the practical need to produce timely information within a limited budget. Unfortunately, the time problem cannot be solved since the nature of the policy formulation process is such that there is seldom any opportunity to conduct policy analyses in anticipation of future issues (Dreyfus, 1978). Methodological compromises result from these pressures combined with the need to raise the validity of the information and lower the practical costs of a quantitative study (Mead, 1977).

There is some disagreement about the need for timeliness in the utilization of research. Although policymakers (Andringa, 1978b; Wholey, 1979; Wolanin, 1978) and many researchers (Boruch & Cordray, 1980; Caplan, 1978) identify the importance of the accessibility and availability of research results within narrow time frames, studies by Weiss and Bucuvalas (1980) and Patton et al. (1978) dispute the relative standing of timeliness as a determinant. The Weiss and Bucuvalas study suggested that timeliness accounted for less than 1 percent of the variance in predicting perceived usefulness when other variables were considered. Patton's study indicated that the receipt of information in a timely manner was not the most important factor in getting the results used.

In addition, as Levinton and Hughes (1979) suggest, the nature of the potential utilization may determine the degree to which timeliness is a critical factor. It may also depend on the degree to which research addresses specific operational problems or broad policy issues. For example, timeliness may be important for short term instrumental use but less so for conceptual use (in Weiss' framework). The requirements of the legislative cycle often determine the need for immediate information (Woy, 1979).

Client Commitment to the Research Activity

In policy research, there is a "real" client, whereas in science the "client-substitute" is one's peers and the obligation to be scientifically rigorous. Experiments such as that conducted by Stevens and Tornatzky (1980) have established the importance of client participation in the research process in order to enhance utilization. Weiss and Bucuvalas (1980) note that although each individual independently assesses the usefulness of a specific research study, the primary influences on utilization are the research quality, conformity to other research findings, user expectations for research results, the degree of guidance for future action, and a willingness to challenge the status quo. Based on data from 155 mental health, drug abuse, and rehabilitation administrators, Weiss and Bucuvalas argue that policymakers use a "truth" test based on research quality and conformance with previous experience, and a "utility" test based on the degree of applicability for taking action and whether or not the information provides innovative approaches. They also found that when the research results conformed with the decision makers views and prior experience, the technical quality of research was a less important determinant of use, but when the research conclusions diverged from previous experience or expectations technical quality became a more important consideration.

Since there is no absolute criterion for policy relevance, the usefulness of the research depends on an individual's values and needs (Lynn, 1980). As such, the analyst should take advantage of the influence of informal means of communication, such as personal conversations, which are used at all levels of hierarchy to involve decision makers (Rich, 1979b).

On the five clusters of variables that Leviton and Hughes (1979) identified which affect utilization, all relate (or can be enhanced) by client involvement in the research process. These are (1) the relevance of the research to the needs of potential users, (2) the extent of communication between potential users and producers of evaluations, (3) translation of evaluations into their implications for policy and programs, (4) credibility or trust placed in the evaluation, and (5) commitment or advocacy of individual users.

The utilization model encompasses the communication of the findings to policymakers as well as to practitioners charged with its implementation (Uliassi, 1978). Utilization requires a careful planning and execution of the analysis and the involvement of the decision maker client in the intial phases of the activity as well as in the preparation of findings targeted to the appropriate audience (Chelimsky, 1977; Sundquist, 1978). Davis and Salasin (1978) underscore the importance of this involvement from a number of studies linking utilization of results directly with decision maker participation.

With the variety of competing information sources, policy research is seldom sought for its own sake or as an aid to policymaking in general (Halperin, 1978).

Since many decision makers affect every program or issue, including Congressional committees, OMB staff, agency executives, and many interest groups, maximum dissemination and utilization of specific analyses should be encouraged (Aaron, Note 2). Many factors affect subsequent utilization, and these should be considered. For example, although a written report is usually required by most managers, verbal communication is the most effective method for calling attention to research recommendations.

Securing the commitment of the policymaker to use the research findings is a critical factor in subsequent utilization. This entails identifying the information needs and insuring that the analysis provides the needed substance, presenting the analysis in a form that is useful to and understandable by the decision maker. Patton's study of the utilization of federal evaluations (1978) was unable to clearly identify factors within the evaluation that contributed to its subsequent utilization. Instead, the role of the personal factor as a primary influence emerged not only in the utilization of an evaluation but in its impact. The implications are interwoven with the structure of the political system and the placement of policy analysis and policy research within the political process. Patton et al.'s recommendations (1978) for maximizing the use of personal factors are the following:

Identify those decision makers who know what questions can be answered through the research process and how to use the research information once it is available.

Identify strategically located persons who will work enthusiastically towards the implementation of the information. The individual in a formal position of authority may not be the most appropriate.

Clarify the questions of the decision makers and insure that the research will address those questions.

Identify individuals within the decision making structure who will provide necessary and relevant information.

Involve the decision maker to the extent possible throughout all of the stages of the analysis from the initial clarification of the issues to the interpretation of the results.

Maintain personal contacts with a wide range of federal administrative staff to reinforce interest during transition periods resulting from reorganizations and other types of program mobility.

In response to the perceived needs for interaction with the decision makers Wholey (1979), Schmidt and associates (1978), and others have developed and actively encouraged the adoption of exploratory evaluation/evaluability assessment activities in the management and evaluation of programs. During this process, senior managers and policymakers are extensively interviewed to solicit their expectations for program performance. Their views become synthesized into models describing the underlying logic of specific programs. At the same time, the actual implementation of the program is described in PERT chart form. These charts are then compared, information needs identified, and options for program change and policy research and evaluation are identified. The process depends on extensive interactions with policymakers' top management throughout the entire process so that the products of the evaluation represent a consensus. Decisions to conduct any data collection or analysis are made jointly between the analysts and the individuals who have a clearly specified use for the information.

DESIGNING RESEARCH FOR UTILIZATION

As the country moves into the era where programs must justify their continued existence, the policy research field must also meet the increased scrutiny of its critics. Research must demonstrate that its contribution to policy development or program management is not only useful, but that information is provided that would not readily be available through other mechanisms. Four areas for improving the relevance and utilization of policy research will be discussed: 1) defining the problem to address policy relevant issues, 2) the development of mechanisms to address information needs, 3) the development of better utilization and dissemination plans, and 4) improving the quality of the research and analysis.

Addressing Policy Relevant Issues

In times of tight budgets for operating programs, expenditures for activities other than direct services such as policy research or evaluation may appear to be wasteful, especially when these increase the overhead and administrative costs (Beigel & Levenson, 1978). The need for demonstrating the transferability of policy research findings is increased as budgets are reduced. The commitment to divert precious program funds will be dependent on the demonstration that their program can be improved, in cost-effective terms, through the conduct of analysts' activities (Abramson & Wholey, Note 3). The perspective and concern of the research must also be useful in both the short and long-term (Radnor & Holfer, 1979).

It is incumbent upon the evaluator to identify those who will become the users, although this task is complicated by the diversity of participants in policy, administrative, and management positions (House, 1980; Meehan, 1979). For example, those with a range of policy development and budget concerns have much different information needs than those with responsibility for the administration of a specific program area. Marans' (Note 4) experience suggests that a participatory design and advocacy-planning process minimizes social conflicts and sensitizes decision makers to the differing requirements of various population groups. Policy researchers can become aware of shifts in priorities which may eliminate or change information needs and help to avoid or minimize the criticism that the researcher "again" failed to understand the needs of the policymaker, agency, or program (House, 1980).

The development of an information gathering strategy for each operational program would take into account diverse information needs as well as the feasibility of obtaining that information (Atkisson et al., 1978). This strategy will: increase managers' and policymakers' familiarity with the data and their confidence in it; show where further work is feasible and likely to be useful; stop additonal data collection when it becomes clear that further increments of information are unlikely to be useful; and determine the costs in advance of additional data collection (Wholey, 1979). Any specific study will represent one step in the overall analysis of a program or policy rather than a disjointed evaluation of specific components. This strategy will become a mechanism for merging all the information collected about a program, thus maximizing the interchange and synthesis.

The researcher should consider organizational factors and their potential impact on the utilization of the analytical information (Halperin, 1980). This includes a definition of the scope of the problem as well as an identification of the multiple assumptions and expectations which underly any program. For example, a discussion of a long-term-care policy has many dimensions focusing on health care, social service, and residential factors. Not only are there a variety of federal agencies which have issue-specific priorities for different aspects of service delivery, but the targeted client populations are quite distinct. As a result, these issues have different implications for funding as far as sponsorship of programs for the aged, the frail elderly, the chronically ill, the young disabled adult, and the mentally impaired are concerned (Kane & Kane, 1980). As a previous minority staff Director on the House Committee on Education and Labor points out, many federal laws which have an effect on any single program area were drafted, passed, and implemented for other reasons such as sex, age, and race discrimination, pension programs, and consumer protection (Andringa, 1978b).

Developing multi-year research agendas, conducting research-strategy assessments, and increasing the interaction between policy researchers and federal, state, and local policy-makers are strategies to force the policymaker and researcher to consider longer-run issues and the relationship of existing projects and immediate priorities to each other. Within the Food and Drug Administration, the Associate Commissioner for Planning and Evaluation reports that this type of consultation and concensus building activities facilitated   the identification of knowledge gaps and assesses the likely utility of future results (Barkdoll, Note 5). Increasing the interaction among officials at multiple levels of government enables federal level analysts and policymakers to see the issues from the perspective of the state and local level where programs and services are, in fact, implemented. Understanding the implementation process allows assessment of discrepancies between policy intentions and current practice thus proving feedback to the policymakers (Leithwood & Montgomery, 1980).

Development of Mechanisms to Address Information Needs

The researcher often finds himself in a bind created by the need for information within the time demands of the policymaking process rather than by the research schedule (Mead, 1977). Timely information is often more significant than more thoroughly validated results which arrive after a decision has been made (Shortell & Richardson, 1978). The deadlines of the policymaking process must be understood by the researcher who needs to employ mechanisms which will produce useful incremental or intermediate information. As a result of a recent study, Boruch and Cordray (1980) urge federal agencies to create a formal policy in order to establish a regular dialog with Congressional staff in order to address timeliness, relevance, and credibility of the research.

The lack of sufficient data sources, particularly in new programs, affects the ability to quickly generate information on program performance. In such cases, the data gathered on program operations and effectiveness cannot be expected to be reliable although the demands for performance information still exist. As illustrated by the inadequate national statistics in mental health, a needs assessment can only be obtained through triangulation, i.e., use of multiple methods, by using a variety of national estimates (Kiesler, 1980). The mechanisms for collecting preliminary implementation data, ongoing performance indicators, and program information should be components of the program design activities (Schmidt et al., 1978). In addition, the information requirements of the offices with policy and program responsibility are different. It is important to distinguish between the data needed for program monitoring, identifying problem areas for remediation, and determining the overall program effectiveness (Evaluation Utilization, Note 1).

The researcher must also continually monitor the relevance of the research design, which may be influenced by legislative changes in the program, administrative changes in the agency, and the implementation of competing or conflicting programs (Meehan, 1979). Any of the changes could invalidate not only the design of the study but the utilization of the research efforts.

Another consideration is to increase the accessibility of study reports. Boruch and Cordray (1980) document the difficulties in obtaining evaluation and policy-research information on a current basis. The need for a shorter clearance process on research reports and public notification of the availability of studies would foster their utilization.

Development of Dissemination and Utilization Plans

While the involvement and participation of the client is a major factor in the utilization of evaluation research (Levinton & Hughes, 1979), it is only a portion of the effort required to facilitate the utilization of the research results. A specific plan must be developed to insure the visibility of the product within the time frame that the issue is active. Zucker's (1977) estimate of a three year "half-life" of any social problem implies that the research must be executed and disseminated within a three-year time frame to maximize the immediate potential usefulness of the findings.

A simulation conducted by Brown et al. (1980) demonstrated the need for an evaluation to consider an educational role with some audiences. This study underscores the importance of specific action to assure the visibility not only to assist audiences in understanding the potential uses of the information but to increase their level of satisfaction with the overall projects. A well-conceived and executed plan can maximize the usefulness of the research to others who were not the intended primary clients.

Kiresuek and others (1981) suggest inclusion of managers and their staff in programs with overlapping spheres of interest, agencies with shared priorities, and different levels of government.

Cronbach et al. (1980) suggest some sort of collegial mechanisms, such as study groups, to improve the utilization of the research enterprise. The literature is becoming filled with examples of how studies with potential applicability were not accessible or available for routine program planning and management (GAO, 1977). It is useful to think of secondary audiences for the results and develop a planned strategy of "secondary dissemination" (Shortell & Solomon, Note 6). An excellent example is provided by the User Liaison Program developed by the National Center for Health Services Research. This program involves a series of workshops with state and local decision makers in which research on given health policy issues is presented within the context of state and local priorities and possible implementation strategies.

A well-planned dissemination strategy is important given that the lack of certainty in scientific findings is contrary to the expectations of non-researchers who want definitive answers on which to base policy or management decisions. The policy researcher maintains responsibility for clarifying these expectations. Some have suggested that a "research broker" to bridge the worlds of the policymaker and the researcher can facilitate the dissemination of research results (Sundquist, 1978; Bushnell & O'Brien, 1979).

There are several rules of thumb about the presentation of materials that are conducive to stimulating the interest of the non-researcher audience. A well-written executive summary highlighting the basic findings and implications is perhaps the most important part of the entire report. Data should be presented in terms understandable to policymakers, and jargon should be avoided (Andringa, 1978a). Technical materials are best put into an appendix. Simple charts, tables, and graphs are useful. Dialogues with policymakers need to be established to be certain that the message is received (Etzioni, 1977). Oral presentations and briefings are useful tools for enabling the nonresearcher audience to obtain a better understanding of the results and offer the opportunity to suggest alternative explanations and implications as the research becomes a part of the ongoing policy and administrative process. This personal contact is important to clarify specific points and to identify the extent to which the report met the needs of the decision maker (Rich, 1979a). In addition, the role of group forces in facilitating the implementation of recommendations is a powerful tool (Mann & Likert, 1977). A final consideration is that different versions of the reports should be prepared for each audience.

Expanding the Potential of Health Policy Research

A now dated review by Bernstein and Freeman (1975) indicated that only about 10 percent of 152 evaluation projects funded in 1970 by federal agencies met minimum scientific standards. While research quality is not necessarily related to research utilization or policy impact, there is some evidence to suggest that research quality is important, particularly when the findings depart from previous conventional wisdom or imply changes in the status quo (Weiss & Bucuvalas, 1980).

There are four specific ways in which the technical quality of health policy research can be improved. The first involves a set of issues related to the availability and quality of data for analysis (Standards for Program Evaluation, Note 7). Too frequently, appropriate data are not available. A policy researcher needs to know, in advance, the accuracy, reliability, and validity of available data sets and administrative records, as well as the opportunities for collecting accurate, reliable, and valid primary data. One way to achieve this is for researchers to participate in the design of management and program information systems so that information pertinent to relevant policy and evaluation issues can be built-in along with the operational information needs. The Medicaid Management Information System (MMIS) represents a good example of an inability to use existing information for policy research, e.g., to compute population-based utilization rates for purposes of planning of current needs and to assess the impact of policy changes. Record systems which require significant investments of both money and human capital are needed which allow the type of cost-benefit and cost-effectiveness analyses required by health policymakers.

There is also need for further development of standardized minimal data sets at federal, state, and local levels to facilitate cross-site comparisons and small-area analysis. The Cooperative Health Statistics System (CHSS) is one effort in this regard. The Alcohol, Drug Abuse, and Mental Health Administration (ADAMHA) is also attempting to develop a data set which will link client information, services, priority, and costs with epidemiological and outcome research data (Attkisson & Nguyen, 1981).

There is also the need for policy researchers to make greater use of available secondary data, particularly in regard to linking data sets from multiple sources. A prime example is the linkage of hospital characteristics data from the American Hospital Association with quality-of-care and related clinical data available from the Commission on Professional and Hospital Activities. Such data sets can also be merged with population characteristics, and health manpower data available from the Area Resource File. Such merging of data sets and aggregating of data from multiple sources is necessary to address some of the broader policy questions (Rosenthal, 1981) such as assessing the impact of HMOs in different markets.

Second, health-policy research can be improved by becoming more interdisciplinary in approach. Most public policy problems do not occur as simply economic, psychological, sociological, epidemiological, or clinical problems, but rather have components involving all of these various dimensions. As such, a single-discipline approach by itself is not very helpful to decision makers (Bice, 1980).

Considerable disagreement exists over the appropriateness of qualitative and quantitative methods to health policy research. While each methodological stance has its own proponents and schools of thought, improving the technical quality of health policy is dependent on moving away from viewing one approach in opposition to another and substituting an integrated methodological framework (Reichardt & Cook, 1979). Qualitative approaches are necessary for conducting process and implementation assessments, but quantitative methodologies are essential for analyses of impact. *Both* are increasingly necessary for the explication of possible causal relationships. The resulting "triangulation" of approaches, concepts, and methods underscores the importance of interdisciplinary policy research teams noted above. It will also be important for many of these individuals to maintain ties with their respective basic disciplines so that the latest concepts, methods, and theories of the respective disciplines can be drawn upon, as appropriate, for policy research.

Fourth, from a technical perspective, health policy research would also be improved by designing research directly to test policy alternatives (Williams & Wysong, 1975). Analyses of single programs or policies are not very helpful in answering questions of comparison, that is, relative to other possible programs or options. Rand's National Health Insurance Study (Newhouse, 1974) represents an example where policy alternatives have been directly incorporated into the research design. The responsibility for such design alternatives, of course, lies as much with the policymakers and funding agencies as it does with the research community.

In an era when resources and finances are severely limited, establishing and implementing successful public policies is critical. While policy research cannot ensure the success of a specific policy, the analytic process can minimize failure through the provision of a rational framework for the decision. Even under the most ideal conditions, the utilization and impact of knowledge is influenced by many factors, including the style in which the research is communicated, political and organizational factors, the availability and accessibility of information, and the client commitment to the research. The usefulness of policy research can be expanded by addressing policy relevant issues, developing mechanisms to address information needs, developing dissemination and utilization plans and employing mechanisms to maximize the usefulness of existing resources. These suggestions can increase the probability of policy research playing a more significant role in the development and implementation of health policies.

REFERENCE NOTES

1. *Evaluation Utilization in the U.S. Department of Health, Education, and Welfare* (Mimeographed report). Washington, D.C: Office of the Assistant Secretary for Planning and Evaluation, 1979.
2. Aaron, H. Statement of the Assistant Secretary for Planning and Evaluation before the Senate Committee on Human Resources, October 17, 1977.
3. Abramson, M.A., & Wholey, J.S. *The Department of Health, Education, and Welfare evaluation program.* Paper presented at the American Society for Public Administration Annual Meeting, April, 1980.
4. Marans, R.W. *Evaluation research and its uses by housing designers and managers* (Working Paper No. 8014). Ann Arbor, Mich.: University of Michigan, October, 1979.
5. Barkdoll, G.L. *Type III evaluation: Consultation and consensus* (Mimeographed report). Office of the Associate Commissioner for Planning and Evaluation. U.S. Food and Drug Administration, Rockville, Md., September 1979.
6. Shortell, S.M., & Solomon, M.A. *Health policy research and analysis: A selective review and suggestions for improving the art.* Health Policy Seminar presented at the American Sociological Association Annual Meeting, August 1980.
7. *Standards for program evaluation* (Exposure draft). Evaluation Research Society, May 1980.

REFERENCES

Alkin, M.C., Daillak, R., & White, P. *Using evaluations: Does evaluation make a difference?* Beverly Hills: Sage Publications, 1979.

Andringa, R.C. Eleven factors influencing federal education legislation. In *Federalism at the crossroads: Improving educational policy making.* Institute for Educational Leadership. Washington, D.C.: George Washington University, 1978.(a)

Andringa, R.C. The view from the hill. In *Federalism at the crossroads: Improving educational policy making.* Washington, D.C.: George Washington University, 1978.(b)

Attkisson, C.C., & Broskowski, A. Evaluation and the emerging human service concept. In C.C. Attkisson, et al., (Eds.), *Evaluation of human service programs.* New York: Academic Press, 1978.

Attkisson, C.C., Brown, T.R., & Hargreaves, W. A. Roles and functions of evaluation in human service programs. In C.C. Attkisson, et al., (Eds.), *Evaluation of human service programs.* New York: Academic Press, 1978.

Attkisson, C.C., et al. Evaluation: Current strengths and future directions. In C.C. Attkisson, et al., (Eds.), *Evaluation of human service programs.* New York: Academic Press, 1978.

Attkisson, C.C., & Nguyen, T.D. Evaluative research and health policy: Utility, issues, and trends. *Health Policy Quarterly: Evaluation and Utilization,* 1981, *1,* 22-42.

Audits and social experiments: A report prepared for the U.S. General Accounting Office, Committee on Evaluation Research, Social Science Research Council. Washington, D.C.: General Accounting Office, October 31, 1978.

Beigel, A., & Levenson, A.I. Program evaluation on a shoe-string budget. In C.C. Attkisson, et al., (Eds.), *Evaluation of human service programs.* New York: Academic Press, 1978.

Bernstein, I.M., & Freeman, H.E. *Academic and entrepreneurial research.* New York: Russell Sage Foundation, 1975.

Bice, T. Social science and health services research: Contributions to public policy. *Milbank Memorial Fund Quarterly,* 1980.

Boruch, R.F., & Cordray, D.S. *An appraisal of educational program evaluations: Federal, state, and local agencies.* U.S. Department of Education Contract Number 300-70-0467. Evanston, Ill: Northwestern University, June, 1980.

Brandl, J.E. Evaluation and politics. *Evaluation,* 1978, Special Issue, 6-8.

Brown, R.D., Newman, D.L., & Rivers, L. Perceived need for evaluation and data usage as influences on an evaluation's impact. *Education Evaluation and Policy Analysis,* September-October 1980, *2*(5), 67-73.

Bushnell, J.L., & O'Brien, G.M.St.L. Strategies and tactics for increasing research production and utilization in social work education. In A. Rubin & A. Rosenblatt (Eds.), *Source book on research utilization.* New York: Council on Social Work Education, 1979.

Caplan, N. A minimal set of conditions necessary for the utilization of social science knowledge in policy formulation at the national level. In C.H. Weiss (Ed.), *Using social research in public policy making.* Lexington, Ma.: Lexington Books, 1978.

Caplan, N. Social research and national policy: What gets used, by whom, for what purposes and with what effects? In S. Nagel (Ed.), *Policy studies review annual.* Beverly Hills: Sage Publications, 1977.

Caro, F. (Ed.). *Readings in evaluation research.* New York: Russell Sage Foundation, 1977.

Chelimsky, E. (Ed.). *Proceedings of a symposium on the use of evaluation by federal agencies.* (Vol. 1). McLean, Va.: The Mitre Corporation, 1977.

Cronbach, L.J., and Associates. *Toward reform of program evaluation.* San Francisco: Jossey Bass, 1980.

Davis, H.E. & Salasian, S.E. Strengthening the contribution of social R&D to policy making. In L.E. Lynn (Ed.), *Knowledge and policy: The uncertain connection.* Washington, D.C.: National Academy of Sciences, 1978.

Dreyfus, D.A. The limitations of policy research in Congressional decision making. In C.H. Weiss (Ed.), *Using social research in public policy making.* Lexington, Ma.: Lexington Books, 1978.

Elisburg, D. A congressional view of program evaluation. In E. Chelimsky (Ed.), *A symposium on the use of evaluation by federal agencies* (Vol. 1). McLean, Va.: The Mitre Corporation, 1977.

Etizoni, A. Public policy in perspecitve—Social science in the White House. *Evaluation,* 1977, *4,* 13-14.

Falcone, D., & Jaeger, B.J. The policy effectiveness of health services research: A reconsideration. *Journal of Community Health,* 1976, *2,* 36-51.

Freeman, H.E., & Solomon, M.A. The next decade in evaluation research. *Evaluation and Program Planning,* 1979, *2,* 255-262.

General Accounting Office. *Evaluation needs of crime control planners, decision makers, and policymakers are not being met* (GG-77-72). Washington, D.C.: General Accounting Office, July, 1978.

Gideonse, H.D. Improving the federal administration of education programs. *Educational Evaluation and Policy Analysis,* January-February 1980, *2*(1), 61-70.

Gilbert, J.P., Light, R.J., & Mosteller, F. Assessing social innovations: An empirical base for policy. In W.B. Farley & F. Mosteller (Eds.), *Statistics and public policy.* Reading, Ma.: Addison Wesley, 1977.

Glaser, E.M. If Mohammed won't come to the mountain...*Evaluation,* 1978, *Special Issue,* 48-53.

Halperin, S. The educational arena. *Educational Evaluation and Policy Analysis,* January-February 1980, *2*(1), 27-36.

Halperin, S. Politicians and educators: Two world views. In *Federalism at the crossroads: Improving educational policy making.* Institute for Educational Leadership. Washington, D.C.: George Washington University, 1978.

Hargrove, Erwin, C. *The missing link: The study of the implementation of social policy.* Washington, D.C.: The Urban Institute, 1975.

House, E.R. *Evaluating with validity.* Beverly Hills: Sage Publications, 1980.

Hutt, P.B. Public criticism of health science policy. *Daedalus,* 1978, *107* (2), 157-169.

Kane, R.L., & Kane, R.A. Alternatives to institutional care of the elderly: Beyond dichotomy. *The Gerontologist,* 1980, *20*(3), 249-259.

Kiesler, C.A. Mental health policy as a field of inquiry for psychology. *The American Psychologist,* December 1980, *35*(12), 1066-1080.

Kiresuek, T.M., et al. Program evaluation and knowledge transfer. In R.A. Levine, et al. (Eds.), *Evaluation research: Comparative and international perspectives.* Beverly Hills, Calif.: Sage Publications, 1981.

Knorr, K.D. Policymakers' use of social science knowledge: Symbolic or instrumental? In C.H. Weiss (Ed.), *Using social research in public policy making.* Lexington, Ma.: Lexington Books, 1978.

Leithwood, K.A., & Montgomery, D.J. Evaluating program implementation. *Evaluation Review,* April, 1980, *4*(2), 193-214.

Levine, R.A. An overview of program evaluation and policy analysis in western nations: Report on a pilot project sponsored by the German Marshall Fund of the United States. In R.A. Levine, et al., (Eds.), *Evaluation research and practice: Comparative and international perspectives.* Beverly Hills: Sage Publications, 1981.

Levinton, L.C., & Hughes, E.F.X. *Utilization of evaluations: A review and synthesis.* Evanston, Ill.: Northwestern University Center for Health Services and Policy Research, 1979.

Lynn, L.D. Crafting policy analysis for decision makers. *Educational Evaluation and Policy Analysis,* May-June 1980, *2*(3), 85-90.

Lynn, L.E. *Knowledge and policy: The uncertain connection.* Washington, D.C.: National Academy of Science, 1978.

Majchrzak, A., & Windle, C. Patterns of program evaluation in community mental health centers. *Evaluation Review,* October 1980, *4*(5), 677-692.

Mann, F., & Likert, R. The need for research on the communication of research results. In F. Caro (Ed.), *Readings in evaluation research.* New York: Russell Sage Foundation, 1977.

Mead, L.M. *Institutional analysis: An approach to implementation problems in Medicaid.* Washington, D.C.: The Urban Institute, 1977.

Meehan, E.J. *The quality of federal policy making: Programmed failure in public housing.* Columbia: University of Missouri Press, 1979.

National Research Council. *Evaluation federal support for poverty reasearch.* Report of the Committee on Evaluation of Poverty Research, Assembly of Behavioral and Social Sciences. Washington, D.C.: National Academy of Sciences, 1979.

Newhouse, J.P. A design for a health insurance experiment. *Inquiry,* March 1974, *11,* 5-27.

Patton, M.Q. *Utilization—focused evaluation.* Beverly Hills: Sage Publications, 1978.

Patton, M.Q., Grimes, P.S., Guthrie, K.M., Brennan, N.J., French, B.D., & Blythe, D.A. In search of utilization· of federal health evaluation research. In C.H. Weiss (Ed.), *Using social research in public policy making*. Lexington, Ma.: Lexington Books, 1978.

Radnor, M., & Hofler, H.D. Beyond measurement to appropriateness and learning: Evaluating LEAA experimental programs. In R.F. Rich (Ed.), *Translating evaluation into policy*. Beverly Hills: Sage Publications, 1979.

Reichardt, C.S., & Cook, T.D. Beyond qualitative versus quantitative methods. In T.D. Cook & C.S. Reichardt (Eds.), *Qualitative and quantitative methods in evaluation research*. Beverly Hills: Sage Publications, 1979.

Rein, M. & Schon, D.A. Problem setting in policy research. In C.H. Weiss (Ed.), *Using social research in public policy making*. Lexington, Ma.: Lexington Books, 1978.

Rich, R.F. Uses of social science information by federal bureaucrats: Knowledge for action versus knowledge for understanding. In C.H. Weiss (Ed.), *Using social research for public policy making*. Lexington, Ma.: Lexington Books, 1978.

Rich, R.F. Editor's introduction. In R.F. Rich (Ed.), *Translating evaluation into policy*. Beverly Hills: Sage Publications, 1979. (a)

Rich, R.F. Problem-solving and evaluation research: Unemployment insurance policy. In R. F.Rich (Ed.), *Translating evaluation into policy*. Beverly Hills: Sage Publications, 1979. (b)

Rosenthal, G. Does good health services research produce good health policy? *Health Policy Quarterly: Evaluation and Utilization*, 1981, *1*, 8-21.

Schmidt, R.D., Scanlon, J.W., & Bell, J.B. *Evaluability assessment: Making public programs work better*. Washington, D.C.: The Urban Institute, 1978.

Shortell, S.M., & Richardson, W.C. *Health program evaluation*. St. Louis, Mo.: C.V. Mosby, 1978.

Stevens, W.F., & Tornatsky, L.G. The dissemination of evaluation: An experiment. *Evaluation Review, June 1980, 4*(3), 339-354.

Sundquist, J.L. Research brokerage: The weak link. In L.E. Lynn (Ed.), *Knowledge and policy: The uncertain connection*. Washington, D.C.: National Academy of Science, 1978. (a)

Uliassi, P.D. Research and foreign policy: A view from Foggy Bottom. In C.H. Weiss (Ed.), *Using social research in public policy making*. Lexington, Ma.: Lexington Books, 1978.

Weiss, C.H. Utilization of evaluation: Toward comparative study. In F. Caro (Ed.), *Readings in evaluation research*. New York, N.Y.: Russell Sage Foundation, 1977.

Weiss, C.H. Improving the linkage between social research and public policy. In L.E. Lynn (Ed.), *Knowledge and policy: The uncertain connection*. Washington, D.C.: National Academy of Science, 1978. (a)

Weiss, C.H. (Ed.), *Using social research in public policy making*. Lexington, Ma. Lexington Books, 1978.

Weiss, C.H. Knowledge creep and decision accretion. *Knowledge: Creation, Diffusion, Utilization*, 1980, *1*(3), 381-404.

Weiss, C.H., & Bucuvalas, M.J. Truth tests and utility tests: Decision makers frames of reference for social science research. *American Sociological Review*, April 1980, 45, 302-313.

Wholey, J.S. *Evaluation: Promise and performance*. Washington, D.C.: The Urban Institute, 1979.

Williams, S., & Wysong, J. The uses of research in national health policy: An assessment and agenda. *Medical Care*, 1975, *13*, 256-267.

Williams, W. *Social policy research and analysis: The experience in the federal social agencies*. New York: Elsevier, 1971.

Wolanin, T.R. Congress, information and policy making for postsecondary education: Don't trouble me with the facts. In *Federalism at the crossroads: Improving educational policy making*. Institute for Educational Leadership. Washington, D.C.: George Washington University, 1978.

Woy, J.R. Policy-making for mental health: The role of program evaluation. In R.F. Rich (Ed.), *Translating evaluation into policy*. Beverly Hills: Sage Publications, 1979.

Zucker, L. Evaluating evaluation research: What are the standards for judging research quality? *Sociological Practice*, 1977, *2*, 107-124.

46

Critical Theory and Public Policy

Fred R. Dallmayr

ABSTRACT

In the confines of the study of politics, public policy analysis involves a shift from pure to applied research, a shift which intensifies the problem of the fact-value split inherited from positivist behavioralism. While early public policy literature concentrated on empirical policy-making processes bypassing moral criteria, some recent writings have elaborated on policymaking and policy evaluation as a type of normative inquiry; significant steps in this direction have been undertaken by Duncan MacRae and especially by Jürgen Habermas in the context of "critical theory." According to Habermas, policy evaluation requires a critically reflective "practical discourse" open not only to experts or policy analysts but to the public at large. The paper argues that such discourse is a valuable remedy against the technical-instrumental bent of applied science, but that recovery of a fully non-instrumental "practical" judgment presupposes an evaluation not only of concrete policies but of the status of "policy" itself.

Meandering through the collective memory of the discipline of "politics" (or "political science"), there is still the legacy of a tripartite division between types of inquiry inaugurated by Artistotle: the division between "theoretical," "technical" and "practical" knowledge.   While the first type was meant to provide knowledge for its own sake (and thus is distantly but awkwardly related to modern "pure" science), and while the second supplied knowledge needed for the "making" of artifacts (thus paving the way to modern applied science and technology), the category of "practical" thought was reserved for insights garnered through life experience and through practical conduct preferably in public affairs.[1]   I intend to invoke these memories and precedents in the following discussion of the present state of the study of politics construed as the study of "policy."   After initially delineating the recent rise of policy studies and the chief quandaries besetting "policy analysis," I shall, in a second section, turn to the issue of "policy evaluation" and legitimation, discussing arguments advanced both by American policy students and (especially) by Jürgen Habermas, the leading contemporary representative of a "critical theory" of society. By way of conclusion, I shall argue that policy evaluation needs to be expanded into a critical evaluation of the very meaning and status of "policy."

THE RISE OF POLICY STUDIES.   Within the larger context of the study of politics, the contemporary preoccupation with policy issues constitutes a departure from an earlier consensus which, during preceding decades, had unified professional practitioners (particularly in America) and which had insisted on the primacy of theoretical frameworks capable of explaining and predicting political conduct seen as empirical "behavior."   While the departure obviously resists rigid periodization, there is an event in recent memory which handily pinpoints the "birthdate" of the policy movement (and simultaneously the period of "post-behavioralism"):   This was the presidential address delivered by David Easton in 1969 at the annual meeting of the American Political Science Association, under the title "The New Revolution in Political Science."   The address came at the height of intense intellectual ferment in the social sciences and also in the midst of widespread social and political unrest.   Noting these troubled conditions, Easton found unsatisfactory the focus on abstract explanatory schemes or the simple cultivation of science for science's sake.   As he observed, the well-spring of the "new" or "post-behavioral" revolution was "a deep dissatisfaction with political research and teaching, especially of the kind that is striving to convert the study of politics into a more rigorously scientific discipline modeled on the methodology of the natural sciences." Easton's address urged a "revolutionary" realignment of the discipline, namely, a shift which would channel professional energies toward the solution or amelioration of the major social and political problems of the time--although problem-solving in his view was bound to honor "the findings of contemporary behavioral science."[2]

Easton's call for a "new revolution" would have been entirely ineffectual if it had not somehow meshed with powerful intellectual and social-political trends; in my view, both "endogenous" or internal-professional factors and environmental or social-political motives must be taken into account in this context.   Among the latter primary emphasis should probably be placed on the "increasing social and political crises" mentioned by Easton.   At the time of his address, these "crises" derived mainly from the experiences of the Vietnam War, racial tensions, and urban riots; subsequent years brought to the fore a host of problems revolving around economic stagnation, energy shortages, and unemployment--not to mention "Watergate" and the disclosure of corruption in high governmental circles.   On the whole, the turbulence of the Vietnam era has given way to a time of scarcity and austerity, a situation which tends to place a heavy premium on pragmatic "problem solving" and on the efficient handling of urgent public needs.   These dilemmas, I believe, can and should be seen in conjunction with long-range trends of our age.   Contemporary developments in the study of politics find a distant parallel in the earlier transition from Enlightenment rationalism to utilitarianism and also from classical economics to post-classical and Keynesian economic analysis.   In large measure, the delay or retardation in political inquiry can be ascribed to the marginal or subsidiary status of politics during the era of laissez-faire liberalism.   In our own time, the progressive amalgamation of the "polity" and the economy has as one of its consequences the absorption of the former by the distinctive rationality and concrete "rationalization" processes characteristic of modern social-economic evolution; epistemologically and methodologically, this absorption entails the alternate (and sometimes combined) predominance of pure and applied science or, in Aristotelian language, of "theoretical" and "technical" knowledge.

In terms of endogenous or internal-professional factors, there is ample evidence that the present policy focus is not a sudden innovation but was prepared and nurtured by analytical and methodological initiatives stretching back over the last several decades.   On the level of macro-frameworks, one may point to the progressive replacement of static equilibrium models by models stressing effective systemic "steering" and crisis management, a change evident, for example, in Gabriel Almond's shifting emphasis from the description of systemic "functions" to the stipulation of basic "capabilities" seen as required "output" criteria for handling domestic crises and environmental challenges; the same trend was also manifest in the emergence of political "cybernetics," a perspective which, according to one of its leading spokesmen, was meant to capture "a shift in the center of interest from drives to steering, and from instincts to systems of decisions, regulation, and control."[3] On the level of micro-frameworks, one must mention especially the so-called "decision-making" approach which, in past decades, was developed both along the lines of an empirical scrutiny of decision-making processes and in the direction of a more formalized "rational choice" or decision theory.   The cited approaches bequeathed to policy analysis not only their respective strenghts or merits, but also all their quandaries and ambiguities. One such quandary concerns the status of "politics" or political practice--notions which tend to be submerged, on the one hand, in general management categories and, on the other, in the dimension of individual or social psychology. More directly apparent is the ambivalent character of "steering," "control" and "decision"--labels which, in professional usage, hover precariously between causal "behavioral" processes and voluntary-purposive activities; the "decision-making" model in particular leaves hazy the import of "intentionality" and the role and range of human "rationality." All the listed frameworks are beset by the positivist "fact-value" dichotomy and its implications, especially the unresolved query whether choices and decisions are amenable not only to empirical testing and prediction but also to normative evaluation and judgment.

Given its inherited quandaries and dilemmas, contemporary policy analysis is not an entirely homogeneous enterprise but makes room for different accents and formulations; like the earlier behavioral consensus, the post-behavioral realignment signals not so much a rigid doctrine as a broad intellectual tendency or outlook. Yet, despite internal flexibility and variations, it is not impossible to pinpoint a common denominator or shared thrust linking adepts of this outlook: This thrust consists in a primary concern with "outputs," with pragmatic problem solving, and with applied knowledge. Without venturing too far afield, this affinity is readily evident from a quick glance at some of the literature which inaugurated the policy focus, writings which appeared roughly at the time of Easton's address. Thus, in a book entitled *The Study of Policy Formation*, Raymond Bauer defined "policy" as a "course-setting involving decisions of the widest ramifications and longest time perspective in the life of an organization," decisions designed to cope with internal or environmental problems of any kind. Similarly, Charles Lindblom's *The Policy-Making Process* treated "policy" as the outcome of decision-making processes set in motion in response to existing stimuli or challenges. What is immediately obvious in these examples is the lacking distinction between politics and non-politics or between political and general managerial policies; equally manifest is the non-differentiation (or obscure relation) between empirical behavior and purposive action. Even where the first issue is partially attended to, the second dilemma may still persist. Thus, in his *Public Policymaking Reexamined*, Yehezkel Dror concentrated more strongly on political aspects, defining policy as the "direct output of public policymaking"; but as in the other examples the subject matter "reexamined" were essentially behavioral processes. All three studies demonstrated the effects of the positivist legacy: The focus on empirical behavior for all practical purposes barred normative inquiry.[4]

The abstinence from practical-normative issues which characterized the cited literature soon proved to be a straitjacket. Given the fact that policy "choices" or "decisions" (if these terms are to have meaning) involve options among alternative courses of action, some attention had to be given to the criteria for such options. Yet, at least during the early phase of the policy movement, such attention did not necessarily imply a departure from positivist premises. As a brief illustration, Dror's contribution to a 1975 symposium on "Current Problems of Policy Theory," published in the *Policy Studies Journal,* sketched "Some Features of a Meta-Model for Policy Studies." Features of this meta-model included a combination of "descriptive-explanatory" and "prescriptive" categories and a stress on "preferization" as the major element of policy studies. "The first yardstick to be applied to any improvement-directed policy study," he noted, "is the quality of the relevant policies as they are or would be without that study. If the study can improve policy-results (in some discernible way) so they will be 'preferable' to those otherwise achieved, then the 'preferization' test is met and the policy study should be judged acceptable." While thus seemingly venturing in a prescriptive direction, the author strongly insisted on the "instrumental" and "relativistic" character of the proposed "preferization" test. Basically, relativism meant the re-endorsement of the fact-vaule distinction, this time in the form of the dichotomy between politics and policy science or between subjectively chosen political goals and objective means-ends research: "'Preferization' is to be considered in terms of the values and goals of 'legitimate value judges' who may range from democratically elected leaders to a general assembly of a Kibbutz or, not acceptable in my personal ideology, various kinds of totalitarian leaders." Although policy scientists could clarify politicians' values, they were not to trespass into the latter's domain, since "The values and goals of the 'legitimate value judges' serve as preferization yardsticks--not those of the policy researcher. Here lies a primary distinction between policy studies as a scientific, academic and/or professional activity and other orientations or roles such as advocacy-researcher, social critic, change agent, and social prophet of radical scientists." The same symposium volume contained an essay by Robert Bish who argued that "most policy proposals are supposed to enhance the well-being of identifiable citizens, and policy analysis is used to determine which of several policies may do the better job." However, the paper failed to shed light on "the assignment of 'values' citizens place on the policy outputs." [5]

POLICY EVALUATION AND CRITICAL THEORY. The sketched quandaries and defects did not go unnoticed among observers and participants of the policy movement. One of the strongest indictments of its shortcomings--especially the neglect of normative questions--was issued at its inception by Theodore Lowi, a political scientist known for his contributions both to the elucidation of contemporary politics and to a reflectively seasoned study of public policy. In a 1970 review of "policy-making" literature, Lowi stressed the need for "policy evaluation" conceived as a non-instrumental assessment of policy goals and preferences. As he pointed out, the exclusive focus on means-ends questions and policy procedures rendered policy studies "essentially technocratic and instrumental in values, in analysis, and in ultimate impact. When one assumes that 'policy making is policy *making* is decision making' and therefore does not enter into *a priori* analysis of the character of the choices being made, one almost inevitably becomes incrementalist and manipulative." The tendency was reinforced by the positivist legacy of fact-value segregation: "When the goals of policies are not questioned because they are the values which must be kept separate from facts, the analyst becomes committed to the value context of those policies even if his political ideology would not support them if he looked more carefully at them."[6]

In the meantime, efforts have been undertaken by numerous scholars to overcome the limitations noted by Lowi. In the domain of policy evaluation, one of the most significant developments has been resort to the notion of normative or "valuative discourse" as a correlate and possible antidote to a narrowly empiricist or procedural approach. In the American context, the concept of "valuative discourse" has been articulated primarily by Duncan MacRae in a series of writings, beginning in 1971 and culminating in a study published in 1976 under the title, *The Social Function of Social Science*. The study constitutes one of the major contributions to social science literature during the past decade and certainly one of the most searching and thoughtful publications in the field of policy analysis. MacRae's point of departure in his study was the "post-behavioral" malaise in the social sciences, especially the widespread dissatisfaction with the conception--characteristic of the behavioral consensus--which viewed the social disciplines as self-contained analytical or "nomothetic" enterprises governed by the motto "science for science's sake." In contrast to more ambitious recent ventures trying to banish or exorcise behavioral "scientism" altogether, his proposal was in essence to correlate and reconcile empiricism and "valuation." Bypassing both positivist and radical anti-positivist formulas, the study noted that

> there is another path to follow; that reliable scientific
> knowledge of man and nature is an important resource
> for policy choice but can coexist with rational ethical
> discourse; that some of the values of science may be
> transferred to this ethical discourse; and that scien-
> tific propositions and ethical assertions, while clearly
> distinguishable, may be fruitfully combined in academic
> disciplines concerned with the study of man and society. [7]

According to MacRae, the combination of scientific knowledge and valuation was particularly desirable and appropriate in the field of policy analysis construed as an "applied" social discipline. To implement its tasks, such a discipline could not limit itself to the investigation of empirical conditions, but had to probe normative questions; it had to be guided by the conviction "that science should serve human welfare, not simply scientists' satisfaction or the discovery of truth as an end in itself." While advocating the strengthening of "applied" inquiry, one should note, MacRae's study held no brief for technocracy and was careful to differentiate its proposals from an instrumental model of "social engineering." Positivism and academic specialization, he observed, had produced either an infatuation with "pure science" divorced from values and purposes, or else a narrowly technical or instrumental type of applied analysis. In the latter case--where research was typically the handmaiden of economic or political organizations--ends or values were treated as fixed or given and thus removed from critical scrutiny and discussion. As the author commented (echoing some of Lowi's concerns), the engineering model was damaging both to academic inquiry and to politics, especially to democratic politics. Operating instrumentally science betrayed its own rational ethos by subservience to non-rational dictates: "To separate valuative questions from science is perhaps to strengthen science, but also to weaken applied science by making it totally dependent for its guidance on unreflective standards and modes of valuation. The values that guide the application of science are thus deprived of the rational component that is so essential to science's own internal functioning." At the same time, definition of values by client organizations--or by such organizations in conjunction with experts or applied scientists--encouraged elitist and undemocratic proclivities, in particular the tendency to bypass the views of "informed citizens" described as "the ultimate decision makers in a democracy."[8]

Despite the concern for democratic participation, MacRae's study did not entrust the formulation of values and policy goals entirely to the "educated public" or to generally informed citizens. To overcome the opacity and "sluggishness" of public opinion and to facilitate the rational resolution of policy issues, ethical argument in his view had to partake of some of the qualities of scientific discourse. It was at this point that his conception of the "function of social science" came most clearly into view: Social scientists were accorded a special role in the discussion of values both because of their empirical knowledge of social conditions and because of their attachment to rigorous canons of inquiry and communication. The specific recommendation of the study was "to transfer to valuative discourse some of the norms that a well-organized scientific community imposes on its own communications." With the exception of empirical testing, the norms of ethical argument were said to be "analogous to those that govern the discussion of scientific theories and hypotheses." The central yardstick of valuative discourse was that "before anyone enter into ethical argument he first render his own ethical system clear, consistent, and general--modifying it in detail if necessary." Apart from stipulating standards for each individual participant, MacRae also outlined a set of rules governing normative debate: first, that such debate be conducted between proponents of "ethical systems" or "ethical hypotheses" which are "specified in writing in advance"; secondly, that "each discussant have equal opportunity to argue for his own system, and against the opposing one, by pointing out presumed shortcomings in the other system"; and thirdly, that after each exchange "the proponent of the ethical system under criticism decide whether he wishes to alter his ethical system or make the choice dictated by it."[9]

In my view, MacRae's study was distinguished by numerous impressive qualities: including its interdisciplinary outlook, its sober and careful mode of presentation, and the cogency of many of its proposals; one of its strongest virtues was its appeal to the "common good" as ultimate yardstick of policy choice, in lieu of the separate interests either of (detached) academics or of politicians and client groups.[10] Unfortunately, such merits were marred by several drawbacks affecting both the status of ethical discourse and the range of public deliberation. In stressing the affinity between

science and ethics and the role of "ethical hypotheses," the study
injected into policy evaluation some of the contingent qualities of
empirical research: Treated as heuristic frameworks, normative
propositions can yield at best hypothetical, not "categorical" obligations.   By treating policy analysis as an "applied" discipline implementing the canons of scientific research (canons which themselves
are rarely open to debate), MacRae's approach also courted the danger of instrumentalism--a peril which was reinforced by his own
ethical preference for utilitarianism, a doctrine traditionally associated with instrumentalist premises and convictions.   The preference
for utilitarianism or efficient utility calculations may also have something to do with the study's deemphasis of citizen participation in
favor of social-scientific discourse.   As John Ladd has noted:
"Like utilitarianism, policy studies often operate with a very limited
picture of what morality and politics are all about; namely, they
conceive of morality and politics as principally concerned with the
production and (just) distribution of *consumer goods* for society."
In Ladd's view, such a conception easily encourages moral "pater-
nalism," that is, a "functional division" between moral producers
and consumers: "A clear understanding of the relationship of the
individual to public policy, not as a receiver (consumer), but as an
active moral agent seems to me to present the most important challenge to policy studies from the point of view of morality."[11]

Many or most of these drawbacks, I believe, are remedied in
a second example drawn from the Continental European setting:
the version of "critical theory" articulated by Jürgen Habermas in
in a series of writings during the past decade.   Broadly speaking,
Habermas' perspective parallels MacRae's approach with respect to
the juxtaposition or combination of empirical science and moral
evaluation; the parallel extends to the stress on disciplined normative deliberation, termed by Habermas "practical discourse."   By
contrast to MacRae's focus on application or applied analysis, however, Habermas intensifies and broadens the significance of practi-
cal-moral argument vis-à-vis empirical-scientific inquiry.   While
empirical science is ultimately geared toward the goal of human
mastery or "control" of the environment and thus guided by a
"technical interest," ethical evaluation is rooted in interpersonal
contacts and communicative interaction which, in turn, are governed
by a "practical interest" in mutual understanding and in the maintenance of just or justifiable norms of conduct.   As used in this
context practice and practical interaction are not synonyms for a
blind activism opposed to thought, but rather are closely linked
with the capacity for radical "reflection" and self-reflection--a
capacity described in Habermas' earlier writings as man's interest
in "emancipation" and later as the basis and mainspring of rational
"discourse."[12] Two studies are particularly relevant to policy
issues: *Toward a Rational Society* (first published in 1970) and
Legitimation Crisis (whose English translation appeared in 1975).
The first volume contains three essays which are particularly pertinent here.   Taking its cues from Lord Snow's "two cultures"
theme, an essay on "Technical Progress and the Social Life-
World" explores the complex relationship between empirical science
and cultural understanding and self-understanding fostered by the
humanities.   In our technological era, Habermas observes, this

relationship is "only one segment of a much broader problem: *How is it possible to translate technically exploitable knowledge into the practical consciousness of a social life-world?"* What emerges in this question is a "true life-problem of scientific civilization" which can be couched in these terms: "How can the relation between technical progress and the social life-world, which today is still clothed in a primitive, traditional, and unchosen form, be reflected upon and brought under the control of rational discussion?" The essay then links this problem to the life-world of politics, particularly democratic politics, where it yields this query: "How can the power of technical control be brought within the range of the consensus of acting and transacting citizens?"

In probing this query, Habermas rejects as too facile two customary responses: that science and technology are the automatic harbingers of democracy, or else that technology necessarily destroys democracy. "Today, in the industrially most advanced systems, an energetic attempt must be made consciously to take in hand the mediation between technical progress and the practical conduct of life in the major industrial societies, a mediation that has previously taken place without direction, as a mere continuation of natural history." To accomplish this mediation, it is not sufficient that society match "the conditions of technical rationality"; since "even if the cybernetic dream of a virtually instinctive self-stabilization could be realized, the value system would have contracted in the meantime to a set of rules for the maximization of power and comfort; it would be equivalent to the biological base value of survival at any cost, that is, ultrastability." Thus, the contemporary "challenge of technology cannot be met with technology alone"; rather, it is a question of "setting into motion a politically effective discussion that brings the social potential constituted by technical know-how into a rationally defined and controlled relation to our practical knowledge and will."[13]

Another essay in the same volume probes the relation between the "scientization of politics" and democratic "public opinion," starting from the premise that if such "scientization" is not yet a reality, it is today "a real tendency for which there is evidence": "It is only recently that bureaucrats, the military, and politicians have been orienting themselves along strictly scientific guidelines in the exercise of their public functions--indeed this practice has only existed on a large scale since World War II." Three theoretical accounts or construals of the relationship are discussed in the paper: a "decisionistic model" dating back to Hobbes and Max Weber; a "technocratic model" deriving from Bacon and Saint-Simon; and a practical-dialectical (or "pragmatistic") model. In the first account the politican is the ultimate authority making arbitrary political choices while employing technical expertise only in the selection of means, while in the second "the dependence of the professional on the politican appears to have reversed itself" with the result that the latter "become the mere agent of a scientific intelligentsia which, in concrete circumstances, elaborates the objective requirements of available techniques and resources as well as of optimal strategies and steering regulations." Habermas' own preference is clearly for the third model in which "the strict separa-

tion between the function of the expert and the politican is replaced
by a critical interaction" and where the transposition of technical
recommendations into practice is "increasingly dependent on mediation by the public as a political institution." As he recognizes,
the feasibility of this model today is hampered by numerous obstacles, including the erosion of the "public sphere" and the pervasive collusion of bureaucracy and expertise. The integration of
technology into social self-understanding--and thus the interpene-
tration of "political will" and scientific rationality--could be effectively pursued only "under the ideal conditions of general communication extending to the entire public and free from domination." This
emphasis on unconstrained communication recurs in a third essay
which distinguishes "two concepts of rationalization," a symbolic-
communicative and a truncated technocratic type. "At the level of
subsystems of instrumental action," we read, "scientific-technical
progress has already compelled the reorganization of social institutions and sectors, and necessitates it on an increasingly larger
scale." On the other hand, *rationalization at the level of the
institutional framework* can occur only in the medium of symbolic
interaction itself, that is, through *removing restrictions on communication.*" In the latter context, "public, unrestricted and unconstrained discussion of the suitability and desirability of action-
orienting principles and norms in the light of the socio-cultural
repercussions of developing subsystems of instrumental behavior--
such discussion at all levels of political and repoliticized decision-
making processes is the only medium in which anything like
(genuine) 'rationalization' is possible."[14]

Public discussion of alternative courses of social action, one
should add, is meant here to entail not only the stipulation and con-
frontation of hypothetical maxims, but the articulation and clarification of valid or categorical yardsticks--whose binding character, to
be sure, derives not from dogmatic acceptance but from the cogency
of a "practical discourse" yielding a rational consensus among all
participants. Elaboration of the character and implications of such
discourse is one of the central themes of *Legitimation Crisis*. As he
points out, norms have obligatory effects and thus raise validity
claims, claims which cannot be redeemed on a strictly empirical or
voluntaristic basis. For, "if only empirical motives (such as inclin-
ations, interests, or fear of sanctions) sustain an agreement, it is
impossible to see why a party to the contract should continue to
feel bound to norms once his original motives change"; the same
situation obtains if reliance is placed on arbitrary will. In general
terms, "we cannot explain the validity claim of norms without taking
recourse to a rationally motivated agreement or at least to the conviction that consensus on a recommended norm could be brought
about *with reasons.*" Consequently, the "model of contracting
parties" merely enacting preferences or heuristic maxims is inadequate: "The appropriate model is rather the communicative community of those affected, who as participants in a practical discourse
test the validity claims of norms and, to the extent that they accept
them with reasons, arrive at the conviction that in the given circumstances the proposed norms are 'right.'" The "rightness" or
validity of norms, from this perspective, is predicated on the
rational structure of the validating discourse--its openness to all

affected parties and the absence of extrinsic constraints: "Discourse can be understood as that form of communication that is removed from direct contexts of experience and action and whose structure assures us that possible validity claims of assertions, recommendations or warnings are the exclusive object of discussion; that participants, topics and contributions are not restricted except with reference to the goal of testing validity claims; and that no force is exercised except that of the better argument."[15]

POLICY EVALUATION AND NON-INSTRUMENTAL ACTION. Critical theory as formulated by Habermas--and especially his notion of "practical discourse"--undoubtedly goes a long way toward overcoming the pitfalls of technocracy and toward giving policy evaluation its proper due. There are reasons for holding that critical evaluation should extend not only to the assessment of substantive policies, but to the status and role of "policy" itself. Despite the stress on interaction, Habermas' arguments carry overtones of instrumentalism which are evident in his commitment to broad-scale "rationalization" and a "rational society"--notwithstanding the distinction between symbolization and technological progress. This is also manifest in the frequent emphasis on human (thought not purely technical) "control," particularly the need to "bring under control" the traditional relation between technology and social life-world. Primary preoccupation with rational action and goal-oriented human designs cannot entirely avoid instrumentalist effects; even when endorsed by a consensus of participants, such designs are liable to reduce the environment--and potentially other human beings--to the level of means. Against this background, political scientists should be reluctant to submerge their discipline in policy analysis or to identify "politics" with policy-making. In a radical sense, non-instrumental action must be construed as action unconcerned with outcomes or goal attainment and even receptive to (what one may call) the inroads of "non-action" into purposive designs.

    Some guidance along these lines may be obtained from Michael Oakeshott's study *On Human Conduct*, a book which has been poorly received by students of politics but probably deserves another look.[16] In his study, Oakeshott differentiates between two main aspects of human conduct: substantive conduct or performance concerned with the pursuit of substantive goals or satisfactions; and rule-governed practices in terms of which particular goals are pursued and among which the most important are non-instrumental or "moral" practices. Building on this distinction, the volume further opposes two modes of interpersonal relationships, termed respectively "enterprise association" and "civil association" or *civitas*. While in the first case agents are "related in the joint pursuit of some imagined and wished-for common satisfaction"--that is, in the pursuit of "some common purpose, some substantive condition of things to be jointly procured, or some common interest to be continuously satisfied"--members of the second type (termed *cives*) are "not partners or colleagues in an enterprise" nor are they "individual enterprises related to one another as bargainers for the satisfaction of their individual wants"; rather, they are related in terms of a non-instrumental practice "which has no extrinsic purpose and is not related to procuring any substantive satisfaction."

Correlated with these modes of association is the difference between "policy" and "politics." In a joint enterprise, Oakeshott observes, "the associates are related in terms of their choice to pursue a common purpose and of their continuous agreement upon a 'policy'; that is, upon 'managerial' decisions concerned with the actions and utterances in which, from time to time, this purpose shall be pursued." Politics, by contrast, has to do with the maintenance or modification of the "practice of civility"; it is "concerned with determining the desirable norms of civil conduct and with the approval or disapproval of civil rules which, because they qualify the pursuit of purposes, cannot be inferred from the purposes pursued."[17] Whether or not one agrees with Oakeshott's separation of the two associational types (or with his dichotomy of matter and form), the distinction between substantive pursuits and a non-purposive matrix permitting such pursuits seems worth pondering. What the distinction suggests is that the "good life" or "good society" is not simply a goal to be implemented, but depends on, or is intimated by, an ongoing cultivation of civility.

NOTES

1. On the legacy of practical wisdom, seen against the background of the rise of scientific explanatory models especially in the American context, see Bernard Crick, The American Science of Politics: Its Origins and Conditions (University of California Press, 1964); on the Aristotelian tradition compare Wilhelm Hennis, Politik und praktische Philosophie: Eine Studie our Rekonstruktion der politischen Wissenschaft (Luchterhand, 1963).

2. David Easton, "The New Revolution in Political Science," 63 American Political Science Review 1051, 1057 (1969).

3. Karl Deutsch, The Nerves of Government: Models of Political Communication and Control (Free Press, 1963), 76. Regarding structural functionalism compare especially Gabriel Almond, "A Developmental Approach to Political Systems," 17 World Politics 183-214 (1965).

4. See Raymond Bauer and Kenneth Gergen (eds.), The Study of Policy Formation (Free Press, 1968), 2; Charles Lindblom, The Policy-Making Process (Prentice-Hall, 1968), 4; Yehezkel Dror, Public Policymaking Reexamined (Chandler Publishing Co., 1968), 35.

5. See Yehezkel Dror, "Some Features of a Meta-Model for Policy Studies," and Robert Bish, "The Assumption of Knowledge in Policy Analysis," 3 Policy Studies Journal 248-250, 256 (1975).

6. Lowi, "Decision Making vs. Policy Making: Toward an Antidote for Technocracy," 30 Public Administration Review 318-319 (1970).

7. Duncan MacRae, Jr., The Social Function of Social Science (Yale University Press, 1976), 5. For some of MacRae's earlier writings see "Scientific Communication, Ethical Argument and Public Policy," 65 American Political Science Review 38-50 (1971); "Normative Assumptions in the Study of Public Choice," 16 Public Choice 27-41 (1973); "Justice, Normative Discourse, and Sociology,"

2 _Contemporary Sociology_ 129-132 (1973); and "Policy Analysis as an Applied Social Science," 6 _Administration and Society_ 363-388 (1975). For a more detailed review of _The Social Function of Social Science_ compare my "Knowledge and Commitment: Variations on a Familiar Theme," 12 _Polity_ 291-302 (1979).

8.   MacRae, _The Social Function of Social Science_, xi-xii, 52.

9.   Ibid., 51, 80, 87, 92-93.

10.   "The social function of social science," the conclusion stated, "is thus not simply to serve the interest of any particular class in a given period of history, nor is it to serve the interests of academics themselves. Rather, it is to provide guidance to society, through research, reasoned discourse, and education as to what interests should be served in particular circumstances and as to the means to do so." Ibid., 306.

11.   John Ladd, "Policy Studies and Ethics," 2 _Policy Studies Journal_ 42-43 (1973); compare also his "The Ethics of Participation," in J. Roland Pennock and John Chapman (eds.), _NOMOS XVI: Participation in Politics_ (Atherton Press, 1975).

12.   Regarding the theory of cognitive interests compare Jürgen Habermas, _Knowledge and Human Interests_, trans. by Jeremy Shapiro (Beacon Press, 1971); for the turn to "discourse" see "A Postscript to Knowledge and Human Interests," 3 _Philosophy of the Social Sciences_ 157-189 (1975). The broader relevance of "critical theory" for public administration is discussed in William Dunn and Bahman Fozouni, "Toward a Criticial Administrative Theory," in _Administrative and Policy Studies Series_, vol. 3 (Sage Publications, 1976).

13.   Habermas, _Toward a Rational Society: Student Protest, Science, and Politics_, trans. by Jeremy Shapiro (Beacon Press, 1970), 52-53, 57, 60-61.

14.   Habermas, "Scientization of Politics and Public Opinion," and "Technology and Science as 'Ideology'," ibid., 62-64, 66, 68, 75, 118-119.

15.   Habermas, _Legitimation Crisis_, trans. by Thomas McCarthy (Beacon Press, 1975), 104-105, 107-108.

16.   Michael Oakeshott, _On Human Conduct_ (Clarendon Press, 1975). The study has been reviewed and strongly criticized by Hanna Pitkin, Sheldon Wolin, and David Spitz in 4 _Political Theory_ 301-352 (1976).

17.   _On Human Conduct_, 59, 112, 114, 122, 160, 174.